HIDDEN TERRORS

HIDDEN TERRORS

BY
A.J. LANGGUTH

PANTHEON BOOKS, NEW YORK

Library of Congress Cataloging in Publication Data

Langguth, A. J., 1933–
Hidden Terrors.

1. Mitrione, Dan. 2. Intelligence agents—
United States—Biography. 3. Police—United
States—Biography. 4. Kidnapping—Uruguay—
Case studies. 5. Murder—Uruguay—Case studies.
I. Title.
JK468.I6L35 1978 327'.12'0924 [B] 77-88769
ISBN 0-394-40674-5

Design by Kenneth Miyamoto

Manufactured in the United States of America

FIRST EDITION

For Arthur Langguth
(1906–1976)

HIDDEN TERRORS

CHAPTER

1

ON THE DAY that Dan Mitrione's body was brought back to lie in state in his hometown, President and Mrs. Richard M. Nixon sent a commemorative wreath both large and patriotic—red carnations, white chrysanthemums, and blue cornflowers. The city's officials agreed that a tribute from the Chief Executive took precedence over all others, and they put it at the head of Mitrione's coffin. A wreath of white carnations from the Secretary of State was set to one side.

Around Richmond, Indiana, people were still stunned by the calamity in Uruguay. Only three days had passed since the news of Dan's murder first reached them; and now, as though by miracle, his body was back from South America and on display in the lobby of the new Municipal Building. Hundreds, thousands, of the men and women who had known Dan were lining up, many with their children, to pay their last respects.

On reaching the head of the line, however, the mourners found that they could not see the body. The Uruguayan government had tried to demonstrate its profound regret by returning Dan's body sealed in a beautifully carved antique coffin.

But Henrietta, the widow, asked for another casket,

something made at home. Dan's brother Ray, who wanted very much to oblige her, went to the funeral directors and spoke to them about his sister-in-law's wishes. While the morticians agreed to make the change, they requested that someone from the family be present when the old coffin was unsealed. Ray asked his older brother, Dominic, to be the witness, but Dom refused.

So it was Ray who stood by, dreading the ordeal, as they pried open the lid. Inside was yet another coffin, this one of heavy metal. The funeral directors had already sent over to a neighborhood casket maker for a coffin—Richmond had once been a center of the coffin industry—and now they asked also for the loan of a hacksaw.

All the while, they were warning Ray that because his brother's body had not been embalmed in Montevideo, the opening of this inner box was apt to be extremely disagreeable. Reluctantly, Ray took that information back to Henrietta; everyone had always called her Hank. Today, though she looked tense and drawn, she was bearing up remarkably well after ten days of waiting and then the long flight from Montevideo. She listened to Ray's explanation and said that they should just forget the whole thing.

Meanwhile, late word had come from Geneva, Switzerland, that Father Robert Minton was on his way home and would arrive in time to conduct the funeral. The family had never doubted that, if they could only reach him, the priest would cut short his vacation to say a final mass for Dan.

Dan's murder had also brought Ray back early from a vacation, and his isolation upstate at Lake Chapman explained why he had been just about the last one in the family to hear the news about his favorite brother. Like many bachelors, Ray turned on his radio each morning as soon as he woke up. But on that particular morning, he had glanced out the window of his cabin and seen his Chrysler listing in the yard.

That flat tire distracted him for the next hour. Afterward, he wondered why no one around the gas station at the crossroads had told him the news. Either they had not heard it themselves or they did not connect it with Ray. That would be understandable. He had bought his cabin only a few months earlier, and had been urging his brothers to make the cabin their retreat too. Dom could come up for his days off from his work as a greenskeeper, and Dan would relax there when he came back on leave from his government job down in South America.

Around Richmond, men who did not know the brothers very well said that both in temperament and looks, Ray, who was forty-two years old that summer of 1970, was a lot like Dan, who was eight years older. To Ray, such a claim would have verged on sacrilege, and he never made it for himself. He was just pleased that when Dan came back home and looked over Ray's wardrobe, he would think enough of a sports jacket or a necktie to wink and walk off with it.

The flat tire fixed at last, Ray headed back to his cabin. He was sorry to think that this was the last day of July and his vacation was already half gone. Possibly he did not guess that there were people in Richmond who asked one another why Ray Mitrione needed a vacation. What Ray deemed a job struck them as little more than a paid hobby.

Every Monday morning, Ray loaded up a station wagon with sports equipment and set off cruising around Wayne County to call on his friends who coached at different high schools. Between the joshing and the speculation over the coming games, Ray took orders for footballs and baseball gloves. Nights and weekends, he relaxed by refereeing at basketball games around the county, a form of moonlighting that had made him a minor celebrity.

If his two jobs meant that nearly everybody knew Ray, his manner insured that they would like him. The worst anyone could say was that he was just an overgrown kid, and why should anyone take offense at that?

In the last year, his thatch of black hair might have gone

a bit gray, and his body was decidedly thickening. But his smile was nearly as broad as his beam, and from behind black-rimmed glasses, Ray's ruddy round face shone on his corner of Indiana like a Wabash moon.

Ray did not have a telephone at the cabin, but as he pulled into his yard, he found his neighbors waiting to flag him down. His sister Rosemary had called, they said. Long distance from Richmond.

Ray first thought of his mother. Maria Mitrione was seventy-seven. In the years following her husband's death, she and Ray had lived together. When she started needing more care, she moved in with Rosemary and her husband, Dick Parker. Then, last March, Maria's condition had worsened, and the family had no choice but to put her in a nursing home. The doctors diagnosed Parkinson's disease. Ray had his own opinion: after a lifetime of hard work, his mother's body had just worn out.

Ray said something to the neighbors about his mother, but they reassured him on that score. The message had specified that there was no emergency, that Ray was not to worry; but he should call Richmond right away.

When Ray got through to Rosemary, she asked him, "You haven't heard about Dan?"

As she spoke, Rosemary was dazed. She had first received a call from Dom's wife, passing along what a man from the State Department had said. Rosemary could not believe it, and she called Washington herself for confirmation.

For the moment, Ray was still more curious than alarmed. "No," he said, "I haven't heard a thing. What about Dan?"

"Dan's been kidnapped."

Usually the drive south to Richmond took Ray three hours. Today, pushing hard, he bent the speeding law and burst into Kessler's Sporting Goods store sooner, desperate for details.

Before Ray got there, a clerk had taken a call from a radio station in one of the big cities near Richmond—Indianapolis to the west or Dayton over the Ohio line. The newsman had reported that Dan had been murdered, but he had already retracted the story by the time Ray got home. Not that Ray would have believed it. Dan did not have an enemy on earth.

But then Ray knew very little about his brother's life since Dan had resigned as Richmond's chief of police. He knew that Dan had been in Uruguay these past thirteen months, advising the country's police force. Now it appeared that a band of thugs or Communists in the capital city of Montevideo had kidnapped Dan that morning on his way to work.

Ray began trading information with the newsmen who called for background material on his brother. Until today, Ray had never realized how many reporters there were in the world; and between taking calls from New York and Chicago, he was trying to help the local boys put together their story, around the corner at Richmond's own daily, the *Palladium-Item*.

As the radio bombardment went on through the afternoon, Ray got accustomed to hearing the family name mispronounced. Every announcer sounded the final *e*—Mit-tree-own-nee—instead of leaving it silent, as his parents had done. The radio's way sounded more Italian, more foreign. Ray learned, too, that his brother's abductors called themselves Tupamaros, another name strange to his ear. Thinking over their last talk together when Dan was home in the spring, Ray was sure his brother had never mentioned the group.

In his entire life, Ray could remember meeting only one Uruguayan, and that was just about a year ago. A clean-cut, well-dressed fellow—suit and tie in the middle of Indian summer—had come into Kessler's and introduced himself as Billy Rial. He was visiting his sister, Rial explained. She had married a teacher from Centerville, down the road. He had heard that Ray's brother was working in

Montevideo, and Rial wanted to leave his address. The next time Ray wrote, he should tell his brother that he would be welcome any time he stopped by. In all, a pleasant and mannerly young man.

Ray thought again about their mother at the Heritage Nursing Home. Frail as she was, the shock of hearing the news could carry her off. But he checked and found that the nurses had anticipated this possibility; they were turning off the radio at the start of each news bulletin.

A newsboy delivered the *Pal-Item* to the nursing home but that mattered less, since Maria Mitrione could neither read nor write. In times past, her family had regretted that she had never learned. Today Ray took it as one more sign that the Good Lord looked after his own. Overnight, their mother's handicap had become a blessing.

Their father, Joseph Mitrione, had been born in the village of Bisaccia, sixty miles southeast of Naples. He had gone through the fifth grade before being sent out to work in the vineyards of Avelino province. When his bride, Maria Arincello, joined him in the fields, she had never been to school.

Because Joseph Mitrione had been working in the vineyards, when he decided to gamble on a trip to the United States, he thought first of California. With the Napa Valley as his goal, he set forth not long after the birth, on August 4, 1920, of his third surviving child and second son. The family would follow afterward. Once in the United States, Joseph changed his plans. From a relative in Indiana, he heard that the Pennsylvania Railroad was hiring men in Richmond, and he decided that picking grapes in central California held little more promise than picking grapes in the south of Italy. The railroad meant industry, development, the future.

Summoned to join her husband, Maria arrived in New York, a twenty-eight-year-old immigrant, with a little daughter, Anna, a younger son, Dominic, and a baby. In their first concession to the new culture, the Mitriones

Anglicized the baby's name to Daniel Anthony Mitrione.

Over her child-bearing years, Maria was pregnant four-teen times. Eight children either were miscarried or died in infancy. The other six lived, and sometimes they inherited a name: before Ray, there had been another baby Ray-mond, and another baby Josephine before the Josie who survived.

Although she had left a twin sister behind in Italy, Maria never showed an interest in going home. To go back, she said, to see the poverty again, knowing that she would soon be escaping for a second time to America, would be too cruel, for herself as well as for her relatives.

Economic considerations had dictated where Joseph Mitrione's family would settle, and their new life in Indiana was far removed from anything Italy had prepared them for. The community of Richmond, Indiana, had been set-tled in 1805 by soldiers of George Rogers Clark, the Revo-lutionary general and brother of the Northwest explorer. But it was a band of Quakers who gave the town its distinc-tive character by establishing in Richmond the Friends Boarding School—later Earlham College—an institution pledged to oppose all war and oppression.

After the Quakers, it was the German migration of the mid-nineteenth century that came to the midwestern tun-dra. Eighty years later, when the Italians began to arrive in force, they found the banks and department stores in com-petent, if not notably cordial, Teutonic hands.

But the land itself was marvelously hospitable. From New York to the Rocky Mountains, the United States had annexed a vast plain capable of feeding a nation, a hemi-sphere; if necessary, a world. Indiana was one of the states marked out across that rich soil. Yet the same sweeping horizon that made life fruitful for the farmers could prove less nourishing to the spirit. The broad, empty spaces that yielded corn and wheat in such abundance rarely seemed to liberate the people who settled there. Instead, the very unbroken low edge to the sky could cramp the better part

of them. Abraham Lincoln spent his rail-splitting years in
Indiana, and he called it "as unpoetical as any spot on
earth." Lincoln tried all the same to fashion a poem out of
his feelings about returning there:

> I range the field with pensive tread
> And pace the hollow rooms;
> And feel (companion of the dead)
> I'm living in the tombs.

More than a hundred years later, Father Robert Minton
was sent to found a Catholic parish in Richmond. In his
younger years, he had traveled the world; as he surveyed
Indiana's limitless vista, he asked himself whether any man
who had seen a mountain or the sea could ever be happy
there.

Not only could this ocean of solid land leave a man
feeling both strangled and stripped bare, but if the newcomer had grown up in a gentler climate, he learned
quickly that the weather would be an enemy for the rest
of his life. Against the raw winter wind and summer sun,
the farmer raised thick roofs and stayed beneath them.
Every planting and harvest, every journey out and trip
home, was at the mercy of the wet snow or searing heat,
and so a midwesterner learned to calculate his life, to avoid
whim or sudden change. Nature had reserved for herself
the right to be capricious. It was only prudent for man to
be steady and long-headed.

Endured long enough, that necessity came to seem a
virtue. Booth Tarkington was already beloved for his stories of the impish Penrod when he stood up in the Indiana
State Legislature to oppose Franklin Roosevelt's New
Deal. Tarkington offered a testimony to the rigorous life:
"Hardship, it seems to me, is a part of life, a test and a
builder of character."

Other native daughters and sons rejected that lifelong
challenge. Leaving Indiana behind, they emerged from
their protective cocoons in a dazzling new guise. Irene

Dunne, from Madison, Indiana; Carol Lombard, from Fort Wayne; Clifton Webb, from Indianapolis; Cole Porter, from the town of Peru.

For those who stayed behind, the physical isolation, the distances between the farm and a meager cluster of shops, sometimes bred suspicion of any new arrivals, or fear and then intolerance. Writing about the time the Mitriones arrived in Richmond, Irving Cobb poked fun at the enthusiasm with which Hoosiers were embracing the Ku Klux Klan. Cobb claimed that the Klan had swept the state like a hurricane, that the situation had become so bad in some Indiana towns that there was hardly an extra sheet in case company came.

Richmond called itself the City of Roses; a botanist, E. Gurney Hill, had built thirty acres of hothouses that sent fresh roses across the entire country. But even half a million rose bushes near the city limits could not brighten Richmond itself. When one mayor printed on his official paper the slogan "Richmond the beautiful," residents took it for the wistful gesture it was.

Given the wariness and rancor of their new neighbors, Italian immigrants tended to group together near the railroad tracks on the north side of Richmond. Joseph Mitrione's children grew up in a section called Goosetown. Sixty years ago, a settlement's name could be both fond and derisive. Besides Goosetown, poor Hoosiers lived in communities called Needmore and Lickskillet.

Richmond's blacks also lived in Goosetown but south of Hibbard Street. There were more of them than there were Italians, and they were quiet and polite. Each Sunday on their way to 5 A.M. mass, Ray Mitrione and his mother passed groups of black men, Saturday-night revelers lingering on the street, sorry to see the dawn. They gave Ray no cause to be nervous as they cleared a path and greeted his mother respectfully. "Hello, there, Mrs. Mitrione! How are you today?"

The Mitriones' first house on North Twelfth Street was

in a neighborhood of clapboard sidings and tar-paper roofs, with every wall either gray or faded green. The house stood scarcely two blocks from the railroad loading platform; and even though more trash cans than trees lined the street, scrap still piled up in the gutters, and all that sparkled in the dusty front yards was the tin foil from gum wrappers.

But the elder Mitriones' feeling for nature and warm colors survived the drabness. Maria loved flowers and surrounded her house with them. During the time Ray was growing up, his father rented a vacant lot a mile away, and in the evenings the whole family would walk out to work in the vegetable garden.

If Ray's had been a temperament inclined to bitterness, it might have soured him that his father never once came out to watch his sons play ball. Joseph Mitrione preferred to spend the time in his garden. Part of that dedication may have been homesickness; more of it was the economic good sense of raising vegetables for a family of eight. He raised corn, hot mangoes and lettuce, potatoes and cabbage, tomatoes for canning, and always one row of garlic for Maria's cooking.

Ray's father also had a winter refuge. Down the street on North Twelfth was the Italian Club, and there Joseph Mitrione retired every Saturday and immediately after Sunday mass. The members were fellow immigrants; the language and practices, exclusively Italian. The Mitrione boys hung around the club and, when they were old enough, became members. With the club and the family talk at home, they all grew up speaking Italian before they learned English.

The clubhouse was one unpretentious room with a small bar at the rear. In the basement a shower was available to members who did not have a bathroom at home.

Italian Club members worked late. They all had big families. If they saw each other on a week night, it was liable to be at a funeral home, paying respects to someone's infant daughter or aged parent. But each weekend, they gathered faithfully to drink beer and play cards. The winner became the club's padrone, the man to decide who got a bottle of beer.

The men worked with their hands. At Dille-McGuire they made lawn mowers. At International Harvester, they ran lathes and key punches and turned out cream separators and tractors. Joseph Mitrione worked a punch for I-H.

One day he came home early. He had lost a finger in his machine. Whatever the doctor had been able to do for him had not eased his suffering. Ray and the other children listened, horrified at the groans, and never forgot his misery.

The life of his children would be better. To fulfill that promise the young Mitriones were sent to a school to be Americanized in classes where English was the language and British law and custom were the rule. If some Italian children came out still talking a bit louder than Richmond thought appropriate or gesturing too expansively with their hands, the schools were not to blame.

With Dan Mitrione, the transformation seemed efficient and painless. He spent his first eight years at St. Mary's Elementary School, under the charge of a band of nuns who could wield a knitting needle until the knuckles stung. It was a Catholic education, and a good one. Teachers at Test Junior High School said the students from St. Mary's arrived better prepared than pupils from the public schools.

But it was not an Italian education. At Morton High, Dan was playing football, not soccer, and he was preening himself in a way no village boy in Bisaccia could afford. Lamenting more than complaining, their mother told Ray how Dan demanded a shirt freshly washed and pressed for every school day. He wanted to look just right, and with his stocky body and dark good looks, he usually did.

Morton's football team was made up of strong, willing, and mediocre players, boys like Dan, who played guard.

For them, it had to be a game for its own sake. There were no scouts watching, no athletic scholarships to crown a winning season. Dan's one tangible reward was his photograph in the high school yearbook, with the caption: "Our tall, dark and handsome football hero."

Since the patterns of American life were strange to his parents, Dan tended to take over for his father with Ray. Parents of the elder Mitriones' generation respected authority; they were aghast to hear that any child of theirs talked back to a teacher. If a neighborhood boy pocketed a candy bar, he was headed for a life of crime. So while Ray heard his mother threaten, "Wait till your father gets home," it was Dan who usually dispensed justice. Ray, idolizing his brother and modeling himself on Dan as best he could, accepted those spankings, thrilled that if he had to be spanked, it was Dan who was doing it.

When his high school days came to an end, Dan may have given a thought to college. He had been only an average student, but conscientious and disciplined. Some of his classmates were heading for Indiana University with no better qualifications except that their fathers could afford to send them. Instead, Dan went to work at International Harvester.

A year passed. Anyone might have predicted that Dan Mitrione was firmly launched on the path his father had laid down for him in the new country. Dan would marry an Italian girl from the neighborhood; he would work at a machine until the day he retired. If he profited from his father's misfortune and stayed alert, he would not lose a finger. Otherwise, that was the die that Dan seemed cast to fit.

But his future proved very different. The new year brought the Second World War and, in Richmond as throughout the country, young men flocked to enlist in the armed services, impelled by patriotism, joblessness, or a sense that this could be their deliverance.

A Hoosier named Ross Lockridge, Jr., spoke for generations of those men in a novel set in a mythical section of Indiana—Raintree County. One of his male characters, Lockridge wrote, "was bounded by a box, the country, inside a box, the state, inside a box inside a box inside a box. . . ." To trapped men, the worst that war could do was to send them home in one last pine box. Catching the national mood, Dan Mitrione joined the navy.

Indiana's recruits did their duty. Typical was Tommy Clayton, whose actions were written by a neighbor, Ernie Pyle, of Dana, Indiana. Clayton, the mildest of men, had killed four of the enemy for sure and probably dozens more that he could not account for. And through the carnage, Pyle said, Tommy remained just a plain old Hoosier.

Reading every day of such heroism, the men not called upon to fight could feel, depending on their characters, lucky, guilty, or cheated. Dan apparently felt cheated. Years later, when he was sent to Latin America, he said that his belated duty overseas might make up for missing action during the war.

He served out his time at a naval base in Grosse Ile, Michigan, tame duty compared to the adventures of other young men from Richmond, but significant enough to consolidate the change in his fate.

He had worked his way to the verge of promotion to chief when peace was declared, and along the way he had been assigned as sergeant of the guards. It was his first taste of patrolling, and he took to the duty naturally. Growing up in a stern Italian home had prepared him for discipline. Now government directives, not simply a personal need, demanded that he follow the rules and devote minute attention to his dress and grooming. It would be another year or two before he knew it, but Dan had found his career.

And in the nearby Michigan town of Wyandotte, he also found his wife. He asked Henrietta Lind to marry him, and she accepted. The marriage was held in Richmond. To the elder Mitriones, nothing was said about Hank Lind having just converted to Catholicism. There were concessions to life in the United States that a dutiful son could spare an Old World family.

In Goosetown, opinion divided over Hank Mitrione, and hometown girls who had fancied Dan could be excused a touch of malice. But she was a serious girl, and Dan, for all his surface pleasantry, was a sober man. Hank worshipped her new husband: the Protestant gentry around town granted that much, even when later they scorned her obedience to her new church and complained that Hank Mitrione had kids like a cat had kittens.

A cruel observation with some truth to it. Eleven months after the wedding, Hank produced one daughter. By the time the war ended eighteen months later, she was pregnant with another. The pattern held over much of the next twenty years, until Hank had given her husband nine children.

When he was discharged from the navy, Dan had for the moment no better thought than to return to International Harvester. He moved his new family into his parents' frame house on East Twenty-first Street. By now they had escaped the railroad tracks and were living near a large park.

On the first day of December 1945, Dan went to police headquarters and filled out an application to join the force. One of the top lines asked for the candidate's political affiliation. Boldly or ignorantly, Dan wrote Democrat.

Later, like most patrolmen, he changed his registration to Republican. But just as he had shielded his parents from learning that Hank had been born outside their faith, he also kept this news from his father. Seeing his son don a police uniform had brought Joseph Mitrione great pride, and there was no point in clouding his pleasure.

In the style of the day, the form asked other bald questions: "White or Colored?" Dan checked white. "Read?" Dan wrote yes. "Write?" He wrote yes again. On the appropriate lines, he listed his past employment, the names of his two children, his Italian birthplace, and his one ailment —the repair, five years earlier, of a left internal hernia.

He was hired, accepted as one of Richmond's finest. Police forces in Indiana might be notoriously underpaid and boneyards for inept political appointees. Those drawbacks could not stop Patrolman Mitrione from going out on the street each day to give the job his professional best. He would treat the police as an extension of the navy and do his duty. To be his partner, Dan drew an easy-going cop named Orville Conyers.

Given his coloring, his dark-red hair and flushed red cheeks, Conyers was destined never to be called by his Christian name. Red was five years older than his new partner. Assigned to ride in the same squad car in 1946, Red and Dan were partners for thirty months and friends long afterward.

By big-city standards, their duty was undemanding— drunk drivers to book, breaking and entering cases to investigate. Richmond did not have a dog warden in those days, and a patrolman sometimes had to shoot a stray dog. It was the one use the average cop had for his Colt .38 special.

For Red, their most dangerous calls were those times they would be sent out to quiet a family squabble. It was worse when the trouble came from the north side of town. They would enter the house, Red glad to have such a solidly built partner, and whatever the couple's complaints they could usually resolve them and get out by repeating, "Just settle down now, just settle down."

Sometimes a man or his wife might say, "You're here only because I'm Negro." That was Red's cue to say, "I don't care what color you are. Just calm down."

It was the era of easy G. I. mortgages for $6500 bungalows and hamburger at three pounds for a dollar; yet Red and Dan found it hard to raise their families on something less than $180 per month and felt compelled to moonlight.

Off hours, they went down to Dille-McGuire and loaded lawn mowers onto the railroad siding. They also cultivated such private patrons as the manager at Sears, who would let them wash his car during the day so that it would be dry and ready for simonizing at night. For a three-hour waxing chore, Dan and Red picked up nine dollars apiece.

Throughout the time Dan was washing other people's cars, he could not afford one of his own. When he pulled the night shift, and there were no buses and not enough traffic so he could hitch a ride, he would set out from the south end of town hunched down in his leather coat, the temperature at zero, and walk the two miles to headquarters.

The days following the kidnapping kept Ray feverishly excited. In deference to the throng of television cameras and photographers, Ray wore a suit every day, and that was strange for him. The family had expected Dan to dress up but not Ray. Years ago, Ray had come home wearing a Stetson, and his mother had mistaken him for Dan. Now he was temporarily out of his sports clothes and possibly the change touched a chord in his mother's memory, for when he visited her at the nursing home, she asked, "Have you heard from Dan?"

Ray said, "Oh, yeah, Mom. Just the other day."

"Well, say hello for me when you answer him."

It pained Ray to lie to his mother, and he may not have been good at it, for two days later, with the biggest *Pal-Item* headlines still about Dan's abduction, Maria Mitrione asked again, "Have you answered Dan yet?" And then, "Is something wrong with Dan?"

For Ray and the rest of his family, it was a time of helplessness. The Tupamaros had announced that they would free their kidnap victims, Dan and the Brazilian vice-consul in Montevideo, only after the Uruguayan government had released its 150 political prisoners.

From the news accounts, Washington and Brasília were each pressing Uruguay to make the trade. But the president down there, a man named Jorge Pacheco Areco, seemed to be stubborn. He was quoted as saying he would never negotiate with criminals.

Yet there were hopeful signs. Representatives of the Vatican in Uruguay were trying to start negotiations to free Dan. Ray also received a call from a man who identified himself as Cesar Bernal. Bernal said he had been an associate of Dan's in Uruguay, and he spoke lightly about the Tupamaros. From spending four years in Montevideo, he knew them like a book, he said, and they were not bad people. That was the phrase Ray remembered, "not bad people."

In addition, the newspapers sometimes recounted the fate of other kidnap victims, particularly in Brazil, where the U. S. ambassador had been seized and sequestered until the Brazilian government agreed to exactly the sort of swap the Tupamaros were demanding. That ambassador—his name was Charles Burke Elbrick—had been released with nothing worse than a bruised skull.

The family knew that Dan's condition had to be more serious than that. Wire services reported that he had been shot during his capture; a communiqué from the Tupamaros said the bullet had entered his upper right chest and gone out through his right armpit. At the State Department, a spokesman protested that by not getting Dan to a hospital, the Tupamaros had "magnified the inhumanity of the act."

But the Tupamaro bulletin had been couched in medical language and specified that no vital organ had been damaged. It sounded as though Dan might be suffering some discomfort but would survive.

When the *Pal-Item* commented that Dan's kidnapping was unbelievable, it was one of the rare times Andrew

Cecere could agree with an editorial. Unlike the Mitrione boys, Cecere had chosen to live in Richmond; he had not been raised in Goosetown. Perhaps that was why he, among the Italian-American community, had been the one to challenge Richmond's old-line politics.

Stocky and frizzy-haired, outgoing and amiable enough to star in productions at the local little theater, Cecere graduated from law school at the University of Michigan, served in the marines, and settled in Richmond in 1949. The Italians accepted him readily. He was invited to the club-house on the north end, where he played cards and met a lot of Italians his own age. One was a young cop, Dan Mitrione.

But the powerful men, the wealthy and conservative leadership of the town, were not interested in one more ambitious young Italian who had forsaken his native Pitts-burgh to dwell among them. After two years of practicing law and another tour of duty in the Marine Corps, Cecere came back to Richmond in 1953, in a fighting mood.

By then he knew who ran the town. It was a short list. Hill of Hill Floral Products; McGuire of Dille-McGuire; Lontz, who had sold the local telephone company to General Telephone; Rudolph Leeds, the publisher of the *Palladium-Item*. Those men shopped for a public official as they might hire a caretaker for their estates. Of the qualities they esteemed in a public servant, an independent mind ranked at the bottom. When Andy Cecere made his assault, the occupant of the mayor's office was Lester Meadows, a barber.

In 1955, Mayor Meadows announced that he would be laying down the burdens of public office, and the down-town businessmen chose a florist as their candidate. Cecere, who had become city chairman for the Democratic party, saw his chance and encouraged the Democrats to pick, for the second time, Roland Cutter, an insurance man from a family sufficiently old and respectable to have made a strong showing against Meadows four years earlier.

Cecere knew the Democrats had to overcome years of lethargy and outright intimidation. Around Rudy Leeds's *Pal-Item*, very few employees had the courage on election day to ask for a Democratic ballot. They voted Republican or they stayed home. The hearts of policemen like Dan Mitrione might be with the new Democratic coalition, but when Cecere thought about it at all he assumed that in the last presidential election Dan had voted for Eisenhower over Stevenson.

This year, Cecere's coalition took hold. The schoolteachers joined. Labor was showing an unexpected militancy. At the International Harvester plant, organizers for the United Auto Workers were ready to challenge the city's anti-labor policies, which had guaranteed for years that during any strike the pickets would clash with a line of truculent cops.

Three days before the election, the sitting mayor made labor the central issue. He endorsed the entire Republican slate on the grounds that "none of the Republican candidates are obligated in such a way as to prevent them from preserving 'law and order' when and if in labor disputes the need arises." That candor, together with Cecere's organizing efforts, led the Democrats to a victory that even the *Pal-Item* called smashing. Cutter beat the Republican candidate by nearly two to one and became the first Democratic mayor in twenty years. To reward Cecere, the new mayor appointed him city attorney.

Sometime later, an old-timer cornered Cecere and asked him plaintively how it could happen that foreigners came in and took over the town. By that time, Andy Cecere was not offended. He laughed and said, "There's been such a void in Richmond that even somebody like me looked good."

Other times, speaking before a civic group, the new city attorney tried to explain what he felt about being part of a minority. The United States was a colossus, Cecere would say. It had great biceps and bulging thighs.

But, he would add, it was we Italians who gave that giant a heart.

A week had passed with no yielding on either side. For Dan's brothers and sisters, it was becoming harder to believe that this horror could end with his being restored to them. News accounts made it sound as though the Uruguayan government was putting hundreds of suspects in jail. But President Pacheco went on refusing to free the original 150 Tupamaro prisoners, and only their release could save Dan.

In Richmond, they had proof that Dan himself wanted the United States to act on his behalf. The editors from the *Pal-Item* called Ray, and he went to the newsroom to inspect a facsimile that had come over the wire, a note from Dan to Hank. Ray looked it over and said there was no doubt that the handwriting was his brother's.

The note had been found after a Tupamaro called a newspaper reporter in Montevideo and told him to look around the toilet of a bar in the center of the city. There, taped to the tank, he found this message:

> Dearest Henrietta,
>   I am recovering from the wound I received when I was taken. Please tell the ambassador to do everything possible to liberate me as soon as possible.
>   I have been and am still being interrogated deeply about the AID program and the police.
>   I send all my love to you and the children.
> Love ya,
Dan

In view of that appeal, the wire stories speculated that President Pacheco would now declare a general amnesty for the political prisoners. But another day passed, and still the Uruguayan government did nothing. In Richmond, Ray and his family knew that their nerves were raw. There was, however, a worse effect to the delay: the kidnappers were giving signs that their patience had run out. In a note delivered to a Montevideo radio station, the Tupamaros said they would wait until midnight Friday, August 7, for the authorities to announce the release of their comrades. "If there is no official announcement by then, we shall terminate this affair and do justice."

The Associated Press reported that it was not clear whether the last sentence constituted a threat; but in Richmond they understood plain talk, and they could not read it any other way.

By the weekend, there was a feeling throughout Richmond that events in Uruguay were now out of control. A new note from the Tupamaros accused Dan of being a spy for the United States. If the family had not been so apprehensive, that far-fetched charge might have left them indignant. The message continued: "He is representative of a power that has massacred entire populations in Vietnam, Santo Domingo and other places." Then came the explicit threat the family had been dreading. Unless the Uruguayan government agreed to release its prisoners, Dan would be killed at noon on Sunday.

The deadline came and went. No prisoners were released. The Tupamaros issued no further communiqué.

At about 4:30 A.M. Monday, Ray's telephone rang in his apartment above Kessler's. It was a UPI reporter from Indianapolis. He had spoken with Ray on Sunday, and Ray had asked him to call back the minute the bureau got any news.

"We just heard," the reporter said. "They found his body in the north part of Montevideo."

"Is it confirmed?" Over the past week, Ray had had his fill of rumor and speculation.

"Not yet. Do you want to make a statement?"

Maybe it wasn't true. Maybe it was propaganda. Maybe they had killed someone else. "I have nothing to say at this time."

Ten minutes later, a call came through from David Dennis, the congressman from Ray's district, who had been solicitous throughout the ordeal. "Have you heard about Dan?"

"Well," said Ray, "it wasn't confirmed."

"I'm confirming it, Ray."

With good reason, Roland Cutter believed that he had launched Dan Mitrione on the career that would end at St. Mary's Catholic Cemetery. Until this past week, the part he had played was a matter of pride to him—and some puzzlement—as he watched Dan use the helping hand Cutter had extended to him to pull himself nearly to Cutter's level and then out of Richmond altogether.

Cutter's grandfather had come to Richmond from Germany in the last century. Henry Cutter had spoken no English, but he learned the names for different foods and opened a grocery. Roland Cutter had inherited a burgher's face, to which he added a dapper mustache. After Indiana State, he returned to Richmond to settle into the insurance business.

Cutter was one of those men—the parish priest, Father Minton, was another—who admired the way the Italians over on the north end raised their children. For years, Cutter had seen Dan around town, always neat and well-behaved, and he knew that the young man had come out of the tradition that what Poppa says, goes.

In recent years, two Italians had won seats on the city council, and they had proved to be so patriotic that their oratory could be shaming to the third- and fourth-generation Americans. Cutter and his friends used to agree that some of those Italians appreciated their country more than they did.

In 1955, when Andy Cecere's coalition put Cutter in office, the new mayor prided himself on being politically naïve, and he would say that he did not know a precinct from a bale of hay. A week or two after the election, Cutter was down on the Indiana University campus, visiting a son at the Delta Epsilon house, and it was weighing on him that he would soon have to name a fire chief and a chief of police.

Although it was Sunday, the new mayor went to the university's School of Police Administration. He found the director in his office and appealed to him: How do you go about picking a police chief, anyway? The director thought Cutter was joking. In Indiana, chief of police was a prime patronage job. Until wealthy men ran out of indolent nephews, there would be no need to ask for the university's help in filling the post.

When he was convinced that Cutter was serious, the director dispatched a team of researchers to Richmond. The mayor rented a hotel room, and the university staff called every member of the force to the room for aptitude tests. Some men grumbled that many of the tests seemed far afield from police work, and in his heart, the mayor agreed. But he continued to support the mysterious method, counting on it to produce the very model of a modern police chief.

The team first gave Cutter advice about the kind of chief he did not want. You're not looking for a so-called brave cop, they kept repeating. You don't want to name a great hero. Remember that the chief's job is administrative.

Then, after all the suspense, and to a reaction from the other cops that ranged from surprise to outrage, the team nominated a young juvenile officer with barely ten years' experience on the force. Mayor Cutter appointed him.

The new chief was no hero, nor did he pretend to be. He was, however, the first scientifically selected professional chief of police Richmond had ever had, and he would amply vindicate the mayor's faith in the process that chose him. Yet Roland Cutter could never help but think of his chief, fondly, as little Danny Mitrione, the Italian boy from Goosetown.

. . .

After the strange official silence while Dan was alive, his murder seemed to have triggered a thousand mimeograph machines in Washington, D. C. Public officials were queuing up to denounce the Tupamaros. Some of them even remembered to send condolences to the Mitrione family.

The two highest-ranking responses did not come from men but from buildings. "The White House said Monday," began an Associated Press account, "the kidnap-murder of U. S. official Daniel A. Mitrione in Uruguay is 'a despicable act that will be condemned by men of decency and honor everywhere.' " The Vatican, in an unsigned article on the front page of *L'Osservatore Romano*, condemned crimes committed in the name of fanatical ideologies. Pope Paul VI a day earlier had called all political kidnappings "vile."

The political figure to speak at greatest length on the killing was House Minority Leader Gerald Ford, of Michigan. Although the murder had led some voices to suggest that the United States should not be engaged in the activities that had taken Dan to Uruguay, Ford took the murder as proof of how important it was for the United States to persevere. Ford also expressed confidence that the Uruguayan government had done all in its power to obtain Dan's release. On the U. S. side, Ford singled out for special commendation Dan's boss, Byron Engle, the director of the Office of Public Safety.

Louis Gibbs owed his job to Dan Mitrione and, he realized on a day like this, much more. Gibbs had applied to the police force six times, and each time when he had come to the line at the upper right corner of the form that asked his political affiliation he had left it blank. Someone in the department was not appeased by his reticence. Six times Gibbs was rejected.

In April 1956, on Gibbs' seventh application, the new chief summoned him to his office. Mitrione's doubts about the young applicant were not political, only economic. Working as a meat cutter, Gibbs made $9,000 a year. A patrolman's salary was little better than half of that.

Mitrione asked him, "Are you sure you want to join the force? You know you're making more than I am."

After seven applications, Gibbs was sure. His application was approved.

Until Mitrione took office, experienced officers in Richmond had trained their new colleagues with a casual apprenticeship. The rookie got in the back seat of a patrol car, and the two veterans in front told him: Keep your ears open and your eyes open and your mouth shut. But the chief had benefited from a modern approach to police science, and he wanted to extend that advantage to his department. Mitrione himself had overcome some resistance on the city council to go off to the FBI training program in Washington. Back home, he arranged for Indiana University to offer recruits a six-week training course on its campus.

After his training, Gibbs found that life for patrolmen under the new chief was rigorous. From the start, the older men had not liked Mitrione, but then they had been passed over for his job. Gibbs granted that the chief was tough. There was only one way to do things: his way. But in a showdown, Gibbs and the other new recruits decided that the chief was usually right.

Mitrione told his troops frankly, "That door swings in and it swings out. You either play the game or you don't play at all." Sometimes an older cop got drunk on duty or would be caught out carousing. The chief was hard-nosed. "Sign this resignation and get out."

Later, the policemen started to negotiate their contracts through the Fraternal Order of Police, and an offending officer was guaranteed a formal hearing. Although in his day, Mitrione held absolute power over his men, he

strained to use that power fairly. Once Gibbs was patrolling with a partner who outranked him, a sergeant, when
they captured a man who had held up a gas station. The
tip said the robber was carrying two guns, and the sergeant
kept slapping the man, trying to find out where he had
hidden them. When Gibbs could take no more, he said,
"You hit that man once more and you'll have to hit me."

Humane motive or not, Gibbs knew that he was being
insubordinate, and he was not surprised to be summoned to
the chief's office.

"You were right," Mitrione told him, "and you were
wrong. You were right about the slapping. But never talk
that way again to a piece of brass."

Another reprimand even less equivocal came after a Sunday night call: a complaint from a black neighborhood
about a drunken girl. Trying to subdue her, Gibbs slapped
her hands, her head. He had not yet returned from the
women's jail when the complaint reached the chief. Mitrione decided from the sound of it that Gibbs had used too
much force. Take care of him, the chief told the captain
on duty. Get him cooled down.

Although in those days most Richmond cops carried a
blackjack, Mitrione dissuaded young Gibbs from taking
one out on his beat. "You don't need it," the chief said.
"You're young. You don't know your own strength."

Most of the time the patrolmen, especially those the
chief had hired, did not worry about displeasing him. They
had come to understand his quirks and aversions. Trim and
neat himself, he expected his officers to look equally pre-
sentable. Around headquarters, appearance was important.

One experience Gibbs would never forget occurred at
2 A.M. on a rainy night. Calling in from his beat, Gibbs was
told to hurry over to a certain room at the hotel. He got
to the corner, saw the chief's blue car at the curb, and
thought, It's a raid! What else could it be on a night like
this?

Gibbs charged upstairs, his wet shoes squishing, and

found Mitrione conducting a surprise inspection for the third shift. Citizens who see patrolmen on the midnight trick, the chief was saying, pay the same taxes as everybody else. They deserve to see neat, clean officers.

Below their raincoats, every cop was soaked—trousers, socks, shoes. But when they unbuttoned those coats, the chief expected them to be sharp from the knees up. Gibbs passed the test. But Mitrione caught one man with a faulty weapon and sent him home.

The rules could be bent but only in a good cause. One year Richmond experienced what it regarded as a juvenile crime wave. It was during the late fifties—the advent of the curled lip, duck-tail haircuts, and rock 'n' roll—and the elder citizens did not like the way teenagers were scoffing at the law by staying out after curfew. Some minors were drinking beer, others stood on corners and yelled offensive remarks after the cars of older drivers. A couple of stores were broken into, and a few dollars taken from the cash drawers.

Mitrione knew the respectable people of town were looking to him for action. He went to Mayor Cutter. "I may make some people mad, but I can clean this thing up."

"Go ahead," said the mayor.

Over the next weeks, the police rousted groups of teenagers wherever they congregated. When the curfew sounded, they ran stragglers into headquarters and called their parents. The teenage nuisance abated. Stern but fair, the chief himself was a model parent. If other fathers shirked their obligations, then it was up to the police to demonstrate how children should be handled.

Ray's first impulse after Dan's murder had been to fly to Montevideo and help bring Hank and the youngest children home; however, the State Department reassured him that all was being taken care of. Dan's four oldest daughters and sons, who were living around Washington,

D. C., were flown to Uruguay to accompany their father's body and the rest of the family back to the United States.

The air-force jet carrying the family landed a little past 8 A.M. Wednesday morning, August 12, at the nearest jet strip to Richmond, Cox Municipal Airport in Dayton. City officials had planned to have Dan's body lie in state all day Thursday; but Hank, who had endured this tension for nearly two weeks, wanted the speediest possible end to it, and a day was cut off the period of mourning.

An honor guard, forty airmen from Wright-Patterson Air Force Base, used a hydraulic lift to bring the body down from the cargo hatch. Traveling at a solemn 45 miles per hour, they provided an escort for the ride back on I-70 to the interchange and along U. S. 27 into Richmond. State troopers from Indiana and Ohio joined the entourage, and police blocked the intersections, allowing the caravan to pass.

The procession pulled into the Stegall-Berheide-Orr Funeral Home, where, for two hours, Hank received Dan's family and friends. Part of the time John, her youngest, sat on her lap.

Hank had boarded the plane in Uruguay wearing a tweed coat as a shield against the August winter wind. In the humid heat of Richmond, she slipped it off, but the sunglasses remained, barely disguising the redness of her eyes.

By 1 P.M., Dan's body was lying in state at the new Municipal Building. Red Conyers was outside the building with a police guard that lowered the flag to half mast while thirty-three Boy Scouts stood at attention.

For six hours and fifteen minutes, Dan's coffin lay on display. According to the *Pal-Item*, nine thousand persons came to pay tribute, an expression of grief unmatched in Richmond's history. The pastor of Reid Memorial Presbyterian Church was among those who stopped by, and he told of the day Dan had come to address an ecumenical youth service. "At that time, Roman Catholic and Protestant relations were not very cordial," the clergyman recalled, "but I told him he was welcome to sit in on our service. Dan said, 'Give me a hymn book.' And he sang as lustily as anybody."

On Thursday morning, the homage and the public mourning reached their climax. Shortly before 10 A.M., Secretary of State William Rogers and his wife arrived at the Holy Family Parish together with the Uruguayan ambassador. President Nixon had also sent his son-in-law, David Eisenhower, who, uncharacteristically glum, tagged at the end of the official party.

A few minutes later the family arrived at the church, and the five hundred other worshipers took note of the dignitaries in their midst, gratified by the honor to Dan. Promptly at ten o'clock Father Minton appeared in vestments of red and gold, and the mass was under way.

That Father Robert Minton stood two inches over six feet tall may have contributed to his theory about the Italians in his parish. The priest had decided that with their round faces and their diminutive size, Italians—indeed, all small people—had a childlike way of looking at life. It was easier for them than for bigger people to believe that they were the children of God.

Father Minton did not mean to be patronizing, and he exempted men like Dan Mitrione who were only three or four inches shorter than he was. But along with many others in Richmond, he regarded the Italian community as a people apart. The Mitriones were definitely what Father Minton considered "good Italians." They went to church, paid their bills, and disciplined their children. The good Italians from the generation that produced Dan's father had a method that Father Minton thought American men envied: they taught their wives to love them and their children to obey them. Some of the rest—ah, they seemed to think that no matter what they did, God would understand.

Father Minton had founded the Holy Family Parish

seventeen years earlier. When he arrived in Richmond, the
town had felt strange to him. He had been a chaplain in
China during the war, an exciting time in his life, and he
found himself falling back on his memories. Tame or not,
the years passed. At parochial school, he began to get students whose fathers he had taught, and that gave his life a
stability, a continuity, that a professional bachelor like himself found warming. He was getting spoiled by the greet-
ings on the street. Everyone, even Protestants, knew him
and called out at the sight of him.

The people of his parish were much like Ray Mitrione,
simple and unspoiled. Among the five hundred families
at Holy Family there was only one professional man, a
dentist. Dan, however, had been different. In any community, Italian or not, he would have been considered
promising.

Dan had his faults, including that quick anger he had to
learn to control. But when he spoke before a service club
or the chamber of commerce, he left behind an impression
of competence without being in any way spellbinding or
giving his audience the feeling he was leagues ahead of
them.

Once—it was before Dan became chief, when he was
still a juvenile officer—he told a church group that the
United States was like a jigsaw puzzle: put all the pieces
in place, turn the puzzle over, and there on the back was
a boy, symbol of American youth. The imagery was not
Father Minton's style, but over the years he had remembered it.

Then Dan left Richmond for Belo Horizonte, beautiful
horizon. On his trips back, first from Brazil, then from
Uruguay, he seemed to be taking on with his years a new
urbanity. He came home fatter and grayer; in that he was
no different from other men. At the end of the visit, Dan
would bring to the rectory a box of the half-empty bottles
he had bought for entertaining his friends. The priest accepted the bottles gladly and took their exotic labels—

Cherry Heering and that coffee drink, Kahlúa—as further proof that travel was indeed doing Dan good.

It struck Father Minton that Dan might even have been developing a touch of charisma, one of those modish qualities that had emerged during the Kennedy years. Not, he thought, that Dan could compete with the Kennedys. Father Minton knew; he had met both Jack and Bobby when they came to town for a Jefferson-Jackson Day dinner in April of 1960. Those were the days before big motels had circled Richmond with their easy anonymity and lascivious billboards: TRY US ON FOR SIGHS. The Leland Hotel downtown was still the select gathering place, and Senator Kennedy met at the Leland with a band of local Democrats. Since Holy Family had the largest open space, the dinner was held there.

This was three months before Dan left for Brazil, and he was still police chief and charged with traffic control and the local security arrangements. Hank came to the church with the other parish women who had volunteered to serve the gala dinner. John F. Kennedy may have been no more than a senator, but he was marching resolutely toward his party's presidential nomination, and a thousand curious Democrats bought tickets.

While stumping Indiana, Jack had lost his voice. In the town of Seymour, he compensated by handing out cards on which was written: "Sorry, I have a sore throat and cannot talk, but please vote for me anyway." The senator's administrative assistant, Theodore C. Sorensen, read Kennedy's prepared address, an attack on the Soviet Union tailored to the conservatism of the farming community.

"For the first time in history," Sorensen read, as Kennedy stood mute at his side, "Russia has its long-sought political foothold in Latin America." He meant Cuba.

Later, at Earlham College, the senator's voice had come back sufficiently for him to read the prepared text himself. "We have been complacent, self-contented, easy-going. I think we can close the gaps and pull ahead. But we must not minimize the Red threat. We know from experience that we cannot rely on their word."

Ten years later, on the day of Dan's funeral, Father Minton could not remember the exact words Jack Kennedy had spoken at Holy Family, but their effect still lingered. As he had listened, he thought, If that man asked this audience to go up on the roof and jump off, they would do it. That was charisma.

The time had come for Father Minton to open the mass. He believed in funerals. They were occasions for the Catholic church to speak out, to affirm that the world is not everything, to say that Dan should not have been afraid to die, and wasn't.

Those were the thoughts Father Minton had been putting together since he received word in Geneva of the murder. He managed to say most of them, though three times he was so overcome that his parishoners wondered whether he would be able to go on.

The week after Dan had been buried in the shade of a silver maple in St. Mary's Cemetery, Ray was out of his business suit and back on the road in shirt sleeves. Returning to Kessler's late one afternoon, he got a message: "You're supposed to call the chamber of commerce office. Frank Sinatra wants to talk with you."

"Yeah," said Ray, "I'm sure of that."

But people were not yet back to joking much with the Mitriones. Ray went ahead and checked with the chamber. Be here tonight at 7:30 P.M., he was told. Ray followed instructions and took the call when it came from Frank Sinatra's agent.

Sinatra had read of the double tragedy—the murder, and the plight of a widow with five of her nine children left to raise on a government pension. The singer proposed flying to Richmond and sponsoring a benefit for the children's education. He had invited Jerry Lewis to join the show;

and along with his own nineteen-member stage band, he would bring a seven-piece rock group, Orange Colored Sky.

(Hank Mitrione got a similar call. Her temperament had always been less ingenuous than Ray's; she had been exposed for ten years to the machinations of federal bureaucracy and had lost her husband to a conspiracy. At 11 P.M., Hank called Dan's old boss, Byron Engle, to check out any hooks to Sinatra's offer.)

Sinatra's one free night was August 29, so despite the muggy summer heat and the people away on vacation, the concert was set for 9 P.M. that evening.

Tickets went on sale at the major banks, Kessler's, and Phillips Drug Store. Since the Civic Hall seated 4,200, tickets were also made available in Dayton, Cincinnati, and Indianapolis. Richmond High School's football jamboree had already been scheduled for the same night. Its time was moved forward an hour so that everyone could be at Civic Hall by nine o'clock.

Dan's kidnapping and murder had been crowding other news off the front page of the *Pal-Item* for nearly a month; the aftermath was covered on the *Pal-Item*'s inside pages, where the newspaper ran a series on the background of the Uruguayans who had murdered Dan. One headline ran, "Tupamaros, Financed by Russia, Are Trigger Men for Castro." On the same inside page, George Smathers, a former senator from Florida, revealed that the late President Kennedy had frequently discussed ridding the hemisphere of Fidel Castro through assassination.

In Washington, the director of the Catholic Conference held a press conference to demand an international investigation of charges that U. S. officials from the Agency for International Development (AID) were instructing police in Brazil and Uruguay in the techniques of torture; he mentioned Dan by name. The *Pal-Item* printed the article on a page with news of Sir Laurence Olivier's recovery from a thrombosis.

More prominently placed was a story from Montevideo: a death squad of vigilante Brazilian policemen was vowing to avenge Dan's murder by killing twenty relatives of the Tupamaro guerrillas. With Dan back and buried, however, Richmond's interest in Latin America and its problems had dwindled considerably.

And on the day of the concert, nothing could compete with the imminent arrival of Frank Sinatra. The basketball floor of the hall had been covered with folding chairs; and in the upper reaches of the bleachers, two immense spotlights were already in place.

Sinatra himself was the liveliest topic. Around Wayne County, some people were vocal in condemning him for the way he lived, for his women, for the hints of dubious associations. To his critics, Sinatra represented the antithesis of Hoosier values, and although they lowered their voices around Dan's family, they were sardonic about this one *paisano* coming to town to help out the family of another, as though they felt the American-Italian Club was overreaching itself.

Most of the county felt differently. Only a few advertisements had run in the *Pal-Item*, but the concert was heading toward a sellout, helped along when Sinatra himself paid for 450 tickets to be passed out among servicemen in the area and another batch for Richmond's policemen and firemen. With no fanfare, his corporation also absorbed the $27,000 in operating costs. All proceeds would go to Dan's family.

Shortly before 8 P.M., the stars arrived on the flagship of Cal-Jet Airways, a charter service owned by Sinatra Enterprises, and they faced the five hundred fans who crowded the runway apron. Interviews had been denied to the press, but one Dayton television announcer drew from Sinatra that he felt "we owe a debt of gratitude for men like these who work for our country."

Lewis clowned for the crowds, but when the newsmen caught him, he turned taciturn. "Just play back what Frank said and you know how I feel."

One reporter persisted, "Are you glad to be in Richmond tonight?"

Lewis stared straight ahead. "Of course I'm glad to be here. If I wasn't, I'd be back in Los Angeles."

But then a photographer yelled, "Hey, Jerry! Look this way!" The comic walked directly into his camera, treating viewers at home to a screen filled with nose. At that, everyone laughed and wrote off any touch of sulkiness to an understandable fatigue.

That night, Sinatra's performance was as generous as the impulse that brought him to Richmond. By the time he took the stage at 11 P.M., the temperature inside Civic Hall was 110°. Sinatra wiped away the sweat and did a dozen of his standards, ending with "My Way."

The audience responded with a standing ovation. The houselights came up, and Sinatra stepped forward to deliver a statement prepared for the occasion: "I never met Richmond's son, Dan Mitrione," Sinatra began. "Yet he was my brother. Just as you and I and Jerry are brothers. As all of us in America are brothers."

Sinatra checked off the problems that currently beset the United States: smog, campus revolt, muggings in the street, polluted water. But then he said, "You sit back and think of Dan Mitrione, and you know that things ain't all that bad."

Sinatra exhorted his audience to put its trust in love and "a genuine belief in the Man Upstairs," and he ended, "I've got this hunch that there's a lot of the Dan Mitrione quality in you folks. And believe me, in my book of human beings worth knowing and remembering, Dan Mitrione is really something else."

CHAPTER

2

DAN MITRIONE WENT OFF to Belo Horizonte as part of the team that Dwight Eisenhower was fielding against the nation's newest and most potent villain. In the Soviet Union, Joseph Stalin had been dead for seven years, and Nikita Khrushchev was proving too earthy, too much the rustic uncle, to frighten the American public for long. The China of Mao Tsetung, though a sworn enemy, remained separated from the United States by its extreme poverty and the Pacific Ocean. But since 1959, Fidel Castro had been ruling over an island so close to the U. S. that John Quincy Adams had considered it an apple that gravity would ultimately bring into our hands.

In fact, at the height of the 1960 presidential campaign, the one sure fact most U.S. voters knew about Latin America was the distance of Cuba from Florida's coast. Taking note of the nation's obsession, Castro commented, "You Americans keep saying that Cuba is ninety miles from the United States. I say that the United States is ninety miles from Cuba, and for us that is worse."

Castro had barely routed the dictator Fulgencio Batista when conservatives within the U. S. government launched a propaganda campaign against him. In April 1959, Vice-president Richard Nixon met with Castro in Washington and afterward wrote a confidential memorandum to the CIA, the State Department, and the White House, stating flatly that Castro was either a Communist dupe or a disciple and should be treated accordingly. At the FBI, J. Edgar Hoover told Nixon he agreed with his view. Eleven months later, President Eisenhower ordered the CIA secretly to prepare an invasion of Cuba that would depose Castro and his band of bearded reformers.

The Democratic presidential campaign of 1960 reflected the confusion in the electorate's mind over Castro's revolution. John Kennedy began the year by referring to Castro as a fiery young rebel in the tradition of Simón Bolívar. That was before those U. S. investors who controlled 40 percent of Cuba's sugar land expressed outrage over Castro's reforms.

When Castro expropriated the larger cane fields, including those of his own family, he offered in payment twenty-year bonds yielding 4.5 percent annual interest. Slyly, he proposed to pay for the land at the value the U. S. owners had placed on it when they paid their Cuban taxes. To the companies involved, the offer was not a fair one; and in protest, Washington cut off a sugar quota that had been advantageous to Cuba.

As mistrust of Castro spread, Senator Kennedy, now the Democratic nominee, changed tactics. He suggested that the Eisenhower administration should have avoided Castro's revolution altogether by using its influence on Batista to cause him to relax his dictatorship and permit free elections.

Between the time Kennedy was elected and his swearing in as president, Eisenhower broke diplomatic relations with Cuba. As a result, the new president entered office with a bipartisan foreign policy. Even such domestic liberals as Arthur Schlesinger, Jr., now perceived Castro's policies as a perversion of the Cuban revolution, and Democrats and Republicans were united in their resolve that Castro's success not contaminate the rest of the continent.

. . .

Before the decade had ended, Dan Mitrione, along with hundreds of other Public Safety advisers, had been sent into combat against communism in Brazil and elsewhere in Latin America. Yet the battle they entered, unlike Vietnam, was no shooting war. Since U. S. policy makers saw communism on the continent as a hidden enemy that would subvert a society from within, they prepared what they felt to be an appropriately secret counterattack.

In Vietnam, the Green Berets often defined war as months of boredom illuminated by moments of sheer terror. That characterization was truer still of the hidden war for which Mitrione had volunteered. Even when the shooting in Brazil began, Mitrione's routine remained comparatively calm, filled as it was with inspection tours and conversations in outlying police stations, requisitions for weapons and supplies, speech making, and daily paper work. He left for his office early in the morning and usually returned home before dusk to be with his family. His most difficult ethical dilemmas, at least in public, came when he served as umpire in local baseball games and had to decide whether or not to call his oldest son out at home plate.

Police advisers like Mitrione were the foot soldiers in Latin America; the CIA officials were the officer corps; the ambassadors, the ranking military attachés, and the CIA station chiefs from the upper echelons of each U.S. embassy were the field commanders. Until Mitrione was given his own unit to command in Uruguay, the CIA officials and the ambassadors overshadowed and ignored him. These were the men, with no need to know Mitrione's name, who were laying down the strategies and pursuing the courses of action that would later take his life.

Had Mitrione chosen to stay in Indiana, today he would still be years away from his retirement, and his youthful days would interest no one but his own devoted family. His upbringing, the degree to which he was typical of his generation, became important only when he took the atypical step of shipping off to a foreign land. His service in Brazil and Uruguay happened to coincide with a critical period in both countries. In a way no one could have predicted, his modest biography became intertwined with Latin American political history. Yet, throughout many significant chapters of that history, Mitrione deserves no more than a footnote.

Then, in death, Dan Mitrione became a symbol. Internationally, he was treated as the embodiment of United States policy in Latin America, even though it was a policy he never had the slightest voice in formulating. As a result, to understand the significance of his life, the message behind his killing, requires turning away from his everyday routine, from his many months of boredom, to examine instead those men and policies that brought him to his moment of terror.

It was not considered usual behavior for a Midwesterner on the threshold of forty who had never traveled abroad to quit his job, crate his belongings, uproot his wife and children, and set off to live on a new continent; and because it was not usual, the citizens of Richmond speculated on Dan Mitrione's abrupt departure. Some said that after four years as chief of police, he had run out of challenges. They detected in Dan a desire to serve that was too compelling to be satisfied in one small Indiana town.

Hank knew the truth was more practical: Dan wanted more money. He had asked the city for a pay raise; and when it was turned down, he felt he had to look elsewhere. Even as chief he had been driven to accept such odd jobs as painting offices at midnight, his car parked around the block so no one would know that the dignity of the chief's office was being compromised.

Contacts he had made during his term at the FBI school

informed him that through the foreign-aid program, the State Department had begun to recruit advisers to train police forces overseas. Quietly, in case he was rejected, Dan sent in an application.

The head of the program was Byron Engle, a former personnel director from the police department in Kansas City, Missouri. Engle tried to keep the federal salaries between $8,000 and $10,000, roughly 10 percent higher than what an officer was being paid at home. But for recruits from a few states, especially Mississippi and Indiana, that was not a fair ratio, their salaries being so much lower than the national average.

By enlisting with Engle, Dan received more money than he had been refused by the council, plus housing and other allowances, and at the end of his working years, the prospect of a better pension. Here at last was a chance for a man with seven children—and no guarantee there would not be more—to draw a living wage. Almost as important, he would be recognized by his government nationally, even internationally, as a professional in his field.

In May 1960, a month after John Kennedy came campaigning through Richmond, the International Cooperation Administration interviewed Dan in Washington and indicated that the job was his.

Back in Richmond, Dan went in to speak with Mayor Cutter about a leave of absence. It would have to be long: two years and four months was the length of the temporary post that was being offered him. Such a leave would be unprecedented. Was it legal?

Andy Cecere reported back that Dan could not be granted leave as chief of police, and that the loosest reading of Indiana law indicated that if Dan ever hoped to be chief again, he would first have to serve five years as a patrolman. There was no alternative. With trepidation but with encouragement from Andy and his other friends at City Hall, Dan resigned the post that had come his way so unexpectedly.

Standard training called for five weeks in Washington and three months studying Portuguese in Rio de Janeiro before Dan would take up his duties in Belo Horizonte, an industrial city northwest of Rio. The authorities recognized the limitations to any cram course, particularly in Portuguese, a language which, more appealing sung than spoken, could sound, if badly rendered, at once mushy and guttural, like drunken German. So Dan, along with most other U. S. Public Safety advisers, would come to depend heavily upon an interpreter. Still, though not exactly boasting, Dan later let friends in Richmond know that those years of speaking Italian at home had proved a boon after all, and that he had passed with remarkable speed through the language training.

July found Hank packing for the long sea voyage. The children's attitude toward Brazil ranged with their ages. When Dan had called them together for the sort of family conference rare to their household, the novelty had aroused everyone's interest.

"I want to talk to you about moving to South America," Mitrione began. The children knew he had already decided on the change. They had been brought up equating respect with love, and they attempted no serious mutiny. In fact, the older girls found that their father could make their future home sound highly romantic. Dan had been strict with his daughters, not allowing them to date until they were sixteen; and for them, the snobberies of a small town cut closer than for their parents. Dan, Jr., was dismayed to hear that the Brazilians favored soccer over baseball, but he confined his carping to neighbors along his newspaper route.

Joseph Mitrione had lived long enough to rejoice when his son put on the police chief's hat. Now his widow watched with misgivings as Dan prepared to leave the United States. Maria Mitrione, too, had once left her homeland and had never seen her family again.

Hank and the children landed in Brazil in September of

1960, and the girls, at the right age for it, succumbed to the country unconditionally. South of the equator it was winter, but they did not mind the rain. Brazil was so alive, so vivid; and after the dusty plains, it was like seeing life through a freshly washed window.

Possibly no new home their father might have chosen could have contrasted more sharply with Richmond. From the time of the first Portuguese explorers, foreigners had found Brazil rich in more than spice and precious stones. Missionaries and adventurers alike told the world that the temperament of the handsome natives was unlike anything to be found in Europe.

That difference persisted through the centuries of colonization. Stefan Zweig, an Austrian novelist, was one of many who tried to describe it. "A certain softness, a mild melancholy," he wrote, contrasted strongly with the dynamism of the North American. The violent, the dangerous, qualities of man had seemed to dissolve in the racial mixing of native Indians, slave blacks, and immigrants from southern Europe.

Some Portuguese explorers—Padre Fernão Cardim, for example, in 1585—had taken that passivity for nothing more than *remissa*, laziness. The Brazilians themselves did not entirely disagree. They told of the explorer Pedro Alvares Cabral first stepping onto the Brazilian coast in 1500 and hearing a voice from the depths of the jungle call, "Tomorrow!" to which the echo answered, "Patience!"

Zweig argued, though, that the quality he described was a virtue. "Anything brutal, cruel or even slightly sadistic is foreign to the Brazilian character." Brazil's history supported his observation: the country had separated itself from Portugal without a war of independence, and it ended slavery tardily but also with no bloodshed. Brazilians themselves pondered this peaceable strain in their national character. One student of Brazilian art from the colonial days noted, "In Brazil, even Christ hangs comfortably from the cross."

Portuguese Brazil was not the same as Spanish America, but north of the equator, the nations of Latin America melded in the popular mind, and the combined stereotype was seldom favorable.

Latin Americans were voluble. ("Oh, my God," cries an Englishman in a Rebecca West novel when his wife tells him whom she has invited to dinner. "South Americans. They will never go home.") Latin Americans were volatile. Seven years before Russia's revolution, Mexico staged a social revolution, and the example proved addictive to its neighbors. Political reports from south of the Rio Grande were always chaotic. (James Thurber, at his fussiest and blindest, described himself as being "more troublesome than Argentina.")

Latin America was dirty. Here the popular conception had some foundation. Until the 1920s, Rio de Janeiro was the most unhealthy of the world's large cities, with raging yellow fever, a high incidence of tuberculosis, and syphilis a badge of honor among the city's young men.

Even after those epidemics were brought under control, Latin America remained intellectually contaminating. For reporters at *The New York Times,* the continent was a notorious graveyard. At Harvard University the dean of the faculty was understood to have been referring to Latin America when he remarked, "Second-rate subjects attract second-rate minds." Six months after Dan Mitrione arrived in Brazil, that dean, McGeorge Bundy, went to the White House as John Kennedy's foreign-policy adviser.

Perhaps the continent's Luso-Hispanic background was to blame. Another Harvard professor, Henry Kissinger, confessed later in his career that his interest in world politics stopped at the Pyrenees. Even Edmund Wilson, insatiable in his erudition, admitted to one blind spot: "I have been bored by everything about Spain except Spanish painting. I have made a point of learning no Spanish, and I have never been able to get through *Don Quixote.*"

When South America did arouse fleeting interest, it was

usually proprietary. In 1899, the *Literary Digest* reported
a strong sentiment in the United States for annexing Cuba.
Campaigning in 1920, Franklin Roosevelt told crowds that
as assistant secretary of the navy he had helped to run a
couple of the continent's smaller republics. "The facts are
that I wrote Haiti's constitution myself, and if I do say it,
I think it's a pretty good constitution."

Lanier Winslow, once a first secretary at the United
States embassy in Mexico City, told friends that Mexico
had the makings of a great country, "if it could be dipped
in the sea for half an hour and all the Mexicans drowned."

Latin Americans bore this neglect and contempt with a
mixture of anger, resentment, and, especially in Brazil, self-
deprecating humor. Brazilians mocked not only themselves
but their colonial inheritance: "Brazil is the country of the
future and always will be"; "The Portuguese language is
the tomb of thought."

Brazilians acknowledged their aversion to labor with the
slogan, "Work is sacred, don't touch it." While other Latins
valued that trait called machismo, Brazilians told a joke
about the man who had been grievously insulted but refused to fight for his honor: "You're a man, aren't you?" his
friends demanded. "Yes," he replied, "but not fanatically
so."

With their sweetness of disposition and genial humor
went the melancholy that Zweig observed, and that may
have finally reached him: Zweig killed himself in Petropolis, the mountain town that had once been Brazil's royal
capital.

Despite a penchant for poetry, the classic sounding of
the Latin American soul was done in prose. At the turn of
the century, a young schoolteacher in Uruguay, José Enrique Rodó, wrote an essay called *Ariel.* The book swept
through Spanish-speaking America, producing a mild defiance of those values that had shaped the Protestant Colossus to the north.

Invoking the spirit of Ariel from Shakespeare's *The Tem-*

pest, Rodó cautioned his readers against false and vulgar ideas of education, those aimed solely at utilitarian ends. Such materialism, he said, mutilates the mind's natural fullness, and young people should hold instead to a single principle: to maintain the integrity of their humanity.

Rodó then expanded his attack: the enemy was a United States democracy preoccupied with its own materialism. Untempered by other values, such democracy extinguished respect for any superiority that cannot be turned to self-interest. Rodó saw his continent, seduced by the greatness and strength of the United States, voluntarily making over its society in the northern mold.

Do not, he pleaded, yield to that temptation. Hold to the sense of beauty you were born with, for it is more powerful than a steam-driven engine. Hold to your own virtues, to your capacity for heroism, because the other way, the northern way, produces monsters. Let the United States, if it must, be Caliban. It is your duty to save the hemisphere, to save the world. Be Ariel.

In Argentina, Mexico, and the Dominican Republic, poets and politicians—very often the same young men—took up the challenge, proclaiming themselves Arielists. Yet in New York and Washington, Rodó went untranslated for many years and unread.

By the early 1960s, the United States was more convinced than ever before that its technicians—engineers, agronomists, and now policemen—had vital knowledge to import to the less progressive nations of the world. In Washington, Byron Engle had been charged with putting together a task force that could train police in Asia, Africa, and particularly in Latin America. He had been chosen because of his experience both in training Japanese police after the Second World War and in setting up a police advisory board in Turkey. His was also a genial yet foxy manner that disarmed even those people conditioned to distrust cops. He had an avuncular way about him, a bland reasonableness, that served him well at staff conferences and at those times when the press could not be avoided.

It was President Eisenhower who first proposed adapting the training of German and Japanese police to meet the needs of the Cold War. Eisenhower told a meeting of the National Security Council: "We're building up military forces that we all know wouldn't last a week or ten days in a hot war. But what are we doing about the constabulary forces?"

The meeting adjourned in confusion. What, the council members asked each other, does he mean? The urban police? Or is he speaking literally of the rural force, the constabulary? Like other oracles, Eisenhower had to be interpreted, and one adviser divined that the President had just returned from the Philippines, where policemen were called constabulary. Ike merely meant police.

With the decision ratified, the project had to be brought under the aegis of an advisory agency. Police advisers in Okinawa and Japan were under army control, along with those in Korea and the Philippines; Berlin's police advisers reported to the State Department; and the four-man group in Iran came under the Foreign Operations Administration.

Officially, the new advisory unit was given to the State Department to be administered as part of the foreign-aid program, but Engle had other allegiances. He had been recruited by the CIA after it was established in 1947. If council members had misgivings about selecting a CIA man to head the program, Engle disarmed any criticism. In 1955, he was given a title and a secretary, and Washington launched itself on its efforts to improve the Free World's police.

From the start, some officials within the foreign-aid program disliked Engle's operation. Economists were the most outspoken, complaining that they were trying to shape a new social structure, and here was this other group, repressive by definition, doing its work under the same banner.

Engle believed that the executive arm of a government —its police and military—were the last to change. But change itself—at least orderly change—depended on stability, and Washington was not prepared to underwrite any other kind of change. Since order required policemen to enforce the law, it served the interests of the United States that those officers be efficient.

If Engle was not finding much support at the State Department, neither was the FBI proving cooperative. J. Edgar Hoover told associates that the police program was simply one more CIA cover—Engle's appointment proved as much—and that he did not intend to pump his life's blood into a competing bureaucracy.

At the CIA, the advantages to putting U. S. operatives in close contact with the local police were obvious, but as late as 1960, with the CIA immersed in training men in Guatemala for an invasion of Cuba, Engle's operation was still allowed to struggle along under the unfriendly cover of the State Department.

When Dan Mitrione applied to the program in the spring of that year, he was put through a rigorous security check. Since Engle was only fielding eighty advisers world-wide, he could draw on his intelligence sources to be sure that each recruit was stable, competent, and loyal to his country.

It was easier in those days to define positive loyalty than to determine precisely who the enemy was. Until 1959, Engle's outline had called for "combatting communism and subversion." But then the King of Iran was assassinated by an armored unit said to owe its fealty to Nasser of Egypt. More alarming, two hundred bearded men sent by Fidel Castro landed in a mangrove swamp for a botched invasion of Panama; yet, in 1959, it was still a moot question whether Castro was a Communist. As a consequence, the words of the police mission were changed to read "combatting interests inimical to the United States."

When the Kennedy-Johnson team moved into the White

House, Engle's program, rather than being dismantled by the liberals taking over Washington, acquired its premier patron. Investigating his duties at the Justice Department, Robert F. Kennedy was impressed with the way the FBI trained policemen from around the country and thought the time was right to expand that ecumenical approach to foreign lands.

At the same time, his brother, as president, was confronted by stirrings in Southeast Asia and throughout Latin America. To seek solutions to the unrest, he convened a number of high-ranking officials and called them the Counter-Intelligence Group. The members agreed that it was not an inspired name. Too negative. Given the time, they would have worked "nation building" into their title, but for now C-I would have to do.

The first chairman, Maxwell Taylor, was an army general who had dropped from favor during the Eisenhower years for warning the country against the Pentagon's reliance on nuclear weapons. He had written a book setting forth his views, and on the New Frontier he was regarded as that most elusive hybrid, an intellectual general, and as a useful counterweight to bombardiers like Curtis LeMay. Later Taylor was named ambassador to South Vietnam.

With his ability to convert passion into energy, Robert Kennedy actively prodded the C-I Group. Its key mission was to develop methods for promoting internal order around the globe. Cabinet departments were represented, and a delegate from the CIA sat in. At no time did any of its members question the C-I Group's goals. As one participant recalled, "We knew we were acting from damn good motives."

Out of the C-I Group's deliberations came Jack Kennedy's Special Forces; new training in counter-insurgency at military schools from the National War College down; and new courses at the Foreign Service Institute to make officers from the State Department, the CIA, and military branches more alert to insurgency problems in the field.

Furthermore, the C-I Group saw early on how important the police would be in a country's battle against its rebels. So it set up a Committee on Police and Police Training, and as chairman appointed a career diplomat, U. Alexis Johnson.

Johnson resembled the British politician Edward Heath, having one of those long faces that are bland but not always reassuring. When Lyndon Johnson became president, he sent Johnson to South Vietnam as deputy ambassador. His job would be to steer Taylor through the complexities of Vietnamese politics, while Taylor would guide General William Westmoreland to victory on the battlefield.

Alexis Johnson's committee recognized immediately that there had to be a new central and more powerful police office, and that decision led to the committee's thorniest discussions. The Pentagon argued that any expanded police effort should come to them. A State Department veteran, Johnson found it easy to insist that the training of police was a civil function. After all, he said, we aren't training MPs.

Having won that battle, Johnson was not concerned that the officials of the police program had been turning to the CIA for the help they could not get through the aid bureaucracy or from the FBI. Perfectly natural, Johnson thought. In an ideal world, he might have preferred a program director without Byron Engle's involvement with the CIA. But Engle's credentials seemed so superior to those of his rivals—hadn't he once trained 100,000 Japanese policemen in only two months?—that Johnson talked with the CIA director and got permission for Engle to assume the expanded job.

Next came the setting of standards for recruits to this newly prestigious program. Engle had been sitting in on the Johnson committee meetings, and he moved adroitly to hold the committee's interference to a minimum. A senior member brought up the subject: "What kind of person do we need?"

That was Engle's cue. He produced a tablet and tore off sheets he passed around the table. "Gentlemen, here are some blank pieces of paper. I'd like to see what you think we should require. So please write down the minimum attributes for a chief police adviser."

On the papers Engle collected, one member had written that the man must be young and, since the work would be arduous, physically fit. Another demanded a college degree, preferably in the social sciences. Another stipulated at least one foreign language; another, a military background. Engle then elaborately calculated the various requirements. "Gentlemen, your minimum standards add up to some ninety years of experience. And yet you don't want our recruits to be over thirty-five."

The committee members, all expert bureaucratic infighters, recognized a master. All right, they told Engle, you know more about it than we do. And he went on exercising sole authority over hiring.

A police academy was another of Engle's deferred ideas whose time had come. Until then, the State Department had been importing promising young officers to the United States. But once on hand, they were often shipped off to Kansas City to sit around a station house.

The first alternative, for Latin American officers, had been the Inter-American Police Academy. Theodore Brown, a former police chief from Eugene, Oregon, and then the director of a Public Safety program on Guam, ran that school at Fort Davis on the Isthmus of Panama. Captains and majors from around the continent, but particularly from Central America, spent eight to twelve weeks learning how to be more effective officers. They then spent another week or two at nearby Fort Gulick, learning counter-insurgency. But police officers from the larger and more sophisticated cities, particularly in Brazil, found the courses in Panama simple to the point of being insulting. Although a few could be placated with invitations to stay on at the academy as guest instructors, most of them shunned the school entirely.

Then, too, with the issue of the pronounced CIA role in past police training already raised within the C-I Group, it was now agreed that the school should be moved to the continental United States. There the civilians could keep a better eye on it. Already reports were filtering up to the mainland that the training in Panama was rougher than the United States would tolerate on its own shores.

To these accusations, the CIA formulated an answer that it employed later, with modifications, when those stories began to appear in print. From 1955 until today, ran Byron Engle's denial, we have been teaching nonlethal riot control in Panama. Before that, Latin American police were equipped with submachine guns. Every year there would be deaths in the streets. We disapproved, and we introduced instead the use of tear gas and stressed its advantages. Tear gas may not be pleasant, but it isn't fatal. You can scrub it off.

In August 1962, Jack Kennedy approved the C-I Group's report; however, a year later, the police academy was still functioning in Panama, turning out seven hundred graduates, and pressure was building to move the school to the United States. Engle tried to explain that finding an appropriate building was no overnight job. In Japan, he had put his academies in bombed-out buildings, but in Washington Engle had personally checked eighty buildings before, on the edge of Georgetown, he discovered the Car Barn.

The barn, more than two hundred years old, had been first a tobacco warehouse and than a turnaround point for streetcars in the District of Columbia. O. Roy Chalk, the owner of the transit system, planned to reserve a part of the ground floor for his law offices. Otherwise, the cellar would do for a firing range, and the remaining three floors of the solid red brick building seemed a natural spot to train police.

But to protect his flank, Engle called Michael V. Forrestal in McGeorge Bundy's office in the White House basement. Forrestal had served on Johnson's committee. With his proximity to the president, if he approved the location none of the committee's nay-sayers could prevail.

The two men toured the premises. The elevators designed to take the streetcars upstairs were still there. A lot of work would be needed before it would look like an academy. But Forrestal, playing the graybeard at thirty-six, said "You guys are young and full of piss and vinegar. You can get it in shape." Then he paused. "It brings back a lot of memories. I used to get my butt spanked for sliding down that hill."

Only then did Engle realize that the site he had chosen was next door to the James Forrestal estate, where Harry Truman's secretary of defense once lived, in the days before the menace of the Cold War helped to unbalance his mind and lead to his suicide.

Drawing on the Inter-American Police Academy, Engle imported the twenty instructors as the nucleus for his new school. They all spoke Spanish, and that was an asset, since Washington's chief concern remained Latin America. Grudgingly, J. Edgar Hoover donated one man to the staff.

Although the move out of the Canal Zone had been set for nearly a year, when it finally took place, it coincided with the Panama rioting of 1964. The U. S. adviser to Panama's police called Engle on the night a Panamanian was killed to say, "Well, they got their first martyr."

Among CIA propagandists, it was widely held that the Marxists—and everyone else with interests inimical to the United States—followed a standard technique for agitation, which they taught around the world: first, get one of your own supporters killed in the rioting. That's why Engle advised the police of other countries against using bayonets: in a crowd, it was too easy for the Communists to push a demonstrator onto the point of one. Next, get physical possession of the body. Carry your dead martyr through the streets. Stage a public funeral. Lastly, hold a public commemoration.

to work with the local police departments. That program provided cover for some CIA officers. The other police advisers, the ones without Company ties, were to be kept ignorant of the clandestine work of their associates.

After Agee had completed his term at the farm, his chief CIA contact suggested strongly that he volunteer for duty in Latin America, where Castro's revolution was causing the CIA to expand its operations. Agee had dreamt of Vienna or Hong Kong. Among the various CIA divisions, the Western Hemisphere (WH) enjoyed the lowest prestige. A number of former FBI men, veterans of the anti-Nazi years in Argentina and Brazil, had moved over to the CIA upon its creation in 1947, and Agee was embarrassed to find himself allied with them in something called the gumshoe division.

Coming to know the WH Division better, Agee's doubts were confirmed. He found a prevailing disinterest in either Latin American history or culture. Fluent Spanish was valued; it was a tool for a man to do his job. Otherwise, Agee was conspicuous for the way he dug into his new assignment and read widely about Latin America. His older co-workers assured him that to operate anywhere a man needed only a few well-placed contacts.

In August 1960, Agee heard exciting news: the branch chief of his division had approved him for an assignment in Ecuador. The CIA was arranging a full-time tutor in Spanish and wanted to get Agee to Quito as soon as possible. His cover would be assistant attaché in the U. S. embassy's political section. The job was a tribute to Agee's potential. Only one other member of his training class had been assigned earlier to the field, and that man was going no farther than New York. Under State Department cover, Christopher Thoron was appointed to the U. S. mission to the United Nations.

At last, in December 1960, Phil Agee and his wife, Janet, were flown first-class from Washington to Quito and arrived in the midst of Ecuador's Independence Day fiesta.

Agee's first working day was a heady one. He saw a bullfight and deplored the butchery. In the evening, he and Janet, along with Jim Noland, the CIA station chief, attended a party at the home of the Ecuadorian family that controlled the country's movie theaters. Every guest that night seemed to be rich and related by blood and marriage. Agee had the chance to meet an important contact, a nephew of the country's president and an undercover agent for the CIA.

That man, Jorge Acosta Velasco, had lately proved his worth by passing along information to the station about a CIA man, Robert Weatherwax, who had been operating in Quito under the cover of a Public Safety adviser. Weatherwax had recruited the chief of Ecuador's intelligence department, who was later exposed as the leader of an illegal secret society of young police officers. Weatherwax dropped from sight to avoid being tarred by his protégé's actions. Now Acosta was advising the CIA that Weatherwax could return safely.

Phil Agee had come to the end of a stimulating day. In a room of sleek men and expensively groomed women, he was not the least important person. And these were people who wanted to get along with him. To cope with the others, the working-class Ecuadorians, he had a drawerful of money for bribes and payoffs. There were also the Indians, but no one troubled about them.

Agee might not have the world in his pocket, but he had Ecuador, and at twenty-six, it was world enough.

During the time that Dan Mitrione was making a mild political gesture by permitting Hank to serve at Jack Kennedy's dinner in Richmond, a fellow alumnus of Kennedy's was holding himself aloof from all forms of politicking—a strategy that eventually secured for him the ambassadorship to Brazil.

Since 1955, Lincoln Gordon had been serving as professor of international economics at the Harvard Graduate School of Business Administration. He particularly prided himself on remaining untainted by Massachusetts' gamy local politics: throughout 1960, he neither met John F. Kennedy nor involved himself in his presidential campaign.

The most significant fact in Gordon's life may have been that he began it acclaimed as a boy genius. He had enrolled early at Harvard and graduated in three years, at the age of nineteen. Along the way, he had developed a phenomenal memory for detail and a reputation as a man who could devote an hour to answering a single question. By the time he went off as a Rhodes Scholar to Balliol College, Oxford, he might have outgrown that precocious need to shine, but he remained a compulsive talker, a tireless explicator—a chatterbox.

Gordon's career after Oxford was respectable. He taught at Harvard and served in government, always on important missions but seldom as the top man. He assisted Paul Hoffman in the agency that administered the Marshall Plan; he was a part of a delegation to the United Nations Atomic Energy Commission; and during the Eisenhower years, he served as a consultant to NATO, but on the alliance's nonmilitary aspects.

Then John Kennedy was elected. The academic ranks around Cambridge began to thin. Although Gordon was not immediately tapped, he tried to remain optimistic. Waiting for the president's men to call, he began by setting the proper value on his worth. There were only three jobs he would take. But Paul Henry Nitze was appointed assistant secretary of defense for international security affairs, and George Ball was named undersecretary of state for economic affairs. That left only national security adviser, and McGeorge Bundy received that post. Bundy was not only six years younger than Gordon, but he might fairly be considered a Gordon protégé, since Gordon had hired him after the war to work on the task force for the Marshall Plan.

For a while, it looked as though Gordon might be left behind at the business school in Cambridge, grinding out a two-volume study on Brazilian investment. But salvation appeared in the autocratic person of Adolf Berle. Before his inauguration, Kennedy had set up a Latin American task force to establish broad lines of policy, and he named Berle as its chief. Gordon thought that Berle suffered from the small man's Bonaparte complex, but he was used to his ways. When Berle called and asked, "Heard from Sorensen yet?" Gordon understood that it was not a question.

He hedged, however. "About what?"

"You know, you know. Lots of names are floating around, but there's only one task force and I'm it." With that, Berle invited Gordon to join his committee as an economist. Gordon protested, as sincerely as he knew how, that despite his Brazil project at the business school, he was a newcomer to Latin America; others had devoted their lives to its study. Berle convinced him that the committee would not take much time, and Lincoln Gordon at last was aboard the New Frontier.

During the campaign, Jack Kennedy's aides had suggested that he take an initiative in Latin America as substantial as Franklin Roosevelt's, and, if possible, with a title as winning as The Good Neighbor Policy. Richard N. Goodwin, who had a talent for capturing Kennedy's cadences, had been assigned the job of concocting that program. Riding a campaign bus through Texas, Goodwin picked up a discarded copy of a magazine published in Tucson called *Alianza*. He took the name to Kennedy, who agreed that it was a start.

A Cuban who had broken with Castro and gone to work in Washington came up with two possibilities: Alliance for Development was instantly discarded because Goodwin was sure his chief could never cope with the Spanish word *desarrollo*. That left Alianza para el Progresso. Goodwin tried shortening the title to the more euphonius Alianza para Progresso, but objections from the U. S. Information

Agency convinced him that even south of the border there were purists who cared about grammar. Rhetoric was Goodwin's specialty, and he set to work on a speech that would match his fine title.

Gordon was asked to look over the speech for substance. He read through the first draft and protested the phrase in which Goodwin promised, within ten years, to close the economic gap between the United States and the nations of Latin America.

Gordon said, "Dick, this is ridiculous. If the United States worked at full speed to impoverish itself, we could probably meet that goal. Otherwise—"

But through eight drafts that unrealistic pledge kept appearing, and it was still in the final draft that Goodwin and Gordon took in to the new president. Trained in speed reading, Kennedy whisked through the draft at a pace that dazzled Gordon. Then he asked, "Any comments?"

Gordon said, "There's one phrase that I've been trying to get Richard to take out."

"What is it?"

After Gordon had explained, Kennedy turned to Goodwin.

"Sure, Linc is right," Goodwin said. "It's just rhetoric. But in ten years, we'll be out of office anyway."

When the president read the speech to an assembly of Latin American ambassadors, Gordon was relieved to hear him omit the offending phrase.

During those early months of the New Frontier, Gordon was given to understand that he would be the next ambassador to Brazil; and to prepare himself, he broadened his reading on the country. From U. S. intelligence estimates, it was clear that Communist infiltration in Brazil was now Washington's overriding concern.

It had once been different. During the Second World War, Brazil's president had been a dictator, Getúlio Dornelles Vargas, who had proved his allegiance to the United States by sending a regiment to fight the Axis in Italy and by allowing the United States to build huge aircraft staging bases on Brazil's northeast coast.

Vargas had first come to power in 1930, the beneficiary of a popular rebellion led by coffee growers protesting a drop in world coffee prices. Forming a military coalition that could challenge the industrial power of Minas Gerais and São Paulo, he ousted the president and became dictator.

Franklin Roosevelt, who came to office three years later, found Vargas an easy colleague who had also embarked on a program of deficit spending to rouse his country from the Depression. There were other parallels between the personal life of Vargas and that of his new friend in Washington. The dictator's legs had been crushed when a falling rock destroyed his car. Marrying late in life, Vargas produced five children; his wife, Dona Darcy, was admired for her good works. But it was known that the two led separate lives, and his partisans insisted that at seventy Vargas was still visiting a mistress once a week.

The two men seemed to enjoy gossiping together. One indiscreet joke to Vargas during the war about Charles de Gaulle helped to earn Roosevelt the French leader's lasting enmity. In the course of another candid meeting, Roosevelt told Vargas that he would not accept for the United States the degree of control that foreign companies exercised over utilities in Brazil.

It seemed a broad hint. In 1938, the Mexican government had nationalized the U. S. oil companies, and the oil executives had appealed to Washington for armed assistance. Theodore Dreiser once explained their thinking: "The whole principle behind intervention by the United States is that when one of her citizens buys property in a foreign land, that property is no longer subject to the law of that foreign land."

The response of the Roosevelt administration had been legalistic, only assisting in negotiating a long-term settlement. Given that background, Vargas might have expropriated the Brazilian utilities owned by U. S. corporations. He did not; however, he was determined that no other sector of Brazil's economy get itself so indebted to foreigners.

During his fifteen-year reign, Vargas faced a number of armed challenges. The middle class of São Paulo revolted in 1932; the Communists rose up in 1935. Vargas responded by banning the Communist party and sending its leader, Luís Carlos Prestes, to jail. In 1938, the Integralists, Brazil's fascists, tried unsuccessfully to storm the presidential palace.

For Brazil's industrial workers, the Vargas years were marked by hope. The dictator instituted a social security program and sponsored a labor movement. The unions were subservient to Vargas's Labor Ministry; but with his support, men and women who had worked from twelve to twenty hours won an eight-hour day with two-week vacations, children under fourteen were banned from industry, and women went from half pay to full pay. Yet Vargas did little for laborers on the farms and great fazendas. They were disorganized and still considered by the landowner to be his personal property.

Nor were the Vargas years at all democratic. The dictator, in fact, had even forbidden the newspapers to print the inflammatory word "democracy." However, the end of the Second World War witnessed an outcry for the return of parliamentary democracy. The officers' corps that had installed Vargas now put him out and called an election for the presidency.

Democracy had returned to Brazil but only by the grace of the army. Once again the generals showed that they took seriously their right, inherited from the Portuguese emperor, to serve the national interest as the *poder moderator*, the moderating power.

Though literacy laws prevented Brazil's majority from voting, three major political parties quickly sprang into being. The most popular was a conservative alliance.

Formed, for the most part, by industrialists and landowners, it called itself the Social Democrats. Next in strength was the National Democratic Union, Vargas's right-wing and middle-class enemies. Finally there was a workers' party, Partido Trabalhista Brasileiro. The Brazilian Communist party was then legalized as the fourth party, a legitimacy that proved temporary. In 1947, it was outlawed again when Brazil broke diplomatic relations with the Soviet Union.

The landowners of the Social Democrats and the workers' party each owed debts to Vargas, and they entered into a coalition that gained in strength until, by 1950, the old dictator could assume the presidency again, this time through elections.

Vargas soon found it was the harder way to govern. Without restrictions on the press, he had to bear a daily onslaught from his opponents; and in a young journalist named Carlos Lacerda, Vargas met his fate.

Gifted in elegant vilification, Lacerda increased his attacks until it became impossible for Vargas and his loyal friends to bear them. One night in August of 1954, an army friend of Lacerda's was murdered in front of Lacerda's apartment building. The evidence implicated one of Vargas's security men, called the black angel of death.

The resulting uproar left Lacerda in the enviable position of being not only a martyr but a living one. Vargas saw that he could not continue as president, and he retired from the scene in a way that none of his North American counterparts had chosen. On August 24, 1954, he took his own life.

Behind he left a remarkable document, bold and pleading, in which he blamed outside forces for helping to create the circumstances that killed him: "The foreign companies made profits of up to five hundred percent. They demonstrably deprived the state of more than a hundred million dollars by false evaluations of import goods."

Vargas, a son of the pampas of Rio Grande do Sul, was

acting from a *gaúcho* code of honor. He ended his message: "Serenely, I take the first step on the road to eternity and I leave life to enter history."

After a caretaking period, a politician named Juscelino Kubitschek took over the presidency in 1955 and was confronted by another period of rising inflation and falling coffee prices. Every penny drop in the world price of coffee cost the Brazilian treasury $25 million. Kubitschek sought to convince foreign capital to invest in Brazil by offering concessions that neither Vargas nor Franklin Roosevelt might have approved. The new president canceled the ceilings on profits and allowed foreign investors to take their profits home. Factory equipment could come untaxed to Brazil. When a foreign investor launched a company, no percentage of Brazilian participation was required. By 1959, the U. S. Department of Commerce was reporting that the investment climate in Brazil was one of the most favorable in the world.

Brazil paid heavily for that expression of confidence. One local economist, Eugenio Gudin, calculated that Kubitschek's regime had given away $1 billion to foreign firms through tax credits and assistance in locating in Brazil. Yet, Gudin was no propagandist for the Left, and in a newspaper article he wrote that "to say that every man has a right to a decent life is a proposition worthy of a donkey."

In another study, the privileges extended to the new automobile industry—Volkswagen, Mercedes-Benz, General Motors, Ford—were shown to equal Brazil's national budget. In those same years of the late 1950s, Kubitschek's ministers cut off support to the National Motor Company, one of the state enterprises created by Vargas.

To some Brazilians, the foreign-aid program of the Eisenhower years, and even the Alliance for Progress, was a sham so long as five times more dollars were leaving Brazil in the form of earnings, dividends, and royalties than were entering the country as new direct investment. Those men, nationalists, joked that it was Brazil that was giving foreign aid to the United States.

But undeniably the infusion of capital had the nation booming, and Kubitschek celebrated the growth by creating a symbol, a city he called Brasília.

For generations, popular wisdom had held that Brazil would never be a great nation so long as it remained a collection of coastal cities with a jungle at their backs. In North America, the plains had been reward enough to draw settlers west. But Brazilians needed an incentive and a proof of the country's commitment to development, a capital city far away from the distractions of Rio de Janeiro.

No one questioned that Rio was a hindrance to hard work. It was said that municipal buses were never routed within a block of Copacabana Beach because the expanse of white sand caused office workers on their way downtown to jump from their seats and defect to the sun.

As Kubitschek built Brasília, the Gross National Product for five years kept going up a healthy 7 percent annually. In this harmonious union of Brazilian politics and foreign business there were only a few discords. Inflation was also on the rise and threatened the value of foreign investments. Then, too, Kubitschek, like Vargas, was assisting the large landowners through coffee subsidies while ignoring the peasants outside the industrial cities. His neglect led to several reformist movements in the arid and poverty-ridden northeast. From Washington these movements came to look dangerously radical.

As the elections approached, there was another difficulty. Brazil's electoral laws did not permit a president to succeed himself, nor were presidential candidates empowered to pick their running mates as Eisenhower had chosen Richard Nixon. In Brazil, the people's second choice became vice-president, and when Kubitschek won, the runner-up had been João Goulart.

A rancher from the south of Brazil, Goulart had been so cherished by Vargas that rumors spread that he was the dictator's illegitimate son. Even in the largest nominally Catholic land on earth, suicide had only enhanced Vargas's standing. In Washington, it was clear, and displeasing, that Goulart might win the next election.

The problem was ideological. As Vargas's minister of labor, Goulart had been credited with the regime's reforms. Some U. S. intelligence reports found him perilously open to Communist influence. But the alternative was little better. Washington rated the other major contender, Jânio Quadros, nearly as susceptible. Between those two imperfect options, a choice was made, and Brazilian journalists had no trouble discerning from briefings with the U. S. embassy staff that Quadros was Washington's choice.

Throughout his term as governor of São Paulo, Quadros had won the affection of the workingman. Now campaigning for president, Quadros repeatedly assured crowds that he was no plutocrat.

Forty-eight percent of the Brazilian voters believed him, the largest majority vote in Brazil's history. Once again, João Goulart was elected vice-president on the labor ticket.

On taking office, Quadros swung his rigid broom erratically. He sharply devalued the cruzeiro, Brazil's unit of currency. That pleased foreign investors more than it did the Brazilians living on fixed incomes. In a campaign to restore morality to Brazil, he banned the bikini from Rio's seashore, a decree honored only in the breach.

A recent trip around the world had convinced Quadros that Third World countries should move to a middle ground between the capitalists and the Communists, and he tried to retire Brazil to the sidelines of the Cold War. In that intuition, public-opinion polls seemed to support him; one survey found that 63 percent of the Brazilians preferred neutrality. The polls also showed that the higher a person's income, the more friendly he felt toward the United States.

Quadros met complaints about his shift to the political

center by saying his foreign policy was "grown-up, vaccinated and old enough to vote." But it was not inoculated
against Washington's disapproval or against the venom of
Carlos Lacerda.

As criticism from the conservative press grew strident,
Quadros sequestered himself in the presidential palace, isolated from his natural allies and lacking a way to build
bridges to the Vargas coalition. In line with his opening to
the Left, Quadros proposed legislation that would have
raised taxes on foreign firms to 50 percent. When Ernesto
(Ché) Guevara went to Uruguay for a conference of the
Organization of American States, Quadros invited him to
stop in Brazil on his way back to Cuba.

At that conference in the sea resort of Punta del Este,
Richard Goodwin, who had promised to end the economic
disparity between the Americas, met the man sworn to
hold Goodwin to that promise. By the time of the conference, relations between the United States and Cuba had
reached their nadir; four months earlier, Washington had
tried to overthrow Castro's government.

Consequently, Goodwin was not expecting to receive in
his hotel room a polished mahogany box inlaid with the
Cuban seal and filled with a commodity increasingly prized
in the United States. The note accompanying the Cuban
cigars read: "Since I have no greeting card, I have to write.
Since to write to an enemy is difficult, I limit myself to
extending my hand."

Goodwin brought the cigars back to the White House
and offered them to the president, who took one and lit it.
After he had puffed awhile, he said to Goodwin, "You
should have smoked the first one."

Goodwin recorded the episode seven years later, after
John Kennedy and Ché Guevara had both been assassinated, Guevara tracked down in Bolivia with the help of
the U. S. Special Forces. Another seven years after his
memoir, it was clear that Castro would have had more
reason than Kennedy to be wary of a gift, what with the

many attempts on the Cuban's dignity and life by the CIA, including a plan to cause his beard to fall out.

Goodwin and Guevara met discreetly at Punta del Este for a long midnight talk. According to Goodwin, Guevara warned him that "there would be either leftist revolutions or rightist coups leading to leftist takeovers, and that there was a strong chance that in some countries the Communists would come to power through popular elections." Writing two years before the election of Salvador Allende in Chile, Goodwin added, "None of this has come to pass."

Guevara put forth a number of suggestions to ease relations between the two countries, including a promise to pay for the U. S. property that Cuba had expropriated. Thus, it was not an intractable foe of the United States who left the Uruguay conference and stopped in Brazil to meet with Quadros.

During Ché's visit, Quadros confirmed his "grown-up" and independent policy by presenting Ché with Brazil's highest award for foreigners, the Cruzeiro do Sul. In Guevara's life, it may have been a minor honor, but to Carlos Lacerda, the presentation was an affront to Brazil and a splendid opportunity for a fiery rant. He went on the air to accuse Quadros's minister of justice of preparing a coup d'état that would give Quadros greatly expanded powers. "The man we elected doesn't want to be president," Lacerda told a television audience seven years after he drove Vargas to suicide. "He wants to be dictator."

Lacerda spoke on a Thursday. When Quadros made his move at three o'clock the next afternoon, he might have expected that the weekend would give the nation time to rally behind him. Whatever his thinking, Quadros resigned the presidency. His message had echoes of Vargas's suicide note: "I feel crushed. Terrible forces have risen against me. I wanted Brazil for Brazilians and I confronted in that battle corruption, lies and cowardice which subordinated general interests to the appetites and the ambitions of groups of individuals, including ones from abroad."

Quadros was to learn that committing political suicide
did not engender the guilt and regret that Vargas stirred
by putting a bullet through his head. Both men denounced
the interests arrayed against them, but in Quadros's case,
rival politicians joked that while they could not identify
the domestic interests, the foreign ones were Haig and
Haig, Teacher's, and Johnnie Walker.

Signs of support for Quadros were few and desultory.
Several labor leaders urged him to return to office. A
crowd understood his references to foreign influence well
enough to stone the United States embassy. But the military moved to place Quadros under guard, which stopped
him from making any rallying speeches. As public attention swung to his successor, the former president was heard
to ask, "Where are the six million who voted for me?"

Whether cunningly or not, before resigning Quadros
had dispatched his leftist vice-president on a good-will tour
of the People's Republic of China. Now it fell once again
to the military, who considered themselves the supreme
political arbiters, to decide whether João Goulart, freshly
contaminated by his exposure to Mao Tsetung, should be
permitted to return and assume the presidency. The minister of war, Odilío Denys, said Goulart should not take
office. The ministers of the various military services agreed
with him.

At this point, the provisional president, Pascoal Ranieri
Mazzilli, told Congress of the military decision and
proposed legislation to keep Goulart from office. There
was a precedent for such a law, but Goulart, half a world
away, had a potent ally in his brother-in-law, Leonel
Brizola, the governor of Rio Grande do Sul.

No one, least of all Brizola, would deny that he was a
man of the Left. At the Punta del Este conference, he had
urged Brazil to side with Ché against the Alliance for
Progress; but as a governor, he could bring pressure on the
commander of the Third Army, stationed in the state capital of Pôrto Alegre, and the heads of the country's three
other armies were wavering.

There could easily have been a civil war. Goulart's enemies claimed that he had put Communists into sensitive labor jobs. But the real threat—to the army, to the industrialists, and to the foreign investors—was the likelihood that under Goulart organized labor would become the dominant force in Brazilian politics. In neighboring Argentina, Juan Perón had shown even better than Vargas how sturdy a base the shirtless ones could provide for an ambitious politician.

After ten days of uncertainty, Congress passed an amendment that reformed itself on a parliamentary model. Goulart, waiting in Paris to hear his fate, would be allowed to come back as president, but his powers would be more those of a prime minister. When the military indicated that the compromise satisfied them, Goulart flew on to Brasília.

Given the Brazilian fondness of the *jeito*, the face-saving fix that circumvents every difficulty, the agreement brought an unearned luster to all participants. The army was credited with restraint and devotion to democratic principles, when all the episode proved was that the plotters against Goulart were not yet strong enough to resist him.

Goulart, accepting the compromise but chafing under it, seemed to demonstrate a defter political touch than later events would bear out. Meantime, he was burdened with an agreement that, among other curtailments of presidential perogative, allowed Congress to remove his ministers without consulting him.

Not surprisingly, the uproar clouded Lincoln Gordon's pleasure in his appointment as ambassador. President Kennedy had sent his name to the U. S. Senate one day before Quadros resigned.

Lauren J. Goin, usually called Jack, appreciated early in his tour of Latin America how crucial it was for a police adviser to be simpatico. Very likely, it was a quality of the heart, and no one could set out to learn it. But if a foreigner made an effort to be kindly and soft-edged, Latin Americans broadened their definition of simpatico enough that he could qualify—even when, as in Goin's case, the harder outlines of his native character sometimes showed through.

Before coming to Brazil early in 1960, Goin had set up the first police advisory team in Indonesia, and served on the advisory team in Turkey. Before that, he had directed the crime laboratory in Pittsburgh. It was this varied background that led Byron Engle to send him to Rio as an adviser in scientific investigations.

Goin's work took him up to the state of Minas Gerais, where he could evaluate the neophyte adviser in Belo Horizonte. They had long discussions about the job, and Goin was able to caution Mitrione against several pitfalls. Goin had seen men isolate themselves within the U. S. embassy compound, spending their off-duty hours exclusively with their countrymen. Such advisers did not last long in Engle's program.

Mitrione would heed that message. He was eager to make good—nine lives depended upon it—but even if he had not been ambitious, he would have found little reason to seek out his compatriots. Those from the State Department often shared their superior's opinion that the police program did not belong under the aegis of foreign aid, and probably did not belong in Brazil at all. Others, from the Central Intelligence Agency, whom the police adviser might have expected to be his natural allies, often let the policeman know that if a partnership existed, the ex-cops were very junior partners.

Sometimes the distinction between the CIA and the police adviser was made even more peremptory. Arriving in São Paulo in 1960, Maurice E. Calfee, a retired officer from the Los Angeles Police Department, was immediately set straight about the limits on his duties. He was told to stay away from the military police: the CIA was working with them. He should deal exclusively with the civil police. But in Brazil the Policia Militar, despite its name, was the main law-enforcement body in the civilian sector. Calfee understood that he was being shut out from any useful work, and after two frustrating years he resigned.

The attitude of the natives, the *brasileiros,* was entirely different. Not only was their tradition hospitable, but they could profit materially from a hearty friendship with their advisers. The Yankees brought a cornucopia of equipment to lavish upon them. Just reading through the catalogues about radios and radars and fingerprinting kits could make a police lieutenant see himself, if not a master detective, at least equal to apprehending a devious and resourceful criminal.

A strain of inferiority ran through the Latin American police departments, and it was particularly so in Brazil. Pay was low, nepotism was taken for granted, prestige was nonexistent. The young Brazilians around Belo had a saying: If you're too clumsy to be a soccer player and too stupid to get into the university and too ugly to play in a rock band, you can always join the police.

Brazilian officials acknowledged that their patrolmen were not of top quality, yet they could not help teasing these powerful North Americans who came to improve their performance. Sometimes it even seemed that the U. S. advisers were the pupils, that they were being measured continually against the ethic of the host country. Were they tough? Gentle? Intelligent? Humble? A few years later, thousands of young U. S. lieutenants and captains faced that same judging process in South Vietnam.

Jack Goin had warned Mitrione of the polite hazing he would receive. To minimize his gaffes, Mitrione conducted official business through an interpreter, a nineteen-year-old student, Ricard Pedro Neubert. To Ricard, everything about the Mitrione family was attractive, particularly the two teenaged daughters. But he knew his station and never approached either girl.

Other young people were also drawn to the bustling

household. At first they could not see past Mitrione's imposing bulk and his big cigars, and they called him the Mafia Chief. Once he ceased to scare them, they hung about the house every day.

Ricard had found that house, clean and pretty, in Belo's Anchieta district. The yard was surrounded by a low wall with an iron railing, which was for decoration, not security. Very few Brazilians knew that the United States had sent a police chief to Belo, and those aware of Mitrione's presence were entirely friendly.

Set near the top of a hill, the house had been faced with blue-and-cream-colored tiles and built around an inner patio. There were four bedrooms, which required some doubling up, and two more rooms were set aside for the maids. Outside, the road was made of cobblestones, and there were three lime trees and a mango. The flowers bloomed purple and pink.

Yet Hank Mitrione was not always happy. Buying meat at an outdoor stall did not meet a Midwestern mother's standard for hygiene, and running the drinking water through a charcoal filter was a daily nuisance. She was not always silent about the discomforts. To Brazilians, who believed that the price for peace was never too high, her complaints were sad to hear, and they felt that Mitrione was very patient with her. Only once did an outsider hear him say, aggrieved, "In the States, I couldn't make fifteen thousand dollars a year, and you couldn't have two maids. Here in Belo, we can."

At the office, Mitrione's routine ran smoothly. His duties were clear-cut: to assist the police of the state of Minas Gerais in making their investigations more scientific, to improve communications throughout the state, and to develop a new regional police academy.

In Brazil, with its history of military takeovers, the civil police were under the wing of the army. The Policia Militar (PM) might be only the regular cops on the beat, but their commander was a political appointee, generally a career army colonel.

Back home, Mitrione had seen the effect of the Republican party's stranglehold on the police. It became his announced creed that in Brazil, policemen must be apolitical, and he expounded to the Brazilians the virtues of disinterested policemen enforcing the law impartially. His listeners, applauding the ideal, could not always see how Mitrione's sermon applied to life in Belo Horizonte.

Mitrione himself could not at all times meet his own high standards. In the police laboratory there worked a Brazilian chemist who, if not formally a socialist, believed that Brazil's wealth had to be radically redistributed before the social system would be a just one. Conversations with that man invariably left Mitrione infuriated. Although he had learned to harness his hot temper, once back in his own office, he would stew over their latest exchange and complain to Ricard Neubert, "That man's impossible! He's all wrong about it! He's not thinking right!"

Dealing with Richmond's city government had taught Mitrione how to extract increased funds for his department and the off-duty time for him and his officers to further their professional education. In Belo, he refined those skills until, by 1961, the Brazilian police were awed by the equipment arriving for their new police academy and criminalistics lab: $100,000 worth of expensive cameras, projectors and screens, fingerprinting kits, and photographic equipment. At the FBI academy, Dan had acquired an enthusiasm for practice shooting. Now the AID program was sending targets and ammunition. For crime-scene training, there were kits of tools and bags for taking soil, wood slivers, and hair back to the laboratory; and at the lab itself, a new spectrograph, worth thousands of dollars, for analyzing raw material.

The traffic department first received simple gear, such as tubes to lay in the street to measure speed. Within a few months, Mitrione had produced for them electronic equipment, and radios for each of the few police cars. There was not much that could be done for the cop on the beat. He still had to call headquarters from the public phone on the corner.

Mitrione had kept his faith in the value of appearances. When the police in Belo received new uniforms, he considered the news worth writing home about. He had been sending occasional letters to the *Pal-Item* that could be converted to news stories, a way of keeping his name alive in Richmond should he want to return when his tour ended. Now he told the folks at home that in their new uniforms, the Brazilian police "will look like Richmond's finest."

He added, "Our public relations program includes changing the traffic uniforms from a plain sack-type cloth to blue, made of a better material. The public will have more respect for the police and we expect morale to be higher."

Other advisers, visiting Belo, very occasionally lured Mitrione out to explore the local night life, but left to himself, he preferred to stay home with his family. Though Hank now had maids, she was one of the rare U. S. wives without a Brazilian cook. This was the result of her desire to please her husband. In Richmond, she had mastered the succulent dishes that Maria Mitrione had brought from Bisaccia, and Dan wanted her to continue doing the cooking.

As a result, Mitrione was getting stout in the languid Brazilian sunshine. To his Brazilian hosts, he remained the model of professional behavior: a democrat who never failed to greet the elevator operator by name; a Catholic who never missed Sunday mass; a family man, and yet not above taking a peep with the other men into the windows across the street from his office.

Oscar Niemeyer, the architect who designed Brasília,

had begun his career in Belo, and the curved walls of one
of his futuristic apartment buildings seemed to undulate
like waves of the sea. To preserve the line, and disdaining
prudery, Niemeyer drafted tiers of unshielded bathrooms,
and all work stopped in Mitrione's office whenever a
woman worth coveting decided to shower during office
hours.

About this time, political tensions were rising elsewhere in Belo, unnoticed by Mitrione, who did not read
the local papers. In the fall of 1961, a division commander
of Brazil's First Army gave a speech in Belo before a conference of the state's Commercial Association. Although
the First Army was based in Rio, its crack fourth division
made its headquarters in Belo, and its commander, João
Punaro Bley, was a figure to contend with.

The meeting of businessmen and factory owners had
been underwritten by a right-wing chain of newspapers,
the *Diarios Associados*. Their publisher, Francisco de Assis
Chateaubriand, was being given funds by the CIA to pro-
mote anti-communism; predictably Punaro Bley gave an
anti-Communist speech. But its partisanship went beyond
even what a conservative audience expected to hear publicly from a general on active duty. Punaro Bley claimed
that Communists had penetrated every level of Brazilian
society and posed a serious threat to democracy.

A fierce young socialist, José María Rabello, published
a weekly paper in Belo Horizonte called *Binomio*, Two
Names. Intrigued by the coverage given the speech by
Estado do Minas, the leading newspaper of the chain sponsoring the conference, Rabello assigned a reporting team to
check into the general's background.

Binomio attracted young leftists reveling in the freedom
that the press had been enjoying since the Vargas dictatorship. Rabello's police reporter for a time was Fernando
Gabeira, a nineteen-year-old from the provinces, who was

using Belo as a way station on the road to a newspaper career in Rio.

As a boy, Fernando had watched the men of his town who owned small looms forced out of business by the textile corporations. One by one, the men had to sell their tools and go to work in the factories. Sometimes they struck for higher pay; always the police took the side of the mill owners.

In high school, one of Fernando's teachers had mused aloud about how it happened that some men were rich and other men poor. If you were to put them all on an island, the teacher said, the same men would become rich again because they worked hard. The poor were lazy.

Fernando had raised his hand and said, "I can only say that in my town, the poor work very hard."

That was the shared attitude at *Binomio,* and the reporters sent to investigate the general undertook the task gleefully. Among other things, they found that in the early stages of the Second World War, he had been active in the fascist Integralists. *Binomio* published the details of the general's background, including the fact that as governor of the state of Espirito Santo, he had constructed concentration camps for his political enemies—the liberals and the anti-Nazis. The dispatch was headed: "Who Is the General Punaro Bley? A Democrat Today, a Fascist Yesterday."

Soon after the story appeared, the general rang Rabello and demanded to see him. "You have published an article injurious to me," he said. "The affair must be resolved."

Rabello agreed to meet him but only at the newspaper office.

General Punaro Bley arrived within the hour. Rabello had prepared some remarks on the freedom of the press. The general interrupted him. "I don't want an explanation," he said. "I've come to give you a lesson."

With that, he bolted around the desk and grabbed Rabello by the neck.

The general, at fifty-three, was a bull of a man. He

seemed to expect that the twenty-four-year-old editor, with horn-rimmed glasses and an intellectual brow, would be intimidated by his age or his rank or at the least by his indignation. Instead, when the general threw a punch, Rabello returned it, blackening Punaro Bley's eye and cutting his lip.

The general had left an aide in the hall. Now, alerted by the tumult, the captain burst in, followed by Rabello's editorial staff. All of them became witnesses to Punaro Bley's ignominy. Worse still, the presence of photographers guaranteed that the general's wounds would be on the front page of every newspaper he despised.

More cursing followed, and more shouts. When Punaro Bley finally retreated, Rabello called the police. He wanted to be sure that they understood that the general had been the aggressor. He had not been reassured to hear the captain vowing as he led his bloodied superior to the elevator, "This is going to continue."

It took about two hours before three hundred junior officers from Belo's army barracks surrounded the block around *Binomio* and stopped traffic in every direction. Shock troops raced up the stairs, threw open the door, and set about destroying the office. It was nearly Christmas; they ground the staff Christmas tree into the floor. When the typewriters were demolished, they broke the toilets. Outside on the street, bazookas had been set up near the machine-gun installations. The entire military action took two hours.

The governor of Minas Gerais, an elderly and conservative politician named Magalhães Pinto, wanted to avoid a showdown with the army, but he did promise the *Binomio* staff that Belo's police would protect them against further reprisals. The damage had run to $150,000, but Rabello knew he could never win a judgment against the general or his troops.

However, he had one ally, who proved better protection than a pledge from the governor. Shortly before the episode, João Goulart had unexpectedly become president. When any Brazilian president spoke, especially Goulart, he could not take for granted that the nation's generals would heed him. Still, he decided to move against Punaro Bley. To punish the general's abuse of power, Goulart transferred him to a less prestigious post and somehow made the demotion stick. Punaro Bley chose instead to take an early retirement.

For the leftists of Minas Gerais, the *Binomio* affair had been an ugly reminder of the hostility the military felt toward them. Yet there was one redeeming aspect: Brazil was still a democracy, and Brazil's president had acted to uphold the rights of one civilian.

When a team of undergraduate scientists journeyed up from Rio to Minas Gerais, Dan Mitrione was already deep in his efforts to improve the Belo police. The students composed another sort of advisory mission: they wanted to find ways to make the state's iron-ore deposits, the largest in the world, turn a healthier profit for Brazil.

One team member was a small, round-faced, wavy-haired student named Marcos Arruda. Enrolled in the school of geology at the University of Rio de Janeiro, Marcos did not look like either a revolutionary or a martyr; and certainly during the years of the Goulart regime, his questioning of Brazil's social order was tentative and very respectful.

For example, Marcos and some friends mentioned to the director of their school that because geology courses always ran from 7 A.M. to 5:30 P.M., poor students, those who had to work to sustain themselves, were automatically barred from the profession.

"Yes," agreed the director, Othon Leonardos, "it is elitist. But geologists must be cultured. They must have money enough to travel.

"You talk about the poor," the director continued, pursuing a favorite subject, "they are good for nothing, consuming and never producing. They should jump from the hills, kill themselves.

"But," Leonardos concluded, chiding them for the question, "geology has nothing to do with politics. Our role is to go up in the hills and see how beautiful the Earth is and say, 'I understand it.' "

Lofty words, but to Marcos not inspiring. Nor could he quite accept the distinction the director drew between geology and politics. Leonardos was both a member of the commission within the Ministry of Education that laid down policy for the teaching of geology throughout Brazil and a director of Mannesmann, the German mining company.

What to make of this? When Petrobras, the federal petroleum company, offered the school two scholarships, Leonardos made the selection and gave one grant to the son of a general and the other to the son of Brazil's vice-president. Once again a student delegation called on the director and asked why he had chosen those recipients. "They need money, too," the director replied, no doubt being mischievous, "to put gas in their cars."

That answer drove Marcos into student politics. He joined his classmates in making independent mining studies; and by the time they traveled to Minas Gerais, they had uncovered some troubling statistics: 97.3 percent of Brazil's iron ore was being mined by companies controlled abroad—from the United States there was Hanna Mining, U. S. Steel, and Bethlehem Steel; from Germany, Mannesmann; from Belgium, Belgomineira.

In Minas Gerais, Marcos's assignment was to survey the iron-ore deposits. At first look, the ownership in Minas belied the earlier findings, for the bulk of the deposits belonged to a Brazilian municipal company. Probing deeper, Marcos and his team discovered that the best ore, the ore of the middle layers, had been bought up by Hanna. For the past ten years, the United States had been sending geologists to the region. During that same period, the foreign companies were bidding on concessions. Hanna had selected areas that the Brazilian government seldom visited, areas not known to contain ore at all. When the survey was finally released, it turned out that Hanna controlled the choicest deposits. Marcos could only conclude that the U. S. companies had enjoyed access to surveys in progress while the Brazilian government had not.

Armed with their findings, Marcos and the other students campaigned for a state monopoly, like Petrobras, to be called Mineirobras. It would mine the nation's ore for the good of all the people. Even in the Goulart era, that idea sounded radical. It was true that the group included two or three members of the Communist party. For that matter, Marcos, as a practicing Christian, considered himself an equally legitimate heir to heretical opinions.

CHAPTER

3

IN MID-OCTOBER 1961, Lincoln Gordon, his wife, and their youngest daughter finally arrived in Brazil. From the day that Goulart made his first cabinet appointments, Gordon had begun to take heart. He considered several of the new ministers mediocre—Tancredo Neves, for example—but others, particularly Roberto Campos, a former student of his, looked extremely promising.

Had the professor been grading Goulart's appointments publicly, Brazilians might have noticed that the further to the Left a nominee leaned, the less chance he had of receiving a passing mark. The apolitical Democrat from Massachusetts was suspicious of reformers with too much zeal.

Despite the creation of Brasília, foreign diplomats had proved loath to leave Rio. The U. S. embassy continued to operate in a ten-story building with a heart-stopping view of Guanabara Bay and Pão de Açúcar, the mountain the Brazilians saw as a sugarloaf. But President Goulart was in Brasília, and after a few days Gordon traveled there to introduce himself.

Whereas Goulart has never published his opinion of the ambassador, Gordon has given freely of his first impressions of Goulart. His countrymen called him a *primitivo*. Gordon's translation would have been closer to lout. The

Brazilian president may have had a law degree, but Gordon sniffed to himself that he had probably bought it.

Goulart was extroverted. He was crude. He was a *gaúcho*. Such was Gordon's first summation, and he never found reason to change it. Gordon also detected that pleasure in manipulating men which had made Goulart so valuable to Vargas. In short, Gordon found the president of Brazil just the sort of ignorant political boss he despised.

Even had Goulart been more polished, those early conversations would still have been rough-hewed. Gordon had just begun Portuguese lessons; yet Goulart, trusting to intimacy and fellow feeling, preferred to talk without an interpreter.

For Gordon, even the president's cordiality could be awkward. "I'm coming down to Rio, and I hope you'll come and call on me," Goulart told the ambassador. "I really want to talk with you, not just as president but as the leader of a great popular political party."

Gordon took that last remark for a touch of presumption, as though Goulart were comparing himself to John Kennedy and suggesting that the workers' party (PTB) was comparable to the Democratic party. The invitation also suggested that Goulart wanted to confide candidly in the ambassador about the political considerations that would be guiding his administration, and Gordon was leery about being drawn into that sort of intimacy.

Perhaps most important in shaping Gordon's attitude was the fact that Goulart was not trusted, either by Washington or by those proven friends of the United States, the Brazilian military. Gordon consequently held the president at arm's length while, at the same time, striving to be correct with Goulart's enemies.

The opposition lost no time in making itself known to the new ambassador. One foe, a right-wing admiral named Sílvio Heck, had a social connection to Gordon. In 1946, his niece had met Gordon at a United Nations meeting on atomic energy, and they had renewed acquaintance thirteen years later when Gordon toured Brazil on a Ford Foundation assignment. Now she called to say that her uncle wished to meet with him privately at a party she was giving. Gordon agreed.

At the right moment, the ambassador and the admiral withdrew to a side room, and Heck came quickly to the point. "You know," he said, "when I was the Navy Minister with Quadros, I opposed Goulart. He's a Communist, and he wants to deliver the country to them. To you, he may appear as a moderate. But the sooner he's thrown out, the better.

"We've polled the services," Heck continued, "and seventy-five percent of the army, much of the air force, and eighty percent of the navy feel that way about him. We are organizing. We do not need help. But we are hoping that when the day comes, the United States will take an understanding view."

"That's very interesting," said the new U. S. ambassador. Admiral Heck, having had his audience, did not press then for a commitment.

The next day, Gordon called in his deputy and the CIA station chief, and told them to check the validity of Heck's estimates. They reported back that there was no powerful coup brewing, that Heck represented a handful of officers. Gordon filed that information. He did not then, or later, as the approaches became more frequent, inform Goulart or any of Goulart's advisers about the conspiracy being plotted against Brazil's democracy.

It had been predictable that the sort of Brazilians Gordon had met over the years would oppose the government to which he was now accredited. His acquaintance with a man named Paulo Ayres, Jr., dated from 1959, when Ayres was head of the Brazilian-American cultural center in São Paulo. He was also a businessman, young and very personable, with the added grace of speaking good English.

When Gordon was asked to suggest a Brazilian delegate to a multinational business conference, he remembered his young friend, and he and Ayres had a pleasant reunion in Washington.

Now, back as ambassador, Gordon looked up Ayres and met his friends from São Paulo's corporate life. In good time, Ayres described to Gordon a political organization he was sponsoring with the cumbersome but innocuous name of the Institute for Social Research Studies (in Portuguese, IPES).

Had Gordon's interests at home been more political, the structure and goals of IPES might possibly have sounded familiar, for in 1958, a Massachusetts candy maker had founded an organization of businessmen who were concerned about communism, especially three years later, when a new administration replaced the old. That was Robert Welch's John Birch Society and the administration was John Kennedy's.

In Brazil, the motivating spirit of IPES was Glycon de Paiva, a clever mining engineer from Minas Gerais. From the day of Goulart's inaugural, de Paiva had known that the new president was a menace who must be removed.

De Paiva was often said to look like a Protestant minister, a comparison meant to underline his austerity and zeal. As he made the rounds of Rio's major industrialists, spreading his warning, he made many converts, but he never deluded himself that these men, although they made lavish gifts to his crusade, shared his ideological hatred for communism. Theirs was a different motive, and he got his best results by keeping the message simple and pungent: Goulart and his kind want to take away what you have.

Sounding that alarm, de Paiva had no trouble raising each month the equivalent of $20,000. He began to expand the scope of his organization. Paulo Ayres, Jr., became a chief IPES representative in São Paulo. In Belo Horizonte, as notoriously conservative as Dallas, Texas, de Paiva also recruited fruitfully.

De Paiva's greatest inspiration was to hire as his chief of staff a retired army general, Golbery do Couto e Silva.

Taking over half of the twenty-seventh floor of an office building in central Rio, de Paiva encouraged the general to compile dossiers on everyone he considered an enemy of the nation. Before they were done, they had files on 400,000 Brazilians.

Their standard method was to put informers on the IPES payroll, many of them soldiers on active duty. Given the army's role in Brazilian politics, de Paiva wanted to be sure that key men throughout the services remained loyal to the abstraction called the Brazilian nation rather than to the president who temporarily led it.

De Paiva also paid informers in factories, schools, and government offices. Petrobras, the state oil company, was his special target because he suspected Goulart of riddling its organization with his own supporters. As for the universities, they suffered from an affliction that de Paiva diagnosed as "too much freedom."

The priesthood was another disappointment to de Paiva, largely because of the influx of foreign clerics. By his calculation, half of Brazil's 13,000 priests were not Brazilians at all. They were outsiders from countries like Belgium and France, which could not support the number of priests their seminaries were graduating. These men brought alien ideas to Brazil. At the very time that the Brazilian masses seemed to be losing their devotion to the Church's high spiritual principles, these radicals arrived to hasten the process. Sadly, de Paiva had come to conclude that in his struggle against the forces of communism, religion was a negligible ally.

To evade detection and possible reprisals against IPES, its directors tried to represent it as an educational organization and, in fact, gave money to a campaign to reduce illiteracy among poor children. Such donations were only to shore up its façade. IPES's real work was organizing against Goulart and maintaining dossiers.

De Paiva acknowledged that his reaction against state socialism was largely visceral, and as IPES flourished he felt the need for a crash course in economic theory. To instruct him, he occasionally imported Delfim Neto, a distinguished economist from São Paulo. For airfare and fifty dollars, Delfim lectured one hour on the merits of the free enterprise system.

IPES could afford the tutorial. In Brazil, printing the telephone business directories was a lucrative private business; and its owner, Gilbert Huber, Jr., was one of the men who supported de Paiva handsomely. Huber was also financially involved with American Light and Power, of which 80 percent was owned by U. S. interests. Brazil's banks and large construction companies were equally open-handed.

Nor did de Paiva meet resistance from the most significant embassy in Brazil. Through Paulo Ayres and General Golbery, de Paiva was introduced to Ambassador Gordon, and the two men would meet from time to time. Gordon found de Paiva a smart fellow who was managing IPES with great skill, whereas de Paiva decided that Gordon was a very simple man who, pressed too hard over cocktails or dinner, was sure to retreat into, "Put yourself in my place. I'm the ambassador here." De Paiva felt Gordon meant that he would be helpful so long as he was not embarrassed publicly.

Aristoteles Luis Drummond, a student in Rio and an aspiring comrade-in-arms to de Paiva's cause, tapped an even wealthier treasury than Gilbert Huber's. By chance, Drummond stumbled on the Central Intelligence Agency.

Skinny, intense, proud of his middle-class heritage, Aristoteles was an ardent conservative, and his hero was Silvío Heck. If de Paiva brought to mind a sharper Robert Welch, Drummond had his parallel in the William F. Buckley, Jr., of the 1950s, the precocious young man who attacked Yale University as a morass of liberalism and rose to the defense of Senator Joseph McCarthy.

At eighteen, Aristoteles founded an organization of like-minded youth, Grupo de Ação Patriotica (GAP). Its natural enemy was the national student union (UNE). Since students world-wide leaned toward the political Left, GAP was not a magnet for new members. Aristoteles found it wise to pass out his leaflets selectively, and when he used spray paint to cover walls with the message *GAP with Heck*, he did it at night. Although it was calculated that GAP had 130 "hard-core" members and about five thousand "sympathizers," these persons seldom donated money to their cause. While de Paiva was taking over expensive suites in a skyscraper, Aristoteles was operating from his parents' apartment on Ipanema Beach.

One day a local radio show interviewed him for ten minutes, during which time he expounded on GAP's determination to defend liberty and property, and his conviction that only the military could be trusted to secure either commodity. The Voice of America re-broadcast the interview.

That exposure brought Aristoteles a call from the U. S. embassy requesting an appointment. Two men duly arrived at the Drummond apartment; and although in Latin America CIA operatives were seen and sworn to in the least likely places, Aristoteles had no doubts that these particular men were from the agency. They questioned him closely about his political views, then they went away. A few days later, they returned. Aristoteles observed that they committed nothing to paper and considered them worthy of 007, the popular fictional spy.

"Can we help you?" one man asked. Aristoteles said he would appreciate their help. "We'll get books for you to distribute."

It was a commitment less trifling than it sounded. A few weeks later, a truck delivered to the Drummond apartment a load of 50,000 books. True, they were not thick—paperback tracts with such titles as *China: Communists in Perspective*, by A. Doak Barnett; *The Political War: The Arm of*

International Communism, by Suzanne Labin; and best of all for paying off intracollegiate enmities, an attack on the national students union, *UNE: Instrumento de Subersão.* GAP put this free literature into the hands of high school and college students throughout the industrial triangle.

As Aristoteles labored to change the complexion of the campuses, de Paiva was beginning to recognize that house- wives were particularly receptive to warnings that godless communism was destroying Brazilian society. He set up women's societies in the major cities. In Rio, it was the Women's Campaign for Democracy (CAMDE). He gave the women rumors to spread, stories about outrages that Goulart and his cronies were supposed to be planning. "Good gossip," de Paiva called it.

Although de Paiva concentrated on disaffected mili- tary men and pious housewives, civilians were also enroll- ing in the conspiracy against Goulart through a front, organized by the CIA, called Instituto Brasileiro de Ação Democrática (IBAD). Writers on the Goulart era later puz- zled over how much Ambassador Gordon knew of the CIA's varied activities. The agency rule called for provid- ing an ambassador with as much or as little information as he showed a willingness to tolerate. Some operations could not be disguised; during this period, the United States in- creased the number of its consulates around Brazil to pro- vide cover for the CIA's expanded operations.

Certainly, Gordon knew all about IBAD, which, founded in 1959, was older than either IPES or GAP. He was aware that not only was IBAD the CIA's means of channeling money into local political campaigns but that such clandestine contributions were an absolute violation of Brazilian law.

IBAD passed on money through its two branches, Democratic Popular Action and Sales Promotion, Inc. During the elections of 1962, Popular Action underwrote the campaigns of more than one thousand candidates. In some cases, IBAD actually recruited candidates to run for office. They were given to understand that their loyalty was to IBAD, not to the political ticket with which they might be associated.

Most of the CIA's candidates, some six hundred, ran for state deputy. Another 250 ran for federal deputy, and fifteen for the federal senate. Eight ran for governorships in one of Brazil's twenty states. In Pernambuco, IBAD underwrote João Cleofas de Oliveira's campaign for governor. It was an important race because the alternative was a leftist, Miguel Arraes; and the hardscrabble northeast, while no prize in itself, was the sort of impoverished region that Washington regarded as ripe for revolution.

One indication of the Kennedy administration's concern had been a visit in June 1961 by the president's youngest brother, Edward Moore Kennedy, a twenty-nine-year-old assistant district attorney from Massachusetts. Kennedy was scheduled to meet with representatives of the Peasant Leagues, although the best-known organizer of the leagues, Francisco Julião, was out of town.

Francisco Juliano Arruda de Paula had been born into a family of sugar plantation owners, but he was no typical *senhor de engenho*, gentleman of the mill. In his adolescence, he had read a book by Friedrich Engels, and from that time on he considered himself a "man of the Left." As one of the few lawyers in the northeast who would represent the poor, the young man, nicknamed Francisco Julião, built a following and went to his state legislature in 1954 as the Brazilian Socialist party's sole successful candidate.

Landowners in the northeast still took the kingly view that God had decreed them to be wealthy, and they resisted any effort to organize the workers on their estates. The more harassed and threatened the peasants felt, the more radical their league became.

During the Eisenhower years, politicians from Brazil's

large southern cities had persuaded U. S. foreign-aid officials that the northeast was so destitute that any money spent there would only be wasted. To Lincoln Gordon, the best solution was a massive resettlement that would lure farmers hundreds of miles south and west to better land. The ambassador's wife encountered the prevailing spirit at a dinner party when she heard wealthy Brazilians speak of a town in the northeast. "It doesn't exist!" they said and laughed contentedly.

The U. S. intelligence apparatus took Julião's constituency more seriously. Equally suspect was an educator named Paulo Freyre, who, under the guise of teaching farm workers to read, was instigating them to question their condition as chattel on the land. Were these men more Fidel Castros? Lincoln Gordon agreed that there was no reason to mix literacy with politics.

CIA operatives began to distribute leaflets promoting Julião's appearance at rallies he knew nothing about. The farmers would come out in droves to see their champion but he would not appear, and somehow a fight would break out. Rumors were also circulated painting both Julião and Goulart as cuckolds. Ambassador Gordon was not averse to gossip and readily passed along stories about Goulart and his wife: that he had blackened her eyes, that she was having an affair with an air-force major. Gordon knew how such stories wounded a man of Goulart's honor. As for Julião, although he and his wife, Alexina, living in a land that did not recognize divorce, apparently had agreed on what came to be called an open marriage, stories of her affairs had never circulated until Julião became a security risk to the CIA.

(Years later, a Brazilian journalist traveling in Pernambuco heard of the CIA's compiling and printing of false documents to prove that Julião was a Communist. Other events overtook that particular strategy.)

For the CIA, there were many enemies in Pernambuco besides Freyre and Julião. By early 1962, the agency had two full-time men working out of the consulate in Recife, the state capital. Other CIA agents were placed within such seemingly straightforward groups as the Cooperative League of the United States of America (CLUSA) and the American Institute of Free Labor Development (AIFLD).

AIFLD was a creature of the early sixties, a merger of talent and funds from the CIA, the AFL-CIO, and some sixty U. S. corporations, including the Anaconda Company, I. T. T., and Pan American World Airways. Its purpose, according to President Kennedy, was to stop Castro from undermining the Latin American labor movement. Yet, at least one U. S. embassy labor attaché, a veteran of the union movement in the United States, felt a pang in watching AIFLD disrupt Brazil's progress in labor organizing under the guise of protecting the workers from communism. By 1963, in addition to its field work, AIFLD was arranging a training session in Washington for thirty-three trustworthy labor leaders, who then returned to Brazil and took clandestine roles in the anti-Goulart conspiracy.

The farm workers of the northeast, then, had reason to be suspicious of outsiders and particularly of all police, whom they regarded as the agents of their enemies. During Ted Kennedy's visit, their spokesman asked that his brother withdraw the U. S. police advisers.

When Miguel Arraes won the governorship the next year, he let it be understood that he did not want Byron Engle's men in his state. The Office of Public Safety took a mild line officially: We don't have enough advisers to cover all of Brazil in any event. Of course we shall limit them to more friendly states. But in Washington, the incident confirmed Arraes as an enemy.

Despite differences in age and occupation, most plotters against the Brazilian president shared a common estimate of their fellow citizens. Aristoteles Drummond said gently that Brazilians did not understand politics. De Paiva was blunter: Brazil was not ready for democracy.

The military, whether on active duty or in the reserve, found de Paiva's thinking congenial. At Listas Telefônicas Brasileiras S. A., printers of the Yellow Pages, Heitor Herrera, a retired general active in the campaign against Goulart, felt it was inevitable and only proper that he and his fellow army officers lead the nation to its destiny. Perhaps it was only an accident of history, but they were better equipped for the task than any other element in society. Herrera did not maintain that military officers were smarter, merely that they were better trained; and that training, which fitted them best to cope with the modern world, they owed largely to the United States. Herrera was proud enough of his stint at the U. S. Command and General Staff College at Fort Leavenworth, Kansas, to keep his diploma framed on an office wall.

Few Brazilians would dispute that training at the hands of the United States left Latin American officers, whether from the army or the police, with a new sense of direction and authority. One reason was the care and attention that U. S. training programs lavished on their political thinking. For instance, under Byron Engle's direction, a student at the police academy devoted 165 class hours—about one third of his total studies—to internal security and methods of investigation. Of those hours, fifty-five were given over to warnings about the Communist party and its techniques.

In Belo Horizonte in 1963, a group of nationalistic high school students were amazed to find the young policemen in their neighborhoods, once the butts of so many jokes, returning from the Inter-American Police Academy in Panama with a new swagger. One such student questioned a recent graduate and found that he now saw himself as marching in the front line against communism. He had also brought back a profound distrust of President Goulart.

These attempts by Washington to instill pride and duty

into Brazil's uniformed forces dated back more than forty years, from the moment the first U. S. Naval Mission in Latin America was established in Brazil in 1922. Until then, Brazilian officers had trained either in Germany or with the French, who maintained a mission in Brazil between 1919 and 1940.

The Second World War gave Washington a justification for expanding its influence even more widely in the Brazilian forces. Military planning was coordinated by a Joint Brazilian–United States Military Commission (JBUSMC). By the war's end, Brazilian training and equipment so thoroughly followed the U. S. model that nationalists protested that the only thing Brazilian in their Independence Day parade was the flag.

In the first years of peace, the United States unloaded surplus infantry and air-force equipment on Brazil at about 10 percent of cost. Among other things, the Brazilians bought more than one hundred combat aircraft. At that discount, naturally they could hardly expect the latest models, and it had been standard practice from the early days of the Krupp dynasty for munitions makers to dump their obsolete equipment on the dictators of Latin America. The weapons, after all, were more likely to be a caudillo's means for keeping his own people quiescent than for waging war across his borders.

In 1949, the Pentagon helped Brazil to set up and staff a copy of the U. S. National War College, the Escola Superior de Guerra. JBUSMC had outlived the war; and in 1954, it was registered with the United Nations as a permanent agency for the handling of military sales and assistance.

At the same time, the U. S. began creating a military-training infrastructure for the continent as a whole. In 1949, the School of the Americas opened at Fort Gulick in the Panama Canal Zone, giving courses exclusively in Spanish and Portuguese. So many of its ambitious graduates went home imbued with a fervor that brooked no civil interference that the school became known throughout the continent as *escuela de golpes,* school of coups.

In 1952, a jungle warfare school was opened at Fort Sherman, also in Panama. Training courses for Latin American flyers at Albrook Air Force Base in Panama dated back to 1943, though student pilots had to await the onset of the Vietnam war to be instructed in the dropping of napalm.

The most prestigious of all training went on at Fort Leavenworth, and many of the officers who were conspiring now to challenge Goulart had trained there. "Those men left Leavenworth," remarked a U. S. general who once served there, "with a burning ambition to identify with the United States and to be loved by their American counterparts."

With such support from the world's strongest power, serving in the Brazilian army or navy became a desirable middle-class way of life. After the home-grown military academies, a promising officer went for graduate work to a Brazilian military college or one in the United States, where he would be exposed to economics, social sciences, and administration. Men like Herrera never questioned that those years of training outstripped anything a man could receive at the civilian universities, which were hidebound, traditional, stuck in the liberal arts of the last century. Only the military was training men for today and tomorrow; the proof was the speed with which a retiring officer could find a well-paying job in industry, either Brazilian or foreign-owned.

Even when an officer did not get to the top school at Leavenworth, training in the United States could change his life. Alfredo Poeck, the son of a physics professor, went to the Special Warfare School at Fort Bragg in 1961, after he graduated from the Brazilian military academy. His three-month course in propaganda and psychological warfare at Bragg opened a whole new career to him.

Poeck was tall for a Brazilian officer, the inheritance of

German parents. He had a receding hairline, his eyes were weak and his chin negligible. He was also methodical and hard-working, and he found the twelve hours of training each day at Bragg pleasurable, even at their harshest.

Poeck was especially struck by the competence of the CIA men he met, then and later. He decided it was the best intelligence service in the world and regretted that Brazil had no counterpart. Poeck was starting to believe the adage "Man is an unviable social product," but in the chaos of Goulart's democracy, it was hard for an officer like young Poeck to see how he could use his psychological warfare training and his dedication to better his country.

The strong government that appealed to many military officers was not the sort that Goulart had in mind. He had always warned that he did not intend to be a Queen of England, a mere figurehead; and by 1962, he had resolved to sponsor a referendum that would restore his full powers. To marshal support, or at least to defuse Washington's hostility, Goulart went to the White House in April to call on Jack Kennedy.

In their talks, Goulart and Kennedy discussed the ballot initiative to return his full authority. Goulart also put forth a plan for the peaceable buying up of the foreign utilities operating in Brazil. He seemed to want to avoid the outright expropriations that had helped to sour relations with Cuba. When the talks adjourned, Kennedy agreed to a visit in July.

Upon Goulart's return to Brazil, he may have felt that his politics of conciliation with Washington had gone too far, and he compensated with a rousing May Day speech that caused any small hope around the U. S. embassy to wane once more. Nonetheless, Lincoln Gordon had to go on meeting with Goulart; it was his job. And he found the Brazilian president, if seldom admirable, full of surprises.

At the time of the Missile Crisis in October 1962, Gordon went to brief Goulart on the presence of Soviet missiles in Cuba. He took along Lieutenant Colonel Vernon A. (Dick) Walters, the new military attaché. Through his service with the Brazilian Expeditionary Force during the Second World War, Walters was the best-connected U. S. official in Brazil, being particularly close to an army general named Humberto Castelo Branco.

Walters possessed a natural flair for languages. He had been Richard Nixon's interpreter during the trip to South America that saw the vice-president insulted and stoned. Sometimes Walters would worry aloud to his friends that his extreme facility as an interpreter had slowed down his promotion to more substantial assignments.

Goulart listened to the ambassador's report, interrupting only to say "I thought Rusk said lately that those arms were purely defensive."

Gordon thought, So he is aware of what's going on. "Yes," he replied, "but now we have evidence to the contrary."

"Well, Ambassador," Goulart said, "if that's true, it's not just a threat to you; it's a threat to all of us. Be assured of our solidarity in this matter."

This momentary rapport was not enough to temper Gordon's conviction that the Brazilian president himself was the greatest danger to his country's democracy. Goulart might not be a Communist, but he would try to emulate Vargas and stage a coup within his own government to obtain even greater powers. Since he was so erratic and inept, that move would only open the way for a Communist takeover of the country.

Because men who already hold their country's highest office rarely overthrow their own government, there was no word Gordon and his advisers could find to describe what they accused Goulart of plotting. It fell to the ambassador to invent a term, and he took pride in its aptness and ingenuity. Anyone working from beneath a government to overthrow it was engaged in "subversion." Therefore, Goulart's plot was "superversion."

John Kennedy chose not to repay Goulart's visit. Instead, he sent his brother Robert to Brazil in December of 1962. Gordon sat in on the meetings between the attorney general of the United States and the president of Brazil, and he saw that Bobby Kennedy had neither the time nor the talent for Latin indirection.

It's been a turbulent period, Kennedy told Goulart. But now with your plebiscite, you'll have a fresh start, a real opportunity for moving ahead. (A few weeks later, by a margin of 4 to 1, the voters returned full presidential powers to Goulart.)

Kennedy continued: We can offer our cooperation and support. However, should you flirt with romantic left-wing causes and give weight to the Communists and their friends—should that mood dominate—then it will be difficult for us to cooperate. That will be bad for you and bad for Brazil.

In a Brazilian phrase, Goulart asked for particulars: "*Da nomes de bos,*" he said. Give names to the bulls.

Kennedy and Gordon mentioned Almino Afonso, the labor minister, whom the U. S. embassy considered radical, and a general at Petrobras, the national oil company.

When Goulart shuffled his cabinet early the next year, he left in office the men whom Gordon had considered too far left. At dinner, Goulart asked the ambassador, "You remember the visit of Roberto Kennedy? How do you think he'll like my new cabinet?"

"It's a mixed bag," Gordon replied dryly. Once again he listed the men his embassy regarded with suspicion.

"Oh," Goulart said cheerfully, "I can keep an eye on them."

With the help of the CIA, however, Gordon had begun to put together his own file—a prosecution brief—against Goulart's government. He kept track of those unions that

Goulart was seeding with suspected Communists: the petroleum workers, the merchant marines, the railroad unions, the communications workers, the bank clerks; and Walters kept him informed of potential subversion within Goulart's military household.

Thus began a time of intense rumor. Gordon was told that Goulart confided to visitors how enormously he envied Juan Perón because in his day the Argentinian dictator was supposed to have had a button on his desk that he could push and send the port workers, for example, out on strike. And there was another button to send them all back to work. Gordon granted that the story might be apocryphal, but what a potential for despotism it revealed!

On the surface, the antagonism seemed to be one-sided. As late as mid-1963, Goulart was still sounding out the U. S. ambassador before he went forward with any reform. "What would you think," he asked Gordon, "if I were to decree that all of ten or twenty kilometers adjoining any federal public works—roads, dams, anything—would be expropriated and subdivided among the people?"

Gordon replied at measured length that if the president was truly interested in land reform, that method would seem both arbitrary and inadequate. "You'd just be left with some peculiar patterns," Gordon concluded.

Goulart agreed, but he explained that the plan would infuriate his political opponents. It was the gleeful remark of a reformer paying off old scores against his conservative opposition. All Gordon saw, with considerable disgust, were Goulart's limitations: that he would weigh an issue for its political advantages.

Meantime, Goulart's enemies continued to meet with the ambassador, not only Gordon's personal friends like Ayres and de Paiva, but others whose language seemed extremist to the ambassador, even though Gordon himself had mastered the vernacular of the Cold War, and these days was regularly tossing off phrases like "parlor pink" and "playing footsie with the Communists."

Within the Brazilian military, traditional political terms were being redefined to satisfy Goulart's opponents. By any usual measure, General Pery Constant Bevilacqua, the commander of the Second Army in São Paulo, was a conservative. Yet word soon passed through the higher echelons that he was critical of the scheming of men like Silvío Heck. Goulart might indeed be a menace, General Pery told his fellow officers, but he had been voted into office, and it was up to the people, not the army, to put him out. That earned General Pery a reputation for being disloyal.

Increasingly, the lines were drawn: the Brazilian military officers on one side and, on the other, Brizola, the labor unions, the Peasant Leagues, the majority of enlisted men, the Communists.

The showdown came in March 1964. Though the U. S. military attachés respected Silvío Heck, they knew that a successful coup could not be led by the navy but would require the army. It would especially require those commanders who were either friendly to Goulart or hesitant to see democracy overthrown.

One key figure was General Amaury Kruel, who had replaced General Pery as commander of the Second Army. Kruel's intimacy with Goulart created a problem, since São Paulo's forces were essential to the success of a coup. Walters was quoted as telling Brazilian officers that if they really wanted to be helpful, they should prevail on Kruel to join the conspiracy.

In February of that year, Philip Agee, the conscientious CIA officer from Notre Dame, had been in Washington preparing for a change of assignment. He had received two promotions in Ecuador, bringing him to GS-11, about the rank of captain in the army. His successes in Quito had included bugging diplomats' houses, suborning and bribing local officials, and disseminating lies through the Ecuadorian press. He was being rewarded with a transfer to Montevideo, with the bonus, for a Floridian like Agee, of its famous beaches.

During his stopover in Washington, Agee spent the night in McLean, Virginia, at the home of the chief of the Brazil branch of the CIA's Western Hemisphere Division. The chief, Jim Noland, briefed Agee on Brazil, the most serious problem the United States was facing in Latin America.

One pressing concern was the Brazilian parliamentary investigation into the CIA's corruption of the 1962 elections through IBAD and ADEP. The CIA had spent as much as $20 million, and everyone involved at the U. S. embassy, from Lincoln Gordon down, was worried about the incriminating evidence that might be made public.

A scandal was averted only by three lucky developments: five of the nine members of the investigating committee had themselves received CIA funds; three of the banks involved—First National City Bank, the Bank of Boston, and the Royal Bank of Canada—refused to reveal the foreign sources of money deposited in the IBAD and ADEP accounts; and best of all, President Goulart, still hoping to get along with Washington, saw to it that the final report was laundered. The offices of both IBAD and ADEP were closed. But to the disappointment of the leftists, no detailed indictment of the foreign agents who had broken Brazil's election laws was supplied.

Throughout the spring of 1964, a Pentagon specialist on Brazil was astonished at the impatience of liberal Democrats around Washington who kept nagging at him, When will your army people finally get going? But the Kennedy years had already proved that distinguished liberals, given authority overseas, could surmount their domestic principles. For example, as early as 1961, John Kenneth Galbraith had urged President Kennedy to undercut President Diem in South Vietnam and prepare the way for a more efficient regime headed by the army.

The embattled Goulart tried to hang on to the presidency with his only weapon, the support of the people. He scheduled a series of public addresses to reassure the population that rumors about his tyrannical ambitions were false. Whatever effect that strategy had on his countrymen, it only further alarmed the intelligence operatives in the Department of Defense, who saw him borrowing his tactics from Fidel Castro. "Going out to the rabble," one influential DOD analyst called it. "Inciting them. Practicing public-square democracy."

The president's brother-in-law tried to buttress Goulart's position by announcing the formation of Groups of Eleven. These groups would be armed, and should the military attempt a coup, they would be prepared to resist it.

Fernando Gabeira, the former police reporter for *Binomio* in Belo Horizonte, had come to Rio to work for *Pamfleto*, a newspaper published by Leonel Brizola. Fernando joined one of the Groups of Eleven and saw at once that Brizola's movement was all bluff. If a coup comes, each cell was told, try to resist it. But how? With what? The groups had been quickly organized; they lacked both training and equipment; and like the Peasant Leagues, they were immediately swarming with informers. Fernando was sure that the embassy knew how ill-prepared and ineffectual the Groups of Eleven were; and when he heard later that Gordon had cited them as one more excuse for the military takeover, he marveled at the ambassador's cynicism. When Gordon first arrived in Brazil, Fernando and his socialist friends had underestimated him. Just an academic, they thought, puffing on his pipe to hide his befuddlement. Now he was at the center of a plot to overthrow the government of the fifth largest nation in the world.

Goulart called a public meeting for March 13. Besides delivering a speech, he was expected to use the occasion to sign his patchy land expropriation bill. For two weeks, the opposition papers attacked the coming rally as perilous to the public order. In Rio, anonymous callers were spreading the message: "Don't go to the Communist meeting."

Out of Washington came news of the creation of the Business Group for Latin America, a linking of U. S. business and U. S. government, with David Rockefeller, president of the Chase Manhattan Bank, presiding over thirty-seven executives of such corporations as Standard Oil, United Fruit, U. S. Steel, Ford Motors, and E. I. Du Pont de Nemours and Company. The group would not be official nor was it seeking publicity. Rather than involve itself only with AID projects, it would attempt to deal with the continent's "political troubles." Late in January 1964, the members had met at the White House with President Johnson; AID Director David Bell; and Johnson's Latin American coordinator, Thomas Mann, who was no partisan of the Kennedy administration's Alliance for Progress. The businessmen reported being received with a warmth they had not felt at the White House for three years.

In the press, Goulart's enemies were now finding it ominous that he had chosen Friday, March 13, for his rally. Not, however, for superstitious reasons. Congress adjourned on March 7 and would reconvene on March 15; and the possibility existed that Goulart, in his demagogic speech, planned to declare a state of siege and keep Congress closed.

One concern of the conservatives was that if Goulart intended to inflame his audiences with the injustices of their daily life, he did not have to search for evidence. Every day the newspapers had fresh examples. The minimum wage was $23 a month; the old and disabled had to get by on even less. One pensioner who had lost his leg in a railroad accident won a slight increase in compensation when Rio's zoo director testified that it cost five times more than the man's monthly pension to feed an adult chimpan-zee.

Prior to the rally, Goulart was floating new proposals: requiring corporations to make loans in order to expand credit for workers; pegging rentals on apartments to the level of the minimum wage; launching an inquiry into all government-controlled business. He had also signed a de-cree compelling manufacturers to add a line of shoes and fabrics priced low enough for the poor to afford. Carlos Lacerda, now the governor of the state that included Rio, protested that the result would be a uniform look, like that of women in Russia. "Choosing colors at will," Lacerda said, "is one of the rights of a democracy."

Everyone seemed to understand that a battle was loom-ing. A spokesman for Rio's Industrial Center proposed to train families in the use of arms, since in the state of Guanabara alone, he said, there were nine thousand Com-munists. Other reports noted that Goulart intended to speak from the very grandstand where Vargas had pro-claimed his dictatorship.

At last the evening of March 13 arrived. Brizola spoke first and attacked the Brazilian Congress as "do-nothing." This statement was designed to contrast with Goulart's action taken before the rally—his signing of the land ex-propriation bill. Besides the swaths along railroads and irri-gation dams, the bill applied to holdings of five hundred hectares or more but only if the land was not being prop-erly used. He also announced plans to take over the last seven private oil refineries, all Brazilian-owned, which had not yet been brought under federal control.

In his speech, Goulart reached out to his opponents on the Right, observing that General Douglas MacArthur had carried out a more radical distribution of land in Japan after the Second World War than anything in the Brazilian plan. To his supporters on the Left, Goulart pledged that this was only a first step. To all the Christian crusaders, especially de Paiva's housewives, Goulart remarked that "Christendom should not be used as a shield for privilege."

Watching Goulart's address on television, Lincoln Gordon was not mollified. First of all, those oil takeovers might not be legal. Secondly, the man standing directly behind Goulart was Darcy Ribeiro, the former rector of Brasília University, head of Goulart's domestic policy advisers, and a dangerous man. Ribeiro had amassed a number of black marks with the embassy. He had attacked the *clube dos contemplados*, the privileged ones, whom he estimated made up five million Brazilians. The other seventy-five million, Dr. Darcy said, were excluded from that club. He also announced that while he himself had no intention of joining the Communist party, it should once again be legalized in Brazil. Furthermore, he had shown the effrontery at diplomatic receptions to let Gordon understand that he felt the ambassador's meddling in Brazil's affairs had overstepped proper diplomatic limits.

Now there he was at Goulart's side. It was perfectly obvious to Gordon that Ribeiro had even written the president's speech. Gordon was flying to Washington for consultations over the weekend. As he listened to the last two thirds of Goulart's speech over the radio on the drive to Galeão Airport, he decided that the situation had finally become untenable.

In the final days before the coup, Washington was being kept well informed. Walters wired a report to the Pentagon, and Secretary of Defense Robert McNamara called in his advisers, including a senior analyst from the Defense Intelligence Agency with good contacts in Brazil. McNamara was not debating the merits of a military coup against a civilian president in a Latin American democracy. He was convinced that many confirmed Communists—or socialists; it was not important what these leftists called themselves—had a powerful influence over Goulart. McNamara was worried, however, that Goulart had already "superverted" the military, having packed it with so many of his supporters that the army would not be able to rise up against him. Gordon had recently coined another phrase for that process: "overmining" the government.

McNamara's only other misgivings seemed to concern the success of the coup. Six months earlier, the United States had collaborated with the anti-Diem forces in South Vietnam to bring down a civilian government and substitute a military man. The first, and regrettable, choice had been the hulking, easygoing general Big Minh, who was popular with his people but an anathema to the more energetic and heads-up U. S. advisers. It took a second small coup three months later to transfer power to a U. S. favorite, Nguyen Khanh.

In Brazil that particular problem would not arise. Walters had remained extremely close to Humberto Castelo Branco, who would head up the proposed coup. But would it succeed? McNamara's analyst from the Defense Department assured him it would.

The secretary then turned to General Joe Carroll for guidance. Did this fellow from army intelligence know what he was talking about? The analyst spoke up again, pointing out that in any case the United States did not want to be openly involved.

Yes, McNamara agreed, that's the ideal. Let them do it. But I'm getting gloomy reports—this general has a Communist wife, that one is a Goulart hack.

It was decided that the Brazilian military should proceed as planned. Tentative arrangements were made for secret help if that became necessary: clandestine arms dropped in by air, tankers docking at Santos with U. S. oil if the Communists succeeded in seizing Petrobras. There was even a contingency plan in the unlikely event the Russians made a move; and a Chilean journalist later reported another commitment: during his stopover in Rio in early March, General Andrew P. O'Meara, the commander of the U. S. Southern Command, had promised to fly paratroopers out of the Panama Canal Zone and drop them into any pockets of resistance left. Washington officials later stressed that two possibilities were never considered seriously: the clandestine use of U. S. troops and an attempt to talk the military out of the coup.

In Brazil, the generals themselves were getting jittery as the time neared. Goulart was obviously popular among the enlisted men, the mechanics, and technicians of the air force. What if the officers found themselves with no flight-worthy aircraft? For that matter, how loyal to their commanders were the army sergeants? Or the navy's seamen?

The generals believed that the civil war they were planning could drag on for three months, even longer, but they believed their assurances from Gordon and their other U. S. contacts: if they could hold São Paulo for forty-eight hours, Washington would recognize them as Brazil's legitimate government.

The week of the coup saw a huge march against Goulart, organized by IPES. In São Paulo, tens of thousands of people walked from Praça de Republica to Praça de Sé in a March of the Family with God for Freedom. The march ended with a manifesto of São Paulo women on behalf of Christianity and democracy. However, not every Christian joined in; the archbishop of São Paulo forbade his bishops to join the march because he said it had been organized by McCann Erickson, the U. S. advertising agency.

Goulart's temperate speech had neither brought him friends nor bought him time. At a Labor party lunch on March 19, some party members asked him to close the Congress. Goulart refused categorically.

The next day, Goulart pledged to the liberal wing of the Social Democrats that he "would not agree to be a dictator even for a single minute." He wanted only to hand to his successor "a new Brazil."

But the rumors kept engulfing him. On March 22, Goulart was forced to assure the public that he was not planning to alter the constitution to extend his term. And Glycon de Paiva churned emotions further with an unproved charge that Goulart had appointed twenty-eight hard-core Communists to key positions in his government.

On March 23, when Gordon returned from Washington, Goulart's days were nearing their end. But Goulart had one last pluck at the eagle's feathers. He asked Brizola to become president of the Brazilian Labor party, perhaps hoping to bank his fire with responsibility. Brizola's faction was to form a front with the country's workers and students to retain mining concessions for Brazilians, extend the vote to illiterates, legalize the Communist party, put all foreign aid under federal control, nationalize foreign banks and insurance companies, and create a monopoly for coffee exports.

The conservatives responded by announcing an immense anti-Communist rally in Rio on April 2. That was also the target date the military had chosen to depose Goulart.

By the night of March 27, Walters was able to remove any doubt about Castelo Branco and assure the State Department that the general was firmly committing his prestige to the plot: "It is now clear that General Castelo Branco finally accepted leadership of forces determined to resist Goulart Coup or Communist takeover ... Mar. 13 meeting and tremendous response to São Paulo March for God and Freedom have instilled new vigor into plotters."

The president was spending the Easter holidays at his vast ranch in Rio Grande do Sul. Gordon had always been a bit nettled that Goulart so clearly preferred fishing and hunting with his sons to the duties of office, that he favored the company of uncouth *gaúchos* to the conversation of diplomats. In Goulart's absence, thirty sailors had been arrested for making political statements, and three hundred marines were dispatched to arrest their protesting comrades, which they could not or would not do.

Upon his return from his ranch, Goulart set the sailors free. They marched through the streets, shouting: "Long Live Jango!" To the senior military men it verged on mutiny, and the navy minister, known for his discipline, resigned in protest.

Then, unrepentant, Goulart met on the night of March 30 with a party of more enlisted men and used the forum to attack the international oil trusts, the greedy owners of apartment houses, the dishonest tradesmen, and the foreign drug manufacturers. Those were the interests, Goulart said, like Vargas and Quadros before him, which were financing the campaign against him.

That happened on a Monday night. Early the next day, Gordon, Walters, Gordon Mein, the deputy chief of mission, and the CIA station chief gathered in the ambassador's office. The army generals of Minas Gerais were unwilling to wait another day. At 9:30 A.M., Tuesday, March 31, 1964, the U. S. embassy got word from an army contact: "The balloon is up!"

The generals marched their troops down from Minas Gerais to join what surely would be a bloody war. Some units of enlisted men were told they were heading for Rio to secure the city against Goulart's enemies, and they marched willingly, nervously, to preserve democracy.

In Washington, an array of the top representatives of the United States government (USG), were also edgy. The March 31 telcon to Gordon came from Dean Rusk, Robert McNamara, General of the Army Maxwell Taylor, General Andrew O'Meara, CIA director John A. McCone, George Ball, Thomas Mann, and special presidential assistant Ralph Dungan. The message granted that such an "opportunity" might not recur but urged the embassy not to "get the USG out in front on a losing cause."

The telcon also posed some belated questions: "Who are the possible civilians who might lay claim to presidency of new government? This does not rule out possibility of military junta as last resort but that would make U. S. assistance much more difficult. What information do you have as to military plans for action? What plans are there for interdicting possible 'break-out' of First Army from

Rio? We assume interdiction should occur in the escarpment area on road between Rio and São Paulo and also on road between Rio and Belo Horizonte. Do you have any information as to what friendly governors and army commanders in northeast area are planning?"

The final question removed any possible misconception about which side the United States had chosen: "Would it be necessary for U. S. to mount large materiel program to assure success of takeover?"

Later "Top Secret" communiqués from the Joint Chiefs of Staff indicated how much the Pentagon was relying on Gordon and his staff to direct the U. S. role in the coup. One message stated that a 110-ton package of arms and ammunition was being held at McGuire Air Force Base pending Gordon's determination that the Brazilian military or police required early U. S. support. In addition, a carrier task force was continuing toward the South Atlantic awaiting Gordon's word that port calls or other U. S. demonstrations of naval power were definitely not wanted. The ambassador was also asked to determine how much of the petroleum shipment should be continued.

That night, March 31, Gordon called on Juscelino Kubitschek. For all the accusations of corruption and the indisputable inflation during his regime, Kubitschek remained a popular politician. Now with Goulart on his way out, Gordon wanted Kubitschek to lobby with the Brazilian Congress to give an appearance of legality to the new regime.

An hour before midnight that same night, General Kruel, the most reluctant of the coup makers, finally joined with his colleagues. Had he held out any longer, very likely he would have been arrested by the officers around him.

If Goulart knew that the United States government was not seamless, if he appreciated the deep division between speeches by Kennedy or Johnson supporting social reform and the resistance to those reforms by the U. S. business community, the intelligence services, the Pentagon and the police advisers, he may have assumed that a president in Washington spoke for the stronger impulse. On the night of March 31, Goulart learned otherwise.

That division was a long-standing puzzle to the politicians of Latin America. Rómulo Betancourt of Venezuela once tried to convince Ché Guevara that the United States had two faces. One could look repressive and imperialistic, Betancourt maintained. The other face was friendly and devoted to social justice. No, said Ché, there is only one face, and it is the repressive one.

On April 1, as the coup became general knowledge, Gordon worried about securing the embassy. Situated only a couple of blocks from the large square in front of the opera house, it could never be protected completely. Gordon remembered hearing that when Quadros resigned, a crowd hurling rocks had broken a dozen of the irresistibly large green-tinted windows. These windows were always sealed, and because there were equally tall buildings on three sides, Gordon ordered the blinds drawn against snipers.

Although it was a hot, humid day, he ordered the air conditioner turned off. Otherwise, if the rebels—anyone loyal to the civilian president—succeeded in starting a fire on a lower floor, smoke would spread throughout the building much more rapidly.

The ambassador also sent home most of the staff and prepared to await reports from the battlefield with a handful of men he called his "executive action group" in his stifling, dark office on the eighth floor. The ninth floor belong to the CIA; the tenth was given over to communications. Gordon ordered that documents be sent up to those three floors, and he posted the embassy's full complement of twenty marines.

But there was no battle. Some students massed to protest the coup in Cinelandia, the square facing the major movie theaters; others gathered at a student cafeteria. One crowd charged up the stairs at the Military Club. The guard shot into their midst and killed two students. The crowd fell back.

Around the country, many commanders were proving watchful and slow to rally to the example of Minas Gerais. But neither the Communists, the labor unions, the enlisted men, nor Brizola's Groups of Eleven mounted a resistance: they were waiting for word from Goulart.

At the main air-force base in Rio, Santa Cruz, the enlisted men, having heard early reports of a coup, seized the base and put their officers under arrest. The chief of the air-force general headquarters was rumored to sympathize with the Communists. Now the mutineers called him, asking what action should be taken. Bomb the army columns coming down from Minas? Some officers were willing to fly, and the others would fly with guns at their necks. But the officer, Major Brigadier Francisco Teixeira, said, Keep organized. Release your officers. Wait and see.

Carlos Marighela, a former deputy in parliament and a leader in the Communist party, ordered Teixeira to bomb the columns coming down from Minas and, at the same time, Governor Lacerda's palace. Teixeira refused to take such an order from Marighela. It would have to come from either Luís Carlos Prestes, the head of the Communist party, or from Jango Goulart.

Prestes did nothing. Earlier in the year, Nikita Khrushchev had reportedly told him that he should work to have the Communist party legalized. The Soviet Union, Khrushchev added, did not want either to finance Brazil or to tangle with the United States over the country.

Goulart proved himself to be more *brasileiro* than fiery *gaúcho*. He flew south to Pôrto Alegre and met with Brizola, who tried to persuade him to stand and fight. Their argument was long and loud. Finally Brizola accused his brother-in-law of being a coward.

No, said the president, I don't want to be responsible for bloodshed among Brazilians.

. . .

For Carlos Lacerda, the coup meant a great opportunity. Under the law, Vice-president Mazzilli could serve 120 days. Then, given Washington's preference for a civilian front man, the military would need someone in mufti to complete Goulart's term. Kubitschek would never take the job. Constitutionally, the interim term would bar him from seeking a full term next year. But the U. S. embassy had allowed Lacerda to understand that he would be a natural temporary choice.

Taking to the airwaves, Lacerda gave one of his most impassioned speeches. He ringed his palace with garbage trucks and urged everyone hearing his voice to rush there and join the barricades against the supporters of Goulart.

At the U. S. embassy, all that Ambassador Gordon and his team could know on the afternoon of April 1 came from the runners they sent into the streets. These agents returned to say that the army had broken up the crowds of students. The siege was ended. It had lasted ninety minutes.

Everyone in the room, aware that a historic moment had passed, looked to the ambassador to provide the fitting phrase. He might fairly have congratulated his staff on their success at "destabilization," but that word did not enter popular usage until Salvador Allende was overthrown in Chile, and it was not coined by Lincoln Gordon.

Still, the ambassador sensed the challenge and rose to it. For years afterward, Walters would chuckle and tease Gordon by repeating his memorable words: "Turn on the air conditioner."

There was one more nervous day for Gordon to pass; but by nightfall on April 2, it was clear that the military had Brazil entirely under its control, and President Johnson had already sent a congratulatory wire to the new government. About twenty people had died in the coup d'état, a low enough figure for its backers to characterize it as bloodless. They also termed it a "revolution."

For Lincoln Gordon, it was as though a nightmare had ended. He went home to the official residence, and for the first time in months he enjoyed a solid night's sleep.

When Gordon returned to Washington, he found the prevailing mood as jubilant as his own. Everyone wanted to share in the credit. William C. Doherty, Jr., director of AIFLD, did his boasting in a radio interview: "What happened in Brazil did not just happen—it was planned—and planned months in advance. Many of the trade-union leaders, some of whom were actually trained in our institute, were involved in the revolution, and in the overthrow of the Goulart regime."

Gordon, who was more discreet, felt that Thomas Mann, in seeking to impress Congress with the administration's sagacity, had bragged a bit in the claims he made for U. S. involvement in the overthrow.

In their responses to Mann's testimony, the congressmen appeared willing to give Mann and his colleagues at the State Department a healthy measure of credit. Representative Wayne Hays, the Ohio Democrat, called the quick approval of the coup the best thing that had happened in Latin Armerican policy in a long, long time.

General O'Meara reminded congressmen of the record in Latin America since John Kennedy was elected president: in nine instances, military juntas had replaced elected governments. But the general was not pointing a critical finger. "The coming to power of the Castelo Branco government in Brazil last April," O'Meara said, "saved that country from an immediate dictatorship which could only have been followed by Communist domination."

Congressman Harold Gross, the Iowa Republican, inquired, "It is a dictatorship today?"

General O'Meara replied, "No."

While in Washington, Ambassador Gordon ran into Robert Kennedy. The attorney general was still grieving over the murder of his brother, but he found cheer in the events in Brazil.

"Well, Goulart got what was coming to him," Kennedy told Gordon. "Too bad he didn't follow the advice we gave him when I was down there."

CHAPTER

4

VERY FEW OF the U. S. citizens in Brazil deplored the coup, the police advisers least of all. The closer their ties to Brazil's business and military circles, the more strongly they believed that the coup was long overdue. Nor did it trouble the advisers that there was an overnight change in their role, that they had been training the police in a democracy and now would be training the police of a dictatorship. That distinction, and the different assignments that might be in store for Brazil's police, also failed to disturb either U. Alexis Johnson or Byron Engle.

In February 1963, Dan Mitrione had been transferred to Rio, where he began to spend more time with the police colonels and thus became less accessible to the average policeman around the barracks. Most junior officers liked what they saw of him, and word spread around headquarters that he got results—more hardware, including reloading machines for revolvers, radios, riot control equipment; and more men accepted at the police academy in Washington. He also introduced the policeman's notebook, standard procedure in the United States, for keeping track of activities on the beat. He urged officers to cut back on ceremony and spend more time on supervision, to get out of headquarters and check their patrolmen.

Mitrione's job expanded even further when the new head of the Guanabara state police, an army colonel, approached him at headquarters. "I've driven a jeep all my life," the colonel said. "Now, they've given me a sedan to drive. Will you show me how?" From that favor, a friendship developed.

Each morning Mitrione spent four hours with the new commander, discussing budgeting, distribution, equipment, the assigning of men. After they had run through the major topics, he would repeat the discussion with the commander's top twelve men. When his lectures were over, he expected the men to take twelve of their own men and brief them with the same material.

Mitrione and his secretary worked out of a small office in the downtown *cuartel*, the police barracks. The office was white stucco, and lights behind an overhead glass gave the cubicle the look of an aquarium. Mitrione's door opened onto a cement basketball court. At its far end rose a small chapel, Nossa Senhora das Dores, Our Lady of the Pains.

That name later took on a sardonic, hurtful meaning for civilians brought to headquarters. Before the coup, however, officers around the barracks believed that the pain was theirs alone. Police the world over, ran the lament, are the same: underpaid, overworked, never supported by the people. Mitrione himself, now sufficiently fluent in Portuguese, joined in the constant griping, whereas his predecessor had never ventured a word in the language.

For months before the coup, the officers had nursed special grievances, each day sharing the most recent outrages committed against them by Goulart's supporters. Their children were abused in school, left-wing teachers grading them low because their fathers were *gorilas*, police or military officers. The policemen did not need W. S. Gilbert to tell them their lot was not a happy one. An adviser stationed with Mitrione in Rio used to say that a policeman was a repository of hurt, and his listeners did not jeer at that striving after poetry.

They all had their stories, *brasileiros* and *norte-americanos:* how the press misused its freedom, how every story about the police was either slanted or snide. There was always room to report that police officer Mauricio Guimarães had been caught stealing a basket of flowers from a florist's shop, or that Severino Bezerra da Silva, a plainclothesman in the theft section, had his pocket picked in the post office. Once, in fact, the police had held a shootout with revolutionaries—dangerous men who had killed two policemen—and the press reported the incident as an assassination of political protestors.

"I'll tell you how that headline should have read," a Brazilian policeman complained to his adviser. "It should have read: 'The Forces of Good Won Over the Forces of Evil.' Instead, the press just murdered us. Why not tell the press to get out of here?"

The adviser hearing that complaint was not the man to defend a free press. Back home, he had once given the publisher of a small newspaper a traffic ticket and subsequently found himself called a liar in print; Dan Mitrione could also remember the bludgeon that Rudy Leeds had made of the *Pal-Item;* and many other advisers had at some time also run afoul of a local newspaper. As the military regime tightened controls over Brazil's press, few U. S. advisers around the police *cuartels* were arguing that the censorship set a dangerous precedent.

As for social programs, most advisers thought that the military regime's leading economist, Roberto Campos, was sensibly ordering the national priorities by favoring industrial development over all other goals. Coming from the world's leading industrial nation, they knew they foresaw better than the impatient Brazilian students the rewards that would one day accrue to every citizen. At police headquarters, one adviser paraphrased approvingly what he took to be the junta's philosophy: "The generals are saying, 'Sure, share the pie. But let's make it a bigger pie before we divide it.' "

Over the early years of the police program, under Kubitschek, Quadros, and even Goulart, most U. S. advisers, unless they were CIA officers using the AID program for cover, had not faced the problem of political subversion. Now there was a new class of criminals, the political rebels; and had their sympathies not lain so totally with the local police, advisers like Mitrione might have faced a dilemma. Officially, the line was clear-cut and antiseptic: police work was concerned with homicides, bank robberies, and kidnapping. The motive was not important.

But in their hearts, policemen from both Brazil and the United States knew better. Subversives were trying to infiltrate the established institutions: schools, labor unions, the Church. One officer returned from a raid on a monastery suspected of harboring dissidents, and reported seeing a photograph of Ché Guevara superimposed over Christ's face. At headquarters, it was hard to determine whether the outrage over that blasphemy was more religious or political.

The danger might be clear, but the means for dealing with it was not. General Golbery had gone to Brasília with his hundreds of thousands of files to set up Brazil's first national intelligence service, the SNI. But sometimes the material in those dossiers was hard to prove, and court procedures were still cumbersome and slow. Thousands of men and women, according to the police, were escaping their just punishment in the wake of the coup. Was there no recourse?

As it turned out, there was a solution at hand. In Washington, students at the International Police Academy would later be shown Gillo Pontecorvo's *Battle of Algiers*. The film portrayed policemen loyal to France regrouping at night into secret squads that wreaked reprisals on Algerian nationalists, bombing their homes and killing their families.

Brazilian police already had a similar blueprint in the actions of their own less scrupulous members. For years, in the tough suburbs of Rio, like Caxias, gangs had contested for control over drugs and whores. When a gang leader needed to eliminate a rival, he sometimes paid a policeman to do the job for him.

The U. S. advisers knew of that practice; and in the years before the 1964 coup, they used it as one more argument for raising a policeman's pay. Mitrione and the others had argued that if the rookie was given more money, headquarters could demand a higher standard of performance.

Yet the practice of off-duty murder was never stamped out, only channeled to new purposes. The year of the military takeover, a Rio policeman named Milton Le Cocq was murdered by a criminal nicknamed *Cara de Cavalo*, Horseface. Le Cocq's friends on the force vowed to avenge him by killing ten gangsters. In a short time, it became clear that their zeal outran mere vengeance. The bodies of thirty petty criminals—*marginais*, in Brazilian slang—were found dumped at roadsides and in remote fields. Pinned to the bodies were hand-lettered notes of explanation: "I was a thief." "I sold drugs." All were signed E. M., for *Esquadrão da Morte*, Death Squad.

Even under a military regime, which was substituting army trials for civil ones, the police found justice lagging and capricious, so the quick, sure judgments of the E. M. spread to other cities, where the police pooled their intelligence. This was not a competitive effort; on a wall at police headquarters in Rio hung a flag, a fraternal gesture from the Death Squad in São Paulo.

Le Cocq's killer, Horseface, was finally trapped on a farm. After he was shot to death, each policeman in the posse stepped forward and fired into his corpse. Such a ritual killing had been clean, in its way: but bodies began turning up with marks of torture—cigarette burns on the skin, knife marks in the flesh. The Death Squads also started courting publicity for their executions. In Rio, a man calling himself Red Rose alerted newspapers to where they could find the latest "ham." In São Paulo, public relations were handled by an officer with the code name White Lily.

Although some members of the Death Squads maintained a formal fiction that they themselves were not involved, they let their identities be known among elements of the public they believed would admire them. One such officer was Sergio Fernando Paranhos Fleury, thirty-one years old at the time of the coup and very ambitious.

The son of a coroner who had died when the boy was eleven, Fleury, with his slicked-down hair, remote eyes, and mouth like a purse's clasp, was not prepossessing. Through the Death Squad, however, he made himself famous, as word of his exploits circulated through São Paulo and then all of Brazil. Fleury seemed to enjoy the attention, although he protested to the newspapers that he was not a violent man, that he cried at the movies.

The São Paulo police was only one of several branches of government in the city that had begun to collect information about subversives. Each of the armed forces had been expanding its own intelligence unit until some conservative businessmen became concerned that the competition among these offices was leading to duplication and, worse, inefficiency.

Henning Albert Boilesen, the president of a liquid gas company, acted on these concerns. Boilesen had come to Brazil from Denmark as an official of the Firestone Rubber Company. Seventeen years later, he became a naturalized Brazilian citizen. He moved easily through São Paulo's prosperous society, picking up a host of influential friends: former minister Hélio Beltrão; Ernesto Geisel, the president of Petrobas; General Siseno Sarmento. He occupied a house on Rua Estados Unidos, and for years it was widely believed that this was not the only sense in which Boilesen lived on the United States.

The suspicion that Boilesen was a CIA agent grew when he began soliciting money for a new organization to be called Operação Bandeirantes (OBAN), in honor of the *bandeiras*, the explorers and treasure hunters who had once trekked across Latin America. OBAN united the various military and police intelligence services in a crusade that went beyond normal jurisdictions.

Boilesen and his cohorts put heavy pressure on fellow businessmen for money to support OBAN. Their message was not so different from de Paiva's. But Boilesen could draw on a squad of volunteers from the military and police; he could guarantee results.

It was not long before the United States subsidiaries based in São Paulo were calling the U. S. consulate asking for guidance. Should they contribute to OBAN? Use your own judgment, the political section replied. We're staying out of this. Despite this show of neutrality, at least one U. S. businessman, after making such a call, did receive a follow-up visit from a consular officer, who told him approvingly about contributions that other U. S. companies in São Paulo had made to the cause of civil peace.

In 1965, another development helped to reinforce the interest of Brazil's military in the Communist threat to the hemisphere. At Lyndon Johnson's urging, Castelo Branco joined the United States in sending troops to the Dominican Republic. Among the Brazilian units to go north were two marine battalions, the Riachuelo and the Humaita.

Since the U. S. military command understood the difficulty Brasília would face in explaining casualties, the Brazilian role was largely defensive. U. S. troops were to hold and expand an international corridor, while the Brazilian marines were to do their part by demonstrating hemispheric unity for the invasion. They were kept well back of those boundaries.

To the young Brazilian troops, the situation soon became demoralizing. They had come to save a sister republic from the communism they themselves had averted only the year before. Yet instead of welcoming them with flowers, the people were inexplicably hostile.

Even when a woman seemed friendly, a Brazilian marine had to be cautious. From the U. S. camp came stories of GI's who would go out dancing with attractive women and be found the next morning with their throats slit.

One incident involved a band of Dominican boys who came to an edge of the Brazilian encampment and pelted the marines with stones. At first the Brazilians ignored the volley. The second day, when the boys returned, the troops called out to them with friendly jokes. They were only children of nine and ten; they could be won over. But the boys shouted back insults and ran away. The third day the boys returned with grenades. Several Brazilian troops were killed. At home, they were listed as military accidents or traffic deaths. From that time on, the Brazilian marines opened fire on any stranger who came too close.

Whatever other effect on the Dominican Republic, the 1965 invasion led to an outpouring of U. S. aid to the right-wing government, some $100 million, and to an expansion of the Public Safety program. Within three years, one third of the eighteen police advisers there were CIA officers operating under OPS cover.

In Washington, the Office of Public Safety had remained immune to public embarrassment as it went about two of its chief functions: allowing the CIA to plant men with the local police in sensitive places around the world; and after careful observation on their home territory, bringing to the United States prime candidates for enrollment as CIA employees.

Besides the courses at the IPA, the CIA was sending foreign police officers to its own clandestine center, a four-story townhouse on R Street in Washington. There, under the name International Police Services, Inc., Asian, African, and Latin American policemen were trained in surveillance, the use of informants, and other police methods. They were processed as though this course were also administered through U. S. AID. Along with foreign students, the institute trained U. S. officers destined for South Vietnam.

As head of the Office of Public Safety, Byron Engle was more sensitive than his CIA colleagues to the need for keeping his program uncompromised by the overt spying. His new associates at OPS heard him arguing heatedly with CIA officers at the agency's headquarters in Langley, Virginia, as he tried to retain a measure of respectability for the IPA.

Throughout the early sixties Engle succeeded, although his efforts did not end the campaign within U. S. AID against his police program. One AID official was sufficiently concerned about the first reports of torture in Brazil to start checking the requisition orders from the Office of Public Safety. Electric shocks, he knew, were usually administered with military field telephones, and over those he had no control. But he could try to prevent generators being sent out with the U. S. AID decal if they were going to be used for torture.

This official soon came to believe that his watchfulness was useless. There were many legitimate purposes for small generators, and to ban them on the assumption that they were going to be abused would be to cripple the AID program. Ultimately, he decided, one had to trust the humanity and discretion of the police advisers. They had been raised under the Bill of Rights, and they could be expected to respect it.

But when put to the test during the Kennedy administration, the Office of Public Safety quickly demonstrated that there were few hesitations about breaking a rule or two if success was at stake. Since the irregularities were in the best of causes, Engle had not feared reprisals from either the president or his liberal advisers.

In 1962, for example, a group of Venezuelan leftists, inspired by Castro, formed the Armed Forces of National Liberation (FALN) and set out to discredit the elected

president, Rómulo Betancourt. The FALN wanted to persuade voters to boycott elections the following year. Although the group never totaled more than five hundred
members, by fanning out they were able to bomb a luxury
hotel, burn a Sears Roebuck warehouse, and attack the
U. S. embassy. When Franco loaned several Impressionist
paintings for an exhibition in Caracas, the FALN carried
off one work each by Cézanne, Van Gogh, Picasso, Braque,
and Gauguin, choices that contributed to the suspicion that
the FALN might include artists as well as students and
writers.

The Venezuelan police seemed helpless to act, even
when patrolmen were being shot down on the street. Under pressure from the Kennedys, Engle borrowed four
Spanish-speaking officers from the Los Angeles Police Department and quietly sent them to Caracas to give intensive
classes in police work. Had the mission been exposed, the
Kennedy administration might have been forced into a
round of excuses and apologies. Had any of the Los Angeles cops been killed, there would have been no provision for
compensating their families. Engle was thus much relieved
when the secret operation ended and the men were back
in California.

That was behind the scenes. The public image of Engle's
program remained positive. Robert Kennedy, now a senator from New York, had been happy to address the first
class that completed its training at the Washington police
academy. Graduation came one month before the military
coup in Brazil; and in his remarks, Kennedy warned the
class that "the world today is buffeted by winds of change."

At the academy, however, most of the actual training
seemed aimed at preventing that change, although that
intention was seldom committed to paper. The training
syllabus, which was not classified, had never been released
to the press; and one IPA official explained that "the Communists might even pay a little more for it. And we don't
want to help them." Yet, any Soviet or Cuban agent who

did pay out cash for the printed materials might have felt short-changed. More perhaps to protect the IPA from onslaughts by the U. S. Congress and the liberal press than to preserve its secrets from foreign enemies, the training sheets were relentlessly high-minded and vague.

The foreign policemen themselves understood why they were being sent to Washington. Even before the coup d'état, in July 1963, one Brazilian officer described the academy program to the governor of São Paulo as "the latest methods in the field of dispersion of strikes and striking workers." He would learn, he said, how to use dogs and clubs and "to modernize the mechanism of repression against agitators in São Paulo."

The basic academy course ran fifteen weeks and was offered twice a year in French, several times in Spanish and, for Africans and Asians, in English as well. The first two and a half months were spent in a standard introductory course, whereas the last four weeks offered advanced training in any of ten specialties, including immigration and customs control, protection of dignitaries, and "Criminal Violence Control," which dealt with airline security, bomb threats, kidnapping, extortion, and assassination.

Candidates were expected to be between the ages of twenty-one and forty-five, and—a provision often waived —to be high school graduates. Women could be accepted at the IPA, but their selection was discouraged. If a country nominated one female officer, it was told it must send two of them.

In Belo Horizonte, and later in Rio, Dan Mitrione had become skilled at screening applicants for the program. His successor in Belo was not so adept. An amiable and lazy cop from the Southwest, he assured every Brazilian policeman who inquired about the program that he was sure to be accepted. When the adviser was finally transferred, the Brazilians found his desk drawers stuffed with applications he had never bothered to forward to Washington.

Brazilian officers attending the IPA often came away

believing that the courses, like those which had been offered in Panama, were beneath them. Sixty percent of the student body came from Central and South America, and some Brazilians felt degraded to be grouped together with Costa Ricans and Guatemalans.

If the training was not always valuable, it could be entertaining. The highlight of each course was an exercise first developed during the school's days in Panama: Operation San Martin. San Martin was an imaginary country with an equally nonexistent capital, Rio Bravos. Its neighbor and enemy was called, somewhat less mythically, Maoland. Few foreign students recognized that the map of Rio Bravos was only an aerial photograph of Baltimore with an overlay of imposing government buildings and its streets renamed in Spanish.

The warm-up exercises were simple. A dignitary was arriving from a friendly country. How would the students deploy their policemen to protect him during his visit? The final problem offered more chances for miscalculation. Infiltrators from Maoland were staging a national disturbance. The villains—and every semester this delighted the students—were instructors from the IPA faculty, their mug shots emphasizing their sinister aspect. Resisting fashion, one instructor kept his hair crewcut, and every semester he was nicknamed The Nazi. Other instructors passed for Communists or university rebels.

A dozen IPA students were divided into three groups: one joined the instructors in creating the problem, writing the Communist propaganda, plotting the disruption; one faction made the decisions for putting the insurrection down; and the other group was composed of onlookers and judges. The chief of police from Somali, an accomplished player, complained afterward that the exercise was harder than any comparable situation in real life because at the IPA he was judged by his peers.

The exercise was held in the Police Operations Control Center, a room of muted grays and greens with four raised rows of seats. The magnetic map of San Martin covered the front wall. Students chosen to suppress the demonstration were connected by telephones and teletype to a control booth. Such direct communication they found to be a burden. One line connected directly with the "Prime Minister," who demanded action, provided it did not embarrass his party in the forthcoming elections. If an operation was going too smoothly, the instructors called from the control booth with snags: "My problem is the reporters on the scene. They're getting in the way and interfering with our police work."

"Do the best you can," said one student commander.

From the control booth, the instructor called two more times about the reporters, and finally he exploded, "God damn it! You've got to do something!"

"All right," said the student chief. "Arrest them! Bring them in!"

That answer won him only a ten-minute respite. Then the Prime Minister was on the line: "What in hell is going on?"

No one had to instruct a police officer how to stall for time. "What do you have reference to, sir?"

"I'm getting calls from AP and UPI. I'm catching hell."

As the Prime Minister passed along some of that hell, the student police chief had to improvise a way out of his bungling. In one case, the student telephoned for a bus, ordered the reporters released, briefed them on the rioting, then drove them back to the scene to let them see it for themselves. His fellow students agreed that for a makeshift remedy his had not been a bad one.

Besides the training exercises, San Martin was the locale of a film shot in Panama, *The First Line of Defense*. The instructors memorized a short introduction in Spanish: "The events you will see take place in the mythical Latin American republic of San Martin. But they are not fictitious events; they 'really happen.' You will see that the people of San Martin are mostly favorable to their government (else it could not stand), and that the police work with the people and are truly the first line of defense."

In the film, the center of subversion was the National Committee for Agrarian Reform (CONTRA). Once an organization of student reformers, it had fallen into the hands of strangers well past college age. Across town, more strangers, possibly Communists from Cuba, disrupted a meeting of striking workers from a fertilizer factory. The plot involved a police spy, a Czechoslovakian gun smuggled in a box marked SUGAR, and a riot outside the factory that became too frenzied for the police to handle alone. The chief ceded responsibility to the military, and the army dispelled the protestors with tear gas, flying wedges, and fire hoses.

At the film's end, two policemen drew the moral for several smiling children: "A new day dawns over the city of Rio Bravos." If other subversives were plotting against the security of the people, they were not likely to succeed as long as the civil police enjoyed the people's confidence and had "confidence in their own ability to enforce the law!"

IPA officials anticipated that some students might object to the film. To cope with them, the instructor was told to break in at any sign of restiveness and assure the class that the film presented only suggestions on how to proceed, not absolute directions. In most cases, if any objections were raised at all, they pertained to the amount of equipment at the disposal of the Rio Bravos police chief.

The inequality between U. S. supplies and what the students had at home was even more glaring when the students were taken outside of Washington to Fort Myers for field training in riot control. Invariably, they came back impressed by the plethora of gas masks, shields and batons, riot guns that fired pepper shot and rubber bullets; and they would grumble about their own meager means.

The instructor was expected to turn any shortcoming into a challenge. "You don't have radio cars for your police? Class, any suggestions?" A student might say, "How about putting up a light bulb at the highest point in town and telling the patrolmen that whenever it was lit, they should call headquarters for instructions?"

The academy also showed more conventional training films: a twelve-minute film, *The Police Baton,* from the Los Angeles Police Department; *The Third Challenge,* made by the Department of Defense; *The Use of Tear Gas to Preserve Order,* a bit of public relations by the Lake Erie Chemical Company. In Brazil, local advisers also used a film on interrogation made by the FBI. Until they could have it dubbed into Portuguese, U. S. advisers turned off the soundtrack and offered their own pungent commentary.

During class hours at the IPA, discussion of domestic politics was discouraged. The academy's officials liked to point to the time the Somali Republic was fighting Ethiopia, yet policemen from each country had roomed together.

Given the films and the tone of the courses, few students missed the purpose behind the IPA. The academy had been set up to train the police to fight communism wherever it existed. Even students not considered sufficiently qualified to be passed on to the CIA for professional intelligence work were instructed in what Jack Goin called "preventive law enforcement."

You're a rural policeman, Goin's illustration went, and you've stopped to talk with a farmer about his sick cow. In the course of your conversation, he mentions that lately a stranger has passed through his pasture. That could be a matter of internal security. It's up to you as a policeman to recognize that it could be important.

Overseas, the U. S. advisers had coped with local customs with varying degrees of ingenuity, and foreign policemen coming to the United States similarly found the native practices confounding. At first, grading at the academy was a problem. One police colonel arrived with his aide, a major. The junior officer sat in on the classes with him and outshone him in every category until the colonel did not want to go home at all. That was in 1965, and grades were abandoned soon afterward.

A Third World student was arrested for shoplifting from a self-service drugstore. He later said that he had waited some time for a clerk to approach him. When none did, he stuck a few items in his pocket and left. He intended, he claimed, to return the next day and pay when everyone was not so busy. Officials from the academy had the charges dropped, but it took hours of persuasion to keep that affronted student from taking the next flight home.

Once an African student was picked up on a rape charge. During a line-up, the white victim made a positive identification. The District of Columbia police investigator then asked what the rapist had sounded like. "Just like any other nigger," the woman replied. The IPA student was asked to say a few words, which he did in his decidedly British accent. Once again the case was dropped. This time the African policeman was more amused than embittered.

Yet many black students arrived at the IPA certain that racism was going to blight their stay. Most were agreeably surprised by the welcome they received in Washington, where the population was becoming increasingly black. But having the academy in the capital irked some of the white instructors who felt that the visitor would get a more representative picture of the United States had the academy been located somewhere in the Midwest.

"We're only here," one said, " because the civilians in the State Department don't trust us."

That much was true. The Office of Public Safety had been sending police-training teams to South Vietnam; and as the years passed, the stories that reached Washington were increasingly disturbing. Around the U. S. embassy in Saigon, there were allusions to the torture and murder of political prisoners, sometimes in the presence of agents of the United States. Similar reports had started to come in from Iran and Taiwan, then from Brazil and Greece.

Torture ran counter to the official instruction at the IPA. A number of instructors fervently spoke against it, less because it was morally indefensible than because they considered it self-defeating. Their students, however, sometimes had different opinions. Interrogation was a crucial subject and a source of lengthy debate among students and staff.

Before discussing the procedure of questioning, students were briefed on what were the best physical surroundings in which to conduct the interrogation. The room should have one door and no windows. If a window was unavoidable, there should be no view. The room should be soundproofed. The telephone should not ring but signal instead by flashing lights seen only by the questioner. All of this, including the blank walls, were to emphasize the prisoner's sense of isolation.

Important interrogations were to be recorded, the microphone hidden somewhere in the room, perhaps in a "live" telephone. The room should have a two-way mirror. If the interrogator wore civilian clothes, he was more likely to inspire confidence.

As the questioning proceeded, the interrogator should look for changes in his prisoner that might indicate lying: sweating, loss of color, dry mouth, racing pulse, heavy breathing.

That had been the preliminary instruction. But during the mid-sixties concerns began to shift. Until then, interrogating a murder suspect had required only experience and a few timely tricks:

INSTRUCTOR (off-handedly, as though it didn't much matter): Would you like a cigarette?
STUDENT SUSPECT: Yes, thank you.
INSTRUCTOR: May I use your lighter?
SUSPECT (fumbling): I don't seem to have it.
INSPECTOR: Where did you leave it then?

But simple ploys like that worked only with amateurs. Policemen arriving at the academy now had tougher questions about defiant rebels and dedicated subversives.

The instructors, particularly those who had served in a country fighting an insurrection, knew that most political activists would try to stall for twenty-four hours, to give their colleagues time to move to safer quarters. The students wanted to know what to do about those professionals. "If a man thinks he's smart," one instructor answered, "bluff to make him think you know even more than he does."

"No," another instructor told another class, "act dumb. Keep him talking. He may try to justify himself. If he does, just go on listening. In the midst of his tirade, something may come out that will be helpful to you."

"Or," another instructor suggested, "bait the prisoner a bit."

But the same question always arose: "Why not beat the shit out of the guy?"

Although the official response was negative, the students could detect which instructors were genuinely opposed to beatings and which were a bit more realistic.

One instructor argued that any torture was ineffectual because some people did not feel pain. Others, he suggested, could be reduced to pleas and trembling without a hand laid on them. Another instructor, a former policeman from the Southwest, advised students to say clearly, "Bring in the transformer and the electric wires." Of course, he added, there were no transformers or wires. It was merely that people responded differently to different stimuli, and the interrogator had to find out what turned the key.

"The first man who hits a prisoner is a coward" was the opening statement of one adviser to an IPA class. He seemed to believe what he said. A Latin American student then asked, "Even if he spits in your face?" It was moot which was the more intolerable, being spit upon or being called a coward.

The adviser nodded emphatically. "Even if he spits in your face."

"Jesus Christ," said another student. "That's a pretty strong statement. There are circumstances—"

"No, he's in your custody and he's your responsibility."

Another time, a Brazilian policeman interrupted that sort of sermon: "Let's cut out the bullshit. If I can get you to swear that no policeman in the United States ever slapped a prisoner, I'll kiss your ass." The instructor could not guarantee that every policeman in the United States lived by the rules.

By the mid-sixties, enough of the students had been exposed to U. S. intelligence methods in their own country to take the IPA's instruction about nonviolence more lightly. Given the difference in signals that IPA students received from their advisers, it was not surprising that when they were asked near the end of their course to sum up what they had learned, their essays were guarded.

Nguyen Van Thieu, a South Vietnamese police officer, began his list of three methods of interrogation with torture, but he said it did not usually bring satisfactory results. But he thanked the free world, "the U. S. most of all," for making interrogation more effective with "technical and equipment aid."

Milciades Espita Ovalle, a detective in Colombia's Security Department, said that a government must kill or capture guerrillas in order to reassure the population that the rebel cause would not prevail. He did grant, however, that Communist propagandists would make the guerrillas out to be victims of the police.

Inspector Madhav Bickrum Rana of Nepal wrote that an interrogator could extract valuable information either by getting a subject drunk or by injecting him with a truth drug, such as sodium pentathol. He also discussed starving a man, hitting him, or subjecting him to steady drops of water on his head. But he concluded that the use of threat and force was justified only as a last resort, when every other technique had failed.

Kula Nand Thakur, also of Nepal, reported to the IPA faculty that he had beaten suspects after he became district inspector for Nawakot in 1964. He had seen other interrogators grow careless, though, and hit tender parts of the body so that the suspect died and "thereby created another trouble."

One Brazilian officer sent to the United States in 1967 brought along memories of a discussion he had had in his police *cuartel* the year before. A police squad had just brought in a young mulatto suspected of belonging to Leonel Brizola's resistance group. The suspect had been beaten during his capture, though not severely enough to require hospitalization. In 1966, this particular police barracks did not use equipment to torture a prisoner, but if a suspect refused to speak, he could expect more kicks and punches.

The Brazilian officer watched the bloody man being brought in and knew what was in store for him. Visiting his office that day was an official from the United States, a pleasant sandy-haired man in his forties who spoke excellent Portuguese.

When he first began to call, he had introduced himself as a political officer from the U. S. embassy. He had not asked about anything at all sensitive. Instead, he seemed willing to talk for hours about soccer and movies. He had come back three times, never in a hurry, never with anything specific on his mind.

Now the Brazilian policeman said to him, "I don't like seeing a prisoner brought in with a black eye and cuts on his head. It reminds me too much of what I heard from my father about life under Vargas."

"I agree with you," the embassy man said. "But you policemen have a very bad job. Other people just don't know. They want protection from men like Brizola and his gang, but they won't see how dangerous they are. This man they brought in could have a lot of information that would save innocent lives."

"Yes," the Brazilian agreed, a little surprised. He had only made the remark because the sight of the prisoner had left him feeling uncomfortable. He had no intention of interfering with the arresting officers or of offering them unsolicited advice about doing their jobs.

"I was in the military police stationed in Germany after the war," the embassy man said. "We used to talk about what we'd have done if we'd ever got hold of a Nazi."

"That was war," the Brazilian said.

"So is this," said his guest.

Bull sessions similar to that discussion went on regularly at the IPA. After class, an instructor talked only for himself, not for the academy. Some of the faculty stuck to the IPA line. If they were not personally outraged at the thought of torture, they argued that word of it always got out and hurt the cause of the men who practiced it.

It was apparent that the men who espoused that soft line, even over a beer several blocks away from the Car Barn, were rarely men who had been stationed in a country with a serious threat to its internal security. They were also— it was a feeling about them—not going far in the hierarchy of the Office of Public Safety. On the other hand, there was the adviser who returned from South Vietnam with sympathetic stories about the perils of the Saigon police. On the ground in South Vietnam, U. S. advisers complained loudly about the timidity of the Vietnamese policemen and repeated their demeaning nickname for them, the White Mice. Part of the name was inspired by their white uniforms, part by their uncombative attitude.

Since Vietnamese and other Asian police came to the IPA as students, the instructors held back on jokes and insults, and spoke instead about the viciousness of the Vietcong, how they planted bombs in crowded restaurants and movie theaters, where they did not kill U. S. troops but their fellow countrymen. The Vietnamese police were en-

titled to take any measures, no matter how severe, to prevent that slaughter. At least, that was the message some
Brazilian students took away with them.

Other Brazilian police had begun to wonder whether
there was a decent way to resolve the conflict facing their
own country's intelligence services. Indisputably, a rebel
movement was growing in Brazil. The government of Artur da Costa e Silva, the hard-line general who had assumed
the presidency on the retirement of Castelo Branco, was
depending on his intelligence network to break up the
movement before it became a real threat to the military
regime.

Inevitably, that new intelligence apparatus, SNI, turned
for help to its powerful counterpart from the north. In the
police barracks, it was well known that many Brazilian
officers worked closely with the CIA and were suspected
of accepting pay from their CIA liaison officers. That exchange of money, more than the exchange of privileged
information, could infuriate those officers who had not
been recruited by the agency.

Sometimes these officers would remark—even in front
of political prisoners—that it was too bad certain *brasileiros*
had sold out their patrimony. The complaints never went
far, since the commanding officers seemed to favor cooperation with the CIA, which brought praise, promotions, and
an access to the CIA's special stores of equipment. A well-
connected police commander who wanted new supplies of
tear gas did not have to fill out the involved U. S. AID
requisitions. Within a few days his friend in the CIA could
obtain what he needed directly from the Panama branch
of the Technical Services Division (TSD).

In that gray area between AID's open program and the
CIA's special needs, Mitrione had functioned so capably
that many Brazilian officers thought he was a CIA officer
working under the cover of the OPS. By 1968, the rumor
had traveled far enough that when an East German publisher named Julius Mader brought out a book entitled

Who's Who in CIA, he listed Dan A. Mitrione. This was a case where common knowledge was mistaken. Mitrione was merely smart and ambitious enough to cooperate with the CIA to the fullest. Brazilian police officers at his headquarters were alert to the distinctions within the U. S. hierarchy, and they took reflected pride in their adviser's evident closeness with the men who came by his office, ostensibly from the embassy's political section. Mitrione's predecessor in Rio had not enjoyed that rapport, nor had he spoken Portuguese.

In 1966 and early 1967, Brazil's police were hard-pressed for information about subversives. Though the Brazilian navy had amassed comprehensive files, they were not sharing information with the other services. It was about this time that the police and army began to use coercion on their prisoners.

Older policemen briefed the younger officers on the ways in which they had extracted information during the first Vargas years. Their techniques, often brutal and effective, usually involved beating a man until he was near death, at which point he either talked or died. One policeman remembered that when Mitrione heard a story like that he had commented that a dead prisoner could not tell anyone very much. Yet what was the alternative? The U. S. advisers who had become close enough to their counterparts to hear these discussions now had to settle the question for themselves. The CIA and SNI were pressing the police for results, and nothing loosened a prisoner's tongue quicker than pain.

Some police advisers argued that intense but not lethal pain was more humane than indiscriminate beatings. Their CIA contacts endorsed that view. At least in one case, when Brazilian intelligence officers began to use field telephones to administer electric shocks, it was U. S. agents who informed them of the permissible levels the human body could withstand.

Word was passed that the CIA could supply more than

tear gas, that the laboratories of the TSD in Washington, and its branch in Panama, were developing devices to make the pain so sharp that a prisoner would break quickly and not force a police interrogator to hurt him repeatedly. But the Brazilian police who heard those reports did not immediately receive the new mechanisms, and those who gave in and used torture had only their field telephones to work with.

The men charged with getting information knew that they were not sadists. They had been given a responsibility, and they would meet it. They did not want sermons from their U. S. advisers, and Mitrione was not one to lecture them. He was their guest. He always told new advisers not to forget that.

From the point of view of the policemen, however, Mitrione was also their patron, their mentor, the keeper of their professional conscience. Stories came up to Belo Horizonte from Rio about the torture of prisoners, and his former Brazilian colleagues debated what Mitrione would do if a police officer began to abuse a prisoner in front of him.

"He'd leave," said one officer.

"Leave the country?" another asked.

"No," said the first. "Leave the room."

In the middle of 1967, Mitrione was called back to teach at the IPA. It was a lucky time to be leaving Brazil. The rebel movement was growing and counter measures would have to be more severe.

Mitrione had spent five years in Brazil. Among his Brazilian students and his fellow advisers, he was leaving as a widely known and well-regarded professional. Later, the Office of Public Safety would claim to have taught 100,000 policemen in Brazil, one sixth of the country's total police force, and Mitrione had trained hundreds of them.

He knew what some of those policemen had started to do. They discussed the problem with him and told him what they had seen—the wires, the water used for near-drownings. His very success as an adviser had won him that intimacy and trust. Hearing of the torture, he was—at least as they remembered it much later—noncommittal.

There would, however, be no torture at the IPA. In Washington, an instructor could talk about police work as it should be done, not about the methods forced on a conscientious cop in a compromised world.

But Mitrione was to find that in conversation over coffee during each IPA term, the question of torture persisted. Another popular instructor settled the queasiness of one Brazilian student with an anecdote. The police officer, who was promoted many times since his student days, remembered it years afterward.

"If anyone ever asks you what you do to prisoners," the U. S. adviser began, "tell them this story: Right now, as we're talking, my fellow policemen are holding a man involved in a kidnapping. He and two of his accomplices took a little five-year-old blonde girl who belongs to a businessman in this city. They're saying that if they don't get two million dollars, they will kill that little child tomorrow at noon.

"We picked up the man while he was leaving instructions. We've had him now for ten hours, and he's told us nothing. The businessman doesn't have two million. He's wealthy but not in that league. The deadline is getting closer. What do we do next?"

"There is no little girl," the Brazilian student said.

"The person who asked you the question can't be sure of that. Somewhere every week or month if not every day, police officers have to face that kind of problem. It might not be a little girl. It might be a policeman standing on a corner that some nut has decided to shoot. But it's the same principle.

"And if the man who asked you about torture doesn't agree that you should use any means to find out where that little girl is being held, then don't answer any more of his questions, because he'll never understand what you tell him anyway.

"He's got his mind made up, and he hates the police so much that he'd sacrifice an innocent child to put you in the wrong."

CHAPTER

FOR LINCOLN GORDON, the coup had first seemed to fulfill his every expectation. Mazzilli, the civilian vice-president, was a dignified lightweight. If the military agreed to let him serve as president for the four months specified by law, that would have satisfied the ambassador. Instead, Gordon was informed that the new president would be General Humberto Castelo Branco, which seemed to satisfy Dick Walters, the military attaché, even more.

The first clue that things might take a bad turn came when Francisco Campos, a lawyer whom Gordon regarded as an unintelligent old fascist, drew up the First Institutional Act. Under its provisions, the government, by decree, could create *cassação*, a political death, a deprivation of all political rights for ten years. Its victims would have neither a hearing nor an appeal. Moreover, they were being identified by General Golbery's SNI. The SNI very much resembled the CIA, except that since Brazil's enemies were inside her borders, Golbery was not burdened by those restrictions the U. S. Congress thought it had placed against domestic activity by the CIA.

Gordon was displeased with the act but took comfort from Castelo Branco's inferences that it was distasteful to him as well. Then, just as the act was about to expire, it was invoked against Juscelino Kubitschek, which was a shock to the U. S. embassy, or at least to the civilians there. According to òne U. S. scenario, Kubitschek was to be elected to the next full civilian term as president.

As it turned out, there were not going to be any more true elections. The military decreed that Castelo Branco's term would be extended for an additional year, which frustrated Carlos Lacerda's hopes of becoming president of Brazil for that year by appointment. The bitterness of his disappointment led eventually to his being made *cassado*, too.

Gordon sought out a friend in the new government, Milton Campos, to protest the military's high-handedness. Since the ambassador had urged Castelo Branco to appoint Campos as justice minister, Campos was obliged to hear out Gordon as he denounced the Institutional Act. What would Washington say? Gordon demanded. Or the world? "At least create a special court," Gordon told Campos, "to preserve the appearance of legality."

Campos promised Gordon that something would be done. Two weeks later, Campos resigned from his post.

Hearing of the ambassador's disquiet, Castelo Branco called him into his office in Brasília. He had been president slightly more than two months. He assured Gordon that the *cassação* of Kubitschek also troubled him, but he pointed sorrowfully to a massive document on his desk. Gordon took it to be a bill of indictment against Kubitschek.

"If we were to publish the reasons for this *cassação*, the degree of corruption is so shameful that it would be devastating to Brazilian pride."

Gordon accepted the explanation. As a diplomat, he felt he had little choice; and Dick Walters, whom the ambassador considered a sophisticated student of Brazilian political history, did not seem much troubled by the Institutional Act.

Eighteen months after the coup, there was a Second Institutional Act. This time Gordon made notes in Portuguese of his long protest so that he would not forget a trope.

I was uncomfortable with the first act, he told Castelo Branco, but it had been for a limited duration. I assumed that when the emergency powers expired, we would get back on the road. Now, after a year and a half, there is this Second Institutional Act, and as a precedent it is very dangerous.

Castelo Branco said he was not happy either, but the ambassador had to understand that he had accepted the emergency powers only from the highest democratic principles. Two politicians from the token opposition party had recently been elected to governorships. If Castelo Branco had not agreed to accept these new powers, he said, the hard liners within the military would never have allowed those two men to take office.

Gordon took his leave. By the time of the Fifth Institutional Act, which shut down Congress, suspended habeas corpus for political crimes, and gave full autocratic power to the president, Gordon was no longer ambassador to Brazil. From the United States, he signed a telegram of protest.

Gordon's successor, John W. Tuthill, considered a number of reprisals against that latest act. One, which was not taken, would have withdrawn all U. S. police advisers from Brazil.

Robert Kennedy visited Rio in 1965 and agreed to meet with students at Catholic University. By that time, few Brazilian officials would risk visiting a campus, and Kennedy got good marks for courage. Otherwise his rally drew a mixed response. Looking on, Jean Marc Von der Weid observed that the more his classmates knew about Brazil's recent history, the less susceptible they were to Kennedy's undeniable presence.

Jean Marc was a bookish boy whose only previous burst of political ardor had been touched off the night of the 1964 coup, when Carlos Lacerda asked his supporters to rally at the governor's palace. Sure that Goulart intended to become another Vargas, Jean Marc had dashed to the palace, where he had been chagrined to find no sign of a threat to Lacerda's life or property, only a few hundred retired military men joined in sedate revelry.

Jean Marc's conservatism came naturally to him. His father, a Swiss chemical engineer who worked for a Brazilian subsidiary of U. S. Steel, had lived in Brazil for many years, married a Brazilian woman, and raised four children in Rio. Jean Marc's mother came from a prominent political family, the Sodres. Her father had been a deputy during the early Vargas years and later a political exile in Argentina.

But although as a high-school boy he had welcomed the coup, Jean Marc's college experiences were leaving him disillusioned with the military government. He had resisted blaming the United States for Brazil's dictatorship, but when the leftists around him called the new influx of foreign capital and control a proof of "U. S. imperialism," Jean Marc asked himself whether they might not be right.

For all his intelligence, the young man was somewhat retiring, following along his father's path by studying chemical engineering at the federal university. He was working with a select unit, charged with studying a means of developing Brazilian mineral oil; and by 1966 it was apparent that if he avoided political involvement, he could look ahead to a decidedly profitable and possibly distinguished career.

Instead, Jean Marc was drawn into his first student demonstration. Out of curiosity, he showed up at the scene and someone put a placard in his hand: AMERICANS OUT OF VIETNAM. Jean Marc laid it down. "That's not our problem," he said and chose another: DICTATORSHIP OUT OF THE UNIVERSITY. In the course of that protest meeting,

Jean Marc was clubbed by a couple of the police, whom U. S. advisers were teaching to be more efficient.

Jean Marc's next political lesson was bloodier still. A boy named Edson Luis de Lima Souto was shot to death during a demonstration that had first seemed trivial but proved to be a turning point in Brazilian politics. Edson Luis died for better food.

The locale was Calabouço, a student café in downtown Rio owned by the state's student union. Its food had never been appetizing, but then few three-star restaurants served seven thousand meals a day. Whenever Jean Marc ate at Calabouço, he considered the meal another sacrifice to his growing political commitment.

In 1967 the state of Guanabara decided to close the restaurant for reasons that had nothing to do with the quality of its meals. The International Monetary Fund was due to convene in Rio at the Museum of Modern Art. Hardly a stone's throw away stood the café, which was also an informal headquarters for those student critics who believed that the fund was more interested in protecting foreign capital than in feeding the world's hungry. It was not surprising then that the governor should abruptly find the Calabouço unattractive and unsafe.

To prevent the café from being closed, the students resolved to occupy it. The leaders set two limited goals: to keep the restaurant open and to serve better food. The governor tried to send in the police, and each day there were clashes between the two groups. Both sides understood that the issue was not half-baked meals at one café. The government was simply not about to submit to the protestors; and that intransigence led to more pamphlets, more protest meetings, and finally to demonstrations that brought out the Guanabara state police in force.

At this point, the police either panicked or merely followed orders. In any event, they opened fire on the students; and Edson Luis was shot to death. There was a struggle for his corpse, and the students won. Hundreds of young people then bore Edson's body through the streets. One of them was Angela Camargo Seixas, a first-year engineering student at Catholic University in Rio. Like Jean Marc, Angela was new to political protest, but this day's demonstration would not be her last.

The students carried Edson's body to the steps of the state legislature and took over the building. Some members of the opposition party supported the demonstration, and their influence kept the police at bay.

Jean Marc arrived at the scene to find the mood hysterical. Most students had been in high school when Goulart's government fell. The 1964 coup had produced at least forty casualties and many vengeful reprisals, particularly in the northeast; but the generals had always boasted of their victory as a bloodless one. Now there was blood everywhere and the corpse of a seventeen-year-old boy to make the students aware that this was no light-hearted game the government had been playing.

The students proclaimed a day of mourning, shut down the schools, and prepared a mass demonstration for the day Edson would be buried. The leaders knew nothing about Byron Engle or his theory of a Communist master plan to create martyrs. Instinct warned them, however, that the police might break in during the night to seize Edson's body so that the sight of it would not inflame passions even more.

They resolved to keep vigil with the body, while a delegation toured the city alerting people to the horror that had been committed. Some went to the cinemas. Jean Marc went to six legitimate theaters around Copacabana and Botafogo beach, interrupting the performances to tell his story. Other students spent the night canvasing *boites* and street-corner bars throughout the city. Rio has no fixed hours for its clubs; they close when the last customer leaves. The students continued until dawn, soliciting money for the burial and for printing pamphlets about the killing. They returned to the parliament building having collected over one million cruzeiros.

One disturbance had occurred during the vigil. An intrepid policeman in plainclothes had infiltrated the wake and was somehow identified. The mob shouted, "String him up!" indicating the nearest gallows, which was a lamppost on the street. Jean Marc and five colleagues linked arms and held the crowd inside the building, while other students surrounded the infiltrator and hustled him out onto the street.

The next day, April 4, five thousand students marched the three miles to the cemetery of St. John the Baptist in Botafogo. There, packed among bone-white tombstones and ornate marble crosses, the mourners were waiting. Edson Luis's family, who lived along the Amazon in Manaus, were poor and could not afford the flight to Rio. But 60,000 of the boy's countrymen had turned out to pay their respects as his body was lowered into its grave.

The police did not try to intervene. In an ill-advised peace gesture, the governor had sent a car and police escort to bear the coffin to the cemetery, but the sight of the uniforms inflamed the crowd, and the officers backed away.

The day of the shooting had been emotionally draining for the students; the day of the funeral proved devastating to the police. Until that afternoon, the public had treated them with good-natured contempt. To the average man, the army, not the police, was to blame for the repression. But the day the state police killed a high-school boy, they became a target for civilian frustration and hatred.

(Three years later, a police psychologist told Jean Marc that the week after Edson Luis's funeral there were officers lined up outside the psychologist's office. Some men wanted transfers to desk jobs; others wanted to resign from the police entirely. Jean Marc paid heavily for that gratifying information; he was in prison at the time, and the psychologist was part of the team interrogating him.)

The day after the funeral, President Costa e Silva, the hard-line general named by the military to succeed Castelo Branco, used the rally as his reason for banning a political movement called The Front. It had been put together by Carlos Lacerda as one last attempt, should civilian presidential elections ever be restored, to win the power denied him after the 1964 coup.

Lacerda responded that the ban demonstrated that Costa e Silva's regime was a "military dictatorship in the worst Latin American tradition." His invective was officially silenced as he was made a *cassação*. Ambassador Tuthill also came under attack when it was revealed that he had been meeting with Lacerda and listening to his fervent, belated protests against close ties between the U. S. government and the Brazilian military.

Jean Marc now enrolled in a drive to change Brazil's entire system of higher education. In 1968, only 250,000 students from across the nation—1 percent of all children who began the first grade—were entering the universities. In May of that year, Jean Marc and his colleagues called a strike in which they were asking for more money for the school of engineering. That strike was nearly as parochial as the Calabouça demonstration.

To generate support, Jean Marc was chosen to speak on television. At that time, television and the press were not yet totally censored. On their screens, viewers were confronted by Jean Marc's long, ethereal face, his delicate yet resolute manner. He now spoke warmly about opening the university to the poor, increasing its funds, keeping it free from government intervention.

That last point interested the former union organizers, who were forbidden to speak so directly. Jean Marc's group attracted a wider and more aggressive following, until, by the end of May, students from the other faculties voted to expand the protest into a general strike. Before calling their walkout, however, the students tried to petition the minister of education with their grievances.

The police blocked them at the ministry steps. When the

students came back in force, they found 20,000 police from all over Rio at the ready. The city looked on, edgy but exhilarated. Drivers snarled in traffic beat rhythm on their horns to show support for the demonstrators.

Jean Marc had been organizing the rear guard at the university and arrived late to a clearly tense situation. Across the main square from the ministry lay Cinelandia, the sector of large first-run movie houses. That wide street was jammed with students and their sympathizers, perhaps seven thousand. Before Jean Marc could reach them, they rushed the police and took control of the ministry steps.

Jean Marc fretted that the students had not adequately explained their position. Climbing up the steps in front of a movie house, he tried to spell out the grievances. Few people heard him.

Meanwhile, the police brought up their reinforcements and gave an order to disperse. Most people obeyed, but some three hundred demonstrators elected to stay. In the milling and confusion, an army jeep was rolled over and set on fire.

Both sides in a political dispute know the power of a symbol: during this same period, anti-war protestors in the United States were sewing the Stars and Stripes to the seats of their blue jeans. The jeep was the first piece of army property attacked during a student demonstration. To Jean Marc, the soldiers at that point seemed to lose control. Although he had not been near it when it was set afire, Jean Marc now stood alongside the smoldering jeep, trying to persuade jubilant students to go home. He was clearly one of the leaders; and when the soldiers and police finally broke through the crowd, he was among those they wanted to arrest.

But being born to a prominent family in a class-ridden country gave him a certain manner. Tall for a Brazilian, Jean Marc drew himself up when the first policeman approached. To that small and timid man, Jean Marc presented his credentials as a reserve officer in the Brazilian marines. Improvising, he said, "I can be arrested only by a marine officer of the rank of captain or above."

Perplexed, the policeman went away. When he returned, he was accompanied by a less gullible police captain, who arrested Jean Marc on the spot.

The arrests made that day provoked another demonstration at which those who blamed the United States for Brazil's despotism led a march on the U. S. embassy. There, throwing rocks at the embassy's inviting windows, they once again identified plainclothesmen in their midst and spotted other armed men on the embassy roof. From the ground, no one could say whether those security guards were from Brazil or the United States. Whatever their nationality, they began sniping at the crowd.

The number killed that day was never resolved. Jean Marc's friends later showed him where two victims—a public official and a shopkeeper—were buried. Medical students and workers at the morgue calculated that perhaps three dozen others had been shot to death. Their estimate became more credible the next autumn, when an air-force officer said that the Parachuting and Rescue Service of the air force had killed many demonstrators that day, collecting their bodies and disposing of them in the ocean.

After the shootings, the student leaders retreated to the university. But most of the demonstrators, including some of the wounded, rioted through the streets, shouting that the government was guilty of murder. From noon until 9 P.M., fighting raged through the center of Rio. Cinelandia, the museums, the opera house, the imposing office buildings, all were in the hands of the demonstrators.

The police were equally out of control, shooting up at office windows along Avenida Rio Branco, the route each year for Rio's joyous carnival. Wherever the police went, people flung down ashtrays, lamps, chairs. One U. S. police adviser never forgot the sight of a policeman, sitting on the curb, crying because he had been stoned. Here it was, the adviser thought, the earliest, the Biblical, way of killing, and the Brazilians were doing it to their own policemen.

Eventually, with the police driven entirely from the center of Rio, the demonstrators went home for dinner, and Bloody Friday was at an end.

Jean Marc heard about the riot from his jailors at the army's First Armored Brigade. All day, the brigade had been on alert. Then the wires to the headquarters were cut and the officers, with no outside contact, considered themselves in a state of war. But headquarters issued no call to arms.

It was a restraint, Jean Marc learned, that disappointed some army officers. During his imprisonment, he was questioned at length by an army colonel, Helvecio Leite, who was notorious as a torturer. Leite threatened Jean Marc with beatings and worse, but on that occasion he was only blustering. After the interrogation, he stayed on to discuss politics.

According to Leite, President Costa e Silva had proved too weak to purify the country. Brazil needed a blood bath, which should have come in 1964, when Leite and some fellow officers were ready to kill the Communists. However, because Goulart and his supporters had refused to fight, that opportunity had been lost. It would come again.

In the week after the rioting, Rio's professors called their first protest meeting and sent their own delegates to the minister of education. The students set their largest demonstration yet for Wednesday. Mindful of the impact of de Paiva's Women's Campaign for Democracy, the students rounded up 1,500 mothers to join their protest. There were also movie actors and musicians and bank employees, along with a few union leaders, although after four years of dictatorship most unions were staffed with docile men.

The demonstration, which lasted five hours, brought 100,000 people into the streets. At the police *cuartels*, at the army barracks, at the U. S. embassy, it looked as though Brazil was finally on the verge of civil war.

Aristoteles Drummond, a little less lithe four years after the coup but still fighting leftists where he found them, received word that the president wanted to speak with him. He took it for a joke, the only humor on that menacing day. Then Costa e Silva himself called. Come to Brasília tomorrow and speak with me, the president said. At 9 A.M., Drummond boarded a military aircraft and flew to the capital with several other conservative spokesmen. They spent an hour with the president, during which time Drummond assured him that Jean Marc and the other student leaders were Communists who did not represent the majority on their campuses.

The next week was quiet, each side weighing the strength and probable response of the other. Believing the future of his government to be at stake, Costa e Silva agreed to meet with a delegation: one priest, one professor of psychology, one tractable student. The group drew up four proposals. Their vagueness caused Jean Marc in his jail cell to despair.

After a month in jail, Jean Marc was released pending his trial, the result of normal legal procedures, not a gesture by Costa e Silva to the demonstrators. Four months later, Jean Marc went on trial in a military court.

The government had one star witness: the driver of the jeep, who testified that he had heard Jean Marc exhorting the students while the jeep burned. The defense had something better: television films of the jeep being set afire with Jean Marc nowhere in sight.

When the court adjourned to deliberate, Jean Marc was ordered to return for the verdict. From the tenor of the preliminaries, he was convinced there would be only one outcome. Besides, he was now running for the presidency of the national student union, and that alone guaranteed a guilty verdict. Consequently, he decided to disappear. His fellow defendant, who was also not guilty, demonstrated his faith in military justice by showing up for the verdict; he was sentenced to two years in jail. In absentia, Jean Marc drew the same. By then it was September of 1968.

A month later, the outgoing UNE leaders decided to hold a clandestine meeting at a farm near Ibiuna, a town outside of São Paulo. Jean Marc argued against the secrecy. Let the meeting be public, he said, and let the police, if they dared, break it up. The resulting publicity would only win the students more converts. But the vote went against him.

By this time, the students had reached a private pact with the governor of São Paulo, a Sodre and a distant relative of Jean Marc's. The governor had opposed the crackdown on the universities, and he promised the students security for their congress. So, from all over Brazil, a thousand delegates streamed into Ibiuna. They faced a three-hour walk to the farm, but for a secret march there was much singing and laughter.

Army intelligence managed to locate them. The local commander called Governor Sodre and told him that the students were armed guerrillas. He was not entirely wrong, for ten or fifteen students had brought along handguns, mostly .22 caliber revolvers. Since the farm abutted a forest, they thought those guns could hold off any raiding party long enough to let the delegates gain cover in the woods. Jean Marc argued unsuccessfully that bearing arms conflicted with their role as students.

The army was threatening a massacre. To avoid that, Governor Sodre decided to arrest the students with his own police, whom he dispatched to Ibiuna. When the students heard of the impending raid, there was panic at the farm. But the São Paulo state police were even more terrified. They believed the propaganda about these fanatical guerrillas, who would fight to their last man.

The police approached the farm shooting. Yet as they drew closer, there was no answering fire. The students had decided that they were not gunfighters after all. Finally holding their fire, the police rounded up the students and poured out stories of how scared they had been. One officer confessed that before he got into the police van, he had drawn up his will.

In the uproar of marching so many prisoners three miles

to the road, the police had no time for identity checks. Once in jail in São Paulo, the students learned that their arrests were already setting off street demonstrations in every state capital. President Costa e Silva tried to lower the fever by announcing that although the students would all be charged, the maximum possible number would be set free immediately, pending trial. Then, too, Governor Sodre was eager to defuse the potential for a riot in São Paulo by getting the prisoners from other states out of his jail. He ordered his men to work round the clock, identifying the students and packing them on buses for home.

Prior to the raid, Jean Marc had been elected UNE's new president. Because he was also the only one among the thousand delegates who was a fugitive from the police, his situation required some inventiveness. In case informers were describing him, Jean Marc traded clothes with one student within the jail. Another gave him a pair of glasses, and he combed his hair into a different style.

The police knew he had been caught somewhere in their net, and officers flew in from Rio with his photograph. As they approached the cells, the students banged on the bars and shouted so ferociously that the Rio team decided not to enter the cells but wait instead until squads of students were led out to the buses.

It was 4 A.M. before Jean Marc was brought from his cell for processing with forty-nine other students. He had concocted a false name to match his new appearance, and he claimed to be from the state of Paraná, south of São Paulo. The governor there was reported to be reasonably liberal.

While the students were being questioned, Jean Marc heard an officer from the Rio detail vow, "He's here somewhere, and I'm going to find him." But as he said it, the policeman yawned, and he passed by Jean Marc without recognizing him.

Once Jean Marc reached the bus, he knew that in a few hours better-rested intelligence officers would be taking up the search. He napped during the ride. Then, as the bus pulled into Paraná's capital city and stopped for a red light, he pushed open the emergency exit, jumped off the bus, and ran down a side street.

During the trip south, he had accumulated the names of people who might help him. His first calls let him know that CENIMAR, the navy's intelligence section, had discovered that he had boarded the Paraná bus. Officers were already checking all traffic out of the city.

Jean Marc considered the size of the town. It was small. His was not the native accent. It would take all his wit to stay a step ahead of the police.

The next day, striking bank clerks had called a mass demonstration in Paraná, to be joined by professors, workers, and the city's poor. A cadre of students surrounded Jean Marc and called on him to address the crowd. He was a wanted man, but he was also a celebrity, and though not the most passionate of Latin orators, he had become diffidently eloquent.

Twice Jean Marc tried to speak, and each time a plainclothes officer in the crowd took a shot at him. Seeing the danger he was posing for the other demonstrators, Jean Marc slipped away to a friendly house, where he borrowed a suit and tie. From another student, he borrowed a car and, newly respectable, drove to the airport.

Some habits resisted even the new technology. Police were stationed at the train and bus depots, and along the roads they were making motorists get out of their cars to open the trunks. However, they were not watching the airport, where Jean Marc boarded a plane for São Paulo. Once lost in its teeming industrial quarter, he lived the next year underground.

Throughout the world, 1968 was a year of demonstrations. Back in Washington, Dan Mitrione was finding the United States far different from the country he had left eight years earlier. Brazilian students at the IPA sometimes asked him why he had not stayed in Brazil, and Mitrione joked with them, "I had to come back so as not to forget I'm American."

But the lawlessness he was finding at home troubled him deeply. IPA instructors in Brazil agreed among themselves that the streets at night were less dangerous than the streets of New York, and Mitrione could feel that he had contributed to the quiet that had fallen across Brazil.

The contrast was so strong that three years later, when Senator Frank Church's foreign relations subcommittee began to probe the rumors of torture coming out of Brazil, the senators called in Brazil's chief U. S. police adviser and asked him where he had felt safer, in Washington, D. C., or in Rio.

The adviser, Theodore Brown, took the bait: "I would feel safer in Rio."

"If that is the case," Senator Church asked, "then how is it we are so well qualified to instruct the Brazilians on adequate police-protection methods?"

It was a debater's point, and the perfunctory committee hearings turned up no hard evidence against the Office of Public Safety, its Washington academy, or the U. S. advisers in the field.

If Nelson Rockefeller wondered what sort of young hooligan organized the protest demonstrations against him in the spring of 1969, one answer was the studious and well-mannered son of a Swiss chemist.

Rockefeller was still governor of New York when Richard Nixon sent him to Latin America to prepare a policy report. The governor was scheduled to spend only a few hours in any one capital, but even the short duration of each stay did not mollify the protestors. In Latin America, the governor was not widely perceived as the beaming egalitarian who ate blintzes and pizza on the streets of New York City. For two generations, long before the prison riots at Attica had tarnished Nelson Rockefeller's liberal standing at home, his family's name had been handy political shorthand throughout South America for imperialism and repression.

The average U. S. taxpayer might find it mystifying that since the 1964 coup, Washington had pumped $2 billion into Brazil to protect U. S. investments totaling only $1.6 billion. But in Latin America as a whole, the stakes were much higher. U. S. investors controlled 85 percent of Latin America's sources of raw material. U. S. investment had doubled from $6 billion in 1960 to $12 billion nine years later, and the Rockefeller interests remained among the most visible of those investments.

At the time of the governor's trip, Standard Oil of New Jersey, part of the trust put together by Rockefeller's grandfather, controlled 95 percent of Venezuela's largest oil company, Creole Petroleum. Below the equator, another Rockefeller family corporation, IBEC, showed assets of well over $50 million. There were also Rockefeller-controlled industries, banks, and supermarkets. Not unexpectedly, then, Rockefeller met riots in Colombia. In Ecuador, the police killed six students demonstrating against him. Faced with public protests, the governments of Chile and Venezuela withdrew their invitations.

Given the scope of Rockefeller's inheritance and the hostile reception he received, the liberals of Brazil were not surprised that his report to Nixon followed a very hard line. According to Rockefeller, workers were largely under Communist domination. The same was true of students, but perhaps they were merely dupes. The report praised the hemisphere's police and its armed forces. The army had enabled each country to deal with "a growing, covert Communist threat to their internal security." As for the police, the Rockefeller report chided the people of the United States for not appreciating the importance of their role. True, the police had been used for political repression, and that was "unfortunate." But if anything, Rockefeller's report concluded, the Latin American police must be strengthened.

That spring, there was more than the Rockefeller mission to occupy Jean Marc. In February, the government had issued Decree 477, forbidding all political activity within the university. The authorities also closed most student centers. In Rio, only Catholic universities were exempt. Many student leaders were expelled, and Jean Marc found growing company in the underground.

Torture was also becoming more systematic. In the earliest aftermath of the coup, a number of men and women had disappeared; their bodies were later found in fields and gullies. The cases of torture had been isolated—a couple of actors; a former army sergeant, Raimundo Suares, tortured to death. Even the leftist students were inclined to blame that torture on a few brutes among the police and military. Their respect for the presidency died hard, though the office was now occupied by usurpers, and torture was far removed from the Brazilians' own view of themselves.

But in June 1969, people in São Paulo were speaking guardedly of a paramilitary organization called OBAN, apparently a collection of intelligence agents from the police and the military. In the war against the Left, OBAN considered itself to have a free hand, and its financing came from industrialists around the city who funneled their money through a man named Boilesen.

Jean Marc spent many months underground without being forced to resort to false documents. Challenged for identification, he would either show his Swiss passport or his card as a marine officer. With a glance at either of those elite documents, policemen would wave him past. Twice when Jean Marc's name was on "wanted" lists, he was scooped up by a police dragnet; but the officers failed to check each name against their lists, and he was let go.

Life underground affected the hunted differently. For

some, the constant movement and daily fears weighed so heavily that they sighed with relief at the clasp of the police hand on their shoulder. Jean Marc was not one of those. When his night came, he was no half-willing accomplice in his own capture.

It was August 31, 1969. Such were the tangled loyalties of that era that Jean Marc was hiding in the house of a physician who was also attending the president of Brazil. In that way, Jean Marc heard that Costa e Silva had suffered a stroke, which the military high command was covering up while his potential successors jockeyed for his position.

It was news too explosive to hoard for himself. Jean Marc set off for the house of friends. They were not at home. Still excited, he broke one of his own security rules and went to a house where fellow revolutionaries were living. Before, he had always met them on the street.

As Jean Marc approached, instinct warned him that something inside the house was not right. Listening at the door, he heard strange voices. Quietly he began to back away.

It was a trap. Minutes earlier, the house had been raided. Now police on the street were watching the door. When they seized him, Jean Marc told the officers that he was simply a student who had come to the wrong address. The police may or may not have believed him. Under the procedure that was evolving, it did not matter. The government had discovered that random beatings created a climate of quiescence at the universities, and the generals much preferred that stillness to the riots of the previous year.

Jean Marc was taken first to the headquarters of the Departmento de Ordem Politíco e Social (DOPS), where he found six other suspects already waiting. They were all told to stand with their feet far from the wall, then to lean forward and press their palms against it. For half an hour they were beaten on their kidneys with clubs. It was not punishment for refusing to answer questions. No questions had been asked. It was a preliminary lesson, to impress on them the consequences of being arrested.

During this first round of beatings, Jean Marc was not blindfolded, and looking around he saw twelve men in the room. Later, he learned that half were from CENIMAR. The other six were civilians from DOPS who specialized in torture.

The main CENIMAR prison was in the basement of the Ministry of the Navy, near the docks of Rio's lovely harbor. Whenever possible, the intelligence agents on the fifth floor of the ministry waited to do their torturing at night, when the staffs were gone from their offices. U. S. Navy officers based at the naval mission in the building sometimes heard screams from across the court. Their attitude was one of wry distaste; but none of them, not even missions commanders—like Rear Admiral C. Thor Hanson, who told aides of overhearing the screams—raised the matter with their hosts. It was an internal matter and none of their business.

Sometimes they saw men, obviously fellow countrymen wearing civilian clothes, around the intelligence office. If anyone was to object to the torture, it was they. Since the screams indicated that the torture was continuing, the information being gathered must be extremely vital to Brazil's security and, by extension, to the security of the United States.

Occasionally Brazilians who had undergone torture at CENIMAR managed to interest a foreign journalist in their ordeal. Once, their story reached William Buckley, Jr., the conservative columnist, as he toured Rio. They complained to him that they had heard English-speaking voices next door to the room in which they were being tortured. If they could hear conversation, why had the North Americans not heard them screaming?

Buckley, who had once worked for the CIA in Mexico City, reported later to his readers that there were radio monitors in the ministry. He said that what the prisoners had heard were not U. S. intelligence officers in the next room but rather transmissions from U. S. ships moored in the harbor.

Jean Marc, when he heard Buckley's explanation, thought that an excuse so transparent would only confirm the accusation in any neutral mind. But who was listening? Either to the charge or to Buckley's rebuttal?

After being held at CENIMAR, Jean Marc was shipped across Guanabara Bay to a prison on the Isle of Flowers, a dot of land in the Atlantic Ocean as beautiful as its name. A battalion of Brazilian marines kept the low white buildings and the grounds immaculate. Also on hand were interrogators who specialized in torture.

For twenty-four consecutive hours, Jean Marc was beaten with clubs and shocked with electric wires. At first the torture was simply administrative, the first stage in the prison's routine. But on the third day, his captors discovered his identity, and the brutality of his beatings intensified.

The island's commander was Clemente José Monteiro Filho, a marine commandante and graduate of the U. S. course in military intelligence in Panama. Monteiro came only twice to watch Jean Marc being tortured. The prisoners were blindfolded, but Monteiro's distinctive voice gave him away. Women prisoners said he looked in more often on them, especially when they were stripped naked.

Among the torturers themselves there was a division, an acknowledgment that a few were sadists and the others merely career men who were following orders. One man who enjoyed his assignment was an agent from DOPS named Solimar. Half admiringly, the other guards called him Doctor Bottleopener for his skill in extracting the last bit of information from the most stubborn prisoner. Solimar was very small, but his energy was prodigious. Jean Marc wondered whether he used drugs. Other torturers often complained of being tired, but Solimar could go on for six and seven hours.

Yet he was not the leader. That man was Alfredo Poeck, the navy commander who had been so impressed by his U. S. training in psywar at Fort Bragg. Poeck tried to protect his reputation by using the alias Doctor Mike.

The fury of the assault of these men on Jean Marc astounded him. He saw how unprepared Brazilians of his generation were for a political war. In Vietnam, fighting had gone on for a quarter of a century; to be a young Vietnamese meant arming oneself for war. But after the first Vargas regime, Brazil had enjoyed nearly twenty years of peace and democracy. Torture had no place in Jean Marc's universe. Until the Isle of Flowers, his greatest pain had come at the hands of his dentist. Now he found himself isolated in a room with men who let him know that they hated him and felt not a trace of compassion for his suffering.

These men routinely wrapped wires around his penis and his testicles, betraying no embarrassment at the intimacy of handling his genitals. With the end of one wire attached to his sex, Jean Marc had the other stuck into his ear, and both were connected to a battery-operated field telephone. Jean Marc recognized the telephone. His marine reserve unit had used equipment like it, supplied by the United States through the military assistance program.

When the crank was turned, voltage leapt between the wires, shocking Jean Marc's tenderest skin. When they wanted to apply the shocks to his mouth, a torturer first put on a rubber glove to hold the wire in place.

Other times, wires were attached to Jean Marc's fingers or, with clothespins, to his nipples. Brazilians called the pins crocodiles because of their wooden jaws. Jean Marc found it disturbing to see those harmless adjuncts to the family wash now appear as instruments of suffering. It was one more proof that the world was mad.

There was another torture Jean Marc hated even more.

The guards took paddles—flat pieces of wood with holes drilled through them—that were normally used to discipline schoolboys. A swat or two left a nasty stinging, like a nun's knitting needle, but until the Island of Flowers the paddle had been nothing for Jean Marc to fear. Now the torturers used them hours at a time, repeatedly beating his head, his kidneys, his sex.

Those beatings and shocks went on for seven days, the first four without interruption. Jean Marc was sure he would not live. What offense justified this fury? Setting fire to a jeep? Giving a few speeches?

On the seventh day, blindfolded and beaten on the ears until his eardrums seemed about to burst, until the inside of his head ached worse than any bruise on his body, Jean Marc learned the answer. He heard Commander Monteiro translating into English the questions put to Jean Marc: "What groups did you belong to?" "Where are its members?"

Jean Marc also heard a man speaking to the commander in English with a United States accent. At the time, Jean Marc was hanging upside down, trussed like a roasting chicken, his wrists and ankles tied to a pole called the parrot's perch. The guards were giving him electric shocks on the inside of his ears. Yet he heard the astonishing news and understood the frenzy that went into his beating.

The U. S. ambassador to Brazil had been kidnapped.

CHAPTER
6

CHARLES BURKE ELBRICK, recently appointed as ambassador to Brazil, was a diplomat of the old school with an air and interests that led younger political officers at the State Department to find him stodgy and unimaginative, to find him, in the words of one very junior colleague, "an old fart." To the more earnest men of his own age at State, everything about Elbrick's life was an irritant. He seemed to them a caricature of the impeccably dressed careerist who selected his political opinions with a bit less care than his neckties.

Elbrick's family, comfortably fixed in Louisville, had sent him off to Williams College. He graduated the year the stock market crashed. Joining the diplomatic corps two years later, he edged his way upward—through Panama and Haiti, and just before the war, Poland. At each of his stations, Elbrick and his wife, Elvira, were indefatigable patrons of the ballet, the local symphony orchestra, and the opera.

As an adult, Elbrick shifted his undergraduate allegiances from Phi Delta Theta to the Metropolitan and the Chevy Chase clubs in Washington. Abroad, with fewer such retreats available, he was a conscientiously good fellow about showing up at embassy picnics and joining in the group sings. He could very nearly seem to be enjoying himself.

During Lyndon Johnson's administration, Lincoln Gordon's service in Brazil had been rewarded with the job of assistant secretary of state for Latin American affairs. John Tuthill, his successor as Brazil's ambassador, was less complaisant about Brazil's dictatorship and had seriously antagonized the country's generals. Now, to ease Elbrick's way, Gordon took him in hand before his departure from Washington and administered a cram course in Brazilian history. Gordon, older now but no less loquacious, talked until Elbrick felt the facts were coming out of his ears. On July 8, 1969, not remembering a thing Gordon had told him, Burke Elbrick arrived in Brazil.

At the embassy, Elbrick's reputation had preceded him, and the fears of his new staff were not eased when Mrs. Elbrick explained firmly that a charity reception previously scheduled for the residence would have to be canceled. "Oh, my dear," she was quoted as saying, "my house is not a public place."

Yet Elbrick and his wife could be gracious indeed, when it pleased them, and there were few qualities that most Brazilians valued more. Perhaps, his staff thought wishfully, when he settles into the job, he will work out after all.

Although Brasília had now been the nominal capital of the country for a decade, the embassies were still loath to relinquish Rio's glitter for the new city's bleak geometry. Elbrick went on living in the official residence in Rio's Botafogo district: 388 São Clemente was the address, and he would return there each noon for an unhurried lunch.

On September 4, 1969, a Thursday in the Brazilian spring, the ambassador followed his habit, dined agreeably, and a little before 2 P.M. set off in the ambassadorial Cadillac to return to the embassy. At the wheel was his Brazilian chauffeur, Custodio Abel de Silva.

The residence was set in the middle of narrow one-way

streets. Making its way down one of them, the Cadillac was suddenly blocked by a Volkswagen that seemed to be stalled. As Elbrick looked to see what was wrong, four men yanked open the doors of the limousine shouting, "We are Brazilian revolutionaries!" They pointed .45 automatics at the ambassador and pushed the driver to the middle of the front seat. In the back, they forced Elbrick to lie down on the floor. To everything he asked, one man kept repeating, "Shut up!"

They reached a deserted spot in the hills above Botafogo beach. The man told the ambassador to close his eyes. They are going to kill me, Elbrick thought.

The year before, John Gordon Mein, Lincoln Gordon's deputy who had been promoted to ambassador to Guatemala, had been assassinated fighting off rebels from his embassy car. Elbrick would not fight, but he would not close his eyes either. Instead, he raised his hand, a reflex, to push away the gun from his face. When he did, another of the men hit Elbrick with a gun butt. The blow stunned him and sent blood running down his face.

His captors prodded him out of the Cadillac and into a Volkswagen bus. Again, he was ordered to lie on the floor while they covered him with a tarpaulin. The man who had told him to shut up sat over him with a .45.

The men spoke to each other but not to Elbrick. They drove for fifteen or twenty minutes. Under the tarpaulin Elbrick began to relax. He puzzled over their intentions, but he no longer thought they were going to kill him. If that had been their plan, they would have done it at the deserted spot in the hills.

The kidnappers drove into a building and stopped the engine. The four of them got out of the Volkswagen. One said to Elbrick, "You can get up now, and if you face forward you can sit on the seat. But if you turn around, we'll shoot you."

Elbrick raised his head. It looked as though they were in a tiny box of a garage. Two men had stayed with him, one on the seat behind him, one just outside the garage door.

It was hot. Very gingerly, careful not to look around, Elbrick slid out of his jacket. He asked for water to wash his wound. Someone brought a bucket and a pitcher of filtered drinking water.

Elbrick assumed that they were waiting for it to get dark so that they could smuggle him safely from the garage. It was only a little after 3 P.M. With springtime's late sunset, Elbrick prepared for a long wait. He pondered his circumstances. Who were these men? What did they want with him?

One of the kidnappers inside the house was Fernando Gabeira, the former police reporter for *Binomio* in Belo Horizonte. Fernando was now twenty-eight, and his rapid advancement as a journalist in Rio had been matched by his evolution as a man of the Left. He had been working as research editor of *Jornal do Brasil*, an influential conservative daily in Rio and teaching journalism at the federal university. He had watched the military coup brewing for years in Belo; yet, when it finally came, it demoralized him.

After 1964, Fernando saw Brazil's Left fall into three major movements. The PCB, Brazil's old-line Communist party, still looked to the Soviet Union for direction. The Partido Communista do Brasil (PCDB) leaned toward Mao Tsetung. Politica Operaria (POLOP) recruited among the Trotskyites. As often happens with articulate revolutionaries, there were many other splinter groups.

The conservative PCB leadership preached that Brazilians must win back their rights through elections. The other groups all saw the only choice as armed revolution. But revolution of what sort? The Catholic Popular Action, the PCDB, the National Liberation Action (ALN), and others favored a revolution of national liberation. MR-8 was different. Movimento Revolucionario do Outubro 8 had been named to honor the day that Ché Guevara was shot. It was an offshoot of the Communist party's student group, and it favored a socialist revolution. Fernando was a member of MR-8.

In his heart, Fernando believed that he and his fellow Brazilian Communists were far from being ideologists. They were Catholics who had lost their formal faith and were now trying to justify Christian concerns by passing them off as Marxist. If they owed their allegiance to any manifesto, it was the Sermon on the Mount.

The members of MR-8 expressed contempt for the idea of working to restore elections to Brazil. One chief grievance against the Communist party was that the Communists in Goulart's day had cooperated with him in peaceable reforms rather than organize an effective resistance against the inevitable military coup.

At its zenith, MR-8 never attracted more than a hundred men and women. The previous July, navy intelligence had swooped down and arrested twenty-seven of them. The small size of the remnant explained the attempt for a grand effect.

Fernando had been steeling himself for this moment by testing his nerve with lesser dangers. He got up mornings at 5 A.M. to leave his expensive apartment in Leblon and race through factories outside Rio, hurling down political tracts. To be caught would have meant arrest, jail, torture, the end of his career.

Then someone in the group proposed a political kidnapping. In 1969, it was not a shopworn idea. They would abduct an important man and hold him for ransom. But not for money. That would not stir the hearts of the average *brasileiro* whom they were trying to reach. It would be better to kidnap a man and demand in exchange the release of political prisoners who were being tortured while they were held for months without a trial. It was a good demand; humane. But how many prisoners? It had to be a reasonable figure. They settled on fifteen.

That much of the planning took six weeks of discussion. As the hectic debates continued to spin out over the same ground, Fernando would think to himself, "We are, after all, intellectuals."

Suddenly it was drawing near to September 7, Brazil's national independence day. Everyone agreed they should take advantage of the symbolism, and the abstract discussions became more urgent. They realized that they had no jail for their victim. However, they had rented a house on Barão do Petropolis in a northern section of Rio to serve as headquarters for an underground newspaper Fernando was supposed to edit. An MR-8 member, Elena Bocayuva, was taking her small children there every day so that the neighbors would think it was a normal household. As soon as her presence was taken for granted, Fernando would launch his paper. Now, with no better place at hand, they decided to use that house to cage Burke Elbrick.

Not that Fernando or most of the others knew Elbrick's name. They knew only that the United States maintained an ambassador in Rio and that kidnapping him would guarantee the largest headlines and the greatest willingness on the part of the Brazilian government to negotiate his release.

(Later, when abducting diplomats became commonplace, Brazilians, joking about the relative status of the victims, agreed that to get one prisoner released, the Haitian ambassador would have to be kidnapped twice.)

To familiarize themselves with the U.S. ambassador's routine, the plotters took a venerable approach. They sent to the embassy a pretty girl who flirted artfully with the young Brazilian in charge of security.

"Oh!" she exclaimed. "I'm fascinated by the way your complicated embassy runs." The security man puffed up and answered her every question.

All at once, it was the night before the kidnapping. Since they did not have much experience in political action, the MR-8 cell had voted to contact the ALN in São Paulo. That group, founded by Carlos Marighela, a legendary figure among the Brazilian Left, also comprised alumni of the Communist party. ALN had agreed to send half the twelve-member crew needed for carrying out the action. Of that dozen, six would actually seize the ambassador on his morning ride to the embassy. The others would stay behind at the house. Fernando had begun living at the address, so he was among those chosen to wait.

It was night when the ALN reinforcements arrived from São Paulo. Marighela was not with them. Later some Brazilians argued that his absence showed cowardice; others saw it as proof that he had never approved of kidnapping as a tactic.

Although Marighela had not come, another revolutionary almost as renowned did join them. Toledo was the code name of Joaquim Câmara Ferreira, a seventy-eight-year-old veteran of the Spanish Civil War who had broken with the Communist party in 1964. Within the ALN he ranked second behind Marighela. Toledo would pretend to be Fernando's father.

There were last-minute arrangements to attend to, including the procurement of four freshly stolen cars. Several men left the house and rounded up three cars and a Volkswagen bus. The revolutionary tactic was to point a pistol at a driver and tell him, "We're going to need your car for an action."

In the early days of the resistance, there had sometimes been room for negotiation. "Do you really need this car tonight?" one young man had protested. "I'm supposed to take my girl to the movies." That would send some rebels moving on, looking for a driver with a less legitimate excuse. License plates were always changed immediately.

Most MR-8 members had been kept ignorant of the kidnapping. They had only been told: Tomorrow, be a little careful. Something is going to happen. But the others, the dozen, went to bed exhilarated by their secret. They knew that tomorrow all of Rio would be talking about them. Or they would be dead. But they did not think seriously about death, and certainly not Elbrick's. Of course, they might have to threaten to kill him. That was the way their hand was to be played.

The next morning, the six set out on their mission. One would linger up the street and signal when the ambassador's limousine approached. Another would block the narrow street with the stolen Volkswagen. Four would leap in with drawn pistols and subdue Elbrick and his chauffeur.

But nothing went right that morning. The kidnappers had scarcely left the house when there was a loud crash on the street. One car had banged another, and the accident blocked the garage so that nothing could get in or out. Then, upon leaving the residence, Elbrick's driver apparently acted on caprice and took a different route. The desperate men of the ALN and MR-8 waited an hour for a car that never came.

So it was important there be no mistake in the afternoon. The tension was too great to be endured another night. Later, talking over why an ALN man—Virgilio Ferreira, code name Jonas—had given Elbrick the crack on the head, the rebels agreed that Virgilio had probably thought Elbrick was making a move to escape and that he had been even more scared than his victim.

At the house, two hours passed. Then four of the six men came tramping up the stairs; and from the exultant look on their faces, Fernando knew that this time everything had gone as planned.

When dusk finally settled, Burke Elbrick was blindfolded and led out of the garage and into the house. "What's happening?" he kept asking. "I want to get in touch with my wife. What's become of my chauffeur?"

The revolutionaries had anticipated Elbrick's concern for his wife. The night before, they had agreed that one agonizing aspect of their life was to have a comrade disappear and not know his fate. Was he dead? In the hands of the police? Had he acted on a tip and fled the city? They resolved to spare Elbrick's family that particular anguish. Immediately upon the ambassador's arrival in the garage, Fernando had gone to a pay telephone on the street and called William Belton, the minister-counselor at the embassy, to assure him that Elbrick was all right.

Fernando could not know that their plan for buying time had misfired. After they placed a threatening note on the front seat of the Cadillac, the kidnappers had taken the driver's keys away from him. His walking down from the deserted hill they thought would take an hour. But Custodio carried duplicate keys. As soon as the van pulled away, he drove down to the first house with a telephone. Within minutes the embassy knew of the calamity, and Belton was contacting the intelligence office: "The ambassador was kidnapped seven minutes ago."

Within half an hour, Belton and the staff had copies of the three-page manifesto the kidnappers had left on the car seat. It was not reassuring. The rebels demanded the government meet two conditions: the release of fifteen political prisoners, their names to be supplied after the government had agreed in principle; and the reading of the entire manifesto over all radio and television networks.

By censoring the press, the military had tried to keep the population ignorant of the rebels' bank robberies and raids on the arms caches at military barracks. Now, on the night of its most daring strategem, MR-8 was demanding its due.

If they received no answer within forty-eight hours, the kidnappers said, they would execute Burke Elbrick. "Each of them," the manifesto added, referring to the fifteen political prisoners, "is worth one hundred ambassadors...." The message ended with a broader threat: "Finally, we would like to warn all those who torture, beat, and kill our comrades that we will no longer allow this to continue. We are giving our last warning.... Now it is an eye for an eye and a tooth for a tooth."

Reading that statement on the air would prove no real

problem, distasteful as the government found it. But the broadcast would satisfy only the simpler of the two requirements: the prisoner exchange looked all but insurmountable. Thus, from the time of the driver's call the entire embassy staff was, in the words of one ranking diplomat, "crapping in our pants to get Elbrick back."

Elbrick, meantime, had no idea that his life had been threatened. In his makeshift cell, he was getting his bearings. They had taken him up many twisting stairs to a top floor and shut him in a room about nine feet by twelve. The shutters were closed, but from the cracks he would be able to tell night from day. Hanging from the ceiling, a single electric bulb burned continually. The furniture was a folding cot and one stool.

The kidnappers told him that he had only to ask permission when he wanted to cross the hall to use the bathroom. Then they took off his blindfold and left him alone. One armed man took up sentry duty beyond the door, left slightly ajar.

Downstairs, Fernando was reproaching himself for not laying in provisions for dinner. For the first time in his life he was responsible for feeding a prisoner, and he did not know what the ambassador might like to eat. Fernando decided on pizza.

In Brazil, pizza is the ubiquitous snack at the small corner bars, their version of the hot dog. For fifteen cents a man can buy a wide slice of pizza fresh from the oven to eat with his glass of draft beer.

The nearest pizzeria was far enough away that Fernando had to take a cab. He picked up the pizza and hailed another taxi for the trip back. As he got in, the driver said, "Do you know that they got that man?"

"Which man?" Fernando asked.

"The man! The boss of everything! The American ambassador!"

"Oh," said Fernando, "I didn't know."

"It's a pity," the driver reproached him, "that you are so

unconnected with reality. Many things are happening in the world."

At the house, the rebels were consulting about the ambassador's head wound. When Elbrick complained of a headache, they called in a revolutionary in his final year of medical school.

"It looks all right," the young man told them. "But if complications develop, you must bring a doctor here."

Although the others wanted to believe that the headache was more likely the result of tension than a concussion, they agreed to frequently check on his condition. Now, however, they wanted to question him. Here he was, the boss of everything, in their power. They would collect the proof for what until today they had only suspected.

Upstairs, Elbrick was growing equally impatient. He called to his guard, "What in the world are you up to?"

The man said, "You'll see, you'll see."

After an hour, Elbrick was ordered to re-tie his blindfold. When it was in place, two men entered the room. Their voices sounded older to Elbrick than those of the men who had grabbed him, and when they spoke it was in the fusty language of Karl Marx. Elbrick asked himself whether one of them could be Marighela. It was tempting to speculate that he was in the hands of the country's most notorious revolutionary. However, it was Toledo who led the questioning. If his intention was to terrify the ambassador, he succeeded.

"Mr. Elbrick, we know all about you," he began, speaking in Portuguese. The rebels had agreed before the abduction that even though several of them spoke English, they would not make the work of the intelligence services easier by using it with Elbrick and narrowing the list of suspects.

"We've studied your career," Toledo went on, "and we know you have long been a prominent member of the CIA."

Elbrick took it for a bluff, a way of unnerving him. "No," he said, "I've been in the diplomatic service for thirty-eight years."

"We know otherwise."

The truth was that in the two months Elbrick had been in Brazil he had not yet requested his briefing from the CIA station chief. Others might call it indifference to duty. Today it looked most fortuitous. Elbrick really did not know much. Even if they were to torture him, he could not betray any profound secrets.

But would they torture him? "We don't like to treat our prisoners the way the Brazilian police treat theirs," one man said. Was that supposed to be reassurance or a threat?

Whatever their intention, whenever Elbrick replied that he did not know an answer, one would say, "Come now, Mr. Ambassador, you don't expect us to believe that. Tell us who the CIA men are."

It was after that repeated hectoring that the ambassador committed an indiscretion. For some time, the CIA station chief in Brazil had been, as Elbrick put it primly, "misbehaving." The CIA man was maintaining a wife and child in Rio and a girlfriend, also from the United States, in Brasília. In Elbrick's view, the man had simply been stationed in the country too long. He had not been seduced by its women, but he had certainly succumbed to its mores.

A few days before the kidnapping, Elbrick had called this station chief to his office. They both understood that such philandering ran counter to CIA rules. But when Elbrick told the chief that he would have to recommend a transfer, the man had pleaded so plaintively that Elbrick had said he would think it over.

Now, pressed by his captors repeatedly for CIA names, Elbrick said, "One officer in the political section maintains contact with the intelligence services, and he briefs me." He meant the CIA station chief. Naturally his questioner said, "Who is he?"

Elbrick gave them the name. The man, after all, had already made a muddle of things. But as soon as he had spoken, the ambassador regretted it. What if they got that man too? With their knowing about his CIA connection, the man would surely be finished. What Elbrick had done made him sick with remorse.

His regret, could Elbrick have known it, was wasted, for his earlier answers had been so uninformed that the kidnappers had stopped paying much attention to what he said. To the Brazilians, Elbrick appeared to be a well-meaning man, even a liberal, who was as contemptuous as they were of the ruling generals. When they kept coming back to the CIA, Elbrick suggested names of Brazilians who might be CIA agents, but it was merely the same speculation they had engaged in among themselves. It was clear that unless he was playing an extremely clever game, Elbrick was simply musing aloud.

The kidnappers decided to open Elbrick's briefcase. Fernando saw that as taking a considerable liberty with the ambassador, but they all agreed that they would read only his official papers, nothing that was personal. Here they had better luck than with their direct questions. Elbrick was carrying no documents stamped SECRET, but he had been planning a trip to São Paulo the following week; and the embassy's political section, drawing on CIA files, had put together a series of profiles on the businessmen and politicians he was due to meet. Elbrick heard the kidnappers going through those papers, and from their exclamations he knew they had found the dossiers engrossing.

For one thing, the language and attitudes of the Cold War permeated the biographical sketches. Was Elbrick going to meet with the minister of mines? Then it behooved him to know that the man's sister was a bit left-wing. Other ministers were described as being flexible; in CIA terms, that was a compliment. Hélio Beltrão, one example, was praised for being very open to U. S. advice.

With that ammunition, the rebels went back to soliciting the ambassador's personal opinions. What did he think of José de Magalhães Pinto, the foreign minister?

This was not idle conversation. Several days before Elbrick was abducted, President Costa e Silva had suffered the stroke that sent Jean Marc Von der Weid rushing to imprisonment. With the president disabled, the country was being run by a military triumvirate.

Elbrick was new to Brazil, but he had no special fondness for generals; and he thought that the vice-president, a law professor and civilian named Pedro Aleixo, had been slighted. Elbrick went to the Foreign Office and asked Magalhães Pinto, "Isn't the vice-president supposed to take over?"

The minister had seemed disconcerted by Elbrick's bluntness. Casting about for an answer, he finally explained that the country was being ruled by Institutional Acts, under which the military triumvirate was perfectly legal.

Elbrick had found it an odd reply. Now, trying to strike a sympathetic chord, he repeated that he had not been satisfied with it. He did not know that the rebels were recording their questions, as well as his answers, on tape.

It was about 11 P.M. before they left him. When Elbrick removed the blindfold, he was sweating, and it was not simply from the warm spring night.

In his briefcase, the rebels had also come across a roll of tablets. These they carefully put on the window sill next to his cot. They think I have a heart condition, the ambassador decided, amused that there was at least one thing he knew that they did not. They were just antacid tablets. Tonight, strangely, he did not feel a need for them.

Elbrick habitually smoked little cigars, cigarillos by Robert Burns, and had been carrying a box of five in his briefcase. He had run through them in the first hour of his interrogation. Now he found that without consulting him, one of his kidnappers had run out and bought him a supply of little Brazilian cigars from Bahia.

The ambassador lit one. It was strong. Strong but good. His captors were peering in the door to watch him, and they seemed gratified by his enjoyment.

Elbrick felt like reading in bed. He called for reading material, and one rebel disappeared and returned with a copy of *Manchete*, the Brazilian picture magazine. He also brought an English-language edition of Ho Chi Minh on revolution. They had given Elbrick a T-shirt; and wearing that and his own undershorts, the ambassador settled down for his first night in captivity.

He read for a while. Then he turned on his side, away from the light bulb burning at the ceiling, and with no trouble at all he fell asleep.

At the U. S. embassy, the mood was not so tranquil. At 5 P.M., the staff official deemed to have the closest ties with the ruling junta went to see Magalhães Pinto. The foreign minister would only say, "We're taking appropriate action." His response was purposely vague because at the moment, the military triumvirate was racked by dissension.

One year earlier, with their riots in the streets, Jean Marc Von der Weid and the student union had come closer than they realized to bringing down the government. Only the police, their U. S. advisers, and the highest embassy and military circles recognized the disarray among the leaders of the junta and the thinness of popular support for Costa e Silva. Tonight, those U. S. agents close to the ruling generals were alarmed that Elbrick's kidnapping would strain once again the uneasy agreement among the military services and reveal to the world their dissension.

It was the army minister, General Aurelio de Lyra Tavares, on whom the embassy rested its hopes and brought the greatest pressures. At sixty-three, a veteran of the engineer corps, he had a reputation for detached analysis, and the embassy trusted that he would foresee the propaganda defeat for the junta in the U. S. Congress were Elbrick to die because of Brazil's intransigence.

The other two ministers, Admiral Augusto Rudemaker Grünewald of the navy and Brigadier General Marcio de Souza e Mello of the air force, were regarded as spokesmen for the hard liners within their commands. Of those two services, the navy seemed the more unbending. In fact, the hard line was demanding that until Elbrick was released, a political prisoner already in custody be taken out every hour and publicly shot. No doubt the kidnappers would retaliate by killing Burke Elbrick, but that sacrifice would be preferable to the humiliation of meeting the rebels' demands.

The U. S. embassy staff saw matters differently. There was no precedent to guide them; nothing like this had happened before. In the absence of any contrary instruction from Washington, they were bringing to bear all their leverage, calling in every debt, to get Elbrick freed.

Once MR-8 had decided to set the number of prisoners at fifteen, the group wanted to free those men and women who were being tortured most savagely. They made room on their final list for one sick seventy-year-old Bolshevik, Gregório Bezerra, to show respect for his twenty years of imprisonment under various regimes. Bezerra had also been one of the first political prisoners abused after the coup of 1964. A Brazilian army major had tied him to the back of a jeep and dragged him bleeding through the streets of Recife.

Jean Marc Von der Weid would almost certainly have been on the MR-8 list, although he and Fernando Gabeira, in their few contacts, had never found each other simpatico. But the same anonymity that had served Jean Marc well in the past now worked against him. Those three days it took the military intelligence to learn his identity were enough to prevent word of his arrest from reaching the outside. By the time his imprisonment became known, Fernando had already dropped the fifteen names into the suggestion box of a supermarket in Leblon.

On his first morning as a prisoner, Elbrick woke up ready to talk. He had found Ho's tract fascinating, and he

wanted to discuss it with his guards. Wasn't it a blueprint
in reverse for what these young men were doing? Ho
wrote about rural warfare, and they were engaged in urban
war. There were so many interesting points to cover.

The kidnappers found Elbrick's naïveté as he spoke of
Ho hard to believe. As revolutionary ideas they had not
been startling for twenty-five years or more. Yet here was
a veteran U. S. diplomat eager to probe and debate them
as though Mao had never lived, as though Ché had never
written, as though Ho himself, who had died just the preceding week, had published his manual yesterday.

Elbrick's colleagues in the State Department could have
assured them that his guilelessness was genuine. And in
Elbrick's defense, the *Minimanual of the Urban Guerrilla*,
Carlos Marighela's contribution to revolutionary literature, had only circulated within the ALN three months
earlier.

Marighela had dedicated his booklet, which later won
support among revolutionaries in the United States, to
three victims of the Brazilian military and police, and to the
prisoners "subjected to tortures that even surpass the hor-
rendous crimes practiced by the Nazis."

The ideas themselves, whether from Ho or Marighela,
struck Ambassador Elbrick as misguided but eminently
worth discussing. The rebels had agreed among themselves
that Elbrick's guards would stand outside his door, not in
his room, and would speak the minimum to him.

Fernando watched as one by one they succumbed to the
temptation to air their opinions before their distinguished
visitor. Well, he thought, resigned to it, we are Brazilians.
But much more of this behavior, and we'll be inviting him
out to dinner.

After Fernando's first excursion for pizza, Toledo had
cooked up a mess of rice and beans and macaroni, and that
was what they were ladling out to the fastidious ambassador. *Feijoda*, the Brazilian national dish, is a mixture of
beans and meat so heavy that many restaurants serve it only

at Saturday noon, when their patrons can go home immediately afterward to sleep off its effects. Properly prepared, *feijoda* is a delicacy.

What the ambassador found on his plate was an abomination. Eating the same slop, Fernando and the other rebels agreed with him. Sympathetically, one said, "You don't eat much."

"I don't seem to have a revolutionary appetite," Elbrick answered. Those who heard him laughed loudly and repeated what he had said. The camaraderie that was developing among them would change Elbrick's life more than his kidnapping.

One young man, six feet four inches tall and exceedingly handsome, was the ambassador's favorite guard. Not only did he have a *brasileiro*'s full complement of charm, but he spoke English far better than Elbrick spoke Portuguese and was willing to breach the ban on speaking English in the hope of making the ambassador understand.

Elbrick asked the fellow whether he ever saw his family.

"No," he said, "I couldn't possibly. They disapprove of what I'm doing."

As they talked further, it became obvious to the ambassador that this boy came from what people once termed—and Elbrick still considered—"a good family." He was a natural heir to wealth and position. Yet rather than exercise those options, he was here, existing on beans and rice, sleeping on the floor of this ramshackle house, ready at any moment to have his head blown off.

Fernando was a tradesman's son. He himself might be proud that as he had advanced as a journalist, he had never lost his sympathy for the poor. But Fernando's was not a story to impress the ambassador. It was this other boy—so attractive, so favored at birth—whose sacrifice made Elbrick begin to understand, even to respect, the depth of the revolutionaries' dedication.

That boy and the other guards came in, some with bandanas over their faces, and talked fervently for the duration of their one-hour shifts. "You are in a dangerous business," Elbrick would remind them. "You can be killed at any minute."

"You're right," one young man answered. "But a bullet is better than being in jail. We've declared war on the Brazilian government. It may take ten years or twenty or thirty, but we will win. For every one who falls, there are a hundred to take his place."

Arrant nonsense, Elbrick thought, but they seemed to believe it. None of his young guards was a Communist, they told him, although they granted that there were Communists in their organizations. They seemed particularly proud of Carlos Marighela—for his skill, for his courage, for his having been a deputy in the parliament.

Although he was warming to these boys, Elbrick continued to be put off by their hatreds. He asked about the rash of bank robberies. Over the past month they had averaged almost one a day. "Yes," said one guard, "we're responsible." Elbrick had to laugh at his coolness and nerve.

Before his capture, Elbrick had known in an abstract way about the repression in Brazil. Now here were men who said they would not hesitate to shoot a policeman. "No, no," the ambassador protested. "No, that's not the right way to go about things. You may have legitimate grievances," he went on, still unaware of the tape recorder, "but violence never solves anything."

They answered him: We have no freedom of speech or expression. We have no free press or trade unions to represent the aspirations of our people. We have no elections, no forums, no rights. If we want to change things, this is the only way.

To that, Elbrick had no rebuttal.

While his colleagues stood guard duty, Fernando maintained communication between the house and the world's press. Elbrick had been allowed to write a note to his wife, and Fernando left it at a church, Nossa Senhora da Gloria. Then he called *Ultima Hora*, instructing the editors where to find it. His own paper, *Jornal do Brasil,* lost the scoop because he was sure someone would recognize his voice.

As Fernando was dealing with the press, another of the rebels, Cid de Queiroz Benjamin, ran information between the house and other members of MR-8 and the ALN. That job took him out regularly among the people of Rio, and he was buoyed up by the festive air in the streets. Three months earlier, Neil Armstrong had stepped onto the moon. Now a taxi driver told Cid there were two groups of men he admired: those who had gone to the moon, and those who had abducted the ambassador.

Another MR-8 member overheard passengers on a bus agreeing that for the first time in its history, at least some Brazilians were acting independent of the United States. Everywhere, people walked with radios pressed to their ears as though it were the week of World Cup soccer.

Cid's message-passing all went smoothly. It was the house, never intended to be a people's prison, that gave the intelligence services the break they needed.

Elbrick first knew there was trouble when he heard a whistle up the stairs. His guard picked up his pistol and pointed it at Elbrick's chest.

Downstairs Fernando was answering a knock at the door. On the step were two men in civilian clothes. They asked for someone Fernando had never heard of. He said, "No one by that name lives here."

"That's strange," said one of the men. "We were invited to dinner."

They apologized and left. Fernando wanted to know whether they were truly lost or whether they were intelligence agents. He waited a few minutes, then slipped out of the house and into the garden of the house next door. Through the wall, he could hear one of them talking on the telephone. From the low monotone, it sounded as though he was making a routine report.

Fernando went back to warn the others. It may have been only a house-to-house check, he said, but we have to face the possibility that they know about us and are planning to come back with troops.

They waited. After an hour, the men had not returned. At last, they whistled up the stairs again, and Elbrick's guard relaxed and lowered his gun. But the ambassador realized with a jolt that had it been a police raid, he would have been the first man killed.

Fernando's suspicions had been correct. The two men were agents from Brazilian army intelligence. Neighbors had reported an unusual amount of activity at the house; and after their brief glimpse past Fernando's shoulder, the men decided that the ambassador was probably somewhere inside. What the men did not know was that CENIMAR had received an earlier tip about the house and had sent a car to park across the street and monitor all activity. Those agents recognized the army operatives; and for one heady moment as they watched them approaching the house, the navy men were sure they had unmasked double agents within the rival service.

(The navy agents also photographed everyone who went in and out of the house. Once Fernando went out to place a message for the press, and an agent had cruised along behind him. Later, in jail, that officer reminded Fernando of the episode. When Fernando looked blank, the agent asked, "Didn't you see me?" "No," said Fernando. "Ah, foolish me," the navy man said with a sigh. "I thought you did, and when I came back to change cars, I lost you.")

While this sleuthing was under way, Lyra Tavares, acting for the junta, decided to meet the kidnappers' demand and fly the designated fifteen prisoners to Mexico. Magalhães Pinto's office announced that he would address the nation. The U. S. embassy staff was jubilant. Lyra Tavares received a barrage of compliments on his wisdom and courage.

Then, late Friday, perhaps because of the success of

CENIMAR in locating the house, a rumor spread that the hard liners had forced a reversal of the plan, and there would be no release of prisoners. When Magalhães Pinto canceled his speech, the rumor seemed confirmed. Then CIA agents around Rio picked up the story, and a CIA officer hurried to William Belton with it.

Belton's dedication to embassy security had been less dogged than the military and police advisers would have wished. Once a thief fished out a woman's purse from a stall the woman was occupying in an embassy toilet. The U. S. police advisers used the episode to argue for beefed-up patrolling, but Belton had said, No, when people entered the embassy they should feel a sense of calm and not be surrounded by uniforms. Given that attitude, Belton's desperation over Elbrick's abduction touched few hearts among the police advisers.

By the time the rumor of a deadlock reached Belton, it was 3 A.M., Saturday morning. He called Colonel Arthur Moura, a diminutive and snappy army man who had succeeded Dick Walters as ranking military attaché at the embassy. A veteran of army intelligence, Moura had never been overwhelmed by either the CIA's sources or its evaluations. Now he scoffed at the report and assured Belton that the trade was still on.

Belton kept calling back. By 6:30 A.M., he was agitated enough to tell Moura, "If he dies, it's on your hands."

Moura capitulated to that moral blackmail. Still grumbling, he got dressed and drove to the suburb of Santa Teresa and the house of a friendly Brazilian general who laid the rumor to rest: "When I left the office late last night, they were rounding up the guys. A C-130 is supposed to be warming up to get them off at two-thirty this afternoon."

By Saturday morning, the kidnappers also started believing that the government was indeed going to meet their demands. Some of them wondered why they had not asked for more prisoners, not knowing that to release even the fifteen had strained the military's hard line almost past endurance. It was not widely publicized within Brazil, but forty Brazilian paratroopers had seized a government radio station on the outskirts of Rio to denounce the release.

For the first time, the rebels permitted Elbrick to see a newspaper. To his chagrin, spread across the front page of *Journal do Brasil* was a facsimile of his reassuring note to his wife. The ambassador taxed the rebels with this breach of his privacy, and they apologized. "But if we had sent it through the mail, it would have taken a week."

"Dear Elfie," Elbrick had written,

> I am all right, and I am hoping that I shall be liberated and see you soon. Please don't worry—I am trying not to. The Brazilian authorities have been informed of the demands of the people who are holding me. They should not try to find out where I am, which might be dangerous, but hurry to meet the conditions for my release.
>
> The people, of course, are very determined.
>
> All my love, darling—hoping that we shall be together soon, Burke

Elbrick joked afterward that his only dismay had been the sight of his stiff handwriting exposed for the world to see. Yet, to the Brazilian hard line, his message was somewhat less than a ringing defiance of his captors.

The sight of the letter, like the taxi driver's remarks to Fernando, reminded everyone within the house that this was no private interlude in their lives. All of them now figured in a world-wide drama whose last scenes were yet to be written, and not entirely by them.

Late Saturday, fifteen prisoners were taken from cells at their various prisons. Two men had overheard radio bulletins about the kidnapping and the exchange. The rest left their cells not knowing what new ordeal awaited them.

Magalhães Pinto's speech to the nation was rescheduled for 3 P.M. At 3:30 P.M., he went on the air to announce that the C-130 was in the air and on its way to Mexico. This was not true. Two hundred navy men, shouting that the exchange was a national disgrace, had surrounded the plane and blocked its departure. The navy high command finally called them off, and the plane left a few minutes after 5 P.M. The four-engine turbo prop flew at 360 miles an hour; and with stops for fuel in Recife and Belem, it was estimated the prisoners would travel the 4,700 miles in about sixteen hours.

On Sunday afternoon, Fernando and his group received confirmation that the plane had landed in Mexico City and that the prisoners had been set free. Relaxing with them, Elbrick watched the young men capering around his room. They came to him, patted his shoulder, and said, "You'll be released soon."

Once more they waited until nightfall. As an extra precaution, they wanted to release Elbrick in the midst of a crowd. There was a major soccer game that night, and the logical spot was around Rio's immense soccer stadium. By now they had spent better than three days and nights with the ambassador, and they understood his crotchets. One man cleaned the blood spots from Elbrick's suit and pressed his trousers. He also washed Elbrick's expensive silk necktie. Accepting his tie, the ambassador appreciated the gesture and did not have the heart to say that of course it had been ruined.

When darkness came, they blindfolded Elbrick for the last time and led him downstairs to a Volkswagen. "Now we're going to drive you to a corner," one rebel told him. "You are to stand on that corner for fifteen minutes without communicating with anyone. Then you're at liberty."

"Fifteen minutes!" Elbrick protested.

"You've been here three and a half days," the rebel reminded him. "Fifteen minutes isn't so long."

There were six of them again—a driver, another man in back with a pistol, and four men in a backup car. Sitting in the dark, Elbrick heard a lot of complaining about the heavy Sunday-night traffic. Then the man in the back said, "We're being followed!"

The driver asked, "Should we get out and run for it?"

"I don't think so."

They speeded up, snaking through the lines of cars. At last Elbrick felt the tension dissolve, and he assumed they had lost their pursuers. Behind the blindfold he could not know that this had not been accomplished through a spurt of daredevil driving. When the navy intelligence officers saw Elbrick being taken from the house, they gave chase. Through the snarl of cars they had managed to keep pace with the two-car convoy. Then at a red light the two navy men pulled alongside the backup car. One officer raised his hand until his pistol showed in the window. At that, the rebels stared at his weapon, and then each slowly lifted his own gun. The navy agents were brave but not fanatically so. They dropped back, returned to headquarters, and reported that they had suffered a flat tire.

The lead car pulled to a quiet corner, and the driver told Elbrick to remove his blindfold. They shook hands all around, ambassador and desperados. Clutching his briefcase, Elbrick stepped out of the car. He made out bright lights a block or two in the distance. Feeling disoriented and more than a little foolish, he walked to the intersection and found crowds of spectators on their way home from the soccer match.

Elbrick went up to the first man he saw and asked where he was. Tijuca. It was a cheerless barrio, and the ambassador had not been there before. He asked where he might find a taxi, and the man said, "There's one right behind you."

The driver let out two women fares, circled around, and opened his door to Elbrick.

"Three eighty-eight São Clemente, please."

"You're the ambassador from the United States, are you not? Get in!" He saw Elbrick's head wound. "*Pobrezinho!*" he exclaimed. Poor little thing.

Turning on the radio, the cab driver picked up an announcer saying, "No word yet on the fate of the ambassador." He turned around and grinned: "Do you hear that?"

It took twenty minutes to reach the residence. A crowd had collected outside—the curious, the thrill seekers, and the police. When Elbrick drove up, there was a wild shout. Enough policemen surrounded the cab that they could have picked it up and carried it to the front door.

Elbrick stuck out his head. Newsmen from the U. S. television networks crowded around and pushed microphones through the window. Elbrick said, "Later."

On the steps of the residence, a man from the U. S. Information Service was waiting with a tape recorder; and Elbrick did not feel, as one State Department employee to another, that he could brush him aside. So he said that he was very grateful to the Brazilian government, and he added, to coin an understatement, he was glad to be back. But he could not bring himself to denounce his kidnappers. He could say that they were misguided, that their tactics were wrong. What he could not do was deny their bravery or their dedication or the consideration they had shown him.

At the U. S. embassy, some men who had striven hard for Elbrick's release were appalled by those mild remarks. They knew the strains on the junta, that at any time over the past seventy-eight hours the military rule could have come unstuck. Now the victim was saying that these terrorists, these criminals, were really nice young men who had gone astray. If Elbrick's own staff was disturbed, the Brazilian military command was enraged—and this was before they found the tapes that had been made.

Elbrick did not know that his diplomatic career was over. When an aide told him that there was a message for him to call the Western White House, the term puzzled an old Washington hand like himself. What could that mean? he wondered. Was it the western side of the White House? In due course a call was arranged from São Clemente Street to San Clemente, California, and Elbrick spoke for a moment or two with Richard Nixon. Everyone was curious about their conversation, but all Elbrick remembered was a formal exchange of appropriate platitudes.

With any luck, releasing Elbrick might have ended the chapter for Fernando and his colleagues. Since Toledo was the most notorious of their number, they had let him out in the soccer crowd to make his way back to São Paulo. Their showdown with navy intelligence had resolved any doubts about the house being identified. The two cars would not return there, and the other occupants were out looking for safer lodgings.

One of those young men made a careless move. He was paging through the classified advertisements of *Jornal do Brasil* for a cheap *pensione*. When he found one that sounded right, he tore out the address, threw down the paper, and packed his bag. After they heard that the ambassador was home again, intelligence agents raided Fernando's house. Although it was empty, they found the torn classified section and went to the *Jornal do Brasil*'s office to see what address had been ripped out. Within hours, they arrested the fugitive.

Another young revolutionary had left an old coat behind, a cast-off from his uncle. After a few days the police traced it through the tailor's label, and the nephew was picked up.

For Fernando, Cid, and the others, their ordeal was only beginning. For the fourteen men and one woman who arrived in Mexico City, the suffering seemed to be over.

In small ways, the air-force guards on the flight had shown their disgust for the exchange, not permitting prisoners, for example, to speak for the duration of the flight. If Flavio Tavares Freitas had not smuggled aboard a newspaper to pass silently among his fellow prisoners, most of them would have known nothing about their release.

Tavares was a journalist, and his early exposé of the ties between IBAD and the CIA had earned him a file in General Golbery's office. Later he joined Leonel Brizola's National Revolutionary Movement (MNR), which drew recruits from the PTB and the PSB, the workers' party and the Socialist party, and shared some members with Catholic Popular Action. A prison guard had told Flavio that Christian nationalists such as he were more dangerous to the regime than Communists because their appeal was broader.

Flavio had been arrested by a Death Squad led by a police inspector nicknamed Chinês for the almond shape of his eyes, then taken to Pelotão de Investigaçoes Criminais (PIC), at the police headquarters at Barão de Mesquita in Rio. True to their new procedures, the police tortured him for three days and nights with no serious questioning. Afterward they asked for the names of revolutionary bombers and saboteurs. Flavio knew no names. He was tortured again, by officers from the army, the navy, the police.

In the torture room, the guards administered electric shocks with a small gray generator about a foot and a half long. On the side facing Flavio was a familiar symbol: the red, white, and blue shield of U. S. AID.

His guards wrapped wires around his penis. They stuck wires up his anus. They jammed wires into his ears. Somewhere, they obtained extremely fine wires to fit between his teeth.

The pain was excruciating. What was worse was knowing that when he could not answer a question, he would be shocked again before the burning from the last spasm had subsided.

For those first three days and nights, Flavio was not allowed to sleep or to eat more than a little bread. His torture went forward in shifts. On the fourth day an army doctor came to examine him. For an idealistic prisoner, the arrival of a doctor could be the most dispiriting part of his ordeal. At first the heart filled with hope. Here was a

professional man dedicated to healing; he would put a stop
to this misery. Then the prisoner learned that the doctor
had come only to be sure that the victim was strong
enough to endure further torture. He might give a prisoner
drugs to make him more compliant, or he might advise the
torturers how to keep welts and bruises to a minimum.
Despite that guidance, Flavio came off the plane in Mexico
City with scars around the little finger of his right hand,
burns from the electric wires.

The journalists on the ground sought out Flavio. As a
former reporter for *Ultima Hora*, he would speak their
language. He tried to impress upon them that for all their
air of celebration, the prisoners were entering upon a
forced exile.

"I am certainly not here of my own free will," he said,
a little stiltedly. "Certainly you realize that I came to Mexico by an imposition." But then his balding head began to
bob and his serious expression gave way. With a grin, he
said, "But I think this is a pretty happy imposition."

From the questions they were asked, the prisoners knew
that the press, while friendly, had no grasp of conditions
in Brazil. "Do my parents know I've been released?" one
student repeated a reporter's question. "They don't even
know I've been arrested."

Soon after his release, Burke Elbrick was summoned
back to Washington for consultations with Secretary Rogers and other State Department officials. In their meeting,
Elbrick asked them whether the department really wanted
him to serve out his tour in Brazil.

His superiors agreed that Elbrick's kidnapping had given
the United States a political advantage. Inside Brazil, it
seemed to have generated a degree of sympathy, for the
embassy had received hundreds of letters apologizing for
the indignities the ambassador had endured. Why shouldn't
he go back and capitalize on those feelings?

Within the week, Elbrick was flying back to Rio. He was glad at least that he was not giving the appearance of quitting under fire. But once on the job, he found nearly everything unpleasant. The ruling junta was not going to risk a repetition of the kidnapping, so everywhere he went he was encircled by military guards.

Elbrick had always thought of diplomacy as a peaceable occupation. Now here he was, the U. S. ambassador, roaring through the streets like a proconsul with uniforms at every side. Although suspicion had fallen on Elbrick's timid driver because the kidnappers had turned him loose unharmed, Elbrick himself never believed his chauffeur had been involved. Now a huskier man had replaced him, and Brazilian security installed another man in the front seat to keep an eye on Elbrick for his superiors. Behind the limousine followed a car bearing three men with machine guns.

Worst of all, the sympathetic feelings that the kidnappers had aroused in the ambassador would not go away. Elbrick deplored violence. He knew they were going about their crusade in the wrong way, but he recalled their desperation, and he still had no answer to their question, *What other way is there?*

Behind the scenes, the junta was agitating for Elbrick's recall. On his side, Elbrick was not making the slightest effort to atone for his tepid public condemnation of the rebels. Art Moura, as well connected to the Brazilian military as anyone in the embassy, saw the ambassador only at the Friday staff meetings. Elbrick never requested a military briefing.

One day Moura ran into Elbrick in an embassy corridor and seized the opportunity to ask, "Mr. Ambassador, would you consider hosting a luncheon for the commander of the First Army? It might be useful to us."

Elbrick said, "I don't have time for those people."

It could not go on. Within three months, Elbrick was letting friends in the State Department know that while

Brazil was a lovely country, he had developed an irrational feeling about it and would like to move on. When an embassy doctor recommended that Elbrick return to the United States for tests, most embassy officials felt that the doctor was practicing more diplomacy than medicine.

Elbrick went home. As his doctor in Georgetown was examining him, he suffered a stroke along the right side of his body. When he came to, he was in an intensive-care unit. His recovery was complete, but there was no thought now of returning to Rio.

Elbrick retired from the diplomatic service to divide his time between Washington and a house in upstate New York. Occasionally he agreed to appear on television, once along with Reg Murphy, a Georgia editor who had also been kidnapped. Another time, Dick Cavett, the television host, invited Elbrick to share the stage with Steven Weed, the fiancé of Patricia Hearst, after she had been abducted by the Symbionese Liberation Army. There was a slight link between the kidnappings of Elbrick and Ms. Hearst: members of the SLA said they had adopted the tactics of Carlos Marighela's *Minimanual.*

CHAPTER

7

WHILE BURKE ELBRICK was serving out the end of his career, Fernando Gabeira was living underground, trying to organize an effective labor movement. He had eluded the police dragnet in Rio, reached São Paulo, and moved into a house with several workmen. One day in January of 1970, while he was at the corner bar for a Coca-Cola, police raided the house and arrested one of the workers.

As he drew near the house, Fernando saw that it was surrounded. When he tried to edge away, a policeman ran up and put a machine gun to his belly. "Move and I'll shoot!"

Instead of freezing, Fernando reached out and pushed aside the gun barrel. Then he ran. More policemen caught up and surrounded him. He feinted from side to side. They opened fire, and Fernando took a bullet low in his back.

As he lay bleeding, he heard the policemen standing over him debate their next move. "Shall we finish him off or not?"

"No, we want to interrogate him. We'll take him to the hospital."

Fernando spent the next two months in a São Paulo military ward. The first night, intelligence agents came to his room. The military doctor protested: Fernando's condition was far too delicate. They ignored the doctor and began their questioning. They did not know Fernando's identity, only that he had been living with men committed to the resistance. The questions yielded little information, because Fernando was too weak to talk. Nonetheless, the agents continued to return at different hours, sometimes pulling their pistols and pretending that if he refused to talk, they would shoot him.

Fernando believed that they were injecting him with drugs to make him dizzy. He was also being fed intravenously through a tube running up through his nose. It was uncomfortable for him but evidently worse for an officer, Captain Homero. "When you speak, blood fills that tube," Homero complained. "I may be a torturer, but I'm not a doctor. It makes me sick to look at you."

When the police judged Fernando sufficiently improved, they took him to the OBAN jail in São Paulo. Because they were too eager to begin the torture, after one day of electric shocks they had to send him back to the hospital. He had begun to bleed from his penis; and during his stay in the hospital, he had lost thirty pounds from a body with no flesh to spare.

By the time he was returned to the police, they had learned Fernando's name and had stepped up the interrogation in hopes of rounding up the rest of Elbrick's kidnappers; and Fernando had discovered that the police had found the recordings the rebels had made with the ambassador. Although Elbrick's open contempt for the military government enraged them, the police destroyed the tapes because his sentiments could have proved damaging to the regime.

The torturers interspersed their shocks and beatings with a good deal of joking and horseplay among themselves. Lighter-skinned men would tease the mulattos: With your blunt features and dressed as badly as you are, you've got "cop" written all over you. You'll never be able to go out on undercover work. Or they would mock the United Nations declaration on human rights. "Time to

apply the declaration again," they would say, tying a prisoner back on the parrot's perch and fastening the wires to
his body.

To Fernando, it was a revelation that the men who tortured him were not monsters. Many wore their hair long.
Off duty, they went to the same night spots he had known.
Some even came to his cell to confide their troubles with
women. But they had been trained to detest him. "You are
a son of a whore!" a man would shout, while his face
clenched with hatred. Then someone would call, "Dr.
Paulo, telephone!" As he crossed the room and picked up
the receiver, his face would open up again, and he would
be smiling and smoothing his hair and murmuring endear-
ments.

Nor could Fernando console himself that the men who
applied the wires to his testicles were depraved. They
seemed to practice sexual torture only because it was most
efficient.

Fernando began to distinguish a hierarchy within
OBAN, one that confirmed his Marxist view of society.
The poorest men, often also the most courageous, were
sent to the streets to make the arrests. The torturers were
usually from the middle class. Some had pretentions to culture. Once Homero, the squeamish captain, came to Fernando's cell with a newspaper, ebullient and ready to talk.
Fernando saw he was a man who, because he had tortured
a prisoner, felt they had established an intimacy.

Homero held out the newspaper. "Would you like to
read?"

Warily, Fernando held out his hand. This was strictly
against the rules. "All right."

"There's nothing new or important in it," Homero said
apologetically, "but this whole experience is incredibly
boring for me. I never have anything to discuss with these
other torturers. God!" he exclaimed, leaning against the
bars. "What I'd really like to do is get away for a weekend
in Santos."

Sometimes the middle-level officers, the ones entrusted

with the torture, boasted to Fernando that they had been trained in the United States. One army officer had once reminisced in front of Fernando about going on a raid against a group of Brazilian rural guerrillas. Much to his disgust, the other men in his party had gone stomping loudly across the fields. "It was obvious," he said, "that they had not been trained in the United States."

The torturers found one sardonic way to honor their North American patrons. They would cut open a sardine can and force a prisoner to stand with the sharp edge of each half cutting into the soles of his bare feet. They would then put something heavy in his hand and make him raise it aloft. He had to hold that pose until he collapsed. The police called that torture the Statue of Liberty.

In most cases those men who had graduated from a U. S. military or police school were the analysts and intelligence specialists, and they were chary about appearing inside a torture cell. They were also the men Fernando feared most. They read transcripts of the interrogations and picked out contradictions, either within his own answers or among the responses of other prisoners from MR-8. They gave lists of trick questions to the torturers and outlines of what they wished to know before the day's torture could end.

Within the jail, prisoners compared notes, and some told of seeing U. S. markings on the field telephones and the electric generators used for electric shocks. But all of them attributed the new Brazilian efficiency to United States training. Before the U. S. advisers helped to centralize information, it had taken days to discover whether a new prisoner was a leader in the rebel movement. Now it took hours.

The subject of retribution came up often among the prisoners. Some took an impotent pleasure in describing the tortures they would inflict on their guards after the revolution, when the electrical generators would be in their hands.

On the Isle of Flowers, cell mates tried to convince Jean Marc Von der Weid that torture, however repugnant, might be required at that future day when they were running the country—but only in extreme cases.

"Maybe I am a purist," Jean Marc answered them, "but from the moment you accept one exception to the rule, you accept all. And, speaking practically, torture is a weapon that always backfires against those who use it."

The others said, "The Brazilian government has managed to keep the scope and cruelty of its torture muffled for several years. We will keep it secret, too."

"All things secret are wrong," replied Jean Marc.

At DOPS in Rio, at least one investigator agreed with the revolutionaries who tried to convince Jean Marc that torture was a neutral tool, useful to either side. "I'm here," the officer, whose name was Massini, told a prisoner, who passed along the offer to Fernando Gabeira. "I'm a serious professional. After the revolution, I will be at your disposal to torture whom you like."

With their religious sentiments never far beneath the surface of their politics, most revolutionaries believed that they could never do to others what had been done to them. One navy captain who tortured Fernando also saw it as a difference in character: "I'm a torturer," he taunted Fernando, "but you are not. If the socialists ever come to power, I'll be in a good position, because you're a coward, and you won't torture me."

After two months in São Paulo, Fernando was shipped to Rio and taken by motor launch to the Isle of Flowers. He had never recovered from the shooting and torture. Now he was having trouble urinating. He was too weak to protest himself, but as he lay on his cot, he was touched to hear the other prisoners risk more beatings by pounding on the bars and shouting, "Do something! This man is going to die!"

He was sent to another hospital, then back to an isolation cell on the island, where he stayed for two months, cut off from all contact. But he did hear occasional stirrings in the next cell. For fifteen days, Fernando tapped on the wall. His sound had to be loud enough for the prisoner to hear, yet low enough not to alert a guard.

At last he persuaded the other man to put his mouth close to a crack in the wall and speak to him. "I'm alive," the man whispered. It was the only thing Fernando understood. The man was mad.

Once out of isolation, Fernando came in contact with common prisoners besides the revolutionaries. Homosexuals were usually forced to clean the corridors. At night, as relief from the prevailing drabness, they staged fashion shows, modeling filthy uniforms with a high-fashion commentary on their elegance and taste. It was no carnival ball, but the other prisoners whistled and stamped their feet.

The poor and out-of-work were often run into prison, as were the deranged and incompetent. To Fernando, it seemed that the police had arbitrary arrest quotas to meet. Not every lunatic was as reticent as the insane man in isolation. Schizophrenics tended to scream through the night.

One evening the police hauled in a young man with an obsession. When he could hold a job, he had assisted a truck driver. The duty that must have weighed most on his mind was parking the truck, because during his first night in jail, he became convinced that his cell was a potato truck. He was crying with frustration as he tried to maneuver it into place.

Across the cellblock, the others all began to help him park. "No! Attention! That's it! To the right! No, not yet! Wait! Slowly!" When they finished, the man's truck was safely at the curb.

The main question for Fernando, for Jean Marc, for

every political prisoner, was whether or not to answer the interrogator's questions. Saying nothing—not a word—was called Turkish behavior. Most men freely admitted that such stoicism was beyond them. A woman, Angela Camargo Seixas, was one of those who adhered to it.

Much had happened in Angela's life since the day she helped to carry Edson Luis's corpse to the parliament building. The experience had made a public speaker of her. And she stopped smiling quite so easily. Her less political friends considered that a pity, for her smile had been wide, a little daft, and very endearing.

Angela spoke before the Communists and Popular Action, but she joined PCBR, the dissidents who in 1967 had followed Carlos Marighela out of the Brazilian Communist party. For a year or two, the group had been undecided about armed struggle; but by the time Angela became a member, PCBR was as far left as any other student movement in Brazil. Its hero was Ché Guevara.

PCBR had both a military arm and a political one. The decision was not Angela's to make: she was assigned to the political side. The military members took the risks—stealing weapons, commandeering automobiles, robbing banks.

Then, in December 1969, the armed group of PCBR staged a bank robbery. One revolutionary was captured. A policeman had been shot during the raid, and the torture of that prisoner was unrelenting.

For the intelligence units, the man had been the best sort of catch. As chief of logistics, he knew the entire chain of command and every house where members took shelter. However, he did not know Angela, and her photograph had never appeared in the newspapers. Thus, it fell to her to arrange new rooms for the fugitive PCBR members, as well as quarters for an allied group called MR-26.

Angela heard of a flat in Copacabana, Rio's celebrated three-mile strand of white beach. Many years and songs ago, Copacabana had been fashionable. Now, although its

shops and apartment houses were a bit shabby, it remained
the most vital part of the city.

The police had received a tip about the apartment Angela was coming to inspect, and at 10 P.M. they were hiding
behind the door when she came up the stairs with an immense black comrade named Marco Antonio. Even for
Rio, a city proud of its indifference to race, the two formed
a notable contrast, Angela being so slight, her skin so very
pale.

As they reached the landing, there was another of those
power failures that the *cariocas*, the residents of Rio, had
been laughing about since the invention of the electric
light. Throughout the district, everything went dark. The
police may have suspected a ruse, for they burst from the
apartment and began shooting. Marco Antonio returned
their fire and wounded two policemen before he was shot
in the head. Angela was struck low in her back. She passed
out.

When she came to—it could have been only a few seconds later—the hall was still dark. The police were gone,
perhaps to treat their wounds. Angela was alone on the
stairs with Marco Antonio's unconscious body.

Then began a sequence of terror that most people know
only in their nightmares. Marco Antonio was breathing,
but when Angela tried to lift him, he was far too heavy and
slipped from her arms. Instinct told her to hide. Along the
landing she ran from door to door, knocking softly, knocking louder. Everyone had heard the gunshots. No one
would open a door. She ran up a flight of stairs. Just as she
reached the top, power was restored and the lights went
on.

She thought, Maybe I can just walk away. From its hum,
the elevator was running again. She pushed the down button and waited for it to reach her floor. The door opened.
Two policemen got out. Angela pressed a handkerchief
deep into her wound to stanch the bleeding.

Blithely she asked, "What was all that noise?"

"Go home," one officer told her. "Go back to your apartment."

"No," she said, "I must go to the street to use the telephone."

It was a plausible excuse even in an expensive apartment building. Customers in Brazil bought their telephones, often paying $1,000 or more, and even at that price, there were still long waiting lists.

Downstairs, one policeman was standing guard at the entrance. Angela slipped past him. She was on the street. She started walking faster. She was nearly out of danger when a voice called, "Stop her! No one can leave the building!"

Policemen on the street grabbed her and brought her back to the building. Marco Antonio's body was surrounded by police. "Who is this man?" they asked her.

"I don't know."

They hit her with hard, random blows and asked again.

A police car took her to the headquarters of the Operational Center of Internal Defense (CODI). When the officers stripped off her clothes, they saw the wound and said, "If you don't give us your name, you will die."

Angela's mind told her that she must say nothing at all. For the past week she had known the names of almost every member of her party. The very next day she had been scheduled to meet fifteen of its leaders. If they could frighten her into giving her own name, whose name would she give next?

Her wound sent Angela to the hospital for ten days, frustrating the interrogators. When she was moved it was to PIC, the small building within the downtown police headquarters where Flavio Tavares had been tortured.

She was held there naked to be beaten and shocked with wires. One of the torturers was Costa Lima Magalhães, a distinguished name in Brazil. This Magalhães was a very small man with a large head and an appetite for torture. Some prisoners attributed his zeal to the wound he had received in the spine during a shoot-out with revolutionaries.

But his torture in this case proved self-defeating. Angela's wound opened and blood poured out until she had to be returned to the hospital. From that time on, she regarded the wound as her ultimate protection. If the torture became unendurable, she could force open the wound and they would have to send her back to the infirmary.

The torture room was being painted a bilious and unsettling lavender. The lights were hot. Noises were piped in from the ceiling, screams and gunshots to add to the sense of impending disaster. Angela told herself that the sounds were a composition by Stockhausen, a composer she admired, and after that the noises stopped bothering her.

The interrogation technique followed the lesson plan from Panama and the IPA by presenting one officer as friendly, one as hostile, the classic method of "good guy, bad guy." They brought in the man who had been picked up during the bank holdup. The torture had shattered him, but he said, "I hope you can hold out. I couldn't."

She also heard news about Mario Alves, a founder of the PCBR. The police had stuck a broomstick so far up his rectum that it ruptured his spleen. Trying to make him talk, they had pulled out his teeth, a technique that both revolutionaries and police could recognize from *The Battle of Algiers*. The police also injected Alves with sodium pentothal.

One day, after Angela had been beaten terribly with rubber truncheons and bare fists, a doctor who saw her asked, "What happened to you?"

She told him about the lavender room. His surprise and indignation did not seem feigned. He had never seen a woman tortured, and he was vulnerable to her being a college student and only nineteen years old.

"Do you know who tortured you?" this doctor persisted. "Give me his name. I'm going to report him."

Angela was able to tell him. When the police were torturing, they usually pasted masking tape or a bandage over their nameplates and called each other by an alias. At other times, around a prisoner but not torturing him, they were often slipshod and their nameplates were exposed. She said, "Costa Lima Magalhães."

The doctor reported that Angela had been whipped and sexually abused, that electric wires had been inserted into her vagina. His charges were impossible to ignore, and Magalhães was reprimanded for the record. During the next six weeks Angela stayed unmolested in the infirmary. Except for one lapse when she admitted to being a member of PCBR, she revealed nothing.

Two events, however, sent her back to the lavender room: now that he was aware of the continuous torture going on around him, the doctor was so sickened that he applied for a transfer; and two more prisoners from PCBR were brought in. After severe torture, they outlined the important duties Angela had assumed before her capture.

The next day at 3 P.M., the hour that her torture had usually begun, the police brought Angela back for another session. This time they warned her that if she refused to talk, they would turn her over to the Death Squad.

They told her about uncovering a cache of explosives and kept demanding to hear what she knew about it. Staying silent that day was easy. She knew nothing. But she heard stories about other prisoners: a union organizer, Manuel de Conceição, was being tortured at the same center. As a fellow prisoner with Fernando Gabeira, Manuel had once had his testicles nailed to a table. Now, because his new wounds were not treated, the military doctors amputated a leg.

Throughout her hours in the torture cell, two voices fought a steady battle in Angela's head. One said, "They'll kill you if you don't talk." The other voice said, "They'll kill you if you do." Although the pain was always intense, Angela discovered that the torture never reached through to her subconscious. Every word she spoke to the police was rehearsed and rational. The spasms of pain never caused her to blurt out an answer.

The torture brought with it another reaction, mystical in its way. Angela would faint and awake to find her mind clearer than ever before. She seemed to be floating above her body, and she could look down and watch herself being tortured. The sensation of being outside her body, the distance between her mind and the pain, helped to stop her from talking.

In the lavender room, Angela realized how simplistic her own attitude and that of her comrades had been about torture. They had all agreed that none of them would ever speak, whatever the provocation. If you don't keep your mouth shut, they said, you deserve to die.

Now, after a two-hour beating, she understood why the man arrested in the bank robbery had spoken. She could forgive him. But she would never forgive the United States for its role in training and equipping the Brazilian police.

Since the 1964 coup, Marcos Arruda, the geology student who had protested foreign control over Brazil's mineral wealth, had lived a scrambling sort of life. For the two weeks after Goulart fled to Uruguay, Marcos left Rio for the country and waited there until friends assured him that he did not seem to be on one of General Golbery's lists.

In Brazil, employers had no use for an outspoken student leader. To stay alive, Marcos tutored students and translated technical papers. After a few years, this life was not satisfying his reformer's urge, and in 1968 he applied under his own name for a permit to do manual work in a factory.

Marcos's one deception was listing his highest education as elementary school. Had he been exposed as a university graduate, his motive would have been suspect. Neither the factory owners nor the government would have risked his contaminating fellow workmen with his discontent.

The company that hired Marcos was a foundry and smelting group owned by Mercedes-Benz. The three thousand workers there manufactured parts for wagons and tractors. Marcos was a machine operator, and each day he turned out a thousand molds. Despite the labor laws passed by the democratic regimes, a worker was required to work twelve hours a day. The overtime accounted for $3 or $4 of a $15 monthly wage.

Since college, Marcos had been married and separated. As a single man once again, he could pay rent, eat, and even ride a bus to work on his meager salary. Married men, however, ran through their pay before the month ended. For the last week or ten days, they had to get up in the middle of the night to walk to work and plead to put in fourteen or fifteen hours a day for the extra bit of overtime pay.

The job itself was arduous. The building was open at each end, and in the winter the workers stood burning before the ovens while their backs froze from the São Paulo cold. Iron dust filled the air so densely that even on sunny days a man who took a few steps away from his machine was gone from sight, swallowed up in the gray murk. Marcos discovered that company doctors recommended that men contracting tuberculosis be laid off before they became a burden to the company.

It was little different from conditions forty and fifty years earlier in the United States, except that every Brazilian John L. Lewis and Eugene Debs had been killed, jailed, or hounded underground.

Marcos met with his fellow workers each day for coffee. They needed no lectures about injustices in the system. They felt those in their muscles and in their lungs. Their question was what they could do about them.

Certainly a man acting alone had no recourse. One worker who fell sick with lung disease was told by his doctor to recuperate in the cleaner air of the south. The factory owed him back pay; and before he left for Rio

Grande do Sul, he went to collect it. A guard stopped him at the gate.

The man said, "I need the money the company owes me."

"Wait here." The guard went to the personnel office and came back. "You're not a worker here any longer. I can't let you in."

Frustrated beyond his endurance, the man drew a knife, stabbed the guard, and ran from the scene. No one heard of him again.

Such were the minor grievances, the disputes a union might have settled with one telephone call. The Metal Workers Union of São Paulo, however, was controlled by men named by the military after the 1964 coup.

Marcos and his friends collected evidence that before mass meetings some union leaders met privately with agents from DOPS, the secret police. Together they arranged that if a delegate they did not control took the floor and forced a vote against the official company-union position, the DOPS men would provoke a fight, thereby giving the union president cause to suspend the assembly.

Since the union held no answers, Marcos and other workers formed a committee to meet with delegates from other factories in the area. They would discuss mutual problems and weigh possible solutions. They were seeking change; and by the prevailing definition, that made them subversives.

In May 1970, Marcos was introduced to Marlene Soccas, a woman from the resistance who was not only out of work but living in a house compromised by earlier police raids. Marcos volunteered to find her a job and a safer place to live. By now he was not working either, having developed a spot on his lung and a case of sinusitis. The doctor at the public health service told him he must give up his job in the factory.

"I cannot," said Marcos. "I must work to eat."

"Then you must work only the regular schedule, eight hours a day."

Marcos asked for a statement to that effect and presented it to his supervisor. A week later he was fired. "It's not the quality of your work," the supervisor told him. "It's that you can't work long enough. There are a hundred people out there waiting for this job."

Marcos spent the next week hunting for work, and he felt guilty about not helping Marlene. He stopped by the house of a mutual friend and left a message: "I don't know how you're getting along. Let's have lunch." He named a small restaurant in São Paulo's Lapa district.

Marcos did not know that Marlene had been arrested four days earlier and tortured continuously. Police agents now intercepted the note and brought her to the café to point Marcos out to them.

When he arrived, five policemen were waiting, their shirttails outside their trousers to conceal the pistols in their belts. Surrounded, Marcos tried to rip up a schedule he was carrying, names and places of others in the movement whom he had planned to see that day.

In front of patrons and passers-by, the police fell on him, kicking and punching to get hold of the scrap of paper. Marcos was small and slight, with hands barely larger than a child's. They got his list away from him. They then shoved him into the back of a station wagon. Marlene was sitting in the front seat. "Show him your hands," one of the agents commanded. "Show him your hands so he'll see what he's going to go through."

Marlene raised her hands. Beneath their bandages, they were swollen to twice their normal size. The tips of each finger and the heels of each hand were black. From that moment, Marcos did not blame Marlene for betraying him. He told himself, I am no judge of what she has endured.

As soon as the station wagon pulled into the courtyard of OBAN, the three policemen in the back with Marcos began to beat him. Once inside, they beat him for hours before they asked a question.

Then the interrogation started. They wanted to know who was listening to the workers at the factory and advis-

ing them on their problems. Marcos decided that although
he knew very little, he would not reveal even that much.
Instead, he tried a tactic that occurred to most prisoners
early in their torture. He would stall, buy relief from the
beatings, by giving them valueless information that would
take several hours, perhaps a day, to check. It was time
dearly purchased. When the police uncovered the ruse,
their torture would become even more punishing; but for
a day it might stop the pain, and tomorrow Marcos might
be dead.

He gave them the address of his ex-wife's aunt. It would
be obvious at once that the old woman was no revolutionary. All she would be able to tell them was that Marcos
stayed with her for a few nights. She knew nothing of his
activities.

The respite was very brief, and Marcos had not died
before it came to an end. The policemen tied his knees to
his elbows and ran a pole through to connect them. They
lifted him into brackets that held his back suspended four
feet off the ground. With the paddle full of holes, they beat
his buttocks a hundred times on the same place, until the
skin under his flesh was black with blood. As they flailed
away at him, they called him "Bastard!" and "Son of a
whore!" The way he was hanging exposed his anus, and
they threatened to rape him.

Marcos heard all of this very distantly. The threats and
excoriation seemed more for their own ears, to goad them
on with the work of beating him raw.

They connected the wire of an electric field telephone
to Marcos's small toe and the other wire to his testicles. The
electricity shot up and down his legs. Marcos did not know
he was screaming until a guard shoved a cloth into his
mouth. The guards themselves laughed at his shouts, but
neighbors around OBAN had been complaining of the
noise. Later they put on a record by Roberto Carlos, a
leading Brazilian pop singer. "Jesus Christ," the song went,
"here I am."

Marcos thought, I have no regrets. My friends and I were struggling for something good, humanly good. I am playing a little part in bringing about a new society. In the Gospels, Jesus had lived among thieves and prostitutes. In the factory, I was living a life as Christian as Christ's life.

Sweat was pouring off Marcos's body. Under the gag in his mouth, his tongue felt crooked. Even without a gag, his voice was gone. His eyes were swollen shut. He heard a voice say, "Let's have some fun."

The policemen washed his body with water. To make the circuit longer and send the shock farther along his body, they moved the wire up to his belly. Then to his throat. To his mouth. Into his ear. When they lowered him at last to the floor, Marcos went into convulsions, which did not stop. For the next month and a half, Marcos could not stop shaking. The police sent him to a military hospital and called in a priest to administer the last rites.

Sometimes, even as the convulsions went on, Marcos fell into a sleep. The police appeared at his bedside and woke him. "You are not a worker," one said. "You are a geologist. That means that you were in the factory to spread subversion. When you get better here, you'll go back to that place again."

But Marcos got no better, and the army doctors had no remedy to stop his convulsions. Two nuns came to his bedside. Marcos was grateful to see them. They were women. The idea of women soothed his spirit.

"How horrible," he heard one murmur. "How can they do that? It is so sad."

Marcos thought, They understand nothing.

The police came again to his bed and called him a Communist. "What is your organization?" "Who are your comrades?" "Why do you work in a factory when you could get a job that pays better? It must be to subvert the others, to make them strike for higher wages."

"Don't you want higher wages?" Marcos asked, but mildly. He did not wish to provoke them to more torture.

"Don't try to sell us your Communist arguments," a policeman said, and Marcos stopped trying to explain.

When his shaking subsided, the police brought him back to OBAN headquarters and told him he had three days to prepare a full confession. They said Marlene had told them he was a member of a subversive group.

Marcos took the three days but gave them nothing. "This is worthless!" they said when they saw the little he had written.

They took him to see Marlene. Marcos heard a policeman tell her, "Get ready to see Frankenstein."

Marcos came hobbling in, a broomstick for a crutch. One leg had no feeling in it, one eye was still shut from the beatings. He asked her, "Did you say I was in a subversive organization? It's not true."

"Shut up, you two," said a guard. "Who's asking the questions here?"

They led Marlene next door and gave her more electric shocks. Marcos could hear her screaming. For himself, his feeling about torture was almost peaceful. He had survived two terrible sessions. They had no worse pain in store for him. But now it was Marlene and not him they were causing to scream.

"We're going to kill her if you don't speak," a policeman said. It was the worst anguish Marcos ever knew.

They brought her to face him in a cubicle. An army captain was there with two lieutenants. "You skunk!" the captain said. "Making her suffer this way! You stink!"

"You are beating her," Marcos said. "Not me."

"You know what we want," the captain said. "You must be stupid, working for that shit wage. You're a geologist. You could have an apartment. A car. Women. You must be out of your head. Look at her." He pointed to Marlene, bruised and sobbing. "Isn't that right?" he asked her.

"No, he is right," said Marlene, indicating Marcos. "I wish I had the courage he has."

They pulled her out of the cell and began to beat Marcos

again. One of them held the broomstick to Marcos's throat from behind and pulled so hard that Marcos thought he would strangle to death and this would all be over.

But there was a wooden door to his cell, and from behind it Marcos overheard one guard whispering to another, "What are we going to do? This guy won't talk." At that, Marcos felt his spirit soar. His enemies were powerless. They had electricity, wires, and clubs, but it was he who had the power.

A general came to see Marcos in his cell. He was also a medical doctor, an old man with white hair. He talked about plankton. Ah, said Marcos to himself, he wants to see whether I really am a geologist. The general seemed to be a cultured man. Patiently Marcos answered his questions. Finally the general asked Marcos why he was in prison.

Marcos told his story, ending with the way he had been tortured and crippled.

The old general grew furious. "That's not true!" he exclaimed. "Nothing like that happens in these army units."

"Stay one day, just one day," Marcos said. "I am not here by choice."

The general called to a captain. "This man is telling me lies! Suspend all salt from his diet. And give him no medicines."

Marcos had been receiving treatment for epilepsy. He was not an epileptic, but it was the only prescription the hospital's doctors had devised to end his shaking.

The captain was even angrier than the general: "We'll suspend his food."

The fury of each worked on the other. The general said, "See that he gets as little water as possible."

Within two days, the shaking had resumed, and Marcos was drooling uncontrollably. He returned to the hospital. In another bed was a prisoner who had been shot; then, with the bullet still in his body, he had been tortured until his flesh rotted. Down the hall, on the edge of insanity, was a sixty-year-old woman, her face deformed from beatings.

Another woman, this one twenty-one years old, had been arrested for distributing leaflets to workers outside a government steel mill. The police administered their ritual beatings. Then they learned she was pregnant. They laid her down and stomped on her abdomen, and succeeded in making her miscarry. But she continued hemorrhaging and was brought to the hospital.

Through the hospital's network of whispers, the prisoners exchanged news from other wards. That was how Marcos heard of two friends who had been tortured in the presence of men who spoke only English.

Later, in a security cell, an army corporal remarked to Marcos how odd it was that Marcos should be in jail with the corporal, an uneducated man, standing guard over him. "It's weird," the soldier said as he offered Marcos a cigarette. "Many of the prisoners are students or professional men. It's funny."

Marcos did not smoke, but he thanked the man gratefully. He had found that army-enlisted men sometimes showed human feeling. The police were worse than animals.

"Doesn't that tell you something?" Marcos said. "We've studied, we've read books. We have something in our heads. And we don't accept the situation in Brazil. Doesn't that tell you something?"

"You have strong arguments," the corporal said. "Let me go away or you'll convince me."

Murilo Pinto da Silva had been a schoolboy in Belo Horizonte when Dan Mitrione arrived to show the police how to be more effective. Nine years later, as a member of the Commandos of National Liberation (COLINA), Murilo was trapped with five comrades in their Belo hideout by a police cordon. In the exchange of gunfire, two policemen were killed. None of the rebels was hit.

Murilo was charged with four crimes: unlawful possession of a gun; being a member of an illegal association; armed actions; assassination. As a result, he also played a role in the training of Brazil's police.

In August of 1969, Murilo and his colleagues were transferred from prison in Belo to the Policia Especial of the army's Vila Militar, a jail for political prisoners in Realango, on the outskirts of Rio.

On October 8, Murilo was led from the jail with nine other prisoners and ordered to wait in an open courtyard. Seven of those nine were also political prisoners from Belo, including a fellow member of COLINA, Irany Campos, who had taken the code name Costa. Two of the others were Brazilian soldiers who had been court-martialed. One had stolen a gun. Murilo did not know the offense with which the second soldier was charged.

Being taken from the cell was always a bad sign. But the mood among the guards in the courtyard this day was jovial, and Murilo began to relax. There would be no torture today.

Then one soldier passed by carrying a heavy stick of the kind used for the parrot's perch. Another carried a metal box about eighteen inches long, which Murilo recognized as a generator for electric shocks. It was capable of greater precision than the field telephone.

Still, Murilo was not alarmed. It all looked so routine, so passionless. Then he overheard a corporal asking, "Are they the stars of the show?"

A soldier laughed and said, "I think they will be."

The joke alerted him. Something bad was going to happen after all.

The prisoners were led single file into a low building and told to stop outside a closed door. From beyond the threshold, Murilo heard the laughing and talking of many men. It was high-pitched and sounded expectant. The prisoners stood very still, a guard beside each of them.

From inside the room, Murilo heard an officer giving instructions. He recognized the voice of Lieutenant Aylton, an officer who had greatly impressed Murilo over the weeks he had spent at Vila Militar. As Aylton oversaw the beatings and shocks, he displayed a calm and control that a less assured college student could only envy. Setting up the tortures, Aylton always seemed so—odd description but true—serene. Now Aylton was displaying that same poise before a crowd of men, speaking with absolute self-confidence. Who could hate a man like that?

Murilo could make out only a little of what he was saying. "Approach them as though we are their friends. As though we're on their side." That was followed by what seemed to be a lengthy explanation of interrogation methods, but Aylton's voice rose and fell, and Murilo missed most of the details.

The lieutenant then raised his voice to say, "Now we're presenting you with a demonstration of the clandestine activities in the country."

There was a stir at the door, and one by one six of the prisoners were led inside. Each young man had his own guard, an army private or a corporal. The room looked to be an officer's mess. Six men were seated at each table. Murilo guessed there were about eighty men in all. They wore uniforms, some from the army, some from the air force. They seemed young: lieutenants and noncoms, sergeants.

At the front was a stage that made the room look like a cabaret. The impression was heightened by the skillful way Lieutenant Aylton was using the microphone. One side of the stage was bare except for a screen. The prisoners were lined up on the other side. Aylton called out a name and gestured to the man so that the audience could identify him. From dossiers, Aylton read aloud everything the intelligence services had supplied about the prisoner: his background, details of his capture, the charges against him.

As he spoke, slides on the screen showed various tortures, drawings of men strapped to the parrot's perch or wired for electric shocks. When Aylton finished, the guards turned to the six prisoners on the stage and told them to take off their clothes. The men stripped to their shorts. Then, in turn, each guard forced his prisoner into position for the demonstration.

Pedro Paulo Bretas had his hands bound together. His guard put triangular pieces of metal twenty centimeters long and five centimeters high through the four spaces between his fingers. The soldier pressed down hard on the metal bars, then ground them to one side. Murilo had never experienced that torture. He noticed that when the torturer turned the sticks one way, Bretas screamed and fell to his knees. When he turned them the other way, Bretas screamed and leapt into the air.

Murilo was forced to stand barefooted on the edges of two opened cans. The edges cut into his soles, and the pain rose up along the muscles of his calves.

The next guard attached long wires to the little finger on each hand of a prisoner named Mauricio. Those were connected to the generator that Murilo had watched being carried through the courtyard.

One of the army prisoners was put into the parrot's perch. Another was beaten with the *palmatoria*, the long-handled wooden paddle with the little holes. To illustrate, he was beaten on his buttocks, his feet, and the palms of his hands. At the microphone, Aylton said, "You can beat with this for a long time and very strongly."

Nilo Sergio was forced to stand on one foot with his arms outstretched like the Christ of Corcovado. Something heavy—Murilo could not see what—was put in each hand.

A prisoner was kept on display while Aylton moved on to discuss the next method. He wanted to impress on the audience that these tortures need not be used singly, that the parrot's perch, for example, was even more effective when combined with electric shocks or beatings from the wooden paddle.

The parrot's perch seemed to be Aylton's favorite, and he explained its advantages to the crowd. "It begins to work," he said, "when the prisoner can't keep his neck strong and still. When his neck bends, it means he's suffering."

As Aylton spoke, the prisoner in the perch let his head fall backward. Aylton laughed and went to his side. "Not like that. He's only faking the condition. Look"—Aylton grabbed the prisoner's head and shook it soundly—"his neck is still firm. He's only shamming now. He's not tired, and he's not ready to talk."

There were other refinements. Use the electricity where and when you like, Aylton said, but watch the voltage. You want to extract information from the prisoner. You don't want to kill him. He then read out numbers—a voltage reading and the length of time a human body could withstand it. Murilo, his feet cut and bleeding, tried to remember the figures, but the pain was driving everything else out of his mind.

There's another method that we will not be demonstrating today, Aylton said, but it has been most effective. It's an injection of ether into the scrotum. Something about that particular pain makes a man very willing to talk.

The lieutenant also recommended, but did not show, an improvement, the *afogamento*—pouring water in the nostrils while the head is hanging backward. To prove that water on the surface of the skin intensified the shocks, one guard poured some over the prisoner in the parrot's perch and resumed the shocks so that they could all see the increased writhing of his body.

As the water strengthened the current, the prisoner in the perch began to scream. Aylton gestured to the guard, who stuffed a handkerchief into the prisoner's mouth. "Normally you shouldn't use a gag," Aylton said archly, "because how can he give you information when he cannot speak?"

The class had been in session forty minutes, and the tortures had proceeded continuously while Aylton spoke. Now it became clear that Mauricio, strung between two long wires, was suffering unendurably. The soldier assigned to him had been forcing the generator faster and faster until, as Aylton had warned, too much voltage was coursing through Mauricio's body.

Mauricio fell forward onto the nearest table. From the army men, there was a roar of outraged laughter. They pushed him off and hit him and kicked him with their boots. All the time, they kept laughing and shouting jokes at each other.

Murilo came out of his pained trance long enough to have it register with him that these men, the eighty of them, had been laughing throughout Aylton's lecture. Not so boisterously as when Mauricio fell onto the table, but steadily, loudly. Their wisecracking had formed a counterpoint to the demonstration.

I am suffering, Murilo thought, and these men are having the time of their lives.

Or perhaps not every one of them. Sargento Monte became nauseated during the torture and bolted from the room to vomit. It surprised Murilo, this show of sensitivity, because Monte had once ordered a lower-ranking sergeant to give Murilo his daily electrical shock.

The class was coming to an end. Murilo wanted to remember who else was there, joining in the tortures. He might not emerge from prison alive, but if he did, he would remember. There was Aylton and Monte, and Sargento Rangel, from Vila Militar.

Murilo particularly remembered Rangel because of the day Murilo returned from the visitors' room with cigarettes that had been palmed to him. Rangel got a tip that either Murilo or his brother, Angelo, had received the cigarettes, and he ordered each of them beaten with the paddle until he found the cigarettes and pocketed them for himself.

Aylton asked whether the class had any questions about the tortures they had seen. No one had a question.

Murilo was jostled off the sharp edges of the cans and led

away with the others. In the anteroom he saw his brother
and another prisoner, Júlio Betencourt. They were being
led in as an encore. Júlio suffered the torture called the
telephone: a guard cupped his hands like shells and beat on
Júlio's ears until he could no longer hear. Murilo found
that out later. He never did learn what use Aylton had
made of Angelo.

Back in the cells, none of the guards mentioned the class;
but the prisoners who had gone through the experience
with Murilo were consumed with hatred and disgust. On
his cot, Murilo heard one shouting to the universe, "Son of
a whore!" Another kept repeating, "Well, that's the end of
the world." Others traded back and forth a Brazilian
phrase, *"É o fim da piada!"* It meant, It's the end of the joke.
It's unbearable for me to think about.

On his bunk, Murilo considered the ordeal. His greatest
concern had been that if he did not appear to be suffering
enough, he would be taken off the sharp edges of the cans
and moved to another torture. The cans had cut and stung,
but they were bearable. The electric wires were not. So he
had grimaced with pain and hoped that his torture would
not be traded for Mauricio's.

He had no emotions left over. He felt no shame at being
put on display as a guinea pig. No rage at the men laughing
at him. No sympathy for Mauricio. Only self-protective-
ness. That he would not be taken off the open cans and
shocked insensible.

He had got through another day. His feet would heal.
He heard a man shout, *"É o fim da piada!"* Murilo felt calm,
at peace. He knew that after today, whatever his provocation or the justice of his cause, he would never hurt another
human being.

CHAPTER

8

WHEN DAN MITRIONE asked Byron Engle to give him another overseas assignment, Engle knew that the reason once again was money. A man with six of his nine children still living at home had a difficult time getting by on the pay of a five rating in the Foreign Service Reserve—the equivalent to a GS-11, which paid $12,000 to $13,000 a year. In addition, at home in the United States, Mitrione was paying his own rent on a house in Wheaton, Maryland, whereas overseas there had been living allowances and temporary duty pay.

Mitrione had been a good instructor for IPA. Not brilliant, but solid and sympathetic. He had a gift for remembering a student's name after only one introduction, and the Spanish and Portuguese surnames came especially easy to him. But he was restless. In the spring of 1969, Engle called Mitrione to his office and gratified the adviser's wish to return to Latin America.

"We've been thinking about an overseas assignment for you," Engle began.

Mitrione brightened but said, "I love the academy."

"Yes, but what about Uruguay?"

"Boss," Mitrione said, dropping all pretense, "when do you want me to leave?"

Six years after Mitrione's murder, Engle would deny that in 1969 he had even heard of the Tupamaros, the growing rebel movement in Uruguay, or that he had chosen to send Mitrione there because of his experience with the Brazilian police. Engle preferred to be seen as an ingenuous, even inept administrator than as a knowledgeable professional deploying a tough cop where he would be most effective in carrying out U. S. policies. Looking back, he claimed that he had pictured Uruguay to Mitrione not as a troubled country, but as "one of the nicest, most peaceful places" on earth.

Yet, if Engle's account were true, he would have had to blind himself to the field reports from Uruguay passing across his desk every month. Those U-127 forms marked CONFIDENTIAL and sent in by Adolph Saenz, the chief adviser whom Mitrione would be replacing, treated Uruguay's political problems in exhaustive detail—the labor strikes, the student unrest, and the revolutionaries who called themselves Tupamaros. When the Tupamaros stole 40-odd weapons or made off with 140 kilos of dynamite or distributed a stack of propaganda leaflets, Saenz immediately informed Washington. When suspected Tupamaros were arrested, their full names were passed along for U. S. intelligence files.

Despite later disclaimers, it is clear that Mitrione was heading for Uruguay entirely aware that his main assignment would be to improve the capacity of the nation's police to put down the insurgents. Certainly, Uruguay was no sinecure; in fact, the easy assignments were becoming increasingly rare. As rebellion spread around the world, criticism of the tactics U. S. advisers employed was becoming harder for the Office of Public Safety to shrug off. Ugly reports had come in from Athens, where the Greeks believed the CIA had conspired to bring a military junta to power; from Portugal, where Washington had supported a dictator for generations; and from South Vietnam, where reports of savagery were the most persistent of all.

In Portugal, officers from the intelligence agency called PIDE were boasting to their victims that a grade-school education was no longer sufficient for their work. The new interrogation methods were too complicated. The source of PIDE's improved technical expertise seemed clear enough. U. S. officials from the Lisbon embassy called in regularly at PIDE headquarters; the director of PIDE's investigative branch was the Portuguese representative of Interpol; and in the late sixties, four senior PIDE inspectors toured Brazil.

In Vietnam, although civilian victims were often nameless to the U. S. troops, there were exceptions. Ms. Nguyen Thi Nhan, a widow, was arrested several times in Saigon, the first in 1969, and charged with being a member of the National Liberation Front. At police headquarters, she was given electrical shocks, and an iron rod was forced up her vagina. Three Westerners in U. S. uniforms watched her being tortured, and the police told her that they were CIA officers. One of them ordered a Vietnamese interrogator to ram needles under Mrs. Nhan's fingernails.

Another woman, Mrs. Nguyen Thi Bo, was taken into custody that same year in Danang because she had neither an ID card nor money with which to bribe the police to release her. At the police station, Mrs. Bo had a stick poked into her vagina; then her face was held in a toilet bowl filled with shit. She was next moved to Non Muoc station, where she was questioned by five U. S. agents wearing green fatigues. After they tied her up, three of the men kicked her.

Stories like these were beginning to discredit the U. S. intelligence services, and there were worse to come. Although it was not yet public knowledge, the United States had been running torture camps, which were always passed off as schools for survival. Two such secret installations, in northwest Maine and in California, near San Diego, were run by the navy. One torture technique involved strapping the navy men face up and pouring cold water on towels placed over their faces until they gagged and retched. A navy doctor stood by to prevent them from drowning.

On the army's side, Donald Duncan, a Green Beret, went through training at Fort Bragg, where the sergeant giving a lesson in hostile interrogation described in detail a number of tortures, including the lowering of a man's testicles into a jeweler's vise. Finally a soldier in the class interrupted: "Are you suggesting that we use these methods?"

The class laughed, and the instructor raised a solemn face with mocking eyes. "We can't tell you that, Sergeant Harrison. The mothers of America wouldn't approve." The class burst into more laughter at his cynicism. "Furthermore," the sergeant said with a wink, "we will deny that any such thing is taught or intended."

Torture training was not restricted to North Americans. On the island of Niterói, across the bay from Rio, the Brazilian military had set up a camp modeled after that of the *boinas verdes*, the Green Berets. The students were kept awake, starved, and caged. They were hung on beams in mock crucifixions. As a way of breaking a man, it proved too effective. After eighteen hours, the Brazilian soldiers were confessing to crimes they had not committed.

As a result of all this, the Office of Public Safety faced serious problems in 1969. Its connections with the CIA, the war in Vietnam, and the similarities in the accounts of torture turning up around the world were rendering the advisory program politically vulnerable. Worse yet, the rebel movements, especially in Latin America, seemed to be growing. In the eyes of OPS and the U. S. military, the Tupamaros of Uruguay presented a particularly grave threat to established order throughout the hemisphere.

That Uruguay should become a breeding ground for revolutionaries seemed to be one of history's incongruous accidents, like Switzerland being the birthplace of Jean Paul Marat. Indeed, though Uruguay was more than four times the size of Switzerland with half the population, it was most often compared to that country. For one thing, it was wedged between Argentina and Brazil, very much as the Swiss Confederation separated Germany and France; for another, its very existence depended on its being a good and mild neighbor.

Of the two nations, nature had been kinder to Uruguay, giving it a gentle climate and a seacoast with ports for commerce and attractive beaches for tourism. In place of the forbidding Alps, Uruguay had a broad plain for the growing of wheat and vast, temperate grasslands for the raising of cattle and sheep.

To cultivate the Uruguayans' garden, fate sent an idealist named José Batlle y Ordóñez, a newspaper publisher who came to power in 1904, after a punishing civil war. Perhaps as a consequence of seeing Uruguay divided, Batlle was determined to treat the small nation as one family, with labor occupying an honored place at its table. The preceding fifteen years had seen waves of Spanish and Italian migration, but Uruguay's Italians did not settle meekly into communities like Goosetown. They brought to the New World their militant syndicalist ideas, and with Batlle's support they created a powerful labor movement.

Batlle resisted relying upon foreign capital to build his nation, because he believed such dependency led inevitably to foreign control. Instead, he fostered a benign statism, with utilities and industries owned by the government but incorporated as separate entities. Their goal was not to amass profits but to provide inexpensive services to the public and high salaries to their employees.

Batlle sought to temper Latin America's predilection for dictators by proposing a nine-member executive, six from the majority party, three from the minority. That idea met more resistance than his plans for universal schooling, pensions, and health care. It was not until 1951 that Uruguayans at last agreed to being governed by a nine-headed executive.

During the first half of the century, Uruguay seemed to fulfill most of Batlle's other utopian dreams. It was a one-crop country; but the crop, rather than sugar or coffee, was cattle; and since Europe had both the money and a taste for Uruguayan beef, the economy flourished. Cattle were an ever-renewable resource, which encouraged Uruguayans to take life with more than customary Latin ease. They began to joke that in their country, the only one who worked was the bull.

Occasionally, there were warning signs of trouble. Even when the price of beef dipped, pension costs kept rising. In addition, the government spent the bulk of its money on the cities; but since more than half of Uruguay's 2.7 million population lived in Montevideo, that seemed no injustice. Over the years, however, the system had neglected the farm workers, particularly those who harvested sugar cane. The cane cutters received their pay in vouchers good only at the plantation's store. They had to build their own huts at the edge of the plantations. When the harvest was in, the plantation owners would have the huts set on fire, forcing the cutters to move on. They were compelled to work as many as sixteen hours a day. Every attempt to organize or strike was broken up by the police.

The cane cutters formed a mute and helpless underside to Uruguay's model democracy, that statistically negligible 9 percent who could neither read nor write. When they found their voice, it was in the person of a young socialist, Raúl Sendic Antonaccio.

Like Jean Marc Von der Weid in Brazil, Sendic was one of those men marked for the good life. His family were small landowners in the department of Flores; but Sendic, indifferent to his surroundings, chose to live in a poor section of Montevideo. A member of Uruguay's Socialist Youth, Sendic was only one examination short of getting his law degree when he abruptly dropped out of school.

He went instead to Artigas, 450 miles north of Montevideo, and volunteered to be a legal adviser to a new union of cane cutters. Possibly he expected that once the plight of the cutters was brought to the attention of his enlightened fellow citizens, they would rally against the injustices; or he may have worked solely from a sense of mission. Men who knew him early in this crusade said that Sendic never thought his cause would prevail, but he intended to go forward just the same.

Whatever his expectation, in 1962 Sendic led a march of cane cutters to Montevideo. They asked for a law to limit their working day to eight hours, the standard shift among office and factory workers. Uruguay's press gave the march wide coverage. A legislative investigating team went to Artigas and reported that conditions were as bad as the marchers claimed.

Yet no law was passed. The middle class in the cities had its own problems: inflation, unemployment, a growing foreign debt, corruption. Especially corruption. Citizens who neglected to bribe the right official could wait up to ten years for government documents to be processed, establishing welfare eligibility. The banks, the highest levels of industry, the courts, all were believed to be bilking the people and the federal treasury.

Sendic tried another march but found that his demands sounded too radical to an urban labor movement that had comfortable ties to management. Having become an increasing embarrassment to the complacent Socialist party, he broke free from both the unions and the socialists. His goal became to blast through Uruguay's smug indifference.

In 1963, Uruguay's newspapers reported an event incomprehensible to most readers. A group of burglars broke into the Swiss Club, a hunting lodge outside Montevideo, and made off with some old and worthless weapons.

(Five men were involved. One was Sendic. Another was a medical doctor, a club member nicknamed Loco.)

That was the beginning. Then other brazen criminals held up customs officials at Uruguay's borders and took their weapons away from them. Although the police intelligence unit began to suspect these arms thefts were somehow connected, it was not until 1965 that their scraps of information fit into a pattern.

The final clue was a convention. Those Communists who wanted to stay within the law and work through elections, as Salvador Allende was doing in Chile, agreed to meet with dissident leftists who took recent events in Brazil as a portent for all Latin America. Out of that meeting came the Tupamaros, officially the Movement of National Liberation. Police spies called them "the most intelligent and clever of the group."

In time, the Tupamaros produced their share of revolutionary literature. But at the start, their approach was to put results before theory, and they took as their slogan, "Words divide us; action unites us."

That decision to forego manifestos in favor of guerrilla action was shrewdly calculated to win over Uruguay's liberals. Throughout 1965, the Tupamaros bombed a number of subsidiaries of United States corporations. They did not try to maim or kill. Their bombs were only noisy public-relations devices to introduce themselves, and at each site they left behind leaflets on which the name Tupamaro was printed. The name derived from an Inca Indian chief, Tupac Amara, who had led a rebellion against the Spanish in Peru in 1780. A noble name, a revered cause. Yet that revolt had failed, and Tupac Amara had been drawn and quartered in a public square.

At first, the new band sought to avoid confrontations with the police, a tactic that earned Byron Engle's contempt. Cowardly, he called them, because they did not stand up and fight. Half a world away, General William Westmoreland was making the same complaint about the National Liberation Front.

When the Tupamaros did appear in public, they took the guise of public benefactors. One December, ten young people stole a food truck, drove it into a run-down quarter of Montevideo, and passed out turkeys and wine to the poor. Breaking into armories, the Tupamaros stole police uniforms and wore them to hold up banks around the city. If customers were waiting in line, the Tupamaros insisted that the clerk enter each deposit so that the bank, not the customer, would be liable for the losses. On one occasion, they burst into a gambling casino and scooped up the profits. The next day, when the croupiers complained that the haul had included their tips, the Tupamaros mailed back that percentage of the money.

On August 7, 1968, the Tupamaros tried a new tack. They kidnapped the closest friend of President Jorge Pacheco Areco, Ulises Pereira Reverbel, and held him captive in what they called a people's prison. From a public-relations standpoint, the Tupamaros could hardly have chosen better. Pereira, who once killed a newsboy for selling a paper attacking him, had been denounced as the most hated man in Uruguay.

The Tupamaros held Pereira a mere four days. But it was long enough to set the Uruguayans laughing at him, at their police department, at the president. When Pereira was released, not only unharmed but apparently a few pounds heavier, the poor in Montevideo were quoted as joking, "Attention, Tupamaros! Kidnap me!"

While the Tupamaros were staging this popular guerrilla theater, the government of Uruguay was, in fact, undergoing changes very different from any the Tupamaros were promoting. Since 1950, Uruguay had been a part of the International Monetary Fund. Disregarding Batlle's admonitions, the country had been accepting foreign loans, many from the United States, to see the country through droughts and drops in the price of wool or meat.

Although the Tupamaros were dramatizing the need for reform, more Uruguayans were probably convinced of

that need by an inflation rate of 136 percent. To overhaul
the government, voters decided to do away with the nine-
member executive and return to a single president. In
March 1967, they elected as president General Oscar Gestido, whom both supporters and detractors compared to
Dwight Eisenhower. Before the year was out, Gestido
died.

Almost as soon as he took office, the vice-president,
Jorge Pacheco Areco, began to cry "Communist." An
Uruguayan joke ran that they had voted for Eisenhower
and got Nixon.

Philip Agee, seasoned by nearly six years of field
work, put in a productive term in Uruguay, helping to
achieve one of the CIA's major goals. The agency had
already installed much of its usual apparatus in Uruguay,
including an active arm of AIFLD, the labor front. In
addition, a special branch for police intelligence work, secretly underwritten by the CIA, had been set up in Montevideo.

Its chief was an ambitious young police commissioner,
Alejandro Otero. By scoring well on police aptitude tests,
Otero had advanced past many men with more seniority.
He was Agee's age, thirty or so; and although within his
department Otero was regarded as a spoiled child, the two
men got along well.

Slender, dark, nearly handsome, Otero was no less intelligent than Fleury in Brazil, but his campaign against the
revolutionaries never took on the same deadly earnestness.
For all his energy and determination, something about
Otero, perhaps his wide-eyed solemnity, usually made people smile. In addition, he was too preoccupied with the
fortunes of his fellow officers, always sure that the ones he
had outstripped in promotions were plotting against him.
So Montevideo's police headquarters roiled each day with
new tales of Otero's noisy feuds and his displays of ego.

In the spring of 1966, the CIA sent Otero to the United States for a course at its International Police Services School. He was supposed to believe that the school was run by U. S. AID. After that course, Otero was transferred for several weeks of special training directly under CIA control, and not being ignorant, he presumably saw through the IPSS cover.

By that time, Otero was himself on the CIA payroll. Phil Agee knew that his superiors in Washington trusted any foreign contact far more once he was accepting U. S. dollars. With Otero, as with other police officers contacted, the CIA followed a tested procedure. A CIA officer would first comment on the heavy expenses of a new office or process and suggest that since much of the information was useful to Washington, it was only fair that the United States pick up a portion of the bill. When he handed over a sum of money, it was more than any reasonable estimate of the added costs, and he would remark easily, "Don't worry about it. What with inflation and the costs of raising a family, a policeman is never paid enough anyway. Keep it for those expenses that aren't covered by your expense account." Guided by the reaction of the officer being bribed, the CIA officer increased the monthly payments until there could be no question in either man's mind that the local official was now accepting a salary from the United States.

Otero had succumbed to those blandishments. After his training in the United States, the CIA station hoped he would return to Uruguay ready to do battle with the new urban guerrillas who called themselves Tupamaros. But Otero was not notably political except in advancing his rank within the police. In a short time, he was mired once again in intradepartmental intrigue.

The experience with Otero ranked only as a qualified success. But with another assignment, the Montevideo station scored much better. For years, the CIA wanted to introduce U. S. Public Safety advisers into Uruguay. Now at last the Uruguayan government had agreed. But when the OPS sent as chief a man named Adolph Saenz, he proved something of a pest for Agee and his colleagues. To their dismay, he was forever dropping by the CIA office to shoot the bull.

This simply was not done. At best, the Public Safety advisers enjoyed low prestige around the CIA; and Saenz, a former cop from Los Angeles, enjoyed none at all. At each intrusion, the CIA men would try to convey the message: You worry about the police, and we'll take care of intelligence. Most police advisers responded by becoming even more deferential, but not Saenz. Whenever he left their office, John Horton, the CIA station chief, would shake his head despairingly. Then Cesar Bernal arrived, also from the Southwest and a veteran of Panama, and the CIA officers agreed that he was even less prepossessing than Saenz.

Although Saenz was not welcomed at CIA headquarters, he could turn his office at the *jefatura*, the Montevideo Police Headquarters, into a hub of sociability. He always seemed ready to drop work for a story or joke, and the local policemen enjoyed hanging around his office.

The *jefatura*, at the intersection of San Jose and Yi streets, was a large pile of stone with shallow columns to relieve its façade and windows shaped like portholes. As the threat from the Tupamaros grew, the police chief ordered small wooden guard posts installed at each door. Inside, the walls were shabby pink and green, reflecting better than the imposing exterior the policeman's status in Uruguay. A beginning policeman—an *agente segunda*— drew about $36 a month. Even given Uruguay's generous social benefits, that was poor pay.

The U. S. police advisory office was only a small room divided into four cubicles. Everyone understood that William Cantrell would not be there often. A CIA operations officer under the cover of the Office of Public Safety, Cantrell could not reach Uruguay as speedily as the station wished. He was coming from Vietnam and had to stop over in Washington for intensive Spanish lessons. His assignment in Uruguay would be primarily field work; his Uruguayan driver would be Nelson Bardesio.

It was in March or April of 1967 that Colonel Santiago Acuna, head of the police general staff, put Bardesio in touch with Cantrell. Uruguayans who knew the comic strip "Mutt and Jeff" laughed at the sight of Cantrell with his squat little driver. Around the Office of Public Safety, however, the other employees regarded Bardesio coldly. Officially he was only a police photographer; but within the *jefatura*, the Uruguayans knew he had been singled out for more important duties, and they simply could not understand how the U. S. had ever lit on Bardesio.

As it happened, the more Uruguayans got to know about the Montevideo branch of the police advisory program, the greater their questions about North American judgment. Cantrell—quiet, tensely ungiving—was widely known to be a CIA officer, and he strode around the city with the air of a man pleased with his performance. But how could he be pleased when he had teamed up with both Bardesio, a man of obvious weakness, and with Manuel the Cuban?

Manuel was supposed to be an exile from Havana. Whenever he came to the police advisers' office he said little but sat silently doodling. He was said to be separated from his wife and children, who had stayed behind in Cuba. That was why he drank heavily. He was also reputed to detest Fidel Castro.

But modest Uruguayans, clerks with no CIA training, noticed that while Manuel never defended Castro, he never spoke against him; and fishing through his scratch paper in the waste basket, one secretary discovered that Manuel's drawings most often consisted of outlines of the Cuban isle. Then one day Manuel decamped for Havana, and the

Uruguayans heard that he had been a Cuban agent all along.

Saenz had complained privately that he did not trust Manuel. But, as Bardesio had observed, although Saenz was a notorious busybody, he did not dare stick his nose into Cantrell's operation. Cantrell also had his own money, which came directly through the U. S. embassy, not through U. S. AID.

Bardesio had begun to work out of the headquarters of the Department of Intelligence Services at the corner of the Eighteenth of July and Juan Pallier avenues. Through Cantrell, Bardesio and other Uruguayans—some policemen, some merely friends of the police—obtained photographic equipment, a radio, and other supplies for an "Office of Information."

Each morning, Bardesio picked up Cantrell in an embassy jeep and took him to this new intelligence office. At noon, he took Cantrell to the embassy, then home again at five or six.

Copies of the work done by the Office of Information were sent to the U. S. embassy on a daily basis. Both the chief of police and the minister of the interior knew about the arrangement. Both also knew that under Uruguayan law it was illegal.

Cantrell often visited Inspector Antonio Pirez Castagnet, a CIA agent, at his office. Other prominent CIA agents around the *jefatura* included Colonel Ventura Rodriguez, Montevideo's chief of police; Carlos Martin, the deputy chief; Alejandro Otero, of course. And Inspector Juan José Braga, a torturer.

Torture was not a total novelty to Uruguay. Even before President Pacheco's war on communism, gangsters and petty thieves had been slapped around in jailhouses. But the use of violence against political prisoners was a barbarity that Uruguayans thought they had put behind them along with the death penalty.

Philip Agee learned otherwise when he went with his CIA station chief, John Horton, to call on Colonel Rodriguez, Montevideo's police chief. The purpose was to involve the chief in a CIA plot that would pressure Uruguay to break diplomatic relations with the Soviet Union.

The CIA plan was inventive. Dick Conolly, an operations officer, had chosen four Russians from the Soviet embassy and concocted for them a history of subversion within Uruguay's labor movement. Another CIA man, Robert H. Riefe, made up stories about leftist officials in Uruguay's unions to interlock with Conolly's fiction, thereby suggesting a conspiracy. The fabricated report was to be slipped to an Uruguayan politician who would use it to justify severing diplomatic ties with the USSR. First, though, to give it an appearance of authenticity, Horton and Agee took the CIA handiwork to police headquarters.

As Rodriguez leafed through the false report, Agee heard an odd sound, low at first but gradually growing louder. Agee listened more closely. It was a human voice crying out. Probably a vendor on the street, he thought. Rodriguez told his aide to turn up the radio. A soccer match was in progress. By then the moan had become a scream. The chief called again for the radio to be turned up, but the screaming drowned out the broadcast.

Now Agee knew that a man was being tortured in the small room above Rodriguez's office. He suspected that the victim was a leftist named Oscar Bonaudi, whom Agee had recommended to Otero for preventive detention. The screaming continued. Rodriguez finally accepted the CIA report; and with their mission accomplished, Horton and Agee walked out to their Volkswagen for the drive back to the embassy.

To most CIA officers, the Uruguayan police were an unending source of amusement—their ineptness, the hopelessness of ever making them efficient. That was what made a man like Saenz so pathetic, that he was so sincere, so straight, that he could never see the humor of the situation.

John Horton was a prototype of the sardonic CIA operator. Now on the drive back, he referred to what they had
heard from upstairs and gave his usual nervous laugh.

Shortly afterward, Otero confirmed that Bonaudi had
been the man Agee had heard screaming. Braga, the deputy
chief of investigation, had ordered the torture when
Bonaudi refused to talk. His beatings had gone on for three
days. Agee resolved that he would never turn over another
name to the police as long as Braga stayed with them.

This was not the first time Phil Agee found himself
troubled by his work. Secrecy no longer seemed so glamorous; and the aliases, with their surnames always capitalized,
struck him as less larkish: Daniel N. GABOSKY for Ned
Holman; Claude V. KARVANAK for Bob Riefe; Jeremy
S. HODAPP for Philip Agee.

Other aspects of the job also disturbed him. In Washington, one training duty had been to run name checks for
Standard Oil to reassure the company that it was not em-
ploying leftists or subversives at its overseas plants. The
lists came in each week from Caracas, where the security
officer of a Rockefeller subsidiary, Creole Petroleum, was
an ex-FBI agent with close ties to the CIA.

The checks had been only part of the game in those days.
Now, in the field, those same security checks went on
informally for the local branches of U. S. corporations. A
club of seven or eight U. S. businessmen met weekly in
Montevideo with the U. S. ambassador and the CIA station
chief. The head of the General Electric subsidiary sat in,
and the man from Lone Star Cement. (But not the International Harvester representative; he was considered a loud
mouth.) The subversive checks were run for them out of
the CIA station's local files.

Faced by both the direct and indirect evidence of how
his various identifications were being used, Agee could
come up with no better solution than not to give the police
any more names. What if he had protested the torture?
Agee was sure that they would not have listened to him.

To have an impact, any protest would have to come from either the CIA station chief or from the U. S. ambassador. Horton's dismissive laugh suggested that he would not be the one; and safe at the embassy, the ambassador never heard the screams.

Not long before Mitrione's arrival in Uruguay, Cantrell's position within the U. S. mission began to erode. He had survived the debacle with Manuel the Cuban, but now rumors spread that money irregularities were at the root of his troubles. Substantial funds had been made available for intelligence work in Montevideo, especially for bribes to informers who could supply information about the workings of Uruguay's Communist party. Since those payoffs could hardly be subjected to close auditing, every conduit for funds came under suspicion. Was Otero pocketing more than his share? Was Cantrell slack, or worse, in his accounting?

Usually the CIA did not want to waste one of its own officers as chief police adviser. There was too much paper work to the job, too many public ceremonies to attend. But in Uruguay, Cantrell was being recalled, and it had not worked out to have an easy-going man like Saenz as chief adviser. Although Mitrione was not a CIA officer, from his first day in the office, the Uruguayan employees knew at once that their routine was going to be tightened.

U. S. businessmen who had dropped by to pass an hour with Saenz found that his successor was all business. Sparing a minute to be sociable, Mitrione might complain about his pay, how low it was compared to his responsibilities. Mostly, though, he was hard at work; and by the time Cantrell was recalled in February 1970, Mitrione was clearly in charge of police operations in a way Saenz never had been.

That change in the top spot at the Public Safety office had intrigued everyone around the *jefatura*, but no one took a keener interest in Mitrione than a young officer, Miguel Angel Benítez Segovia.

Benítez had risen to the not inconsiderable rank of sub-commissioner, only two grades below inspector. As he advanced, he had distinguished himself as one of the most vocal enemies of the Tupamaros. Around police headquarters, Uruguayans and U. S. advisers alike called them *Putamaros,* the pun being the Spanish word for whore. But Benítez seemed to take the rebel movement as a personal affront. He would snarl and say, "We really ought to get those bastards!"

Such crudity was not Otero's style. As his associates saw it, Otero was still charging out against the Tupamaros like a knight gallant going to do battle with a worthy adversary. They observed sardonically the respect with which Otero treated the outlaws, the esteem he showed for their sly and elusive tactics. It was quite all right with them if Otero wanted to play Don Quixote, but they tried to remind him that he was tilting with true enemies, not with windmills.

For their part, the Tupamaros found Otero the perfect foil. He lamented their daring; but whenever a tip came into his office, the police moved so sluggishly that the Tupamaros could almost always escape.

The Tupamaros were still stealing cash from banks. They were also "liberating" records from finance companies and publishing what they found, records that indicated tax evasion and fraud in high places. Pacheco's government was falling in public esteem, and the pressure for change continued to spread. Pacheco responded by invoking emergency security measures. Newspapers were forbidden to use the words "Tupamaro" or "Movement of National Liberation." Reporters responded by calling the group "the unmentionables."

Those were the conditions of Dan Mitrione's nice and peaceful new assignment. Once again, as in Rio, the surface of his life seemed agreeable. The Mitriones moved into a two-story house on Pilcomayo, a quiet residential street. As wife of the chief adviser, Hank took Spanish lessons and involved herself in community affairs, particularly a thrift shop run by the women of the U. S. community.

Yet, the Tupamaros allowed the new chief adviser no time at all for settling in before they made another dramatic strike. It had been more than a year since Pereira Reverbel had been released. Now the Tupamaros carried off another wealthy victim, Gaetano Pellegrini Jiampietro, and extorted about $60,000 for his return. Mitrione reported to Washington that they had probably been inspired by the recent kidnapping of Burke Elbrick in Brazil.

The police themselves were vulnerable. When the police chief decided that the children of Jorge Batlle, grand-nephew of the great Batlle, should be protected, he sent around two policemen armed with .38 Colt revolvers. Batlle spoke with the men and learned that they had never fired their guns. Policemen had to pay for their own ammunition, and these two could not afford the cost. Batlle bought each of them six bullets.

Mitrione also had to deal with another Uruguayan custom. Confronting a criminal, the policeman was trained to fire in the air. He was justified in returning gunfire but never in initiating it. That restriction had to be removed.

With Mitrione in charge, Montevideo, like Belo Horizonte and Rio de Janeiro, experienced a marked increase in U. S. equipment, especially tear gas, gas masks, and police batons for crowd control. More important, however, was the change in attitude.

When a police commissioner named Juan María Lucas had studied at the IPA, Mitrione had been one of his teachers. Upon hearing of Mitrione's appointment to Montevideo, he called together his assistants, including Benítez, and told them, "Now we have someone who will support us in our activities."

As it had in Brazil, Mitrione's assignment also led to an

increase in the number of Uruguayans sent to the United States for training. But these days all students did not spend their time entirely at the IPA or the CIA's IPSS in Washington. In their fifth week, some were sent to Los Fresnos, Texas, where they were taught to build bombs.

The instruction at Los Fresnos became particularly embarrassing to the Office of Public Safety later on, when the press learned that the CIA had been running those courses. OPS said that it had asked the U. S. Army to give the training but the Pentagon had refused. "Maybe they didn't have room for it at any of their bases" was one OPS official's best explanation.

The obvious answer was more accurate. Intelligence agents at the Pentagon had picked up traces of what the CIA was doing, and they wanted to keep the army uninvolved. The instructors at the Texas school, however, were Green Berets.

Except for one detail, OPS could have had an unassailable explanation for sending students to Los Fresnos. By now the world had entered upon a time of bombs and bomb threats. Public opinion might have readily accepted the argument that any nation's policemen needed training in the defusing and demolition of bombs. The problem for OPS was that the CIA's course at Los Fresnos did not teach men how to destroy bombs, only how to build them.

The instruction was called T.A.I.; in English, Investigation of Terrorist Activities. The students were required to sign oaths of secrecy, and to live at the camp, under permanent guard, in tents on the isolated Texas plain. Their course began with a review of various explosives, including C-3 and C-4 plastic bombs, and a scientific analysis of TNT. The students were instructed in fuses—how to light them, how to time them. To overcome their fears, they were made to put dynamite under their shirts and walk toward the camp with the detonator set.

Next the students had to race the clock, setting a charge against a gas tank or a telephone pole in a specified number of minutes. They learned to catapult bombs. Practicing on the camp fence, they were shown how to cut through steel. In the clear Texas air, they blew up jeeps carrying cans of gasoline.

The students were called guerrillas, and they were told, This is what guerrillas do. Given that instruction, it was not surprising that Byron Engle later denied that IPA students had been shown *The Battle of Algiers,* with its scenes of policemen excusing themselves from a dinner party to go off to bomb a rebel's house.

Then grenades: ten or so for each student to lob at gasoline cans or old cars. Next: the Claymore anti-personnel mines, a staple of the Vietnam war. Filled with long nails, one mine could wound a dozen men at five hundred yards. Finally, the thirty students of the course, all from Central and South America, were given a major assignment: blow up a convoy of trucks; hit a gas depot surrounded by booby traps; interrupt enemy communications by slipping past sentinels and knocking over telephone poles. The director of the IPA and a cadre of Green Berets sometimes oversaw these commencement exercises.

At the end of the course, one student who asked his hosts why the training had been given was told: "The United States thinks that the moment will come when in each of the friendly countries, they could use a student of confidence—who has become a specialist in explosives; that is why the different governments have chosen their favorite persons."

Mitrione sent at least seven men to take the CIA's course in Los Fresnos. Among them was Inspector Lucas, who had hailed Mitrione's arrival in Montevideo. Another was Subcommissioner Benítez, who hated the Tupamaros from the bottom of his heart and at the top of his lungs.

During this period, the CIA stations of Latin America's Southern Cone entered into a period of even greater cooperation. The Western Hemisphere Division had always been an active liaison office. In 1964, when the CIA's Office of Finance in Washington could not secure enough Chilean escudos for its election campaign against Salvador Allende, it set up regional purchasing offices in Buenos Aires, Rio, Lima, and Montevideo.

Helping out in that emergency, Philip Agee had contacted the assistant manager of the Montevideo branch of the First National City Bank of New York, who was also a CIA agent, and he sent men to Santiago to buy $100,000 in escudos. Those bills were then sent back into Chile via the U. S. embassy's diplomatic pouch.

In the late 1960s, that CIA network began handling matters more sensitive than illegal money. The agency was putting Brazilian, Argentinian, and Uruguayan military and police officers in touch with each other for training in wire tapping and other intelligence procedures, and for supplies of explosives and untraceable guns. Those contacts also led to the surveillance, the harassment, and finally the assassination of political exiles. Between the time Allende was elected president of Chile and his overthrow in 1973, the CIA arranged similar meetings between the Brazilian right wing and Chilean army and police officials opposed to Allende.

Members of Brazil's Death Squads were introduced to the police in Montevideo and Buenos Aires. After he shot Carlos Marighela in November 1969, Sergio Fleury of São Paulo became celebrated among Uruguayan police. He met with groups of them, on at least two occasions through CIA contacts.

One Uruguayan police official, proudly nationalistic, resented the way in which U. S. intelligence operators seemed to be melding the intelligence services of the Southern Cone into one interlocking apparatus. He was convinced that given Uruguay's small size and its position between Argentina and Brazil, this surrendering of autonomy would one day prove harmful to his country. If this work was so valuable in stopping communism, he wondered, why did the CIA officers take such care that their role be secret? For example, a high-ranking official from Argentina's Ministry of Justice arrived in Montevideo to discuss ways of monitoring the two countries' political exiles. A CIA man had arranged that particular meeting, then found an excuse for not attending it.

The Uruguayan, who understood the concept of "deniability," wondered why a U. S. intelligence officer should feel his country's reputation was more valuable than Uruguay's. Another point gnawed at him as well. The turning over of Uruguayan intelligence to the CIA was treason. Despite the motive, despite its expressed goal of allowing the CIA to help protect Uruguay against subversion, it was still treason.

But the official, until he retired, never spoke out. When he did, many years later, it was nervously and after exacting repeated promises of anonymity. Had he complained earlier, he could never have been sure whether a colleague agreed with him or pretended to agree and immediately picked up the phone to call his CIA contact.

William Cantrell's former driver, Nelson Bardesio, seemed to have no doubts about the virtue of the CIA's anti-subversive methods. After Cantrell's departure, Bardesio readily accepted an assignment to a secret team under the control of the Ministry of the Interior. Of his five fellow team members, three came from the traffic police and two from the police institute.

The director of the effort was President Pacheco's personal secretary, Carlos Piran, who later sent the Uruguayans to Buenos Aires for training with the Argentinian Information Service (SIDE). While in Buenos Aires, Bardesio called on a SIDE captain who gave him three charges of gelignite to deliver to Piran.

Bardesio and his associates then formed an Escadron de

la Mort, which bombed the houses of lawyers and teachers considered sympathetic to the Tupamaros. On at least one occasion, they killed a suspect they had kidnapped. Bardesio's crew rode to and from their bombings in police cars. After the bomb was exploded, Bardesio would tell the central radio operator at police headquarters where he was leaving the getaway car.

The importance of his illicit life turned Bardesio's head. In fact, once when he decided the car issued to him was not adequate, he refused the mission. The minister of the interior ordered the Montevideo police chief from that time forward to give Bardesio whatever he wanted.

During his first year in Uruguay, Mitrione's duties became increasingly arduous, but he took time during his first year in Uruguay to enjoy himself on the golf course and to keep in touch with his family in Richmond. Early in 1970, he wrote to Ray, asking him to send a set of irons and numbered cloth wood covers; he enclosed a check for $158. The condition of his present set had brought out Mitrione's jocular humor: "... the war-clubs that Daniel Boone used to hunt bears with that I bought second-handed back in 1948 are not doing much for my game."

The clubs and covers were missent. When he inquired about their whereabouts, Mitrione also supplied Ray with innocuous observations about his life: "I came back yesterday from a two-day trip of about 700 miles. Sure is pretty country."

The jaunt had actually been part of Mitrione's effort to improve the efficiency of Uruguay's interior police departments and to scout the countryside for potential IPA recruits. The Tupamaros were an urban group with their foco in Montevideo. If the battleground later shifted to the country, Mitrione wanted the rural police to be prepared.

"The country situation is still calm," Mitrione wrote Ray in February 1970. "However, when summer is over and everyone starts thinking about something else besides the beach, it may get a little livelier. I hope not." He added that he could now work at home. "I have an office they furnished for me all set up." At the *jefatura,* the policemen noticed that Mitrione was spending less time in the OPS office.

Benítez once visited Mitrione's embassy office, where his camera eye swept the room. Mitrione's office had thick green carpeting, a bulletin board covered with white nylon, two armchairs, a small sofa. It was air conditioned. Benítez admired three photographs of waterfalls, decorative touches supplied by U. S. AID. Mitrione, he noticed, sat at his desk with his back to the window; and although he was on an upper floor, he seemed to present a tempting target.

"Don't you worry," Mitrione explained. "Those window panes can stop a .45-caliber bullet." Mitrione, however, was now carrying a pistol, a .38-caliber Smith and Wesson. In Belo Horizonte and Rio, he had felt secure without one.

In March 1970, his family in Richmond informed him that his mother's condition was deteriorating. He replied that it would take forty-eight hours from the time he left Uruguay to make the connections and arrive in Richmond. He also reminded his brother that although he was now a chief by title, he was still only a non-com in the Office of Public Safety: "It would also be well to advise Dr. Mader that he is the one that has to convince Washington that Mom's condition warrants my being there."

He ended his next letter: "Take care and God bless, as ever," and then added a postscript: "Things could get a little 'hot' here in the next couple of months." One word had been crossed out and changed. He had first written: "Things should get a little 'hot' here . . ."

Late in March, the worsening news from home caused Mitrione to fly to Richmond alone. It was the last time he saw his mother. Still, except for the sadness underlying his return, Mitrione had a fine time. He was back with people who admired him and away, for the first time in eight months, from the tensions of his work. To his closest friends from the Richmond police, he confided something of the dangers he was facing in Montevideo. With his brothers and sisters, as with his wife and children, Mitrione was less forthcoming.

His reticence with the man who cared most about him may have troubled Mitrione, for a month after his return to Uruguay he wrote Ray: "The situation here is still pretty (you know what), and I wish I could have told you more when I was home with you. I am not trying to alarm you, because you know what it's like in most Latin American countries at this time."

On April 13, 1970, a band of Tupamaros shot Inspector Héctor Romero Moran Charquero to death with a machine gun as he was driving to work. In his monthly report to Washington, Mitrione noted that Moran was a graduate of the International Police Academy and was head of Montevideo's Special Brigade to fight terrorists. He also wrote that one Uruguayan newspaper, an "extreme leftist daily, had been carrying out a week-long press campaign vilifying Moran as one of the principal police 'torturers' of terrorist suspects." He added that Pacheco's government had closed the newspaper in a "quick-reaction to [its] smear campaign."

Near the end of the report, in the section marked EVALUATION, Mitrione wrote: "It is felt that the police will continue to be a target and that there may be other attempts to kidnap and/or kill key police officials."

For Benítez, the predictions about Mitrione from Lucas had turned out to be accurate. Mitrione brought a new spirit of dedication and expertise to police work. In the land of mañana, he never postponed today's work to tomorrow.

That much had been true of Mitrione ten years ago, but he was different in 1969, heavier, tougher than he had been in Belo Horizonte, very knowing about the ways of U. S. intelligence overseas, and totally committed to the policeman, his miseries, his poor pay, his war on subversives.

Over the years, Mitrione had raised his sights. Measuring himself against the average police adviser had given him considerable confidence, and in Brazil he had learned to cooperate with those CIA officials who he felt were the real leaders in the fight against communism. He could believe that in Rio he had earned their respect, as in Montevideo Adolph Saenz had not.

Was it far-fetched to speculate that when J. Edgar Hoover finally retired from the FBI, his successor might be a former Midwestern police chief with international experience? Mitrione's loyal family saw nothing impossible about that vision. Naturally, any such extraordinary promotion would depend on Mitrione's success in quelling the Tupamaros. He was now forty-nine. This assignment could be the best, the last, chance of his life.

Mitrione had been chief police adviser only nine months when a respected Uruguayan weekly ran an issue with one word on the cover: *Torturada.* The magazine, *Marcha,* was reporting the results of an investigation by liberal members of the Uruguayan Senate who had found that the police were systematically torturing suspected Tupamaros. The methods would not have surprised a Brazilian prisoner— electric needles under the fingernails; electric shocks along the body, particularly on the captive's sexual organs.

Mitrione filed a report of the Senate's findings to the Office of Public Safety in Washington without explanation or elaboration. But in the EVALUATION section, he wrote: "One major problem seems to be that the general public considers the fight one between the police and the extremists, and are not too concerned about it. Until they realize that the activities of the extremists threaten their pursuit of social, political, and economic betterment and assist the police by providing information and stop playing ostrich, the situation will not improve in the foreseeable future."

Under RECOMMENDATIONS, Mitrione wrote: "None."

One day a story about Mitrione's toughness passed through the ranks at the *jefatura*, and Benítez noted it. Mitrione had watched a trade-union official, the head of the bank workers, come to the *jefatura* during a strike and observed the man in his dealings with the police clerks. Then Mitrione offered his ideas on how to break a man like that.

He had always emphasized finding out as much as possible about a prisoner before the interrogation began. Learn the suspect's breaking point and reach it quickly, he told the interrogating officers. Like them, he was not a brute. He wanted the questioning over as soon as possible.

In the case of the labor leader, Mitrione said: Undress him completely and force him to stand facing the wall. Then have one of the youngest policemen goose him. Afterward, put him into a cell and hold him for three days with nothing to drink. On the third day, pass through to him a pot of water mixed with urine.

In Richmond, Indiana, it was hardly credible that Dan Mitrione would advocate that kind of behavior, particularly with its sexual overtones. But Mitrione had been out of the United States for most of ten years, and the police forces of Latin America were filled with youngsters barely out of their teens. Sexual joking was endemic, along with what sergeants in the U. S. Army called grab-assing. Standing guard duty at the *jefatura*, a young Montevideo policeman could expect his colleagues to make false passes at his genitals, to tease him about being attracted to men, to pat his buttocks mockingly. It went on all the time. So when Mitrione urged a method for breaking the control of an arrogant suspect, he was only talking to his students in the terms they knew best.

For all his curiosity about Mitrione, Benítez never saw him torture a prisoner. He knew, though, that Mitrione directed certain interrogations; and as the equipment for torture became more sophisticated, he gave credit for the change to the chief U. S. police adviser.

According to the notes Benítez was keeping, when Mitrione arrived in Montevideo, the police were torturing prisoners with a rudimentary electric needle that had come from Argentina. Mitrione arranged for the police to get newer electric needles of varying thickness. Some needles were so thin they could be slipped between the teeth. Benítez understood that this equipment came to Montevideo inside the U. S. embassy's diplomatic pouch.

Philip Agee could have informed Benítez that the CIA routinely sent its equipment through the pouch. Even a lie detector, large as a suitcase, came to a CIA station trussed up and sacrosanct from Uruguayan inspection within the pouch. Audio and bugging equipment came the same way.

The Technical Services Division made ingenious use of the abundant technological skills in the United States, giving support to every agency division and supplying experts in listening devices, lock-picking, and photography. It also supplied containers with hidden compartments, methods for secretly opening and closing letters, tools for invisible writing. It provided disguises, as the world found out when a former CIA officer named Howard Hunt wore a red wig supplied by the agency to call on an ailing female ITT executive.

Under the direction of psychologist James Keehner, TSD had devised personality tests with geometric designs to merge with other data and form psychological profiles. The CIA maintained 30,000 of those dossiers. (The one on Fidel Castro noted that he kept his pants on while having sex.) The tests could establish a good deal more about a person: whether or not he was moral; whether he would be more loyal to a person than to a cause; what sort of torture would be the most effective against him. TSD also tested hallucinogenic drugs; the news of those experiments, and the death that resulted from them, was revealed only after two decades of secrecy.

Keehner observed that most CIA employees were the type of people who could compartmentalize their work in their minds. "They can do horrible things all day," he told a reporter, but only after he had left TSD, "and then go home and forget about it."

In the Montevideo *jefatura*, it was a badly kept secret that TSD maintained a support office in Panama, which supplied emergency riot guns and tear gas to Latin American armies and police forces. Under Pacheco, Montevideo's Metropolitan Guard was shooting so much gas that its leaders were constantly badgering their U. S. contacts for more from the Panama depot. The weaponry was secretly stowed aboard the military aircraft that flew to Montevideo, flights that often also carried groceries—eggs and bread—for U. S. officials who refused to eat the local products.

It was less well known that the Technical Services Division operated another office in Buenos Aires. Only a few Uruguayan police officers learned that the improved torture equipment, the wires and the generators, as well as such explosives as Bardesio's gelignite, passed through that TSD office in Argentina.

When it came to the interrogation of Tupamaros, Mitrione conveyed his instructions through a few such high-ranking Uruguayans as Lucas. But if Benítez never saw Mitrione actually inside the torture room at the *jefatura*, others did. After Mitrione's murder, male and female prisoners at Uruguay's jails traded stories about his participation in the torture. Usually those were secondhand accounts repeated to convince a doubter that the Tupamaros had been justified in killing Mitrione.

The more reliable information about his activities came from Uruguayan policemen themselves. One officer later recalled Mitrione coming into the third-floor room, probably inadvertently, while the police were administering electric shocks to a Tupamaro suspect. Mitrione had come in only for a minute, to ask for other information. The prisoner heard Mitrione's voice and shouted a vile insult against all Yankees.

The officer who observed the incident said that Mitrione did not seem angry. It was for that reason that his behavior was talked about, as evidence of his admirable control. He simply glanced over at the man getting the *picana* applied under his fingernails. The Uruguayan police officer took that look to mean: They can say what they like, but we have our own ways of answering them.

Another time, the Montevideo police unwittingly brought in a young woman who, while in fact a Tupamaro sympathizer, was also a friend of Alejandro Otero's. In the course of the interrogation, she was tortured severely. Upon her release, she contacted Otero and told him that Mitrione had watched and assisted in her torture. For Otero, that was the breaking point. For four years, he had known of intermittent torture; but with Mitrione's arrival, it had intensified. Otero rejected torture on pragmatic grounds: it only radicalized both the police and the Tupamaros. Some of the police supported that reasoning; others, the chief of police among them, sided with the *norte-americano*.

After all, Otero's methods had not worked. Once, as he was standing beside Secretary of State Dean Rusk on a ceremonial occasion in Montevideo, his squad had allowed a young man to dash up to Rusk and spit in his face. The Tupamaros had been spitting in the face of Uruguay's police long enough.

All the same, Otero, who was vain, who was troublesome, who could be lax and indolent, was not a torturer. Philip Agee had never heard of him torturing a prisoner, nor had anyone else. He was no hero, and sometimes he had turned his back while other policemen beat a prisoner. But torture seemed to offend Otero, and he was doubly affronted when he went to Mitrione to complain about the abuse of this woman, his *amiga*.

Mitrione heard him out impassively. He had the weight

of his own government, and Otero's, on his side. Soon after their meeting, Otero—in his words—was put on ice.

Only a few months later, Otero gambled his career on one reckless attempt at vindication. He told a man, a reporter, about the torture of his *amiga,* and that indiscretion began an unraveling that would shut down the entire U. S. police advisory program.

On July 30, 1970, Don Gould, the information officer at the U. S. embassy in Montevideo, received his first telephone call from a Tupamaro. After that, the calls came every day of the week but Sunday.

"Mr. Gould," a man's voice said, using the English salutation but delivering the rest of his message in Spanish, "get out of Uruguay or you will be killed."

No U. S. official could serve long in Latin America without receiving some threat to his life. In Gould's case, he had been in Honduras when revolutionaries shot up his hotel. This call, however, was more specific, and he went to Mitrione's office to discuss it.

Gould had lately used the facilities of the U. S. Information Service to print posters for a police campaign, so he knew Mitrione and regarded him as a good corner cop who had probably come overseas for the living allowances, being a Catholic with God only knew how many kids.

After Gould reported the threat, Mitrione explained his own philosophy: "I'm in danger and I carry a gun. But if I were approached, I'd size up the situation. If I could get away, I'd use my gun. Otherwise, I'd go along with them."

The next morning, Nathan Rosenfeld, the embassy's cultural attaché in Montevideo, called the apartment of Gordon Jones, a young member of the political section, to say that he was ready to leave for work. The two men lived in the same building, and most mornings they drove to the embassy together.

Jones said he was on his way, and Rosenfeld went ahead to the garage. He was walking toward his yellow Ford convertible when he saw a tall man in the shadows. Rosenfeld took him for Jones and called, "How the hell did you get down so fast?"

With that, two men jumped Rosenfeld from behind. They were waving .45- or .38-caliber automatics and seemed very nervous. "Don't say anything," one warned Rosenfeld. "We're Tupamaros."

Swarthy and balding, wearing tortoise-rimmed glasses, Rosenfeld was twice the age of his assailants. The most aggressive thing about him was his flashy wardrobe. He was certainly not going to try to overpower them.

"Are you Gordon Jones?" a Tupamaro demanded. Rosenfeld said he was not. Jones, twenty-seven years old, could have been his son.

They pushed Rosenfeld to the wall. "Get your hands up," a voice commanded. Rosenfeld was wearing an overcoat and scarf. During Montevideo's July winter, temperatures could fall to freezing.

When he felt metal connecting with his bald spot, Rosenfeld gave the Tupamaros what he considered his best Lee Strasberg fall. His heavy overcoat softened his impact on the cement floor.

They aren't professionals, Rosenfeld thought. No one has come over to kick me in the ribs to see whether I'm shamming.

Meantime, Gordon Jones had come into the basement and saw Rosenfeld's body on the floor. As he ran over to examine the body, the Tupamaros jumped him. While they were tying him up, Jones puffed out his chest enough so that when he exhaled, the ropes went slack. They then rolled him in a blanket and laid him on a bed of sand in the back of a small truck.

Once on the street, Jones shouted for help. At the sound, a Tupamaro clouted his head with a gun butt hard enough to rip the skin. But at a stoplight, Jones was able to throw his feet over the edge of the truck, jump down, and hop to the curb screaming, "Help! Help! Help!" The truck roared off without him.

Jones wriggled free and called the embassy from a wine shop. The first thing he said was, "Nate's dead!" "No," an embassy staff man assured him, "he's all right."

At the garage, Rosenfeld had waited until he was sure the Tupamaros were gone. Then he called the security office and reported the kidnapping attempt. "Yes," said a security guard. "They've also taken Dan Mitrione."

Mitrione's driver, a police sergeant named González, left the garage of the *jefatura* that morning in a white Opel. He drove out to the Malvin district and parked in front of Pilcomayo 5398. Mitrione never kept him waiting more than a minute or two.

With Mitrione inside the car, González turned down Alejandro Gallinal. There, on a grade, with the muddy winter Atlantic in the near distance, the Opel was cut off by a white truck with a red sun visor.

An eyewitness told the newspaper *El País* that four young men jumped from the truck and took Mitrione away at gunpoint in a second truck. It happened so quickly that the onlooker could not offer a detailed description of the kidnappers.

Sergeant González, who had been struck on the head, located a telephone and called the *jefatura*. Sometime during Mitrione's ride to a people's prison, he was shot in the shoulder.

The Brazilian vice-consul, Aloysio Mares Dias Gomide, had been abducted that same morning by four Tupamaros pretending to be telephone repairmen. His wife and six children were elsewhere in the house and were not harmed.

Had the Tupamaros' plan succeeded, they would have held three prisoners to bargain with, because for the first time in Uruguay's history, the rebels were about to emulate the tactics of Fernando Gabeira and his Brazilian colleagues by demanding that a group of political prisoners be released in exchange for their captives. They had chosen Dias Gomide much in the spirit that the MR-8 had Burke Elbrick, more for the country he represented than for anything in his background. Dias Gomide turned out to be a singularly disagreeable captive, but the Tupamaros could not know that in advance.

For the last six years, Uruguayan liberals, even those with no admiration for the Tupamaros, had apprehensively watched the developments in Brazil. Arriving in Montevideo, their Brazilian friends would step from the plane and breathe deeply. "It's wonderful," they would say, "to be in a democracy again." But with the Tupamaros as his excuse, President Pacheco had been using the police and the army to tighten his control over Uruguay, until these days the air in Montevideo was not so free. Moreover, looming above the Uruguayans was the constant threat of Brazil's powerful military apparatus. Already Brazilian agents disguised as shepherds and farmers had crossed the northern border on scouting raids. The Uruguayans knew that if one morning Brazil were to invade them, their country could be subdued before lunch.

Yet that same harsh Brazilian government had shown on four separate occasions that it was willing to trade political prisoners to save a diplomat's life. If Pacheco balked at this trade, surely Brazil could bring enough force to change his mind.

The Tupamaros also expected that when Mitrione's activities with the police were exposed, even apolitical Uruguayans would concede that he was as natural a target as Moran Charquero or Inspector Juan María Lucas, who had been badly wounded by a Tupamaro bullet.

After the exchange of prisoners, Mitrione would be sent back to the United States in disgrace, and U. S. assistance to Uruguay's police would be at an end.

The case of Gordon Jones was different. A young man of considerable self-confidence, he had stirred himself out of the embassy's closed society to meet with a range of Uruguayans. Given Montevideo's temper at the time, many of his acquaintances were either Tupamaros or their friends, who expected that Jones, so knowledgeable and opinionated, would have a great deal to tell them during his days of captivity. Also, Jones had just become the father of twins. The Tupamaro cell, which did not foresee a bloody ending any more than Elbrick's abductors had, thought that the large families of two of their victims, and this new family of Jones, would be another reason for the Uruguayan government to yield to their condition.

Left to himself, Jorge Pacheco Areco probably would not have agreed to release the 150 prisoners the Tupamaros were demanding. Even his political backers did not claim that he was a compassionate man. Consequently, he announced that his government regarded the Tupamaro prisoners as common thieves and killers. Constitutionally, he said, he could not release them. However, better lawyers than Pacheco pointed out that since the president had the power of pardon, the 150 prisoners could be on the next flight to Algiers.

But the decision was not entirely Pacheco's. At the time that Elbrick was kidnapped, Richard Nixon's administration was less than a year old, and it had not formulated a policy for dealing with this new guerrilla tactic. In urging the prisoner exchange for the ambassador's release, the U. S. embassy in Rio had acted largely on its own. Its pressures were taken as representing Washington's policy when Washington had no policy.

Now the seizing of Dan A. Mitrione set off a great deal of discussion at the State Department about establishing one standard line for these cases. At first, Secretary Rogers and his chief aides considered this criterion: If the host country had carried out normal responsibilities for protection, then Washington would discourage the payment of any ransom.

But that still left the U. S. government judging each

kidnapping separately. What Washington needed was an iron-clad rule, especially since individual victims were likely to be well known to the top echelon at State—or, rather, the ambassadors and the CIA station chiefs would be known. As Alexis Johnson said afterward, there would never have been occasion for him to meet Dan Mitrione.

The dilemma was resolved when word came down from the White House that President Nixon adamantly opposed any trade or deal with the rebels of any nation.

The United States now had a policy. Held beneath the earth in a basement prison in Montevideo, Dan Mitrione did not know that he would be the first sacrifice to Richard Nixon's show of strength.

CHAPTER
9

THE TUPAMARO who entered the cell sounded like a son worried about his sick father. Tentatively he asked, "Are you sleeping?"

"Yeah," said Dan Mitrione, "I was, yes."

"Well, I'm sorry."

"No, that's great."

"Would you like to have a meeting?"

"Huh?"

"Yes," said the Tupamaro. "Would you mind?"

"I'd be happy to."

"All right. Okay." Anyone overhearing them, catching the young man's skittishness and the older man's self-assurance, would have assumed that Mitrione was the jailer. The Tupamaro seemed to be deferring to his prisoner because of Mitrione's age or because he was an Uruguayan and Mitrione was a Yankee.

"You have—how many sons do you have?"

"I have nine."

"Nine sons and daughters?"

"Well, four sons and five daughters."

"Gee," said the Tupamaro. "I see. Are some of them here?"

"Four of them are here, yes."

The Tupamaro seemed to remember that he had come for information. "Tell me, you had some important, um, work in the States while you were there?" He spoke fluent English. The pauses were from embarrassment, not from a groping for words.

"Well," said Mitrione with a slight chuckle, "I don't think it was."

The Tupamaro laughed politely at that deprecation.

"I think it's a matter of what—what is important." Mitrione's hesitations seemed to come from finding the right, the blandest, phrase to convey his meaning with no possibility of giving offense. "It was advisory. Advisory—"

"Yes?"

"We used to advise the men who came to the States in the latest techniques. Of course, this has been going on for, oh, gosh, twenty years."

"Twenty years?" Not disbelief, simply a reflex, a verbal nodding to encourage the other man to say more.

"Yeah, at least."

"That must be around—?"

"Because I remember some people from Iran and Tunisia and every place, over twenty years ago."

The Tupamaro, who was obviously young, laughed in admiration of the idea of a program twenty years old: a lifetime. "Did they go and learn?"

"Well, they—they—they learned some of the things," Mitrione said with an anxious stutter. All the same, his manner was one of an IPA instructor spelling out the basics to an incoming class of mixed abilities. "They can't learn everything. They can't use everything they learn because every society is different."

"I agree with that." The Tupamaro's voice was thoughtful, investing Mitrione's commonplace with another level of meaning.

"But the main thing is to, ah, teach them possibly the better ways or the newer ways to do things."

"What kind of 'things'?"

This was the heart of the interrogation, and Mitrione's laugh acknowledged it. But he said nothing. The Tupamaro had not been trained in interrogation in Panama or at the IPA or anywhere else. Later, when the tape was played back, other revolutionaries groaned to hear him moving on to another subject.

"And, ah, you have been chief—of police, or something?"

"Yes. I was chief of police."

"I heard that. Where was that?"

"In Indiana."

"Indiana?" The Tupamaro turned the word over on his tongue.

"Indiana, yeah." As Mitrione said it, it sounded very far away, and very dear.

"Is it a large state?"

"No." Almost a sigh. "Well, about four million population. Four and a half million."

"Is it hard to be chief?" Reporters would recognize that kind of question as something to ask until a better question presented itself.

Mitrione took up the answer vigorously. This was safe ground to linger over. "Well, I wasn't chief of the state. I was chief of a city in that state."

"Oh, I see."

"And my city was only about fifty thousand population."

"Umh," said the Tupamaro, sounding a bit bored. "And, ah, which city was it?"

"Richmond."

"Richmond?"

"Mmm."

"And how is it? Difficult work?"

"No. No, it's pleasurable work. It's . . . to me, it's the same thing as a schoolteacher and the people who pick up the *basura*." Mitrione used the Spanish word for garbage. "It's a little bit of everything around the city. Some people work in a factory." That was his father. "Some people work out in the fresh air." That was his brother, Dom, tending the golf links. "It all depends."

"That's right."

"But police work is a little bit different. Very much different in many instances. But in a city like that, it's not too bad."

"Is it—it was too long ago?" The Tupamaro meant very long ago.

Mitrione heard the mistake but understood the question. "When I was chief?"

"Yes."

"Nineteen sixty, I left there."

"Nineteen sixty. Well, things change."

"Oh, yes." From Mitrione a comradely laugh.

"Probably now you have a different kind of work, being a chief of police in the States."

"Altogether. Altogether different." Mitrione repeated it again, wistfully. "Altogether different. You're right."

"There are different kinds of works for the police?"

Mitrione, tired and resigned, said, "Yeah."

"And you know things change. And how about your work in Brazil?" The Tupamaro was sounding more sure of himself, but he was only angling for some chance indiscretion. Mitrione had been an adviser in Brazil for seven years. The Brazilian police had preceded Uruguay's police in the use of electrical torture. The Tupamaro had those two parts of the equation, and he seemed to expect Mitrione to draw for him the logical, damning conclusion.

"I was a, a, a *asesor*." Again Mitrione used a Spanish word, this one for adviser. "I worked in the interior of Brazil, and I worked with the—I was an adviser to the military police. And we worked on, uh, training."

"Oh, I see."

"You know how the . . . in Brazil and in Uruguay, the way things are, they walk, how a policeman walks when he's on duty. Well, we try to teach a way that will be a little better for them and a little better for everyone, to walk a little more. How to stand."

The Tupamaro picked up the word "interior," although Mitrione meant only Belo Horizonte, away from the coast. "Have you been in the jungle then?"

"No, no, not *that* kind of walking." They both knew the stories of official atrocities committed against the Indians in Brazil's remote forests, and they laughed together at Mitrione's eagerness to clear himself of that stigma. "And we also try to teach them better maintenance, better maintenance of equipment."

"Yes, well, very often, you know, we stole about seven hundred weapons." The Tupamaro laughed modestly as Mitrione said with a sigh, "Yes, I know."

"They cannot take care of them." The Tupamaro was complaining to the U. S. adviser about the habits of the Uruguayan police. "And some of them were very badly, you know—"

Mitrione sounded sympathetic to this protest against an abuse of firearms. "Bad shape, weren't they?"

"Oh, yes, all dirty." It was the guerrilla's turn to sigh. "We had to work a lot to put them in condition. You know, all those guns—"

"Yes."

"But the guns were all right, but the long arms, you know—"

"They weren't taken care of, huh?"

"We have to do it now." Again the Tupamaro laughed, and Mitrione joined in at the absurdity of the rebels being forced to clean up the policemen's weapons. "We have them pretty good now."

"I'll bet." Mitrione's tone was low-keyed but flattering.

"Fortunately," the Tupamaro concluded. "And how about your work in Uruguay, tell me."

"It's about the same. It's about the same. We have—we have an office in the *jefatura,* and we work with, ah, the Ministry of Interior and the, ah, chief of police, the head of the *jefatura,* and we work on communications in the interior. You know, for the states of the interior, a basic— a basic network. And they bring in automobiles for police cars, but Uruguay buys them. We don't buy the cars."

"Oh, I see."

"On the radios, it's fifty-fifty on some." Mitrione was giving away nothing they could not read in the transcript of any year's appropriation committee hearings. "But on others, Uruguay buys them all."

"I see. But I think that the Uruguayan police learn very fast. Do they?"

"Oh, I don't know, I think the Uruguayan, the Uruguayan young man, is a pretty smart young man. I think he is better than any place else in Latin America, because of your good education system here."

Mitrione's words were measured, analytical. Nothing in his manner suggested that he was trying to ingratiate himself and thereby pull himself out from the tightest hole of his life.

The Tupamaro took his praise for Uruguay's schools as no more than their due. "Yes," he said.

"You have schools, and the other thing, I think, is wrong is maybe the desire." Pressure caused Mitrione to garble Uruguay's assets with its liabilities. He also seemed to forget for the moment that he was not giving a pep talk to a class of rookie cops. "You know, you need a little more will and a desire to do a better job."

"Yes," said the Tupamaro to this misdirected lecture.

"And because they don't pay very much." It was the recurring complaint of Mitrione's adult life. "That would help, if they paid them more."

"And what can you say about those guys like Moran Charquero and all that?" A crucial question. Moran was the guerrilla fighter, trained at the IPA, who had acquired a reputation as a torturer and had been assassinated the previous April.

Mitrione's voice went higher as he answered. The strain

to sound offhand was becoming more apparent. Moran's work had figured favorably in Mitrione's U-127 reports to Washington, but now was not the time to recount the successes of Moran's Special Brigade. "I didn't know Moran Charquero too well. I never worked with him. I met him when he went to the States, 'cause I went to the airport to say good-bye and, ah, when he came back I saw him. But I never—never worked with Moran Charquero or with . . . what was the other fellow's name? From Canelones? That went to school at the same time?"

"Legnani?"

"Who?"

"Legnani?"

"No, Legnani's the chief up there. The other one, ah, the one who went for training with Moran Charquero at the same time."

"Oh, I see. I can't remember his name."

"I can't either." They shared a light laugh at this mutual frailty. "I never worked with any of those men." Mitrione went on, pressing his advantage. "I knew them when I saw them, you know. I never worked with any individual police because I worked in the administrative part."

"And in which department?"

"Well, I worked in my office in the embassy."

"Oh."

"I spent ninety-nine percent of my time in the embassy."

"Yes." The Tupamaro's "yes" was a Latin American "no." He wanted Mitrione to know that he was not going to be deceived. "I think my mates know that. Because they've been checking everything about you for a long time." This last was said with a laugh that was apologetic but boastful too.

"Meaning your who?" "Mates" was more Australian slang than Midwestern.

"My friends."

"Oh, yes. About me, you mean?"

"Yes."

"You'll find that I spend most of my time in the . . . well, I haven't been in the *jefatura,* to be exact. I haven't been there for . . . for two and a half weeks. Maybe three weeks."

"Though you have a place to park your car, down there in the garage, you know."

"At the *jefatura?*" A debater's question, a stalling for time.

"Yes."

"That's not for me. That's for the other *asesores.*"

The Tupamaro asked matter-of-factly, "Who are they?"

"We have three other men here."

In exactly the same tone the Tupamaro repeated, "Who are they?"

Mitrione answered with a challenge. "Well, you know their names, don't you?"

The Tupamaro laughed deprecatingly.

Then Mitrione, weary with the fencing, said, as though scolding one of his children, "Well, I think you know their names."

"Yes, I do. But"—a gentle reminder that Mitrione cannot take that fatherly dismissive tone—"you know we changed the place. Now I'm the police."

Mitrione gave an open-throated laugh. If it was not a mirthful sound, it was, given his situation, a gallant attempt.

The Tupamaro met the laugh with a new persuasiveness. "No, you should tell me the names, really."

"I should tell you the names." Mitrione was not arguing, only trying to get the rules straight.

"Yes, please."

"What advantage would they be?"

"Just to know that you are really . . . willing."

"Well, there's no need for me to lie," Mitrione said briskly, "because you have their names."

"Yes."

"One man's name is Martinez, Richard Martinez."

"Yes."

"Another man's name is Richard Biava."

"Yes."

"Another is Lee Echols."

"One of them is Cuban, isn't he?" The Tupamaro may have meant Manuel, who had disappeared by this time. The Tupamaros' network was not infallible, nor did they always distinguish between the police advisers and the CIA officers operating under police advisory cover.

"No, Mexican."

"Mexican."

"Mexican. Yes, Mexican descent. He is from the United States but Mexican descent."

"*Muy bien.*" Very good. "And how do you think the Uruguayan government will behave now? You know, what do you think they'll do?"

"About me?"

"You and the others who are in prison now. We have some of you."

The Tupamaros had set President Pacheco a deadline of midnight, Friday, August 7. He had remained obdurate; and to press him further the Tupamaros kidnapped another *norte-americano*, Dr. Claude Fly, a sixty-five-year-old agronomist from Fort Collins, Colorado.

Most guerrillas did not suspect the mild Dr. Fly, with a distinguished reputation as a soil analyst, of being a CIA officer. But one Tupamaro was well acquainted with his laboratory in the suburb of Colón, and Dr. Fly was easier prey than other U. S. staff members, who were now taking such elaborate security precautions that the embassy resembled an arsenal.

The Brazilian government was making a concerted effort to have Dias Gomide released. Washington seemed less concerned about Mitrione, and some Tupamaros were wondering whether the Nixon administration, for its own purposes, was prepared to let Mitrione die. Possibly so obvious a political innocent as Dr. Fly would improve the rebels' bargaining position.

Mitrione said, "I hope they—I hope they bargain with

you." He knew nothing of the U. S. policy against trades and deals. The State Department had polled its ambassadors world-wide on the issue, and those gentlemen had supported Nixon's hard line overwhelmingly.

The Tupamaro said, "Yes, we hope it too. We don't like it."

"Yeah."

"We don't like this mess. We're terribly sorry about your wound, you know, but we helped—"

Mitrione cut in to say, judiciously, "That was a mistake, I think."

"Yes, yes. We are making an investigation about that."

"I don't know why he shot me," Mitrione said. "I really don't. I was laying on the floor of the truck."

"Yeah, we're trying to find out, and there is already people trying to find out that." Then, playfully, "You know who is your roommate here?"

"No, I do not." He was separated by a wall from Dias Gomide. "I heard you call him 'consul.' "

"Yes, he is with you."

"No, I don't know him."

"Well. Ah, and how about your government? What will they do?"

"I, you know, I cannot answer that. I think that the government will definitely talk to the Uruguayan government and ask them to—to intercede. But I don't know just what they can do, what the pact is, I—I have no idea."

The deadline clearly weighed on the guerrilla's mind. "But you think they will do some pressuring, don't you? They should, at least."

"Well, I would hope so, definitely hope so. I would guess that they would say, yes, please, put some pressure, do something."

"Yes," said the Tupamaro, "we hope so. We've done it in our country."

"That's right." Perhaps Mitrione knew what his interrogator meant, perhaps he was merely being agreeable. He paused and asked, "How long will something like this take, you know?"

"Hmm?"

"How long would a situation like this take?"

"Well," said the Tupamaro, "that doesn't concern us, you know. We have everything prepared to have you months here, here and in different places."

The Tupamaro could not know that his mates would hold Dias Gomide for 206 days; Dr. Fly for 208; and the British ambassador, Geoffrey Jackson, for eight months, from January 8, 1971, to September 9.

"But we hope to, you know, to do it short," the Tupamaro added. "That's for the best for everybody."

"Lord, I hope so."

"We also want our friends free."

"Yes."

"You understand that?"

"I understand that, yes."

"Probably, the government will do some pressure. Some of the people who is now in prison with you is very important. We think that you are very important too. Really. So—"

"I'm glad somebody thinks so." Again they laughed together.

"Yes, you probably would. Well, now tell me something about the CIA." He said it as Latin Americans often did: cee-ah. "You know, we like James Bond. About the CIA, what can you say?"

"Well, you know you're not going to believe me—"

"Yeah."

"And no matter what, what, ah, I have to convince you that I tell the truth: I know nothing about the CIA. Absolutely nothing about the CIA."

"About the FBI?" As soon as Mitrione was captured, the Tupamaros found three identification cards in his pocket. One was from the Department of State, Agency for International Development, and signed on the back with a facsimile of David Bell's slanting signature and Mitrione's careful penmanship signing his own name. There was also a card from the Montevideo Police Department, and one identifying Mitrione as a member of the FBI National Academy, Associates, of Indiana. The Tupamaros had released copies of that card to the press as evidence in the case they were building that their prisoner was not just one more U. S. AID technician.

The Tupamaro may not have expected Mitrione's enthusiastic response. The FBI training had been the real launching of his professional career; and even here, in enemy hands ten feet under the ground, he was a proud alumnus.

"FBI? I know very much about the FBI because I went . . . I graduated from their academy."

"I see."

"I know everything about . . . well, not everything. I know lots about the FBI."

"What are the names of the FBI in other departments of —" The Tupamaro apparently meant Uruguay's other states. In fact, the FBI did maintain agents overseas in several U. S. embassies under the transparent cover of Legal Officer.

But Mitrione had an opportunity to instruct his questioner on a subject close to his heart. "Well, one of the reasons why I know a lot about the FBI is because the FBI is a—a very open—a very open information-gathering investigation department. There you have agents all over the United States, and they work right in with the police departments. However, the FBI is only allowed to work, ah, on certain cases. For example, in my city, if there was a— a burglary of two thousand dollars or three thousand dollars, the FBI couldn't work on that. The FBI, it has to be a certain amount of money, or it has to be somebody that they think ran away and ran into another state."

"I see, I see. That's federal." It was an odd word for the Tupamaro to use unless he had studied in the United States.

In the Montevideo jails, the prisoners joked about the fact
that both political factions had been to the United States.
The Tupamaros had gone as students on scholarships from
the American Field Service or Youth for Understanding;
the police had gone as guests of the IPA.

"That's right," Mitrione said. "Because they only come
into the picture on federal laws. They have nothing to do
with the protection of people. That's the Secret Service.
They have nothing, with that. That's the Treasury Department."

"How come that you can say that you really know
nothing about the CIA? You must know something."

"Well, let me say that I know the CIA is just like every
other organization that every other country has." It was an
accepted answer at IPA, where a student's questioning of
the CIA was met with horror stories about the Soviet
Union's KGB. "Every country has an organization like
that." Mitrione did not add, if he knew, that neither Brazil
nor Uruguay had had such an organization until the
United States helped to establish one. "But the interior
parts of the CIA, I am sorry I know nothing about it. And
I'm speaking sincerely."

"Well, I believe you. I think—"

"I'm speaking sincerely because our work, the four people here, our work is strictly on top of the table, everything, on top of the table."

"Um hmm. Um hmm. Though," the Tupamaro said
speculatively, "they must have some—"

"Well, I'm talking about my division," Mitrione said
quickly. "I don't know anything about anything else." He
added it so forcefully there could be little doubt that there
were other things to know. "If there is anything else, I'm
sure I don't know about it, and I—"

The Tupamaro talked over him. "We know some," he
said, and missed Mitrione's conclusion, which sounded later
on the tape like, "and I don't want to know about it."

"We have a pretty good CIA ourselves, you know," the
Tupamaro continued, with his modest, bragging laugh.

"Well, I would think so. I would think so. But we both know . . . we are smart enough to know that every country has its own intelligence-gathering unit."

"Well, I don't blame them."

"But I am not part of ours. That's what I am trying to impress on you."

"Well, we will have the last word. You know. But we have the means to know it."

"Sure." It was noncommittal, neither an admission nor an agreement.

"Ah, well, what do you think about us?"

It was a question every traveler from North America to South America was likely to hear. What do they think in the United States about Rio? Or Lima? Or Santiago? There were as many diplomatic answers as there were travelers. But the only truthful answer was, They don't think about you at all.

Now the Tupamaro was trying to put Mitrione at his ease, another technique that an IPA graduate might have handled better. "I mean I don't want to . . . just, you know, chat."

"Tupamaros?"

"Yes, you know pretty much about us. At least, you have been here for long. How long have you been here?"

"One year."

"One year?"

"Yes."

"Long enough."

Mitrione said in a sincere voice, "You do a pretty good job." He repeated it. "You do a pretty good job. You're well organized. You must have good leaders."

"Well, that I must tell you, and I hope *you* believe me"—the Tupamaro laughed—"we don't have leaders at all. We have people who is more important than others. But we don't have anything like being chiefs, you know. We don't receive orders."

"Is that right?"

"Yes, we discuss everything. You know, we are absolutely nonimportant, at least me, you know. But there are some here who are pretty important, and, you know, they are just names."

It was as romantic a view of the rebel movement as Mitrione's assurance that the FBI was a very open agency. As it happened, on Friday, August 7, the Montevideo police had captured thirty-eight Tupamaros, including its most important member, Raúl Sendic. All of the prisoners denied knowing the whereabouts of Mitrione, Dr. Fly, or the Brazilian diplomat.

Later, in jailhouse debates, some Tupamaros argued that the capture of Sendic and others from the top leadership had doomed Dan Mitrione. Not only did their arrest persuade Pacheco that his guer-illa war might be nearing an end, but it removed from the deliberations those more experienced Tupamaros who might have vetoed killing Mitrione.

Mitrione listened to the Tupamaro deny that his group had leaders. Then he said, "Uh huh. Well, it is very evident, to me, that your organization is a good organization. I would say that you have very good discipline."

"We try to."

"Because you have been very successful."

"We probably are the first Uruguayans that don't leave for tomorrow things that can be done today."

Mitrione said, "Sure, sure."

"And what do you think about what we think . . . politics and history?"

"Well, I don't know. I find it very hard to know, to know enough about . . . you have to live with the people a long time before you know what the real—the real problems are. I would say there are problems here, and I would say in some of your—your points you are right. But I don't think, I can't agree with the way you are doing it. I think that is a very common statement that many people would make."

Then, as the guards from MR-8 in Brazil had explained

the realities of their political life to Burke Elbrick, the Tupamaro tried to reason with Mitrione: "You know, I will tell you something just for you to be informed. Today —I mean, yes, today—because we read in the newspapers this morning—two newspapers have been censored, for ten days, you know, and that makes ... I don't know how many. You see?"

Mitrione was no Elbrick. The Tupamaro found no spot of common ground. "Two papers censored today?"

"Yes," said the Tupamaro, "because—"

"Two more?"

"Besides the other yesterday and the day before yesterday. They can't tell why, really. They inform something they shouldn't inform. And you know there are many political parties who are forbidden here. You know that."

"Sure." Then, more tentatively, "I suppose. I don't know much about it, but—"

"Well, you met Zina Fernandez. Did you?"

He was speaking of the army colonel who had been named Montevideo's chief of police. Romeo Zina Fernandez's tenure as chief was an unhappy one. First, a group of female Tupamaros escaped from prison through an unlocked door. Then police officials were exposed as having spent thousands of pesos on birthday parties and other amusements at their station houses. Worst of all, despite restraints on the press, the torture by the police was gradually becoming known, and the opposition in parliament was making it an issue. After the assassination of Moran Charquero, Pacheco forced Zina Fernandez to resign.

"Yes, yes, I met Zina Fernandez, sure."

"What did you think about him?"

"Well"—a slight laugh—"I knew him as a police chief and as a colonel in the military. That is the only thing I knew. I've never been to his house."

Slyly: "Or his parties?"

"No, I know nothing about his parties. What was he?"

"What was he?"

Mitrione meant which political party. It was hardly a germane question. Perhaps he had misunderstood his captor. "Yeah, was he a *Blanco* or a *Colorado*. Or—"

"I really don't know."

One more bond of ignorance. "I don't know either."

"But you know that he wasn't so honest, really."

"According to what I read, he wasn't."

"He was a chief of police, and I bet you are far more honest." Both sides could try a bit of discreet flattery. "I mean, I feel that you are, you know, engaged in something you believe and you are paid for and you just—"

"Well, you're right," said Mitrione, passing over any implication that he was a fanatic or a mercenary. "I feel strongly that way. I feel that if city government people can't be honest, how can you expect anyone else to be honest?" It was a popular theme at the police academy, where morality sometimes seemed defined entirely as the taking or not taking of bribes.

"We are fighting that," said the Tupamaro. "We hate to be violent, you know. You noticed the way we treat you after you were injured, the way we tried to bring you doctor. You have the doctor very fast."

"You were very kind. I must say that."

"There have been many doctors here to take care of you, and we have ... everything to avoid, you know, any surprises. And we really don't like to kill people at all but"— the Tupamaro gave an apologetic snort—"we will. And we do, when it's necessary, you see. We killed Moran Charquero with a smile, you know, because we knew that we were doing something some mates will, you know, will thank. Because he really was a tortu—I don't know, how do you say—tort-too-er."

"Torturer."

"*Si.* And there are many, and we will kill everyone of them, sooner or later, you know, and, ah—"

"I hope—let me say this—I hope you get the problems solved before you have to kill any more on either side." It was Mitrione's abstract public voice again, as though he were not at all involved. "That doesn't accomplish anything really."

"Ah, we hope it too. But we don't see it very soon."

"I hope so. Miracles have happened before."

"Hmm?" asked the Tupamaro.

"Miracles have happened before. The thing I say is that the Tupamaros—the MLN—are not people from Mars. You are all Uruguayans, and you are not strangers from outer space or enemies. You are Uruguayans that want to see your government do things. What you consider better, and that is why I say you ought to be able to get together, because it isn't a case like in the United States, where we do have a very definite separation between the black and the white."

"Yeah, that's a pretty rough problem, isn't it?"

Mitrione had spent two years in the environs of Washington, D. C., and his response was emphatic. "Oh, yes, my goodness! Is it a rough problem! But here you don't have that. Everybody is an Uruguayan, but the philosophy and the ideology is different, that's all."

"Yes. Yes. And it's pretty hard to do it without violence, you know. Pretty hard. I've been trying for long before I decided to work with violence, you know. I didn't care about my life. I cared more about hunger and exploitation. So we wouldn't care to die, really. We have been chosen for that, you know, because we really give our lives for something we feel is important. You see?"

Something told the Tupamaro to drop his attempts at conversion and get back to the questioning, this time about the connection between the Policia Militar and the Department of Political and Social Order. "So when you were working with the PM there in Brazil, ah, what kind of relations do they have with the DOPS?"

"With the DOPS?"

"Yes."

"Oh, I think the DOPS back in those days—I didn't know too much—DOPS are the political police, right?"

"Yes."

(Nine months later, Senator Frank Church's subcommittee asked Ted Brown about OBAN, Operation Bandeirantes. "I have heard that expression," said the chief Public Safety adviser in Brazil, "and it slips my mind right at the moment what it is.")

Mitrione said, "Yeah. Um, I think one of the problems that they had was the political police—the DOPS—were more ... mostly political appointments, and the military police were, you know, people who came up from the ranks, came in and they were—"

"Disciplined?"

"Yeah, like army, you know. Like military. I had very little to do with DOPS. I didn't know much about them."

"Well, I understand that the training—the training to the military police now is mainly against guerrillas, because, you know, that's the main problem now."

"Well," Mitrione sounded insistent about clearing himself at least of the worst excesses of the era of OBAN and DOPS, "back in those days we didn't do that, because guerrilla problems were not the news—the thing—then. All we trained for was how to handle, ah, ah, labor strikes, you know, labor problems and, ah, maybe demonstrations of people and how to use humane methods and how not to hurt anybody if you could help it. And how to be ... how to fight if you had to, too. You know—"

"Yes." The Tupamaro sounded knowing. "We read all those documents you sent to the police department in Latin America, you know."

"Ah, yeah. Yeah, well, they're changing now. You know that."

The Tupamaro laughed again in the way that suggested he was embarrassed to know things that Mitrione wasn't admitting. "We've been reading special means on, you know, interrogation. That's very interesting." He paused. "And when are you planning to retire, I mean, if—if everything runs well and we can go out free and all that? Go back to family?"

Mitrione answered with conviction. "Well, if I go back to my family, I'd like to gather up my family and finish my days in my country."

"Yeah." The Tupamaro seemed to understand what the last week had meant. "That's pretty rough."

"As quickly as possible."

"We hope it too. We been . . . and, uh, you go to Indiana?"

"Yes, well." Mitrione seemed to mull his options at the age of fifty. "Yes, I'd have to go to Indiana. That's my home."

"What about the universitarians there in Indiana?"

"University?"

"Yes."

"They're having their problems too. They're having demonstrations, and the hippies—"

The Tupamaro snorted again. Revolutionaries of any country seldom approved of the flower children.

"And the Yippies," Mitrione continued, "and the Students for a Democratic Society, and—"

"Weathermen?"

"Weathermen. But they're not all wrong. They're not all wrong. They have some good ideas too."

"Do you think?"

"Yes, I'm sure. There are a lot of smart people there. They're not all dummies. I think some of them are lazy." Mitrione's prejudices died hard, even in a *carcel do pueblo,* a people's prison. "But I think some of them have some ideas, and I think the older people ought to listen to them a little more."

"Yes, that I understand," the Tupamaro said. "They made enough noise to be listened to, at least."

"Yeah, well. Well, just like you said a while ago. They tried to talk but you finally had to resort to violence because nobody would listen."

"Have you seen *Zabriskie Point,* the film?" The

Tupamaro referred to Michelangelo Antonioni's vision of youthful disaffection in California's Death Valley.

"No. I haven't been to a film here, a movie, in . . . I think the last one I saw was *Funny Girl* about—a long time ago."

"Pretty good movie."

"Very good film," Mitrione said heartily.

"Yes," the Tupamaro agreed with no enthusiasm.

"What's *Zabriskie Point* about?"

"Well, about violence in the States."

"Is it?"

"Yes."

"Oh, boy," said Mitrione.

"It's pretty interesting."

"Well, I stay home with the children and the family. I don't go out too much at night. Sometimes we have to go to cocktail parties, that type of thing."

The Tupamaro snorted, this time sympathetically.

"Most of the time we're—I'm home with the family."

"A lot of diplomatic work?"

"Not too much, not too much."

"Have you met the president?"

"Of what? Of—of Uruguay?"

"Yes."

"No, no I haven't."

"You should. Nice guy." The Tupamaro's deprecating laugh took in President Pacheco.

"I never had the pleasure."

"Pleasure? I would like to meet him too. Under the same circumstances I met you. Or even worse, really. I don't feel that . . . bad about him, really, but about what he's doing, you know. That's a nice talk. I mean, I think you are very smart. You chose the best way of dealing with us, you know. You know you are, really, under our power and can't do anything so—"

"I'm strictly at your mercy," Mitrione said, as though he were saying, I'm entirely at your service. "Really. And I understand that."

"Well, it's not mercy. Well, I don't know the word in English, but I'd translate it . . . I wouldn't call it mercy, you know. It depends on your government, and the pressure it can do, and ours—our government—and . . . But, uh, you know your neighbor." He meant Dias Gomide. "He makes a little more noise."

Mitrione said, "Well, the only thing I regret all about this, I—I—I don't like the thing and that is too many innocent people suffer." His voice came strong and indignant. "My wife and children at home, there's no reason for them to be suffering."

The Tupamaro now sounded halting and very young. "I—I—I have wife and children too. But you know, you do it for money and I don't. You even said it before. You choose your work, and the States choose a political way to do things, and you are engaged with your country, and so you are under your own, you know, law."

"Um," said Mitrione.

"I'm sorry about them too. I'm sorry about other families of our friends who are in prison, being tortured or killed."

"Well, that's true too," said Mitrione.

"There are many, really. Many innocent people have to suffer. But do you know that about one million boys and girls under five years die every year in Latin America?"

"Of hunger?"

"Yes, sir! And that is not a way of control, birth control, you know."

"No."

"And how do you feel about other guerrilla movements? You know, we don't work all the same way. You have seen that."

"Well, every one of them has to work according to his surroundings. Whatever he can work best. From what I have read, I think the Tupamaros are . . . a little smarter than some of the others because the Tupamaros don't kill unless they have to. I think they shoot and then ask questions later."

"Well, you know"—with a laugh—"what happens probably, ah, I feel a little the way you feel. But it's the conditions there are different than here. You know the Uruguayans—and Uruguay—has a different history than other countries."

"Oh, I'm sure that's true."

"Violence in Brazil is harder than in Uruguay. Or in Bolivia or in Guatemala. You know."

"It's accepted, isn't it?"

(Not much later, José Yglesias, the novelist, was in Rio to interview Brazilians for a magazine article. One historically minded Brazilian told him, "I wonder if you know that all this—these tortures, the death penalty for subversive acts, the terrorism of the underground groups—is new to our country? We have had coups and coups but they have never involved this.")

"Yes," said the Tupamaro, "I feel human life is cheaper than here. So—"

"Yeah, yeah."

"So—"

"In other words," Mitrione yawned. "Excuse me. Uruguayans, I am sure, are different."

"But they torture here too. Brazil is horrible, you know. I would kill—I would *like* to kill Monsieur Fleury, you know. Fleury, chief of—"

"Of the police there? Chief of police?" They were fencing once again. The Tupamaro's question could not have been so careless as he tried to make it, and though Fleury operated out of São Paulo, his exploits were well known to men far less involved than Mitrione in Latin America's police campaign against guerrillas.

"No, you know they have this special—"

There had been a third person, perhaps a guard, in the cell as Mitrione was being interrogated. Now he prompted in a whisper that the Tupamaro and Mitrione both ignored. "Death Squad."

"What is his name?" Mitrione asked.

"Flowry. Floo-ree. I don't know how they pronounce it."

"I don't know either. In Brazil? In Rio? In Brasília?"

"All I know is Brazil. He has been here, teaching, too. About four or five months ago."

"Oh, yeah?"

"Yes. You know, the Death Squad or something."

"Oh, yeah."

"He's been here. In Punta del Este. We couldn't meet him." He laughed.

Mitrione, who had chuckled, said, "But you met me, huh?"

"Yes. All—we've been doing everything to meet you. Not myself, I didn't know who you were until you told me and the mates told me. Yesterday morning we met you really." It may be that Mitrione was transferred for safe-keeping to a different cell. "Because we don't have any information we don't need to have, so we can't talk too much. But that's the way it works. But you should talk more than me."

"Can I have another glass of water, please?"

"Yes." When the water was fetched, Mitrione took a deep swallow and sighed.

The Tupamaro asked, "What do you think is going to happen with all Latin America?"

"Well," said Mitrione, "Latin America is going to be all right. I don't care. I don't know how long it is going to take. But there are people here that love life, there are people in every country that love life. Governments have problems, but some day it's going to be solved. You mark my words."

"It is." From the Tupamaro, it was a vow.

"It's going to be solved. It's going to be solved. All these buildings and all these stores and all these schools and foot-ball fields are not accidents. They were built by intelligent people. They're not going to be destroyed overnight."

"No. We hope not."

"No, I *know* they're not. It's just going to be a case of how long it is going to take. Some countries will take longer than others."

"You know, there are some people who love very much the things they have, and they have very much, and they have too many things, though. Then it's very difficult to take them out, you know."

"This is true. This is true. That's one of the problems in Latin America."

"You know, there are a few people who are holding so many interests, you know: The Bank of America, the First National City Bank, and the Manhattan—the Chase Manhattan Bank. You know they are very strong."

The guard had filled Mitrione's cup again. He said, "Thank you," and took another swallow.

"They are really very strong," the Tupamaro repeated.

"This is something that's been going on for hundreds of years. It isn't just—"

"Yes. But we have to finish it."

"What I mean is, something that's been old. It isn't something that's just started."

"Will you excuse me a minute?" The Tupamaro stepped away. When he came back, he said, "Well, I have to do some other work now, so we'll keep talking later." They had been speaking together for half an hour. "All right?"

Mitrione said, "All right. Fine."

These were the last words his family heard from him, and they heard them many days after his death.

CHAPTER

10

AT 4:25 A.M. on Monday, August 10, 1970, Dan Mitrione's body was found on the back seat of a stolen 1948 Buick convertible. He had been bound and gagged and shot twice in the head.

At 9:00 A.M., President Pacheco decreed a period of national mourning for Mitrione.

At 11:30 A.M., the Uruguayan General Assembly ended a discussion of individual rights and reconvened ninety minutes later to approve extensions of Pacheco's executive power.

At 5:15 P.M., seventy-six of the 106 members of the General Assembly voted to waive temporarily the rights guaranteed under Article 31 of Uruguay's Constitution. Declaring a state of emergency, the assembly suspended for twenty days the rights of property, assembly, personal liberty, and free expression.

The killing of Mitrione had allowed Pacheco and his security forces to assume dictatorial powers over Uruguay. The government now had 14,000 troops and policemen on the streets searching for Dr. Fly and Dias Gomide.

The extinction of Uruguay's democracy had been threatening for two years. One man who understood that his country would never be the same was Alejandro Otero.

He was no longer the leading specialist in combating the Tupamaros, having been replaced months before, when the CIA and the U. S. police advisers had turned to harsher measures and sterner men. Otero still rankled from the indignity of being replaced.

Artur Aymoré, a Brazilian journalist, had come to Montevideo to report on Dias Gomide's kidnapping for the *Jornal do Brasil.* From informants, Aymoré also had been gathering material about the Uruguayan police and their handling of the Tupamaros. He had learned that Dan Mitrione had bestowed technical equipment on the security police; that the United States had introduced a system of nationwide identification cards, like those in Brazil; that torture had become routine at the Montevideo *jefatura.*

But none of that was why Aymoré had been sent to Uruguay. His assignment was to report on the prolonged holding of Dias Gomides, for the Brazilian people were incensed at the heartlessness of the Pacheco government in not agreeing to the terms that would free their consul. (The consul's wife ultimately raised a quarter of a million dollars; and after six and a half months in captivity, Dias Gomide was released, on February 21, 1971.)

But the kidnapping story began to slow down after Mitrione's body was found; and Aymoré asked one of his contacts to put him in touch with a mutual friend, Alejandro Otero, so he could learn more about the U. S. police advisory program. Otero had been teaching at Montevideo's police academy, and a meeting was arranged in his office. To this foreign reporter from a distant newspaper, Otero confided all of his resentments.

Otero began by granting that in conducting an interrogation, the police were justified in many deceptions. It was a duel of wits, and the policeman's weapons included lies and tricks; but the U. S. advisers, especially Mitrione, had introduced scientific methods of torture that violated Otero's philosophy of life. The advisers advocated psychological torture, Otero told Aymoré, to create despair. In the next room, they would play tapes of women and children screaming and tell the prisoner that it was his family being tortured. They used electrical shocks under the fingernails, on the genitals. He told Aymoré about his friend, the woman who had been tortured, and about the way Mitrione ignored his protests. Mitrione had been very hard in his methods, Otero said.

Aymoré stood up, ready to go off to file his story. "One last thing," Otero said. "I must not appear in your story." Aymoré agreed. He sent out a story quoting "police sources," but he added a memorandum to let his editors know where the accusations against Mitrione had come from. When Aymoré made his next routine call to the newspaper, his editor got on the line: "We can't publish this without Otero's name."

Aymoré called Otero and explained the problem. "If anything happens," Otero said, "you have to tell them that I didn't talk with you. I could lose my job."

How Otero thought his name might be used without compromising him was hard to understand. The *Journal do Brasil* played the story conservatively on an inside page, but such damning accusations could not be buried.

The day after Aymoré's story appeared in Rio, two Uruguayan intelligence officers and an agent from Interpol came to his hotel with written authority to question him. Aymoré was not in his room at the time; when he learned of the visit, he spoke with the Brazilian ambassador, who promised him diplomatic protection but advised him to go willingly to the police.

Aymoré and a colleague, Alberto Kolecza, presented themselves at the prison. They were locked in a small cell with no seats, where they remained for four hours. Kolecza was the first to be led away for questioning. Then Aymoré was called in.

"Why am I here?" he asked.

The chief of the three-man unit replied, "We are conducting an investigation to determine whether Otero said what your newspaper reported. Kolecza has told us everything."

Aymoré knew that much was a bluff; he had not told Kolecza anything.

They put a piece of paper in front of Aymoré and told him to sign it unread. He refused. "I want to read it. I might sign it if I can read it."

The chief tore up the statement.

Aymoré, small but bearlike, had his country's embassy behind him, as well as one of the continent's major newspapers. Still, he was worried. It appeared that Otero was not denying having talked with him, only that he had criticized Mitrione.

"Where and when did you speak with Otero?" the chief asked.

Aymoré answered that although he had talked with him, he could not say where or who had arranged the interview.

The chief asked Aymoré about his own political philosophy and how he regarded the Tupamaros. Aymoré responded in monosyllables. The chief grew angry and warned Aymoré that he would suffer the repercussions of his silence. For two hours, the police repeated the same questions.

At 4 P.M., Aymoré was released. At 7 P.M., the Brazilian ambassador informed him that Uruguay had declared him *persona non grata.* He suggested that Aymoré stay at the embassy until a flight could be arranged. Aymoré slept on a couch and flew to Rio at 6 A.M.

Being home did not end his difficulties. His editor at *Jornal do Brasil,* Alberto Dines, called him in to say that the U. S. embassy was bringing immense pressure on the newspaper to fire him.

Dines asked, "Aymoré, do you promise me that what you wrote is true?"

"It's true."

The *Jornal do Brasil* resisted the embassy's demand, and Aymoré kept his job.

In Washington, Byron Engle may have reasonably expected to see Dan Mitrione transformed into a martyr. The case met all the classic requirements: there was a victim; Engle's men got possession of the corpse; other policemen paraded Mitrione's coffin through the streets of Indiana; there had been a public burial; commemorative services were scheduled; even *The New York Times* had joined the cause with an editorial calling Mitrione's killing "absurd" and accusing the Tupamaros of using the techniques of Hitler. Consequently, Engle was taken aback by Aymoré's news story and the treatment of the entire affair in the *Jornal do Brasil.* Engle offered a tale of conspiracy to explain the situation: "The three Brazilian reporters in Montevideo all denied filing that story. We found out later that it was slipped into the paper by someone in the composing room at the *Jornal do Brasil.*"

In Uruguay, the war with the Tupamaros intensified after Mitrione's murder. The rebels blew up the Carrasco bowling alley patronized by the U. S. community. On one night-club wall they scrawled their most pungent slogan: *O Bailan Todos O No Baila Nadie*—Everyone dances or no one dances.

On January 8, 1971, Tupamaros snatched the British ambassador, Geoffrey Jackson, who had been disdainful of his personal security. He paid for his hauteur with eight months in an underground cell. At the U. S. embassy, the political staff watched with fascination when an agent from the British secret service arrived and set to work to free Jackson. Then, early in September of 1971, more than one hundred Tupamaros made use of an old fifty-yard tunnel, broke out of Punta Carretas prison, and escaped through a neighboring house.

At first, journalists treated the incident as one more example of the incompetence of Uruguay's police. When the Tupamaros released Jackson, however, it began to look as

though the kind of trade that Pacheco had refused for Dan
Mitrione had been accomplished covertly on behalf of the
British ambassador. Certainly it was evident that the career
of the colonel responsible for prison security had not
suffered from the jailbreak. He was promoted to the job of
chief aide to General Gregorio Alvarez, one of the four
leaders of Uruguay's powerful emerging junta.

In Richmond, Ray Mitrione read of the jailbreak
and noticed that one of the occupants of the house through
which the Tupamaros escaped was named Billy Rial.

Since Ray first received a tape of the interrogation between his brother and the English-speaking Tupamaro, he
had been playing it over and over, listening for clues. This
obsession went on so long that his family urged him, for his
own sake, to give it up.

To Ray, the voice on the tape sounded like that of the
young Uruguayan who had called on him at Kessler's
Sporting Goods. Now he saw Billy Rial's name in print,
connected with the Tupamaros in that suspicious way, and
he called Washington to tell them the whole story.

In Montevideo, Billy Rial, a convert to the Church of
Latter Day Saints, was arrested and jailed. The Montevideo
police granted that although Mormons were almost never
revolutionaries, possibly Rial was an exception. But Ray
had been mistaken about the voice he heard interrogating
his brother. Most likely, the voice belonged to a Tupamaro
named Blanco Katras, who had studied in the United States
and was killed in a Uruguayan police raid in April 1972.

In March of 1971, Dr. Claude Fly suffered a heart
attack in his underground hiding place. The Tupamaros
first took him to one of their sympathizers, a heart surgeon,
who examined him and insisted that he be sent immediately
to a hospital.

Dr. Fly was left outside an emergency room at the British Hospital with a sheaf of electrocardiograms and a prescription for suggested treatment. Those instructions were clearly expert, and the hospital staff followed them. Dr. Fly survived and returned home to Colorado.

By tracing the machine that matched the EKG graph paper, U. S. investigators were able to track down Dr. Jorge Dubra, the Uruguayan heart specialist who had examined Dr. Fly. Dr. Dubra was arrested and imprisoned.

Morris Zimmelman, an elderly U. S. businessman in Montevideo, was shocked by the news, because that same Dr. Dubra had pulled him through his own heart episode. You never could tell, Zimmelman and his wife agreed, just who those Tupamaros were. But like most of the U. S. community, they were impressed by the skill of the intelligence officers from Washington. If they had not been able to save Mitrione's life, at least they had caught the man who had saved Dr. Fly's.

In Brazil, the kidnapping of Burke Elbrick had gone so successfully that the rebels employed the same tactic on three more occasions. In June 1970, while Fernando Gabeira was in prison on Rio's Ilha Grande, a broadcast was interrupted by a news bulletin announcing that Germany's ambassador to Brazil had been seized by rebels who were demanding the release of forty prisoners.

Within five minutes, prison guards stormed through the cells and stripped away all radios. One prisoner managed to hide his under a pillow, and he lay awake all night waiting for the next bulletin.

In that prison alone were 120 political prisoners. They debated until dawn about which of them would be on the list. Fernando expected to be one of the names. Most of the other prisoners were serving shorter sentences and could look forward to being released. Without a prisoner exchange, Fernando had no hope at all.

No one slept. At the first light, the prisoner with the radio shouted out four names, and after each name he yelled, "Good-bye!"

Then he cried, "Fernando Gabeira! Good-bye!"

Even the sound of his name could not make Fernando rejoice. He knew how many obstacles stood between him and freedom. For example, the police could find the house where the ambassador was being held. It had happened to him.

Within half an hour, the police rounded up the forty prisoners. While they were having their hair cut, the police confiscated their wrist watches and any other personal property. With only the clothes they wore, they were taken to a cell at CODI.

When Fernando's turn came for a final interrogation, he was questioned about a suspected escape plan from Ilha Grande. There was no plan. However, because the guards decided to give him a few last electrical shocks, Fernando made up a story that would satisfy them.

It was nearly over. The police blindfolded the prisoners and placed them in a circle around an outside courtyard. As one man called out a prisoner's name, several policemen fired into the air. Another policeman moaned and gasped as though in the agonies of death. The supposed victim spoke up loudly enough for the others to know that this was only a mock execution, one final harassment. They were then herded back inside into a tank of water, where they were forced to shave with razors that gave them electrical shocks. With that, the police ran out of things to do.

At 9 A.M. on June 16, 1970, Fernando and the others were taken to the airport in police cars. They waited on an air-force base for six hours while the authorities took their pictures and fingerprints. At 3 P.M., on a jet from Varig, Brazil's national airline, they left for Algiers.

Colonel Fontenel, a particularly vicious torturer, made the flight with them. On the journey, he told jokes and recalled episodes from their life in prison together. Fernando thought, It is all very Brazilian.

The plane arrived in Algiers at 5 P.M. Journalists were waiting, along with a crowd sympathetic to the rebels. The Brazilian guards had expected to go shopping with the U. S. dollars they had been issued for the flight, but the crowd's hostility kept them aboard the plane until it made the return flight to Rio. This hostility they could not understand. After all, one policeman told the prisoners, nothing we ever did to you was personal.

When revolutionaries seized the Swiss ambassador on December 3, 1970, it seemed fitting that one of the hostages they should demand for his release was the son of a Swiss father, Jean Marc Von der Weid. It was Christmas Eve before word of the trade reached Jean Marc, and then the news came from a prison official who was suddenly solicitous of Jean Marc's well-being.

"We don't want anyone to be forced to go," the guard said. "If you want to stay, you can stay."

In prison, Jean Marc had been judged a hopeless agitator, and after eleven terms in solitary confinement, he had been transferred from the Isle of Flowers to an air-force base at Rio's Galeão Airport. Now João Paulo Moreira Burnier, the base commander, called for him. This was some months before Burnier was exposed for his role in the killings of the 1968 riots.

"If it were my choice," Burnier said, "you'd all be shot. I don't give a damn about the Swiss ambassador. But let me tell you, if he's killed, I guarantee you that you'll be killed." By then it was a more menacing threat than it would have been when Fernando Gabeira was awaiting word of his exchange. In the interval, Dan Mitrione had been executed.

Negotiations limped forward into the new year. The Brazilian government was haggling over some of the seventy names on the list, and the Swiss were not pressing as hard for their ambassador as the Germans had done. Throughout his days of waiting, Jean Marc was visited regularly by military men trying to persuade him to refuse to leave Brazil. They played on his patriotism. An air-force major named Silva, one of the worst torturers, now came to say that, after all, he and Jean Marc were both nationalists first.

Finally, on the eve of the exchange, a colonel arrived claiming to represent President Emílio Médici, an intractable army general who had replaced Costa e Silva.

"I can't convince you that the government is good," the colonel said. "But if you refuse to leave, you'll be released in one year and back in school and free to resume your protests."

"The students would see it as a vote of confidence in the government," Jean Marc said.

The colonel had an answer for that: "You can write a short letter giving your reasons, which we'll release later."

"No, no matter what I said, it would appear that I trusted this government."

"All negotiations are ended," the colonel said. On his departure, an air-force torturer came into Jean Marc's cell and made a few desultory threats. Jean Marc then composed a statement, as the military had requested. He wrote: "Freedom is the most important thing for a person or a society. I am leaving Brazil for my freedom, but I will continue to fight for the freedom of my nation."

Amnesty International, an organization formed in London to protest the torture of political prisoners, launched a campaign to free Marcos Arruda from prison. This was accomplished in February 1971, when he was abruptly released, pending his trial. On his attorney's advice, Marcos left the country. He was tried in absentia, and found innocent of subversion.

Later that year, sponsored by Catholics in the United

States, Marcos applied to the Vatican for an audience with the Pope. Marcos regarded himself the spokesman for the thousands of other Brazilian victims who had not been as fortunate as he. Pope Paul sent Marcos a note assuring him that through his sufferings, he was becoming more like Christ. Bear your sufferings gladly, the Pope added.

In Brasília, President Médici contacted a distant relative of Marcos's, to whom he complained that Marcos was damaging the image of Brazil. Tell that young man, the president said, that if he ever—ever—tries to come back to Brazil, he won't get out of the airport alive.

Throughout the early seventies, liberals in the Uruguayan Senate had tried to form a united front. When this attempt failed and the dictatorship became ever more oppressive, they were forced to flee, usually to Buenos Aires. There the leaders were murdered by Death Squads operating unhindered by Argentina's police.

Before the Tupamaros were exterminated and Uruguay's democracy snuffed out, Nelson Bardesio was kidnapped by the rebels and compelled to tell his story. He disappeared on February 24, 1972; and in a series of interviews held underground, he confessed to police bombings and described the link between the police and military in Uruguay and Argentina. *Marcha*, before it was finally suppressed, printed a transcript of his statements.

The Tupamaros had deleted names of Bardesio's colleagues, intending to conduct their own investigation and mete out their own justice. Even with the substitutions of *X* for the names of police and military officers, Bardesio's confession confirmed that Uruguayan Death Squads had been bombing and strafing the houses of lawyers and journalists suspected of being sympathetic to the Tupamaros. He also cleared up the mystery surrounding the disappearance of Héctor Castagnetto, a student whose two brothers were Tupamaros.

"I arrived at the house just in time," Bardesio's statement read. "I saw them put Castagnetto, who was blindfolded, in X's auto [Bardesio provided a description, which the Tupamaros deleted] that had a broken windshield and belonged to the Ministry of the Interior. Castagnetto and the two functionaries of Department 4 sat in the back, X drove with José [an official of the Interior Ministry] beside him. . . . X got into my auto. . . . The three autos then went to the harbor, to the entrance beside the central railway station. I believe this is the entrance for the Rowing Club. X's auto turned in and we turned back. I took X to Department 5 and went to the house of a friendly couple on Canelones Street, where I then lived. One hour later, around 2 A.M., X phoned me to tell me the house on Araucana Street was to be 'cleaned out' because it would be searched by the police because of a neighbor's complaint, and also if I might keep some parcels that they didn't have any place to keep. X came to take me with his auto, and we went to the corner of Rambla and Araucana streets, where we met a small lorry normally used by the two functionaries trained in Brazil. In the lorry there were two people I didn't know and who were part of José's team. X told me to keep absolutely secret about them. They took me in the lorry to my studio, where I put the two parcels and box taken from the house on Araucana Street. . . . I later opened the two parcels and found machine guns, .45 caliber, without brands or numbers [they were filed clean] and some explosives. These were colored cubes with a place for a detonator in one of the extremities. They were enclosed with sheets of paper on which was written CCT [Command to Chase the Tupamaros]. . . . I understand that Castagnetto was interrogated and tortured in the house on Araucana Street and later murdered and thrown into the river. This final part of the operation was carried out by the two functionaries who went with him into the harbor."

Later, Bardesio disappeared entirely. He was first reported in Canada; but when questions were raised about the propriety of giving him sanctuary, he was sent elsewhere, apparently to Panama.

The Tupamaros were even more interested in the whereabouts of Héctor Amodio Perez. Amodio had ranked high in the rebel movement; but when his prominence as a leader was challenged, he had seemed to act from spite, providing the police with the locations of thirty Tupamaro hideouts. Raúl Sendic had escaped once from Montevideo's sievelike prison. Now he was captured again and shot through both cheeks. Sendic lived, but his jaw was destroyed.

In the spring of 1972, a young Uruguayan returned from studying law in Buenos Aires and found life in Montevideo hellish. Families were reduced to whispering to each other in their own homes. Everyone was taken for being a spy. The student himself knew two Tupamaros, reason enough for his being arrested and confined to an army jail.

There, like prisoners in Brazil, he was appalled to find doctors—young doctors, doctors his own age—cooperating in the torture. They asked him whether he was asthmatic, to know whether to use electricity on him or near-drownings in water. They measured his blood pressure to see whether he could bear more pain. They gave him stimulants to permit the torture to go forward. It was as though the police, the soldiers, and the doctors were all crazed. "I torture you," one army officer shouted at him. "Someday you will kill me! But I don't care!"

The doctors miscalculated, and the student had to be sent to Montevideo's central military hospital to recuperate. The sheets were stamped U. S. NAVY. His robe, the nicest robe he had ever worn, was dark-blue terry cloth and marked U.S. MEDICAL DOCTOR.

Back in prison, the young man was roused one day by a great din in the passageway. Guards were rushing by, excited and jubilant. One stopped long enough to tell him:

"Hey! We got one of you, and he was in our own ranks!"
The traitor was Subcommissioner Benítez.

At the *jefatura*, the other Uruguayan officers suddenly recalled peculiar episodes with Benítez. For all his cursing and threats, he had never managed to shoot a Tupamaro; in fact, on one raid, he had claimed that his weapon jammed.

During that same period, Benítez had been supplying the Tupamaros with information about the police. In the course of a police raid, copies of Benítez's notes were found. Knowing everything could be traced to him, Benítez sought out a judge and threw himself on the court's mercy. He was jailed and beaten nearly to death.

Exiled in Switzerland, Marcos Arruda kept alert for news of his former jailers. One officer who had tortured him was a captain named Dalmo Cirillo. Late in 1975, Marcos read in the newspapers that a metal worker had been killed in the torture rooms on Rua Totoya. One of the men implicated in the death was Cirillo, who had recently been promoted to the rank of lieutenant colonel.

Two of Jean Marc Von der Weid's chief torturers had also met with rewards and professional recognition. Clemente Monteiro, the graduate of U. S. training in Panama who had overseen torture on the Isle of Flowers, was named commander of the National Police Academy in Brasília. Under Monteiro's leadership, that academy, which had been subsidized by U. S. funds, was enlarged to train police cadets from other Latin American nations.

Alfredo Poeck, the navy officer who found his vocation during his training at Fort Bragg, left the Isle of Flowers to accept a promotion with SNI, the national intelligence service established by General Golbery after the 1964 coup. Poeck's new work gratified him, and he hoped to help SNI achieve the high standards of its U. S. counterpart, which he still felt had no peer throughout the world.

Poeck told SNI recruits that the most important quality in a good intelligence officer was natural curiosity; one should never be satisfied. As an instructor in propaganda analysis, Poeck now had access to the dossiers on Brazil's guerrillas, and he informed his students that a high percentage of the rebels came from parents who were legally separated, Brazil's compromise with divorce. Fully 85 percent of the revolutionaries, according to Poeck, suffered from serious psychological problems.

When outsiders asked about his earlier career, Poeck said at first that it was shameful the way honest military men could be besmirched for simply doing their duty. Worse yet, he added, he himself was sometimes confused with a Commander Alfredo who had worked at CENIMAR some years ago and called himself Mike.

If his questioner did not seem to believe this story of mistaken identity or asked where this other Alfredo was living, Poeck grew solemn. It would be a great unkindness to track him down, Poeck said. He had been a top-notch pilot in his day, a real daredevil, but now he was very sick. They say it's cancer—a tumor—and to ask him to speak about the past would only be to remind him that he was not the man he once was.

In the spring of 1973, a member of Brazil's tame opposition party sought out U. S. Senator James G. Abourezk of South Dakota in his Washington office. Under a pledge of secrecy, the Brazilian poured out grisly stories of torture and laid out fragmentary but persuasive evidence that the United States was implicated in it.

Since his election to the Senate, Abourezk had been seeking an issue, a crusade, and he now began looking into the Office of Public Safety. He was not its first critic, only its most determined one. As early as 1966, Senator J. William

Fulbright had expressed doubts about the program, but he had caused no particular alarm at OPS. Fulbright was emerging as a critic of the Vietnam war; and among the police advisers who supported the U. S. intervention, that position alone was enough to discredit him.

During his years as president, Lyndon Johnson had not taken a stand on OPS. Officers at the police academy attributed this to his two preoccupations, the Vietnam war and his Great Society, and to the absence of much attack against the police program. It was not crucial that he show support at that time.

During Nixon's first term in office, the president told Byron Engle that the advisory program was a good one, and in good hands. In 1971, while Brazil's third military president, General Médici, was visiting Washington, Nixon had summed up his Latin American policy by praising Brazil as a model for the continent. By the time the drum-roll of accusations began against OPS, however, Nixon was expending his energies on a burglary at the Watergate apartments.

John Hannah, the U. S. AID director, supported OPS in a letter to Congressman Otto Passman. But Hannah had been president of Michigan State University at the time the university took on secret CIA contracts for advisory work in South Vietnam, and that connection undercut his authority with the Senate's liberals.

Overseas, the U. S. police advisers waited for a high-ranking government official to stand up for them. None ever did. The CIA, adroit at lobbying for itself, let OPS go down without a struggle. When Senator Abourezk publicized the Texas bomb school, the agency cut its losses rather than wage a campaign that might have led to Congressional hearings.

In 1974, the CIA was still months away from the forth-coming barrage of leaks and charges and investigations that would devastate its reputation. "You must believe that we are honorable men," CIA director Richard Helms once told the Washington press corps, and in the main they believed him.

When OPS was abolished, its funds cut off, and the Car Barn doors locked, some advisers retired entirely from government service. Some entered into private security work. Jack Goin, for example, opened a Washington office called Public Safety Services, Inc. Other, better-connected men made an easy transition to the Drug Enforcement Agency, which put them back in touch with police overseas.

Many advisers had never served in a country where torture was the accepted means of extracting information. Others, although stationed in Brazil or Uruguay, had never taken part in a torture session. Some knew what went on; others claimed ignorance. But whatever their background, in the years following Mitrione's murder, they found themselves publicly soiled, disavowed by their government, and usually out of a job.

An early omen that three decades of preferential treatment were ending for the CIA was the word out of Paris that Philip Agee was writing a book. While at his last post in Mexico City, Agee had swung far to the political Left. He divorced his wife, a serious step for a Catholic; he left the CIA, equally serious for a man nearing forty with no training except in dirty tricks; and he began his memoirs, most serious of all for a man who valued his life.

Exercising the prudence he had been taught in Langley, Agee was able to finish an immensely detailed reconstruction of his years with the CIA. The very documentation— or the prospect of long legal battles with the agency— discouraged most U. S. publishers. But Agee's story had two happy endings. The book was published with great success in London and then New York. And in Paris he met Angela Camargo Seixas, who came to live with him.

. . .

In July 1970, Angela's guard had told her that if she
would sign a confession they had prepared, she would be
brought before a three-man military court. Although Angela had not told them anything, she signed the paper just
the same. Tell about the torture, the guards warned her,
and you will be back here with us.

The judge she faced was sympathetic. One of Angela's
school friends was close to his son. Even after she had told
the judge about the torture, when she returned to prison
to await the next step she was not molested.

The trial itself came a full year later at the Vila Militar.
Angela was found guilty of violating one article of an
institutional act and was sentenced to two years and one
month. Both prosecution and defense filed appeals. By the
time the Military Supreme Court set her sentence at twelve
months, she had already served thirty.

Upon her release, she tried to live in Brazil and exercise
the freedom that had been promised Jean Marc Von der
Weid if he refused to go abroad. Instead, the police followed her everywhere, and she saw that she was only
compromising anyone she met.

Angela went to Paris to study economics at the Sor-
bonne. Early in September 1972, she attended a party of
mostly Frenchmen and Brazilians. One of the guests was
Philip Agee, then at the emotional and financial nadirs of
his life.

When Agee's book was finally published, his dedication
read: To Angela Camargo Seixas and her comrades in Latin
America struggling for social justice, national dignity and
peace.

Burke Elbrick, in retirement, attended the funeral of
Cleo A. Noel, Jr., an ambassador killed in the Sudan with
his counsellor and another diplomat. After Richard Nixon
had made a statement that the United States would not

succumb to blackmail, the terrorists had shot the three men to death with machine guns.

Watching Noel's coffin being carried out of Washington's National Presbyterian Church, Elbrick thought, There, but for the grace of God . . .

Upon the election of Richard Nixon as president, Lincoln Gordon left his post at the State Department and served for a time as president of Johns Hopkins University, where he sometimes was badgered by the students about his role in burdening Brazil with a military dictatorship. Gordon countered by pointing to an economic boom that Brazil enjoyed for several years. The students rebutted with statistics proving that the prosperity had come at the expense of the nation's poor: during the first ten years of the dictatorship, real wages declined by 55 percent. Gordon then argued that since the military had held power only since 1964, it was too early to assess its rule. The dictatorship tortured political dissidents, true, but at least it was not a Communist regime.

Throughout the seventies, tales of torture coming out of Brazil's prisons had not changed greatly; and the relevance of Lincoln Gordon's last defense was considerably diminished during the first two months of President Jimmy Carter's administration, when the police in São Paulo arrested 28,304 persons "on suspicion."

Occasionally, a commander whose excesses were too flagrant was asked to retire. That happened in the aftermath of the death in prison of a journalist, Vladimir Herzog. The outcome was different, however, for the commander responsible for troops who tortured a U. S. clergyman named Fred Morris. Eighteen months after Morris was released, the commander was promoted to Brazil's highest military post, despite publicity about the torture.

In Uruguay, a politician named Juan María Bordaberry had replaced Pacheco Areco as president. Before
Bordaberry's term had run out, Uruguay's generals had
stripped him of his power; then, in 1976, they put him out
of office altogether. In hardly more than a decade, the
Tupamaros had made good on their threat: in Uruguay,
the former model of democracy, there was now no dancing for anyone.

In the spring of 1977, a military court finally sentenced
a suspected Tupamaro for the killing of Dan Mitrione. For
the shooting, and his alleged part in the kidnapping of
Geoffrey Jackson, Antonio Mas Mas received thirty years
in prison.

Around the police barracks in Rio de Janeiro, Brazilian officers trained at the International Police Academy
remembered Dan Mitrione fondly as a symbol of the era
before Washington lost its will to fight the Communists.
The United States was decadent, the officers said; it
suffered from too much freedom. The torch had been
passed to the military and police of Brazil. It was now their
task to defend the hemisphere, and they would not falter.

In the police garages of Rio stood black, impregnable,
rolling fortresses, built at a cost of $100,000 each, designed
to carry troops with machine guns into the densest crowds.
They were bulletproof and so squat that they could not be
tipped over. They could withstand Molotov cocktails.
They were air conditioned against the fumes of their own
tear gas.

If Brazil's students ever dared to throw another stone,
the police would not be sitting on the curb of downtown
Rio crying.

The *coup de grace* in the campaign against the Office
of Public Safety was delivered by a motion picture. Costa-

Gavras, the Greek film director, hired an Italian, Franco Solinas, as his script writer, and together they set off for Latin America to make a film about the death of Dan Mitrione. Solinas, a member of the Italian Communist party, had written the script for Gillo Pontecorvo's *The Battle of Algiers.*

When Costa-Gavras visited Montevideo in 1972, he side-stepped questions from the local reporters about the kind of film he intended to make. Privately, though, he was collecting documents. Through Alain Labrousse, a French writer, Costa-Gavras obtained blurred photocopies of the material from Benítez.

Solinas traveled to the Dominican Republic, where he tried to meet secretly with the head of the country's Communist party. Although that attempt failed, a party functionary briefed Solinas on the police terror in the Dominican Republic and assured him that Dan Mitrione had set up the apparatus in Santo Domingo after the U. S. invasion of 1965.

From that time on, Mitrione acquired a reputation as his country's foremost expert in torture. *The New Scientist,* a British publication, described a device called the Mitrione vest. Designed for interrogations, it slowly inflated until it crushed the ribs of its victims. The vest itself was no more horrifying than other well-documented methods of torture used in Brazil and Uruguay and later in Chile. Yet, no prisoners, at least none who lived to testify at the Bertrand Russell Tribunal in Rome or at hearings of Amnesty International, had ever heard of such a vest, and Mitrione's friends never claimed for him the ingenuity of an inventor.

Hank Mitrione and her children could only meet the accusations with equal hyperbole about the Dan Mitrione they had known. "A perfect man," his widow said. "A great humanitarian," said his daughter, Linda.

Mrs. Mitrione withdrew to a suburb of Washington to

finish the job of raising her children. She kept a large portrait of her husband on the wall, and a photograph of Frank Sinatra on the piano. She did not keep much in touch with her husband's former colleagues. They had been very kind to her, but she found it hard to respond to their notes and Christmas cards.

Costa-Gavras included in *State of Siege* every undocumented rumor about Dan Mitrione from Santo Domingo or Belo Horizonte because his aim was a composite indictment of U. S. policy throughout Latin America. He and Solinas named their central character Philip E. Santore, and Costa-Gavras cast Yves Montand in the role. Montand was slim and continental; he smoked cigarettes. Mitrione had been corpulent and Midwestern; he had puffed, sometimes, on big cigars.

In the film, the interrogation sequences omitted the Tupamaro's incessant use of "you know" and Mitrione's sententious repeating of his remarks. "You are subversives, Communists," Santore tells his captors in the movie. "You want to destroy the foundations of society, the fundamental values of our Christian civilization, the very existence of the free world. You are an enemy who must be fought in every way possible."

With speeches of that sort, the film explained lucidly Santore's motivation; and in public statements Costa-Gavras extended the same analysis to Mitrione, who was, he said, "as sincere as the judges of the Catholic Church during the Inquisition. . . . He is convinced that one must cut down everything that is liberal or Communistic and by any means possible. He thinks that ordinary liberalism can plunge society into chaos."

But very few police advisers, least of all Mitrione, shared such certainties. Their mission in Latin America was not only secret but vague. Dan Mitrione went there to stop the

Communists. As did Philip Agee. As did Lincoln Gordon. In the years after Castro came to power in Cuba, no administration, Republican or Democrat, felt that it could afford another Cuba in the Western Hemisphere. And no one resisted the Communists more fervently than the local military and police officers, especially those who returned from Panama, Washington, or Fort Bragg persuaded that they were the Free World's first line of defense.

Philip Agee, college-educated, of the middle class, a divorced father of two, came to see the result of his official lying and cut free, a decision that took courage and perhaps a degree of fanaticism. Had Dan Mitrione been the inquisitor that Costa-Gavras painted him, his character might have equipped him for the same sort of dramatic conversion. Instead, Mitrione was self-educated, of the working class, a devoted father of nine, and dedicated to his work. In the White House and the U. S. embassies, there were brilliant men to set his nation's policy; in the CIA, there were arrogant men to interpret it.

With the overthrow of Goulart on April 1, 1964, Mitrione's job in Brazil had changed drastically. He had been working for democracy; henceforth, he would be working for a dictatorship. If no one in Washington or Brazil saw the difference, why should Mitrione?

In Uruguay, young men and women who considered themselves idealists began to shoot policemen who were often Mitrione's good friends. The U. S. government had developed harsh methods in South Vietnam for combating that kind of subversion, and some of those techniques and devices had found their way to Latin America. Mitrione merely made use of them.

In the twelve years of the Office of Public Safety, a total of seven police advisers were killed, six of them in Vietnam. Around the International Police Academy, at Fort Bragg, in Panama, the professionals agreed that Latin America would be the next Vietnam. Dan Mitrione, they felt, was a premature casualty of that Vietnam.

. . .

At Test Junior High School in Richmond, Indiana, in the mid-1930s, Dan Mitrione's advisers had filed the usual reports about his character. Their evaluations were uniformly favorable: "Honest." "Modest." "Tries to do what others would like." "Has a serious attitude toward work."

By the time he reached high school, Dan was majoring in English and Vocational Machine Shop, and he reported that he expected to work in a factory. One questionnaire called on him to list the abilities and knowledge he would need for that vocation.

"Know math," Dan wrote. "Know something of machines. Must not loaf. Have to be alert. Must take precautions. Know all the safety rules."

Then the form, designed to establish a student's talents and interests, asked, "What likes or dislikes have you developed in High School?"

And Dan Mitrione from Goosetown, who wanted to do what others would like and knew that he faced a life where he must not loaf and must know all the rules, answered, "I like all my subjects."

Acknowledgments

To name many of those men and women who contributed to this book would be to jeopardize their jobs, their pensions, or their status as exiles. It could also mean prison, torture, perhaps death. Zelmar Michelini, an Uruguayan senator in exile in Argentina, was murdered by a death squad three days before I arrived in Buenos Aires for our interview. Scores of people helped me in Europe and South America, and to them I want to express my thanks and admiration.

In a different category are those men accused of torture who demanded anonymity as a condition for talking with me. As a result, I have been required to withhold from the reference notes the identities of these informants. In some instances, the reader may be able to deduce my sources; the persons involved understood that likelihood and asked only that they not be conclusively identified.

There are other contributions that I can acknowledge freely and gratefully. Not all of the people on this list will agree with my conclusions. But in every case, they were generous with their time and assistance:

Philip Agee, Rennie Airth, Eva Ållander, Captain Ray Alvardo, Miguel Arraes, Marcos Arruda, Leilo Basso, Jorge Batlle, Cid de Queiroz Benjamin, Jan Knippers

Black, William Brown, Tim Butz, Mauro Calamandrei, Irany Campos, Luis Felipe Carrer, Carlos Castelo Branco, Andrew Cecere, Al Chvotkin, Calvin Clegg, Orville Conyers, Senator Alan Cranston, Roland Cutter.

Arnold Dadian, Tom Daschle, Kader Dehbi, Glycon de Paiva, Aristoteles Drummond, Maruja Echegoyen, Fred Ekton, C. Burke Elbrick, Byron Engle, Charles Fleming, Myles Freschette, Albert Friedman.

Fernando Gabeira, Eduardo Galeano, Colonel Raúl Garibay, Louis Gibbs, Fred Goff, Lauren J. Goin, Lincoln Gordon, Donald Gould, David Halberstam, Bruce Handler, Joseph Hanlon, Maria Hennequin, Robert Hernandez, General Heitor Herrera, Rinard Hitchcock, Linda Hoff, Claudia Hutchins, Paul Ingels.

U. Alexis Johnson, Edy Kaufman, Michael Klare, Alain Labrousse, Doris Langguth, Jerome Levinson, John Lindquist, John Marks, John Metelsky, Father Robert Minton, Henrietta Mitrione, Ray Mitrione, Fred Morris, Ethel Narvid, Lucy Neill-Kendall, Ricard Pedro Neubert, Joanne Omang, Dick Oosting.

Richard and Rosemary Parker, Susan Pierres, José Magalhaes Pinto, Murilo Pinto, Louise Popkin, Michel Puéchavy, Thomas Quigley, José María Rabello, Robert Rockweiler, Christopher Roper, Nathan Rosenfeld, Anthony Ruiz.

Ginetta Sagan, Harrison Salisbury, John Salzberg, Robert Sandin, Jay Scott, Angela Camargo Seixas, James Shea, Enio Silveira, Franco Solinas, Thomas Stephens, Dan Taher, Gary and Linda Tarter, Flavio Tavares, Richard Tiernan, William Tuohy, Brady Tyson, Jean Marc Von der Weid, Stephen and Susan Watkins, William Wipfler, Louis Wiznitzer, Morris and Edna Zimmelman.

At Pantheon Books, I would like to thank André Schiffrin, Tom Engelhardt, Donna Grusky Bass, and Wendy Wolf; at International Creative Management, my agent, Lynn Nesbit.

I also received valuable assistance from Amnesty International, the Bertrand Russell Foundation, the Catholic Conference, the U. S. Department of State, the Institute of Cultural Action, the National Conference of Churches of Christ, the North American Congress on Latin America, the Office on Latin America, and the U. S. Senate.

Finally, I wish to acknowledge gratefully a grant from the John Simon Guggenheim Memorial Foundation.

References

CHAPTER ONE

Details of Dan A. Mitrione's funeral service and burial: *Palladium-Item* and Sunday *Telegraph*, 12–14 August 1970. Uruguay providing an antique casket, Ray Mitrione's response to the kidnapping, meeting with Billy Rial, Mitrione family background: interviews, Ray Mitrione, Richmond, Indiana, March 1976. Lincoln poem: Ross Franklin Lockridge, *The Story of Indiana* (Oklahoma City: Harlow Publishing Corp., 1953), p. 231. Famous men and women from Indiana: Irving Leibowitz, *My Indiana* (Englewood Cliffs, N. J.: Prentice Hall, 1964). Cobb on the Ku Klux Klan: Irvin S. Cobb, *Indiana* (New York: George H. Doran Co., 1924), p. 51. Tarkington quotation: Leibowitz, *My Indiana*, p. 246. "A box": Ross Lockridge, Jr., *Raintree County* (Boston: Houghton Mifflin Co., 1948), p. 17. Pyle writing about Clayton: Howard H. Peckham and Shirley A. Snyder, eds., *Letters from Famous Hoosiers* (Bloomington, Ind.: War History Commission, 1948), pp. 123–25. Dan Mitrione's navy service: interview, Henrietta Mitrione, March 1976. Dan Mitrione's police application: personnel files, police headquarters, Richmond, Indiana. Dan Mitrione's early police work: interview, Orville Conyers, Richmond, Indiana, March 1976. Developments in the Mitrione kidnapping: *Palladium-Item*, 2–9 August 1970. Democratic party's 1955 campaign: interview, Andrew Cecere, Richmond, Indiana, March 1976. "Smashing" victory: headline, *Palladium-Item*, 9 November 1955. Dan Mitrione's note: *Palladi-*

um-Item, 3 August 1970, p. 1. Calls from UPI and Representative David Dennis: Ray Mitrione interviews. Selection of Dan Mitrione as police chief: interview, Roland Cutter, Richmond, Indiana, March 1976. White House reaction to the killing: *Palladium-Item,* 10 August 1970, p. 1. Other official responses: *Ibid.* 13 August 1970, p. 6. Dan Mitrione as police chief: interviews, including Louis Gibbs interview, Richmond, Indiana, March 1976. Richmond's teenage crime wave: *Palladium-Item,* 6–7 July 1956; and Cutter interview. Father Minton's background and reactions: interview, Father Robert Minton, Richmond, Indiana, March 1976. John Kennedy's Indiana campaigning: *Palladium-Item,* 21 April 1960, p. 1. Sinatra call: Ray Mitrione interviews. Sinatra's preparations and concert: *Palladium-Item,* 21, 30 August 1970. Sinatra's statement: *Palladium-Item,* 30 August 1970, p. 3.

CHAPTER TWO

John Quincy Adams on Cuba: Teresa Casuso, *Cuba and Castro* (New York: Random House, 1961), p. 31. Castro on the ninety-mile distance: Herbert L. Matthews, *Fidel Castro* (New York: Simon and Schuster, 1969), p. 198. Nixon memorandum, Hoover's agreement: Richard M. Nixon, *Six Crises* (Garden City, New York: Doubleday & Co., 1962), p. 352. Eisenhower ordered invasion: Matthews, *Fidel Castro,* p. 162. John Kennedy comparing Castro to Bolívar: John F. Kennedy, *The Strategy of Peace* (New York: Harper & Row, 1960), quoted by Nixon, *Six Crises,* p. 351. U. S. holdings, Castro's land policies: Samuel Shapiro, *Invisible Latin America* (Boston: Beacon Press, 1963). Sugar quota suspended: *Facts on File,* July 5, 1960. Kennedy charges: Nixon, *Six Crises,* p. 351. Eisenhower breaks diplomatic relations: Matthews, *Fidel Castro,* p. 163. Schlesinger's "perversion of the Cuban revolution": Arthur M. Schlesinger, Jr., *A Thousand Days* (London: André Deutsch, 1965), p. 201. Two hundred advisers in Brazil: *United States Policies and Programs in Brazil,* Hearings Before the Subcommittee on Western Hemisphere Affairs of the Committee on Foreign Relations, 92nd Congress, 1st session, Table VI, at 10 (May 4, 5, and 11, 1971). Mitrione refereeing softball games: Brazil *Herald,* 1 March 1964, p. 5. Mitrione denied a pay raise: Henrietta Mitrione interview. Engle's background and beginnings of police advisory program: interview, Byron Engle, Washington, D. C., March 1976. Mitrione's talk to family, the daughters' response to Brazil: interview, Linda Mitrione Tarter, Richmond, Indiana, March 1976. "A certain softness": Stefan Zweig, *Brazil: Land of the Future*, translated by Andrew St. James (New York: Viking Press, 1941), p. 9. "Remissa": *Ibid.*, p. 141. "They will never go home": Rebecca West, *The Thinking Reed* (New York: Viking Press, 1961), p. 140. "More troublesome than Argentina": Burton Bernstein, *Thurber* (New York: Ballantine Books, 1976), p. 549. Bundy on "second-rate minds": John Mander, *The Unrevolutionary Society* (New York: Alfred A. Knopf, 1969). Henry Kissinger: Later, as Secretary of State, Kissinger acknowledged that U. S. holdings in Latin America shaped his policies; not only did U. S. subsidiaries remit profits, but they were major customers for U. S. exports: Richard Armstrong, "Suddenly It's *Manana* in Latin America," *Fortune*, August 1974, p. 216. Edmund Wilson bored by Hispanic culture: Brendan Gill, *Here at The New Yorker* (New York: Random House, 1975), p. 254. *Literary Digest* on annexing Cuba: *Literary Digest* April 1899, pp. 363–64, cited in Ernest S. May, *American Imperialism* (New York: Atheneum Publishers, 1968) p. 208. Franklin Roosevelt on Haiti's constitution: Ernest Gruening, *Many Battles* (New York: Liveright, 1973), p. 160. Mexico "dipped into the sea": *Ibid.*, p. 109. "Work is sacred": John F. Santos, "A Psychologist Reflects on Brazil," *New Perspectives of Brazil*, edited by Eric N. Baklanoff (Nashville: Vanderbilt Press, 1966), p. 249. "Not fanatically so": *Ibid.*, pp. 244–45. Zweig's suicide: J. C. Thorne, ed., *Chambers's Biographical Dictionary* (New York: St. Martin's Press, 1962), p. 1396. José Enrique Rodó, *Ariel*, translated by F. J. Stimson (Boston: Houghton Mifflin Co., 1922). Responses to Rodó: Jean Franco, *The Modern Culture of Latin America* (New York: Frederick A. Praeger, 1967). Eisenhower on constabulary, Robert Kennedy's support for police program: Engle interview. Background on C–I Group: Engle interview; interview, U. Alexis Johnson, Washington, D. C., March 1976. Latin Americans offended by Panama courses: interviews. Forrestal touring Car Barn: Engle interview. Agee's background: interview, Philip Agee, Cambridge, England, May 1976; Philip Agee, *Inside the Company: CIA Diary* (Harmondsworth, England: Penguin Books, 1975). Lincoln Gordon as "boy genius": *The New York Times,* 12 April 1967, p. 16. Gordon's background, named to Berle task force, Richard Goodwin and Alliance speech, appointment as ambassador to Brazil: interviews, Lincoln Gordon, Washington, D. C., March 1976. U. S. aircraft bases on Brazilian coast: Gerhard Masur, *Nationalism in Latin America* (New York: The Macmillan Co., 1966). Vargas's personal life: Tad Szulc, *Twilight of the Tyrants* (New York: Henry Holt, 1959). Roosevelt's joke about de Gaulle: Robert E. Sherwood, *Roosevelt and Hopkins* (New York: Harper & Brothers, 1948), p. 970. Roosevelt not accepting foreign control of utilities: John Gunther, *Inside South America* (New York: Harper & Row, 1966), p. 21. Dreiser on U. S. holdings abroad: Theodore Dreiser, *Tragic America* (New York: Liveright, Inc., 1931). Vargas on nationalism: Masur, *Nationalism in Latin America,* p. 128. Threats to the Vargas regime: Herbert Wendt, *Red, White and Black Continent* (Garden City, New York: Doubleday, 1966). Post-Vargas political parties: James Kohl and John Litt, *Urban Guerrilla Warfare in Latin America* (Cambridge, Mass.: MIT Press, 1974), p. 33. Carlos Lacerda: John Dos Passos, *Brazil on the Move* (Garden City, New York: Doubleday & Co., 1963), p. 142. Vargas suicide note: Wendt, *Red, White and Black Continent,* p. 443. Kubitschek's policy on foreign investment: Steven J. Rosen, "Rightest Regimes and American Interests," *Society,* September/ October 1974. Eugenio Gudin's statistic: Eduardo Galeano, "The Nationalization of Brazilian Industry," *Monthly Review,* December 1969, p. 19. Gudin on "a decent life": Gary MacEoin, *Revolution Next Door* (New York: Holt, Rinehart and Winston, 1971), p. 47. Five times the amount of foreign aid leaving Brazil: Galeano, "The Nationalization of Brazilian Industry," p. 23. Goulart susceptible to Communist influence: Peter D. Bell, "Brazilian-American Relations," *Brazil in the Sixties,* edited by Riordan Roett (Nashville: Vanderbilt University Press, 1972). Quadros vulnerable to Communists: Lieutenant Colonel Edward King, quoted in Jan Knippers Black, *United States Penetration of Brazil* (Philadelphia: University of Pennsylvania, 1977), p. 40. Quadros campaigning: Wendt, *Red, White and Black Continent.* Brazilian poll on neutrality: Keith Larry Storrs, "Brazil's Independent Foreign Policy, 1961–64," Cornell University's Latin American Studies Program Dissertation Series No. 44 (January 1973), pp. 248–49. Quadros's term: Irving Louis Horowitz,

Masses in Latin America (New York: Oxford University Press, 1970); Donald E. Worcester, *Brazil from Colony to World Power* (New York: Charles Scribner's Sons, 1973). "Grown-up, vaccinated, and old enough to vote": *Ibid.*, p. 219. Richard Goodwin's meeting with Ernesto Guevara: Richard Goodwin, "Annals of Politics: A Footnote," *The New Yorker,* 25 May 1968. Lacerda's attack on Goulart: Dos Passos, *Brazil on the Move,* p. 167. Quadros's resignation: Worcester, *Brazil from Colony to World Power,* pp. 221–23. Goin's background: interview, Lauren Jackson Goin, Washington, D. C., March 1976. CIA's attitude toward police advisers: Agee interview. Calfee resignation: correspondence, Maurice E. Calfee and Senator James Abourezk, U. S. Senate files. Belo Horizonte attitude toward the police: interviews. Mitrione's service in Belo Horizonte: interviews, including Ricard Neubert interview, Belo Horizonte, August 1976. "Mafia chief": Tarter interview. Belo Horizonte police "like Richmond's finest": *Palladium-Item,* 12 March 1962, p. 12. Mitriones had no cook: Tarter interview. Niemeyer building: Neubert interview. Assault on *Binomio* by Punaro Bley: interviews, José María Rabello, Paris, May 1976. Gabeira's background: interviews, Fernando Nagle Gabeira, Stockholm, May 1976. Arruda's background: interviews, Marcos Arruda, Geneva, April 1976.

CHAPTER THREE

Ambassador Gordon in Brazil: Gordon interviews. IPES: interview, Glycon de Paiva, Rio de Janeiro, July 1976. GAP: interview, Aristoteles Drummond, Rio de Janeiro, July 1976. IBAD background: Eloy Dutra, *IBAD: Sigla da Corrupcao* (Rio de Janeiro: Editora Civilização Brasileira, S. A., 1963). IBAD underwrote Pernambuco campaign: letter, Miguel Arraes, May 1976. Edward Kennedy in northeast Brazil: Joseph A. Page, *The Revolution that Never Was* (New York: Grossman Publishers, 1972), pp. 120–21. Background of Francisco Julião: *Ibid.*, pp. 38–43. Paulo Freyre's method: *Ibid.,* p. 173. CIA in northeast: interviews, Washington and Rio de Janeiro, March–August 1976. AIFLD: Black, *United States Penetration of Brazil,* chapter 8, pp. 111–24. Background of General Herrera: interview, Heitor Herrera, Rio de Janeiro, July 1976. Escola Superior de Guerra:

"Resistance to populism had been a mainstay of the military's Superior War College [ESG] since its inception as focus and fountainhead for the nation's military elite in 1949": Kohl and Litt, *Urban Guerrilla Warfare in Latin America*, p. 39. JBUSMC: Black, *United States Penetration of Brazil*, pp. 162–66. For a detailed discussion of U. S. training in Panama: Michael T. Klare, *War Without End* (New York: Alfred A. Knopf, 1972). Brazilian desire to be loved by U. S. counterparts: interview, Rio de Janeiro, June 1976. Poeck background: interviews, Brasília, August 1976. Gordon's relations with Goulart, Cuban Missile crisis: Gordon interviews. Pery Bevilacqua: interviews, Rio de Janeiro, July 1976. Robert Kennedy's visit to Brazil, Goulart's envy of Perón, Goulart's land reform: Gordon interviews. Walters soliciting Kruel's support: interviews, Rio de Janeiro, June–July 1976. Agee's experience: Agee, *Inside the Company;* and Agee interview. IBAD: Black, *United States Penetration of Brazil*, pp. 72–77; and Agee and Gordon interviews. Galbraith on undercutting Diem: William Bundy, "Dictatorship and Foreign Policy," *Foreign Affairs*, October 1975. "Going out to the rabble": interview, 1976. Gabeira in Brizola's Group of Eleven: Gabeira interviews. "Don't go to the Communist meeting": Brazil *Herald*, 4 March 1964, p. 3. David Rockefeller's business group: Brazil *Herald*, 3 March 1964, p. 4. Brazil's minimum wage, comparison to feeding a chimpanzee: Brazil *Herald*, 7 March 1964, p. 4. Lacerda on choosing colors: Brazil *Herald*, 13 March 1964, p. 4; three days earlier the newspaper (p. 2) had quoted Lacerda as saying that one of his first acts as president would be to repeal Goulart's agrarian reform law. March 13 rally: Brazil *Herald*, 14 March 1964, p. 1. Gordon's reaction: Gordon interviews. Darcy Ribeiro on legalizing the Communist party: Brazil *Herald*, 4 March 1964, p. 3. "Clube dos contemplados": Brazil *Herald*, 1 March 1964, p. 3. Robert McNamara briefing: interview. O'Meara's alleged offer: Robinson Rojas, *Estados Unidos en Brasil* (Santiago, Chile: Presa Latinoamericana, S. A., 1965) pp. 72–73, quoted in Black, *United States Penetration of Brazil*. Jittery mood among generals: interviews. U. S. would recognize military in São Paulo: Jerome Levinson and Juan de Onis, *The Alliance that Lost Its Way* (Chicago: Quadrangle Books, 1970), p. 89. March of the Family: Brazil *Herald*, 20 March 1964, p. 1. Archbishop forbade marching: Rojas, *Estados Unidos en Brasil*, p. 198. Labor party asked Goulart to close Congress: Brazil *Herald,* 19 March 1964, p. 2. Goulart's pledge not to be a dictator: Brazil *Herald,* 20 March 1964, p. 3. De Paiva's charges about communism: Brazil *Herald,* 22 March 1964, p. 4. Walters' telegram: Gayle Hudgens Watson, "Our Monster in Brazil," *The Nation,* 15 January 1977, pp. 51–54. Goulart's March 30 speech: Brazil *Herald,* 31 March 1964, p. 1. U. S. embassy on day of coup: Gordon interviews. Soldiers told they were fighting for Goulart: interview. Telcons from Washington to U. S. embassy: Watson, "Our Monster in Brazil," pp. 51–54; fuller documentation from the Lyndon B. Johnson Memorial Library in Austin, Texas, appeared in *Jornal do Brasil,* 19, 20 December 1976. Gordon's call on Kubitscheck: Gordon interviews. Ché Guevara's "There is only one face": Ricardo Rojo, *My Friend Che,* translated by Julian Casart (New York: Dial Press, 1968). U. S. embassy on April 1: Gordon interviews. Teixeira's hesitation: interviews. Khrushchev to Prestes: Brazil *Herald,* 6 March 1964, p. 4. Goulart not wishing to be responsible for bloodshed: Gordon interviews. Lacerda on day of coup: interviews. "Turn on the air conditioner": Gordon interviews. Doherty's testimony on AIFLD training: Black, *United States Penetration of Brazil,* p. 117. Wayne Hayes, General Andrew O'Meara, and Representative Gross comment on the coup: Foreign Assistance Act of 1965, Hearings Before the Committee on Foreign Affairs, House of Representatives, 89th Congress, 1st session, pp. 345–57.

CHAPTER FOUR

Unless otherwise credited, the information in Chapter Four came from interviews with U. S. police advisers, Brazilian police and military officers, journalists, diplomats, and others who requested that they not be identified.

No change in U. S. police advisory role after the 1964 coup: U. Alexis Johnson, Byron Engle, and other interviews. Brazilian policemen stealing flowers, plainclothesman having pocket picked: Brazil *Herald,* 3 March 1964, p. 4. Esquadrão da Morte: Jeff Radford, "The Brazilian Death Squads," *The Nation,* 30 July 1973; Edwin McDowell, "The Murderous Policemen of Brazil," *The Wall Street Journal,* 1 November 1974. Sergio Fleury: *Visao* (Brazilian magazine), 12 November 1973. Boilesen background:

Jornal do Brasil, 22 April 1971, pp. 23–24. OPS advisers in Dominican Republic were CIA agents: interview with David Fairchild, assistant program officer, U. S. AID, "U. S. AID in the Dominican Republic," *North American Congress on Latin America* [NACLA] *Newsletter*, November 1970, p. 8. Dominican Republic: Norman Gall, "Santo Domingo: The Politics of Terror," *The New York Review of Books*, 22 July 1971; Juan Bosch, the former president of the Dominican Republic, summed up the 1965 U. S. invasion: "This was a democratic revolution smashed by the leading democracy of the world, the United States": quoted by Seymour Martin Lipset and Aldo Solari, *Elites in Latin America* (New York: Oxford University Press, 1967), p. 181. CIA's International Police Services, Inc: John Marks and Taylor Branch, "Tracking the CIA," *Harper's Weekly*, March 1975. Los Angeles police officers sent to Venezuela: Engle interview. Robert Kennedy's speech to the IPA: press release, Agency for International Development, 9 July 1965. IPA exercises with mythical Rio Bravos: interviews; and Peter T. Chew, "America's Global Peace Officers," *The Kiwanis Magazine*, April 1969, pp. 22–24; David Sanford, "Agitators in a Fertilizer Factory," *The New Republic*, 11 February 1967, pp. 16–19. "First Line of Defense": *Ibid.* IPA students' essays on torture: U. S. Senate files. Le Van An, redacteur of the South Vietnam police wrote in his IPA paper: "Despite the fact that brutal interrogation is strongly criticized by moralists, its importance must not be denied if we want to have order and security in daily life": U. S. Senate files. Dan Mitrione listed as CIA agent: Julius Mader, *Who's Who in CIA* (Berlin: Mader, 1066 Berlin W66 Mauerstrasse 69, 1968), p. 364. Training of 100,000 Brazilian police officers: "Through December, 1970, the Public Safety project in Brazil has assisted in training locally over 100,000 federal and state police personnel. Additionally, approximately 600 persons received training in the U. S.": Project data for 1971 budget hearings, Table III, Brazil, Public Safety, U. S. AID.

CHAPTER FIVE

Except for the following references, material in this chapter was drawn from interviews with Jean Marc Von der Weid, Paris, May 1976.

Ambassador Gordon's protests after the 1964 coup: Gordon interviews. Angela Camargo Seixas in protest demonstration:

interview, Angela Seixas, Cambridge, England, May 1976. Lacerda's "The Front": Kohl and Litt, *Urban Guerrilla Warfare in Latin America*, pp. 44–45. Lacerda's criticism of the "military dictatorship": *Facts on File*, 17 July 1968, p. 279. Student protests: João Quartim, *Dictatorship and Armed Struggle in Brazil*, translated by David Fernbach (New York: Monthly Review Press, 1971), pp. 139–42. Policeman sitting on curb: interview. Aristoteles Drummond summoned to Costa e Silva: Drummond interview. For further discussion of Governor Abreu Sodre's conflict with local army commanders: Ronald M. Schneider, *The Political System of Brazil* (New York: Columbia University Press, 1971) pp. 291–92. Mitrione's "I had to come back": interview. Theodore Brown before Senator Frank Church's subcommittee: *United States Policies and Programs in Brazil* (Washington, D. C.: U. S. Government Printing Office, 1971), p. 36. Earlier in the testimony, Senator Church asked Brown, "In light of the many reports that we hear of torture in Brazil, do you think you have been successful in inculcating humane methods in restraint?" Mr. Brown: "Yes, sir; I do, Senator." *Ibid.*, p. 18. Nelson Rockefeller's tour, report: Nelson Rockefeller, "Quality of Life in the Americas: Report of a U. S. Presidential Mission for the Western Hemisphere" (Washington, D. C.: U. S. Government Printing Office, 1969). Rockefeller holdings: Gary MacEoin, *Revolution Next Door*, pp. 146–53. OBAN: interviews; also, Riordan Roett, *Brazil in the Sixties*, pp. 43–45. CENIMAR and U. S. Naval Mission, Rear Admiral C. Thor Hanson overhearing screams: interviews. Buckley column: "Torture in Brazil," from syndicated column "On the Right." After Buckley attempted to explain away the allegations, he added, "If Brazil were Uruguay, or Bolivia, where the political Mau Maus roam, one might understand the use of torture as an instrument of war." But since Brazil's dictatorship was secure, the economy booming, and the political opposition perfunctory, Buckley protested the "humiliation and disgrace" of torture. Clemente Monteiro's U. S. training in Panama: personnel records, Brazil's federal police academy, Brasília, August 1976.

CHAPTER SIX

Much of this chapter came from interviews with Charles Burke Elbrick, Washington, D. C., March 1976; and Fernando Nagle Gabeira, Stockholm, May 1976.

"An old fart": interview. Elbrick's background: "A Sturdy Ambassador," *The New York Times*, 8 September 1969, p. 2. Tuthill antagonized Brazil's dictators: interview. Mrs. Elbrick saying her house was not a public place: interview. The Haitian ambassador would have to be kidnapped twice: José Yglesias, "Report from Brazil: What the Left Is Saying," *The New York Times Magazine*, 7 December 1969, p. 165. Belton called intelligence offices: interviews. MR-8 manifesto: *The New York Times*, 6 September 1969, p. 1. "Crapping in our pants": interview. U. S. embassy negotiations with Brazil's junta for Elbrick's release: interviews. Marighela's Minimanual: Carlos Marighela, in *Tricontinental Bulletin* (Havana, Cuba), no. 56 (November 1970), pp. 1–56, and quoted by Kohl and Litt, *Urban Guerrilla Warfare in Latin America*, pp. 86–135. Taxi driver admiring Neil Armstrong and kidnappers: interview, Cid de Queiroz Benjamin, Stockholm, May 1976. Army and CENIMAR rivalry: interviews. Moura checking on exchange: interview. "Dear Elfie": *The New York Times*, 6 September 1969, p. 1. Mrs. Elbrick commented, "Even the bad guys are good. They are letting my husband write me a letter." *Ibid.* Two hundred navy men tried to block the airplane: dispatch, Joseph Novitski, *The New York Times*, 7 September 1969, p. 1. U. S. embassy staff dismay at Elbrick's remarks: interviews; "Elbrick has been having a bad time of it with the [Brazilian] Foreign Office ever since Brazil had to give up 15 political prisoners in ransom for him. Many officials of the military-dominated regime have felt Elbrick presented his captors in far too good a light after his release, and they resented it": Jeremiah O'Leary, "Elbrick's Return to Post in Brazil Is Doubtful," *The Evening Star* (Washington, D. C.), 12 June 1970. Prisoners' arrival in Mexico City: interview, Flavio Tavares Freitas, Buenos Aires, Argentina, June 1976. "They don't even know I've been arrested": Miami *Herald*, 9 September 1969. Elbrick's "I don't have time": interview.

CHAPTER SEVEN

As indicated in the text, the material in this chapter came from interviews with Fernando Gabeira, Stockholm; Jean Marc Von der Weid, Paris; Angela Seixas, Cambridge, England; Marcos Arruda, Geneva; Murilo Pinto and Irany Campos, Paris.

CHAPTER EIGHT

Engle's interview with Mitrione: Engle interview. U-127 field reports: responding to a request made under the Freedom of Information Act, the U. S. State Department supplied reports, formerly classified CONFIDENTIAL, from January 1969 through December 1970. Greek and Portuguese tortures: files, Amnesty International, London. Vietnamese torture: files, U. S. Senate. U. S. Navy torture camps: *Newsweek*, 22 March 1976. Donald Duncan's training at Fort Bragg: Donald Duncan, *The New Legions* (New York: Random House, 1967), p. 159. Brazilian camp on Niterói: "O Limite de Resistência," *Jornal do Brasil*, 6 August 1969, Section II, p. 1. Tupamaros presented a grave challenge: interviews. Batlle's benign statism: a fuller description in Martin Weinstein, *Uruguay: The Politics of Failure* (Westport, Conn.: Greenwood Press, 1975). Raúl Sendic's background: interviews. Bribery in Uruguay: Gunther, *Inside South America*, p. 233. Raid on Swiss club: interview. "The most intelligent and clever": police intelligence reports, Montevideo, Uruguay. Tupamaros: Alain Labrousse, *Los Tupamaros*, translated by Rodolfo Walsh (Buenos Aires: Editorial Tiempo Contemporáneo, 1971); Kohl and Litt, *Urban Guerrilla Warfare in Latin America*, pp. 173–95; Arturo C. Porzecanski, *Uruguay's Tupamaros* (New York: Praeger Publishers, 1973). "Words divide us": Carlos López Matteo, introduction, *Generals and Tupamaros* (London: Latin America Review of Books Ltd., 1974), p. ii. Tupamaro bombings: interviews. Tupa Amara: Captain Bactasardo Ocampo, *The Execution of the Inca Tupac Amaru* (Cambridge: Hakluyt Society, 1907), p. 230. Engle calling Tupamaros cowardly: Engle interview. Westmoreland on NLF: briefing by General William Westmoreland, Saigon, 1965. Tupamaro Christmas raid: Major Carlos Wilson, *The Tupamaros* (Boston: Branden Press, 1974), p. 30. Pereira killed a newsboy: interview. "Attention, Tupamaros! Kidnap me!": Wilson, *The Tupamaros*, p. 32. President Gestido: Porzecanski, *Uruguay's Tupamaros*, pp. 56–57. Voted Eisenhower, got Nixon: interview. Agee's relations with Otero, CIA's bribing techniques, reaction to Saenz: Agee interview. Uruguayan response to Saenz: interviews. Bardesio put in touch with Cantrell: *Marcha* (Montevideo), 28 April 1972, translated into English and quoted by Wilson, *The Tupamaros*, p. 106. Uruguayan employees' reaction to Bardesio, Manuel the Cuban: interviews. Bardesio's routine: Wilson, *The Tupamaros*, p. 107. Uruguayan CIA agents: Agee, *Inside the Company*, Appendix I, pp. 599–624; before Agee overheard the torture of Bonaudi, he had received reports (p. 443) of Braga torturing a young waterworks engineer, Julio Arizaga, suspected of belonging to the Movement of the Revolutionary Left. Gangsters and thieves beaten by police: interviews. Agee and Horton overhear torture: Agee interview; and Agee, *Inside the Company*, pp. 455–59. CIA aliases: Agee interview. CIA running checks for Creole Oil: Agee, *Inside the Company*, p. 103. CIA checks for businessmen in Montevideo, weekly meetings with them, International Harvester representative excluded: Agee interview. Cantrell and CIA funds: Bardesio's testimony described Cantrell receiving money apart from the U. S. embassy and Cantrell giving Bardesio 11,000 pesos to cover shortages from the intelligence office's petty cash; quoted in Wilson, *The Tupamaros*, pp. 106–08. Subcommissioner Benítez wrote: "Although an attempt was made to hide the reason, people heard about certain 'financial' matters [a good part of the money poured out by the CIA and FBI had disappeared without any justified cause]": cited, in English translation by Raymond Rosenthal, by Costa-Gavras and Franco Solinas, *State of Siege, Documents* (London: Plexus Publishing, 1973), p. 169. Mitrione's complaints about pay: interviews, including Morris Zimmelman interview, Montevideo, June 1976. Miguel Angel Benítez Segovia: interviews and Benítez documents. "Putamaros": interviews. Otero as Quixote: interview. Pacheco's government falling in esteem: *Generals and Tupamaros*, p. 1. Newspapers forbidden to use "Tupamaros": interviews. Hank Mitrione's life in Montevideo: interviews, including Henrietta Mitrione interview. Pellegrini kidnapping: *Generals and Tupamaros*, pp. 6, 9. $60,000 ransom: interview. Police protection of Jorge Batlle's children: interview, Jorge Batlle, Montevideo, June 1976. Mitrione's effect on police, comment of Juan María Lucas: Benítez documents. Los Fresnos bomb school: interviews, Benítez documents. Engle denying *The Battle of Algiers* shown at IPA: Engle interview. Agee's financial transactions with First National City Bank: Agee, *Inside the Company*, p. 382. CIA Southern Cone network, Fleury in Uruguay: interviews. Bardesio's Death Squad: interviews; Wilson, *The Tupamaros*, pp. 92–113. Mitrione's letters: correspondence with Ray Mitrione. Mitrione's office: Benítez documents. Mitrione carrying pistol: interviews, including interview, Don Gould, U. S. consulate, Rio de Janeiro, June 1976. Attempting to refute the contentions of the film *State of Siege*, Ernest W. Lefever, then a senior fellow at the Brookings Institution, stated erroneously (p. 5) in a paper, "The Unmaking of a 'Documentary'—Film vs. Fact," that Mitrione never carried a gun overseas. Lefever reversed Mitrione's Brazil service, writing (p. 13) that he spent five years in Belo Horizonte, two years in Rio de Janeiro. Lefever calls "the torture school scene" in Costa-Gavras's film "highly implausible and appears to be a figment of his [Costa-Gavras's] imagination." Mitrione confided dangers: interview. Moran Charquero's killing: U-127, Public Safety Report, April 1970, p. 2. Mitrione never postponed work: interviews. *Marcha*'s "Torture" cover: *Marcha* (Montevideo), 10 April 1970. "One major problem": U-127 Public Safety Report, June 1970, p. 6. Mitrione on breaking a man: Benítez documents, quoted in *State of Siege*, p. 180. Sexual joking at *jefatura:* interviews. Electric needles: Benítez documents. Agee on diplomatic pouch: Agee interview. Technical Services Division: Agee, *Inside the Company*, p. 85. James Keehner, TSD psychologist: Maureen Orth, "Memoirs of a CIA Psychologist," *New Times*, June 1976, pp. 19–24. TSD branch offices in Panama and Buenos Aires: interviews, including Philip Agee interview. Mitrione tortures: interviews. Otero turned his back on beatings: Maria Esther Gilio, *The Tupamaro Guerrillas*, translated by Anne Edmondson (New York: Ballantine Books, 1973), pp. 198–99. Threat to Don Gould: Gould interview. Attempt to kidnap Jones and Rosenfeld: interview, Nathan Rosenfeld, Brasília, August 1976. Mitrione kidnapping: *El Dia*, 1 August 1970, p. 1; *El Pais* (Montevideo), 1 August 1970. Dias Gomide a disagreeable captive: interview. "Wonderful to be in a democracy": interviews. Brazilian agents disguised as shepherds: interviews. Jones background: interview. Nixon's guidelines on kidnapping and prisoner exchange: interviews, including U. Alexis Johnson interview.

CHAPTER NINE

After the killing of Dan Mitrione, the Tupamaros released a recording of his interrogation during his ten days of captivity. U. S. government officials supplied a copy of the tape to Ray Mitrione in Richmond, Indiana.

CHAPTER TEN

Chronology of August 10, 1970: *El País* (Montevideo) 11 August 1970, p. 3. Otero's interview with Aymoré: interviews. Dias Gomide release: interview. Aymoré and Montevideo police: interview. U. S. embassy pressure on *Jornal do Brasil:* interview. Editorial calling Mitrione killing "absurd": *The New York Times,* 11 August 1970, p. 32. Byron Engle's explanation: Engle interview. Tupamaros blowing up Carrasco bowling alley: *Generals and Tupamaros,* p. 18. Geoffrey Jackson kidnapping: *Ibid.,* p. 19. Government trade for Jackson, promotion of police colonel: interviews. Ray Mitrione informing Washington about Billy Rial: Ray Mitrione interviews. Rial's arrest: interview. Tupamaro interrogator probably Blanco Katras: interview. Dr. Fly's heart attack: interviews, including Morris and Edna Zimmelman interview. Gabeira's release: Gabeira interviews. Von der Weid's release: Von der Weid interviews. Arruda's release: Arruda interviews. Bardesio's confessions: *Marcha* (Montevideo), 28 April 1972. Bardesio excerpt in English: Wilson, *The Tupamaros,* pp. 116–17. Whereabouts of Bardesio, Héctor Amodio Pérez, and Raúl Sendic: interviews. Montevideo prisoner, Benítez's arrest: interview. Benítez on police force: interviews. Cirillo implicated in death: Arruda interview. Clemente Monteiro, Alfredo Poeck: interviews. Senator Abourezk's concern over OPS: interview, Tom Daschle, Washington, D. C., March 1976. Nixon's praise for Brazil: *The New York Times,* 7–10 December 1971. Richard Helms's "honorable men": *The New York Times,* 22 January 1971, p. 8. Dispersal of police advisers: interviews. Agee's resignation from the CIA: Agee interview. Angela Seixas released: Seixas interview. Agee dedication: Agee, *Inside the Company,* p. 5. Burke Elbrick at funeral: Elbrick interview. Gordon's reflections on dictatorship: interviews, including Gordon interview. São Paulo arrests: *Latin America Political Report* (London), 22 April 1977, p. 3. Torture of U. S. clergyman: interview, Fred Morris, Washington, D. C., March 1976. Brazilian police attitude toward the United States; anti-riot equipment: interviews. Benítez documents: interview, Alain Labrousse, Paris, May 1976. Communist official tells Solinas about Mitrione in Dominican Republic: interview, Franco Solinas, Rome, April 1976. "Mitrione vest": "Building a Better Thumbscrew," *New Scientist* (London), 19 July 1973, pp. 139–41, quoted in *Science Digest* (New

York), December 1973. "A perfect man": Henrietta Mitrione interview. "A great humanitarian": Linda Tarter interview. Film treatment of Santore: *State of Siege* script (London: Plexus Publishing, 1973). Dan Mitrione's school questionnaire: school records, Richmond, Indiana.

Index

About the Author

A. J. Langguth was born in Minneapolis in 1933, graduated from Harvard College in 1955, and spent two years in the U. S. Army. He has worked for several publications; and in 1965, he served as Saigon Bureau Chief for *The New York Times.* Since 1967 he has traveled often to Brazil. He is the author of three novels and one nonfiction book, *Macumba: White and Black Magic in Brazil.*

PRAISE FOR RUS BRADBURD'S *FORTY MINUTES OF HELL*

"[An] excellent . . . biography."   —*Financial Times*

"A combination career retrospective and racial history of Southern college basketball. . . . Establishes Richardson as one of college basketball's most compelling figures."   —*Kirkus Reviews*

"Read *Forty Minutes of Hell* and you'll gain a greater appreciation for Richardson, the man and the coach."   —*Lexington Herald-Leader* (Kentucky)

"Bradburd does an incredible job chronicling Richardson's rise from a high school coach to getting a junior college job. . . . [His] copy shines in the well-researched chapters on the black coaches and the athletes who came before Richardson but never got the opportunity to elevate themselves."   —*SLAM Online*

"*Forty Minutes of Hell* . . . brilliantly details the coach's improbable rise from El Paso poverty to national championship coaching glory."
                    —Dan Wetzel, author of *Glory Road*, on Yahoo.com

"Nolan Richardson's extraordinary life and his success as the University of Arkansas coach are an important chapter in the history of our country's struggle for racial equality, with all the excitement of the Final Four. What an incredible journey! I am grateful that I got to see a lot of it firsthand and to know such an able and remarkable man."   —President Bill Clinton

"This is a great story about America and its hidden histories. Nolan Richardson understands the struggle because he did the heavy lifting. Every black college coach with a good job today owes Nolan Richardson a measure of respect for the fearless way he kicked down doors. Every American should thank him for showing us it was possible."   —Charles Barkley, basketball legend

"I've never read a sports book I would describe as operatic until now. Nolan Richardson's story, both unique and universal, would challenge the most seasoned biographer, but Bradburd's libretto is heartbreaking and inspiring. This is the finest sports biography I've read in years, hands down."
                    —Dave Zirin, author of *A People's History of Sports in the Unites States*

ALSO BY RUS BRADBURD

Paddy on the Hardwood: A Journey in Irish Hoops

CONTENTS

VII

FORTY MINUTES
OF HELL

SOUL ON ICE

My great-great-grandfather came over on the ship," Nolan Richardson said. "I did not come over on that ship. So I expect to be treated a little bit different."

With television cameras and tape recorders rolling, Richardson began giving the people of Arkansas and America a history lesson, although his purpose was not entirely clear. This was supposed to be another ordinary press conference—that's what most journalists had expected—and a briefing on an upcoming game was the norm. Reporters arrived Monday afternoon, February 25, 2002, figuring that Richardson might still be discouraged after Saturday's loss at Kentucky. Richardson had said that night: "If they go ahead and pay me my money, they can take the job tomorrow." Since then, there had been whispers that perhaps the coach was getting ready to retire.

That would have been big news for Razorback basketball fans. Richardson had coached Arkansas to the landmark 1994 NCAA championship. With nearly four hundred wins at Arkansas, he had earned two additional Final Four appearances, led Arkansas to thirteen NCAA Tournaments, and could brag of one of the highest winning percentages in college hoops in the 1990s. Arguably the top black coach in America, Richardson was the first black coach in the old Confederacy at a mostly white university, as well as the first to win the national championship at a Southern school.

On this Monday, however, less than a decade removed from that national title, Richardson would become the kamikaze coach.

After seventeen seasons, he was still the only black coach in any sport at the University of Arkansas, and that bothered him. "I know for a fact that I do not play on the same level as the other coaches around this school play on," he said. "I know that. You know it. And people of my color know that. And that angers me." Richardson glanced toward the door, as if all twenty white head coaches of the other Arkansas Razorback sports were lined up outside.

The journalists scratched their heads in wonder, shifted in their seats. It was a bizarre session, they thought, but not a fatal one for Richardson. The media had heard him rant, privately, about their coverage of him and his program. That kind of complaining is common among college coaches, but on this occasion, the topic veered erratically from basketball.

It was clear that Richardson wanted to talk about race.

He surveyed the media room at the Bud Walton Arena, and pointed out that everyone except him was white. "When I look at all of you people in this room," he said, "I see no one who looks like me, talks like me, or acts like me. Now why don't you recruit? Why don't the editors recruit like I'm recruiting?" The collection of media representatives swallowed hard or scribbled in their notebooks. Although he was not shouting, he used the righteous tone of an Old Testament prophet. Richardson was a bear of a man—6'3" and, at the time, close to 230 pounds—as much a linebacker as a basketball coach. He stood alone on the podium, wearing a flaming-red Arkansas pullover, and the banner behind would frame him in the same color for television viewers.

On that day, Richardson's Arkansas Razorbacks were 13-13 over-all—not the kind of season that normally could be called a disaster. Richardson said as much. "I've earned the right to have the kind of season I'm having." That was likely true. However, it was Richardson's worst stretch since he took the job in Fayetteville. Arkansas was 5-9 in the Southeastern Conference and had lost nine of their past twelve games.

It would be difficult to exaggerate Richardson's cachet at the school, but the coach seemed to do just that, essentially claiming the reason recruits—basketball and football—came to Arkansas was because of him. "The number one thing that's talked [about] in our deal is the fact that the greatest thing going for the University of Arkansas is Nolan Richardson."

Richardson had kept his program, practices, and locker room open to every reporter, but not anymore. "Do not call me ever on my phone, none of you, at my home ever again," he added. "Those lines are no longer open for communications with me."

Richardson must have believed his job was on the line, and yet it seemed as though he both wanted and did not want to remain at Arkansas. He made it clear he would not walk away; that wasn't what he'd meant two days earlier in Kentucky. "I've dealt with it for seventeen years," he said, "and I'll deal with it for seventeen more. Because that's my makeup. Where would I go?"

Nobody in the media had suggested he should be terminated, but Richardson accused them of it anyway. "So maybe that's what you want," he said. "Because you know what? Ol' granny told me, 'Nobody runs you anywhere, Nolan.' I know that. See, my great-great-grandfather came over here on the ship. I didn't, and I don't think you understand what I'm saying."

Then Richardson wheeled, confronted the cameras, and ended the speech by saying, "You can run that on every TV show in America."

A question-and-answer session followed. No journalists asked questions about race, or ships, or his grandmother. The first query: Had he watched the tape of the Kentucky game?

"I thought it would blow over," one veteran Arkansas journalist says. "No way did I think Nolan was going to get fired. Sure, he bristled, but mostly it was surreal, bizarre."

It might have blown over but the highlights, if you can call them that, were indeed run on television shows across the country. The quotes most often broadcast were the most confusing. Why was Richardson referring to his grandmother? And what ships? He must have meant slave ships.

The highlights ran again and again.

The story grew legs: a rich and famous black man was lecturing a roomful of white media about race, reminding Arkansas, and then America, about its racist past.

Several subsequent newspaper and online accounts emphasized how obsessed Richardson had been with race throughout his career. *Sports Illustrated* called the press conference ". . . a bewildering self-immolation."

The endless cycling of the clips brought national attention to the most perplexing forty minutes in college basketball history. How could a black man who was so prosperous come across as so ungrateful?

Of all the basketball coaches who have won national championships, none had the deck stacked against him like Nolan Richardson. He grew up in the poorest neighborhood in America's most remote city; not one black man was working the sidelines in major college basketball when he began coaching high school in 1967.

Richardson was an innovator whose teams performed at a frantic and furious pace. His style of play was nicknamed "Forty Minutes of Hell."

Facing a Richardson team was physically and psychologically exhausting. He recruited players who were overlooked and had plenty to prove; then he conditioned them with a regimen of near-brutality until they were as hard and sharp as swords. During breaks in practice, between workouts, before games and at halftime, his speeches made it clear to his team that no one in the basketball hierarchy respected him—or any of them—and the only possible retribution for the snub had to be found on the basketball court. By game time they were so emotionally wired they seemed to give off sparks.

While most coaches separated their systems into offense and defense, Richardson saw the game as flowing turmoil. Substitutions came often, sometimes en masse, and the rapid rotation of players contributed to the sense that the game was descending into chaos.

His players exerted defensive pressure the entire length of the court, attacking the ball the instant it was passed into play and dogging the dribbler's every step. Traps came quickly and constantly, but rarely at a moment that could be anticipated.

If the opponent managed to split the trap or escape the press with a precise pass, the illusion of an advantage would present itself, and that momentary mirage could be their undoing because Richardson's team had badgered them into playing at a speed at which they were unaccustomed. Endurance became paramount as his platoons of substitutes weighed heavily on the backs of his opponents. His five players were locked in relentless pursuit—pursuit of the dribbler, pursuit of the pass, pursuit of the missed shot, pursuit of the coach's approval. The thronging defense further frustrated the opponent's attack when his players rotated quickly after the double-teams. If his men made a steal, it was often because a forgotten guard trailing the play refused to give up and tipped the ball from behind. They would overcome players ahead of them, overcome halftime disadvantages, overcome their (often imaginary) underdog status.

At times it appeared Richardson must have six players on the nightmarishly cramped court. After a missed shot or a steal, though, when they converted to their fast-breaking offense, the court instantly felt as wide open as a West Texas freeway.

Like his press, the half-court offense was unpredictable by design. His teams slashed, penetrated, and attacked the basket before the opponent could establish their defense. A diagram of his system on a chalkboard looked like a Jackson Pollock painting.

Purists and traditionalists found "Forty Minutes of Hell" to be a violation of everything they'd learned about the sport. It was as if Richardson's teams wanted to destroy the very decorum of the game. And that was indeed precisely what his teams wanted—to confiscate the traditional etiquette of a college basketball game and snap its neck.

Richardson was an instinctive genius who disdained basketball's textbook theories, but he was rarely credited as a brilliant teacher, and this rekindled the resentment: when he was disrespected, his players were also implicated. The only way to shed the shackles and undo the affront was to play the next game as if their very existence depended on it. In this fashion, the paradigm was endlessly renewed.

How was it possible that this pioneering coach, winner of the national championship, whose style of play had altered the way college basketball was played, was going to be most remembered for a press conference?

ONE

A BEWITCHED CROSSROAD

On March 1, 2002, Nolan Richardson was terminated by the University of Arkansas. I was finishing a graduate degree at the time, after ending my own modest career in college basketball. Burned out, I stayed away from the game. Two NCAA Tournaments had come and gone, and I had not watched a single minute. I could not, however, avert my eyes from the train wreck Nolan Richardson's career had become, and I read as much as possible about his fantastic fall. Nearly every piece said that Richardson had brought on his own firing. The coaches I talked to—the white ones, anyway—wanted to know what a guy making that kind of money had to complain about.

Richardson seemed unable to move beyond 1968, determined to fight a war most Americans believed had ended long ago.

To understand Richardson's mindset, I knew I'd have to seriously examine the two most influential people in his professional career. Both of these men were icons in the world of college athletics, but they couldn't have been more different.

One, Don Haskins, was Richardson's own basketball coach, who accidentally began the avalanche that was the desegregation of college basketball teams. The other, Frank Broyles, was Richardson's boss at the University of Arkansas.

A photograph of Nolan Richardson hung above my desk at the University of Texas–El Paso for eight years. My assistant coaching job kept me on the phone constantly, so there was plenty of time to study that photo of Richardson, with TEXAS WESTERN across his chest, soaring above some anonymous white player. Richardson was an El Paso native, who finished his playing career in 1963, the photo's caption said. I wasn't one of those people who thought basketball had much to do with a person's character, but the photo revealed something. Power, maybe. Nerve and confidence. Aggression.

UTEP (Texas Western College until 1967) had a compelling basketball history. Every wall in the basketball office was adorned with black-and-white action shots of players who had survived the decades of Don Haskins's harrowing discipline. These guys had magical names that *sounded* like they were basketball players. Willie Cager. Bobby Joe Hill and "Big Daddy" Lattin. Tiny Archibald and "Bad News" Barnes.

I had stumbled onto that job at UTEP in 1983, an entry-level graduate assistant under the Miners' coach Don Haskins. Haskins was a cult figure then because he had stunned the world of college basketball by upsetting Kentucky for the NCAA title in 1966. What got people excited wasn't simply the shock of a remote school beating a traditional power. The focus was on race. Haskins played only his black players in that final game.

No team in the Southwest Conference, where nearly all the big Texas schools competed, had ever suited up a single black player. Texas Western, however, was an independent with no conference affiliation.

The championship game had been dominated by black athletes before 1966. In 1963, Loyola beat Cincinnati for the national title. Loyola started four black players, Cincinnati three. But as chance would have it in 1966, Texas Western's Miners faced Kentucky, who had never dressed out a black player. Kentucky's entire league, the Southeast Conference, was segregated.

Given that the 1960s were an era of protest, it is tempting to interpret Haskins's move as a political statement. It wasn't. The Black Power movement of the 1960s didn't alter Haskins one bit. He was hard on his players before, during, and after, and wasn't exactly poring over the writings of Eldridge Cleaver. Haskins, who won over seven hundred games during his tenure at El Paso, was distinctly apolitical, and his only quest was to smother opponents with stifling defense. Both in interviews and during private conversation, he insisted that he merely started his best five players.

Haskins's nickname was "The Bear," and he seemed to have ridden on horseback out of the pages of a Cormac McCarthy novel. He preferred shooting pool, smoking, tavern life, and hunting quail to schmoozing with corporate types or doing television interviews. His speech was peppered with Southwestern cowboy-isms, and he rarely asked a question to which he didn't already know the answer. Making big money was of little interest to Haskins, and only once was he even offered another job.

During my eight seasons at UTEP, I became an unofficial expert in the history of the basketball team. Forty years after their historic victory, the 1966 El Paso team would become the subject of the movie *Glory Road*. At the movie's premiere, two ushers shushed me as I pointed out the numerous factual errors in the film.

In fact, the 1966 championship brought Haskins plenty of aggravation. *Sports Illustrated*, in a 1968 series called "The Black Athlete," attacked Haskins for his black players' graduation rate. Then James Michener, in his book *Sports in America*, repeated the claims: none of the black players had graduated. Both *Sports Illustrated* and Michener were off base—all but two of the entire championship team earned degrees—but Haskins's reputation suffered.

I lucked out my first year recruiting at UTEP by finding an unknown point guard out of Chicago, named Tim Hardaway. After college, Hardaway would play thirteen NBA seasons and appear in five NBA All Star games. We signed him early, and I got a reputation for being an astute judge of talent.

Hardaway's high school coach was a guy named Bob Walters. Many blacks in Chicago have ties to Mississippi's Delta; that's how the blues came to Chicago, on the backs of musicians such as Muddy Waters and Howlin' Wolf. But Walters was not from Mississippi. He was from Prescott, Arkansas. Walters had an unusually clear memory of watching the 1966 Texas Western championship and knew details about that historic match-up that only real students of the game could possibly recall.

I would smile sheepishly when people said nabbing Hardaway was a brilliant move. The talk about my shrewd evaluations was flattering; my modesty, however, was genuine. It was beginner's luck. Hardaway took just one other campus visit before signing early at UTEP, fifteen hundred miles from Chicago. I never analyzed our good fortune in landing Hardaway, or the enthusiasm Bob Walters had for UTEP.

Once an older fan, a friend of Haskins, walked in and tapped his knuckles to the photo of Richardson, who was by then a successful college coach.

"He won't shut up about racism," the man said. "Everything is black or white to Nolan Richardson."

That take on Richardson proved to be a common point of view. Even Don Haskins, the Abe Lincoln of college hoops, was occasionally perplexed when Richardson would challenge the newest SAT requirements or media coverage as racist.

I followed Richardson's coaching career closely—he was an older uncle in my new UTEP family. We met a few times, on rental car shuttles, at junior college tournaments, or at airports. In the 1985 NCAA playoffs, UTEP played his Tulsa team. But Richardson's daughter was sick, and he didn't get to the game until minutes before tip-off. We beat Tulsa that night in a fairly close game, and we got a little help from the referees since UTEP set the NCAA record for "Most Free Throws Attempted." It was not the kind of record that impresses anyone, but it was something Richardson emphasized to me when I first began interviewing him twenty years later. Fifty-five free throws UTEP shot that night, he said. He was exactly right, as it turned out, but who remembers getting screwed after two decades?

TWO

BLACK BOY

El Paso, Texas, was known as El Paso del Norte until the late 1850s. A gap between the Franklin Mountains and the Sierra de Juárez allowed travelers a convenient route to journey east to west. Because of this geographical advantage, the border town below attracted nomads and newcomers, and some boundaries blurred.

Black men could find work because four separate railroad lines ran through El Paso at the turn of the century. The railroads provided jobs as well as access. El Paso, at the edge of U.S. territory, was relatively open to working black men and even had a Negro Women's League. Plenty of social and legal pressures, however, kept the races apart, especially black men and white women. In 1893, the state of Texas enacted a law that prohibited interracial marriage.

No obvious black neighborhood existed in El Paso in the early 1900s, and there isn't one today. By the time Richardson was old enough to attend school, close to four thousand blacks lived in El Paso—a mere 3 percent of the population. Some lived near the army base, and others lived close to the border, near downtown. All black children had to attend Frederick Douglass Colored School, which opened around 1890.

In 1911, the school's principal introduced Booker T. Washington, founder of the Tuskegee Institute, to a packed house at the El Paso Theater. That day, Booker T. Washington urged blacks not to fight the forces of segregation and instead to accommodate whites based on their mutual interests—economics. This idea played well in El Paso, a town where blacks were treated a little better than in most of Texas. Around that same time, a chapter of the NAACP formed in El Paso.

The Ku Klux Klan moved into El Paso soon afterward and exerted a growing influence over city hall and El Paso's biggest newspaper.

Nolan Richardson's mother, Clareast, was just twenty-one years old when she withered away from a mysterious disease in 1944. The family was living in Los Angeles, and had little access to medical care. Clareast Richardson left behind three young kids: Shirley was five, Nolan Jr. three, Helen six months old. The Richardson kids had few options but to move in with the children's grandmother in El Paso's poorest neighborhood, the Segundo Barrio.

For years, the Segundo Barrio was the Ellis Island for many Mexican immigrants coming to the United States. Despite the constant influx of newcomers, the neighborhood had a settled and historic feel. Low-slung adobe buildings, hand-painted storefronts, blaring *norteño* music, and lively street life dominated El Paso's second ward.

Nolan's father, Nolan Richardson Sr., had a sporadic career as a prizefighter. He lived in El Paso on and off, working at a car dealership when he was in town. While he stopped by to visit his kids after their relocation, he didn't often live with the family. He battled the bottle much of his adult life.

That left the responsibility of raising Clareast's three kids to their grandmother, Rose Richardson—"Ol' Mama." Ol' Mama was from just outside of Ruston, Louisiana, but had moved to El Paso in her youth. She worked two jobs: one as a cook at Hardees, a family restaurant on Alameda Street; the other waitressing around El Paso.

Richardson's grandfather—Ol' Papa, of course—was a huge man, whose health was already declining when the grandkids moved in. He was born in 1875, ten years before Ol' Mama. He gave young Nolan the nickname "Sam." Sometimes he was "Sweet Sam" and sometimes "Sam Don't Give a Damn."

The expanded family resided in a three-room house, well before the days when air-conditioning made El Paso tolerable. The house was at 1626 Overland Street, a short walk from the downtown bridge that connected El Paso to Juárez, Mexico. Ol' Mama was a peculiarly determined and serious woman, and she made no secret of her belief that young Nolan Jr. was special. She reminded him constantly that he was going to be different from other kids, and she very much meant it. Richardson is still struck today by the bond he had with his stern, diminutive grandmother, despite the fact that the extended family was large. "I had the feeling that she loved *me* more," he says.

The gritty pocket of the Segundo Barrio where Richardson became fluent in border Spanish was called El Pujido. The area was plagued by poverty, but Richardson insists he was never hassled in the Mexican-American neighborhood, despite being the only black boy around.

Outsiders believed the El Paso neighborhood the Richardsons lived in was treacherous, but he only feared two things: Ol' Mama's disapproval, or, worse, her leaving him. His cousins would go out of town for Christmas. Not Richardson. "I'd stay around Ol' Mama because I was afraid when I came back she might be gone," he says. Richardson would sit at her feet and badger her to tell him stories.

When he was small, this meant Bible stories. "I knew the Bible better than any churchgoing friends of mine," he says.

She'd also tell Richardson about her own parents.

Ol' Mama was born in 1885; her parents had been enslaved in Louisiana. This one-person separation from that history had a profound impact on Richardson. "I grew up hearing stories about what slavery was like," he says. "Not from any *book*," he says, a refrain he'd use in his professional life, "but from my grandmother, whose very parents had lived it." A story that stuck with him was about one of the few ways a slave had to rebel: inflicting an injury on himself.

It began to register with Richardson that being black was something of consequence one day, when he was ten years old, at El Paso's Washington Park.

The El Paso summer heat can be devastating, and in the 1940s and 1950s, the only relief was at the local swimming pools. Richardson already knew he was not allowed to swim at the Segundo Barrio's Armijo Park pool: they had a no-Negroes rule. Ol' Mama figured they'd try at Washington Park, where black kids were allowed—one single afternoon a year.

The blistering sun made it almost too hot to stand in place on the cement deck that day. Not that the barefoot kids would have stood still—they sprinted before slanting a dive or cannonball into the cool, blue water.

Occasionally, a splash reached close to Richardson's sneakered feet. He kept his fingers wrapped in a fist around the fencing that kept him from the swimming pool. The yelping of the white children was joyous, but he didn't smile. He could feel the intense heat rise up from the bottom of his shoes, as if the rubber might melt and he'd be stuck watching the swimmers forever. It was over one hundred degrees, as it often was in El Paso.

The dozens of white kids didn't notice him. They shoved and

dunked each other amiably, then ran up close enough to him that it was nearly impolite of them not to say hello, or come on in, the water's fine.

Richardson knew they'd gotten the day wrong, but stood for a while anyway. It was June of 1951, but not Juneteenth, the unofficial holiday that celebrated the end of slavery in Texas. Juneteenth was the single day each year when black kids were allowed to swim. "They'd drain the pool afterward," he says, "and fill it up fresh again."

Richardson often recalls this swimming-pool story when he talks about growing up in El Paso. "Lots of people think that because Texas Western won the national championship in 1966 that El Paso was always a progressive town," he says. "But that's not true." El Paso's theaters, restaurants, and hotels were segregated as well. Mexican-Americans were welcome most places, but blacks were not.

Once-a-summer swimming in El Paso's blazing heat wasn't enough to cool him off. He found the Missouri Street Center, the only pool where black and Mexican-American kids could swim all summer. As he got older, if Richardson felt frustrated in the lagging-behind Texas town, he would head south. With the border only a baseball-throw away, he crossed into Mexico at will by the time he was a teenager. "In Juárez, I always felt freer," he says. "My Spanish was nearly as good as my English, and the folks in Mexico didn't seem the least bit concerned with a young black kid exploring the streets."

When Richardson was twelve, his father died. His grandfather, Ol' Papa, passed away soon after. With the men in his life gone, he grew even closer with Ol' Mama.

Frederick Douglass School was a small building on Eucalyptus Street that housed close to a hundred students. Because of a lack of space and teachers, every classroom served several grades, from first to twelfth. The books were ragged hand-me-downs from El Paso's white schools and included the long list of previous owners' names on the books' inside covers. Yet, by all accounts, Douglass had talented teachers and was the unifying institution for El Paso blacks. It wasn't exactly idyllic, but Douglass provided Richardson with both a sense of place and history.

The social scene for blacks in El Paso, formed at Douglass School, was limited but lively. Shiloh Baptist Church was a hub, as were places like Rusty's Playhouse, Gillespie's Steak House, and the Square Deal Barbershop.

On one scorching afternoon, when Richardson was thirteen, a teacher named Mrs. Johnnie Calvert closed the doors and windows. That got the attention of everyone in the class. "We knew that something important was up," Richardson says.

Mrs. Calvert cleared her throat and spoke softly to her subdued class. "There's going to be a big change coming to this country," she said. "Soon, Negro children and white children will be going to school together, and all of you will have a choice to make." There was a Supreme Court case, the teacher said, in which a Negro family had challenged the laws, hoping their daughter could go to the same school as the white kids. The Douglass students looked at each other but didn't speak. "You can stay at Douglass, or you can go to the school in your neighborhood," Mrs. Calvert said.

Douglass School's 1954 valedictorian, Thelma White, decided to test that Supreme Court decision. With the help of the local NAACP, she applied at Texas Western College, but was denied admission. She took Texas Western to court and won. The following year, she was admitted, along with twelve other black students. But Thelma White, put off by the snub and subsequent delays, had enrolled at nearby New Mexico State University by the time the case was decided.

George McCarty, the Texas Western basketball coach at the time, realized that the college's decision to admit blacks might be used to his advantage. He signed up a junior college player named Charlie Brown in 1956 to be the first black athlete at any mainly white school in the old Confederacy. Richardson, a high school freshman, was intrigued by the news.

El Paso during this era was torn. While the influence of the Klan had long faded, this was still Texas. The town remained segregated and blacks had to ride in the back of city buses and trolleys. Unlike most of the South, though, blacks could shop and feel welcome at premier places, such as the Popular and White House Department Store. They could even try on clothes and hats before making a purchase, something that was denied them all over the South.

The peculiar combination Richardson absorbed—the community and tradition at Douglass School, and his soulful Mexican neighborhood—gave him a unique view of the world. Richardson was the only Douglass student who lived in the Pujido section, part of the Bowie High School district. Bowie was virtually one hundred percent Mexican-American. That didn't worry Richardson. He chose Bowie and became their first black student. "All the kids I'd known forever from the barrio were going to Bowie," he says, "and I knew I'd be fine. I didn't have any kind of chip on my shoulder, because in that neighborhood, I was just Sam."

Richardson loved nearly everything about his time at Bowie. "The Mexican kids treated me so well," he says. "I was an athlete, of course, and that helped."

There were some problems before Richardson established himself as a sports hero, though. During his freshman year, he was called to the main office by an assistant principal, named, of all things, Patton. "Raymond Patton," Richardson recalls. "And he was mean."

Richardson looked down, shuffling in place as Patton chewed him out for an overdue library book. "You're not allowed back in school until this fine is paid and I see your parents," Patton said.

Richardson made the long trek home in the heat to tell Ol' Mama. She grabbed her purse, and the two walked back to Bowie to meet Patton.

"How much do you owe?" Ol' Mama asked midway to the high school.

"Six cents," Richardson said.

Ol' Mama's pace quickened. When they got to Patton's office, Ol' Mama went on the attack, insisting to Patton that the punishment didn't fit the crime. Richardson, who often stared at his shoes when confronted by authority, was quietly thrilled that Ol' Mama had straightened out the most feared faculty member in the building. He didn't expect what happened when they got outside the office.

Ol' Mama turned on Richardson and let him have it, too. "I saw you looking down at the ground in there," she said, poking him in the chest. "Don't you ever put your head down in front of anyone. You look every man in the eye, I don't care what color he is!"

Richardson offered to escort her home, but she declined, and ordered him back to class. But not until she gave him one more earful. "You don't like yourself," she said. "Don't be staring down at the floor ever again."

Richardson, who was fourteen at the time, sees this episode as a crossroads in his life. "She had given me permission to be a man," he says.

As a teenager, Nolan began to see more of El Paso. He had friends who owned *ranflas*, and they wanted to drive these jalopies to investigate more than the town's swimming pools.

"I think my first shock was trying to go to the movies, and seeing how the different theaters operated," Richardson says. "Movies were our biggest form of entertainment, but nearly all of the theaters were for whites only." At the Mission Theater, blacks could sit in the balcony. The Alcazar Theater was the only integrated movie house in El Paso until Richardson attended college, although the army base sometimes hosted integrated audiences at movies then, too. Occasionally, his Mexican-American friends had to be reminded that Richardson couldn't go everywhere they were allowed.

Mexican-Americans viewed Richardson as one of their own, and his status as an unofficial Mexican had its benefits—with perhaps one drawback. "The treatment my dad received from Mexican-Americans is very different than the way he was received by whites," his daughter Madalyn says. "Still, I don't think El Paso's Mexican people fully understood the racial discrimination he was fighting against. It was different for him as a black man. But that's because the Mexican people never assigned the color black to his skin."

During Richardson's history class his junior year at Bowie, a teacher told the students about a high school in the South where the Negro students were having problems. The National Guard had been called in to help a handful of Negro kids enroll at the all-white Central High School. Nine of them, mostly girls, came to Central, and some of those girls had been spit on, even by their classmates.

This was in Arkansas, the teacher said. Then she pulled down a tattered map and reminded the students where Arkansas was. Girls being threatened and spit upon? Richardson didn't know whether to weep or fight.

That night, he and his grandmother went across the street to a neighbor's to see Arkansas on the evening news. "All these troops were coming in, and their governor was on, too," Richardson recalls, "talking bad about President Eisenhower. Nothing like that had ever happened at Bowie. Until that day in class, there was no reason to talk about what was happening in Arkansas. Now I was frightened, scared of Arkansas, Mississippi, places like that. Ol' Mama said it was horrible there for black folks."

Fearing Ol' Mama's fierce glare, Richardson took school seriously, and developed other talents besides athletics. He played the dented trumpet issued by the school for marching band, except during football season. "The coach wouldn't let me march during the halftime shows," he says.

As a young boy, Richardson idolized Rocky Galarza, a Segundo Barrio legend with movie-star good looks. Ten years Richardson's senior, Galarza was one of the heroes on Bowie's state championship baseball team of 1949. Galarza had encouraged him to attend Bowie, emphasizing what a great leader Nemo Herrera was. Herrera coached baseball and basketball at Bowie and was regarded as the godfather of El Paso coaches.

Richardson would surpass Galarza's accomplishments, being named All-City in football, basketball, and baseball. In one basketball game, Richardson sank an incredible twenty-four baskets, missing just five shots.

The spring of Richardson's junior year in high school, the Bowie Bears baseball team won a spot in the district playoffs. A powerful left-handed hitter, Richardson batted .450 that season. He was clearly the Bears' best player, and still the only black kid on the squad. The playoff games would be held in Abilene, an eight-hour drive into the heart of Texas. This would be his first trip with a sports team, and Richardson was beside himself with excitement.

A few days before their departure, Coach Nemo Herrera surprised Richardson by showing up at Ol' Mama's shotgun house. Herrera didn't usually make house calls.

Richardson wasn't allowed to stay with his Mexican-American teammates at the hotel in Abilene, Herrera said. Playing in the games wouldn't be a problem, but the coach was going to find Richardson a family to stay with in Abilene, a Negro family.

Richardson was angry when Coach Herrera left. "To hell with Bowie baseball, then," he said to the only other set of ears in the house. Ol' Mama looked at him hard. "You're going on the trip," she said. "You let your bat do your talking for you. If you don't go, this kind of stuff is going to go on forever."

Richardson started to speak, but Ol' Mama cut him off, listing the enormous changes she'd seen in the world between 1885 and 1958. "Your children will one day get to stay in those hotels," she said.

Richardson knew what was coming next.

"If it wasn't for Jackie *Robinson*," she added, "you wouldn't be able to do this, or anything else." Ol' Mama didn't care much about sports, but she admired the baseball pioneer and would often invoke his name as if it were sacred.

When the Bowie Bears arrived in Abilene, the usually boisterous bus grew silent. The Bowie players filed off, with a nod or handshake offered to their black star, then disappeared into the hotel. Richardson, who was seated on the sidewalk side of the bus, memorized the face of the building. Then the bus driver took him to his accommodation with an elderly black couple, living, of course, on the other side of the tracks. Richardson says, "They were very kind and I had my own bed. Also, the lady's cooking was terrific."

The bus came by the next morning, this time full of Bowie players and coaches. Richardson didn't speak on the ride to the game.

Richardson clubbed two home runs that day, and the Bowie Bears won. He thought that might be the end of it—he'd let his bat do the talking for sure. Instead, he came home to another lecture from Ol'

Mama, who, as usual, was waiting on the porch for him. Somehow she'd already heard the news.

"The only way you're going to make it is to keep going," she said. If he were good enough in sports, she said, he'd get an athletics scholarship. "But you have to keep knocking on that door," she said. "And when it opens a little bit—just a crack—you knock that damn door down, you hear!"

When Richardson was sixteen, he found his own personal Jackie Robinson in Texas Western's first black player, Charlie Brown.

Charlie Brown was a twenty-six-year-old air force veteran when he arrived in El Paso on a basketball scholarship in the summer of 1956. (Jackie Robinson was a twenty-eight-year-old army veteran when he joined the Brooklyn Dodgers.) A native of Tyler, Texas, Brown had played a year of junior college ball in Amarillo.

Only 6'1", Brown paced Texas Western College in scoring and rebounding in each of his three seasons, averaging 17.4 points as well as eight rebounds per game. After he poured in 29 points against New Mexico State, their longtime coach Presley Askew—who had been the University of Arkansas coach in the early 1950s—said, "Charlie Brown is the best basketball player I have ever seen."

When Brown first arrived in El Paso, he was met by one of Texas Western's graduating guards, Alvis Glidewell. The bespectacled Glidewell was an intellectual kid who already professed a desire to coach. He carried the less-than-flattering nickname of "Tweetie Bird," but was respected by his teammates for his dedication and heady play. Glidewell and Brown became best pals. Glidewell recalls, "We tried to go to a movie at the Plaza Theater, but they wouldn't let Charlie in. But everybody liked Charlie and it wasn't just because of basketball. Charlie was the darling of the whole school."

In 1958, Glidewell began coaching at El Paso's Austin High

School, where he'd witness Richardson's final two high school seasons. "Nolan made Bowie good all by himself," he says, "and was likely the best all-around athlete we've ever seen in El Paso, and not just because of basketball. He was dominating three sports." Unbeknown to Glidewell, Richardson began keeping tabs on him as well.

Richardson began playing with Charlie Brown while he was still attending Bowie. A local basketball fan, Saul Kleinfeld, put together a traveling team to represent his company, Union Furniture, and he recruited Richardson to be their youngest member. The rest of the team consisted of players and former players from Texas Western. Kleinfeld's crew would often go deep into the interior of Mexico, and they continued to play together in the summers after Richardson had graduated from Bowie.

Texas Western's basketball coach tried to recruit Richardson to play for the Miners, but got frustrated with his indecision that spring. Richardson believed that since the Miners had no baseball team, the school was not ideal. Just before his graduation, he was offered a basketball scholarship to nearby New Mexico State University, which had both basketball and baseball. That inspired coach Nemo Herrera to honor his only black athlete. Herrera organized a collection to buy a gift for Richardson—his first suit, to be worn at commencement.

On graduation day, Richardson donned that suit, slung the cap and gown over his shoulder, ready for the ceremonies. But Ol' Mama insisted he put on the graduation gown so that everyone who saw him would understand that this was a high school graduate. Richardson complied, and they traveled on foot, Richardson complaining, Ol' Mama beaming.

The following week, Richardson changed his mind about New Mexico State, deciding that he might rather concentrate on baseball. Unsure of what to do, he asked Bert Williams for help.

Bert Williams was an El Paso city alderman who had played basketball at Texas Western after the war. He still played summer baseball, and like anyone involved in El Paso baseball, he knew Richardson. Williams phoned a friend, the coach at the University of Arizona, a baseball mecca. The Arizona coach had done his homework; he knew exactly who Richardson was, and tempted him with talk of a future in Major League baseball.

There was a hurdle, though. He had a 2.6 grade point average, and Arizona required a 3.0 for out-of-state kids. Williams, with the help of the Arizona coach, arranged for Richardson to attend Eastern Arizona Junior College for one season. Richardson didn't anticipate playing basketball, despite his admiration for Charlie Brown. "Ol' Mama wasn't the only one," he says. "By then I was totally enamored of Jackie Robinson, too."

THREE

THE KNOWN WORLD

In September of 1959, Richardson enrolled at Eastern Arizona, certain he'd be gone to Arizona on a baseball scholarship after one year. The basketball coach at Eastern Arizona learned of Richardson's background, though, and convinced him to play hoops. That was a smart move. Richardson was sensational, scoring 22 points and ten rebounds per game before the baseball season even began.

Around Christmas, Richardson married his high school sweetheart, Helen, then returned alone to Eastern Arizona. When Helen phoned to say she was pregnant, he knew that Arizona or New Mexico State could no longer be an option. He needed to go home to El Paso to be near both of their families. Harold Davis, Texas Western's basketball coach, heard rumors of Richardson's situation and offered him a full scholarship. Texas Western still didn't field a baseball team, so it seemed an abrupt end to his baseball career.

Richardson racked up a lot of points his first season at Texas Western. An explosive and determined wing player, he scored 21 a game as a sophomore. The team wasn't too bad that year, either, finishing 12-12. Playing for Harold Davis was a pleasure because the coach allowed Richardson to shoot whenever he got the urge.

Still, something about his time under Davis didn't sit right with Richardson.

The Miners were invited to a three-game holiday tournament at Centenary College in Shreveport, the team's first road trip. Texas Western had won their first five games in a row going into the tournament and expectations were high. Richardson was excited because Ol' Mama was from Louisiana, and he was hoping maybe some distant relatives could attend.

Harold Davis called his high-scoring wing player aside a few days before the team's scheduled departure. Davis was never threatening or aggressive with the players, and he often used his private talks to bolster their confidence, so Richardson figured it was another pep talk.

"You can't play this weekend," Davis told him.

Richardson, who'd been having a bit of trouble with an injury, yelped in protest. "My ankle's fine, coach," he said. He hopped side to side to demonstrate.

His health was not the issue. The tournament at Centenary College had a rule: no Negroes.

Richardson stayed at home, lonely and depressed, while the undefeated Texas Western team flew to Shreveport. The Miners promptly lost all three games. Richardson listened to the games on the radio, pacing back and forth and kicking his couch.

The Shreveport Tournament snub is something Richardson talks about to this day. He was fond of Davis, but was hurt and angry that the coach did not have the backbone to do what was right.

"I think that story really defined my dad," says his oldest child, Madalyn. "He always said that Harold Davis should have forfeited those games."

————

After Richardson's sophomore season in 1961, Harold Davis resigned from Texas Western. His family's oil wells out near Big Spring, Texas, had gone crazy. Money was gushing out of the ground, plenty more than the sorry salary that a Texas mining college paid its basketball coach.

One August afternoon, Richardson was standing outside the Miners Hall dorm in the shade of an overgrown cactus. A football player nudged Richardson and said, "Your new basketball coach is here." It was Davis's coaching replacement, Don Haskins, from tiny Dumas High School in the Texas panhandle.

Haskins, red-faced and cranky from his kids' crying, climbed out of the station wagon, his family's U-Haul in tow. Haskins was annoyed, because he had been straining to listen to the live radio reports as he drove into town. The world's first commercial airplane hijacking had taken place at El Paso's airport.

Richardson couldn't quite remember the new coach's name, but he stepped into the El Paso sunshine to help the man unload his station wagon.

Haskins recalled Richardson emerging from the shade: "He had muscles popping out all over and a tiny waist and just looked like an athlete. I hadn't seen anybody that looked like Nolan Richardson. I couldn't wait to get him into the gym."

Texas Western's athletics director had given Haskins the scouting report on his new team, focusing specifically on the two stars. Al Tolen, a white forward, had averaged nearly as much as Richardson. "The first one of them who got the ball shot it," Haskins said. In fact, Tolen and Richardson took more shots than the rest of the team *combined*. Everyone Haskins talked to concurred that Richardson was a terrific talent but wouldn't make an effort on defense. Haskins reckoned he understood the problem. "Nobody had ever asked him to guard anyone," he said.

When the unloading was done, Haskins got face to face with Richardson and established the terms for their next two years together.

"I heard," Haskins said, pointing a finger in Richardson's face, "that you can't guard a goddamn fencepost."

Like Richardson, Don Haskins chose to play at a college near his home. Haskins had a rocky playing career with the hyper-disciplined Henry Iba at Oklahoma A&M (later renamed Oklahoma State). He'd score a bunch of points one game, then wind up on the bench for his lack of defense or appearing too confident. Haskins even had some academic eligibility trouble, further irritating Mr. Iba.

Haskins was from Enid, where he had befriended an older boy named Herman Carr. They'd pal around or go shoot hoops. Haskins admired Carr and thought it was a shame that he was not playing college ball. Carr did not have a basketball scholarship for a reason. "Herman Carr was black," Haskins said. "Simple." Haskins and Carr would get grief wherever they went in Enid, even in the black neighborhood. "We got ran off several times," Haskins said. "He was just black and I was white and there wasn't much difference between us."

Herman Carr was at the forefront of Haskins's mind when he began interacting with Richardson and Willie Brown, the only black players at Texas Western that August. Haskins was captivated with Richardson's athletic ability, and realized that his versatility might cause him to miss court time in the off-season. "I saw him run a 9.7 hundred-yard dash at Texas Western," Haskins recalled. "He'd beat everybody without even having time to practice, and that was wearing basketball shoes."

Richardson never roomed on campus when he played for the Miners. He and Helen rented a house on Tularosa Street in central

El Paso, using the money he made at two part-time jobs to get by. It was here that Richardson's first three children were born—Madalyn, Nolan III ("Notes"), and Bradley. He was less than a mile away from his old neighborhood and felt more of a connection to the town of El Paso than to Texas Western College. Yet El Paso was still segregated by law, something that continued to irritate him.

Because of his athletic prowess, there were other El Paso businessmen who coveted Richardson for their summer baseball teams. City alderman Bert Williams, who'd helped him get to Eastern Arizona, also moonlighted as a basketball referee. That summer, after a basketball game, he convinced Richardson to join his fast-pitch softball team. After a game when Richardson batted in the winning run, Williams offered to treat him to dinner at a popular Copia Street restaurant, the Oasis. It was the summer of 1961, months before Richardson would play a game for Don Haskins.

"I can't go in there, Bert," Richardson said as they rolled into the Oasis parking lot.

"Why the hell not?" Williams said, popping the car door open. Surely they'd serve an alderman and the college's top athlete, Williams reasoned. The two men took a seat, but the waitress came over without menus or water. Williams asked for a beer, Richardson wanted a Coke. The smell of grilled hamburgers and fried potatoes floated back to their table.

"I cannot serve *him* in this restaurant," the waitress said, refusing to look at Richardson.

Williams tried to force the issue—the owner of the restaurant was Fred Hervey, who had been El Paso's mayor, and Williams mentioned that he knew him. The tables got quiet as a bitter stalemate ensued. Williams grabbed Richardson—who'd kept silent—by the elbow and led him to the door. "I'll be back," Williams warned.

Williams was so upset by the incident that he immediately began drafting legislation to officially end the segregation of El Paso hotels, restaurants, and theaters.

"The city was divided by railroad tracks," Williams recalls, "but the laws were enforced more arbitrarily for Mexican-Americans, and there were places where they could eat without trouble." The laws were nearly always enforced to keep blacks out, though.

Bert Williams became obsessed with integrating El Paso. After rallying his fellow aldermen and revising the wording, the bill was ready. The ordinance—the first of its kind, Williams says, in Texas—passed an initial vote. It would need to pass another, and get the mayor's approval to be turned into law. Both El Paso newspapers, the *Times* and the *Herald-Post*, published editorials condemning the progress. The mayor vetoed the ordinance, but Williams had enough votes to override him.

"It was just by coincidence that Nolan was there that night at the Oasis," says Williams, who was subsequently elected mayor himself. "After I witnessed the way he was treated, such a great kid and the star of the college, I knew I had to do something."

Bert Williams's heroic act made El Paso the first major city in the old Confederacy to officially desegregate. Yet Williams's courage—he ignored numerous threats and enormous pressure—was barely reported nationally and remains nearly forgotten even in El Paso. Don Haskins took notice though. The town's new progressive status would have a profound effect on Texas Western's ability to recruit black athletes. Two years after Bert Williams's legislation passed in El Paso, the United States adopted national civil rights legislation into law.

NCAA rules at the time allowed Richardson to work while he was enrolled in college. Every Wednesday he hauled heaps of wood scrap and planks around a downtown lumberyard. That wasn't as enjoyable as his Sunday job, parking cars at First Methodist Church, not too far from the college. The church was the one Haskins and his family attended, and the coach had arranged for the job. "I'd park cars for white folks coming into church," Richardson says, "and hang around until it was time to retrieve the car. Some people gave me a dollar tip, and that added up." Parking cars stands out as one of the few pleasant aspects of Richardson's time playing for Haskins.

The new coach's mannerisms were perplexing to Richardson. Haskins did not curse the players individually; instead, his invectives involved challenging the collective manhood of the entire group, or included phrases that Haskins considered derogatory. Many of these phrases simply left Richardson amused. "He'd tell us to quit our damn barbershopping," Richardson says. "He meant our gossiping."

Haskins's acerbic tone could be intimidating, yet Richardson believed the team would benefit from the discipline that had been absent under Harold Davis. "You could tell the way Coach Haskins acted—well, it *was* an act in some ways," Richardson says. "But he was different under the surface. I didn't like him much that first semester, though. He was taking away all of my shots."

In order to get his Miners to play with more patience, Haskins instituted a rule for practicing their offense. They had to pass the ball ten times before they shot. The rule didn't sit well with the team, but only Richardson openly challenged the policy.

"Sometimes when the ball came to me, I'd call out 'ten!' and shoot it," he says.

Playing for Harold Davis was more fun, but the Miners started to gain momentum, winning eight games in a row in Haskins's first season. Richardson grudgingly decided to buy into Haskins's system during the streak, recalling a favorite expression of Ol' Mama's—"A raggedy ride is better than a smooth walk." He stopped studying the stat sheet by January. "I tried not to think about my points," he says. "You could feel that the program was going to become something important."

By the end of Richardson's junior season—their first together—Haskins had molded Richardson into the Miners' best defender.

Texas Western finished Haskins's first season at 18-6. Under the new system of stubborn half-court defense and a tightly controlled passing-game offense, Richardson's offensive totals plummeted. A major college player who averages 20 points per game as a sophomore is headed toward basketball greatness and often a professional career. But Richardson went from 21 per game as a sophomore to 13.6, then finally 10.5 as a senior. In fact, in only one game in the two seasons after Haskins's arrival did Richardson again pop in 20 points, during a win against Tennessee. Any player who had his scoring average chopped in half would be sensitive about it, and Richardson was no exception. Only the fact that they were winning made it palatable.

Don Haskins was different from the previous coach in another respect, as well.

The Miners were in Abilene for a game. Haskins had Richardson and Willie Brown, as well as two other black players, Major Dennis and Bobby Joe Hill. (This was not the same Bobby Joe Hill who would star in Texas Western's upset of Kentucky in 1966, but an East Texas wing player.) The team was scheduled to stay at the same Abilene hotel that had denied Richardson a room as a Bowie player. When the Miners walked into the hotel lobby, the manager came scurrying over.

"No coloreds!" he said.

"So I told him to hell with him and his hotel," Haskins recalled. "We all stayed somewhere else."

The Miners rarely played in the South and usually traveled west for road games. But that kind of incident would recur.

"The next year," Haskins said, "we were in Salt Lake City, and the same goddamn thing happened. We got the hell out of there, too. I wasn't going to split my team up." He used the incident to motivate his team in the locker room—everyone was against the little team from El Paso, Haskins reminded the Miners again and again. He had recycled that "everyone is against us" speech since he arrived at Texas Western. The Miners beat both Utah State and Utah.

In August of 1962, Andy Stoglin enrolled at Texas Western. Stoglin was a rugged black kid from Phoenix who would become a key player for the Miners. Richardson and Stoglin weren't immediately tight, but when Richardson wound up in an El Paso hospital with a minor injury, he became friendly with Stoglin's wife, who worked as a nurse. Soon after, the two players—both married—grew close. The friendship between Stoglin and Richardson would endure for over four decades.

Stoglin was an outspoken critic of both overt and subtle racism, and Richardson admired him greatly. In fact, in the privacy of Haskins's office, Stoglin would even challenge Haskins as to why more black players weren't starting. Stoglin could hold a grudge and had little patience for the good ol' white boy system.

One day, Haskins called Stoglin into the office at Holliday Hall, the tiny gym where Texas Western played. "He pulled a drawer open, and showed me several letters saying that Texas Western was starting too many niggers," Stoglin says.

Stoglin says he perused a few of the letters, then looked up.

"Read enough?" Haskins asked him. "That's the reason I don't start you. You can handle that, but I don't want you to tell your teammates."

Stoglin remembers the incident down to the smallest detail. Haskins claimed not to recall either the letters or the talk with Stoglin.

Stoglin was a fine recruit, but Haskins would sign the best big man ever to play for the Miners the spring after Richardson's junior season.

Jim "Bad News" Barnes was raised in Arkansas but moved to Oklahoma, where he had hoped to enroll at Oklahoma State and play for Haskins's mentor, Henry Iba. Academic shortcomings forced Barnes to attend Cameron Junior College in Lawton. Haskins learned that the explosive big man still might not have the grades for OSU.

Haskins's own father was born in Arkansas, and he used that fact to try to get close with Barnes during his recruitment. Haskins spent the majority of his recruiting time and budget trying to convince Barnes to come to El Paso. In April, when he felt Barnes was stalling, Haskins played his last card. He challenged Barnes to a free-throw shooting contest. If Haskins lost, he'd leave the big man alone. If Haskins won, Texas Western got Barnes.

Barnes joined Texas Western for Richardson's final season.

Haskins shared credit for recruiting Barnes. "Nolan talked Jim into coming," he said. "I knew then Nolan would be a good recruiter." There was more than basketball on Barnes's mind. He made it clear he didn't want to live in a segregated city, but thanks to Bert Williams, that wouldn't be a problem.

Bad News Barnes was the nation's dominant big man for two years. In Richardson's senior year, the Miners qualified for the NCAA Tournament for the first time in school history, but they lost to the University of Texas in the first round.

The following year, without Richardson, the 1963–64 season, Barnes averaged a whopping 29.2 points per game. He led the Miners to their second-ever NCAA Tournament and was the first player picked in the NBA draft.

As the team's lone black player with El Paso roots, Richardson was often nominated to take visiting recruits around town. It had worked with Jim Barnes, and Haskins quickly recognized Richardson as the perfect tour guide for black prospects. Even after Richardson's playing career was over, Haskins relied on him to socialize with Texas Western's recruits, including most of the historic 1966 team.

Richardson knew El Paso still had some unofficial Jim Crow sites, and Mexico became the preferred destination.

In Juárez, black men could eat thick steaks, dance with whomever they wanted, and stay out as late as they pleased. Heroes from the 1966 team, such as Harry Flournoy, Orsten Artis, Bobby Joe Hill, and Nevil Shed all socialized in Mexico with Richardson and had a lively time. As such, Mexico as well as Bert Williams hold a place in the history of American college basketball; they were largely responsible for the recruitment and comfort of the historic Texas Western team.

———

While a professional career appeared to be a long shot, Richardson continued to train in order to improve his chances. El Paso barely had a basketball tradition, and few pickup games or playground culture existed. Finding real competition in the off-season was a challenge, so Richardson often trained at Fort Bliss, the ironically named army base. The soldiers, with their stubby beards and thick chests, were not great players, but they offered rough competition, and Richardson loved it.

Kenny John, a local high school star who was heading to UTEP, heard about the games at Fort Bliss and became a regular as well.

"Nolan had no off season," John recalls. John began challenging the older Richardson to play one on one every day, figuring that would help him improve, too. Richardson was incredibly competitive, John says. "He'd get right up next to you and head-check you."

Head-check?

As John began with the ball at the top of the key, Richardson thrust his forehead into John to control his movement. "His neck was so strong and he was so quick," John says, "that he'd stick his head into you to slow down your drive. I've never seen that, before or since. Can you imagine?"

John was no pushover—he could dunk, shoot from long range, and would soon be the starting guard at UTEP along with Nate Archibald. "If you want to understand Nolan Richardson," John says, "just visualize that head-check."

FOUR

NATIVE SON

Texas Western finally added a baseball team Richardson's senior year. He hit .421, with ten home runs. He was among the NCAA leaders in RBIs, and that single 1963 season was enough to get him noticed. The Houston Colt 45s drafted him and offered a signing bonus, but Richardson now had three children. A journey beginning in the Class C minor leagues didn't interest him.

The AFL's San Diego Chargers also drafted him in football, although Richardson had not played a minute of the sport since high school. He went to San Diego to try out but pulled a hamstring the first week and came home. Richardson lacked nearly a full semester of coursework to get his diploma from Texas Western, and he would not have returned to college quickly had the Chargers kept him. When he was waived, he opted to finish his degree at Texas Western.

He went undrafted in basketball but continued to play with a traveling team sponsored by Saul Kleinfeld, the prominent El Pasoan. Their schedule would take them into Mexico, where Richardson's fluency in Spanish came in handy. He could listen in on the opponents' strategy during free-throws and dead balls.

The trips to Mexico would provide him with an important lesson. Kleinfeld's team might have Texas Western players, including stars such as Bobby Joe Hill and David Lattin. They were far better than most college teams, and Richardson thought nobody in Mexico could possibly come close.

He was wrong. Occasionally the black stars from the best program in Texas would be frustrated by the press and fast break of the smaller—and superbly conditioned—Mexican teams. It was an epiphany of sorts for Richardson, and he kept the memory of the racehorse Mexican teams in the back of his mind.

Richardson was hired to teach and coach at Bowie High School in the fall of 1964. The principal, Frank Pollit, must have assumed Richardson's versatility in athletics meant that he was well-rounded in the classroom. Pollit assigned him a vast array of classes over the next decade, including math, English, social studies, history, and physical education. Richardson was given coaching assignments for JV and ninth-grade football, baseball, and basketball, and he stuck with these lower-level posts for three years. His total salary was $4,500 per year.

One day, Pollit asked him what sport he really wanted to build his career on.

Texas high school football, of course, was immensely popular, and the Friday night lights seduced Richardson briefly. He told Pollit that he dreamed of being a head football coach someday.

"Wrong answer," said Pollit. "It will take too long for a black man to get a chance in this town." Pollit had plans for Richardson but knew he might never be a head football coach in Texas. "There's too much of a good ol' boy system. You'll have a better chance in basketball."

Richardson felt no resentment toward his principal, a man he admired for being direct and honest. "I can take something straight up," he says, "and Pollit would tell you right to your face."

"Don't worry about your enemies," Pollit sometimes told Richardson. That echoed what Ol' Mama had told him for years. "It's the people sitting on the fence who might turn against you," she'd say. "That's who you have to be careful of."

In 1967, Richardson was drafted in a third sport. This time it was the young American Basketball Association and the Dallas Chaparrals, and they offered to match his teaching salary at Bowie. Former Kentucky star Cliff Hagan had arranged a job for Richardson at a television station. Richardson hurt his leg, however, and grew frustrated hanging around a hotel. He considered a return to El Paso.

Around this time, Richardson's nephew Butch came down with a bad cold. The boy's mother, Shirley, began to worry when Butch didn't get better. When the cold evolved into a sleepiness that wouldn't go away, the family took Butch to visit an El Paso doctor. Butch was diagnosed with acute lymphatic leukemia, ALL. After a two-month struggle, Butch died. He was seven years old. Richardson began to wonder if this was perhaps the disease that took his own mother, and he left Dallas for good, returning to El Paso in hopes of both counseling Shirley and coaching again at Bowie.

Pollit surprised Richardson upon his return, telling him he could not have his old job back. He did, however, have a new position to offer. Richardson was named varsity basketball coach at Bowie in the autumn of 1967.

Still sensitive about the way his college scoring average had taken a beating, and about the way he felt smothered by his coach, Richardson vowed one thing: he was going to be different from Don Haskins.

Ol' Mama was still prominent in Richardson's life, but her health was visibly fading. She suffered a stroke in the mid-1960s, which left her unable to walk or talk. It also forced her out of her own home. "After the stroke she would try to talk," Madalyn says, "and now I realize that she was so frustrated because her mind was still sharp."

Richardson's grandmother passed away in 1974. The family's memories of this remarkable woman are still vivid. "She was always very stern," Madalyn recalls, "and didn't tolerate a lot of nonsense from the children."

Without Ol' Mama around, the struggle to advance seemed to Richardson more severe, steeper. Head college coaching jobs were out of the question. There were no coaches of color to imitate except at historically black colleges, the closest of which was five hundred miles away. While socializing with the black college players whose teams were playing in El Paso, he began hearing talk of a coach whom he could emulate—a coach who was black and who practically invented fast-break basketball.

John McLendon was the most successful African-American coach from the 1940s through the 1960s. A pupil of basketball's inventor, James Naismith, McLendon won 264 games at historically black North Carolina College from 1940 to 1952. He was not a big or brash man, and tried to repair the racially torn world gradually. His tools were craftiness, dignity, and intelligence.

In 1944, while he was at North Carolina College, articles appeared claiming that the Duke University Medical School team, which was tearing up the intramural competition, was actually the best team in the state. McLendon requested a secret game with the Duke team, which featured a few former stars whose eligibility had expired. Duke and McLendon had an odd relationship. During his glory years at North Carolina College, which was also situated in Durham, he was invited to attend the Duke games and permitted to sit at the end of the Duke team's bench—if he'd wear a waiter's coat.

The game was illegal, and by agreeing to play it, McLendon would put everyone in danger. A challenge was issued by one of North Carolina College's players, and the game—without spectators, but with referees—was played. McLendon's team destroyed Duke by 44 points.

In his last years at North Carolina College, McLendon began petitioning the NCAA to admit the historically black colleges to compete in their national tournament. His numerous requests were denied in writing, so for years afterward the black colleges would compete in the powerful National Association of Intercollegiate Athletics (NAIA), which began including the historically black schools in their national playoffs in 1953. (Teams that were not in either the NCAA's existing University Division or College Division would compete in the NAIA, which up until the 1970s could boast of some of the best black players in America.)

When McLendon moved to Tennessee State, he won 88 percent of his games and three consecutive NAIA championships. He remains one of only four coaches to win three straight national titles. (John Wooden, Kentucky State's black coach Lucias Mitchell, and Dan McCarrell of North Park are the others.)

From 1959 until 1962, McLendon coached the integrated Cleveland Pipers of the National Industrial Basketball League—a postcollege league that was regarded as nearly as competitive as most NBA teams. In 1960, his Pipers handed the best amateur U.S. Olympic team in history—a team featuring Jerry West and Oscar Robertson—their only defeat.

In 1969, McLendon was named the first black coach in the old ABA with the Denver Rockets. He later coached at Kentucky State and then Cleveland State University, where he was the first black head coach at a predominantly white college. (Cleveland State participates in Division I today but was College Division under McLendon.) He won a total of 522 college games at a clip of 76 percent.

In both 1968 and 1972, Henry Iba invited McLendon to be an assistant coach for the Olympics. He was joined by Don Haskins on the 1972 staff.

After those stints, McLendon became America's finest basketball ambassador, traveling to nearly sixty countries to do clinics at a time when the teaching of basketball overseas was practically nonexistent. In 1979, he became the first black coach to be inducted into the Naismith Basketball Hall of Fame—although, in a disgraceful omission, he was not included as a coach, but rather, as a "contributor."

As incredible as John McLendon's success is the way he was ignored by the established white schools his entire career. He was never offered a job at a major state school and was known to only the most astute observers of basketball.

McLendon's story is part of a pattern at American colleges—reaping black talent but not black leaders. This system crushed his career, as well as those of countless other talented black coaches. Nolan Richardson, like many young black coaches in the 1960s, came to know McLendon's story well.

After a coach named Ray Mears won the NCAA's College Division title at Wittenberg College of Ohio in the early 1960s, he was named the University of Tennessee coach. Mears, who was white, was inarguably a fine coach. But McLendon had won *three* national titles in a row, right in the state of Tennessee.

It is impossible today not to look at McLendon's career and wonder what could have been. While McLendon's name is still revered, it is almost exclusively by black coaches and older players.

Richardson understood that McLendon was far from the only black coach whose talents were ignored. Each overlooked black coach was a disturbing body in the road to any young black man starting in the profession.

One of McLendon's contemporaries was the Winston-Salem State coach Clarence "Big House" Gaines. At the time of his death in 2005, Gaines was fifth on the NCAA's list of winningest coaches, with 828 career victories. All forty-seven of his seasons were at Winston-Salem State, a historically black college. His 1967 team, featuring Earl "The Pearl" Monroe, went 31-1, and won the NCAA College Division championship.

A giant of a man, Gaines is a member of eight halls of fame, including the Naismith Basketball Hall of Fame, which honored him as a coach. He and McLendon would occasionally go on recruiting trips together, promising not to lure each other's prospects. Since hotels were not always available to black men, they would often sleep in the car. Big House, of course, got the wider backseat.

Wake Forest University is in the same town as Clarence Gaines's school. During his time at Winston-Salem State, Wake Forest went through seven basketball coaches. At one point, Wake Forest struggled through thirty-three years (1963–1995) without winning a regular season or ACC Tournament title. Yet Clarence Gaines was never offered the Wake Forest job.

Gaines's story is not unique, either. Kentucky State coach Lucias Mitchell won three-straight NAIA national titles in 1970, 1971, and 1972, when he was still in his thirties. He was black and was never offered a job at a Division I school.

The stagnant careers of John McLendon and Big House Gaines haunted Richardson during his early years of coaching. But without the advent of videotapes or cable television, it was only through conversation that he could begin to construct a style contrasting with Don Haskins's system. Naturally, Haskins was his most prominent influence, and Richardson had a difficult time shaking off Haskins's way of thinking about the game. So Richardson's undersized all-

Mexican-American teams his first years at Bowie played patiently. The dizzying pace that would one day be a Richardson trademark was almost a decade away.

"He played a lot closer to Haskins's style those first few years than people think," recalls Alvis Glidewell, who was already making a name for himself as a shrewd coach. "He had much smaller kids than the rest of us."

Richardson was likely doing what most young coaches do—teaching the game the way they've been taught. But he was on the lookout for a specific strategy that suited him. He had no way to familiarize himself with the systems of either McLendon or Big House Gaines. Instead, Richardson first studied, then copied, Glidewell's Austin High School teams.

Glidewell says today, "We all copy off somebody. I'd seen things that John Wooden did at clinics when he was winning at UCLA, but I didn't announce it around town. Nolan certainly wasn't yet pressing the way he'd get famous for in college." Glidewell, who is unknown outside El Paso, was surprised to learn that Richardson now credits him with some of his success as a pressing college coach. "We were never close," Glidewell insists. "He never came over to practice, never let on that he was interested. But he must have been watching pretty close."

Glidewell does recall one particular bus ride to Amarillo for a tournament both their teams were competing in. "We sat together for the first time and really talked. He asked questions about our system, but he never wrote anything down, so I had no idea he was going to use it."

Richardson says, "Glidewell's teams were so disciplined that they could press after a missed shot. That really takes total control, but his guys could do it. Not many people know about him, but he should be in somebody's hall of fame."

While he was trying to find his own voice as a coach, Richardson was also struggling at home. His marriage to Helen collapsed in the mid-1960s, something he attributes today to the couple being too young to sustain the pressures of family life. After their divorce, he raised the two boys, while Helen had Madalyn. Helen became a schoolteacher, too, teaching at Bowie's rival, Jefferson High School, for decades.

Richardson was coaching three sports and teaching several subjects. He had plenty of extra duties, too, one of which was grooming the baseball field at Bowie. When the heat got the better of him on a sunny May afternoon, he recalled that his high school pal, Manuel Davila, lived across the street from the field. Richardson trudged over to beg a glass of water. That's when he met Rosario Davila, Manuel's sister, who was tending to the garden. Like anyone in the Bowie neighborhood, Rosario knew exactly who Richardson was. She also had been married but was now divorced with a daughter of her own, Sylvia. Manuel was not at home, but Richardson stuck around to talk anyway. He asked for a second glass of water.

Soon after, Richardson married Rosario—he called her Rose, which was Ol' Mama's name—and their only child, Yvonne, was born in 1972.

Richardson's first Bowie teams were good, but not exceptional. The Bears were simply too small, and the coach had to make adjustments to be competitive. They were so aggressive that local fans began calling them *Rabia*—Spanish for "rabid dogs."

Richardson's training regimens were a daily test in toughness, and his high school players named the last third of practice "Forty Minutes of Hell." Years later, the moniker would refer to his style of play in college games of that same length. His coaching philosophy was evolving, but his insistence on defensive pressure was like a mantra—"Pressure leads to poor decisions."

Despite the furious pace of Richardson's practices and his hyper-demanding style, he grew close with his players at Bowie. Years later, those players, many from broken homes, too, credit Richardson with

being deeply influential as well as a close friend. Richardson's identification with and love for his scruffy underdogs from Bowie—the
poorest of El Paso's poor—was authentic.

After school one afternoon in 1973, Richardson was taking a
shortcut through the Bowie gym on his way home. A pickup game
in progress stopped him like a forearm to the chest. He didn't recognize the gangly black youngster who was blocking shots and grabbing
rebounds.

Richardson walked into the middle of the game and asked the
new kid his name.

"Ralph Brewster," the boy said. He was an eighth-grader, who
didn't even play competitive basketball, although he was already 6'1".

Richardson looked at Brewster's feet, which were huge. "Aren't
you Joe Brewster's son?" he asked.

"My friends took off when he said that," Brewster recalls, "ran
out of the gym. They thought I was in trouble. So did I. Growing up,
Nolan was like God to me."

Richardson asked the younger Brewster why he wasn't playing on
the junior high team.

"My father won't let me play," Brewster said.

With chores and schoolwork to tackle, not to mention Ralph's
smart-aleck demeanor, sports would be a waste of time, his father
felt. Joe Brewster, a Korean War hero, was a huge man—over three
hundred pounds—and his word was law.

Later that evening, Richardson phoned Joe Brewster and asked
for permission to coach his son.

"My Dad didn't see an athlete in me, although he liked sports,"
says Brewster. "I was just a gawky kid but I hated losing. Any board
game, Ping-Pong, I wanted to win."

The next day Richardson went to the Brewsters' home in Segundo
Barrio's Tays Housing Project and made an appeal to the father. "I've
seen great players come and go," he said. "Trust me with Ralph and
I'll make him something special."

Joe Brewster was surprised Richardson was interested in his sassy son. "If you think he's good," Joe Brewster said, "have at it." But Joe Brewster had one concern—his boy Ralph walking home. Although his mother was Mexican-American, and both parents were fluent, Ralph couldn't speak Spanish. Richardson would be required to drive him home every day, and the coach used the time to gain Brewster's trust.

The long hours Richardson spent coaching, driving, and telling stories to Ralph Brewster would be worth it. By the time he was a senior, Brewster would bless Richardson in a way nobody could have predicted.

Throughout the late 1960s and early 1970s, Richardson was absorbing as much as he could from the area's best coaches. Nobody was more successful than the team three hours away in Hobbs, New Mexico. If Alvis Glidewell's system was enticing to Richardson, the style of Hobbs coach Ralph Tasker must have been like cool water in the desert.

Tasker came to the oil-boom town of Hobbs shortly after World War II. He won an astounding number of games—1,122—and took home eleven state championships. Full-court pressure was his calling card.

Tasker, like Alvis Glidewell, wore glasses, and looked more like a professor than a hoops guru. Tasker preferred his team's bench to be on the baseline, to witness his press as it uncoiled like a diamondback rattlesnake. His lead defender, guarding the inbounder after made baskets, would follow the first pass and trap it; everyone else would rotate. The opponents knew when the predictable traps were coming, but it usually didn't matter. Tasker won seventy home games in a row during one stretch.

"Hobbs would come into El Paso and destroy our best teams," Richardson recalls. "They pressed every minute, but it was more extended, more exciting, than what Alvis Glidewell was doing. So I copied Tasker's system, too. Later I took it a step further by teaching my kids not to trap at the same time or place. I wanted us to be more difficult to prepare for."

Glidewell today says Richardson may have borrowed more than his full-court press. "Nolan started playing faster when he had better players. He had those two guys, Ralph Brewster and Melvin Patridge, and Nolan let them run more. But Patridge lived on our side of the freeway," Glidewell insists. "So we challenged the situation with the school district. Patridge's mother said something like 'Nolan was his uncle.' We were saying 'Richardson is recruiting,' which was illegal [for high schools], but we lost our challenge."

Today, Melvin Patridge laughs about Glidewell's old claim. "We actually are cousins, but didn't realize that until eighth grade, in 1972," he says. "We owned a home in the Bowie district, but didn't always live there." Patridge understands Glidewell's frustration. "We probably could have won state if I'd gone to Austin High School," he says.

Patridge remembers how Richardson would use his own version of shock treatment to get his Bowie Bears' attention. "He would put us on the floor with some of the UTEP players, and they'd kill us," Patridge says. "But then the high school kids we'd face, they were nothing."

Patridge recalls a trip the Bowie team made into central Texas for the state playoffs after winning the city championship. The players filed off the bus to eat a few hours before the game but sat, ignored, for half an hour. "Nolan finally got up and talked to the manager," Patridge says. Eventually the coach returned to the team and said, "Let's go." They bought hamburgers at a McDonald's and ate them in their hotel rooms.

Patridge confronted the coach the next day. "Why didn't we just stay there until we got service?" he asked.

Richardson had remembered Abilene from his high school baseball trip. "I didn't want you guys to have the humiliation that I did," he told Patridge.

"He wasn't often verbal about race at that time," Patridge says. "Nolan might say, 'Look, me being a black coach means that my players are going to have to suffer the same as I do. If a call can go either way, it's going to go against us. I have to prepare you for that.' "

The us-against-the-world mentality became a recurring theme in Richardson's pregame and postgame talks.

According to Kenny John, his former workout partner at Fort Bliss, "Nolan carried that chip on his shoulder, like he had something to prove. He could act during games like the world was against him because he was black. But that worked for him, because he'd sometimes get the calls, and his players seemed to be on a quest. I don't know if Nolan really felt that way, or if he was just trying to help his team any way he could, like all of us."

Patridge sees it differently: "The Anglo coaches could really ride the refs, but the refs would tell Nolan to shut up."

The addition of Ralph Brewster, Melvin Patridge, and high-jump hero Arthur Westbrook radically altered the Bowie team's racial makeup—and success rate. Richardson's teams were 190-80 in his ten-year career at Bowie. The trio of black players, however, would amass a sparkling record of 101-13 in his final three seasons.

Brewster grew to be 6'8" and was Richardson's first and only major college prospect. Patridge and Brewster were the two biggest and strongest kids in El Paso, and they could dominate the boards, allowing them to fast break. "We'd force the issue and push them into submission," Brewster says.

Richardson alternated deliberately between being a harsh task-master and a loving father figure with his team. Once, after a brutal Saturday practice, Richardson took Brewster to Luby's Cafeteria, where the player ate like a famished soldier. When they finished eating, the manager came over and insisted on comping Richardson's check. The manager told Richardson, loud enough for Brewster to hear, that it was an honor to have him in the restaurant.

Back in the car, Richardson turned to Brewster. "That's why I stay on you, because I want to pass that kind of respect on to you," he said. The rides home were always instructive, with Richardson lecturing or telling stories to Brewster or Patridge from behind the wheel of his dilapidated Oldsmobile.

"It was a gold 1968 Tornado," Patridge says, "and it had no shocks. The car would bounce up and down. And the needle on his speedometer would bounce up and down, too. The windshield wipers didn't work, and if it was raining, look out. Coach Richardson would have his head out the window. We were a sight."

"You could get seasick in that car," Brewster says.

Once, Patridge asked his coach why he didn't spring for a better set of wheels.

"I don't care about what people think about a car," Richardson said. "I want them to notice *me*."

Richardson would pontificate on what it took to be a player and why his two stars had to hit the books. "But he never talked about race to me, never," Brewster insists. "He talked about studying and doing well in class. I didn't experience any racism then. I thought it was something from my dad's era."

Brewster claimed an El Paso innocence that would be shattered when he went away to college—and believes the story was similar in some ways for his coach. "Bowie was special," he says, "and ironically, that's because Bowie was considered the lowest you could go. We supported each other, although it was somewhat of a bubble." Brewster believes that 1970s El Paso was far more progressive than the rest of Texas. "When I got exposed to the other Texas," he says, "I started seeing blacks being treated differently. That's what Nolan went through when he left El Paso."

Nolan Richardson's best year at Bowie was 1977, but by the end of the season, he'd made a decision. Although he longed to be a college coach, he needed a backup plan. Richardson quietly resigned, intending to go back to school for a master's degree at UTEP so he could one day become a school principal. Richardson would go out a winner at Bowie, though none of the players yet knew of this decision.

If 1977 was Richardson's best team, it may have been Don Haskins's worst. UTEP finished with a losing record for the first time in Haskins's career. Two losses to hated rival New Mexico really stung. Both schools badly wanted Ralph Brewster, who was only seventeen and didn't understand what kind of tension he was about to stir up. When Texas Tech began recruiting him, things got complicated.

In the days before nationalized scouting services and meat-market exposure camps, Brewster was initially something of a secret. Word began to seep out that there was a big kid at Bowie with a boatload of potential.

"UTEP knew about me all along," Brewster says, "and I liked UTEP. But initially I wanted to go to the University of New Mexico. The coaches offered me a new car, and a UNM coach would give me two thousand dollars in cash when he'd come see me play." This was a shock to Brewster, who was far from a worldly kid.

Brewster's indecision would drag into the spring. One April day, Brewster showed up at UTEP's new arena for a postseason pickup game. UTEP was still actively recruiting Brewster and encouraged him to come around.

"I drove up in a new 1977 Monte Carlo that UNM had arranged

for me," Brewster says. "The first person I see is [former UTEP star] Nate Archibald."

Perhaps the best point guard in the world at that time, Archibald was back in El Paso, rehabbing an injury.

"Wait a minute," Archibald said. "Where'd you get that?" Archibald was used to NBA stars driving fancy cars, but not El Paso high school kids.

"University of New Mexico," Brewster said.

"You'd better get it in your name," Archibald said, according to Brewster.

Not everyone at UTEP agreed with that assessment. When the first pickup game was over that day, Brewster noticed Richardson coming through the tunnel in the arena, motioning with his finger.

"We need to talk," Richardson said.

Archibald had told Haskins about the Monte Carlo. Haskins had phoned Richardson, who was there to put a stop to it. They marched up the tunnel to Haskins's office.

After Brewster admitted the car was a gift from UNM, Richardson spoke up. "You can't take it. People are going to see a $10,000 car being driven by a South El Paso kid?"

Brewster considered whether to pay attention to his skinny wallet or his high school coach. Then, according to Brewster, Haskins said, "I don't care whether you come to UTEP or not. But when you leave here, you take that goddamn car back."

Brewster reluctantly returned the car.

Then something happened that would change Richardson's choice and the course of his life. El Paso's remote location meant that no matter what level of success a local high school coach enjoyed, nobody outside of town noticed. The odds against Richardson advancing to be a college coach were astronomical. Don Haskins, of course, was not going anywhere, and the closest Texas colleges were the two-year schools, which were a five-hour drive away. Under normal circumstances, even they wouldn't care who was doing well in El Paso, a town where no high school coach had ever moved on to a college position.

Western Texas College was a two-year school in Snyder, Texas, nearly four hundred miles from El Paso. Many of the Texas junior colleges were remote, but few were as isolated as Snyder, which was a half-hour north of the newly built interstate. Sid Simpson, their director of athletics, felt it was time for a new direction for his basketball team. After coaching the team himself for a while, he took a chance on a hot young coach named Mike Mitchell. At just twenty-six years of age, Mitchell won the National Junior College Championship.

Simpson, an Arkansas native, found himself in a quandary when Mitchell bolted for the College of Southern Idaho after the 1977 season. Simpson wanted to keep winning, that was obvious, but Mitchell had irritated him with his harsh treatment of players.

Yet Simpson himself was halfway annoyed with the typical I'm-going-to-the-NBA mentality of junior college kids. He wanted a coach who was tough and smart, but also somebody who could emotionally connect with the kind of conscripted kids who populated the rosters of the Texas junior colleges.

When Texas Tech assistant Rob Evans walked in one April day and announced, "I've found your next coach," Simpson was intrigued and assumed Evans was referring to himself. The junior college had never had a black coach—no integrated junior college in Texas ever had—but Rob Evans was clearly head-coaching material.

Evans had played at Hobbs High School for the iconic Ralph Tasker, then starred at New Mexico State in the mid-1960s. Evans had been an assistant coach at NMSU under Lou Henson before going to Tech. He had the demeanor of an ambassador and the reputation for being honest and patient.

"Would you consider hiring a black coach?" Evans asked Simpson.

Simpson sensed it would be a great coup to land Evans. "You might be perfect, Rob," Simpson admitted.

"No, no," Evans said. "It's not me. I'm talking about an El Paso high school coach named Nolan Richardson."

Texas Tech had been hot on the trail of Ralph Brewster, and Rob Evans was leading the recruiting charge.

Around this time, near the conclusion of Brewster's senior season, Richardson had pulled his star into the office.

"You know about Texas Tech?" Richardson asked.

Of course Brewster did. He had a box of letters from Lubbock that Richardson had hand-delivered.

Richardson continued. "Rob Evans is going to offer you a full ride to Tech, and now he's interested in Melvin Patridge as well."

"That made me sit up," Brewster says, "because Melvin and I were close." Brewster began to think he'd decline the offers from UTEP and UNM.

When Tech realized Patridge was on shakier ground academically, they slowly backed off from him. Brewster's academics, on the other hand, were fine—he even had congressional approval for admission into the Air Force Academy. Richardson began hinting over the next few weeks that Tech might be the best fit.

Brewster went on his official visit to Lubbock alone, and he came back disappointed. "There was no basketball spirit," he says. "I could tell by the dirty gym that smelled like cow manure. It was a football school." Brewster decided to hold off on signing anywhere despite pressure from the three universities.

Brewster had been leaning toward taking the UNM deal. "But then Haskins came to my home, and everyone knew he never went out recruiting," Brewster says. "He met with my dad, who mentioned the UNM car."

"When you start giving kids things," Haskins said, "they start expecting that for the rest of their lives. If he wants a car so bad, here's what I'll do. I'll do it legally, but he won't be able to live on campus."

That sounded good to Brewster at first. Haskins outlined his idea. Brewster could live with his parents, then use the scholarship money normally tagged for room and board to make a modest, but legitimate, car payment.

"That got my dad's attention," Brewster says. But not his. It wouldn't be a new Monte Carlo. It wouldn't be a new anything.

When Haskins left, Ralph Brewster took a look around the little apartment. The tiny black-and-white television. The malfunctioning air-conditioning. The noisy neighbors. Keep living there? Not likely.

Richardson leveled with Brewster in the weeks after his visit to Lubbock. Brewster recalls his coach saying, "Ralph, if you go to Texas Tech, I'll get to be the coach of Western Texas College."

"They'd worked out a package deal," Brewster says today. "I was going to go wherever Nolan suggested. I had no qualms with that." And Richardson clearly favored Texas Tech.

"Some of these schools are offering Ralph the world," Joe Brewster had said to Gerald Myers, the Tech head coach, during their home visit.

"We don't do that sort of thing at Texas Tech," Gerald Myers said.

"But when I went to Lubbock," Brewster claims, "every good football player had a Thunderbird or Monte Carlo."

Still, Brewster waited. At the end of April, the Tech coaches cornered the Brewsters again in their living room for a final push. This time the Tech coaches were more direct.

According to Brewster, Rob Evans said, "If you sign, Ralph, Coach Richardson is going to be the next coach at Western Texas

College. Don't you want Nolan Richardson to be a college coach?" Package deals and quid pro quo arrangements were standard practice in college sports, but certainly new to El Paso high schools.

Brewster admitted it would be great if Richardson could be a college coach. He leaned forward on the couch, holding his head in his hands. The apartment seemed to be getting smaller by the minute.

"What if Coach Richardson told you to sign with us?" Evans asked. "Would you sign then?"

Brewster said he would.

"Just a minute," Evans said.

"They went outside and got Nolan," Brewster recalls. "He must have been waiting in the car."

Ralph Brewster signed with Texas Tech. It's possible that without Brewster, Richardson would have either been a school principal or coached his career away at Bowie—although Brewster refuses to stake that claim. "I was a talented player," he says, "although I wasn't any All-American. But sure, I went to Tech because it was good for Nolan."

In retrospect, Richardson insists Texas Tech was the right choice for Brewster, regardless of the junior college job—UNM was about to implode, and UTEP wasn't very good at the time. Neither man would have guessed then how Brewster's career at Tech would unfold.

FIVE

NOBODY KNOWS MY NAME

Snyder, a tiny oil town halfway between El Paso and Dallas, was named after a buffalo hunter, Pete Snyder, who opened a trading post in 1878. Oil was discovered in Snyder in 1948, and the population tripled. Oil derricks seem to outnumber trees.

When Western Texas College opened its doors in 1971, Snyder was home to about twelve thousand people, nearly all of them white. The towns in the Western Junior College Athletic Conference are more similar than they are unique. Odessa, the town made famous by *Friday Night Lights*, is one of those towns. So are Hobbs and Roswell, New Mexico. Throw in Texas towns like Borger, Levelland, Big Spring, Clarendon, and the more upscale Midland, and you have the nation's premier junior college conference. Former NBA stars Larry Johnson, Spud Webb, and Avery Johnson got their start in this league.

Director of Athletics Sid Simpson was quickly building a reputation as a shrewd judge of coaches, but college basketball is often about favors and paybacks. Simpson fielded phone calls from all over about the coaching job. "Bobby Knight even called," Simpson says, "but I figured, what did Bobby Knight know about Snyder? Rob Evans knew our league, had been around it all his life. I trusted him."

Even employees of the junior college had suggestions for Simpson. One man had gotten wind of the fact that Sid Simpson was considering hiring a black coach and wanted to recommend his own coaching pal, but he must have sensed Simpson was leaning toward Nolan Richardson.

"You're going to be sorry if you hire that nigger," the school employee said.

"I didn't worry about any of that," Simpson says. "I wanted a guy who cared about Western Texas College."

Simpson drove to El Paso to interview Richardson and his family over dinner at a steak house, where a procession of people came over to greet Richardson throughout the meal. Whites. Mexicans. Blacks. "It was people of all ages, too," Simpson recalls, "and you could tell they held him in the highest esteem. I could see he could get along with all kinds of people."

Simpson knew coaching could tear up families and render the coach ineffective, so he closely considered Richardson's immediate circle. "I instantly liked Rosario," he says. "She was supportive and captivated by Nolan, but was clearly a strong woman."

One other thing stuck in Simpson's head. Simpson was charmed by their daughter, Yvonne, who was then six years old. "She was the cutest kid," he says, "smart as could be. You could have a conversation with her just like she was an adult. The way Nolan interacted with his wife and child, well, that had a lot to do with why I was impressed with him."

Simpson drove back to Snyder with the radio off. There had never been a black coach at any integrated junior college in Texas, school employees kept reminding him. The next morning Simpson told his president that he wanted to hire Nolan Richardson.

The school's president, Dr. Robert Clinton, ran the proposal by the school's board, but there was plenty of unease. Dr. Clinton wasn't opposed to the idea of hiring a black coach, but knew it was a gamble in Snyder. The business of Rosario, his Mexican-American wife, and their child, had to be considered—an interracial couple and a biracial child in Snyder, Texas? Simpson told Dr. Clinton, "If somebody sees Nolan walking with his wife, it's going to look different."

Simpson asked for a single year for Richardson to prove himself.

Dr. Clinton told Simpson it would be his decision, but added a warning. "If this Nolan Richardson is not what you say he is," Dr. Clinton said, "and we don't win, it's going to reflect on you. You'll have to get a couple one-way bus tickets out of town."

Simpson says, "Dr. Clinton wasn't all that prejudiced, he was just being practical. There was going to be pressure on us both, Nolan and myself."

Nolan Richardson signed on for $19,000 a season, a raise of $2,000. It was 1977, and a historic hire. (Richardson was not, however, the first black coach at a majority-white college in Texas. Bob "Snake" Legrand was named the head coach at the University of Texas–Arlington in 1977, just before Richardson went to Snyder. There were less than a half-dozen black major college coaches in America at the time.)

"Snyder is redneck central," Don Haskins said. "It was about as tough a place for Nolan Richardson to start out as you could imagine. Sid Simpson was gutsy to take a chance on him."

Richardson's first junior college team featured eight El Paso kids whom he'd rounded up and brought along. "They looked like a team from the United Nations," Simpson laughs. "They were white, brown, and black, and all sizes."

Perhaps feeling a little unmoored being away from El Paso, Richardson reached back to his roots, but not to Don Haskins.

Richardson wanted to speed the game up and needed reminders of Alvis Glidewell's system—he'd used parts of it for a few years, but now he wanted more. By November, Richardson had implemented as much of Glidewell's system as he could recall.

Dwight Williams, his new fireplug guard who had played high school ball for Glidewell, would be Richardson's bridge back to El Paso. At Richardson's insistence, Williams sought out Glidewell at Christmas break that first year, with specific instructions: collect the rules, cues, options, and rotations of the full-court pressure.

By January, Richardson's first team had implemented Glidewell's presses, and they tore through the competition during the conference season.

The team adjusted to "redneck central" as quickly as their coach had. Players who are winning make peace with their surroundings, and Dwight Williams was no different. "Snyder had one stoplight, a typical little Texas town, but it was a wonderful place because it was all centered around the college," he says. "Race didn't come into play until my sophomore year, although it was always in our minds."

Sid Simpson was more than just the athletics director. He coached the women's team, too, but he made sure to watch nearly every Richardson-run practice and game. "Nolan would just have his team jump in the other team's face the second they got off the bus," Simpson says. "They'd spread the court with their defense, and run, run, run. There was playing time for everyone. I'd been trying to press and do some of the things that Nolan was doing, but it was funny—when I told my team to do it, they wouldn't respond to me, although I was often saying nearly the same thing Nolan was."

Simpson had neglected to reveal one of the oddities of the job in Snyder during the interview process. The college was outside of town, and it was too far to walk. That was fine with Richardson—nothing to distract his players from school and basketball. But the cafeteria was closed on the weekends. That meant the players would have to cram into a few cars to buy fast food with the minimal meal allowance Simpson could supply.

Richardson realized the athletics department wasn't as frugal as he and Rosario were. He suggested to Simpson that they use the money to buy groceries instead.

"Who is going to cook?" Simpson asked.

"Rose and I will," Richardson said. Rosario had run a barbecue stand and Mexican restaurant in El Paso and could do wonders with a low budget.

The next Saturday morning, shopping for groceries for team meals, Rose noticed the manager taking meat off the shelf and putting it into a large cart. She asked him what he was doing.

"These are pull-backs," he told Rose. "They're still good, but we can't sell them after a certain date."

From that day forward, the Western Texas College team feasted on pull-backs, and the regular weekend meals helped the ballplayers to bond. Richardson delivered the meals to the dorms personally, with Yvonne dragging a basket of her own. It was one thing when the brash new coach hollered at you and ran you to exhaustion for three hours. But when the coach, his wife, and daughter donned aprons, chopped onions, and then hauled out enormous baskets of home cooking every Saturday and Sunday?

"The meals were outstanding!" Dwight Williams says. "Mrs. Richardson used to run the kitchen in The King's X, which is famous for Mexican food in El Paso. Coach would be staggering under the weight of the baskets, and he'd hand-deliver it to our rooms."

"It was a family atmosphere like I've never seen before or since," Simpson says. "Nolan could make a purse out of a sow's ear."

Yvonne would roam from room to room, goofing with the players, pretending to be a waitress taking food orders. Her sense of fun rubbed off on her father. "Coach Richardson can be a very mischievous guy," Dwight Williams says, "and Yvonne brought that out in him. She personified the best parts of Rose and Nolan. Yvonne got her father's fearlessness and her mother's endurance."

Since the family was away from El Paso and their families, Yvonne and her father had time and space to grow close in a way Richardson had not been able to with his first three children. He had been busier and less patient with them; then the divorce complicated things. His youngest daughter understood him, he felt. They were closely matched, personality-wise.

She knew how to push his buttons, as well, especially if she needed his attention. "I want an interview!" she would say.

Richardson, who had mainly lived in El Paso, could immediately sense a different racial mindset in Snyder. He was sensitive to any slight or insult, real or imagined, and occasionally Richardson even misinterpreted Sid Simpson's best intentions that first season. When Rosario and Yvonne were back visiting El Paso one weekend, Simpson learned Richardson was alone. He invited his coach over for dinner. Simpson's son Mike loved to cook, and Southern cuisine was his specialty.

When he arrived at Simpson's home, Richardson surveyed the spread awaiting him. Fried chicken. Corn bread. Collard greens. Black-eyed peas. Sweet potato pie. Even watermelon. "Ahh hah, I see," Richardson thought. "They're feeding me *soul* food." He sat down cautiously, not sure if he was being insulted or perhaps was the butt of a joke.

Simpson recalls, "Nolan had one eyebrow raised up, checking us out."

Simpson slid into his chair and, without ceremony or comment, tore into the fried chicken. His son grabbed a thigh and attacked it.

"I knew Sid was for real when I saw him eat that night," Richardson says.

_____

Richardson learned that coaching in Texas junior colleges could be a rough ride. Once, Western Texas was at Panola Junior College, where Richardson grew more and more incensed with the biased officiating as the first half progressed. After computing the total number of free throws for both teams at halftime, he sent a manager up from the locker room to the scorer's table with an announcement. Western Texas was done. They would not be coming out for the second half, because they were being cheated.

The Panola officials were shocked, then livid; they set up outside the Western Texas locker room to prevent Richardson from exiting to the team bus. Richardson said in no uncertain terms that the referees were prejudiced and wouldn't give a black coach a fair shake. The Panola athletics director tried to calm Richardson down. "We know it's bad out there," he said, only to appease the coach.

"If you know it's bad, why haven't you stopped it?" Richardson said.

"That's just my way," Richardson says now, "to speak out. When I coach, it's me versus everybody. Same with when I played. I kept a chip on my shoulder, and that's something I guess I still carry from Ol' Mama."

Richardson also admits he can be intimidating. "I'm a black man with a big, strong voice. I have a certain physical stature," he says. "There are games within games, psychological games, and that's part of what I'm up to on the sidelines." In characteristic fashion, he adds, "That's something you won't find in coaching books."

Eventually, the Panola boss talked him into bringing his team on for the second half. Although they were behind by twenty points, Western Texas stormed back to win easily. Richardson had proved a point. Or so he thought.

A note was on his door when he got back to school Monday morning: *Please see Dr. Clinton in the president's office, pronto.*

"I heard you had a little trouble in Panola the other night," Dr. Clinton said.

Richardson forced a smile, not sure what to expect. Would he be suspended? Chastised? Fired?

"I'm damn proud of you," Dr. Clinton said. "Don't back down from anybody, Nolan. We don't want you walking on eggshells around here."

It was the first direct vote of confidence Richardson received from his president. "That just made me sure that I could win," he says. "I knew the school was behind me."

It wasn't only the president who was affected by Richardson. "Nolan could have run for mayor of Snyder and won, after his first season," Simpson says.

Later that spring, Richardson began socializing regularly with the employee who told Sid Simpson not to hire the "nigger coach."

One afternoon that first season in Snyder, Richardson called the team into the locker room and singled out a Detroit native, Freddy Davis. Richardson said, "Freddy, that white girl you're dating? You can't be seen in town, at the movies, at a football game. Some boosters have called, and they're going to withdraw their support."

Melvin Patridge recalls, "Nolan put it out to all of us, so we'd know what kind of atmosphere we were in. These are the same boosters that were having us to dinner and smiling in our faces. In El Paso, who you were dating wasn't a big deal. But we saw racism in Snyder, and the look on Nolan's face that day, you could tell it was the hardest thing to tell us."

During Richardson's college days, Don Haskins had called in his friend and teammate, Andy Stoglin. According to Stoglin, Haskins told him to stop holding hands with a white girl around the El Paso campus.

It annoyed both Richardson and Stoglin that Haskins would be involved in this sort of monitoring of their social lives. (Haskins did not recall this incident.) Richardson surprised himself by handling things in Snyder more or less the way Haskins did in El Paso.

Patridge says, "I think that's when the racism thing really raised its head, and he had to adjust. I saw Nolan change there in Snyder, from happy-go-lucky to 'It's me against the world.'"

That pressure carried onto the court. During one game, the Western Texas team was down by eight points at halftime.

"You have to perform," Richardson insisted. "If you don't perform I can't feed my family."

"He had never put it in that context," Patridge says. "That was new."

The family would eat—Western Texas College was winning big, even in Richardson's debut season.

Western Texas qualified for the state playoffs at the conclusion of Richardson's first year. The games were to be in Abilene—the town where Richardson had not been allowed in the hotel with his Bowie baseball team, and Haskins's team had been sent back into the night.

When Simpson gave Richardson his travel itinerary, Richardson had to smile. They had reservations at the same hotel. Every pregame talk takes place in a locker room. This one would take place in front of the hotel. Richardson gathered his diverse squad on the sidewalk and stood on the steps, recounting his shame and anger at twice not being allowed to room in that very hotel. Of course he stressed how he'd hammered two home runs after being insulted the first time.

Then Richardson quoted his ace, Ol' Mama. "There are people who pave roads and others who walk on them," he said. As often would happen over the years, with his us-against-the-world speech, the coach ended with, "Let's go out and beat somebody's ass."

"You feel like you *can* take on the world after Nolan speaks," Dwight Williams says. "First, nobody worked harder than us. We were in incredible condition. Coach talked about pride in our work ethic every day. Second, he instilled confidence in us."

Patridge says Richardson's mindset evolved in Snyder, a town with a practically nonexistent black population. In El Paso, the Hispanic population revered Richardson, considered him one of their own. There was no such comfort zone in Snyder. "When we were at Bowie," says Patridge, "it wasn't ever *us against the world*, but instead it was *us against whomever we played*. Nolan didn't talk about race so much in El Paso."

Western Texas College won the state playoffs, qualifying for the national tournament in 1978. They finished Richardson's first season ranked #13 in the nation.

That summer, Texas Tech assistant coach Rob Evans told Richardson about a high schooler named Paul Pressey. Pressey had quit his Richmond, Virginia, high school mid-career, then returned. As a senior, Pressey was discovered to be too old to compete, and so he slipped under the radar of recruiters.

If Ralph Brewster was Richardson's first great high school player, Pressey was his first college star, first of a long line of versatile wing players who would shine for him. At 6'5", he could dominate inside or out. Pressey later went on to score nearly 8,000 points in his NBA career.

Western Texas would alternate between Glidewell's cat-and-mouse press and Ralph Taskers's full-court frenzy, with Paul Pressey usually on the nose of the press. Richardson's second Western Texas team lost only two games in the regular season. They went back to the national playoffs and made it to the first round of the 1979 Final Four.

Dwight Williams, only 5'9", signed at Texas Tech that spring, leaving behind a more talented team in junior college than he'd join in Lubbock. But Williams, who was friendly with Ralph Brewster from their El Paso days, knew help was on the way. "Paul Pressey, David Brown, Greg Stewart, they were supposed to sign at Tech the next year," Williams says. "That's the primary reason I went there. The plan was those guys were supposed to follow me to Tech."

Lubbock is less than an hour by car from Snyder, and it was impossible for Richardson and Brewster not to keep close watch on each other. Brewster had gotten off to a good start at Texas Tech, but he still wasn't crazy about the town or the basketball arena. "We played at the dingy Lubbock Coliseum," he says. "It was almost like I went back in time being at Texas Tech." Brewster started some games as a freshman, chipping in almost 4 points per game, and 3.1 rebounds. The team was doing reasonably well, too, finishing 19-10.

Brewster often reminded himself of three facts that made Lubbock easier to stomach. First, UTEP continued to struggle through losing seasons, so Brewster could hardly get wistful thinking how much fun he would have had in El Paso—although the Miners certainly would have improved with him patrolling the paint. Second, rumors were swirling about the University of New Mexico program. They were about to go down in flames, destroyed by a transcript-fixing scandal. Finally, Brewster was playing a lot for a freshman. Brewster could just about make peace with himself over his decision.

Brewster's second season in Lubbock was even better. Tech finished 19-11, and just missed the NCAA Tournament. They did earn an NIT bid, but lost to Indiana in the first round. And Brewster was blossoming, scoring 11 points per game to go along with 7.6 rebounds—impressive sophomore stats.

———

Over Christmas of 1979, his third year in Snyder, Richardson returned to El Paso. While attending UTEP's Sun Bowl Tournament, he bumped into the school's director of athletics, Jim Bowden. Bowden was a native of Odessa, not far from Snyder, and knew how difficult the world could be for Richardson in West Texas.

Bowden was out of place as a college administrator. He used the plain language of a ranch hand, and he seemed uninterested in glad-handing El Paso's few rich boosters. He had uncommon common sense, and coaches would seek him out for advice.

When Richardson took a seat, Bowden congratulated him for being undefeated so far that season. "You know," he continued, "the Tulsa job is supposed to open up this year. You should apply."

Richardson told Bowden that he would.

The University of Tulsa's basketball team was in the midst of their fifth losing season in a row. Their coach, Jim King, would resign only eighteen games into the season. His assistant took over, but things didn't get any better. Although no professional teams claimed this medium-size city as home, attendance for the college was less than 3,800 per game. (UTEP, situated in a similar-size city and carrying a losing record that year, averaged more than twice as many fans as Tulsa.)

Tulsa had been sending teams to the court for over seventy years and had garnered exactly one lonely NCAA Tournament bid. They had earned a trip to the NIT on three occasions—in 1953, 1967, and 1969. Tulsa had not won a postseason game in over two decades.

Consecutive bad years can cripple the enthusiasm of boosters, making them desperate to try something new, almost anything to revive hope.

Ed Beshara had hope. Beshara owned a men's clothing store in Tulsa and was closely involved with raising scholarship money for the private university's basketball program. Beshara stubbornly believed the school could compete, although the Missouri Valley Conference was one of the nation's best basketball leagues. A Lebanese-American, Beshara was a relentless worker in his little clothing empire. He was also a stubborn optimist and longed for someone who shared his attitude to lead the Tulsa team.

Ed Beshara's father, Antone Beshara, had emigrated from Lebanon in the early 1900s. Religious persecution of Catholics and the chance for a better life brought "Papa Tony" Beshara and his family to Oklahoma.

But Oklahoma, which became a state in 1907, wasn't always friendly to immigrants or people of color. In Okemah, a lynch mob went after a young black crime suspect in 1911. The mob temporarily settled for the suspect's mother, Laura Nelson, knocking down her cabin door, then accusing her of hiding her son. The image of Laura Nelson, dangling with her son from a steel bridge, was captured on camera, sold as a postcard, and remains one of the few lynchings of a woman on record.

Antone Beshara settled in Haskell County, forty miles from Okemah, where he would raise twelve children. With vigilante justice and white mobs lurking in Oklahoma, Papa Tony Beshara wasn't shocked to find the Ku Klux Klan on his doorstep one evening. The Klan charged him with the crime of running a successful business while not being born in America. But Papa Tony knew how to face down cowards in sheets—he returned to the porch moments later with a loaded shotgun.

The Klan scurried away, lobbing curses and threats over their shoulders. Peering out from behind Tony's leg was his American-born son Ed.

Beshara had a rough time growing up when the family moved to Tulsa. "I would get beat up three times a day on my way to school," he'd say, "and I lived across the street!"

Despite growing to only 5'5", Beshara was a skilled and gutsy football quarterback, who received the equivalent of an athletics scholarship to Washington University of St. Louis. When the Great Depression hit, Beshara's scholarship was rescinded. He was forced to forgo college, moving back to Tulsa to begin working in the clothing business.

In 1950, Ed Beshara Clothing was founded on Harvard Street in Tulsa, where it still stands. Beshara grew to love Tulsa but often struggled with the mentality of the locals and had little patience for racist talk or attitudes.

Blunt and brash, Beshara was well connected around town. He had heard the rumors that Tulsa might consider a black coach, then kept hearing the same refrain from Tulsa business folks—they wanted a white coach. The West Point coach, Mike Krzyzewski, seemed to be the popular choice, and Beshara would have been okay with an immigrant name nobody could spell. But hiring a black coach intrigued him.

"I don't think there's any question that Dad felt sympathetic to a minority coach," his son, Ed Beshara Jr., says.

Beshara, who considered himself a champion of the underdog, got involved.

Richardson's team at Western Texas College rolled on, making it through his third regular season undefeated. Before the junior college tournament even began in the spring of 1980, Nolan Richardson was promised the job at the University of Tulsa—although he had not signed a contract yet.

He went into the playoffs as the most inspired lame-duck coach in history. Western Texas won it all, finishing the year 37-0.

Snyder's fans knew Richardson was Tulsa-bound, but that didn't stop them from having "Nolan Richardson Day" before he left—a mark of both Richardson's charisma and the way he was able to win the town over. But what Richardson recalls most is the drive back to Snyder after winning it all. The team got caught in a blizzard. Fearing for the safety of the kids, Richardson ordered the bus to stop in a remote Kansas town. Doors were knocked on; calls were made. The team was eventually put up in a local church. That's how the championship team celebrated: with hot chocolate, plaid blankets, and cookies in a church basement.

During Ralph Brewster's junior year, as Richardson was winning big in junior college, the Tech team took a step backward. Tech finished 16-13, but Brewster was still a force inside, getting 11 points per game again and pulling in 7.1 rebounds. After three seasons at Tech, Brewster had thrown down 33 dunks, and had big games of 29 points on two occasions. He was also one of the coach's favorites and was often trotted out at Elks Club and Lions Club luncheons as a model Tech basketball player. He was growing into an impressive and self-assured young man.

Brewster was thrilled to learn Nolan Richardson was going to be a major college coach at Tulsa. He was pals with the El Paso players on the Western Texas team, and they kept him informed of their success. Brewster's confusion about choosing Tech—it wasn't exactly remorse—had washed away. His unselfishness and loyalty had paid off for Richardson, and, he now concluded, Tech had, in fact, been the correct choice for him. Brewster even fantasized about Texas Tech meeting Tulsa in the playoffs.

There were problems, though. Brewster heard the first subtle strains of racism. "I'd hear people say to black players, 'You can't major in that,' when someone would express an interest in an academic field." Yet Brewster was reasonably happy. "I wasn't perfect, either," he adds. "I'd oversleep on the road, for example."

Everything pointed to a great final season for Brewster. He was about to have a senior year to remember, but not the one he'd anticipated.

SIX

GOING TO THE TERRITORY

Tulsa has a tangled and tragic history of race relations. Oklahoma earned statehood in 1907, and by 1910, Tulsa numbered ten thousand residents. By 1920, the population had multiplied tenfold. The catalyst for this boom was the discovery of oil nearby, and as the town mushroomed, so did its black population. Many blacks were the descendants of runaway slaves who had fled to Indian Territory. Others came with Native American tribes during the "Trail of Tears." By 1920, more than ten thousand blacks lived in Tulsa. Soon the Ku Klux Klan began to make inroads; a Klan leader from Atlanta attracted a crowd of three thousand as the new decade began.

Most of Tulsa's blacks settled in an area north of Tulsa, which became known as Greenwood. Within the Greenwood district were two newspapers, over a dozen doctors, lawyers, and a thriving black middle class. People referred to the self-sufficient district as "The Negro Wall Street," or, disparagingly, "Little Africa." Tulsa might have been a model for future American cities—although greater

Tulsa was not integrated, both communities thrived independently.

Everything changed on May 30, 1921. Dick Rowland, a black man, was accused of assaulting a white woman in an elevator. Rowland was arrested and held in jail. The next evening the *Tulsa Tribune* ran an editorial with the headline "To Lynch a Negro Tonight."

Sure enough, that evening, a mob of approximately two thousand whites stormed the jail. Fifty black men—many of them World War I veterans—blocked their path. An argument ensued. Shots were fired. The most devastating and deadly race riot in United States history was on.

Given a free hand by Tulsa police and authorities, white mobs terrorized Greenwood, and thirty-five square blocks of buildings were burned to the ground. The *Chicago Defender* reported that a private airplane was used to drop dynamite on Greenwood. Among the destroyed property were six hundred businesses, twenty-one churches, and dozens of restaurants and groceries, as well as a library and a hospital. In all, over a thousand homes were lost, and as many as three thousand blacks, many of them women and children, were killed. The official total of murdered blacks at that time, however, was twenty-six.

No white person was charged with a crime. Neither was Dick Rowland, the accused elevator assailant.

Few towns in America had as horrific an event in their rearview mirror as the Tulsa Race Riots, a black genocide. Many blacks—the ones who survived—left Tulsa. Others lived in tents. Blacks tried to rebuild Greenwood, and it enjoyed a modest resurgence in the late 1920s. Greenwood was partially leveled during the urban renewal of the 1970s.

By then, the Tulsans had made modest progress in improving their ruptured race relations. John Phillips, who later became TU's coach and attended high school in town in the mid-1960s, says, "The races got along pretty well in the sixties and it wasn't really a redneck town by any stretch." The high schools were desegregated by then, and athletics became a place where the races mixed freely. However, there were still powerful elitists resistant to progress.

Tulsa Athletics Director Emery Turner had desperately wanted to hire Lamar University basketball coach and Tulsa native Billy Tubbs to turn the program around. But Tubbs figured Tulsa was doomed to fail and dropped out of the running. Rumors circulated that it was a done deal: Nolan Richardson would be the next coach.

One day in early March of 1980, just before the University of Tulsa offered Richardson a contract, a booster named Evans Dunne appeared in the doorway of Ed Beshara's clothing store. He didn't want a new suit.

"What's on your mind, Evans?" Beshara asked.

What Evans Dunne said became a familiar refrain among Tulsa boosters that spring: "I'll never give another dime to the University of Tulsa if they hire a nigger to coach our boys."

Evans Dunne was one of the University of Tulsa's biggest financial contributors, and he donated huge sums to their struggling sports programs. The Dunnes were considered Tulsa's first family. Evans was the son of an old oil-money family; his wife, Nina Lane Dunne, was the author of *Tulsa's Magic Roots*, a picture book published in 1979 that was on every coffee table in South Tulsa.

Dunne's attitude was indicative of the dilemma in college sports. While students or faculty might have been ready to desegregate, the people pulling the purse strings often were not. Most schools, especially in the South, began adding black players, but not because it was the right thing to do. Rather, they desegregated when they did not want to risk getting beaten on the court or field. It often took a well-established coach, one with a sense of courage and justice, to begin recruiting black players.

An administrator who suggested hiring a black coach would be under enormous pressure. But Richardson's breathtaking junior college teams were averaging over 100 points a game, and that had gotten Tulsa president Paschal Twyman's attention. "Nolan bowled us over with charisma," Twyman told *Sports Illustrated*. "We knew we were breaking some ice here, but we decided to fly with it. We needed to win badly."

Richardson's predecessor, Jim "Country" King, had been a standout player at Tulsa before going on to the NBA. The 6'2" Jim King played plenty for the Los Angeles Lakers, San Francisco Warriors, and finally as a backup on gritty Chicago Bulls teams, their best of the pre–Michael Jordan era.

When Ken Hayes bolted from Tulsa in 1975 for the head-coaching job at New Mexico State, Tulsa asked Jim King, their most visible alum, to take the helm. The school was in a bind, and King—who had no coaching experience—was pulled by loyalty. Only two years into his NBA retirement, and at the age of thirty-five, Jim King agreed to be Tulsa's head coach. After his first season, King was offered an NBA assistant-coaching spot but remained at Tulsa.

King wouldn't enjoy the consistent winning he had helped to generate in the NBA. His best record at Tulsa was in his third season, 1978–79, when he finished 13-14. King even lost eight in a row to its crosstown rival, Oral Roberts University.

By the end of January 1980, Jim King took an early retirement. Bill Franey, his assistant, coached the final nine games of that season. King left Tulsa with a record of 44-82. At the age of forty, his career as a coach was over.

Don Haskins knew a positive piece from popular sportswriter Bill Connors would help smooth the way for Richardson. Connors knew Haskins from his playing days at Oklahoma A&M, took Haskins at his word, and ran a glowing profile of Richardson in the *Tulsa World*.

Richardson continued to make it clear, even to Connors, that he wanted to distance himself from Haskins in terms of coaching philosophy. Richardson never disparaged Haskins personally, but he was quick to criticize the conservative playing style that Henry Iba was credited with popularizing.

Richardson could, however, sometimes be loose with his language. About his El Paso home, he told *Sports Illustrated*, "I'm from a place I never want to go back to." Later, Richardson would clarify this statement. He meant being poor and unknown.

Tulsa's on-court struggles were in stark contrast to the success of its crosstown rival, Oral Roberts University.

ORU was a new school founded by Oral Roberts, the evangelical preacher, educator, businessman, and television personality. The school opened its doors in 1965, and immediately had three winning seasons in a row.

Reverend Roberts was hugely popular in black communities at that time—not only for his willingness to include blacks in his church, but also for his encouragement for blacks to attend his university and play on his basketball team. ORU had three black players on their inaugural team in the fall of 1966.

The state of Oklahoma was relatively progressive in desegregating their college sports teams. Henry Iba desegregated his Oklahoma A&M team in 1957, when he signed Memphis native L. C. Gordon. The other major state school, Oklahoma University, followed suit the next season. Before the 1964–65 season, Tulsa coach Joe Swank signed the school's first black players, a trio of junior college transfers—Sherman Dillard, Julian Hammond, and Herman Callands.

This was a new era, though, and Oral Roberts University fully integrated their team from its inception, putting a premium on black athletes whose style and speed became a hit in Tulsa.

In 1968, a seemingly meaningless home game became one of the most important in ORU history. Middle Tennessee State racehorsed past ORU, putting up 115 points. Reverend Roberts, who was a fixture at ORU games, was smitten with Middle Tennessee's style of play and decided to hire Ken Trickey, their flamboyant coach, the following spring.

Playing in the smaller College Division, Trickey finished 27-4 his first year at ORU. In 1972, his third year, the school entered the University Division and broke out with a 26-2 season and an NIT bid, the school's first postseason playoffs.

But it was more than just the fact that Oral Roberts University was winning. The team was fast-breaking as if the flames of hell were at their heels.

The godfather of Oklahoma basketball was still Henry Iba, whose strict, disciplined style influenced three generations of local coaches. Teams all over the state walked the ball up the court and played a conservative and stifling defense. Nobody, it seemed, wanted to risk irritating *Mister* Iba by playing a fast-paced game. Iba, who retired in 1969, was too diplomatic to speak out about what was happening at the new college in the state, but it must have appalled him.

During Ken Trickey's 26-2 run of 1972, ORU averaged 105 points per game, and even tallied 155 points in a win over Union College.

In 1974, ORU won two games in their debut in the NCAA Tournament. ORU needed to beat Kansas to earn a trip to the Final Four—a remarkable feat, considering it was less than a decade since the college opened its doors. Kansas overcame a 9-point deficit in the game's last few minutes, crushing the hopes of the ORU faithful.

That spring, the Tulsa police busted Ken Trickey for driving while intoxicated. Trickey had already announced his resignation before the arrest, but rumors of a setup spread through Tulsa.

Trickey compiled a record of 118-23 in only five years at Oral Roberts University and was a John the Baptist of the Fast Break—indirectly prophesying the coming of Nolan Richardson to Tulsa less than a decade later.

——

While ORU was welcoming to black players, their administrative approach was typical of the times. Black players were coveted; black leaders were not. Consider that twenty-six players have scored over one thousand points in the school's history. Twenty of them have been black. ORU has had ten head coaches, all of them white.

A few years after Ken Trickey's departure, Oral Roberts himself enticed coach Ken Hayes to leave New Mexico State and return to the city of Tulsa.

Hayes had been successful at New Mexico State, but he decided to return to Tulsa after the reverend made his offer. "You'll be my last coach," Roberts promised. Hayes came back to town just after the NCAA sheriffs penalized ORU with serious sanctions in an effort to get Oral's basketball coach to walk the straight and righteous path.

Hayes kept the pressure on Tulsa University. In his first season, Hayes knocked off his old TU team twice, the eighth win in a row for ORU over Tulsa.

The following spring, Nolan Richardson arrived in town.

Head coaching jobs have always been hard to come by, even for hugely successful junior college coaches. Richardson, who was thirty-eight years old, could not afford to turn his nose up at Tulsa's pauper past.

Tulsa competed in the Missouri Valley Conference, which had been one of the premier basketball leagues in America for years. The MVC at one time featured Cincinnati and Louisville, two teams that had won NCAA titles. Memphis State and Drake had earned berths to the Final Four, while Bradley and Wichita State had illustrious histories.

During the 1960s and 1970s, only one or two nationally televised college basketball games were broadcast a week. The advent of cable television in the late 1980s would slowly strangle the powerful MVC, because none of the schools were in major media centers. They were in Des Moines, Peoria, Canyon. And Tulsa. But before the days of cable TV, the Missouri Valley was a feared conference.

When Richardson arrived, the MVC had just seen Larry Bird at Indiana State lead his team to the NCAA title game. Richardson would face a long list of greats who would later earn jobs in the NBA: Lewis Lloyd, Antoine Carr, Cliff Levingston, Xavier McDaniel, David Thirdkill, Benoit Benjamin, Kevin McKenna, Mitchell Anderson, Hersey Hawkins, and Jim Les.

Nobody believed Richardson could win, especially not win immediately, despite his four fine players from Western Texas College—David Brown and Phil Spradling from El Paso, Greg Stewart, and future NBA star Paul Pressey. They'd be joined by Bob Stevenson, Tulsa's best returning player. Spradling and Stevenson were white.

Richardson still needed a natural point guard, and he settled on Mike Anderson, a relentless scrapper on the Alabama junior college team he'd beaten for the championship. Anderson's team lost any hope of winning when he fouled out. In a classic case of "if you can't beat 'em, join 'em," he signed with Tulsa a few weeks later. Richardson was taken by Anderson's quickness, but it was more than that. Richardson says, "You could tell he was that rare kid, a natural leader and a listener. And tough? He was as tough as could be."

Anderson, who is now the head coach at Missouri, says, "I could see that people just gravitated to Nolan, and he was unique in that way. I was excited about how Nolan played, but my first impression was that Tulsa was the real West, cowboys and Indians."

A decade before Richardson took over at Tulsa, Will Robinson was hired as the first black coach in major college basketball. Illinois

State, also of the Missouri Valley Conference, named Robinson the head coach in 1970, when he was fifty-eight.

Like Richardson, Robinson had begun coaching at the high school level, leading Detroit's Pershing High School to a state title. That team featured Spencer Haywood, who, with Robinson's help, would successfully challenge the NBA's ban on allowing underclassmen into the draft.

Robinson had been a talented high school football quarterback in Ohio and even came in second in the state's golf tournament—although he was not allowed to play on the golf course at the same time the white kids played.

His teams at ISU featured the skinny hotshot Doug Collins, who went on to a long NBA playing and coaching career. Robinson compiled a record of 78-51, and never had a losing season, but got dumped in 1975, his college career over after five quick years. Robinson then hooked on as a scout with the Detroit Pistons of the NBA, but declined an offer to be their head coach in the 1980s. Today, the Pistons locker room is called the "Will Robinson Locker Room of Champions." He died in 2008 at the age of ninety-six.

Neither John McLendon nor Big House Gaines was ever offered a chance to coach at a major white-majority state university. They were seen as Negro coaches at Negro schools and could not liberate themselves from that identity—or, rather, the administrators who hired new coaches at white universities could not free themselves from that prevailing mindset. Ben Jobe has managed to coach at both historically black colleges and majority white universities. Jobe served as the head coach at five historically black schools, the last of which was Southern University. In between those head coaching posts, Jobe was an assistant at two mostly white colleges, as well as the head coach of the University of Denver (then a Division II school).

In 1968, while Jobe was at the historically black South Carolina State University in Spartansburg, campus life was shattered when three young black men were shot in the back by police during a campus bonfire and protest. The incident echoed the killing of students at Kent State University by the Ohio National Guard.

Except that it didn't. Kent State got international media coverage and even inspired a rock 'n' roll anthem. South Carolina State's killings were largely ignored, and this left Jobe mystified and angry. The white media's blindness to State's on-campus slaughter would serve as a twisted metaphor for Jobe's successes. Despite his 524 college wins, he was ignored, too. He was never offered a head Division I job at a white-majority university.

Jobe enjoyed his most publicized success at Southern University, where, in 1993, he defeated an old employer, Georgia Tech, in the first round of the NCAA Tournament. His Southern teams qualified for the NCAA Tournament four times and earned one NIT bid (a rarity for a Southwestern Athletic Conference [SWAC] school).

He won 209 games at Southern, a remarkable total, considering he was forced to play almost ten "guarantee games" a year—games where Southern would travel to play for money, games that would never be "returned" to Baton Rouge, where Jobe's team could enjoy the home-court advantage. Despite this, Jobe never had a losing season at Southern.

An important reason coaches at historically black colleges don't advance to bigger state universities is because their overall won-lost records don't reflect their coaching ability. The Jobes with overall winning seasons are rare. Guarantee games are often necessary for a smaller school's survival. A big state university pays anywhere between $40,000 and $80,000 per game to the smaller historically black college. Never does the big school "return" the game and play on the smaller college's court. (It should be noted that not only the historically black colleges are subject to this prostitution; it might be Sam Houston State or Northeast Louisiana. All these smaller schools very much depend on the guarantee money to keep their programs afloat.)

The big state schools learn that some of the historically black colleges should be avoided. Over the years, teams like Southern and Coppin State have made the big schools regret paying out enormous amounts of money only to get beat on their own court. Because of guarantee games, there will never be a time when, say, two SWAC teams are awarded NCAA bids, since no teams in the league have impressive enough overall records.

Ben Jobe is brilliant, politically conscious, and outspoken. He is also devoid of the verbal clichés required of basketball coaches. He despises the Basketball Hall of Fame, where he ought to be a member—although he claims he'd refuse induction. Jobe lambasts the hall of fame for inducting announcers like Dick Vitale and the inventor of the shot clock. (Jobe: "The man who invented the shot clock should be in the General Electric Hall of Fame, not the Basketball Hall of Fame.") Jobe calls the NCAA a "fascist organization" and blames the NCAA for the destruction of black sports at black colleges.

Like Jobe, Frankie Allen has coached at both historically black colleges and white-majority universities and has some insights in the problems black coaches have advancing. Allen became the first black head coach at a mostly white school in Virginia when he was named coach at Virginia Tech in 1988. He has also been the head coach at Tennessee State, Howard, and is now at Maryland–Eastern Shore.

Allen says that if you want to understand the problems at historically black colleges, follow the money. And not just the guarantee game money. "There is little money coming from the private sector at Tennessee State," he says, "but the white schools enjoy tremendous help from donors." He says that the guarantee games sometimes allow historically black schools to fund the entire athletics department but that the money rarely goes to the basketball programs.

"That all depends on the coach's relationship with his boss," Allen says. "We played at Nebraska and got $75,000, and our AD is going to help us get new lockers."

One of the costs of this bargaining—almost certain losses for guaranteed money—is the sacrificed coaching careers.

The head-coaching jobs in the SWAC or MEAC are mirages at best; graveyards of crushed careers at the worst. Each January, every SWAC and MEAC coach starts his conference season with a losing record after its devastating preseason schedule has been played out. If a coach wins the SWAC, he still might not be above .500 for the season.

Today, a common trend is for big universities to hire a hot coach from a "Cinderella" team that has miraculously made the NCAA Tournament. But no SWAC coach, and just one MEAC coach, has ever gotten that call. One of Nolan Richardson's longtime assistants, Andy Stoglin, got his first head-coaching job at the SWAC's Jackson State University. He made the NCAA Tournament there, but the guarantee games prevented him from having a sparkling record, and he never advanced.

Examining the history of the program at North Carolina A&T affords both a look at the futility of coaching in the MEAC and an insight into how college hoops has evolved ever so slightly.

The MEAC includes schools like South Carolina State, Coppin State, Bethune-Cookman, and the league's traditional power, North Carolina A&T.

Cal Irvin took over at A&T in 1954, and he amassed over three hundred victories at the Greensboro school. He never had a losing season in eighteen years, but never got a chance at the big time either.

During the 1980s, North Carolina A&T was coached by Don Corbett, who led A&T to *seven straight* NCAA bids. His overall record, despite a slew of guarantee games at A&T, was 249-133, including thirty-seven wins in a row at home. Yet no mostly white school in basketball-crazed North Carolina, or anywhere else, would try to lure Don Corbett away—or play on his home court.

Jeff Capel Sr. is the exception that proves the rule. He coached North Carolina A&T for a single season, in 1993–94, and made the NCAA Tournament. He was named the head coach at Old Dominion the next season.

For every modern success story like Richardson's, there are forgotten men, brilliant coaches like Cal Irvin and Don Corbett, whose opportunities were limited by their skin color. Richardson still speaks with respect of his successful-yet-obscure predecessors: Ben Jobe, "Fang" Mitchell at Coppin State, and David Whitney at Alcorn State.

Black coaches, especially assistant coaches, were perceived for years as recruiters who could relate to black players and little more. Recruiting is imperative, but most black coaches consider the label to be belittling at best, as there is a distinct division within the business between recruiters and strategists. The coach who relies on strategy must be smarter, the thinking went, and they were always white.

Reggie Minton remembers those labels well. He was an assistant at the Air Force Academy before becoming the head coach at Dartmouth, then Air Force. Minton attended Wooster College in Ohio, where he began to develop his political consciousness. "In college I had given a speech," he recalls, "and I talked about not only wanting to ride in the front of the bus but wanting to drive and then *own* the bus." It was a speech America's athletics directors and college presidents should have been required to attend.

The Air Force Academy played a PAC-10 school one season when Minton was an assistant. After the game, the coaches went out for beers, but Minton, who doesn't drink, returned to his hotel room. When his boss, Hank Egan, returned, he told Minton what the PAC-10 coach had said.

"Why do you have *that* guy on your staff?" the PAC-10 coach said to Egan, referring to Minton. "Air Force doesn't even have any black guys."

By the early 1980s, Minton was one of the most qualified assistant coaches in the game. That didn't exactly reap huge rewards. He landed the job at Dartmouth for $30,000 a year.

Today, Minton helps direct the National Association of Basketball Coaches (NABC). He thinks today's new generation of African-American coaches simply does not understand their place in history. "They come along and it is all there," Minton says, "and they think of it as a right. In 1980, Nolan Richardson was one of a handful of black coaches outside of the historically black colleges. In 1983, there were eight of us. Eight! It was tight, a brotherhood."

The long-term effects of college basketball's segregated coaching ranks can still be charted. When UCLA icon John Wooden began his long string of championships in the 1960s, not a single black coach was competing for the national title. Today's recently retired coaching legends got their start in a segregated system. Bobby Knight, Don Haskins, Lou Henson, Eddie Sutton, Dean Smith, and Ray Meyer all began their careers well before a black coach could challenge them.

This segregated system has perpetuated itself, distorting the otherwise impressive "trees" of most of these coaches. For example, Bobby Knight had twenty-five assistant coaches who worked under him land head jobs. Only two have been black.

Since no black head coaches worked in powerful places, they were not calling the shots on who might get the *next* promotion, as Eddie Sutton and Lute Olsen did for decades. For a black assistant coach, the wait could be humiliating.

Rob Evans, who helped launch Nolan Richardson's career, worked as an assistant for Lou Henson on highly successful teams at

New Mexico State. Later, after his long tenure as an assistant at Texas Tech, he joined Eddie Sutton at Oklahoma State. All in all, he served as a major college assistant for twenty-four years before he got the call from Mississippi to run their program. Soon after, Evans led Ole Miss to two straight NCAA bids for the first time in school history and was named SEC Coach of the Year.

The system in college ball limited black coaches from even thinking about beginning a career. Imagine a typical black college graduate, who did not come from a middle-class background. Would he sign on as a low-paid assistant coach? Or would he take a job at, say, Marshall High School in Chicago for twice as much money? Since young black coaches did not often have the luxury of calling home for help with the rent, they were simply more likely not to be able to pay their dues. Or, rather, pay any *more* dues.

"Man, they hired that nigger coach."

That became the refrain heard around Tulsa the summer of 1980, and the complaint drove Ed Beshara to distraction. Unbeknown to Richardson, Beshara was able to talk Evans Dunne down, urging him to consider the woeful state of the basketball team, and to not withdraw his support. "Give the guy a chance, let's see how he does," Beshara told anyone who would listen.

Soon after Richardson arrived in Tulsa, Beshara called the basketball office and invited Richardson to stop by for coffee.

Richardson was met at the store with Beshara's standard greeting. "Hoss," said Beshara, "I just want to find out where you stand and who you are." The two men took off for hamburgers.

Richardson and Beshara came back to the store two hours later, laughing like school kids on the playground.

Encouraged by Beshara's upbeat humor, Richardson began looking for fresh ideas to set his Tulsa team apart. He ordered flashy new uniforms, then decorated the dismal locker room. Next, he selected a theme song to be played endlessly: "Ain't No Stoppin' Us." When Richardson learned that some of the few fans would dump their trash in the mouth of the team's bloated mascot, he insisted on a sleeker one.

On Richardson's second trip to Ed Beshara's store, he figured he'd better buy some clothes. He beelined to the sale rack and held a polka-dot shirt to his chest. A row of polka-dot shirts that Beshara could hardly give away lined the wall. Beshara didn't want them ruining the new coach's image. "You don't want that stuff, Nolan," Beshara called, waving him away.

He was too late.

"Check out how these colors look on me!" Richardson said. "How about this? Blue with gold polka dots. Tulsa colors."

"It's totally out of style," Beshara moaned. "We're trying to get rid of those."

But Richardson was grabbing the eye-catching colors by the handful. "I have to entertain, fill the gym with fans," Richardson said, checking for sizes.

"Fill the gym, hoss?" Beshara said. "They only get a few thousand fans a game."

Richardson turned serious. "You better get your tickets now," he said.

"I used the polka dots as an attention-getter, to get myself and my team noticed," Richardson says today. Soon the style—or anti-style—caught on, and a tacky Tulsa tradition was born. The students began wearing them as well, and the fans followed suit. Richardson wore polka dots his entire time with the Hurricane.

"Polka dots became contagious, like a citywide case of the measles," sportswriter Jimmie Tramel said.

Ed Beshara said, "I sold polka-dot shirts like selling ice cream."

In one mid-season contest, Richardson donned a tuxedo, and the team struggled. As he followed his team toward the locker room at halftime, fans implored him to change his outfit. The coach switched to polka dots in the locker room. Tulsa won in overtime. Later, when he again tried to take a detour from the polka-dot path, his daughter, Yvonne, insisted he stick with them.

"That kind of talk—about hiring a nigger coach—wasn't unusual at all back then," Beshara's son says today. "It was my dad who was unusual. He just didn't see color."

Ed Beshara also didn't see basketball. Literally. He rarely went to games at Tulsa, even during Richardson's tenure. "Five games in five years," his son says, quoting one of the few stats he recalls. "Dad wasn't friends with Nolan because he was a coach or famous. If Nolan decided to drive a bus instead of being a coach, they would have still been close."

Tulsa easily won their first two games under Richardson, but on December 4, 1980, Louisville was coming to Tulsa. Louisville was the defending NCAA champion and had four returning starters from the 1980 winners, as well as future NBA star Scooter McCray. It would be Richardson's first big test as a major college coach.

Louisville had swept through the NCAA Tournament field the previous year with a rip-and-run style, beating UCLA for the national title. They were one of the dominant programs in college basketball in the 1980s and an offensive model for what Richardson hoped to assemble: a fast-breaking team that ran its opponents into the ground. Richardson's pep talk to his Tulsa team was simple. The lowly Junior College Champions of Western Texas College were taking on the Division I champions of Louisville. Richardson repeatedly reminded his players of their underdog role, and this was Tulsa's first us-against-the-world challenge.

The fourth-largest crowd in school history went berserk as Tulsa's frantic full-court defense forced Louisville to commit an astonishing thirty-five turnovers. Tulsa won, 68-60.

Two days later, Tulsa beat the University of Oklahoma on its own court.

Tulsa fans were dizzy from excitement. "It was love at first dribble," the *Tulsa World* wrote. Crosstown rival Oral Roberts University was next.

A miracle was unfolding, but not the one Reverend Roberts hoped for. Richardson won at ORU, 72-69.

The ensuing matchup was with the University of Georgia, and future NBA stars Dominique Wilkins and Vern Fleming. Lines formed at the Tulsa ticket office for the first time in decades. But the University of Georgia ended Tulsa's win streak, beating Tulsa by two.

That was okay with the coach—they were going to have to lose sometime. It was not, however, all right with Yvonne Richardson. The eight-year-old did not recall ever seeing her father lose a game. They'd been undefeated the previous year, and rarely lost a home game in Snyder before that. Her father had won forty-two games in a row. When was the last time she saw him lose—when she was five? Six? Richardson couldn't recall either, and Yvonne was disconsolate. She wept for hours.

The Tulsa Hurricane's quick start won over Evans Dunne and his cohorts,

Richardson admits, "It was easy for the fans to say, 'Hey, we've got something here.'" Indeed, Tulsa did have something.

Just before the conference season began, Tulsa beat Purdue, which had been in the Final Four the previous year. The Hurricane cracked the top ten for the first time in their history, and the town was up for grabs. Sportswriter Jimmie Tramel coined the phrase "Rollin' with Nolan," and it stuck.

Polka dots were the most visible change in Tulsa, but something more important was stirring below the surface. Basketball success and improved race relations went together like a screen and roll. In this case, historically white South Tulsa and predominantly black North Tulsa united over Hurricane hoops. For the first time in school history, attendance topped a hundred thousand for the season. Per-game crowds doubled, going from 3,700 a game to 7,300. Tulsa's townies began referring to the Hurricane team as "we."

"A lot of good things happened in Tulsa that had nothing to do with basketball," Richardson says. "Blacks and whites had something to talk about, something good to share."

One fan told Richardson, "I remember going to work and nobody, and I mean black and white, said anything to each other. Now we have a common bond."

"When we beat Louisville," recalls Mike Anderson, "anybody could see that something special was brewing." The Tulsa team and their coach were at the forefront of social change, both on campus and in town. "Nolan used to tell us all the time," Anderson says, "there's just one race. The human race."

In 1982, a Gannett News piece claimed that Tulsa University ". . . may be the number one social phenomenon in college basketball."

Just before Christmas, Richardson would give the fans another gift. Tulsa would complete the in-state sweep by nudging out Oklahoma State.

Nobody seemed to mention the "nigger coach" anymore.

Tulsa finished the 1980–81 season with a record of 11-5 in the Missouri Valley Conference, good enough for a second-place finish. But they lost in the semifinals of the MVC Tournament and got passed over by the NCAA Tournament selection committee, despite their wins over Louisville, Oklahoma, Oklahoma State, Tulane, and Purdue in their nonconference schedule. In fact, Tulsa had finished the regular season at 20-6 against eleven teams that went on to postseason play. It was perhaps the worst snub in NCAA Tournament history.

Only forty-eight teams were invited to the NCAA at that time, and Tulsa was given a bid to the NIT. Because of the sorry state of the Tulsa University facilities, the first few games were to be played on the Oral Roberts campus. Tulsa beat Pan American in their first game to set up a showdown with UTEP and Don Haskins. UTEP was just beginning to recover from three straight losing seasons, the worst of Haskins's career.

The game proved to be an emotionally conflicted one for Richardson, as well as a matchup of contrasting styles. He had, of course, totally abandoned Haskins's philosophy by this time, and it was important for him to have a good showing against his own coach. Richardson's resentment over being smothered on offense by Haskins's system had faded—nearly twenty years had passed, and Richardson was the only former UTEP player who was a major college coach. That made it easier for him to reconcile with Haskins's overbearing control.

With no shot clock at the time, UTEP began the game passing and cutting for a full minute. Tulsa countered by pressing and trapping everywhere, trying to coax UTEP into a faster pace. Tulsa took the lead with two minutes to go. A frantic rally led by an obscure UTEP sub wasn't enough, and Tulsa prevailed.

Tulsa beat South Alabama by one to earn a trip to Madison Square Garden and the semifinals.

New York City was a blur.

Tulsa beat West Virginia by two.

In the NIT championship, Tulsa topped Syracuse in overtime.

It marked the first time in the history of the game that a black coach won the NIT. Tulsa and Nolan Richardson were on the map.

What made the biggest impression on the coach in New York City happened during the cutting-down-the-net ceremony in the midst of the on-court celebration. Somebody grabbed Richardson, embraced him, and planted a kiss on his cheek. Richardson had been getting hugs and handshakes, but no kisses. He turned to see who the hell had gotten his cheek wet.

It was Evans Dunne.

When the team arrived home in Tulsa at 4:30 a.m., two thousand fans were crammed into the airport terminal to welcome them. University president, Paschal Twyman, pronounced Monday an official campus holiday and shut down the college. Governor George Nigh joined ten thousand other fans in downtown Tulsa's Bartlett Square for the victory party.

Richardson refers to that magical year as one of his favorite seasons. "It was maybe the most incredible feeling I've ever had as a basketball coach, seeing how much the city and community appreciated what we had accomplished."

Ralph Brewster, however, was heartbroken in Lubbock, Texas.

He'd grown to tolerate the town, and he very much liked his teammates at Texas Tech. He'd overcome his initial homesickness. Then his patience and dedication had paid off with those two fine seasons in a row, when he averaged double figures as a sophomore and junior. Richardson had steered him to the right place, he believed, because he was a success at Tech.

He'd celebrated privately when Richardson had won the national junior college championship at Western Texas, and he nearly phoned to ask if he could join the guys and transfer to Tulsa. But Brewster knew he'd have some hard explaining to do with his Red Raider teammates. Plus, he'd have to sit out a full year to play just one final season. So he'd stuck around at Tech, anticipating a landmark senior season.

That great season didn't happen. Brewster was shocked to find himself on the bench. Richardson's raucous ride with his crew of El Paso players made him feel worse. Why had Coach Gerald Myers thought the best place for his experienced insider was on the sideline?

Brewster's senior year was a disaster. He was healthy, playing in twenty-seven games that final year, but his playing time was chopped in half, and thus his point totals. He scored only 5.7 points per game. His rebounding also fell off, to 4.1 a game. Brewster was humiliated. He had willingly bought into the Bowie backroom deal, and he'd helped launch Nolan Richardson's career, but he had somehow again gotten caught up in the machinations of college basketball.

With Brewster on the bench, Tech would stumble to its worst record during his four years there, finishing 15-13. "I didn't even understand what had happened," Brewster says, "until years later."

When his college days ended, Brewster played professionally in Mexico, Venezuela, the Philippines, and the minor league CBA. After his professional playing career was through, he became a business-man, traveling all over Texas. Once, he phoned Rob Evans, his old assistant coach, when he had an appointment in Lubbock, and sug-gested getting together. Evans made a tearful confession to Brewster that night, saying that Myers had grown to despise Nolan Richardson and took it out on Brewster. Brewster still didn't get it—why wouldn't Myers like Richardson?

Gerald Myers believed his recommendation had landed Richard-son the job at Western Texas and that there should be another pay-back—signing Brewster out of high school was not enough. "My coaches felt Nolan *owed* Tech," Brewster says. When Myers learned that Richardson was bringing his best players with him to Tulsa—especially Paul Pressey—he took out his frustrations on Brewster. "Whenever he saw me, he saw Nolan Richardson," Brewster says. "Myers suppressed it all, he never said it out loud, but it wasn't the same for me. After that, he was just anti-Ralph."

Brewster remains perplexed by the irony. Tech had essentially *taught* Nolan Richardson to use his best player to advance his career, yet when Richardson took the next step, going to Tulsa, the Tech coach was angry.

Brewster's Tech teammate and El Paso pal, Dwight Williams,

says the contrast in styles between Myers and Richardson was stark, and that made things more difficult for Brewster. "I think Gerald Myers epitomizes college basketball," Williams says. "From the top down, it is a business. But from the bottom up, from the player's point of view, it's a game. Somewhere in the middle you're supposed to meet, but we never got that from Coach Myers." Richardson was different, Williams says. "He will see a man who played at Bowie forty years ago, and know his name."

To this day, Brewster thinks about his decision to attend Tech. "There's a thin line between resentment and wondering *what if*," he says. "Because in truth, the way my career turned out was not to my liking at all. In my adolescent mind, I wondered during that senior season, 'Why did I let Nolan talk me into Tech?'"

Winning the NIT meant the Tulsa program could finally upgrade. Before Richardson arrived, the basketball office didn't employ a full-time secretary; former coach Jim King's wife would volunteer a few days a week. Richardson had only $36,000 to divide among his entire coaching staff his first season. After the big win in New York City, Richardson insisted on raises for his assistants.

The next season, Richardson's team didn't take any chances. They swept through the MVC Tournament by an average margin of 16 points, earning the automatic berth to the NCAA. It was only the second trip to the NCAA in the school's history. Tulsa lost to the University of Houston team, which featured Akeem Olajuwon, 78-74.

Richardson was so confident in his coaching skills that the quick success at Tulsa came as no surprise to him. Besides the breakneck pace his teams played at, there was something else setting Richardson apart. He wanted his players around his home as much as they desired.

This could mean a formal dinner hosting a recruit, a birthday celebration, or simply the guys flopping around his TV room and watching the game of the week, the World Series or the Super Bowl. The
total immersion with the players was in complete contrast to most
coaches—including Don Haskins—who quickly grew weary of their
kids and wanted nothing to do with them once practices were over.

Of course Richardson was winning, and that helped. The open-
door policy meant Rose Richardson was always cooking, and young
Yvonne was balancing trays of soft drinks. He was cognizant of this
void in his earlier years and that plenty of his players came from frac-
tured homes as well. The team quickly learned that Richardson's dis-
satisfaction or anger on the practice court remained there.

Although Richardson was emotionally closer to his players than
the vast majority of coaches, there were occasions where he simply
could not solve the riddle presented by some troublesome player.

Such was the case with a chronically overweight Phoenix player
named Bruce Vanley. Despite his weight, Vanley was a talented and
effective college pivot who once outplayed North Carolina star Sam
Perkins when Tulsa tamed the Tar Heels by 10 points. Regardless,
Vanley's weight remained a problem. Extra sprints. Jump-rope sessions. Laps. Diet restrictions. Lectures and threats. Nothing helped.
It was a mystery to Richardson how an overweight player might
remain fat within his frenetic system. Yet Richardson was fond of
Vanley, and he made it clear that the pudgy post player, like everyone
else, was always welcome at the Richardson home.

One evening, Richardson went to scout a Tulsa high school prospect. By the end of the first quarter, the coach had seen enough. The
player wasn't fast enough for Tulsa, and Richardson slipped out a side
door and headed home.

When he shook open the back door, Bruce Vanley was sitting at
his kitchen table. Below his round face was a pie tin. Half the apple
pie was gone. Vanley looked up, his mouth full.

"What the hell is going on here?" Richardson bellowed.

"Hi, coach," Vanley mumbled.

Richardson sprang forward as if to toss the entire table aside. But Rosario appeared at Richardson's hip, and she slid between the coach and the still-chewing Vanley. She pointed her finger at her husband. "This is my kitchen!" she said. "I'm in charge. I do what I want in here."

Vanley shoveled in another bite. Richardson reached for his own plate.

Tulsa would slip a bit during the 1982–83 campaign, finishing 19-12 and earning a return to the NIT. That the players were now disappointed with the NIT bid revealed how far the program had come. Not out to prove themselves as they had been in 1981, Tulsa lost to TCU 64-62 in the first round.

In 1983–84, Tulsa would finish 27-4. Although it was a few years before the three-point line was instituted, Tulsa averaged a blistering 90.8 points per game. The season marked a new high in excitement for Tulsa basketball, and the team's scoring totals were by far the highest in their history.

Tulsa's fans took notice, too. Attendance under Nolan Richardson is still the high mark for the University of Tulsa. Many of the players who competed for Tulsa during those years allude to the era as a time when nothing could go wrong. The team's success seemed preordained in a way, as if they were destined at Richardson's arrival to become one of the most improved teams in the nation.

Only one thing was nagging at Richardson. Yvonne sometimes complained that she didn't feel well. She was fatigued often, and if she had a fever it seemed forever until it came down.

Richardson would finish his time at Tulsa with a home record of 80-6, and Tulsa would win the Missouri Valley Conference in 1984 and 1985. In Richardson's five seasons, he boasted a record of 119-37, a rate of 76 percent.

Just as impressive, and invigorating to the Tulsa faithful, black and white, was the way Richardson disposed of their non-league in-state rivals. Richardson would amass an astonishing record of 17-1 against Oklahoma, Oklahoma State, and Oral Roberts University. He was 10-0 against ORU, a team that had regularly qualified for the NCAA and NIT. That record of 17-1, maybe more than the NIT title and NCAA bids, is what solidified Richardson's hero status in Tulsa.

Still, Richardson's legacy at Tulsa goes far beyond jump-starting a dormant program. While twenty-three coaches preceded Richardson at Tulsa, only one coach made the NCAA Tournament. There have been eight coaches since Nolan Richardson left Tulsa in 1985, and five of those coaches have qualified for the NCAA Tournament, a shocking turnaround even with the expanded field of sixty-five teams today. One other coach, Buzz Peterson, won the NIT in his first and only season before tripling his salary at Tennessee. The Tulsa job is now coveted nationally, and coaches like Tubby Smith and Bill Self, who would also go on to win NCAA titles, have gotten their starts in Tulsa.

Just as important, Richardson paved the way for three African-American coaches: Tubby Smith, Steve Robinson, and Alvin "Pooh" Williamson, who took over briefly in 2005. Incredible progress has been made in Tulsa since the "nigger coach" complaints of 1980.

In March of 1985, the Tulsa team was waiting to hear their matchup in the NCAA Tournament. When Richardson learned Tulsa would be in the same bracket as Don Haskins's UTEP team, his feelings were mixed. Either Richardson or Haskins would be sent home from the NCAA playoffs after a single game.

The next morning, Yvonne Richardson, who had not been feeling well since February, was diagnosed with leukemia. She was thirteen years old.

A few weeks later, Arkansas coach Eddie Sutton announced he was leaving to accept the University of Kentucky job. Sutton, like Don Haskins, had played for Henry Iba. In an uncharacteristic display of frustration, Sutton said he would have crawled to Kentucky to be the coach there. Something or someone at the University of Arkansas, evidently, had angered him.

Sutton had taken his 1978 Arkansas squad to the Final Four, the first time a Southwest Conference team earned a Final Four bid with black players.

Arkansas athletics director Frank Broyles phoned to gauge Richardson's interest in Arkansas. Broyles played in Ed Beshara's annual golf tournament, and had heard an earful from Tulsa fans about their black coach.

Yet Richardson originally declined to be interviewed for the Arkansas job, citing his daughter's diagnosis. Yvonne's doctor was there in Tulsa, and that was that. But Yvonne reminded her father of his own complaint, that if he'd just had a better on-campus home court he might win the NCAA championship. She encouraged Richardson to at least listen to Arkansas. He had driven Yvonne to Fayetteville when Tulsa played them in football, and she was astounded by Arkansas's rabid crowd and first-class facilities.

Richardson, as it turned out, was not the top candidate. In a move indicating either the nerve or foolishness of Frank Broyles, the job was first offered to that year's NCAA championship coach, Rollie Massimino of Villanova. When Massimino declined, Bobby Cremins and Gary Williams were approached, but none of the three white coaches had a genuine interest. "They all three used Broyles to get a raise at their own schools," one Arkansas sportswriter says. Richardson was the last one standing, front and center, and Broyles offered him the job.

The coach, though, told Yvonne he had decided he was going to stay at Tulsa.

"No, Papi," she said. "We're going to Arkansas."

Richardson relented and accepted Broyles's offer.

"Two hours later," the same sportswriter says, "Broyles was on a plane that went to Augusta National Golf Club. Augusta is an archaic and blind place," he says, "but that's how Frank was raised and he didn't see anything wrong with it." The home of the Masters Tournament was segregated at that time, and the irony of his Augusta trip after hiring a black coach was obvious to some Arkansas insiders.

Richardson still mulls over his decision today. "Everything was there for Yvonne in Tulsa," Richardson says. "Not just her doctors, but her friends, too."

Years later, Richardson would express remorse to the *Tulsa World*. Despite Yvonne's encouragement, he wondered if the move might not have been the best one for her. "When you think about that, going back over things," Richardson said, "you often ask yourself if you had to do it over again, would you do that? I would have probably not done it. No one was more important than my girl. That was a selfish decision . . . what I really wanted was her."

Haskins couldn't recall much about beating Tulsa in the NCAA Tournament in 1985. He claimed not to have any recollection of setting the NCAA record with fifty-five free throws attempted, although Richardson could not forget that statistic.

But Haskins clearly remembered when Frank Broyles phoned for a recommendation on Nolan Richardson a week later. "I told Nolan that I wouldn't go to Arkansas," Haskins claimed. "I asked Broyles, 'If Nolan gets in trouble, are you going to stand behind him?'"

Broyles's answer, according to Haskins, was, "It's a black man's game."

"That's all he kept saying," Haskins said, "the entire phone conversation, *'It's a black man's game.'* He never did answer my question about standing behind Nolan."

Yet no other large state school in the old Confederacy had ever chosen a black head coach in basketball, and it would be seventeen more years until a black man was picked as a football coach in the south. Regardless of Frank Broyles's assessment of the state of college basketball, his decision to hire Richardson in 1985 was daring.

SEVEN

THE SOULS OF BLACK FOLK

Arkansas joined the Union as a slave state in 1836 and seven years later prohibited the entrance of any new free men of color. In 1853, an editorial ran in the *Arkansas State Gazette and Democrat*. God, the newspaper said, had created Africans to be slaves. Slavery was both divinely sanctioned and legal.

On the eve of the Civil War, 111,000 slaves lived in Arkansas, roughly a quarter of the state's population. But three-quarters of Arkansas slaves lived in the southeast half of the state. That diagonal demarcation is still important today. The Mississippi floodplain to the southeast meant flat lands, big plantations, and slave ownership. The northwest half of Arkansas, with the Ozark and Ouchita Mountains, was less suited to cotton plantations. Northwest Arkansas was both whiter and poorer, with largely yeoman farmers scratching out a living.

Just before the start of the war, the Arkansas legislature voted to expel the remaining free blacks, less than a thousand men. When the fighting began, many slaves fled for the North. A lot of them would return. Between five thousand and fifteen thousand black men from Arkansas fought for the Union before the conclusion of the war.

In 1864, Arkansas's "Organic Law" abolished slavery, repudiated secession, and forbade any law "prohibiting the education of any class." Allowing freed slaves to be educated was a surprising development, but voting was another matter. No provisions were enacted for black male suffrage—not for literate black men, for those who owned property, or even for Union soldiers. And blacks not already living in Arkansas could not take up residence in the state, except in the unlikely case of an exception made by the U.S. government.

Radical Reconstruction had hardly been unveiled before the balance of power shifted back to ex-Confederates. The Ku Klux Klan appeared in Arkansas in 1868, and a wave of lynchings followed, with the precise purpose of influencing elections. The sheriff in Monticello was kidnapped and tied to a black man before both men were shot. Then their corpses were posed, embracing, and left to rot, as a lesson.

When Jim Crow segregation became official in the 1870s, the frequency of lynchings declined, although there would be periodic outbreaks, especially in the southern part of the state. Arkansas became a center of the Back to Africa movement, and Liberia was promoted within the black community as a fine place for freed slaves to live.

Arkansas became a national joke (if you could bring yourself to overlook the lynchings) in 1869, with the opening of a popular theatrical production called *The Arkansas Traveler*. The protagonist was a rustic back-hills character with a muddy Southern accent and laconic wit, initiating the hillbilly stereotype. The production traveled around American stages, a success until it closed in 1899.

The damage to the state's reputation continued in the 1880s, when the widely published newspaper column called—surprise—"The Arkansas Traveler" featured more depictions of hillbillies dispensing wit and wisdom. Soon a magazine with the identical name and goal—making fun of Arkansas—was published and stayed in national circulation for over thirty years.

Arkansans began to adopt attitudes of resentment and paranoia about the East. Of course, Arkansas could be its own worst enemy. The well-known journalist H. L. Mencken, in a lengthy article about the South, made a brief reference to Arkansas, writing that residents were "too stupid to see what was the matter with them." The state's General Assembly leaped into action, passing a resolution that demanded an apology from Mencken.

In the resolution, they misspelled the author's name.

The worst post–Civil War racial episode in the state's history occurred in 1919 in Elaine, Arkansas. Whites feared the organization of a black union there, and when a hundred sharecroppers attended a gathering of the Progressive Farmers and Household Union, violence erupted. Five whites and hundreds of blacks were killed; in fact, the exact number of murdered blacks has never been known.

Probably the most publicized lynching occurred in 1927, when John Carter was accused of assaulting a white woman. He was hung from a telephone pole, set on fire, dragged through the streets, then dumped at the corner of Ninth & Broadway in the heart of Little Rock's black community.

During the Great Depression, two western Arkansas residents created the fictional radio characters that became the *Lum and Abner Show*. NBC bought the program and moved the "rural philosophers" to Chicago, where the show aired for twenty-five years. The Arkansas hayseed backwoods image was now a firmly established nationwide joke.

A few years later, *Reader's Digest* published a note that was supposedly found on a bulletin board at a closed factory up North. The note read: "Pair of shoes for sale; moving back to Arkansas." Despite the lighthearted nature of some of the humor, concern about the state's reputation was of growing importance.

In 1953, Arkansas elected a governor with a progressive background, named Orval Faubus. One of Faubus's best moves was to appoint a Rockefeller to oversee the state's economy. In Winthrop Rockefeller's first year, 1956, over five hundred businesses were convinced that Arkansas would be a great place to relocate.

The University of Arkansas opened its doors in 1871 as the state's land-grant institution. Just a year later, the university's board of trustees announced the school was "open to all without regard to race, sex, or sect."

At least two freed slaves attended UA that year. One, James McGahee, is credited with being the first black student to enroll. (The story of McGahee's enrollment was discovered in 2006 by a graduate student.) The university president taught McGahee himself, so as not to embarrass the teachers.

In 1873, the Arkansas State Legislature authorized a university branch in Pine Bluff to be the school for African-Americans. Then, as the state's politics shifted, the University of Arkansas in Fayetteville began excluding blacks.

That policy of exclusion was unchanged until Silas Hunt applied to the UA law school in 1948. Hunt was an army hero who had fought at the Battle of the Bulge, where he was badly wounded. (Hunt was not, however, awarded the Congressional Medal of Honor. No black soldier would be honored for decades.) Through a coordinated effort with Little Rock activist Wiley Brandt, Hunt was admitted to the UA School of Law in 1948. That same year, Edith Mae Irby became the first black to enroll at the University of Arkansas Medical School in Little Rock.

State laws still prohibited integrated classrooms, so Hunt had to attend segregated classes—meaning that he was the only student in his classroom in the basement. In an odd subterranean show of support, a couple of white students decided to join him. Later, Hunt was allowed upstairs, with a single railing separating the wounded World War II hero from his classmates. He died a little over a year after enrolling, at age twenty-seven, likely from tuberculosis combined with complications of his war wounds.

Although the University of Arkansas was the first major school in the South to enroll a black student, the college continued its policy of rejecting all applications from undergraduate blacks until the *Brown v. Board of Education* ruling by the Supreme Court in 1954. That led to the first black undergrads being admitted at Arkansas in 1955.

Fayetteville High School, as well as the Hoxie District in the northeast corner of the state, immediately began implementing the *Brown* decision in 1954. Seven black students were admitted to Fayetteville High School, making it among the very first towns in the South to successfully desegregate without fanfare or controversy.

There would be plenty of controversy, however, coming up in Little Rock.

The Civil Rights movement targeted Little Rock as a city that could, potentially, quietly withstand the desegregation of its schools. Little Rock was not in the Deep South, the state was largely white, and Governor Orval Faubus was a moderate, so the town appeared to be a good bet. Little Rock had become a focal point in 1942, when Susie Morris, a black teacher at Dunbar High School, filed a lawsuit because she was paid less than white teachers. Morris won the lawsuit but lost her job.

The plan was to integrate Central High School gradually, and only nine students volunteered, due to pressure, rumors, and fear. Yet that made the plan easier to implement. Nearly everyone—newspaper editors, businessmen, school administration—expected an easy and peaceful transition.

During his reelection campaign in 1956, Faubus had hardly referred to race. In Arkansas, the law required the governor to go up for election every two years, and by 1957, Faubus was gunning for a third term. He had a stark choice: empower the tide of integration and lose, or challenge the feds and make himself a symbol of segregation.

In the spring of 1957, Faubus pushed through four segregationist bills. He didn't need a weatherman to know which way the wind was blowing. The segregationist bills passed, 81-1.

With school and desegregation at Central scheduled to begin, Faubus could find no middle ground, the salvation for many a politician. That September he indirectly condoned mob violence by publicly claiming that he, the governor, could not maintain peace. Then Faubus decided to call out the Arkansas National Guard to *prevent* blacks from enrolling at Central High School. The National Guard found itself on the side of the white mobs, and despite specific orders from the district court, kept the nine black kids from entering the school.

What happened in the ensuing weeks is well documented. Eight of the students who arrived were abused and threatened before being turned away by the Arkansas National Guard. The mob had its confidence bolstered, as did the segregationists. President Eisenhower reacted by sending in the 101st Airborne Division to aid the integration process, the first time since Reconstruction that federal troops were sent to the old Confederacy.

Most compelling about the Central High School story was what happened to Elizabeth Eckford that first day. A fifteen-year-old, Eckford had not received the message about the detailed plan for the nine students to travel to Central together. Wearing the new dress she had made herself and bolstered by the morning prayers of her parents, Eckford walked to Central High School alone.

The mob spotted her and mirrored her steps, taunting and spitting on her. Eckford had seen the National Guard ahead and figured she'd be safe. When she got to the guard, though, they blocked her path by raising bayonets to her throat.

With the mob closing in behind with shouts of "Lynch her!" Eckford realized she'd have to reverse directions and walk the gauntlet again. Soon she was surrounded on all sides, with the National Guard behind her. She turned toward a bus stop, and the crowd let her pass, giving her an earful the entire walk. After being encouraged by a *New York Times* education reporter and an elderly white woman, Eckford finally got on a bus and was out of harm's way.

Eckford returned to Central the next day and graduated on time a few years later.

The genocide in Tulsa's Greenwood district in 1921, of course, predated a national television audience. While the story of Central High School appeared in newspapers and magazines, it was the newer medium of the television screen where the meltdown in Arkansas had the most impact.

Central High School was the first showdown between a rabid mob and the force of law to play out on national television. According to David Halberstam's book *The Fifties*, "The images were so forceful that they told their own truths and needed virtually no narration. It was hard for people watching at home not to take sides . . . watching orderly black children behaving with great dignity, trying to obtain nothing more than a decent education, the most elemental of American birthrights, yet being assaulted by a vicious mob of poor whites."

It was hard for people at home not to take sides. While surely not everyone in Arkansas had a television, everyone in Arkansas had to make a decision. Especially its leaders. They had televisions. The white students at Central decided mostly to accommodate the nine black kids, especially as the year progressed.

Black teenagers from Little Rock, without the least bit of power, were acting with tremendous courage. How would the state's leaders, with *all* the power, act?

Frank Broyles arrived as football coach at the University of Arkansas in the late winter of 1958. Fayetteville High School had successfully, if modestly, desegregated, as had the university's law school, medical school, and undergraduate student body. Of course, none of those events were nationally televised.

Broyles, no doubt, took note of the fortunes of Governor Faubus, who during the previous summer had looked unlikely to win a third term. But the Central High School crisis ignited his popularity among the majority, the white voters. A white person of voting age could no longer be for segregation yet against Faubus. In the next election, Faubus beat his two opponents handily—their combined votes didn't amount to half of his total.

It wasn't just Frank Broyles who was watching, of course. Future presidential candidate and segregationist George Wallace also learned from Little Rock, according to Halberstam, ". . . how to manipulate the anger within the South, how to divide the state by class and race, and how to make the enemy seem to be the media." A decade later, George Wallace would win Arkansas in the presidential election as an independent. Wallace won only five states, and Arkansas was the only one not in the Deep South.

Some moderates felt the "lessons of Little Rock" meant that violence would scare away business. That would prove to be true. The negative publicity again set Arkansas back in the nation's eye. Not a single new industrial plant opened in either Little Rock or its surrounding Pulaski County in the year following the crisis. Winthrop Rockefeller, who had championed Arkansas as a great business location, resigned.

But another lesson of Little Rock was that clinging to a racist past at the institutional level could be a popular policy.

Desegregating a high school in the biggest city in the state was one challenge. Getting anyone else to follow suit was quite another. By the autumn of 1963, less than one percent of African-American public school students in Arkansas attended classes with whites. As late as 1967, 83 percent of black students still attended segregated schools.

Any leader interested in keeping the world segregated had to *make the enemy seem to be the media*. But it could be taken in a different direction—befriending and controlling the media could be a smart step, too. Nothing in Arkansas received the same media attention given to the University of Arkansas football team.

In 1963, Governor Faubus announced that he opposed lifting the racial restrictions on athletics at the University of Arkansas. The University of Arkansas Board of Trustees agreed with Faubus, instituting policies that excluded blacks from university sports and dormitories.

"When I heard the board of trustees made that ruling," longtime UA psychology professor Phillip Trapp recalls, "I said the faculty should go on record." They did. The college faculty, as well as the student association, officially endorsed the integration of Razorback athletics.

Trapp was asked to serve on the university's faculty athletics council in 1962. What better place to integrate, he thought, than the place where most of the attention was? "The board of trustees was still solidly against integration," Trapp says. "That's why Frank Broyles was so against it, he'd be going against the board."

Trapp's embracing the ideals of integration didn't sit well with one board of trustees member, Pete Rainey. When Trapp was introduced to him, Rainey turned his back on the professor.

Delbert Schwartz chaired the faculty athletics council for years, and Trapp says that Schwartz wanted to groom him to someday chair the group. Just before a meeting, Trapp cornered Schwartz and told him he was going to make a motion that Arkansas should integrate their athletic teams. "I want it to go into the record," Trapp told him.

"Oh, my God," Schwartz said, "if you do that you'll *never* become my replacement."

"I knew the committee was handpicked by Frank Broyles," Trapp says, "and I didn't have much aspiration that it would pass, but our students had voted that way."

Knowing his proposal was likely doomed, Trapp still made the suggestion that Broyles integrate his team. "I can see this giving us a national title in short order," Trapp said. "We'll be the first major school in the South, and we'll have our pick of black athletes." Black athletes were already dominating on the national stage, and that meant bigger crowds, Trapp reasoned, more money. Many of the top black athletes were from the Old South, but Arkansas was now embracing the principle of segregation at the expense of their basketball team—as well as their balance sheets. Arkansas football was certain to be harmed as well, when the SWC integrated, if they didn't follow the trend of sports being at the forefront of racial progress across the country.

Two board members voted for integration; nine voted against it.

But that was not the most disheartening aspect. "I heard [Broyles] say when I made that proposal that it would be 'over his dead body,'" Trapp recalls. "I think he had a strong race card going. That would be pretty obvious, he came from Georgia, and in fairness, he'd been indoctrinated, but at that time Broyles was very strong against integrating athletics."

A few months later, Trapp would get a final reminder of how popular his ideas on integrating football were. He was removed from the faculty athletics council, with which Broyles worked very closely. "I would guess, and this is a guess," Trapp says, "that Frank Broyles said, 'We don't need that radical on that committee.'"

Trapp was gone from the faculty athletics council by the mid-1960s, but more showdowns were on the horizon, ones that would reveal who held the power at the only major university in the state. Would it be the students and faculty? The board of trustees? Or the football coach?

EIGHT

GOD'S TROMBONES

Rosario Richardson was tired of the talk in Fayetteville, and they hadn't even been there a year. Waiting in line at a grocery store, she heard a shopper offering to give away her 1985–86 season tickets. The shopper knew the reason the Arkansas Razorbacks weren't winning. "Because they hired that black coach."

Rose Richardson whipped out her checkbook and tapped the woman on the shoulder.

"I'll buy those tickets," she said.

The lady at the grocery store was not the only disappointed Razorback fan. Former coach Eddie Sutton's crew had won their opening NCAA Tournament game the previous season, and Richardson had two of those starters back. Expectations were enormous—Arkansas was even included in some preseason Top 20 polls. While the team did pretty well in the preseason, once Southwest Conference play began, the Razorbacks stumbled badly.

The team appeared confused under Richardson's system, and they even lost seven games in Fayetteville's Barnhill Arena. Richardson suspended two players for drug use. He realized that he didn't have the talent in place to do much better, and he was already catching heat, particularly from *Democrat-Gazette* writer John Robert Starr. "You have to sweep the house out before you move in," Richardson says. "I didn't do that at Arkansas and it may have been a mistake."

Richardson's time at Arkansas began with a sense of trepidation—he loved Tulsa; Yvonne was sick; then his new team floundered. The traits that made him successful—brazen confidence and his us-against-the-world philosophy—were in stark contrast to Frank Broyles's trademarks. The athletics director was more politic and measured, quick to smile, always positive with his pat answers. Few people were aware then that Eddie Sutton had grown weary of Broyles's strange, overbearing-yet-distant management style.

Richardson found a modest townhouse overlooking a golf course in Fayetteville. The place didn't quite feel like home, partly because the family was returning so often to Tulsa for medical treatment. They kept their house near Seventy-first and Memorial in Tulsa as a base for when Yvonne went in for treatment. Richardson soon came to believe there were not the doctors available in Fayetteville that Broyles had suggested there would be. Little Rock offered better medical care, but Tulsa was an hour closer. The constant return trips to Tulsa reminded Richardson of how content he had been there.

Richardson also came to grips with the notion that leukemia killed the mother he could barely remember, and his nephew Butch was gone just two months after being diagnosed. Richardson badly needed support, but instead felt as though people in Arkansas only cared about whether his basketball team was winning.

Mike Anderson, the point guard on Richardson's first Tulsa teams, joined the staff at Arkansas as a low-level assistant coach. His responsibilities were centered on driving Yvonne back and forth to Tulsa on days when her father could not. Anderson had met Yvonne in 1980, his first year in Tulsa. "She was like my kid sister," he says.

"Yvonne was the inspiration to keep Coach Richardson going," Anderson adds, emphasizing the powerful sway the girl, now in her teens, had over her father.

As her health declined, Yvonne never expressed pity for herself. "She didn't complain," Anderson remembers. "She was optimistic, always thinking God would make a way for her to get well."

Anderson believes Richardson had been so fortunate in his time at Tulsa that the same feeling of optimism initially spilled over into everyone's thinking about Yvonne. "All those championships Nolan had won, all those firsts for a black coach. His life was like a story-book in a way. When Yvonne was diagnosed with leukemia—well, we all just knew she would turn out okay."

As Yvonne deteriorated, she could still find humor in the darkest of times. Occasionally, Anderson would drive Yvonne, along with her mother, to road games on the day the Razorbacks played, so she wouldn't have to be gone as many days as the team. Once, coming back from a loss in Dallas, Anderson found himself in a thick fog. High beams made the fog appear denser. Because he was on a narrow road, Anderson figured pulling over might be even more dangerous. He slowed down then leaned forward over the steering wheel, hoping that might help his vision. Rose, a nervous traveler in good weather, began crying out, "Oh, Lord Jesus!" at every dip and turn.

When the fog lifted, Yvonne began mimicking her mother. Soon, everyone was laughing, even Rose. "Yvonne called me 'Oh Lord Jesus' for weeks afterward," Anderson says.

Yvonne wouldn't let her father—*Papi*, she called him, or *Papito*—pity her, or himself. Instead, she peppered him with inspirational talks or demanded another "interview."

In an attempt to comfort her, Richardson reminded her not to worry, that the Razorbacks would get better and he was doing his best. One day Yvonne told him his best wasn't good enough, a startling thing for a child to tell a father. "You've got to step it up," she said.

When Richardson assured her he would, she let out a sigh.

"I think I can rest now."

Remaining upbeat became nearly impossible for Richardson. The drive to and from Tulsa, which he sometimes did instead of Anderson, gave him plenty of time to second-guess his decision to leave for Arkansas.

On one occasion, Yvonne was retching and vomiting and couldn't stop. Richardson pulled the car over and decided to let her stretch out in the backseat. Tulsa was still over an hour away. Richardson climbed back in and floored the accelerator, figuring if he exceeded the speed limit on a straightaway, perhaps a policeman would pull him over. He could convince the cop to flip on his siren and give them an escort into Tulsa. Instead, he sped into Tulsa unnoticed.

With Yvonne dying, his wife understandably distraught, and feeling pressure from Broyles, the fans, and media, Richardson felt isolated. He was in need of someone who could provide what Ol' Mama did, and he found that guidance and friendship in an old white man named Orville Henry, Arkansas's best-known sportswriter. Henry checked in with Richardson every day during his early tenure in Arkansas.

This is a pattern in Richardson's life, gravitating to older men, who are often white, for advice and friendship. First, Bert Williams, Don Haskins. Then Sid Simpson. Ed Beshara. Orville Henry.

Although Henry was better known as a football writer, he and Richardson became close. Henry was in some ways an Old Southerner but had become more progressive as far as questions about race were concerned. An Orville Henry anecdote: In the late 1960s, Henry and his ten-year-old son Clay went to play golf at the Fairpark Golf Course. On the eighth hole, both Henrys drove their ball from the tee and began walking ahead. Clay saw a black boy about his own age cutting across the fairway.

"Dad," Clay said, "we need to hurry! That boy's going to steal our golf ball."

Orville Henry stopped in his tracks and turned to his son. "You think he's going to steal your ball because he's black, don't you?"

When they got to their golf balls, the black boy, perhaps eight years of age, had passed. They were safe. But Henry called and waved the boy back.

Henry asked the boy if he had ever hit a golf ball. The boy had not.

"Would you like to try?" Henry pulled out his son's five-iron. Then Henry emptied his son's bag of two dozen balls.

"I'm going to give you a lesson," Orville Henry said to the boy—or perhaps both boys. Henry showed the black boy the grip, got him in a stable stance, and showed him the classic shoulder turn, and how to keep his eyes down. Fifteen minutes later, with balls sprayed everywhere, Orville Henry turned to his son.

"Where's your putting ball?" he said. "Let me have it."

Henry presented it to the boy. Then he turned back to his son and said, "Pick up all the balls."

Although Richardson had heard the story on several occasions, he always found it moving. He could have been that black kid cutting across the grass.

One longtime Arkansas sportswriter says that Orville Henry may have been influenced in the same way Evans Dunne was at Tulsa. Although Henry wasn't racist, he says, Henry would have certainly had an older mentality. "At one time, Orville had been asked not to return to Pine Bluff to speak, because of his off-color jokes," this sportswriter says. "Later, Nolan sort of won Orville over. Also, Orville had married a very progressive woman, and that helped."

Richardson's trouble with Frank Broyles began during that first season. Orville Henry was friends with both men, and could sometimes smooth over misunderstandings. More often, though, understanding was beyond Richardson's and Broyles's grasp.

Broyles remembered Eddie Sutton's slower style, and Richardson was radically different. "When Nolan was struggling," one Arkansas sportswriter says, "Broyles was coming down to watch practice, trying to figure out if Nolan could really coach."

Once the disappointing first season concluded, Broyles told Richardson he wanted him to go visit Indiana coach Bob Knight. Broyles felt that Richardson could maybe learn how to teach defense and get his team under control.

Richardson, who was already sensitive about his rabid pressing and *Star Wars*–paced offense being slandered, considered this an insult.

Plenty of coaches still believed Don Haskins to be the best defensive coach in the nation. Knight himself had spent time with Haskins at the 1972 Olympic trials, where Haskins had been an assistant to Henry Iba. "Hell, Knight had all kinds of questions about Mr. Iba's system," Haskins recalled. "Knight could have gone to Nolan to learn my system. Nolan knew it as well as anyone."

Richardson declined to visit Indiana, although he admired Knight.

"Fuck Bobby Knight," Richardson told Broyles. "My daughter is dying and you're bothering me?"

Broyles's pestering Richardson about coaching decisions was not unique to basketball. This was perhaps Broyles's central contradiction—he found great coaches, then could not stop himself from second-guessing them.

One October, football coach Ken Hatfield burst into Richardson's office, fuming, waving a legal pad. "Damn!" Hatfield said. "Broyles is sending me plays to run. First he wants me to fire [assistant coach] Fred Goldsmith, and now he wants me to change my whole attack."

Richardson leaned forward in his chair and smiled at his assistant coaches.

"Let me see those plays," Richardson said. He still loved football and liked to talk the talk with Hatfield. Richardson studied the diagrams for a long minute, flipping back and forth, engrossed in the possibilities. Suddenly he crumpled the pages into a ball and lofted a left-handed shot at the wastebasket. It banked in.

"That's what I do with Broyles's suggestions," Richardson said.

As Yvonne's situation deteriorated, Richardson lost all patience with Broyles. It was one thing to make suggestions about scheduling, the media guide, or uniform styles. But it was quite another to suggest, by offering tactical advice, that Richardson didn't know how to coach.

"I think Frank Broyles had different expectations of black people," Richardson says today. "Look where he came from—the Deep South, Georgia. His ancestors were slave owners, and he had a different view of the duties black people should have."

He finally blasted Broyles over what he believed was his boss's lack of compassion. "You knew I had a sick daughter when you hired me!" he shouted at Broyles his first season. "Don't expect me to ignore her."

Any gesture from Broyles seemed to irritate Richardson. "Broyles did offer Nolan to take a leave of absence with pay," one longtime sportswriter says, "but Nolan misinterpreted that to mean Broyles wanted him gone." Events that would unfold a year later would prove Richardson was right.

Richardson was not the only person who might be baffled by Frank Broyles.

Charles Prigmore was the executive vice chancellor at University of Arkansas Medical Center in Little Rock during the 1970s. Prigmore, a former high school football coach, kept a close eye on Broyles, and sees him as a complex man, a charismatic leader who could border on arrogant and self-serving.

One hot summer day in the early 1970s, Prigmore was in his office at the Medical Center when word began circulating that a Razorback football player, a lineman from South Arkansas, had arrived in an ambulance. He'd fallen out of a pickup truck, and it appeared there might be spinal cord damage. Prigmore hustled down to the neurology floor, where the player had been moved. He was shocked at what he found.

With a whirlwind of commands, the neurology floor came under Frank Broyles's jurisdiction. He lined up the staff as if they were freshmen at fall football tryouts. "Our chief of neurology," Prigmore recalls, "was a quiet and unassuming guy, and he just stepped back when Broyles and his entourage came through. Broyles wasn't trying to medically treat the kid, but he just took over, saying he needed this type of bed and that kind of room, and calling out orders to nurses."

An hour later, without asking anyone for permission, Broyles hosted a press conference in the neurology wing.

The 1986–87 season was a bit better than Richardson's first year, but he was preoccupied with Yvonne. Andy Stoglin would coach the team when Richardson couldn't be in Fayetteville, and the alternating coaches certainly didn't help the Razorbacks. They couldn't get any momentum, although they beat Kansas, Ohio State, and Cal, and were 8-4 before the league season. Then Yvonne got worse.

The back-and-forth trips to Tulsa and St. Francis Hospital, where Yvonne had been nearly full-time, were taking their toll on everyone. Transfusions, bone-marrow transplants, chemotherapy, a journey to the Mayo Clinic—nothing improved Yvonne's situation. At one point, fungus appeared on her lung, and that worried the doctors. They had to break her rib to get to the lung.

After the New Year, Yvonne was allowed home from the hospital. She slept between the coach and Rose. But her condition worsened, and she was rushed back to the hospital.

Yvonne Richardson died of leukemia on January 22, 1987. She was fifteen years old.

Richardson's sense of isolation from the state, the town, the university, and the athletics department was overwhelming. He was so distraught that even when well-wishers tried to console him, he could barely bring himself to feel their sympathy.

People close to Richardson believe Yvonne's death altered his level of compassion. Watching his daughter slowly wither away gave him a more empathetic antenna for others in trouble. Ironically, though, after witnessing Yvonne's resilience, Richardson pushed his players even harder. While he understood emotional anguish, seeing a healthy player who wouldn't fight frustrated him.

His empathy for the underdog was natural—who had had to overcome more obstacles? Starting out as the Bowie coach kept him close to his roots, and he identified with the scruffy Segundo Barrio kids as outsiders. The mindset continued as he became one of the few black college coaches in America, first at Snyder and then Tulsa—and finally as the only black coach in the Southwest Conference.

Through Yvonne's illness, Richardson says, Broyles never acknowledged that these were tough times for his family. That hurt Richardson deeply. Then it angered him, especially when he felt as though Broyles was pressuring him to turn his back on his family and focus on the Razorback team.

A longtime employee of the University of Arkansas athletics department confirmed Broyles's attitude, but thinks the bad relationship that had already surfaced had less to do with race than ego over the years.

"Broyles forced out Ken Hatfield as football coach in 1989," the employee says. Hatfield had amassed over a thousand yards in his playing career at Arkansas as a punt returner—his totals led the nation for two seasons—and he was a hero on Broyles's best team, when he coached football for Arkansas, in 1964. Hatfield's coaching record at Arkansas was 55-17, and he was widely regarded as one of the top football coaches in America.

This employee made an appointment to visit Nolan after he lost Yvonne, although he didn't know him well then. "I brought him a plaque that someone had given me," he says. "It wasn't a fancy gift, but it meant a lot to me and I wanted Nolan to have it." The employee waited outside Richardson's office, the gift in his lap, until the coach emerged. The employee presented the bereaved coach with the worn-out plaque and explained why it had given him strength over the years.

Richardson was clearly touched. He wept, and thanked the man.

"Nolan told me he felt like he was all alone, on an island," he continues. "That really surprised me."

Less than a week later, this employee was at lunch with a table full of Arkansas football coaches when Frank Broyles approached and began openly disparaging Richardson's coaching ability. "It just struck me as out of place," the employee says. "I mean, Yvonne had just died, and he was telling us that [assistant coach] Andy Stoglin was a better coach, that Nolan couldn't coach."

Going into their last home game in 1987, less than two months after Yvonne's death, the Razorbacks were 6-7 in SWC play—not exactly where Richardson had envisioned being, after taking the job two seasons earlier. The opponent for the final game in Fayetteville was Baylor, which had beaten Arkansas in Waco. With only three games to go, Richardson badly needed a win, since he'd be going on the road for his final two league games. Baylor wasn't a great team, but their coach was an Iba—Gene Iba, a nephew of Henry Iba—and that ball-control playing style sometimes meant trouble.

Another concern to negotiate was Senior Night. The last home game for any college usually means a chance to honor the players in the final year, both stars and benchwarmers. The Razorbacks' starting lineup that season did not include a single senior. Richardson's predecessor, Eddie Sutton, had traditionally started as many seniors as he could in the last home game.

Richardson did have one senior, a 6'7" Houston kid named Eric Poerschke, a holdover from the Sutton era. Poerschke was simply the wrong player for Richardson's system, a bad fit stylistically, and he found himself on the bench his last season. It wasn't that Poerschke was a bad player. He'd started a handful of games as a sophomore for Sutton. In Richardson's first season, Poerschke led the Razorbacks in field goal percentage, and scored over fifty baskets for the year.

"I realized I wasn't really in his plans my senior year," Poerschke says, "and that wasn't a great thing to go through. But I knew that this was part of life, so I decided to be a good teammate and pull for our other guys."

The Razorbacks had shown plenty of promise before the holidays, but kept stumbling in SWC play. Poerschke says, "Pressure seemed to come when we started losing. But looking back it didn't have much to do with winning and losing at all. It was Yvonne." Now Poerschke can see that the season was incredibly difficult. "I've got three kids now, and you begin to realize—well, Nolan was at practice more than most people would have been. And being the first black coach, there was already overwhelming pressure."

Richardson respected Poerschke, a brilliant student who would graduate with a business degree, although he rarely played him as a senior. "He never complained, never hung his head," Richardson says. "He worked and fought like he was one of our main guys." Yet, because Richardson's first team at Arkansas had sputtered, he was concerned about a late-season collapse again, so the idea of starting a benchwarmer in an important game made him skittish.

Regardless, Poerschke was looking forward to Senior Night. His parents were coming from Houston to see his last game, and it would likely be his last chance to shine before the home fans.

But Baylor controlled the tempo from the outset and wouldn't let the Razorbacks run their fast break. Richardson's assistants suggested giving Poerschke a try, but he didn't seem to hear. Arkansas held on to win by four, but senior Eric Poerschke didn't play a minute.

"I wasn't that upset," Poerschke claims. "We won."

And that, Poerschke thought, was the end of that.

Arkansas finished that 1986–87 season 8-8 in the SWC, and was awarded an NIT bid. Richardson was fiercely proud of his NIT championship team at Tulsa, so it annoyed him terribly when he began hearing Broyles refer to the NIT as "a loser's tournament."

The NIT bid in 1987 offered an unusual matchup for the Razorbacks. They'd face Arkansas State, which they had not played since 1948.

There's a reason the big schools like Arkansas do not schedule the lower-profile in-state schools—a loss would be embarrassing. The afternoon of the game, the president of the university, Ray Thornton, stopped by with Frank Broyles to see their basketball coach. Thornton told Richardson, "Win, lose, or draw tonight, you are going to be our coach." Then Thornton turned to Broyles, and, according to Richardson, said, "You understand that, Coach Broyles?"

That evening the Arkansas State Indians got off to a fast start and built a 21-point lead in Fayetteville. Razorback fans squirmed. Their press wasn't effective, and the game clearly meant more to Arkansas State. After a couple of steals and blocked shots, the momentum shifted, the *Democrat-Gazette* wrote, and the Razorbacks would rally, sneak by, and perhaps save Richardson's job, just two years after he began.

"Nolan has a sixth sense," Mike Anderson says. "He has a feeling about who wants him to succeed and who does not."

Frank Broyles, Richardson believed, did not.

The *Democrat-Gazette* must have had the same sense, writing later, "Arkansas Athletics Director Frank Broyles, spotted before the game, is nowhere to be seen afterward. There are rumors that Broyles was back at his office calling boosters to buy out Richardson. Years later, Broyles denies he was at the game, saying he was out of town."

According to Richardson, this attempted sabotage by Broyles indicated who was in charge in Fayetteville. It wasn't the president, either. "Broyles ran the show," he says. "They couldn't touch him."

Arkansas lost their next NIT game at Nebraska. Richardson returned home believing what the *Democrat-Gazette* obviously believed, that Frank Broyles wanted him gone. The timing of this—with Yvonne recently deceased—was something the coach never got over. And for Richardson, slights or insults are permanent.

"But that works both ways for Nolan," says his longtime friend, El Paso judge Thomas Spieczny. "Any injustice sticks with him, even if it's one that *he* caused accidentally."

Eric Poerschke, who never stripped off his warm-ups on Senior Night, concurs. "The odd thing is, when I see Nolan, he keeps apologizing for not playing me one game in 1987. I've gotten over it, but he can't. It's been twenty years."

NINE

INVISIBLE MAN

Twenty years might seem like a long time to some, but not to Frank Broyles. He served the University of Arkansas as football coach and then as director of athletics for a total of *fifty* years—nineteen seasons as football coach, thirty-five as AD, and four years as both. His football teams in the 1960s, along with the University of Texas, set a standard for excellence in the Southwest Conference. Arkansas was a member of the SWC from 1915 until 1991, and the only team in the league not from Texas.

Broyles was born in 1924 and raised in Decatur, Georgia, just outside of Atlanta. Like Nolan Richardson, he starred in football, basketball, and baseball. Richardson had done that in high school, but Broyles did it in college too. He was named All-SEC a half-dozen times at Georgia Tech, both as a football quarterback and a basketball star. Broyles's Orange Bowl passing record stood for over fifty years. Of course, Broyles never competed against a single black player.

The state of Georgia in that era set clear lines and values. In the 1940s, Georgia invested $142 per year for each white student, as opposed to $35 for each black student. Eugene Talmadge, who was Georgia's governor for much of the 1930s and 1940s, said, "I like the nigger, but I like him in his place, and his place is at the back door with his hat in his hand."

Georgia passed laws to protect segregation before and after the 1954 Supreme Court decision. One candidate for governor in the mid-1950s wanted children to declare under oath whether they preferred an integrated school. If they did, they would be assigned to a mental institution.

Frank Broyles returned to Georgia Tech to join its coaching staff as an assistant from 1951 until 1956. The governor of Georgia by then was Marvin Griffin, who realized the impact Jackie Robinson had a few years earlier and saw athletics as an important place to fight against racial equality.

Broyles was the offensive backfield coach when Georgia Tech was invited to play in the Sugar Bowl on New Year's Day of 1956. Tech would face Pittsburgh, who had a single black player. Tech head coach Bobby Dodd got Governor Griffin's permission to play the barely desegregated game, but a month before the contest, Griffin changed his mind, saying, "There is no more difference in compromising the integrity of race on the playing field than in doing so in the classroom. One break in the dike and the relentless seas will rush in and destroy us." The governor ordered Georgia Tech to stay home.

In a demonstration more indicative of Tech students' love of football than equal opportunity for Negroes, close to two thousand students marched to the capitol building and burned Griffin in effigy. After the Georgia Tech Board of Trustees approved the trip, Governor Griffin backed down. Tech won the game—their fifth bowl game victory in a row—but the leading rusher was Pitt's black star, Bobby Grier.

In 1957, on the heels of Georgia Tech's success, Broyles was named the head football coach at University of Missouri.

Broyles only coached Missouri for one season before accepting the job at Arkansas. Most interesting about his time at Missouri is the fact that on his watch, his football staff signed the first two black players in school history—Norris Stevenson and Mel West. The pair would star on the best teams in University of Missouri history.

Norris Stevenson knew the town of Columbia was segregated before he arrived in 1957. "For one semester I was the only black player," he says, "and in retrospect, the coaches weren't exactly thrilled with the idea."

Stevenson was joined by Mel West the following semester. "This was another time," Stevenson insists. "You'd have to move everybody, physically and emotionally, to understand it. You'd have to recreate the atmosphere, otherwise things we said today would make no sense. We were kids, and half of us didn't know who Martin Luther King was."

When Broyles announced he was leaving for Arkansas after their freshman year, Stevenson and West stuck around to help Missouri to three fine football seasons. The University of Arkansas had never had a black athlete in any sport.

Frank Broyles had a personal connection to the Little Rock Central crisis of 1957. One of the first moves he made at Arkansas was to lure a man named Wilson Matthews away from his job coaching Central High School to become the Razorbacks' assistant coach.

Playing a whites-only schedule, Wilson Matthews led Central High School to ten state championships in his eleven years there. Matthews had an interesting view of what caused the problems at Central. In Terry Frei's book about the showdown between the Texas and Arkansas football teams of 1969, *Horns, Hogs, and Nixon Coming*, Matthews is quoted as saying, ". . . if a bunch of damn soldiers hadn't showed up and got a crowd around, there wouldn't have been any problems." Whether Matthews meant the Arkansas National Guard, who held bayonets on black girls, or the 101st Airborne Division, who opened the school to them, is unclear.

Matthews helped Broyles with the Razorbacks from 1958 to 1968 and was known as the most influential coach on Broyles's staff. A passionate and foul-mouthed motivator, Matthews assumed head coaching duties for the freshman team, the "Shoats," in 1969. Later, he took over the conditioning programs, then moved into athletics administration soon after. He worked as an assistant athletics director until 1992. Because he moved to administration, Matthews never coached a varsity black athlete at the University of Arkansas.

Broyles's debut at Arkansas in 1958 began badly—he lost his first six games in a row. The Razorbacks recovered by winning their last four. They had phenomenal success after that rocky start, especially in the 1960s.

In 1964, Broyles's all-white squad roared through the season undefeated at 11-0. But Arkansas faced only four teams with winning records, so both UPI and AP, the biggest polls, declared Alabama national champs before the bowl games were played, as was their custom at that time.

Alabama devalued that decision by losing to Texas in the Orange Bowl. Then Arkansas beat Nebraska in the Cotton Bowl, 10-7. (Nebraska was the only team Arkansas faced that year that had black players.) Two smaller polls, the Football Writers Association of America and the Helms Foundation, declared the Razorbacks national champions. Today, both Arkansas and Alabama claim the national championship of 1964.

That same year, a black student named Robert Whitfield won a discrimination lawsuit against UA campus housing, and the federal ruling forced the dormitories to be open to all without regard to race. Whitfield and Joanna Edwards became the first two blacks at the University of Arkansas to be admitted to previously segregated dormitories.

Broyles's all-white 1969 team lost a heartbreaker to Texas in the still-segregated contest called "The Game of the Century" by some. The loss likely cost Arkansas a unanimous national title.

Over his career, Broyles's teams won over 70 percent of their games. His Razorbacks appeared in ten bowl games, usually the Cotton Bowl or Sugar Bowl. He would coach only two losing teams in his nineteen years. Broyles's time at Arkansas straddled two eras—the strictly segregated Southwest Conference of the late 1950s and early 1960s, and the quickly integrating teams of the early 1970s.

The black football phenoms of the 1950s and 1960s college scene include an impressive roster of stars who later earned places in the NFL's Hall of Fame: Jim Brown, Gale Sayers, "Deacon" Jones, Willie Davis, Lenny Moore, Roosevelt Brown, Carl Eller, Herb Adderly, Emerson Boozer, Ollie Matson, Dick "Night Train" Lane, and Paul Warfield.

The closest NFL team to Arkansas, the St. Louis Cardinals, featured black Texas native Johnny Roland—who, of course, had to leave Texas to play major college football.

The best black players from Arkansas flaunted their talent before Frank Broyles could even get a foothold in Fayetteville. Bobby Mitchell, Willie Davis, and Elijah Pitts were Arkansas natives who became NFL stars despite being ignored by the state university in the 1950s. Other black players from the state, such as Jim Pace and Sidney Williams, had been all-conference players in the Big Ten.

Any objective observer could figure out that black kids deserved a chance based on ability alone. Few states have as impressive a tradition of black football players, but with mostly segregated high schools and a separate athletics association for the Negro schools, it was rare that whites competed on the same field as black kids in Arkansas.

Only the biggest Negro schools competed in football, because of the equipment needed to field a team. There might be thirty schools competing for the state's Negro championship in any one year, but there were generally eight well-established high school teams. Those teams often had to leave the state to play games. "Separate but equal" was a joke, with the state of Arkansas spending as much as three times more on educating white kids as it did on black kids in some counties. It wasn't until the 1970s that all the black schools were accepted into the Arkansas Activities Association, the governing body of high school sports in the state.

Broyles would have had to go just a few hundred yards to find a great black player to desegregate his team. Fayetteville High School had a star football player named William "Bull" Hayes, who graduated a few months after Broyles arrived in 1958. Bull Hayes was the first black athlete in the state of Arkansas to play against white competition in high school.

Hayes had to deal with more than the usual high school hassles. When the Fayetteville team bused into Harrison for a game, an effigy of a black man was hanging from a tree in the town square. According to the *Democrat-Gazette*, Harrison star Don Branison said his team was told to stop Bull Hayes no matter what it took. "We tried to kill him. . . . We tried to hurt him real bad," Branison said.

Fayetteville beat Harrison anyway. Branison was awarded a scholarship to the University of Arkansas the following year.

Bull Hayes had offers from Oklahoma State and Tulsa, where Arkansas played regularly. To avoid the embarrassment of a local black player making them look bad, the Arkansas staff arranged a full ride to University of Nebraska for Bull Hayes.

TEN

THE EDGE OF CAMPUS

Richardson's task as the first black coach in the old Confederacy was not fully appreciated, and most newsmen didn't see the significance. "They didn't understand that this was another world," TV journalist Steve Narisi says, "this was the Southwest Conference." The fact that Richardson didn't have the instant success he did in Tulsa compounded the trouble.

Yvonne's decline, of all things, caused Richardson problems with the fans and Broyles. "He'd miss games with Yvonne sick," Narisi says, "and people would get down on him for that. From the very early days Richardson was on the wrong side of some of the fans. I don't think Nolan ever got over that. If he was a white coach under those circumstances, the fans and media would have been far more patient."

Another source of trouble was the speed at which Richardson was pushing his team to play. Wally Hall, whose *Democrat-Gazette* columns irritated Richardson for years, says, "I will be the first to admit that I didn't embrace Nolan's style. He was a pioneer, and it took me two years to appreciate that." Hall says both the media and the fans had grown accustomed to the Iba-influenced style with which Eddie Sutton succeeded.

With two major newspapers in Little Rock, numerous television stations, and his first teams spinning their wheels, Richardson was confronted with a different media presence than that in Tulsa. Richardson's relationship with Arkansas journalists was complicated. During his first few years in Arkansas, there were two statewide papers, the *Democrat* as well as the *Gazette*. An aggressive battle for readership meant inflammatory articles were sometimes the norm. John Robert Starr was especially critical of Richardson, and when the Razorbacks made dramatic improvements over the years, Starr took credit for that in print, claiming his mean-spirited attacks made Richardson a better coach. In the late 1980s, the papers merged, but Starr continued his critiques.

The games at Arkansas brought a surprising yet familiar face on a regular basis—Tulsa clothier Ed Beshara, who had rarely attended games at TU.

Richardson had talked Beshara into a road trip to attend a Tulsa game at West Texas State in the early 1980s and invited him to sit on the bench. With the score tied, and just seconds remaining, Richardson took a time-out. As he started to set the play, he became aware of a commotion in his own huddle. It was Ed Beshara, jumping around, red-faced, yelling, "Get the ball to Ricky Ross!"

Ross hit the winning shot moments later. After that, though, Richardson figured Beshara was too excitable.

Nevertheless, Richardson was comforted to see Beshara appear at every home game in his early days at Arkansas. With Yvonne dying and the team struggling, Beshara was more than a fan. Richardson loved and trusted him.

"Suddenly you're a real supporter," Richardson joked. "Why didn't you come to the games at Tulsa when it was ten minutes away?"

Beshara answered straight away. "You didn't need me at Tulsa. You need me here at Arkansas, hoss."

Everyone deals with death in different ways," Mike Anderson says. "Rose's job, like a lot of mothers' jobs, was to raise her child. Then Yvonne wasn't there. Basketball was going on, and that was Coach Richardson's focus because the players were family, too."

"I don't think I've ever met anyone who gave so much of herself as Rose," says Madalyn Richardson about her stepmom, "especially after Yvonne passed."

Several people close to the couple suggest that Rose in particular is still, twenty years later, struggling with the loss of Yvonne.

When Richardson was gone recruiting or at a speaking engagement, Rose would often remain in her bathrobe all day, living in a corner of their bedroom. She would switch on the television, letting the noise distract her. Sometimes she would go days without even venturing outside the townhouse, let alone into Fayetteville.

Some say, however, that Richardson himself carried the grief around even longer.

"After the loss of Yvonne," one player says, "Coach could always go to basketball, and when you're playing or coaching there's that feeling nothing else is going on. His team could substitute for the family."

After reading about Yvonne's death, Temple University coach John Chaney phoned Richardson. Chaney is in some ways Richardson's northern alter ego. His résumé is another testament to how difficult advancement was for black coaches of that era.

Chaney played ten seasons in the Eastern Basketball League, the only minor league below the NBA, and was named that league's MVP in 1959 and 1960. The MVP awards never led to an NBA career; most teams still had quotas limiting the number of black players.

Temple University hired Chaney in 1982. It was seen as a risky move—he was fifty years old, and despite his incredible success as a Division II coach, he had not a single minute of experience at the Division I level as a player or even assistant coach. The gamble paid off, as his Temple teams were usually nationally ranked.

Chaney has had some controversial moments. During a rough-and-tumble game against Saint Joseph's in 2005, he sent substitute Nehemiah Ingram into the game and ordered him to foul intentionally. Chaney, whose team recorded more fouls that night than field goals, would regret the move. Ingram badly injured a Saint Joseph's player. Chaney suspended himself for the remainder of the season.

Chaney refuses to sidestep these incidents. In the Temple media guide the following season—obviously controlled and written by Temple with his guidance—one of the topics in the "Chat with Coach Chaney" section is "On last year's incident with Saint Joseph."

Chaney can be blunt, charming, and funny. He's part philosopher, part social critic. When questioned about his career accomplishments, he declines to mention the five-hundred-something games he won at Temple. Rather it's "To cause the NCAA to sit down and listen to us about the needs and changes that should be made for many of our young athletes who are predominantly black. That is the fight that I have not stopped fighting."

Chaney and Richardson would cement their friendship in Virginia in the late 1980s, where a new organization called the Black Coaches Association was holding one of their first meetings.

Talks with Chaney helped Richardson regain his focus. By the autumn of 1987, the beginning of his third season, Richardson felt a sense of urgency to get Arkansas back to the NCAA Tournament. His Razorbacks responded, going 21-9, including 11-5 in the SWC. They were rewarded with their first NCAA Tournament appearance since Eddie Sutton left Arkansas.

The Razorbacks drew Villanova in the first round and lost 82-74. Richardson was now 0-4 as a coach in NCAA Tournament games, including his time at Tulsa.

Broyles, still not convinced Richardson could coach, suggested after that season that Richardson hire Bob Weltlich as an assistant coach. Richardson knew the reason. Weltlich, who had stumbled as head coach of University of Texas and was fired, got his start as an assistant to Bob Knight. It exasperated Richardson that Broyles wanted him to hire a coach whom he had little trouble beating.

Instead of a staff change, Richardson gathered his assistants a week after the Villanova loss to talk about intensifying their recruiting. Richardson was blessed with a terrific staff—several of his assistant coaches would one day be head coaches. Andy Stoglin, Scott Edgar, Mike Anderson, and his son, Nolan "Notes" Richardson III, all coached Division I teams after leaving Arkansas.

Richardson had his own style of dealing with prospects. Whether it was at a high school gym or campus visit, Richardson would have an assistant coach gather the recruit or his family and bring them to him. Former Tulsa coach John Phillips says, "Nolan would never get up and go to the player. He was establishing early on that if you want to play for him, it was going to be on his terms."

In the spring of 1988, Richardson and his staff signed one of the best recruiting classes in school history. The group included Todd Day, Lee Mayberry, and Oliver Miller, a trio who would win three consecutive SWC regular-season and tournament titles.

The following year, the Razorbacks finished the 1988–89 season at 25-7, including 13-3 in the SWC. Richardson won his first NCAA Tournament in 1989 over Loyola-Marymount.

Richardson created a new award at the conclusion of the 1989 season, for the Razorback with the best attitude and grades. He called it the Poerschke Award. Eric Poerschke, who was glued to the bench on Senior Night in 1987, was now forever a part of Razorback lore. Richardson recognized himself in the underdog, even if the guy was a well-to-do white benchwarmer with straight A grades.

Richardson's sense of justice was becoming tied to memory—by reminding everyone of past injustices, even his own, he could make things better.

Despite the Razorbacks' gradual improvement, Richardson could still find himself frustrated by the Arkansas mentality. It had been difficult to change old habits, and not only with his players. The university and townspeople sometimes left him flummoxed.

The northwest corner of the state, where Fayetteville is located, still had a far greater percentage of whites than the rest of Arkansas. Many towns in the northwest had unofficial laws forbidding blacks from living in them at all.

The town of Alix had a sign at its city limits that read NIGGER, DON'T LET THE SUN GO DOWN ON YOU IN ALIX until 1970. Nearly one hundred "sundown towns" existed in Arkansas through the 1960s. Towns like Paragould and Springdale—practically a twin city of Fayetteville—were also sundown towns. A Springdale steak house called Heinie's had paper placemats that read, THIS IS AN ALL-WHITE CHRISTIAN COMMUNITY. Harrison, a Klan stronghold, was a sundown town until 2002.

All of these towns are a short drive from the University of Arkansas.

One morning, during Richardson's early years at Arkansas, his secretary, Terri Mercer, announced that he had some visitors: representatives from a black fraternity and sorority. The young lady was crying. "They ruined our social on Saturday," he heard her say to Mercer.

Richardson invited them in. The police had arrived at the party, she sobbed, and brought things to a halt. That wasn't unusual on any big college campus. Richardson handed her a Kleenex and checked his watch. It was a Monday morning, and he had plenty to do.

"Dogs!" she said, finally getting her composure. "They raided the house with dogs!" Police, responding to a call, had cleared out the social event with a K-9 unit, the snarling German shepherds scattering the black college students.

Richardson felt his face get hot. He called his secretary back in and instructed her to find Lonnie Williams, a black administrator on campus.

"It was just a fight after the dance, some pushing and shoving that escalated," Williams recalls. "Since black students had been involved, Nolan felt like we had to go down there and do something."

"I couldn't believe it," Richardson says today. "I'd seen Bull Connor in Alabama on television, breaking up marchers with dogs and hoses. But this was the 1980s."

Williams arrived at Richardson's office minutes later, and they hurried over to the campus police station. Richardson had golfed with police chief Larry Slamons before and got along fine with him, but the coach was seething as he entered the station.

"What is the policy on using dogs to raid a home?" Richardson demanded.

The chief was perplexed. What dogs?

"Do you use dogs to raid white fraternity parties?" Richardson asked.

"Of course not," said Slamons.

"Then you shouldn't be doing that shit with the black fraternity either," Richardson said.

Slamons excused himself, made some calls, and learned that dogs were indeed used to raid the black fraternity. A young campus cop called for backup, and the Fayetteville *city* police brought the dogs.

"Chief Slamons was truly sorry," Williams says, "and just as much in the dark as we were." Instead of the campus police intervening, the Fayetteville police arrived. "They used incredibly bad judgment," Williams continues. "Just the sight of the dogs created bad feelings, and dogs were never needed to disperse that type of a crowd."

Lonnie Williams was inspired, however, by Richardson's response. "Nolan was very animated and authoritative and simply would not budge until we got some answers," he says. "How many coaches do you know would have personally gotten involved, or not stopped at the phone call?"

There was no player accused. No victory hung in the balance. No referee's judgment could be questioned. It was an important moment in his time at Arkansas, an awakening of sorts that had nothing to do with basketball.

Richardson's direct style in confronting injustice in the 1980s contrasts greatly with that of Hall of Fame coach—er, contributor—John McLendon.

When McLendon attended the University of Kansas in the 1930s, the campus was segregated. Degree requirements in McLendon's major included proficiency in swimming and lifesaving. The school had an unusual policy, though. Black kids were given an automatic "A," to keep them from polluting the whites-only pool.

McLendon decided not to accept the free grade and went to the pool anyway to fulfill his requirements. Friends of McLendon collected over a thousand signatures on a petition that said they did not mind swimming with Negroes.

But the word was out, and the attendant had already drained the pool before McLendon arrived. When signs started appearing on campus, reading DO NOT SWIM WITH THE NIGGER, McLendon collected the signs and gave them to his advisor, and basketball's inventor, Dr. James Naismith. Naismith, in turn, took the signs to the university president and said if another sign appeared he would find work at another college.

McLendon then went to the head of the physical education department, who happened to be Phog Allen, the basketball coach. Allen claimed that the pool rules were simply for McLendon's safety. McLendon cut a deal on the spot with the KU basketball coach. Keep the pool open—for everybody—for two weeks. If violence or any ugly incident between races occurred, McLendon would retract his request.

McLendon had a plan. Rather than meet the Neanderthal segregationists head-on, he gathered KU's four dozen black students and instructed them *not* to go near the pool for two weeks.

At the conclusion of the allotted two weeks, McLendon returned to Phog Allen. Since no racial incidents had occurred, McLendon—with the help of Dr. Naismith—held Phog Allen to his word.

McLendon's gentle touch slowly helped make room for more aggressive changes decades later. In 1987, the Black Coaches Association elected a popular assistant coach from Iowa, Rudy Washington, as their leader. One BCA goal was to increase the number of head coaching jobs being offered to African-Americans, especially assistant coaches. The BCA enjoyed enormous growth in the next seven years and wielded surprising power.

The group quickly established ties to Nolan Richardson, John Chaney, John Thompson at Georgetown, and George Raveling at USC—the most visible of the nation's black head coaches. Raveling would later retire to work in the gym-shoe industry, leaving the outspoken trio of Richardson, Thompson, and Chaney.

Another issue was Proposition 48, which called for rising requirements of SAT and ACT standards. Chaney—and many experts—insisted the tests were culturally biased against minority students. The issue of reducing the number of men's basketball scholarships from fifteen was also a concern. Any reduction in scholarships in basketball would have profound effects on African-American high schoolers, who made up nearly two-thirds of the talent in major college basketball. With over three hundred member schools, the NCAA cutting a single scholarship from each team could affect as many as two hundred potential black students across the country.

On January 14, 1989, John Thompson walked off the court at the beginning of a game, protesting the exclusion of black kids from the game due to Proposition 48. Thompson's exit was broadcast nationally. John Thompson was, at that time, the country's most visible and successful black coach in any sport.

Richardson had an epiphany watching the replays of Thompson's exit. "I felt so bad," he says. "I didn't know what to do. I might not have been a college player or coach if I'd have had to pass the SAT back then."

Thompson's dramatic move—along with the police dogs incident—reinvigorated Richardson. By all measuring sticks, he had "made it," but he was beginning to sense that success threatened to distance him from his own past. Thompson's protest somehow made him aware of what his choices might be.

Richardson grew more reflective about his own history. Decades removed, he didn't feel so very far from the Segundo Barrio, despite all his success. Clinging to the fence in the heat at a segregated swimming pool. Watching his Bowie teammates file into a no-Negroes hotel. Listening alone to the radio static of the all-white tournament in Shreveport. These events still felt very current to Richardson.

ELEVEN

TELL ME HOW LONG
THE TRAIN'S BEEN GONE

Frank Broyles's willful blindness in the 1960s became the stuff of legend in Arkansas black communities. The list of qualified black players who prepped in Arkansas *while* Broyles was coach—and refusing to desegregate—is damning. Dozens went on to star at other colleges.

Arkansas natives Willie Frazier, Eugene Howard, John Little, and Clarence Washington all had productive NFL careers. Still, the University of Arkansas clung to its backward policies. None of these talented players were allowed to play at the only major school in their state.

It wasn't just Broyles who was ignoring Arkansas black talent. The basketball coaches at the university were blinded, too. Eddie Miles was good enough to play ten NBA seasons but was ignored by Arkansas. Frank Burgess was not recruited by the Razorbacks but led the entire nation in scoring in 1960 when he racked up over 30 points per game at Gonzaga.

The University of Arkansas did not recruit Oliver Jones of Rowher. He went to Albany State instead, where he grabbed over a thousand rebounds, an incredible total, in the early 1960s. The repercussions of ignoring Oliver Jones were enormous, and expose recruiting cycles—or ruts—and the difficulties in overcoming them.

Albany State named Oliver Jones as head coach a few years after he graduated. He'd win nearly four hundred games at Albany State. And for *eighteen seasons* in a row, one of his younger brothers started at center for Albany State: Melvin Jones, Wilbert Jones, Caldwell Jones, Major Jones, and Charles Jones. The Jones brothers weren't just good college players. They would combine for over twenty thousand career points in the NBA or ABA.

Caldwell Jones, who desperately wanted to attend the University of Arkansas, played seventeen years in the ABA and NBA. When Arkansas went cold on him, it sealed things for the next Jones boys in line. Charles Jones won two NBA championships in his fifteen years in the league.

There's no telling how good Arkansas could have been had they hauled in the best black players—especially the six Jones brothers, who surely would have started a basketball dynasty in Fayetteville.

Yet basketball was far ahead of Frank Broyles when it came to pursuing black players.

In Broyles's autobiography, which was published in 1979, he dances around the issue of integration like Gene Kelly in a cloudburst.

"We did not recruit black athletes until the late 1960s," he wrote. "When I came to Arkansas, there were no black players in the Southwest Conference . . . Nothing written in a Board policy stated that we were to avoid recruiting blacks, but it was very clearly (though informally) conveyed to me that we would not.

"It was a matter out of my hands and I didn't think about it a great deal.

"I assume there was a feeling on the part of some of our board members that if we unilaterally integrated our athletics program, SEC schools would use it against us and open recruiting strongholds in certain areas of Arkansas."

It was the SEC's fault, as well as the enigmatic Board, whom Broyles, sadly, had no influence over. While future NFL players were denied a chance to play at the state's only major university, Broyles used the excuse of protecting his white recruits from those vicious vultures to the southeast.

"We fell behind," Broyles wrote. "All of a sudden it became an issue and people wanted to know why we weren't recruiting black athletes. Our conference had an image to overcome."

All of a sudden it became an issue.

Blacks within the state either resented the University of Arkansas or became apathetic. Broyles's deafness to the Civil Rights movement would come back to haunt him in recruiting.

Lyell Thompson was a professor of agriculture at the University of Arkansas for years. Thompson, who is white, found himself on campus at the same time the new football coach arrived. An army veteran, he tried to spark a desegregation movement as early as 1958.

Working to end segregation at the University of Arkansas would prove to be a discouraging battle. Thompson was surprised to discover one summer that he would not be getting the raise everyone else in his position was entitled to. "I went four years without a raise, and I was told by the dean, and then the vice-president, that I should go north, where people looked on blacks in the same way."

In fact, says Thompson, the president and board of trustees were all strongly against desegregation. So was the football coach. "Frank

Broyles was a Southerner, and he didn't want to integrate at all," Thompson says.

It was his church affiliation, of all things, that got Thompson into hot water. "I had grown up a Methodist, but I had lost my orthodoxy. My Unitarian church group met in the university building on campus. I realize now that we shouldn't have met on campus." Technically, the meeting was against school policy.

What kind of radical plots were these Unitarian zealots up to? "We came out with statements about desegregation," Thompson says, and word soon spread around campus. "Frank Broyles brought up the fact that a religious organization was meeting on the university campus."

The feared Unitarians were exiled and forced to meet elsewhere.

After Texas Western and their all-black starters won the NCAA basketball title in 1966, even the Texas universities began recruiting black athletes. So did the mostly white colleges in the state of Arkansas.

Were they following the leadership in Fayetteville?

Not a chance. Not only would Frank Broyles be slower to desegregate than anyone in the Southwest Conference, the famous coach at the big university was slower than virtually all of the other colleges in Arkansas. Ten white-majority colleges within the state of Arkansas desegregated their sports teams before the University of Arkansas:

1. The College of the Ozarks, which dropped football in the years before they integrated, had a black basketball player in 1963.
2. Ouachita Baptist had a black basketball player in 1965, and had a black football player two years later.
3. Harding College had eight black basketball and football players in 1966.

4. Henderson State added two black basketballers in 1966, two footballers in 1967. (Henderson's Bill Lefear played four seasons in the NFL.)

5. Arkansas Tech had a black football player in 1966; in 1968 they added a black basketballer.

6. Arkansas-Monticello played a black basketballer in 1967; football in 1968.

7. Central Arkansas played a black basketball player in 1967; football in 1968.

8. Hendrix College (with no football after 1960) had a black basketball player in 1968.

9. Arkansas–Little Rock (who had no football team in the 1960s) featured a black basketball player in 1968.

10. Southern Arkansas desegregated basketball in 1967, football in 1969.

Only nearby John Brown University was slower than the University of Arkansas. They added a black basketball player in 1973. John Brown the abolitionist is not, obviously, the school's namesake.

On top of that, Arkansas AN&M in Pine Bluff was sending players like L. C. Greenwood to the NFL. (At the time, three historically black colleges were in the state: Philander Smith College, Arkansas Baptist, and Arkansas AN&M, which today is UA–Pine Bluff.)

The Razorback basketball team finally would sign their first black player, T. J. Johnson, in 1967. When would Frank Broyles and Arkansas football follow the lead of virtually every team in the Southwest Conference and every other college in the state?

The plights of the first African-American athletes in the 1960s Southwest Conference foreshadow the experience Nolan Richardson would have as the first person of his race in a leadership role. While the pressure on Richardson would not be nearly as dramatic, a quick study of the SWC's most important recruit of the 1960s sheds light on the mindset of the league and Frank Broyles.

TCU played the SWC's first black basketball player, James Cash, during the 1966–67 season. Cash led TCU to the SWC title when he was a junior; he would later become a professor at the Harvard Business School.

It was an undersized speedster, however, who changed the face of the Southwest Conference. In 1962, Southern Methodist University hired an assistant named Hayden Fry to be the new football coach. Fry, the least experienced coach in the league, began working to sign an African-American player who perhaps could lift SMU football out of the cellar.

Fry found that player in Jerry LeVias of Beaumont, Texas. While he was not the first black football player to take the field, LeVias was the first superstar in the SWC.

A mere 5'9" and 170 pounds, LeVias was an electrifying halfback and receiver. Like every black kid in Texas at that time, he'd played in the Prairie View Interscholastic League, the Negro poor sister to Texas's all-white University Interscholastic League. Although highly recruited nationally, LeVias chose SMU, which was 1-9 in 1964. He signed with SMU in 1965, but since freshmen were not eligible to compete, LeVias would play for the first time in September of 1966.

Fry knew exactly what kind of impact LeVias would have and appeared to be challenging his SWC rivals. In SMU's press release announcing that LeVias had signed, Fry said, "I hope this signing will open the door for future Negro student-athletes in the Southwest Conference." SMU claimed a total of five black undergraduates on their campus LeVias's first year. He was one of two African-Americans playing varsity football in the SWC in 1966.

LeVias became perhaps the greatest player in the league history up to that time, and without question the most influential. He caught 155 passes and scored 25 touchdowns in his career. On three occasions he was named All-SWC and would go on to play six years in the

NFL despite his small frame. LeVias was also named to the dean's list at SMU.

LeVias was the subject of abuse from students, and that included his teammates in his early days. He overcame myriad obstacles—hate mail, his teammates yelling "get that nigger" at a Purdue running back, and harassing phone calls.

Death threats were common. One game, LeVias was instructed by Fry to stand in the center of the SMU huddle the entire contest so a threatened assassination would be more difficult. The abuse took a huge toll on him. At a symposium in 2002, when asked if he would choose to do things the same way—sign at SMU, become the first African-American player in the league—LeVias said he would not.

SMU put together two 8-3 seasons with LeVias. They tied for the SWC conference title in his first season, and he led the league in points scored.

Jerry LeVias was a consensus All-American after his final season.

Yet Arkansas football still had not put an African-American player on the field.

And SMU's coach, Hayden Fry, had not come from some liberal Yankee school with progressive tendencies. Fry had been Frank Broyles's assistant at Arkansas.

The final two SWC schools to desegregate their football teams were the most powerful programs—the University of Texas and their coach Darrell Royal, and the University of Arkansas.

Former Arkansas appellate judge and UA graduate Wendell Griffen likes to quote Dr. Martin Luther King when the subject of segregation in Arkansas sports comes up: "Cowardice is a submissive surrender to circumstance."

"Had it not been for Jerry LeVias," Griffen adds, "running rings around Royal and Broyles, heaven only knows when black athletes would have been allowed to play at those institutions."

Fate intervened to permit Arkansas to continue their disgraceful segregationist policies. In 1963, the University of Arkansas Board of Trustees came out with a statement of policy. They were shrewd enough not to say "No blacks allowed." Instead they instituted a gentler "Keep things as they are" policy. This was the biggest civil rights story in Arkansas since the Little Rock crisis, and it was announced on November 21.

On November 22, John F. Kennedy was killed, and the Arkansas story disappeared.

TWELVE

THE FIRE NEXT TIME

Nolan Richardson brought a feeling of urgency to the 1989–90 regular season. Arkansas entered the NCAA Tournament as a No. 4 seed in the Midwest Regional. Wins over Princeton, Dayton, North Carolina, and Texas landed Richardson in his first of three Final Fours. The Razorbacks dropped the semifinal game to Duke 97-83, finishing the year 30-5, including 14-2 in the SWC.

The Final Four appearance gave Richardson a new measure of respect, both nationally and within the state.

Arkansas's last season in the old Southwest Conference was 1990–91, and they finished it by winning the regular season at 15-1, then taking the SWC Tournament championship. They scored over one hundred points in an astounding eighteen games. The Razorbacks went into the NCAA Tournament as a No. 1 seed, but Kansas ruined their hopes of a Final Four repeat, beating the Razorbacks 93-81. Arkansas finished 34-4.

Also in 1991, assistant coach Mike Anderson and his wife welcomed the birth of a daughter. They named her Yvonne.

In 1991–92, Arkansas finished its first season in the SEC at 13-3, winning the conference. That first year included a 103-88 rout of Kentucky at Rupp Arena. The final game for the trio of Day, Mayberry, and Miller took place when Memphis upset Arkansas in the second round of the NCAA Tournament. The Razorbacks finished 26-8. Day, Mayberry, and Miller, whose combined four-year record in Fayetteville was 115-24, became first-round NBA draft picks.

Richardson has always had a disdain for what he calls "book coaches," a reverse snobbery. When Larry Gipson was a new assistant at Tulsa, he delivered detailed scouting reports about upcoming opponents in Richardson's office. Gipson was no fool. He'd coach his own national championship junior college team in the 1980s, and years later he'd win the Division II national championship at Northeastern State of Oklahoma.

Gipson recalls, "Nolan would look through the report for a while and snort. Then he'd toss it back at me. 'Book coaches,' he'd say."

Richardson acknowledges that there's plenty to learn from a book about basketball. "But it's getting it from a book to the players' heads," he says. "That's the key. That's coaching."

He pioneered a run-and-trap system, but he may have trapped himself into a stereotype. "For years, the theory has been that if you play fast, you aren't really coaching," he says. "But my experience is that it takes more discipline for kids to play fast. For example, as good as Ralph Tasker's teams were in Hobbs, in some ways his press was predictable. I wanted my players to think on their own, not be robots. It takes *more* discipline, and smarter players, to play with that kind of freedom."

One of the primary paradoxes of Nolan Richardson is that he

disdains an academic approach, yet wants to be respected by "book coaches."

He was irritated by the status bestowed upon Rick Pitino. While Richardson was winning with a *Star Wars* pace before Pitino was ever a head coach, Pitino has put out several videotapes and DVDs about coaching. He's even written self-help books for coaches. Richardson has shown less interest in marketing his playing style or coaching philosophy, but he's never turned down an offer to make an instructional video or book. He simply has never been approached.

Wally Hall of the *Democrat-Gazette* says, "Nolan *was* an X and O coach, but he put it in during practice and had everyone programmed. Then he pushed the button in the game. But you had to go to practice to see the strategy."

Todd Day, who became the school's all-time leading scorer, says, "Nolan was the king of up-tempo, pressure basketball. We hardly practiced offense. It was defense, defense, defense." Day claims that practice was much different than game day. "Nolan was a great motivator on game day," he says, "but the strategy was implemented in practice."

In this respect, Richardson mirrors Don Haskins, whose game-time philosophy was to avoid complicating things—victories were won during practice, Haskins believed. Haskins disdained the concept of "game coaches."

Richardson heard the way successful black coaches were described by the media, and it stung. Black coaches had the talent, the horses. They were great recruiters and could relate to the players. Rarely was a black coach acknowledged as a strategic genius.

"I've studied the so-called X and O guys, and people are now emulating what Coach Richardson did since junior college," says Mike Anderson, listing the prominent programs that are clear descendants of "Forty Minutes of Hell." Richardson rarely gets credit for the changes that he helped bring about. "I know that sometimes hurts him," Anderson says.

This situation—whites getting credit, blacks getting ignored— is not unique to coaching. Pete Maravich adopted a flashy, black playground style—something that Earl Monroe and Nate "Tiny" Archibald from the same era could do—and brought it to a mostly white conference and audience. Maravich became the subject of books, films, and instructional videos. While Monroe and Archibald won NBA championships, Maravich got more notoriety and bigger paychecks.

Richardson responds to this kind of snub by attacking the club that won't grant him full membership. "I remember Jud Heathcote from Michigan State raving to me about his match-up zone defense," he says, "and he was getting all kinds of attention. But I played nearly exactly the same zone."

This is a Richardson trademark. Attacking the attacker, or disdaining the disdainer. In an interview with the *Sporting News*, the writer Bob Hille wrote, ". . . [Richardson] always seems to be saying he doesn't give a damn about what you think of him, yet always finds time to defend himself against criticism or perceived slights."

Richardson could be hypersensitive if the slight came from a rival or antagonist. Frank Broyles sent an interoffice memo to Richardson that, according to Richardson, said, "I envision you being athletics director here someday."

Richardson remains angry about the memo. "He signed his name *Frank*. He didn't even have the decency to write his last name."

Richardson rarely drank and never frequented bars in Fayetteville. Instead, the coach and his wife immersed themselves in laid-back lunches and weekend barbecues during the Day, Miller, and Mayberry years. The team could generally be found hanging out on the couches in their coach's condominium, especially after Yvonne died.

Around that time, Richardson bought a ranch outside of Fayetteville from former Olympic track star Mike Conley. The ranch, with its horses and sprawling hills, also became, for the Richardsons and the players, a place to escape.

"I think Rose wanted some of the team around as much as possible," Todd Day says, "and that was because Yvonne was gone. Rose had less to fall back on, and she was such a long way from El Paso."

Richardson's hands-on approach with his players sometimes had hilarious results. During road trips, bed checks and curfews were routine. One night before an important game, Richardson decided to make the rounds himself. He checked on Oliver Miller's room last.

Miller was not a typical Richardson-style player. Nearly 6'10", Miller tipped the scales at close to three hundred pounds. The Fort Worth native was also unusual in that his parents were moderately well-off compared to most of the team. Miller's weight was as baffling as Bruce Vanley's had been at Tulsa. But Richardson admired Miller, who relished, and often won, his battles with LSU's Shaquille O'Neal.

During that evening's bed check, while Richardson was saying good-night to a couple of freshmen at one end of the hotel hallway, a Domino's Pizza man hurried by.

The deliveryman tapped on Oliver Miller's door. Richardson saw money change hands, as well as four large pizzas.

The coach took a deep breath, walked down to Miller's room, and knocked.

Nothing. Richardson knocked again, louder. "It's your coach. Open the door."

"Just a minute," Miller cried.

Richardson paced the hallway. When the door popped open, Miller scurried back inside and sat down.

"Lights out in ten minutes," Richardson said. "And turn down that TV."

"Sure, coach," Miller said, muting the sound. "I'm almost ready for bed."

Behind Miller was a pile of sweat suits and practice gear. "What's under those warm-ups?" Richardson said, moving around Miller.

"Nothing, coach." Miller stood and shifted, as though setting a screen.

Richardson reached below Miller's feet and uncovered the cardboard boxes.

"Oh!" said Miller. "Right. I ordered those for the rest of the team. They're not even for me."

"Great," Richardson said, sliding the pizzas past Miller. He whipped out his rooming list. "I'll take them down to the guys and you can get some sleep."

"Wait!" Miller cried as the coach closed the door behind him.

Any observer of a Nolan Richardson practice could sit in the back row and be shaken by his booming voice, a tool he would wield like a hammer. He'd demand respect from the strongest kids, instill fear in the weaker ones.

Respect was more important than affection, despite the open-door policy at the Richardson ranch. "I never worried if the players liked me," Richardson says. A major component to his big recruiting pitch was what he'd tell their mothers: "If you send me a boy, I'll send you back a man."

That respect—or fear—doesn't die easily. Todd Day returned to Fayetteville with his agent one year, and as he walked into the arena, Day appeared to be frantically scratching his ears. The agent asked him what the trouble was. "I'm trying to get these earrings out before coach sees them," Day said.

Don Haskins said, "I think there was an element of fear because Nolan got his guys to play so hard."

After Haskins retired, he was invited to come watch the Razorbacks practice. Because of his own grind-it-out style, his typical practice agenda was primarily based on stopping the opponent's fast break. He'd stress both the clogging half-court defense and his annoyingly patient offense. A Richardson practice—the laboratory for "Forty Minutes of Hell"—was as foreign to Haskins as a three-piece suit.

"Everything was done full-court," Haskins said. "Shooting drills, man-to-man offense, hell, you name it. They started on one end, and they raced like hell to the other. There wasn't a single thing that didn't involve the length of the court."

Haskins prided himself on knowing exactly what his players should be doing at all times. "Nolan was different," he said. "He wanted them to rely on their own instincts. That would make them very difficult to scout, because nobody could tell when they were going to trap." The pace of practice, according to Haskins, was exhausting. "I've never seen so many guys running so hard for so long. And they didn't dare complain."

As the Razorbacks began to scrimmage, something happened that initially had Haskins perplexed. One of the Razorback guards caught the ball behind the three-point line. Richardson yelled, "Layup!"

"What in the hell is Nolan yelling *layup* for?" Haskins wondered. "That wasn't a goddamn layup. That was a twenty-footer." Each time the player received the ball behind the arc, Richardson hollered the same thing: "Layup!"

Haskins was aware he had cut Richardson's scoring average in half in the early 1960s—Richardson could now finally joke about that remarkable statistic. But Haskins was unaware that even Richardson's free-throw percentage, something unrelated to style of play, dropped. Before Haskins's arrival, Richardson was shooting a respectable 64.5 percent from the free throw line. Under Haskins that first year, he dipped to 56 percent. His senior year, his shooting confidence further shaken, he finished at an abysmal 54 percent.

Sitting in the second row of the Arkansas arena, Haskins had an epiphany. "Nolan was making that guard think it was an easy shot," he said. "He meant the three-pointer for that kid was as easy as a layup! That stuck with me, the way Nolan can instill confidence."

Richardson's deliberate injection of confidence in his best shooters was a direct reaction to his own career, the way Haskins had clamped down on him.

Richardson would tell the Razorbacks, "I'm an old-school guy. I'm not a damn psychologist."

"But in reality," says Pat Bradley, Arkansas leader in career three-pointers, "Nolan could have had a PhD in psychology."

Richardson wanted his shooters to be brazenly confident. Yet the Haskins-like intimidation remained an important factor. "The team loved him," says a man who was close to the Razorback program for years. "But there was also fear. You can't discount that. Nolan was very, very tough and sometimes mean." Many of Richardson's former players use the word "fear" as often as "love" when describing him.

Pat Bradley says there was another peculiar Richardson trait in practice—his kindness to freshmen. This was also the only time Don Haskins showed any generosity on the court. "He'd encourage the freshmen all season," Bradley says. "Once they were sophomores, though, look out."

Still, at the heart of Richardson's motivation during practice was the constant us-against-the-world speech. How would that sit with someone like Pat Bradley, a white kid from Massachusetts? "I think nearly everyone has inside them," Bradley says, "a feeling for the underdog. I know for me, I was constantly trying to prove I belonged in the SEC, and Nolan never stopped appealing to that. I believed in *him*, because he believed in *me* in a way that nobody else did."

Clint McDaniel, who would star for Richardson's best teams, says the coach's charismatic power pushed the players beyond their limits in practice. "Have you ever seen somebody sprain both ankles at the same time?" McDaniel asks. One substitute, Reggie Merritt, did just that, coming down hard on someone else's high-tops. Merritt, however, refused to be carried off the court by the trainer. "Merritt kept trying to play. He was so pumped up he refused to stop," McDaniel says, "but when he tried to walk, he just kept falling over. That's the kind of motivator Nolan was."

Dave England, the basketball trainer, says, "It's hard for people to understand. The players loved Nolan. *Loved* him."

THIRTEEN

BLUES FOR MISTER CHARLIE

Haskins's hollering and Ol' Mama's wisdom echoed constantly in Richardson's head—his speech, playing style, and career reflected his own history. While he'd play a lot faster than Haskins, and he'd host his players as though they were sons, the aggressive anger his teams played with seemed to be a modern descendant of both Haskins and Ol' Mama. Richardson's past clung to him like a hyped-up defender with plenty of fouls to give.

The same could be said for Frank Broyles, an icon of the Old South, but his past was very different from Richardson's.

Although Jackie Robinson joined the Brooklyn Dodgers in 1947, the South—the white South—was not impressed. Professional sports teams had little or no influence there, even into the 1950s. Atlanta had no professional teams. St. Louis was the closest franchise to many Southern schools.

However, the Civil Rights movement was slowly creeping up on schools like the University of Arkansas and coaches like Frank

Broyles. At times, Broyles must have felt that modern America was encroaching on his tradition of all-white teams, but he clung to his system and his enormous success of the 1960s. As college sports integrated, Broyles became an outsider by the end of that decade. Pressure would even come from the mediocre basketball program on his own campus. In 1966, basketball coach Glen Rose announced to the media that he would be willing to recruit a black player. Broyles refused to endorse those sentiments.

Basketball was more difficult to desegregate simply because of the nature of the game. Football players are covered with helmets and padding, while basketball players have much more skin exposed. The proximity of the fans leaves no doubt as to a basketball player's race, and blacks were also easier to reach with racial taunts or hurled objects. Also, the number of football players—as many as one hundred on a team—should have made football's integration more viable.

Otto "Bud" Zinke was a University of Arkansas physics professor for three decades. He arrived on the UA campus in 1959, a year after Frank Broyles. Although he was a diligent antiwar activist in the Vietnam War era, he does not consider himself to be a radical, especially along racial lines. "I came back from World War II, and it wasn't so much that I was involved with blacks," he recalls, "I simply didn't want to live in a country that had second-class citizens."

He's no dreamer. "I don't get into fights unless I think I can win them," he says. He worked to quietly integrate the Fayetteville swimming pool, as well as the Ozark Theater.

He was a young member of the senate council, the ruling body elected by the faculty senate. Nearly everyone on the faculty was in favor of integration, according to Zinke, or at least the more modest concept of desegregation. Zinke says he will never forget a senate council meeting in the late 1960s.

The university had slowly begun making steps to change the face of the campus, but Zinke and his colleagues knew that football and Frank Broyles were the symbolic center of the university. The senate council decided to confront Broyles.

"If Frank Broyles had said we were going to integrate, nobody would have challenged him," Zinke says. "So we called Broyles in, and asked him to integrate his team."

The room got quiet as Broyles stood. "The faculty was challenging his eminence," Zinke says.

According to Zinke, Broyles said, "I'll go home to Georgia before I have any niggers on *my* team."

A stunned silence followed. "I'll never forget the day," Zinke says. "He just stood there very brazenly, and said that with his slow Southern drawl."

Thomas "T. J." Johnson of all-black Menifee High School signed with the Arkansas basketball team in the spring of 1966, becoming the first black athlete to do so. Freshmen were not eligible to play, but when his sophomore year began in 1967, the coaches decided to "red-shirt" Johnson, holding him out of games while he continued to practice. When an older player on the varsity got hurt, Johnson figured the coaches would change his status. They did not, and Johnson, frustrated, transferred to Central Arkansas, where he led the team in scoring his final two seasons.

His time at UA was mostly without incident, although he told the *Democrat-Gazette* that he hated when the fans in Fayetteville waved Confederate flags. "That always took the wind out of my sails," he said.

Another black player, Vernon Murphy, joined UA during the same semester, but was declared academically ineligible.

After T. J. Johnson and Vernon Murphy did not work out as planned, struggling new basketball coach Duddy Waller set his sights on Fort Smith native Almer Lee to buoy the program. Almer Lee became the first black athlete to earn a varsity letter in any sport at Arkansas. The unassuming Lee had spent a year at Phillips Community College, then transferred to Fayetteville in 1969.

Lee's high school had already integrated, and Duddy Waller believed that would make his transition easier. So would the fact that Lee's high school coach was the highly regarded Gayle Kaundart. Lee had other important pluses. He was a flashy ball-handler, a great scorer, and fun to watch. Lee quickly became a star, pouring in 19.2 ppg in 1969–70. Unfortunately, the Razorbacks weren't very good, finishing 5-19 overall in Coach Waller's final season.

Lee rejects the idea that his first coach in Fayetteville was fired for integrating the team. "Duddy Waller didn't have a very good record," Lee says.

The next year, Lee again paced the Razorbacks in scoring under a new coach, Lanny Van Eman. The team was not very good that year, either, finishing 5-21. As a senior, Lee blew out a knee and never really recovered. A tryout with the Chicago Bulls didn't last long. Lee had a superb, if brief, playing career in Holland.

Lee insists his time at Arkansas was fairly ordinary. No threats. No fights. No name-calling. His teammates liked him, and nearly every Southwest Conference team had a black basketball player by then.

"If there were racial slurs," Lee says, "I didn't hear them. I was treated just like the white players. Of course there was some prejudice in Fayetteville," he says, "but the team stuck together." Instead, Lee took abuse for something he hadn't anticipated.

"The fans called me a hot dog," he says. "They were shocked to see the things I could do with the ball. There was very little behind-the-back or between-the-legs dribble then. They would say 'he's a Harlem Globetrotter!'"

"Almer's style was very suited to the present day," Van Eman says. "He could really handle the ball and shoot, and was like Pete Maravich in some ways."

Van Eman had five black players when his tenure ended in 1974. But it wasn't the challenges of integrating, or the remote location of the university, that presented the biggest struggle. "It was a laborious battle because football was so popular," Van Eman says.

Frank Broyles and Arkansas finally offered a scholarship to an African-American football player named Jon Richardson (no relation to Nolan), a speedster who played from 1970 to 1972. Broyles told the *Democrat-Gazette*, "We wanted to make sure the time was right."

Jon Richardson was an instant sensation. In his debut, a nationally televised game against Stanford, Richardson grabbed a 37-yard touchdown pass for his first of eleven scores that season. But a broken leg in 1971 slowed him, and he became primarily a kick returner the rest of his career—a dangerous and nerve-wracking position.

Jon Richardson got heat from whites and blacks; whites who feared a wave of athletes of color, and blacks who called him an Uncle Tom.

Steve Narisi, an Arkansas native who was later named sports director for Channel 29 in Fort Smith, remembers attending radio-listening parties as a boy whenever the Razorbacks would play. No regional television existed then, and football tickets were gone years in advance. Jon Richardson's debut season still stands out to Narisi. "When Jon Richardson was first there, you'd hear the 'N word' everywhere. He hurt his wrist and he was having trouble, so he fumbled a few times. You'd really hear it then."

FOURTEEN

SOLEDAD BROTHER

Jon Richardson was the first black football player to *play* for the Razorbacks. The desegregating of Arkansas football is complicated by the incredible story of Darrell Brown.

Darrell Brown attended a tiny "training" school—a code word for Negro school with poor resources—in Lockesburg, Arkansas. Brown was the star of the track team, a sport that had little in the way of equipment. He practiced the shot put using a heavy stone; he hurdled over carpenter's wooden horses.

In 1965, his school consolidated with the local white school, and team sports like football were available to the Lockesburg kids for the first time. He wanted the chance to fully experience high school athletics, so he asked his schoolteacher father if he could delay his graduation for a year. But it was too late for Darrell Brown, already in his senior year. His father told him he had to go on to college. Brown was in the wrong place at the wrong time. It would happen again.

Brown knew he had outstanding speed and quickness from his

success in track and field. But he longed to play organized football and got the peculiar idea that he could be the first black football player at the University of Arkansas.

When he arrived on campus, he went straight to the football coaches' offices and asked to try out as a "walk-on," a non-scholarship player.

"I'm Darrell Brown," he announced, "and I want to play football."

No black kid had ever been that bold before. Brown informed the coaches that he was a running back. "After a long pause," Brown recalls, "they finally brought me a uniform and some pants. 'This is great!' I thought. I'm going to walk on."

Darrell Brown was not aware of the 1964 Student Association endorsement of integrating the athletic teams in Fayetteville. He knew nothing about the college faculty or their senate council, which had also voted in favor of integration, or that the governor, the board of trustees, and the football coach resisted.

Darrell Brown just wanted to play football for Arkansas.

Being a college walk-on in a major sport is a difficult road. Earning a scholarship—room, board, tuition, and books—is often · the ultimate goal, but few reach that payoff. During the 1960s, some major college football coaches had the budget to award scholarships to as many players as they saw fit. Anyone whom the coaches truly wanted was usually awarded a full ride before even enrolling. Walk-ons who impressed the coaches might earn a full ride the next year.

Walk-ons are at the mercy of the coach's discretion and sense of fairness.

A coach can directly discourage or encourage walk-ons. In basketball, just sitting a player on the bench during scrimmages sends a message. Benching a player during, say, shooting drills can be even worse. There are plenty of perks that can be used to reward—or withheld to punish—walk-ons. Free shoes, sweat suits, or travel gear go to the most appreciated walk-ons. There are other carrots, as well. Team meals, team pictures, a photo in the media guide, a seat on the airplane to road games, complimentary tickets, off-season weightlifting. Playing time in varsity games, or a full-ride scholarship, means a walk-on has arrived.

It doesn't take a walk-on in any sport very long to get the message "I'm wanted." Or, "I'm not wanted."

"Let me just sum up my history with Arkansas football," Darrell Brown says. "As a running back, I was simply a tackling dummy."

There's nothing more dangerous in football than receiving a kickoff or punt, and Brown was often assigned that role in practice. The assignment was radically different from normal, though.

Brown became the target of a bizarre meanness, something as grotesque and obscene as the "Battle Royal" scene in the novel *Invisible Man*, where twelve black boys were blindfolded and pushed into a boxing ring. "There were times," Brown says, "I'd be placed on the field to run the ball on a kickoff or punt without *any* offensive players in front of me to meet eleven defenders." One player, with the ball, trying to get through an entire team sprinting directly at him.

Brown absorbed both the abuse and the obvious message from the coach. "I was a country bumpkin," he says. "I just wanted to be at the University of Arkansas and break that color barrier, get what I missed out on in high school."

Frank Broyles, of course, oversaw every practice. "He *wanted* them to do what they did," Brown says. "It all came down from the power that Broyles possessed. I remember him being up in the stands when I was running back kicks against eleven of them, and he'd shout out, 'Why is it that you can't catch that nigger?' "

Brown persevered through that hellish autumn despite feeling as though a bull's-eye was pinned on his jersey.

Sometimes he would have ten other players on his side during practice, but that wasn't a big help. "On the practice field and in the few [freshmen] games in which he played," Richard Pennington wrote in his book about the desegregation of SWC football, *Breaking the Ice*, "his offensive teammates sometimes refused to block for him and even engaged in racist group chants."

Brown never advanced beyond his role as the human punching bag, and never made the varsity. "But he might have if Frank Broyles had made it clear to everyone that Brown was to be treated fairly," Pennington insists. Instead, Broyles's silence condoned the cruelty.

Brown says, "I never had a playbook, was never taught a play. I was placed on the field without knowing any part of the system." That didn't stop Brown from working his way to the front of the line. "The coaches might say, 'I need a defensive back!' and I'd just raise up my hand."

No personal interaction took place between Brown and Broyles. "What I heard from Broyles came to me indirectly," Darrell Brown says, "when he talked about me."

Brown became a member of the Shoats, the UA version of the freshmen team, which featured walk-ons, transfers, and players waiting to earn eligibility or varsity action. "I'd get in and say, 'Where am I supposed to run?' I wouldn't ask about hitting the one-hole, or the two-hole. They'd never taught me that. I was just asking if I was to run right or left."

In *Horns, Hogs, and Nixon Coming*, Brown credits Wilson Matthews as being the running-back coach who encouraged him. Today, he's fuzzy on it, and not sure exactly who that coach was. Matthews was never the running backs' coach; he was usually in charge of linebackers. Matthews is quoted in Frei's book as saying that he has no recollection of any Darrell Brown. The Arkansas football media guide names Bill Pace as the running backs' coach that year. "Only one coach was encouraging to me," Brown says today. "That particular one had responsibility over the running backs."

In fact, Matthews would find himself in the Arkansas administration before Frank Broyles finally desegregated his team.

Lanny Van Eman was named Arkansas basketball coach in 1970 and watched as Broyles began signing black football players. Despite Van Eman's endorsement of Broyles ("a great athletics director"), he believes there was a specific reason Wilson Matthews wasn't on the field when integration took place.

"[Wilson Matthews] used the word 'nigger' in his day-to-day conversation," Van Eman says. "It made me totally uncomfortable." Van Eman suspects the reason Broyles promoted Matthews, making him an assistant athletics director, was simple. "To get him away from the players," Van Eman says, when Broyles was forced to desegregate.

As the vice chancellor at the University Medical Center, Charles Prigmore was often around the football team. Prigmore confirms the fact that Matthews used that kind of language. "Wilson Matthews was a crude guy," Prigmore says. "He was on the staff when we played Georgia in the Sugar Bowl, and I was a part of the official travel party. He didn't have the polish that Frank Broyles had. Matthews would always be spouting off."

One former Arkansas basketball coach before the Richardson era says, "Matthews talked like that, but his heart was better than Broyles's." (Matthews died in 2002 at the age of eighty. Today the Arkansas football stadium has a 3,800-square-foot Wilson Matthews "A" Club room for the big-money boosters.)

Darrell Brown resided in Humphrey Hall, one of the first integrated dorms, and he ate at Brough's Commons. The dining hall there closed at six p.m., which was when football practice usually ended. The scholarship players were half a block from their cafeteria, but Brown would have to run uphill for a half mile, then often find his cafeteria closed. He slept without eating the first few weeks. Later, he realized he needed to get to know the ladies in the lunchroom, and he began doing what blacks in the South had known to do for years. "I'd knock on the kitchen door," he says, "and ask if there was anything left to eat." The cafeterias at that time were totally staffed by black help, and they were sympathetic to Brown's plight.

Being the first black football player took a terrible toll, yet in Brown's understated manner, he says, "I had reservations about continuing on the field. It wound up being a positive experience because it opened my eyes. There was a big shield of resistance to having a black player at Arkansas. Their [the players] words were, I heard some of them say, 'Why do we need a black, we just won a national championship?'"

Any fairness on the football field stood out to Brown. "David Hargis was one of the few players who never called me 'nigger,' and he would stand up for me. I considered him to genuinely believe in the right thing. He'd say, 'Give Brown a chance.'"

Hargis came from southern Arkansas and later was accepted to the UA law school, where he was named editor of the *Law Review*. Today Hargis is a successful trial lawyer in Little Rock. He declines to say "nigger," even when quoting someone, always using the phrase "N word" instead.

Hargis recalls Brown's ordeal vividly. "Darrell Brown displayed a whole lot of courage in doing what he did," he says. "The fact that he didn't have a scholarship, that made it even more daring on his part. They were sending a brutal message to Darrell. When the ball was snapped, it was like he was the only player left on his side. He'd come back in the locker room and he'd have been beaten up every day."

Although it appeared a systematic ostracizing of Brown was in place, Hargis believes it was not orchestrated. "Darrell was never exactly singled out and mistreated in an organized manner," he says.

It was often spontaneous, with the players chanting "Get the nigger." "I heard it back then," Hargis confirms. "It'd be when they were trying to tackle Darrell, and sometimes his teammates wouldn't block for him."

Hargis insists on pointing out cultural and historical differences and the danger of judging the past with today's more progressive mindset. He is also sensitive about Arkansas's portrayal in print. "I'd hate to contribute to Arkansas being viewed as backward," he says. "I don't want to condemn anyone. This was a different era. I'm not blaming or faulting anyone, retrospectively. There were people who had not been confronted with these issues, who hadn't thought about these things. If confronted today, I think they'd regret what they had done."

That may be true. Yet it's important to understand that this was the kingdom that Frank Broyles ruled, the athletics program where Nolan Richardson would arrive two decades after Darrell Brown.

It's also true that Elizabeth Eckford and her spit-drenched home-made dress represented enormous courage, regardless of any sociological analysis or historical context. She returned to Central High School the next day, and the next few years. Darrell Brown was the Elizabeth Eckford of college football.

Football, though, is only part of American society, Hargis notes. "Lots of blacks were exposed to far worse away from sports. They were brutalized," he says. "There's a big difference between being called a name on the field and having a Coke bottle smashed against your head in the street. It's difficult to judge Frank Broyles or Adolph Rupp by today's standards. Our own fathers and grandfathers, some of them, without ill will, entertained racism."

The old Razorback football coach has changed some over the years, Hargis says. "Broyles displayed a lot of racism, but he's softened, and he's done some things that are pretty commendable, especially with Alzheimer's research funding." (Hargis also admired Wilson Matthews and defends him, too. "You could count on what Matthews said," Hargis says, and he never heard Matthews use what he calls the "N word." "Why would he? There weren't any black players around to speak of.")

Hargis is quick to apply modern standards to Darrell Brown's situation in one regard, though: "Darrell had superb athletic ability, based on his speed and quickness," he says. "He wasn't big, but he was very strong for his size. In today's world, Darrell Brown would have played for the Arkansas Razorbacks."

"I made it through the year in 1965," Brown says, "then went out again the next fall."

It is nearly beyond belief that Brown would return to the Razorbacks, but in some ways he was luckier the second year. "I got hurt in practice," he says. That gave him time to reflect on the futility of his quest and make a decision. "I turned away, because of my dream being shattered," he says. Brown's hope of being the first black scholarship player, or the first black to take the field in a Razorback uniform, was over.

Brown concentrated on academics. "I remained frustrated," he says, "because I felt I was just as good and fast as anyone who was playing."

Two years later, Martin Luther King and Bobby Kennedy were gunned down, politicizing Darrell Brown. He was accepted into the University of Arkansas law school. After a long career as a Little Rock attorney (he took President Bill Clinton's deposition at one time), he retired to a farm in Horatio, Arkansas, near his childhood home.

Brown's daughter is employed today with University of Arkansas's athletics department. "She played basketball and ran track," Brown says, "and I all but told her and my son *not* to go to Arkansas. But I think they wanted to prove something, prove that they could make it."

The bond that Brown and Hargis forged kept them in touch for years. In the late 1980s, Brown teamed up with Hargis, but not on the football field. This time it was to play a little golf.

At that time, country clubs in Little Rock remained segregated. Hargis invited Brown and two other prominent black lawyers, Les Hollingsworth and Richard Mays, to play at the Pleasant Valley Country Club. Hargis says the three played without incident and, soon after, Richard Mays applied for membership at Pleasant Valley, bidding to become their only black member.

The Pleasant Valley doctor who conducted the application interview asked Mays why he wanted to join the club.

"I like to play golf," Mays answered.

"But who would you play *with*?" the doctor asked.

Darrell Brown can still get emotional when talking about his time as a football walk-on for Arkansas. He says he's had so few personal interactions with Broyles that he remembers them all clearly. "I saw Frank Broyles one time at a function, and I said to him, 'You don't remember me, do you?'" Then Brown explained that he had been practice fodder, a human tackling dummy as a walk-on in 1965 and again briefly in 1966.

"That's right," Broyles told Brown, "you were the first one!"

In *Horns, Hogs, and Nixon Coming*, Frei writes, "Broyles long has said the state board informally made it clear to him when he arrived at Arkansas that he could not recruit black athletes, but he felt integration was inevitable and right." This claim ignores a number of issues, such as the way Darrell Brown was treated. Also, the fact that the basketball coach at Arkansas beat Broyles by three years in desegregating his team. And virtually every college in the state and SWC desegregated before Broyles.

Yet, according to Frei, "Broyles said he didn't ask the university or athletics administration for permission to begin recruiting blacks."

Thus, in manipulating even the modern media, Broyles made himself simultaneously the victim and the hero of Arkansas's belated desegregation. The board wouldn't let Broyles *and* he ignored the board. Frei even states in the opening of one chapter that Broyles's having a single walk-on in 1969—who never played a minute or even suited up for the games—meant that the Arkansas team was "integrated." Frei makes the same ludicrous assertion about Darrell Brown's time in 1965, saying that Brown had ". . . briefly integrated the program."

"Don't confuse integration with desegregation," Judge Wendell Griffen cautions. "They're not the same thing."

"If you played football, you remember those awful days of sweaty football practice," says Richard Pennington, whose *Breaking the Ice* remains the only book on the integration of the Southwest Conference. The coaches start drill, maybe a one-on-one or two-on-one drill. Every player is standing there, watching. The coach asks for a volunteer to go first. "Well, that volunteer is the guy you want on your team," Pennington says. "He has guts and courage. You know who the wimps are? The cowards? They're at the back, hiding from the drill. That's what Frank Broyles and Darrell Royal were both doing in the 1960s, hiding in the back of the line!"

Pennington was never able to get access to Frank Broyles. The Arkansas coach was the only one who stonewalled him. "Royal and Frank Broyles—and, for that matter, 'Bear' Bryant at Alabama and others—were cowards," Pennington says. "They were simply afraid to lead and do what needed to be done, no matter how difficult, and preferred to let people like Hayden Fry take the heat." Broyles finished 1-9 in his last ten games against Texas, which makes it harder to believe that he would not recruit blacks sooner for practical, if not ethical, reasons.

An unknown walk-on who never scored a touchdown or played a single minute of varsity football at Arkansas is in elite company. Jackie Robinson. Jerry LeVias. Darrell Brown. "What these men did

was so very important not just for black people but for whites, too,"
Pennington says. "What all this shows is how incredibly narrow-
minded and parochial white people were back then. If those in power
let these black guys compete fairly, they were going to rise to the top.
Hell yes, they were afraid."

FIFTEEN

GO UP FOR GLORY

The 1992–93 Razorback basketball team went into the season with low expectations—after all, three of the best players in school history now were being fitted for NBA uniforms. However, a surprising group of newcomers, led by freshmen Corliss Williamson and Scotty Thurman, as well as junior college transfers Corey Beck and Dwight Stewart, made it to the NCAA Tournament's Sweet 16 before losing to eventual national champion North Carolina. Arkansas finished 22-9, including 10-6 in the SEC, and celebrated its last win in Barnhill Arena.

Richardson and Bud Walton, one of the founders of Wal-Mart, became better friends around this time, although they had met soon after Richardson arrived in Arkansas. Wal-Mart is based only a twenty-minute drive from the university, and Bud Walton, who loved the Razorbacks fast-break style, often made the drive to Fayetteville for lunch with the coach.

One October, Richardson had an idea for their annual exhibition game. He usually divided the players into a red and a white team and let his assistants coach. Richardson would watch from the stands to evaluate. Since the university was continuously courting donors, Richardson suggested to Frank Broyles that Bud Walton be asked to coach one of the teams.

Broyles told Richardson he'd already invited Bud Walton, and that Bud declined. "But I didn't believe it," Richardson says, "because coaching half the team, even in an intra-squad game, was an honor."

Richardson ignored Broyles and asked Bud Walton himself. Walton accepted and coached that year against one of the Tyson Foods bosses. This invitation to coach brought Bud Walton and Richardson even closer, but pushed Richardson and Broyles farther apart. This incident was one of several occasions where Broyles's pride trumped his wisdom—anything that would have kept Bud Walton pleased with the university would have been worthwhile.

When the University of Arkansas decided it was time to build a new basketball arena, the Waltons were a natural choice to help. Bud Walton reportedly gave $15 million for the construction of the arena, which was ready for the 1993–94 season. When it came time to make decisions about the design of the arena, Bud Walton went directly to Richardson for input. What color tile for the locker room? What kind of seats for the biggest donors?

In building Bud Walton Arena, the university was rolling the dice, hoping Richardson's Razorbacks would double the size of their crowds. One important stipulation from Bud Walton was issued when the arena was built—only Razorback men's and women's basketball could use the facility. No concerts. No pro wrestling. No volleyball. No circus. The one exception could be the annual convention for Wal-Mart.

Bud Walton Arena, with a capacity of 19,200, opened in 1993. The Razorbacks led the nation in attendance in its inaugural season. The arena remains one of the ten biggest for college hoops in the country. Richardson's squad would be ranked in the top ten in attendance eight of the nine years he competed there.

The team's success and its bond with one of the richest men in America may not have helped Richardson, ultimately. "Bud Walton loved Nolan," says Sid Simpson, "but Broyles was afraid of that, resented it."

Bud Walton Arena also became home to Razorback supporter Fred Vorsanger.

Vorsanger had served as vice president of finance and administration, a role that meant all of athletics was under him, including then-football coach Frank Broyles.

In 1989, Vorsanger became mayor of Fayetteville. After his term as mayor was complete, he felt that he still had the energy for another job. But in Fayetteville, Arkansas, few jobs were more prestigious than mayor. In 1992, Broyles offered him the job of managing the new basketball facility. It seemed like a step up.

Vorsanger liked Richardson immediately. When the coach heard how Vorsanger was the son of German immigrants in Chicago, bullied as a boy for his accent, the two got to be friends. They joked and teased each other constantly. Once Richardson was walking outside Walton Arena with a visiting golf pro when he spotted Vorsanger coming out of his office. Richardson whispered to the golf pro, then waved to Vorsanger.

"Fred, I want you to show this golf pro your swing," Richardson said.

The golf pro had his clubs with him and handed Vorsanger a driver. Vorsanger loosened up his shoulders, took his stance, reached back, and swung.

Richardson turned to the golf pro. "What do you think? Does he have any hope?"

"No," said the pro. "There's no hope for this guy."

Richardson grabbed the club and they walked away. Richardson and the golf pro stifled their laughter until they got outside.

Sometimes Richardson would joke with Vorsanger about his coaching situation. After hearing that an NBA coach was being paid lots of money not to coach his team any longer, Richardson said to him, "That's what we need, Federico. A long-term contract, then we screw up and they have to pay us anyway."

"He was joking when he said it," Vorsanger says. "He'd laugh and say, 'I wish they'd just pay me my money and I could go away, Federico.' I never took him seriously."

Richardson prepared the Razorbacks for the 1993–94 season with his usual brutal regimen that forced the players to grow up or go home.

One player, Alex Dillard, nearly joined the Marines out of high school—few options were available for a 5'5" kid in the world of sports. Instead, Dillard took some time off, then enrolled at a local junior college, where he sprouted up to 5'9" and emerged as a hot-shooting guard. He signed with Arkansas and arrived in the fall of 1993, but wasn't fond of the coach at first.

"We're going to be the best-conditioned team in NCAA," Richardson told the team, and Dillard wasn't emotionally prepared for what that entailed. By October of 1993, he was no longer planning on being a Razorback. Dillard instructed his father to call a list of coaches who had been recruiting him before he signed with Arkansas. He was planning on transferring at Christmas. Arkansas was like boot camp, Dillard says. "We ran and ran. The first month we had to be in the locker room at five fifteen in the morning." That was difficult enough, Dillard says, but they had to return in the afternoon for more.

Strangely, Dillard continued to grow that fall, sprouting two more inches in a single semester. That coincided with his evolving attitude.

Dillard decided not to quit. "You had to be tough," Dillard says. "He made Bobby Knight seem like a saint, he was so hard on us."

Instilling confidence and fear simultaneously is a Richardson paradox, and Alex Dillard acclimated, then erupted into the most productive scorer-per-minute in school history. Dillard would later score 19 points in seventeen minutes in a single NCAA Tournament game.

The fear-confidence combo sparked a new nickname for the coach, something the team called Richardson behind his back, and an echo from his past. Dillard says, "For four hours a day, he was the meanest motherfucker—excuse my language—that ever walked. Then afterward he'd open his home to us. We called him 'The Bear.'"

The Razorbacks were unaware that "The Bear" was Don Haskins's nickname.

Richardson had a fine team in place going into the 1993–94 season, but he was focused on more than his full-court pressure. He spent an increasing amount of time advising the Black Coaches Association.

The NCAA had decided to phase in something they called Proposition 16, a stiffening of the standards set by Proposition 48. Under the proposed new rules, a freshman would need a 2.5 grade point average in thirteen core classes. The NCAA was also proposing a "sliding scale" for the college board exams, the SAT or ACT. For example, if a student scored as high as 900, he could be permitted to play with a high school GPA of 2.0. The standards were more challenging, but the NCAA felt that, over time, high school students would meet the raised bar.

The Black Coaches Association rejected the new proposals. The BCA released a statement claiming that the NCAA had "... turned its back on socially and economically disadvantaged people ..." When the proposal was passed, many athletic teams would have higher entrance requirements than the rest of their respective universities.

A challenge was issued back in 1989, when John Thompson walked off the court at an opening tipoff. The NCAA backed down then, and the ruling was rewritten. This time, Richardson and Chaney vowed to appeal to civil rights organizations like the NAACP.

Would higher admissions standards improve the graduation rates of athletes, especially black basketball players? Almost certainly. Fewer top athletes were being declared ineligible over the years, and it appeared that kids were adapting slowly to the new higher standards.

However, the most experienced black coaches relied on their historical perspective. To Richardson, any rule change that would exclude black kids was a disturbing move backward.

The BCA began calling for a boycott of the NCAA Tournament that spring. The target date for the discussed boycott was initially set for January 15, the birthday of Martin Luther King Jr. Members of the Congressional Black Caucus met with the BCA in Washington, DC, and they were able to convince the coaches to delay a protest—the Black Caucus thought it was too strong a move. When the boycott didn't materialize, Richardson was quoted nationally as saying, "I've always been a pioneer myself, and growing up like I did, I learned a lot about surviving. There will be a boycott." The NCAA Tournament was six weeks away.

The Black Caucus agreed to begin dialogue with the NCAA that would address the BCA's concerns. The reduction of total basketball scholarships from fifteen to thirteen over a decade was still a sore spot.

By the end of March, the threat of a BCA-sponsored boycott was a very real possibility—a boycott planned for the midst of the NCAA Tournament. Rudy Washington, the BCA's executive director, told the *Sporting News*, "We have the ability to stop work now . . . the NCAA kept saying, 'Yes, we'll put a committee together. We'll study it. We'll do this, yes, yes.' And then we say, 'We're not going to play basketball anymore.' . . . Call it a crisis, a dramatic gesture, if you will . . . We were forced to do this. This isn't something we wanted to do."

Washington was also critical of how long it took for African-American athletes and coaches to wake up. "Unfortunately, most of our people, meaning African-Americans, will die like they lived their lives: asleep. They never know what's going on around them. I just feel a real need to take a step and make some things work for us."

Reactions to the boycott by some black coaches were not so supportive. Ben Jobe, then coaching at Southern University, was frustrated that some of the most visible African-American men in America found time to battle for basketball scholarships. Jobe rejected the notion of a boycott to the *Sporting News*. "This is not the Civil Rights movement," he said. "This is not the war on poverty. This is not ethnic cleansing. This is not pro-life or abortion. This is not crime. This is not the killing of black youngsters by black youngsters. I'm not going to be wasting my energy . . . on fighting for a fourteenth scholarship for a kid who probably doesn't want to be going to school in the first place. If you have an important issue, call me. If not, don't bother me."

The Black Coaches Association, along with the NABC, began to hammer away at the NCAA in 1994 about four major concerns.

The first concern was the reduction in basketball scholarships. Second was the shocking absence of African-Americans in the NCAA's own headquarters. Third, there were few African-Americans serving in upper-management positions at colleges. Fourth, the BCA noted that more white males were coaching women's basketball than African-American females.

The Arkansas media jumped into the fray, and, as was often

the case, they irritated Richardson. John Robert Starr wrote in the *Democrat-Gazette*, "If the [Arkansas] players play, their chances of winning the tournament are considerably enhanced if Richardson, one of the poorest bench coaches in the land, is back in Fayetteville, sulking in his tent."

The Razorbacks quickly established themselves as a great team during the 1993–94 season. They lost only twice in the SEC season, by a total of three points. They were ranked #1 nationally for much of the year. The state-of-the-art Bud Walton Arena even attracted President Bill Clinton, an Arkansas native and former law school professor, who attended four regular season games that year.

Arkansas lost to Kentucky in the SEC Tournament and went into the NCAA playoffs ranked #2 in the nation. They beat historically black North Carolina A&T, then Georgetown, Tulsa, and Michigan to get to the Final Four.

When senior sub Roger Crawford got hurt, Richardson decided to honor Crawford by having #31 sewn onto the shoulder of every Razorback jersey—a sort of "No Hawg Left Behind" policy.

Three thousand Arkansas fans made the trip to Charlotte for the Final Four, where the Razorbacks would meet Arizona.

Richardson, an outsider all of his childhood and professional life, seemed unable to accept the accolades. Despite the national ranking and the notoriety the team had earned, the coach hammered the us-against-the-world story into their heads over and over. The team came to believe that they were not, in fact, getting the respect they deserved—despite being ranked #1 most of the season.

In the semifinals, Arkansas guards Clint McDaniel and Corey Beck harassed Arizona's backcourt, regarded as the best offensive duo in America, into making just two of twenty-two attempts from behind the three-point arc. Arkansas beat Arizona, 91-82.

Richardson held court after the Arizona game, lecturing the

media. In the *Sporting News*, he was quoted as saying ". . . if I would win games and some of the other black coaches would win, we would never win because of our brains and our techniques and our teachings. . . . it was always because 'Well, they've got the best athletes' and 'Man, look at those athletes that guy's got out there.' Wait a minute, I said, look at my team and look at Krzyzewski's team and put us on paper and just ask how many they want of their All-Americans as opposed to us—they don't know us, they don't know anything about us—and see whose team they're going to pick, whose players they're going to pick. That was the thing that used to bother me more than anything." The Duke coach, Richardson believed, had his pick of the nation's top high school players, while Richardson relied on under-recruited sleepers.

What raised even more eyebrows was what Richardson said on national television to color analyst Billy Packer immediately after the Arizona game. Packer had irritated Richardson plenty in the past; not directly, but through what Richardson felt were his veiled comments about black coaches and athletes—the very same things he would be lecturing the media about a few minutes later.

Minutes after the game ended, Packer lobbed a softball question to Richardson. "Gee, Billy," Richardson said, "a blind man could see that."

Don Haskins believed Packer had an East Coast bias. "If you weren't from the ACC [Atlantic Coast Conference], Billy Packer thought you didn't know anything," he said, but Haskins would never challenge Packer, or anyone else, on live television. Haskins thought Richardson's comments, both with Packer and to the media, were a distraction. "I don't think he needed to do that," Haskins was quoted as saying. "He kicked Arizona's ass, and he should've left it at that." With the NCAA championship still to be played, Haskins in his day would have been anything but political. Richardson had emerged as even more politically conscious and outspoken with the national title at stake.

———

The Razorbacks would play Duke, the NCAA champs in 1991 and 1992. Duke had a host of great players, but their star was Grant Hill, a consensus pick for national Player of the Year honors.

The day before the championship, Richardson grew pensive. He was reasonably proud of his accomplishments, but something was nagging him. Richardson had been the underdog so long that despite his team's yearlong national ranking, he still felt dispossessed. He found himself pondering one of Arkansas's little-used substitutes, a senior named Ken Biley.

Biley was an undersized post player who was raised in Pine Bluff. Neither of his parents had the opportunity to go to college, but every one of his fifteen siblings did, and nearly all graduated. "I had already learned that everybody has to play his role," Biley says of his upbringing.

As a freshman and sophomore, Biley saw some court time and even started a couple of games, but his playing time later evaporated and he lost faith. "Everyone wants to play, and when you don't you get discouraged," he says.

On two occasions, he sat down with his coach and asked what he could do to earn a more important role. "I never demanded anything," Biley says, "and he told me exactly what I needed to do, but we had so many good players ahead of me. Corliss Williamson, for one."

Nearly every coach, under the pressure of a championship showdown, reverts to the basic strategies that got the team into the finals. But Richardson couldn't stop thinking about Biley, and what a selfless worker he had been for four years. The day before the championship game against Duke, at the conclusion of practice, Richardson pulled Biley aside. Biley had hardly played in the first five playoff games leading up to the NCAA title match—a total of four minutes.

"I've watched how your career has progressed, and how you've handled not getting to play," Richardson began. "I appreciate the leadership you've been showing and I want to reward you, as a senior."

"Thanks coach," Biley said. He was unprepared for what came next.

"You're starting tomorrow against Duke," Richardson said. "And you're guarding Grant Hill."

Biley was speechless. Then overcome with emotion.

"I was shocked, freaked out!" Biley says. "I hadn't played much for two years. I just could not believe it."

Biley had plenty of time to think about Grant Hill. "I was a nervous wreck, like you'd expect," he says. He had a restless night—he stared at the ceiling, sat on the edge of his bed, then flopped around trying to sleep.

Richardson had disdained book coaches for years. Now he was throwing the book in the trash by starting a benchwarmer in the NCAA championship game.

On the day of the game, *New York Times* columnist William Rhoden wrote a column titled "A Coach and a Player Climb a Mountaintop." The article profiled Nolan Richardson and Duke star Grant Hill. It was April 4, the anniversary of the assassination of Martin Luther King Jr., and the coincidence was not lost on Rhoden.

Rhoden wrote of the volatile political and social climate that meant college sports were being more closely examined than ever. This was a "basketball season that became a civil rights movement, and a tournament that, largely because of Richardson, has forced the news media to at least hear, if not address, festering sociocultural issues striking at the foundation of college sports." Who would play, coach, write about, and profit from college basketball? These issues were now at the forefront.

Rather than win gracefully, Richardson had used the NCAA

triumphs to ". . . drive home the BCA's message of giving African-Americans the same off-the-court opportunities that they command on the court." Rhoden also called out the media on what he called a "manufactured morality play," something that had bothered Richardson for so long—the perception journalists had helped foster, that Arkansas had "talent" while Duke had "intelligence."

Rhoden marveled at Richardson's influence. "Richardson has talked so often and so loudly," Rhoden wrote, "that athletes are beginning to hear what he's saying." Of course, nobody heard more about it than the Razorbacks.

Near the end of Rhoden's piece, he asked a question that would prove prophetic: "Why do black coaches who get fired have such a difficult time resurfacing, if they resurface at all?"

Ken Biley had admired Grant Hill's skills countless times when Duke played on television. He made a conscious decision—he wouldn't back off Hill or give him too much respect. He'd deny Hill the ball whenever he could, crowd him, and try to overwhelm Hill with aggressiveness. Fatigue wasn't going to be a factor, since he figured he'd get limited minutes. "I didn't want to save anything. I always tried to contribute with defense and rebounding, anyway."

Biley was quite aware that this was not the ideal time for a coach to pay tribute to substitutes with good attitudes. "It was risky," he says. "What might it do for our chemistry and our tone for the game?"

Minutes before the game, Arkansas radio spotter Bob Carver watched to see what the reaction might be with the media as one of Richardson's assistants penciled in Ken Biley as a starter at the scorer's table. "Press row lit up!" Carver says. "You could see them thinking, 'Has Richardson lost his mind?'"

———

As expected, Ken Biley would play less than four minutes and did not score a basket. But he harassed Grant Hill, using his long arms and great lateral movement to hassle the All-American. Hill played point guard at the start, and was off his game. He would throw the ball away nine times that night.

Arkansas guards Clint McDaniel and Corey Beck set the tone with their furious defensive pressure. Corliss Williamson grabbed seven offensive rebounds and put in ten field goals. Scotty Thurman— from Ruston, Louisiana, where Ol' Mama was born—drilled a three-pointer with under a minute to go. That shot sealed the Arkansas victory. Arkansas beat Duke, 76-72. Nolan Richardson had won the national title.

The following week, Curry Kirkpatrick wrote about Richardson's NCAA title run for *Newsweek* and reflected on what he called the coach's manipulation of the media, whom ". . . Richardson plucked like a Stradivarius in motivating his team to overcome what the coach—though seemingly nobody else—perceived as slights based on racism."

Kirkpatrick felt the national polls were enough respect. Richardson insisted the polls were not—it wasn't respect for his team he was looking for. Richardson never suggested it was all a ploy to motivate his team—he remained the defiant outsider, reminding the respected writer of the ugly history in the rearview mirror.

"I know who I am," Richardson railed. "We [black coaches] can recruit, motivate, teach . . . but are we good coaches? I never hear that."

Later, John Thompson told the *Sporting News*, "The game is defined differently for a black coach. Truthfully, it's hard to explain that to a white person. . . . There's no such thing as the game for the sake of the game. It's not a luxury but a necessity; it's a means to an end, it's a means to an end for a lot of people. Nolan understands that."

Thompson was later quoted nationally as saying, "Nolan can never compete as 100 percent coach. He has other responsibilities as a black man. I hear people say they're in it for the love of the game. He can't go in feeling that way; no black man can."

Frank Broyles didn't make the trip to the Final Four in Charlotte because he was hospitalized briefly. He recovered enough to address the crowd at Bud Walton Arena the next week. The two men would embrace in front of the hysterical Razorback fans.

Scotty Thurman says Richardson never discussed his relationship with Broyles, but that the tension was obvious, even after the championship. "You could tell they didn't like one another," Thurman says.

Todd Day, by this time an established NBA star, says, "Frank Broyles had run Arkansas for forty years, and here comes this outspoken black man disagreeing with him. Nolan would stand up for what he thought and challenge Broyles."

There was one powerful person from Arkansas, however, for whom Richardson had no animosity. On June 15, 1994, the Arkansas basketball team was honored in the Rose Garden by President Bill Clinton.

Clinton had made a brief speech in the locker room after the Duke game, and had even posed on the cover of *Sports Illustrated* sporting a sweat suit Richardson had given him. "Nolan Richardson has done a lot of remarkable things in his life," Clinton said to the team, "often against all odds. . . . And so I say to him and all the players, you did your state proud. You made the president happy. But more important, you showed America the best of what college athletics should be. And we are all very proud of you."

Despite the praise from the president of the United States, Richardson had a difficult time enjoying himself. "You create a monster," Richardson told the *Sporting News* after the season. "I know that I've created a monster."

SIXTEEN

IF BLESSING COMES

Nolan Richardson was the first black man in power to openly challenge Frank Broyles, but the ground had been shifting under Broyles's feet since the mid-1960s.

The University of Arkansas campus was not exactly a bastion of radicalism then, but attitudes began changing. The student body and faculty confronted Broyles, and by 1969 he'd been forced to finally offer a scholarship to Jon Richardson. A modest antiwar movement had even emerged on campus, led in part by Professor "Bud" Zinke. In 1969, Gordon D. Morgan and Margaret Clark became the first black faculty members.

The school yearbook reflected the shift on campus. One photograph of Broyles in a late 1960s yearbook had the caption "The best football coach in America. Just ask him." Another photo featured a new group on campus, Black Americans for Democracy (BAD), whose objective was to raise the number of blacks enrolled at

Arkansas. Another full page was devoted to marijuana growing and smoking among white students.

Whether it was because of Arkansas's reputation as a stronghold of segregation or a lack of recruiting effort, Arkansas football just couldn't seem to attract the best black players. After 1967, Broyles would not coach another first-round NFL draft choice.

Broyles claimed to have been handcuffed by the board of trustees, and also to have ignored them on the subject of desegregation. Did he have the power to simply desegregate when he wanted? Or did the board of trustees insist that Broyles be last among colleges in Arkansas and teams in the Southwest Conference?

By 1961, Broyles had won three straight Southwest Conference titles. He was thirty-seven years old and one of the hottest names in all of football. Broyles won at least part of a national championship in 1964 and was named the national Coach of the Year. He was acknowledged by both supporters and detractors as perhaps the most powerful person in the state of Arkansas. The university, dorms, and basketball teams were already desegregating by the time Broyles made a move.

In other words, Broyles likely could have desegregated whenever he wanted to, and definitely after being named national Coach of the Year.

Certainly Broyles lived in a different place than, say, Don Haskins in El Paso, where half the city was Hispanic. Yet Arkansas has never been considered the Deep South. What if Broyles had the courage needed simply to announce he was going to break the color barrier first in the SWC, or look for a job elsewhere?

Fort Smith native Joe Neal, a passionate antiwar activist, rattled the establishment in the late 1960s by leading demonstrations outside UA football games. "The peace movement and the Civil Rights movement were interwoven," Neal says today. "One day we were out trying to stop the war, the next we wanted the campus newspaper to cover black issues."

Neal understood the emotional heart of the university was Frank Broyles's football team, and his blocking of desegregation needed to be challenged. At home football games, Neal and his crew stood in an area outside Razorback Stadium with signs reading WE WANT RAZOR-BLACKS.

"We set up where people were walking into the stadium," Neal recalls, "so they'd have to see us. We operated on the assumption that if Broyles wanted blacks on the team, he could have had them. Broyles was an extreme exemplar of the establishment and Arkansas was way behind the country. But in retrospect, they were trying to always raise money in parts of the state that wouldn't have wanted black football players."

The "Razorblacks" demonstrations were one of a quick succession of events that rattled the slowly awakening campus. Next came the occupation of Hill Hall, which housed the school of journalism and campus newspaper. Black and white students were angry that the school's weekly, the *Traveler*, would not print a letter rebutting an earlier one criticizing Dr. Martin Luther King Jr. Hill Hall later burned, but nobody was ever charged with arson. School president David Mullins's office was occupied by thirty black students who were frustrated with Arkansas's lack of progress.

Not everyone within those progressive movements was in agreement. "There was tension between well-meaning white liberals and others who were closer to the street," says Neal. "There were a lot of people around campus on both sides who felt threatened by black activists."

One of those black activists was former football walk-on Darrell Brown. Brown and a group of other black students bonded together in an attempt to get the school's band to stop playing the Confederate anthem "Dixie" every time Arkansas scored a touchdown or took the field. The song had irritated the first black basketball player on scholarship, T. J. Johnson, and that revulsion was typical of black students. In 1969, black students threatened to storm the field during the nationally televised showdown with Texas if the band didn't stop playing "Dixie."

On the weekend following the Arkansas v. Texas game, Darrell Brown was on the front page of the *Traveler*, along with the Razorback football team. Neither Brown nor the football team had good news to report.

Arkansas had lost to Texas in the white-guy version of the self-proclaimed "Game of the Century."

Darrell Brown had been shot, hit in the leg by an unknown sniper near campus after a meeting about the "Dixie" issue. The president of the university hadn't bothered to check on the wounded student, despite a personal plea from Gordon Morgan, UA's first black professor.

President Nixon was in attendance, as was George H. W. Bush and Bill Clinton. The shooting of a black student was the last kind of publicity the state or university needed. As it turned out, the administration didn't need to worry about Arkansas's image. Darrell Brown's shooting was not mentioned on television. The Razorblack protest didn't make it on national TV. Neither did "Bud" Zinke's antiwar crew.

The band director, acting independently, had decided to quit playing "Dixie" altogether, so black students did not storm the football field. Soon after, the student senate voted to recommend the song be dropped from the band's repertoire.

Brown's law school dean offered a public reward leading to the arrest and conviction of the person responsible for the shooting, but nobody was ever charged with the crime.

Arkansas avoided national exposure when Darrell Brown was hit by sniper fire, and they'd work hard to avoid embarrassment in the future. "I can't say that Frank Broyles was prejudiced," Arkansas's former basketball coach Lanny Van Eman stresses. "But there was one incident where a *Sports Illustrated* writer I knew came down for a spring football game, in 1970 or 1971." Broyles called Van Eman to his office and said, "A friend of yours is coming to town."

Broyles was concerned about the way Arkansas—the state, university, and football team—would be portrayed. *Sports Illustrated* had done a blistering series called "The Black Athlete" a few years earlier, and nobody was safe from criticism.

"Broyles was really scared," Van Eman continues. "He said, 'This is a *Northern* guy.'"

Arkansas was likely to be a top-ranked team in the coming season, so, naturally, ticket sales for the spring game were brisk. Van Eman attended with the *Sports Illustrated* writer, happy to be outside on this sunny spring day. But Van Eman was perplexed when he noticed a small tent set up next to the field.

With no threat of rain, the tent near the sideline seemed strange. Why? Maybe a player had an embarrassing location for a nagging injury—perhaps a pulled groin that would need constant treatment.

"At that time," Van Eman says, "there were just three blacks on the football team. Two were on scholarship and the other was a walk-on. Every so often the walk-on would run into the tent. I just couldn't figure out why."

Then it became apparent. The black walk-on would dash into the tent wearing #23. When he came out, he was wearing #41. Next time it might be #35.

The deceptive costume changes were intended, of course, to make the *Sports Illustrated* writer believe that Arkansas had plenty of black players.

———

The book *Untold Stories: Black Sports Heroes Before Integration* profiles many of the black athletes in Arkansas whose careers were ruined by the segregated system. Darren Ivy edited the collection, which includes many of his own articles, originally written for the *Democrat-Gazette*, researched and written when he was only twenty-four years old. The book was published by the *Democrat-Gazette*, and at first glance seems like a remarkable historical document. Then a pattern emerges—the players were never asked how they felt about being ignored by the University of Arkansas, or what impact segregation had made on their lives.

In fact, in the entire book of nearly a hundred chapters, there is just one single mention of, or quote from, Frank Broyles. His unwillingness to speak about the racist system he empowered, and the inability of the local press to ask him difficult questions, is astounding.

Ironically, the book tries to use Broyles's name to sell copies.

"Now, in this era of equal access," the book's back cover says, "it's difficult for some to remember that at one time there were two worlds of sport, delineated by pigment." Difficult for some, alright.

Just below that is the only Frank Broyles quote, a rather strange one. "It was like a blur," Broyles's quote reads. "It just happened, and you can't remember when it wasn't."

When Darren Ivy was given the assignment to both write and collect the articles by the *Democrat-Gazette*, he had to find his own way. Ivy was just out of school and not even an Arkansas native. Few records and no film could be found about the black sports heroes, and many of the best players only seemed to exist as legends. So Ivy, who worked at the paper from 2000 until 2004, got busy, relying on word of mouth. Outdoor dirt courts, patchwork uniforms, cracked backboards—one story led to another and soon enough, the *Democrat-Gazette* had a series. Ivy interviewed Broyles and used the quote—"It just happened and you can't remember when it wasn't"—in an early piece.

Later, when Ivy asked about Fayetteville star "Bull" Hayes, the black player who was steered away to Nebraska, the conversation with

Broyles came to an abrupt end. "He started getting all defensive and upset," Ivy says. "He got pissed off and he hung up on me."

That article changed everything for Ivy. "After we wrote the story on Bull Hayes, that was one of the most controversial. The series stopped at that one. It made me realize we're living in Arkansas, where racial issues are still pretty prevalent."

The black players during the era of segregation in Arkansas had been stifled. Years later their voices and stories were, in effect, still censored, because the difficult questions were not being asked. Anyone asking uncomfortable questions about that time was being stifled too.

There was a cost to this segregated system of keeping these young men on the outside. Not the touchdown totals or cutting down the nets at the Final Four, but a very real human impact. At least one story was begging to be told, one that connected Frank Broyles and Don Haskins.

Among the first pieces in *Untold Stories* is a profile of Bobby Walters, a running back who scored a mind-boggling ninety-six touchdowns in his high school career. Near the end of the article, it mentions that Walters was the guy who had coached Tim Hardaway in Chicago. A few years later, of course, Hardaway went to El Paso to play for Don Haskins.

Few people knew what kind of football hero Bob Walters had been in high school, because he kept it to himself. Instead, in his adult life, Walters was known as the Carver coach, then as Tim Hardaway's coach.

Walters scored thirty-two touchdowns as a senior, which should have been counted as the state record. Since McCrae High School of Prescott did not have films, or even detailed statistics, they had a difficult time getting colleges to believe Walters's amazing touchdown total. Bob Walters's brother Shelton believes the stats might even be too conservative. "I have to take that as official, since there were no records or films," Shelton says, "but if Bob scored *fewer* than four in any game it would be considered unusual."

The University of Arkansas, where Frank Broyles had just completed his second season, expressed no interest—despite the fact Walters was also ranked #3 in his class academically. Broyles would have never had a chance to see Bull Hayes play; Hayes's season at Fayetteville High School was finished by the time Broyles moved to town, so that would have been a handy excuse. Bob Walters may have been the first great black player in Arkansas whom Frank Broyles ignored.

Northwestern University of the Big Ten took notice, though. Their star, Irv Cross, was a cousin of Walters's coach.

Each school year in Prescott featured their annual talent show and awards ceremony. The spring of 1959, Walters's senior year, would not be any different. There would be all kinds of acts, but the topic on everyone's mind was where Walters would go to play football. When McCrae football coach Joseph Hale tapped the microphone in preparation of an announcement, people got quiet.

"Everyone should know," Coach Hale announced, "that Bob Walters left today on his official visit to Northwestern University." The gymnasium, filled to capacity, roared its approval. "Bob Walters will be the first Negro player from the South to go to Northwestern, and he's going to have the opportunity to play on television." Again, the crowd went berserk.

Distance was not going to deter Walters from taking a shot at the big time. His father, Johnnie Walters, was likely the only black car salesman in the state of Arkansas, and he always had access to a dependable car. "They didn't let him wear a shirt and tie," Shelton says, "but he was allowed to sell cars, mostly to blacks, and that was a big deal."

So was the opportunity to play sports in the Big Ten.

That August, Bob Walters made the journey to Northwestern for preseason football. While he was immediately homesick for Arkansas and overwhelmed by the new surroundings, Walters was happy to be out of Dixie.

But something happened after the first week of practice at Northwestern. One of the coaches told Walters, "I expect you to keep your nose clean and not date the white girls."

Walters was not so much interested in white girls. He was, however, interested in escaping the mentality of the South. The orders from an assistant coach dredged up years of being treated differently because of his skin color. Now Walters realized that the North could be nearly as oppressive. He got discouraged and quietly left campus at the end of the week; a homesick small-town kid, Walters's promising football career was suddenly a wreck.

Walters had few options. Without film or statistics, hundreds of miles from home, he was in a bind. A former Northwestern assistant who'd become the coach at Augustana College asked Walters to go to the small school in western Illinois. Walters went.

Augustana was just as frustrating. "There was absolutely nothing for him to do at Augustana but play football," says Shelton Walters. "Bob had no life at all."

Regardless, Walters played, and his family would pile into a couple of cars and make the journey to see the games. The trips reminded the family of home in a way. The police in Rock Island would follow their car, both going into the city, then again on their way out of town. Shelton says, "Part of it was harassment and part was to send a message. It was to keep you in your place."

Walters quit Augustana after playing just one year.

A depressed dropout from a small college, Walters was running out of options. He bounced around in Chicago in the early 1960s, working odd jobs and attending two junior colleges. In late August one summer, he went back to Augustana for less than a week, but then enrolled at tiny North Central College in Naperville, near Chicago.

Walters was an instant sensation at North Central, and his family again began loading up the family car. But a pattern was emerging, even in Illinois. "Naperville was a small town then, not a suburb," Shelton Walters says. "The police would be waiting at the edge of town, and they would follow us into the city, into the stadium, made sure we left out of town. The police were always in our rearview mirror."

Even at North Central, Bob Walters may have been headed toward a professional career. His coach there had played in the NFL and had the connections to get Walters, by far the best player on his team, a serious tryout. But during the fourth game of his senior year, Walters tore up his knee.

"Bob's talent would have gotten him in professional football," his brother Shelton claims, barring that injury, "if the NFL would have been fair and objective."

With football in his past, Walters began a career teaching and coaching basketball at Carver High School. He rarely mentioned his stellar prep career in Prescott, and being snubbed by the University of Arkansas was nearly forgotten. But Walters would one day get a chance to thumb his nose at Razorback football.

Bob Walters's nephew Danny was only five when he moved from Arkansas to Chicago. The boy was already interested in sports, and over the years he learned bits and pieces about his uncle Bob's high school exploits from family members remaining in Prescott. Meaning, from everyone except his uncle. "Bob never talked about himself," Danny says.

When his parents divorced, Danny moved in with Bob Walters and his wife for a couple of weeks. That experiment went well, so throughout high school Danny would stay with Bob Walters's family on the weekends. During those times Bob would clear the kitchen table, take the phone off the hook, yank the television plug out of the wall, and go over schoolwork with Danny. Danny might try to change the focus to sports, but Bob rarely fell for it—unless it had to do with attitude. Bob's influence and control over Danny mushroomed.

During the Chicago summers, all the Walterses would return to Prescott. Now that he was becoming more interested in focusing on football, the stories Danny would hear about his uncle began to resonate. They always ended with the same refrain—"There's never been anyone as good as Bob Walters."

On these pilgrimages to Arkansas, Danny also became intrigued with the state's big university. Razorback shirts, posters, and fans were more prevalent in Prescott since the team began adding black players in the early 1970s.

In the summer of 1976, before anyone was aware of his own status or potential, Danny wrote a letter. He wanted to express his interest in attending his dream school on a football scholarship. The letter was to Frank Broyles.

Likely, Broyles received hundreds of letters a year asking for a chance to play for the Razorbacks. But Broyles retired from coaching and never wrote back to Danny Walters.

By Danny's junior year in Chicago, he emerged as the star of Julian High School's powerhouse 1977 football team. An explosive hitter with great quickness, Danny was ranked highly by every national recruiting service and was one of Chicago's top prospects.

One day, a letter from Arkansas showed up at Julian High School. Then several more. Lou Holtz, whom Broyles picked as his replacement football coach, sent an assistant named Bob Cope to recruit Danny that year. Cope wasn't the only recruiter to show up. Famed Ohio State coach Woody Hayes came. So did coaches from football factories like Michigan, USC, and Oklahoma. Naturally, Danny began seeking Bob Walters's advice about what school he should sign with.

Bob Walters finally had his chance, twenty years later, to get even with the University of Arkansas.

As the frequency of the phone calls increased, and the pressure was building, Bob Walters came to a realization. He wanted his nephew Danny to play football at Arkansas, despite the way the university ignored his unofficial record-setting career in 1959.

He never suggested stonewalling Arkansas, according to Danny Walters. "Bob wasn't that kind of person," he says. "He wasn't reared that way."

"Bob *encouraged* Danny to go to Arkansas," his brother Shelton says, "because it was something that he could not do himself. Bob felt a sense of accomplishment that someone from his bloodline would play for the Razorbacks, especially after he was not allowed that opportunity."

So Danny Walters did what Bob Walters could never even consider—he signed with the Razorbacks.

Twenty years after his family had driven to North Central College games, Bob Walters found himself on the reverse journey, driving back to Arkansas to follow Danny's Razorback career up close. Legions of the Walters family came up regularly from southwest Arkansas as well.

While Danny was off to a fast start as a cornerback for the Razorbacks in 1980, Bob Walters got bad news. He was diagnosed with cancer and subsequently had most of his colon removed. He continued coaching at Carver the next few years. His enthusiasm for his team got a big boost in 1981, when he first witnessed hotshot freshman Tim Hardaway dribbling the basketball between his legs as though it were on a string.

With the cancer gnawing at him, Walters still occasionally felt strong enough for the six-hundred-mile trip to Fayetteville. The Razorbacks earned three bowl game bids with Danny at defensive back. Danny would later be named to the University of Arkansas All-Decade team for the 1980s, then played five years with the NFL's San Diego Chargers—where, coincidentally, Nolan Richardson had tried out in the 1960s.

When Bob Walters came to Fayetteville, he never referred to his past, and instead was caught up in the excitement of Danny starring for the Razorbacks. "Nobody would have ever known about Bob's high school heroics," Shelton says. "Even Danny hardly knew the exact details."

While Walters remembered how the segregated system had forced him to go north, he didn't dwell on it. "I don't think Bob lost one minute of sleep over Frank Broyles," Shelton says. "Bob never expected to be recruited by Arkansas. That was part of playing in the South." While Danny was one of the team's best players, Bob Walters never met Frank Broyles.

As the cancer got worse, Walters could manage fewer trips to Razorback Stadium. He'd sleep in his car while his wife drove, gathering his strength for the Saturday showdowns. Then the unofficial leader in career high school touchdowns for the state of Arkansas would put on his red sweatshirt and cheer anonymously for his nephew and the University of Arkansas.

By the time Frank Broyles finally decided to desegregate, it was too late for the good of his team. Broyles had blown his recruiting advantage of being the only major school in the state. Terry Nelson, Cleo Miller, Ike Harris, Roscoe Word, and Ike Thomas were all black Arkansans who starred at other colleges before earning spots on NFL teams.

Yet retired professor Phillip Trapp credits Broyles with rapidly adjusting in the early 1970s. "He changed his tune and quickly began to integrate athletics," Trapp says. "I think Broyles dragged his feet, but realized that integrating was the only way he could continue to have a winning team."

And Trapp is correct about Broyles at least trying to adjust.

By 1974, two years before he quit coaching football, his Arkansas team had *twenty-eight* black players on the squad, a huge jump from the lonely Jon Richardson days of 1970. This represented 23 percent of Broyles's team, second highest in the Southwest Conference and a remarkable improvement.

Bud Zinke is long retired from his physics professorship. Today, the reluctant radical is moderately happy about the progress his university made after the senate council meeting when Broyles shocked the faculty with his "I'll go back to Georgia" declaration. "The university integrated pretty gracefully after that," Zinke says. "At that time, the football team was first and everything else was second. But Arkansas has done really well—football is not as popular as it used to be."

Zinke scoffs at any notion that Broyles championed integration at Arkansas, though. "It's really funny. After he realized that he was going to have a second-rate team, he got with it pretty smartly, but that isn't the way he started out."

Broyles was never close to being as successful once he integrated. He won six SWC titles during the Jim Crow era of Arkansas football but could manage only one SWC championship in the integrated 1970s. Regardless of integration issues, by 1976 it was clear that Broyles had become a victim of his own success in the segregated 1960s. In his final five seasons, the Razorbacks were 32-21 with three ties. He lost the last four games of his career.

Broyles still had an incredible run before that to be proud of. His teams appeared in ten bowl games, and his overall record, including his brief time as Missouri coach, was 149-62, with six ties. Within a decade of his retirement he was inducted into College Football Hall of Fame.

The willingness Frank Broyles displayed in changing his team from a publicly racist program to a pretty well-integrated one reveals what some feel is the true nature of the Arkansas icon: everything is business to Broyles. Despite his public statements at faculty senate council meetings, other behind-the-scenes moves, and the brutal humiliation of Darrell Brown, many people think Frank Broyles was mostly concerned about money. Big money boosters didn't want black athletes? Broyles would comply. The rest of the Southwest Conference was passing Arkansas, and it was hurting attendance? Broyles would recruit black athletes.

In any case, Broyles resigned from football in 1976 to concentrate solely on administrative duties. He would reinvent his career by becoming perhaps the most successful and powerful athletics director in college sports.

SEVENTEEN

ONLY TWICE I'VE WISHED FOR HEAVEN

Despite the glow of the 1994 NCAA basketball championship, another misunderstanding between Broyles and Richardson was festering. This one would irritate both men for years. In 1995, Broyles amended Richardson's job title to head basketball coach *and* assistant athletics director. Richardson was thrilled. At first.

Broyles was now in his seventies, and the question of who his successor would be was often a topic of conversation in Arkansas. Broyles told Fred Vorsanger: "If Nolan ever applies for another job, either as a coach or administrator, it will help him."

Richardson asked Broyles what his new duties would entail. Broyles admitted that there wouldn't actually be any extra responsibility. That fall, although Arkansas had a dozen assistant athletics directors and as many meetings, Richardson was never invited. Broyles told him it was a token position. Richardson says, "That was the word he used. 'Token.'"

Vorsanger says, "Broyles thought he was helping Nolan."

Richardson simply did not believe it. "I didn't need a résumé for other jobs," Richardson says. "I wanted to stay at Arkansas."

"This place is not very good at communicating," Vorsanger adds.

On the eve of the next season, with a terrific team in place, Richardson went on the offensive. "When I was playing running basketball, they called it niggerball," he told Alexander Wolff of *Sports Illustrated*. "When Rick [Pitino] did it, it was called up-tempo. If I lose, I can't coach. If I win, it's because my athletes are better."

"He seems to make a system of anger," Wolff wrote. "Players with something to prove identify with his sense of aggrievement and thrive."

Scotty Thurman agreed. "Coach talked about how nobody respected us. He was adamant about that."

Often, before playing a nationally ranked team, Richardson would work his way through the locker room, asking the players one by one if the university they were facing had actively recruited them. Since there were dozens of highly rated programs, the odds were always against it, but Richardson would still rub their collective noses in it—"Did Duke recruit *you*?"—reminding them that they were underappreciated.

Thurman says, "He used our past and under-recruitment in high school, then brainwashed people to get them to do what they needed to do."

In February of 1995, while Richardson was revamping his Razorbacks for another NCAA title run, the BCA got some unusual help from a college president.

The BCA's executive director, Rudy Washington, hinted publicly that the threat level was elevated now. It wouldn't be the coaches who acted as if the boycott planned in 1994 were still to occur. This time it would be the students. More than one hundred students marched onto the basketball court at halftime of a Rutgers game and refused to budge. The game was canceled.

Much of the furor was caused by a statement made by then-Rutgers-president Martin Lawrence, who was quoted in the *New York Times* as saying, "Do we set standards in the future so we don't admit anybody? Or do we deal with a disadvantaged population that doesn't have the genetic, hereditary background to have a higher average?" Naturally, the unfortunate folks with poor "genetic, hereditary backgrounds" were likely 6'9" and could dunk a basketball with either hand. Lawrence later backpedaled on his remarks, saying that he did not believe racial heredity could forecast academic success.

John Thompson was not buying the retraction. "This was a deep statement," he told the *New York Times*, "interjected in conversation that was intended to be handled subtly or privately."

The BCA finally got their wish, yet there was no next step. The coaches were so involved with their own teams as the NCAA Tournament approached that they couldn't muster a unified response. Writer William Rhoden saw it as a wasted chance. ". . . [T]his time the BCA missed an opportunity to ignite a movement it actually predicted. . . . The BCA has run out of threats and, in the case of Rutgers, come up short on providing direction as well," Rhoden wrote. "There was a movement in Piscataway, ready to be ignited. The BCA wasn't prepared to strike the match."

In early spring of 1995, feeling the pressure of expectations for another NCAA title, an obviously frustrated Richardson called Razorback fans "turds and assholes." The *Democrat-Gazette* printed the quote verbatim. Richardson quickly apologized, saying a very small percentage of supporters had upset him. His earlier comments about creating a monster were coming true—the fans, media, and especially the coach, all expected another NCAA title. Nobody from the university administration questioned or counseled him about the "turds and assholes" quote.

In a *Sporting News* interview in 1995 with Bob Hille, Richardson softened his tone. "There are some good, beautiful, wonderful people in Arkansas," he said. "There's a few who are always going to stick—" At this point, Richardson checked himself, concluding, "They don't want me to be successful, so they'll do anything they can or say some things that are going to affect that."

The 1994–95 Arkansas team was the favorite to win a second national title, with nearly everyone back from the 1994 title team, including the usual starters. Arkansas lost in overtime to Kentucky for the SEC Tournament championship, but that didn't hurt their tournament seeding. Then, in the NCAA playoffs, the Razorbacks struggled before beating Texas Southern, Syracuse, Memphis, and Virginia by a total of 15 points to get to the Final Four. Two of those wins were in overtime.

Just as the NCAA playoffs commenced, the United States Basketball Writers Association gave Richardson the award for Most Courageous Coach. The justification for winning the award was as much for the coach's emotional recovery after Yvonne's death as for his pioneering career. Receiving the award, however, left him raw, retrospective, and saddened. He may have been psychologically unprepared for the Final Four.

The Razorbacks beat North Carolina in the national semifinals, but they were denied a second consecutive NCAA title, losing to UCLA 89-78.

Corliss Williamson and Scotty Thurman decided to declare for the NBA draft after the season. Both were juniors, eligibility-wise. This proved to be the right move for Williamson, but Thurman went undrafted and never played a minute in the NBA. In 2007, ESPN rated Thurman as one of the "Top ten players who should have stayed in school" of all time.

The 1995–96 Razorbacks went into the season with a recruiting class that was ranked first in the nation, but the group featured mostly junior college players who would have a rough transition. In January of that season, leading scorer Jesse Pate and leading rebounder Sunday Adebayo were declared ineligible by the school because of allegations their junior college grades were improperly certified. This controversy set off an eighteen-month NCAA investigation. Despite these troubles, the Razorbacks made the NCAA Tournament, barely, as a #12 seed. They defied the odds by making the Sweet 16 after wins over Penn State and Marquette.

"There were questions by the University of Missouri, which had tried to recruit Adebayo and Pate, about their transcripts," one Arkansas insider says. "Arkansas reviewed it all, but by January they still couldn't figure out the transcripts. So it was Arkansas who made them ineligible, and it was Frank Broyles's decision, not the NCAA's. Nolan felt that Broyles had fucked him."

What happened next further angered Richardson.

"When this conflict over Pate and Adebayo became an NCAA investigation," the insider continues, "the NCAA came back and said that those kids, Pate and Adebayo, *should* have been eligible."

The Razorbacks suffered when Jesse Pate went on to the minor league CBA. Richardson believed that the school's compliance staff within the Arkansas athletics department fought for his program, but that Frank Broyles did not.

Arkansas self-imposed some penalties, most of which were mild. But one of the sanctions—no junior college players allowed for two seasons—infuriated Richardson yet again.

The story got stranger when Sunday Adebayo transferred to Memphis during the transcript trouble. While at Memphis, he led them to victory over his old school. Then he petitioned the NCAA to reconsider his grades and won the appeal. Adebayo then transferred back to Fayetteville, where he powered Arkansas to a win over, ironically, Memphis.

The following season, 1996–97, featured a stripped-down Arkansas team without junior college recruits. It also marked the first time in ten seasons that Arkansas did not earn a bid to the NCAA Tournament; instead, they settled for the NIT. They bumped off Northern Arizona, Pittsburgh, and UNLV before losing in the semifinals at Madison Square Garden. Arkansas finished the year 18-14, and 8-8 in the SEC.

In 1997, the University of Arkansas introduced Dr. John White as its new chancellor. Each of the branches within the Arkansas system—Fayetteville, Pine Bluff, Little Rock, and Monticello—has its own chancellor, but the premier job within that system is in Fayetteville. John White was excited about coming back to his alma mater after his combined twenty-two years as a Georgia Tech faculty member and dean of engineering. Nobody speculated that it might have helped White's application that Frank Broyles was a Georgia Tech graduate.

John White was a natural fit; he was bright, congenial, and had strong ties within the academic and business communities. White males, however, have traditionally dominated engineering, and his hiring raised concerns within Arkansas African-American community as to how sensitive White would be to racial issues.

White, an introspective and thoughtful academic, recognized that and understood the problems with race relations were entrenched at the university. Fortunately, White had an interesting background in seeking diversity. He'd attended the National Science Foundation convention in 1988 and looked at the national data in regard to women and minorities in his field. He returned to Georgia Tech with a fresh

reportedly said that Sam Cunningham had done more for integration in two hours than Martin Luther King Jr. had done in twenty years—a statement suggesting the basis for integration in sports was often not idealistic but exploitative.

Getting "some of those" might have been exactly what Broyles was up to when he hired Nolan Richardson. The hottest coach in the nation at that time was John Thompson, who had won the NCAA title in 1984, becoming the first black coach to do so. In 1985, Villanova squeaked by Georgetown. With Villanova's coach Rollie Massimino no longer interested, Broyles began looking for another candidate. Thompson wouldn't leave Georgetown, but Broyles decided to nab the next-hottest African-American coach.

Regardless of Broyles's motivation, his knack for hiring great coaches is nothing less than incredible, and in hiring football assistants, Broyles stands alone. His former assistant coaches have gone on to win five national championships, over forty conference titles and have combined for over two thousand victories in college. He has had forty assistants go on to be head coaches in college or the NFL.

The Rotary Club of Little Rock sponsors the only national award for assistant football coaches, the Broyles Award. The trophy depicts the coach kneeling in front of his former assistant, Wilson Matthews.

The Broyles Award reflects the lack of racial progress in college football. The selection committee members who choose the award winner are nine white men, including Broyles. No black man has ever been on the committee.

The award began in 1996. It took four years before a black man was even one of the five assistant coaches nominated. There has never been a time when more than one black man was a nominee. Sixty-seven assistants have been nominated overall. Six were black. That comes out to 8 percent, while 33 percent of assistant coaches today are black. Only once in the twelve-year history of the award has the winner been a black man. Randy Shannon of Miami won in 2001.

At the time of this writing, Randy Shannon is the only black head football coach at a top sixty-four BCS university. Like the award's namesake in the 1960s, the Broyles Award Committee can't seem to locate qualified black men.

The most obvious sign of Frank Broyles's impact on the Arkansas campus today is its incredible athletics facilities. Razorback Stadium is a breathtaking tribute to the power and place of sports at the University of Arkansas.

Next to Razorback Stadium sits the old Barnhill Arena, basketball's old home. Past that is Bud Walton Arena, the state-of-the-art basketball facility. Then the Smith Golf Center. Next is Walker Pavilion, an indoor football practice field. There is McDonnell Field for the track team, and also the Tyson Track Center for indoor races. Baum Stadium looks like a Major League baseball park.

Don't worry, many on campus assure. Athletics isn't taking a nickel away from academics, and it's not like the money would have been donated for education. "All of the facility improvements have been financed through private donations without a dollar of tax revenues," an Arkansas media guide says. In the past thirty years, with Broyles as boss, the athletics program has spent nearly $250,000,000 on building or improving athletics facilities. Athletics has an annual budget around $40,000,000.

Over the years, Broyles has ingratiated himself to the biggest money people. He is a member of Augusta National in Georgia, one of America's most affluent and exclusive golf clubs. Membership to Augusta, which is on the site of an old plantation, is by invitation only; there is no application process. Only about three hundred people are members at any one time. Augusta admitted its first black member in 1990, nearly seventy years after it opened, and no woman has ever been a member.

Yet money talks at Arkansas and in the world of college sports. After decades of covering college sports in the area, the *Tulsa World*'s longtime sportswriter Bill Connors named Frank Broyles "Best Athletics Director" in his farewell column of 1995.

EIGHTEEN

SHADOW AND ACT

In 1999, the University of Arkansas Press published *Bitters in the Honey*, a book about the Little Rock crisis of 1957 and the civil rights views of Arkansans. Beth Roy, the author, concluded, "One finding of my study in Little Rock is that white racist attitudes continue unabated, their forms and codes changed since the fifties, but not their intensity."

Chancellor John White had plenty of work to do. "Fayetteville was stunning to me," he says. "I started calling out the cheerleading squad and the pep band. There wasn't a single black student involved! I just kept hammering at it."

White set out on what he saw as part of his mission, scoring some major victories in the hiring of African-Americans. The vice chancellor of student affairs. The dean of the library. The dean of the law school. All were African-American. Nevertheless, White knew his best recruiter and spokesman could be his boisterous basketball coach—not just for athletics, but as a representative for the entire school. "One reason I felt so good about Nolan was having him here, and working with him to get across the message of how great an institution it was for everyone; it really didn't matter about your skin color."

The Razorbacks jumped out to an 8-0 start in the 1997–98 season. Their 11-5 record in the SEC scored them a return trip to the NCAA Tournament, where they topped Nebraska before losing to Utah. Arkansas finished the year 24-9. It was a satisfying year, although Richardson's team got beat by his old friend Rob Evans, who had taken over as the first black head coach at the University of Mississippi.

Richardson was already a hero in his native El Paso. Before the next season, El Paso made it official when Nolan Richardson Middle School opened in northeast El Paso.

Some of the glow of the national championship was beginning to wear off in Arkansas, though. The 1998–99 Razorbacks went 23-11 and landed another NCAA Tournament appearance. Arkansas beat Siena in the first round but lost to Iowa. Richardson was now four years past his glorious Final Four runs.

The frustrations of high expectations sometimes became apparent in Richardson's day-to-day dealings. That May, on an airplane flight, Richardson vented to football coach Houston Nutt, calling Frank Broyles both untrustworthy and a "white-haired devil."

In 1999, Head Coach and Assistant Athletics Director Nolan Richardson received a letter citing statistics from the National Association of Basketball Coaches president Jim Haney.

Haney, who is white, was disturbed. "African-American employees are the academic advisors, equipment managers, facility managers, strength coaches, and compliance coordinators," he wrote. "The athletics administration at the core management positions, administrative jobs that have the most influence on the success of the athletics department, are for white men and women only!"

According to Haney's study, African-Americans filled only 6.5 percent of "core management jobs" in Division I schools. (Division II and III were even worse.) Part of Haney's concern was that African-American basketball players, who then made up over 60 percent of the participants, would conclude that their chances for important jobs after their playing days were nearly nonexistent.

At the time of the study, 30 percent of basketball coaches—assistant and head—were African-American. But did core management opportunities actually exist for them? Or was there a ceiling? Haney asked, "Can we name African-American basketball coaches who have had the opportunity to move into athletics administration in the last five years? I cannot."

The only issue the BCA felt had been fairly addressed by the NCAA was that they had successfully sought out African-Americans for management jobs at their own headquarters. Little or nothing had been done at the university level.

Writing in his *Courtside* column for the NABC's newspaper, Haney was astounded. "Rightfully, you may ask where is the outrage? Where are the powerful voices within the NCAA structure that champion legislative changes on this matter? Where are those who would call the NCAA institutions into account for the abysmal hiring of African-Americans and people of color to core management positions?"

Richardson read Jim Haney's column and accompanying statistics, then brooded. With Christmas of 1999 only five days away, he composed a letter to Frank Broyles. In part, Richardson wrote:

During our meeting, you commented that you viewed my appointment as Assistant Athletics Director as a "token" appointment. The more I think about this, the more it frustrates and disappoints me. I viewed my appointment back in 1995 as a significant advancement in my career. I looked forward to learning more about the inner workings of the entire athletics department at the University of Arkansas. As you may recall, I previously served as Athletics Director at Western Texas Junior College, and as Assistant Athletics Director at Tulsa. I particularly looked forward to offering you my services and skills in negotiations, and my knowledge of endorsements to assist the department when you were dealing with shoe and apparel contracts. This of course did not come to pass, and I now understand why.

Richardson wanted a clarification of his assigned role—or, rather, he wanted an authentic role, and not a token appointment. He was now considering whether or not to resign from this appointment, given its lack of substance. His letter continued:

Like you, I love the University of Arkansas and want to help the school in many ways, but not as a token.

I have never looked upon any position I have had in my life in a token way. I have worked my entire career to prove that I deserve every opportunity that I have been given. I would never accept a position just for the sake of appearances.

Three days later, Broyles faxed a letter back to his basketball coach. "I have received your letter and I understand your feelings," he wrote. "I will respond to you after the holidays."

Another burr in Richardson's boots was that Broyles undercut the shoe deal Richardson had with Converse, working out an agreement with Reebok to outfit all of the university's athletic teams. Shoe companies buying up entire athletics departments is common today, but at that time it was a new development. Richardson felt he had earned his shoe money; the lesser sports, which would benefit so greatly, had not. Later, the university would buy out Richardson's Converse deal, which helped monetarily, but the coach could not help but feel sabotaged by Broyles again.

On January 15, 2000, still waiting on a response to his letter from Broyles, Richardson went public about his "token" status as an assistant athletics director. He simply did not want to be used as a statistic if there were no extra duties—or pay. Richardson's complaints were reported only in local newspapers.

Then, on January 17, 2000, Richardson again brought up his situation in the *Morning News* newspaper. When the journalist pointed out that other assistant ADs, the white ones, had been in similar circumstances, Richardson remained unconvinced. "Those guys can go ahead and stay that way because they've got guys their color doing things for them," he said. "What about me? Who sits in that hallway up there to represent us? I don't. Do I help make decisions? No, sir. I've never been asked a question, I've never been in a meeting. So why use me as an assistant AD for affirmative action? I'm not an Uncle Tom."

On January 25, 2000—now the wait for Broyles's written response was gnawing at him—Richardson wrote a second letter. The subject this time was the disparity in pay between basketball and football assistant coaches. Richardson had raised the issue in a 1997 letter, and Broyles had justified the pay differences then by citing experience. Broyles couldn't use that excuse this time. The pay differential had become even greater when Houston Nutt became football coach in 1998. Richardson's top assistant, Mike Anderson, had more experience than any of the football assistants, and had been coaching in Fayetteville for well over a decade.

Richardson copied the letter to both Chancellor John White and University of Arkansas system president Alan Sugg.

Richardson could not have picked a less opportune time to challenge the Arkansas power structure. His 1999–2000 team struggled all year. They finished the regular SEC season at 7-9, Richardson's worst mark since joining the more competitive league.

On February 17, 2000, Broyles addressed Richardson's second letter, admitting to the obvious. Pay disparities existed between Arkansas's assistant football and basketball coaches. Since experience could not logically be cited, Broyles attempted to justify the difference by saying it was "required by the marketplace"—an odd logic indeed from the man who controlled the money within the entire multimillion-dollar business that was Arkansas athletics. There was yet to be a written response to Richardson's pre-Christmas letter.

Broyles also forwarded copies of his own letter to John White and Alan Sugg. But he included a cover letter to them, saying that matters of this nature should be resolved between Richardson and himself. Broyles said that by sending White and Sugg a copy of his letter, Richardson had followed "inappropriate protocol." Richardson was not sent a copy of Broyles's cover letter to his superiors.

That same day, Richardson got into a heated discussion with Wally Hall, the sports editor of the *Democrat-Gazette*. Hall and Richardson often reverted to the usual complaints about each other: Hall wasn't fair; Richardson was too sensitive. Near the end of the argument, Richardson claims he called Hall a "redneck." That is not how it was reported in the next day's news. Hall wrote that Richardson had called the Razorback *fans* "redneck SOBs."

The following day, former football star and board of trustees fixture Jim Lindsey claimed he got a call from an irate fan demanding Richardson be fired for the statement. Lindsey, who was close with Broyles, phoned his former coach to express those concerns. The fan was never identified, but suddenly the feelings of the fans—which had mattered little in the firing of successful UA football coaches over the years—became paramount. Broyles never asked Richardson about

Wally Hall's column, or if the quotes were taken out of context.

The annual banquet for senior football players was that very evening. Broyles approached a table of media representatives—all white, of course—to grumble about Richardson's comments. Just a few days earlier, Broyles had complained to the chancellor and system president about Richardson voicing grievances through inappropriate channels. Now Broyles was about to do the unthinkable.

Broyles asked one of the writers at the table to publish an article that equated Richardson's use of the word "redneck" with a white person using the word "nigger."

The media table was dumbfounded, both at Broyles's public use of the word "nigger" and at his bizarre request. One writer later said that Broyles was animated and raised his voice. Black football players were seated at the next table, and the writer reached for Broyles's arm, asking him to lower his voice. Later that night, Broyles cornered the writer again, saying that the article needed to be written.

Redneck = nigger.

Of course, he emphasized, the comparison should leave out the name "Frank Broyles."

The writer later confided to Richardson that Broyles had tried to push him into doing that article. Richardson asked the writer to record his recollection on tape, and the writer agreed.

What would remain a source of debate in Arkansas was not that Broyles publicly used the word "nigger," and wanted major Arkansas media sources to write about niggers and rednecks. Rather, the question centered on whether Broyles *himself* compared the two terms or if Broyles was *reporting* on the feelings of mysterious "fans."

Paul Eells, the sports anchor for KATV and host of Richardson's weekly television show, later said he was shocked by Broyles's prodding of the journalists and believed the comments to be Broyles's own sentiments. Other media representatives understood the comments to mean Broyles was quoting someone else.

"Frank thought he was made of Teflon," one of Arkansas's longtime sportswriters says. Indeed, Broyles was. Not a single media member wrote about Broyles's bizarre request or criticized him in print.

On February 28, 2000, Broyles wrote back to Richardson again, this time to answer Richardson's letter from over two months earlier. Several factors, Broyles wrote, contributed to this delayed response. ". . . [T]he holidays, the football postseason activity, blocked arteries . . . football stadium debates." Broyles also wrote about ". . . the unexpected nature of your letter, both in timing and content."

Broyles pointed out that Eddie Sutton and successful track coach John McDonnell held the role of assistant athletics director while they were coaching. "In each instance," he wrote, "the title was assigned as a symbolic gesture of respect for contributions to our athletics programs. . . . This title designation . . . has never been and is not currently intended to change any job duties. Given these circumstances, please let me know your decision regarding the title."

In regard to NABC boss Jim Haney's claims, Broyles said that ". . . each and every point is well taken and should be an area of concern."

Broyles could not resist a final parting shot. "One of the virtues of Chancellor White's emphasis on increased graduation rates is the increased availability of qualified former athletes who have attained their degrees."

Was Broyles taking a swipe at Richardson for the graduation rate among black players? Probably. In two years, Richardson's players' graduation rate during his championship years would become a national story. But for Broyles, the solution was simple and easy. If Richardson would simply *graduate* more players, then Broyles would *hire* them as associate athletics directors.

———

Tensions between Broyles and Richardson had reached the boiling point. With the Razorbacks playing their worst ball in a decade in February of 2000, Broyles felt that he had the upper hand. He could have removed Richardson before the SEC Tournament but likely figured the coach would fall on his face—and prove to everyone in Arkansas that he had lost his touch. Just like in 1987, Broyles began quiet preparations to dump the coach, although this time Richardson was acutely aware going into the SEC Tournament that Broyles wanted him gone.

The Razorbacks played Georgia first, but even if they won, they'd have to get by three teams, including powerhouse Kentucky. Despite winning an NCAA title and three Final Four births to his credit, Richardson had never won the SEC Tournament title.

Arkansas rolled over Georgia, then the nationally ranked Kentucky and LSU. In the SEC finals they beat Auburn, and the Razorbacks were the 2000 SEC Tournament champions. The state was awash again in praise for Richardson. Sophomore guard Brandon Dean was voted the tournament MVP, and the team was back in the NCAAs. Despite losing to University of Miami in the first round the following week, Richardson's renewed popularity kept Broyles from firing him.

Broyles likely learned a lesson. With Richardson on the sideline, even a weak Razorback team could not be counted out of the SEC Tournament. He wouldn't make that mistake again. For now, he was stuck with Richardson and forced to sign him to a six-year rollover contract for a million dollars a year just before the next season began. Despite the big money, the tumultuous year had left Richardson cautious, angry, and resentful. His relationship with Broyles—America's most powerful athletics director—was now beyond repair.

Jim Haney, who authored the column that rattled Richardson, has directed the NABC for years. Although championing the cause of minority coaches is not part of the NABC's mission, Haney and his top aide Reggie Minton have helped initiate change, especially within the NCAA's own offices. Haney has witnessed a new emphasis. "In the 1970s there was a big issue as to whether you just had an African-American on your staff in football and basketball," he says.

Haney actually worries about what college basketball players think. "It would have benefited Arkansas and minorities both if there were contributing minority athletics directors at the school," he says. "In the college setting, if I'm an African-American player I might be thinking, 'What will I do, how can I stay involved in athletics?' But when it comes time to make decisions to see about the future, they think, 'I don't see anyone like me within the athletics department.'"

The new breed of young black coaches who were not politically inclined irked Richardson. Within the BCA, there was a fundamental disagreement about the group's purpose. Did the BCA exist to help young black assistant coaches? Or did it exist to use its influence in helping black kids get more scholarship opportunities?

Much of the debate likely stemmed from the background of the group's big three. Neither Richardson, nor John Thompson, nor John Chaney had ever been assistant coaches. The trio never used the BCA to secure job interviews or boost their own standing. Richardson and Chaney had taken the long road at unknown schools. Thompson, while a former Boston Celtic, had landed the Georgetown job when it was considered a graveyard for coaches. None of the three, when they were younger, had heard their names trumpeted on ESPN as deserving of a college job.

John Chaney asked the BCA to take his name off the group's letterhead. Richardson, Thompson, and George Raveling followed suit. Chaney said, "The organization has really deserted the kids as far as I'm concerned."

———

In February of 2000, sportswriter Orville Henry was hospitalized to have his gall bladder removed. Doctors found a malignant tumor on his pancreas. Richardson began checking on Henry every day. It was the most time he had spent around hospitals since Yvonne had passed away.

While Orville Henry was the godfather of sportswriters in Arkansas, some insiders criticize him, calling him a "mouthpiece" for Frank Broyles. Richardson never felt that way about Henry, though, and had great admiration for him.

Until his illness, Orville Henry sat in the middle of the Broyles-Richardson feud, keeping in touch with both men. Richardson claims that Henry told him Broyles had complained about the basketball coach's whopping salary. "That nigger is making too much money," is the way Richardson recalls Henry's account.

Regardless, Henry was another in a long line of older men on whom Richardson leaned for advice and friendship. This seems to dispel another theory heard from time to time in Arkansas, that Nolan Richardson was a racist who hated white people. What person who hated whites would hang around with crusty old guys like Don Haskins, Sid Simpson, Ed Beshara, and Orville Henry? The ways they became friends and the nature of the relationships were varied. They were Richardson's coach, boss, lunch buddy, and scribe.

Even the players noticed the pattern after a few years. Clint McDaniel, whose ball-hawking defense earned him a brief NBA career, says it's ridiculous to insinuate that Richardson is racist. "Nolan hardly had any black friends," he says. "The people who traveled with him and his genuine friends, they were mostly white."

"These are authentic friendships," longtime Arkansas judge Wendell Griffen says. "This notion that Nolan is racist, it's all part of the disinformation campaign. The tendency to believe what isn't true is easier," Griffen adds, "when you don't care what the truth is."

———

The new millennium brought harder times for Razorback basketball, at least by the standards that Nolan Richardson had set.

During the 2001 regular season, the Razorbacks lost their first three SEC games, but turned things around to finish 10-6 in league play. While they were waiting for the postseason SEC Tournament, a strange thing happened.

Richardson continued to enjoy his scenic ranch. The rolling hills and gorgeous views were a tonic for him and Rose, and he relied on the ranch the way other coaches depended on a drink. When the usual pressures of a college season piled up, Richardson resorted to finding solace there. "When I'm worried about things, I get on my horse and clear my brain," he says.

With the SEC Tournament looming that March, Richardson went for a walk. He noticed a path of blood. With sweat pooling in his palms, Richardson tiptoed along the trail until he came upon his beloved horse, Tulula, moaning in the grass. She had been shot with a high-powered rifle.

"Whoever did this knows who I am and where my farm is," Richardson said.

No arrests were ever made after Tulula's shooting. The horse survived, but the incident rattled Richardson, and he made comments to the effect that he would reevaluate his career at Arkansas.

Arkansas was awarded an NCAA bid in 2001, but again lost in the first round, this time in a shocker to Georgetown. The score was tied 63-63 when a Hoyas's substitute barely beat both buzzers—shot clock and game clock—to sink the winning shot. After officials watched replays, the basket was allowed. Arkansas ended the season 20-11. A few weeks later, Richardson's best player, sophomore Joe Johnson, announced he was leaving Arkansas early for the NBA.

A record of 20-11 is a fine season for most coaches, but Richardson was now seven years past his NCAA championship. Chancellor John

White noticed the change in Richardson's demeanor that season, and he met with Richardson privately.

"Nolan would make these statements," White recalls "that in northwest Arkansas there was nothing for black students to do." In an era where a prospective student's social-life options were increasingly important, Richardson's statements irritated the football coaches—and Frank Broyles—as well as the university administration. "I don't think he realized what a negative impact that was having on everybody's ability to try to recruit," White adds, "including our ability to recruit students."

In fact, according to White, football coach Houston Nutt went to Frank Broyles to complain about the statements. Broyles, in turn, discussed Richardson's comments with White. White then met with Richardson and asked him a single question: "What can I do to help you?"

Richardson cited general concerns on the challenges ahead, both for the basketball team and for the entire university.

Then Richardson asked White, "What can I do for you?"

The two men held each other's gaze for a moment. White, more than most administrators, could occasionally step away from his job and shed his suit and job title—the propriety of being an administrator sometimes seemed a burden to White. He leaned across the table, straining for Richardson, although the coach's hand was beyond reach.

"I need you to be *happy*," White said. "I need that to be obvious to the people you come in contact with. I don't think you realize that how you come across has far-reaching implications for what I am trying to accomplish here at the university."

Richardson assured White that he would try to be happy. "I came back and put it in a memo to him," White recalls.

NINETEEN

THINGS FALL APART

With **Joe Johnson** leaving for the NBA, the Razorbacks were bound to struggle throughout the 2001–02 season. Their schedule was rated the most difficult in the country by some experts, and included Wake Forest, Oklahoma, Illinois, Tulsa, Memphis—and Eddie Sutton's Oklahoma State team, which beat Arkansas just before Christmas.

As the season progressed, Richardson's frustration festered. In January of 2002, the Razorbacks lost four SEC games in a row for the first and only time in Richardson's tenure. Soon after, the coach was told by administrators that he had to control his comments on his own weekly television show. "Arkansas attempted to muzzle Richardson," *Sports Illustrated* wrote later, "prohibiting him from speaking out on matters of racial discrimination." The school wanted Richardson to sign a contract stressing that he would ". . . not directly or indirectly, disparage the Producer, the University of Arkansas, the [Razorback] Foundation, or any sponsor of the show for any reason." Such contracts and language are not uncommon, but Richardson took it as a direct attack. "It is this issue that seems to have pushed Richardson over the top," *Sports Illustrated* claimed.

On February 23, 2002, after a loss at Kentucky, Richardson was quoted nationally as saying, "If they go ahead and pay me my money, they can take the job tomorrow. I'm glad I don't have to answer to anyone but myself and my god upstairs. That's the only people I answer to, for real. I'll answer to the chancellor and the athletics director, but fans and things of that nature, I don't answer to those people."

The comments were interpreted by the media as several things— venting frustration, a challenge, a genuine offer to Arkansas administrators, and Richardson's interest in retiring.

Richardson's press conference in Kentucky happened to be the same weekend that the university was hosting the SEC track meet in Fayetteville. When Chancellor John White walked into the hospitality tent on Sunday, the press cornered him.

White said he was not yet aware of Richardson's comments. Newsmen relayed Richardson's claim: "If they go ahead and pay me my money, they can take the job tomorrow."

"It must have been just out of the frustration of the moment," White says, "and losing at Kentucky. I couldn't figure out what it was about. I left the track meet, went to the basketball arena where our women were playing, and saw the arena manager, Fred Vorsanger."

Vorsanger said, "There goes Nolan again. He said the same thing to me before he left for Kentucky."

"You're kidding," White said.

Vorsanger was not, although he himself had joked with Nolan to "take me with you. I'll carry the money."

White now concluded that Nolan's comments were premeditated and that he had not simply reacted in anger. "I had a lot of time to think about it," White says, "and what I came around to was this. If I had a dean or vice chancellor who made that statement, they wouldn't hold their position another week."

With two games to go in the SEC, the critical league tournament was just around the corner. White believed that he and Frank Broyles needed to meet with Richardson in a hurry—the coach was returning from Kentucky that very day—to find out the source of the trouble, and either allow Richardson to resign or get him pointed back in the right direction.

The meeting with Richardson that Sunday never took place. "Here's where I made a mistake," White says. "I said to Frank Broyles, okay, let's meet with Nolan tomorrow morning and tell him we're going to go ahead and do what he says, we're going to pay him his money and he can leave." Barring an all-out apology from Richardson, White says, they were going to accept his resignation.

Broyles told White, "I can't do it. I'm leaving early in the morning to Augusta to play golf."

Broyles was scheduled to return Wednesday night, the same night Richardson would be playing at Mississippi State. Richardson would be back Thursday. They agreed to delay meeting with Richardson until then.

"That was a huge mistake," White says of the missed opportunity for him and Broyles to meet with Richardson. The meeting that never took place, however, would have likely been for damage control. By the end of the evening on that Sunday, nearly all of the board of trustees had been notified. Frank Broyles, John White, and University of Arkansas system president Alan Sugg had decided to end Richardson's tenure. His contract had a clause that allowed the university to terminate Richardson "at the convenience of the University."

Pressure leads to bad decisions, Richardson had told his teams for years. The pressure of losing, his horse being shot, his deteriorated relationship with Frank Broyles, and simple exhaustion culminated in

Richardson's outburst. When Arkansas lost to Kentucky that weekend, they had lost nine of their last twelve games.

"I've earned the right to have the type of season I'm having," Richardson was often quoted as saying that month. Broyles must have disagreed.

Could John White have put out the fire if he had gotten Nolan Richardson alone? Perhaps he could have persuaded him to clarify his comments after the Kentucky game, or even apologize, to admit he was blowing off steam. At the very least, White believes he could have helped to avoid the disastrous press conference yet to come, on Monday.

White adds, "I think John Chaney and a civil rights attorney, lots of people got to Nolan and got him cranked up, frankly. Had we met on Monday, I think it would have been a much calmer kind of discussion and there would have been all kinds of movement on our part to try to negotiate something that Nolan would feel comfortable with." Instead, White huddled with university attorneys. "I just knew that if we didn't handle it well, we'd all be heading to court," he says.

With Broyles on a golf holiday at the historically all-white Augusta National Golf Club, things went from bad to worse.

"That's why I said I made a huge mistake," White says, a rare admission for a college administrator. "Frank [Broyles] had a number of major donors he was taking to Augusta for golf, so I thought, okay, let's just do it on Thursday. But as I look back, I just beat myself up over it. We should have done it on Monday. We should have had the discussion then. It was a contentious relationship all the time that I was here, between Frank and Nolan, and I kind of got tired of it. After a while you just say, my goodness, this obviously doesn't seem like it's going to work out."

Broyles had attempted to remove Richardson in 1987, then again in 2000, after White's arrival at the university—and those seasons went better for the Razorbacks than the 2002 season. As the losses mounted, Richardson knew Broyles would be pushing to fire him once again. The chancellor was a decent and caring man, but that would be of little consequence when it came to controlling Broyles.

On Monday, February 25, with no word from either the chancellor or the athletics director, Richardson hosted the rambling Monday press conference, and his comments were broadcast nationally, as he directed. The vast majority of viewers would have had no sense of Richardson's history, his battles to bust through a segregated profession, that his grandmother's parents had been slaves, or that his director of athletics preferred he fail. Without that perspective, it appeared that Richardson had simply lost his way.

Democrat-Gazette's sports editor Wally Hall wrote, "This season no one in the UA administration or on the board of trustees has been anything but supportive of Richardson." The ensuing trial during Richardson's lawsuit would prove Hall's claim to be spurious—depending on your sense of humor and what your idea of "supportive" was. Yet Hall also added, "Not long ago I wrote in this space that Richardson deserves this as a grace season. That sentiment still holds. If Nolan Richardson really still wants the job."

Wednesday, the Razorbacks played at Mississippi State, where they lost, 89-83. Afterward, Richardson's tone was much more sedate at the customary postgame press conference. He apologized to "99 percent of the fans" and some of the media for his statements on Monday. He admitted he was guilty of stereotyping in the same way he had been stereotyped for years. Richardson was quoted in the *Democrat-Gazette* as saying, ". . . Arkansas fans are the greatest fans in America. . . . If there's an apology, I give that. Because the fans and the people that I've lived around in Fayetteville are great, wonderful people . . ."

Even so, the coach would not retreat from his claim that he was regarded differently as the Arkansas coach because of his skin color. "I'm not treated differently from a fan standpoint," he said. "But everybody who follows college basketball or follows the Razorbacks or are being honest with themselves know that what I have said is a true fact. It's absolutely true. When you think about what I really said, you need to ask the question, is it true? Some will say, 'But he didn't have to say it.'"

Americans are notorious for lacking any sense of history, and white Americans are particularly forgetful—intentionally or not—about issues of race. Should Richardson have kept silent while his team struggled in 2002? While much of Arkansas white power-structure, both at the university and around the state, had heard enough over the years, most of that state's black population and a surprising number of closeted white progressives thought Richardson was both invigorating and important. Richardson could no more change his blunt honesty than he could begin ordering his teams to slow down and play more conservatively.

Would Richardson have been fired if he had been white? This simple question begs asking, but the answer is complicated. The kind of support and patience Richardson would have been given by Broyles, the media, and the fans in the state over the years would have been altered. How would his teams have performed if the coach could have focused his energies on winning, rather than believing that his boss preferred for him to fail? Defenders of Frank Broyles, ironically, like to point out that Broyles fired every football coach over the years—why should the basketball coach be any different?

After that Wednesday's Mississippi State game, Richardson told the press that he had addressed the Razorbacks on the subject of who would be their coach in the future. "I tell my players, don't fret for me, baby. If I get to leave the University of Arkansas, I graduated, and I did it my way."

He also said he believed his tenure at Tulsa and Arkansas "made it a better place for people to live and to have respect, because they know that I wasn't no Uncle Tom and I'm not politically going to tell you what you want to hear all the time." The coach was again both defiant and conciliatory. He mentioned having to answer to the school's president and to Frank Broyles. "I do apologize for things I've done wrong. . . . I'm not above that, and I've done that tonight."

Richardson was looking back, not looking forward. "If it comes to pass they're going to buy out my contract, I'm not going to be disappointed. Not at all," he said. "Because, see, the Good Lord brought me to Arkansas. When I was a kid growing up, I was afraid of Arkansas, Mississippi—where I am right now—and Alabama . . . I'm very proud of the fact that I started with five or six black coaches in the country, and now there's more than thirty-nine."

March 1, 2002. Less than a week had passed since the Kentucky game. Chancellor John White and Frank Broyles came to Richardson's office and gave him a choice. White suggested that Richardson could resign and coach the final home game against Vanderbilt, enjoy the adulation of the crowd one last time. Richardson was defiant. "You're going to have to fire my ass," he said.

White informed Richardson that the university would then be buying out his contract and paying him for six more years. After the meeting, White jotted down pages of notes, and his lengthy transcription was later published, wholly intact. The notes included Richardson saying that if he were fired, blacks would take the UA campus back to 1957—presumably to the Little Rock crisis—and that there would need to be tanks on campus because of picketing.

White denied that the meeting had been tape-recorded. "If you had been there in that meeting, you would have remembered it, too." White told the *Democrat-Gazette* that he didn't take any notes while the meeting was in progress.

White's transcription of the meeting would haunt Richardson

publicly and White privately. "For several days, when I would close my eyes and try to go to sleep at night, it was like it was a videotape, it would just start replaying that whole meeting," White said.

Richardson spent a lot of time during the ninety-minute meeting asking what would happen to longtime assistant coach Mike Anderson. The administrators promised Richardson that Anderson would be interviewed for the now-open job. Richardson knew that this meant a courtesy interview only.

When the meeting was nearly over, White said to Broyles, "Coach, would you mind if I had some time alone with Coach Richardson?"

Broyles complied, leaving the chancellor and the coach alone.

According to both White and Richardson, the chancellor reached out and put his hand on Richardson's. "Nolan," he asked, "would you pray with me?"

Richardson says, "I was surprised. I didn't know what to do." But he bowed his head. Richardson was cognizant of the historical implications of this gesture—the Bible had been used to sedate blacks in the Old South for centuries. And today, Richardson grudgingly admits that there is much to admire about John White. He's caring, smart, and sensitive.

What White was not, however, was more powerful than Broyles. Richardson knew it was difficult to hold that against White. By all accounts, White had attempted to wrestle control of the university away from Broyles, and he was rebuffed by the board of trustees.

As White finished his prayers, Richardson came to understand that White was genuine—he really was asking for help from a higher power. But the entity with higher power had already left the office, at White's request.

ESPN aired a program the same day Nolan Richardson was fired, an interview with the coach that had been prerecorded in January. The timing could not have been worse for him.

The ESPN interview included John White and Richardson discussing the just-published graduation rate of black players at Arkansas. The NCAA had released the study of black players at every Division I basketball program. The results, for black basketball players who entered as freshmen between 1990 and 1994, were based on a formula that evaluated whether a degree was received within six years of enrolling.

Richardson was the focus of the interview partly because the last year of the study was the season his Razorbacks won the NCAA title. ESPN compared the Razorbacks' rate to that of Duke, a private school that had a terrific percentage for graduation. Arkansas had not graduated a single black player during the specified time, 1990–94. Richardson said that the ultimate responsibility lay with each individual player, not the coach or administration.

The list of schools with a graduation rate of 0 percent included a lot more than Nolan Richardson's Razorbacks. Many of the schools were basketball powers with renowned coaches: Georgia Tech (Bobby Cremins), James Madison (Lefty Driesell), LSU (Dale Brown), Oregon State, Texas Tech, Cincinnati (Bob Huggins), Hawaii (Riley Wallace), Louisville (Denny Crum), Nevada, Pacific (Bob Thomason), Wyoming, Utah State, Virginia Commonwealth, Colorado, Long Beach State, Cal State–Sacramento, Cleveland State, Eastern Washington, Georgia Southern, Jacksonville State, McNeese State, Morehead State, Samford, SW Missouri (now Missouri State), Idaho, Memphis, Minnesota (Clem Haskins), UNLV, Oklahoma, UTEP (Don Haskins), Texas Pan-American, Toledo, and Wisconsin-Milwaukee.

The ESPN program did more to damage Richardson's reputation than any other single story and would be used repeatedly to justify his firing.

———

A few days later, *Democrat-Gazette* sports editor Wally Hall wrote a piece in response to all the media requests for the usually low-profile Arkansas press corps. He wrote that many of the inquirers wanted to know, "Has the media in Arkansas treated Nolan Richardson with kid gloves out of fear of being called racist?"

Hall wrote, "What everyone saw Monday night, Nolan Richardson's anger, was something the media in Arkansas has experienced dozens of times. We called it the real 'forty minutes of hell.' This time, though, he did it with cameras running and everyone got to see why he has been stroked and petted by the press for seventeen years. We've walked around on eggshells for years because of Richardson's anger."

The tension was clearly a two-way street between Hall and Richardson. When Little Rock civil rights attorney John Walker was asked by the same newspaper if he would be representing Richardson, he said, "Unless coach asks me to do something for him, then I'm not authorized to say one way or another, especially to the *Democrat*."

There was still one more home game to play, and assistant coach Mike Anderson took the helm. Arkansas beat Vanderbilt, but the following week they lost to Tennessee in the first round of the SEC tourney. In both games, the Razorback players wrote the name of their deposed coach on their sneakers to honor him.

"I was shocked, totally shocked," Temple coach John Chaney recalls. "My president made it very clear that when I got ready to express my opinion, I could." While Chaney was disappointed in Arkansas's chancellor, he likes to remind people that John White was not the only higher-up who did not stand up for the coach. "Neither did [then-governor] Mike Huckabee, and he's an Evangelist! That's the house of righteousness? You can't dismiss the truth that was spoken by Nolan."

Huckabee did, in fact, weigh in. He told the Associated Press, "I think [Richardson is] one of the truly great people I've known, and I have appreciated that he has overcome more than most people. That's one of the things that a lot of people now don't fully comprehend. They haven't walked in his shoes. They haven't taken his journey. They may not fully understand some of the deep feelings that he carries inside. There's a wonderful success story in Nolan Richardson."

Richardson also received a letter of support from Huckabee, which read, in part, "Please don't let the critics and the media wear you down. I know from experience it's exasperating when those with small minds and big mouths seem to have all the answers. I face those types of people every day."

Chaney understands Richardson's refusal to sugarcoat statements during tough times. Before Temple played Xavier, Chaney had criticized the invasion of Iraq. "I made it very clear about Bush," Chaney says. "This man is guilty of treason and guilty of making a decision to kill our kids. In Ohio, they'd lost half a million jobs." Chaney found himself greeted by a hostile crowd, and got an escort to and from the bench by Ohio state troopers.

When Temple returned to Philadelphia, Chaney was pulled out of practice. It was ex-president Bill Clinton calling to thank Chaney for speaking up.

On March 9, the *St. Petersburg Times* ran a piece by Darrell Fry called "Don't Play the Race Card if You Can't Cover the Bet." Fry wrote, "These days the race card is tossed out like worthless lottery tickets." Then Darrell Fry brought out a card of his own, the one that would repeatedly be used to bury Richardson—the graduation-rate card. Zero percent from 1990 to 1994.

NABC director Jim Haney thinks that Richardson's graduation rate for that period is not entirely accurate. "Nolan had guys leaving to go to the NBA early," he says. "The way the graduation rate was determined then, it didn't count freshmen who transferred and graduated! Junior college kids didn't count and weren't factored in at all, and Nolan had lots of those guys. There's simply a high transfer rate among college players, and that can affect the way the percentages are calculated. You have to really study Nolan's circumstances. Now the APR [academic progress report, which factors in junior college players and transfers] gives you a more accurate rate." Corliss Williamson and Scotty Thurman, Haney points out, were the two most visible players, and they left school early for the professional ranks. Others would play pro ball in Europe.

Alex Dillard was the third-leading scorer on Arkansas's 1994 NCAA champs but wasn't as productive off the court, and he did not graduate with his class. Over a decade later, he is completing his degree requirements at home in Alabama. He takes the blame for his delay in graduation.

"Nolan didn't give a shit about us making it in basketball," he says. "He was more concerned about us succeeding in the real world. 'Your skills can only last this long,' he'd say. Now I truly understand what he meant. He was trying to prepare us for life. If we missed a day of class he would run our ass until we dropped."

The media's perception of Richardson's academics and the weak graduation numbers from 1990–94 exposed by the NCAA's study were not indicators of Richardson's priorities, Dillard claims. "Coach *said* it wasn't his job on TV, but that's all he cared about. School." Almost everyone close to the Razorbacks' basketball program—even players disgruntled about playing time—say that Richardson talked about education and opportunity constantly.

Scotty Thurman, whose three-pointer sealed the Razorbacks NCAA title in 1994, left Arkansas before his eligibility was up. The NBA didn't work out, but gigs in Greece and Italy paid nearly as well. When his long career in Europe was over, Thurman finished his degree in English at the historically black Philander Smith College in Little Rock. Today he works for a real estate company.

Thurman believes Richardson's policy of running his players as punishment for academic problems was a mistake, since running does not directly improve academic performance. "Looking back, I feel like there were some things that could have been done differently," Thurman says. "If a guy is coming to school for hoops, running only helps him get better on the basketball floor."

Thurman had both parents at home, and his father had played college ball at Grambling. "But a lot of the players didn't have both parents like I did. A lot didn't have a strong father figure, and they looked up to Coach Richardson." Thurman believes Richardson should have held players out of games for missing class, not just punished them by running. "If your son was coming to play for me," he says, "isn't it my responsibility to get him to go to class? Some of those guys came from tough situations."

Sometimes players were simply not interested in graduating. "Nolan had a player named Arlin Bowers," trainer Dave England recalls, "a great kid whose dream was to be a firefighter." Bowers would often insist that firefighters didn't need a college degree. Today, Bowers is a firefighter near Memphis. "It may surprise some people to learn that Nolan stressed academics all the time," England says.

In this respect, Richardson was a paradox—he stressed opportunity and education to his players daily but lashed out at critics who questioned his graduation rate, saying it wasn't his job to graduate players. Rather than admit to common academic shortcomings during his tenure—dozens of schools were on the same list—Richardson went on the attack. Rather than bragging (as he saw it) that he did indeed stress academic success, he confronted the very premise of their criticism.

TWENTY

MAKES ME WANNA HOLLER

The firing of Nolan Richardson left the black residents of Arkansas and black alumni bitter. After 2002, even moves the university made to diversify were viewed with suspicion. Old wounds opened, reminding the black community of Arkansas of the years of deception and delay at the university.

His dismissal spurred students, alumni, and faculty to consider reforms in the process of how UA recruited African-American students, as well as the manner in which the university hired and promoted minority faculty.

The African-American studies program at the University of Arkansas is part of the school's Fulbright College. J. William Fulbright, president of the University of Arkansas from 1939 until 1941, went on to be a U.S. senator for thirty years. He was one of the first senators to condemn the United States' invasion of Vietnam; before that, Fulbright stood up to the bullying and Communist witch hunts of Senator Joe McCarthy.

Charles Robinson, head of the African-American studies program, says the Fulbright name (and the seven-foot statue of him outside) reminds him of the daily complexities of living in the South. "Fulbright was an avowed racist. He's turning over in his grave right now, over the very existence of my program."

While Robinson admires Nolan Richardson, he was taken aback by the coach's comments after his graduation rate from 1990–94 was revealed, and was confused by Richardson's explanation on ESPN.

Robinson believes the Arkansas story is complicated. He is proud of the university, pointing out that it was the first major white university in the South to integrate. Yet the firing of Richardson left him shaking his head. "After all he's done, this man still can't control his own destiny. His time was up when his boss, the white athletics director, said it was up."

Arkansas did not take long to find a replacement for Nolan Richardson. With a lawsuit likely, the new hire was no surprise— African-American coach Stan Heath. Heath had just finished an incredible run in his first year as coach of Kent State, where they won thirty games and came within a single win of going to the NCAA Final Four.

Many felt the hiring of Heath was a deliberate move to avoid a lawsuit. "Absolutely, Heath was hired to keep the racial tension down," says Fayetteville *Morning News* sports editor Chip Souza. And most blacks in Arkansas believed that the hiring of Heath was cynical and cosmetic. "You can't fix the *Titanic* by changing out the deck chairs," Judge Wendell Griffen told the *Democrat-Gazette*.

In the spring of 2002, the enrollment of black students at UA was close to 6 percent, well below the 16 percent makeup of the state's population. Blacks also made up less than 4 percent of the UA faculty. Judge Griffen believed that the dismissal of Richardson would make things even worse. "Same song, different verse," Griffen said. "If the university didn't deal fairly with Nolan Richardson, then hiring a new [African-American] coach does nothing."

Professor Charles Robinson acknowledges that the bar was set high for Heath, who would have had to win *two* NCAA titles and earn four Final Four berths to surpass Richardson. "I feel the hiring was calculated, definitely," Robinson says. "I'm not saying Stan Heath wasn't a deserving coach, but as quickly as he was hired? And no interest in athletics about hiring other African-American coaches?"

Nobody in Arkansas's black community was surprised by Richardson's replacement. "Stan Heath was hired to appease the turmoil that was rising within the black alumni," says Lonnie Williams, who marched across campus to help Richardson challenge the issue of police dogs on campus in the 1980s.

Hiring a black coach to replace a fired black coach almost never happens, except at historically black colleges, and a small percentage of people viewed the hire as another bold move by Frank Broyles.

Lonnie Williams, who has since moved to Arkansas State University, doesn't buy that. He believes the hiring of Heath was premeditated to coincide with the threat of a lawsuit. "I told African-American staff members at the UA to ask for whatever they needed soon, because they [UA administration] are going to lean over backward to support diversity efforts. If there was a lawsuit that got settled, the well may quickly dry up."

Williams has seen enough to be certain that "America—especially Arkansas—is still afraid of a strong black man who can speak his mind. Nolan Richardson won't bite his tongue, he's still speaking up like a man. America can't handle that."

Stan Heath bristled at first. "I wasn't hired to help in the threat of a lawsuit," he stressed. "We'd won thirty games at Kent State." Yet Heath quickly points out that he knew he was walking into a hornet's nest in Hawg country. "My color was a plus at that particular job because it might calm some of the fire that was brewing because of Nolan's situation. My color helped in those terms, but we'd been to the Elite Eight at Kent State. Yes, the university in some ways was trying to use me to pacify a situation that was difficult. But I looked at it as an opportunity to continue the legacy of Eddie Sutton and Nolan. *Somebody* was going to take the job. All of us feel, as black coaches, we take jobs that are going to have big obstacles. They might not be the Duke or North Carolina job." Heath signed a five-year contract.

Chancellor John White would remain in his position until June of 2008, when he returned to teaching. When asked about the repercussions of the firing, and its effect on his attempts at diversity, he doesn't hesitate. "The difficulty has been, frankly, in getting past the continuing negative feelings within the state after Nolan Richardson's dismissal," he says. "It's still an uphill battle to get parents, particularly in the Delta, to have their kids come to northwest Arkansas and the university."

His remorse over what happened to Richardson seeps into his remarks about the controversy. "We were already there, doing well," White insists. "If anything, the firing set us back as far as the negative publicity associated with it, and as far as faculty and staff. In my eleven years here, we've had two women and two African-American student body presidents. It's hard to say that we're better off today, I wouldn't say that at all. I think it was just a sad chapter in the history of the University of Arkansas and Nolan Richardson, and I'm frankly not able to see what good has come from it. There are still people who have strong feelings on both sides of the issue and time has not ameliorated it the way I thought it would."

White does think there may be positives for Richardson on the heels of his own return to the classroom—as well as the departure of

Frank Broyles. "Maybe it will take Frank being off the scene and me being less visible for Nolan to feel comfortable," he says.

Lonnie Williams has sympathy for White's immense challenge of racial issues in Arkansas. Or some sympathy. "John White *wants* to do right on racial issues," Williams says, "but it's one step forward, two steps back. He can't control the underlying issues. He talks the talk, but when you bring in this many black staff and faculty, and have the same amount leaving? Diversity is always in the top five goals, but we never seem to get much better."

Williams feels perhaps John White's problems are coming from across campus. "John White wanted to move Broyles to a fund-raiser position away from athletics, according to newspaper reports, and some board of trustees members weighed in, then John White was rebuffed."

Broyles remained as athletics director. "That shows where the power is located. Athletics," Williams says.

Judge Wendell Griffen says, "The University of Arkansas is the Southern institution with the longest track record for having admitted blacks and the worst track record for treating them in this century."

Griffen says the number of blacks admitted, their inclusion in college life, the number of graduates, and the number of faculty employed and retained all reveal a deeper problem. "In Nolan Richardson, we have a stellar person, morally, professionally, and personally," Griffen says, "who literally was ousted because people were too unwilling to accept him as the person he is. That's *cultural incompetence* in its most glaring consequences. It is a classic example of what happens when incompetent people are in power and have to deal with cultural issues. The problem didn't lie with Nolan," Griffen insists, "the problem lay with Frank Broyles and John White and the institution that has historically been behind, when it had every reason and chance to be a leader."

While some people believe the firing of Richardson improved things for blacks on campus, that progress has been made, Griffen does not.

"I don't talk about the University of Arkansas and use the word 'progress,'" Griffen says. "I use the word 'movement.' If a student has an average of twenty points in a class, and later has an average of forty, that student has had movement but not progress. The University of Arkansas is still at the 'F' level, but seemingly determined to congratulate itself."

The state of Arkansas took a beating again in the national media—just as it had for decades—when Richardson was fired. "We've a feeling Arkansas won't come out looking too good," the *Democrat-Gazette* wrote in an editorial, and they were correct.

The editorial continued:

> Everybody else has taken sides in this case, so we'll break with our daily tradition and come down squarely in the mushy middle. We're not sure whether Nolan should have been fired, or bought out, or made to apologize, or just sent to his room without any supper. We just know that it was as disheartening to watch a grown man, head coach, and role model make a public ass of himself as it was to watch the consequences: a whole state in a shouting match over race. Again. The one thing Karl Marx was right about is that history happens twice—the first time as tragedy, the second as farce. And in this case all it took was about 50 years—from 1957 to now.
>
> Instead of a rousing debate about whether the struggling Razorbacks need a new coach after 17 years, too many of us got dragged into an argument over Nolan Richardson's skin color—just the way he wanted. Half a century ago, it was the

white demagogues who could speak only of race; now it's the black ones. History has a way of being terribly just.

Their conclusion—"just move on"—was typical within the state, and indicative of the dominant mindset in Arkansas. Any bad news or ugly history, especially where race is concerned, needs to be put behind us as quickly as possible. Richardson's biggest sin might have been his refusal to let anyone forget.

Nearly every writer concurred with the decision to dump the coach. But a small few were sensitive to the dynamic of a black coach being covered by an all-white media. J. A. Adande, who is black, wrote in the *Los Angeles Times*, "I've read some tired columns that sarcastically lament poor Nolan Richardson and his $3 million buyout. These writers will never even have a chance of considering Richardson's perspective. They'll never write in a newsroom in which they're the minority."

William Rhoden of the *New York Times*, who lionized Richardson during his NCAA title run, was less supportive this time:

Upheavals and departures of coaching icons are rarely successful. Longtime coaches like Jerry Tarkanian, Bob Knight and Richardson often assume the stature of pope or ayatollah on their campuses. They often act as though they can trample on rules, behave in the most outrageous manner and make the most outrageous statements. In time, Tarkanian's rules violations, Knight's behavior and Richardson's angry statements became embarrassments that could not be offset by championships.

Other writers used the story to take yet another shot at the state of Arkansas.

Bernie Lincicome of the *Rocky Mountain News* wrote, "Nothing Richardson could have said would bring more discredit to Arkansas than its idiotic school cheer [known as "calling the hogs"], never mind all those reasonable and caring alumni wearing red hog snouts like hats."

Sid Simpson, who hired Richardson at Western Texas College, remains a staunch defender of the coach. But when pressed, Simpson will admit that Richardson has two flaws. Or rather, Simpson stresses, two strengths that can be seen as flaws.

"First, if you get Nolan trapped in a corner, he's going to fight his way out." This is apparent, Simpson says, from his response on ESPN's program about graduation rates. When challenged on the poor graduation rate of his championship team, Richardson could have said, "We always want to improve our graduation rates and we'll continue to stress higher education." Or he could have named several players who graduated before and after that time-specific study. Instead, Richardson insisted that it is not his job to graduate players—a direct contradiction to the way he actually dealt with his team over the years.

"Second," Simpson continues, "he responds from the heart, whether it's the right thing to say or not."

The question at his post-Kentucky press conference in 2002 was, "What were you and [Kentucky coach] Tubby Smith talking about after the game?"

"Hardly a question to make someone offer up a job that no one—let me repeat—no one has asked for," Wally Hall wrote.

Richardson could have said, "That's between Tubby and me," or "Just general stuff about our teams." Or even "No comment."

Instead, Richardson revealed that he and Smith talked about focusing on their paychecks during tough times, which led to Richardson's quote, "If they go ahead and pay me my money, they can take the job."

Richardson made an unusual decision for a fired coach that summer. He decided to stay in Arkansas, on his ranch outside Fayetteville. He'd return home to El Paso for visits, or fly to Birmingham, where Mike Anderson was quickly retooling the UAB program as their new head coach. His refusal to move away indirectly kept the controversy alive in Arkansas.

In March of 2002, black conservative talk-show host and pundit Armstrong Williams wrote his weekly column about the recently fired coach, titled "Nolan Richardson, Adios." The column ran nationally as well as at the Townhall.com Web site.

Armstrong Williams admitted in 2005 to being paid $240,000 by the George W. Bush administration to endorse its "No Child Left Behind" program. This was a foolish business decision on the Bush administration's part, since Williams has consistently championed conservative establishment causes without under-the-table cash. Any journalist who accepts such a payment damages his credibility.

Williams wrote that Richardson had ". . . gained admiration as the first prominent Southern college coach to recruit black athletes . . ." That wasn't even close to correct. Williams, predictably, hammered Richardson for his graduation rate from 1990 to 1994. He also challenged Richardson's claim of discrimination. "It is precisely this sort of culture of victimization that conditions blacks to regard themselves as inferior."

Williams defended the University of Arkansas's decision, writing that the coach's remarks ". . . were plainly racist . . . I mean, can you imagine the outrage that would occur if a white basketball coach calmly surveyed the reporters in attendance at his press conference, then demanded that the local newspapers hire more whites?" This was a strange comparison as there is nowhere in the country a room of all African-American media—TV, radio, newspapers—would be covering the team of a white coach.

Richardson's mindset is common, Williams says. About Richardson's complaints on dealing with an all-white media every day, Williams says, "If writers are fair and objective, and don't make judgments on race, it doesn't matter. Are people being denied the opportunity or are they choosing to do other things? If there is evidence to support that they [blacks] are applying for jobs, and they're denied, that's different. If people choose another profession, that's an issue of choice, not racism."

Williams believes there is a mentality that Richardson and others hold on to that has dragged him down. "[People from Richardson's era] can't relate to the progress we're making. They want to stay stuck in the past. It's difficult, because you become a prisoner of that period. There's some truth [to Richardson's charges], not everybody has clean and pure hands. We are talking about the South."

"There are older people," Williams says, "who feel that, because of racism, they were robbed of something they can never get back. Racism was vicious, it had an impact, and it was systemic. The wounds are still there. When they see Rodney King or Sean Bell, that reinforces things for them that not much has changed. It haunts them and that is their burden."

However, Williams says Richardson was being unreasonable. "Blacks feel they are held to a higher standard, but most of that is imagined."

The key to life for Armstrong Williams: "Forgive people, judge them as individuals, not as a group." He closed by saying, "I've never experienced racism, it has never impacted my life."

"Armstrong Williams is either a liar, a freak, or not intelligent enough to discern racism," former Air Force coach Reggie Minton says. "We study history for a reason. Nobody can take those experiences away from you. You learn from what you've seen and experienced. For anyone to say, 'Why can't he let go?' . . . Well, people can't let go for a reason."

Minton's time as a black man coaching at the ultraconservative Air Force Academy left him with very specific ideas about how the world changes. "I don't buy into the premise that racists are plotting this," Minton says, "but there needs to be somebody around who raises the level of awareness."

Once, before joining the administration at the NABC, Minton was having dinner with three generals from the Air Force.

"Is there anything we can do?" one of the generals asked Minton.

Minton mentioned a new aircraft trainer, the most recent model of plane. "Make the cockpit bigger."

"We could easily do that," one general said. "Nobody's ever brought that up."

"That's because everybody who is sitting at this table fits in the cockpit," Minton answered.

Minton says today, "If not everybody is aware of the problem, things won't change. America should know that only 3 percent of college administrators in athletics are minorities; that is where you start."

Even funerals seemed to be divided along the Broyles/Richardson line. Sportswriter Orville Henry died a few weeks after Richardson was fired, and Richardson delivered the eulogy at historic Central High School in Little Rock. Although Frank Broyles had been close to Henry as well, he was not asked to speak.

A month later, Richardson was back in Little Rock, but this time it wasn't for a funeral. St. Mark's Baptist Church in Little Rock hosted a tribute in support of Richardson, a celebration of his long career.

The list of speakers at St. Mark's included former NBA star Darrell Walker, who had played for Eddie Sutton. Walker was confident of Richardson's place in history. "Anytime you see a [black] coach getting hired whether it's Division I, II, III, think about Nolan Richardson," he said. But his remarks also illustrated the difference of opinions within the state about whether Richardson was out of line or right on. "I'm glad you did what you did," Walker said, looking at Richardson. Everyone in attendance—nearly all African-Americans—rose in a standing ovation.

Lonnie Williams was the only current University of Arkansas employee to speak. Williams said, "He showed us that there are still a few Davids in the world, ready to take on Goliath."

It was Wendell Griffen, an eloquent and charismatic speaker, whose brilliance colored the afternoon. Griffen credited Richardson for his "refusal to let himself be defined by the myths commonly applied to black men and black leaders. He may speak coarsely, but never deceitfully. It may not be the truth we want to hear, but it's always the truth we cannot deny. Thank you, coach, for refusing to sell out your principles and worship popularity at the price of integrity. Thank you for reminding our state that you will not ignore the business of social justice just because you are a basketball coach. Thank you for not allowing yourself to be put on a plantation, even if they do pay you a million dollars."

TWENTY-ONE

BATTLE ROYAL

In early December of 2002, Richardson went ahead with plans to file a lawsuit against the University of Arkansas, Frank Broyles, John White, and the fund-raising Razorback Foundation.

It was a trying time for Richardson and his family. Later that month, Richardson's son—Nolan "Notes" Richardson III—was terminated as the head coach of Tennessee State, where trailblazing coaches John McLendon and Harold Hunter had preceded him. Richardson III had been an Arkansas assistant for ten seasons.

Notes' problem stemmed from a disagreement with his Tennessee State assistant Hosea Lewis concerning practice times on Christmas evening, when many of the TSU players were no-shows. Notes Richardson told police that he went to his car and brought an unloaded gun into the school's Gentry Center in response to threats from Lewis, who, Notes says, had a chain. Although he disputes the circumstances of his firing, in the ensuing days he signed a statement with campus police acknowledging that he used the gun as a threat.

Bringing a gun onto campus in Tennessee is a felony, but the school did not attempt to prosecute Richardson III after he quickly resigned in early January of 2003. Tennessee State's president was quoted nationally as saying, "What he did is something that was beyond belief in terms of anyone in higher education doing something like that."

Richardson's lawsuit didn't go to trial until 2004. His arguments were centered upon allegations of racism and his own freedom of speech—speaking out on racism, which he claimed was a matter of public concern. The judge quickly tossed out everything directed at the Razorback Foundation.

If Richardson proved either racism or the stifling of his right to free speech, he would win. The trial lasted nearly a month, beginning on May 5, 2004, and included forty-four witnesses over eighteen days. Both parties waived the chance for a jury trial. Some legal experts felt that this was Richardson's best bet, since the coach would have had a difficult time finding a sympathetic jury because of the amount of money at stake.

Philip Kaplan, the lawyer representing the University of Arkansas, said in his opening statement that Richardson's lawsuit was based on his hatred of Frank Broyles. According to Broyles, at his February 28, 2002, meeting, Richardson told him, "I will destroy you. You will have no legacy."

UA football coach Houston Nutt testified at the trial, saying that Richardson told him that Broyles "may like you now, but wait until your ass goes 5-6, or 4-7 and see what happens."

Part of Richardson's claims focused on the treatment of Houston Nutt, who, Richardson felt, received favorable treatment. However, Judge William Wilson, who is white, couldn't find substantial difference, aside from the fact that assistant basketball coach Mike Anderson was underpaid.

Judge Wilson did point out that in a written memo Broyles rec-ommended to Chancellor White that Richardson's six-year contract should not be "rolled over." Broyles also added that he thought all contracts should be limited to five years. The rollover, a powerful equivalent of a professor's tenure, was once popular, but the current trend among even the biggest contracts was moving away from them. "However," Wilson wrote, "Broyles failed to mention in his memo that he had recommended a ten-year contract for Nutt in October of 1999, which White approved. This evidence is disturbing . . ."

In his final ruling on the case, Judge William Wilson seemed to struggle for wiggle room, writing how difficult his decision was, and that ". . . some pieces will always be missing." Before going much fur-ther, he stressed that ". . . this case has been hard to decide. Judging, like coaching, often appears easier from the bleachers."

The university took the curious position that Frank Broyles was not responsible for Richardson's firing.

At the trial, Broyles claimed that he regretted using the word "nigger" to a table of media representatives. Judge Wilson, in his written summary, remained troubled by the "redneck = nigger" com-parison that Broyles had hoped to see in print:

> It should ring out loudly and clearly—an African-American calling a Caucasian a "redneck" is nowise the same as a Caucasian person calling an African-American a "nigger."
> Although some may argue that there is no real difference, they are wrong, and I suspect they know it. . . . The fact is that terms like "nigger," "spic," "faggot," and "kike" evolve and reinforce entire cultural histories of oppression and subordination. They remind the target that his or her group has always been and remains unequal in status to the majority group.

Judge Wilson would continue chipping away at Broyles. In his argument about Broyles's comments at the banquet, he reasoned:

> Defendants have argued that Broyles's banquet comments two years before the firing are "too remote" and "stray" to support an inference that Broyles harbored racial hostility toward Richardson. They argue that his remarks are, therefore, insufficient to constitute direct evidence of discrimination because there was no causal link between the remark and the firing. . . .
>
> I disagree.
>
> In this instance, the issue is not Broyles's words themselves, but his apparent desire to use race in a publication, which would create conflict among fans and garner support for firing Richardson . . . Broyles solicited an article making the comparison and [I] can think of no other reason why he would do so . . . Broyles had already attempted to get support for firing Richardson as early as February 2000. This solicitation can hardly be seen as anything but a willingness to "stir the racial pot."
>
> . . . Broyles was animated when making the statement . . . he knew he was sitting between two news media persons, that there was no contention that their conversation was "off the record." [One media representative] testified that he asked Broyles if he wanted to be quoted as a source in the requested article, and Broyles responded with the equivalent of "perish the thought."
>
> These statements were made at a time when Broyles, a decision maker, was considering Richardson's termination. I find that this is direct evidence of discrimination and is sufficient to require a mixed-motive analysis of any employment decisions made by Broyles before October 2000. . . .

Frank Broyles testified that this was the only time in his entire life that he had uttered the word "nigger."

While it seems that it would make a difference whether Broyles was quoting the irate and anonymous fan, or stating his own opinion, Judge Wilson did not think so. The judge felt certain that it was Broyles's own feelings (redneck = nigger) that were being communicated, although Broyles insists he was quoting the all-important-yet-mysterious fan. In his summary, Wilson cited the conflicting testimony of two media representatives who were at the banquet: Paul Eels (who died later in a car wreck) and Mike Nail.

> Paul Eels . . . heard it as a direct statement, rather than as a quote . . . I do not think that it makes any difference whether it was a direct statement or a quote, but everyone interested in the case knew that the distinction was very important to Coach Broyles. Nail testified that, in a private conversation prior to trial, Eels told him that it was a quote. This means that either Nail or Eels lied about this specific point. I am satisfied that Eels told the truth.

Judge Wilson's findings determined that the University of Arkansas's decision to dump Richardson was made on Sunday, February 24, 2002. Wilson relied on the testimony of thirteen witnesses (including all but the lone African-American member of the board of trustees, who was told the following Thursday). This meant Richardson was effectively fired the day after his Kentucky press conference ("They can have this job if they just pay me my money"), but before Richardson's ramble on the following Monday—the televised, scattered lecture for which Richardson became nationally known.

In other words, Richardson's final press conference was meaningless, a moot point—although that fateful Monday was used by fans and media to justify what had already been decided.

Did Richardson know the ax was about to fall, instinctively sense his time was up? He knew he was in trouble, and that Broyles had wanted to fire him in 1987, then again in 2000. Richardson's romp through the 2000 SEC Tournament put out that fire. The coach understood he simply did not have the players to pull off another miracle that March—and save his job. In any case, a host of administrators and trustees knew Richardson was terminated on February 24; the school would wait until February 28 to actually inform Richardson. Judge Wilson wrote, ". . . the decision was not only unfair, but an administrative nightmare."

On February 24, Chancellor White told media representatives that in his view, Richardson was just frustrated after a tough loss, despite the feeling he had after talking to Bud Walton Arena manager Fred Vorsanger. The *Democrat-Gazette* even wrote a piece on February 25, 2002, under the headline, "Chancellor Expects Nolan to Complete Contract," despite the loss and comments at Kentucky. "He puts the most intense pressure on himself," White said. "I fully expect to see him complete his contract at the University of Arkansas."

Then on February 27, with Richardson's fate sealed, White told a local television station that he had no knowledge of a buyout planned for Richardson.

Both of these statements came up at the trial and were commented on by Judge Wilson in his summary, although throwing the media "off the scent" is a common tactic among administrators. Regardless, either John White misled the media, or he was not involved in Broyles's decision.

Richardson's attorney tried to catch Frank Broyles in a similar trap, pointing out that the athletics director had written complimentary evaluations of Richardson, as well as publicly said that Richardson would make a fine athletics director someday. Neither the evaluation nor the statement, he admitted under oath, was true, only intended to be "friendly."

Unless Richardson had miraculously swept through the SEC

Tournament again—and even if he had spoken the usual clichés after the Kentucky loss—he would have been fired. But since testimony indicated the decision to dump Richardson came on the same day that White made his comments, it appeared somebody else besides the chancellor was making the decisions at the University of Arkansas.

Perhaps as disturbing as Frank Broyles's attempts to rally racist comments from the media were the admissions under oath by university board of trustees members Gary George and Bill Clark that they occasionally told "nigger jokes." Gary George was the chairman at that time.

University officials using racist slang, and the implications of such language, disturbed Judge Wilson. He wrote:

> It seems to me . . . that when a person accepts an
> important position of trust with the entire University of
> Arkansas system, he would purge his vocabulary of such
> words—and work on his heart and mind in the same vein.
> Most troubling to me was that neither of these witnesses
> seemed abashed by their admissions.

Neither Clark nor George was asked to resign in the wake of those admissions.

The *Democrat-Gazette's* Wally Hall wrote, "Richardson's attorney, John Walker, was very successful at making Broyles look like an almost 80-year-old man with 50-year-old ideas and very outdated management skills. This suit revealed Broyles's mishandling of several coaches, fading the truth whenever he deemed necessary, his reference to the 'N word' and even how he answers to no one."

In the end, however, Judge Wilson wrote that the University of

Arkansas's claim—that Richardson was canned because of his state-ment after the Kentucky game ("If they go ahead and pay me my money, they can take the job tomorrow")—was both sufficient and accurate. This simple judgment settled things in the University of Arkansas's favor.

> This comment . . . showed a lost interest and lack of commitment to UAF, undermined public confidence and support for the program and had a negative impact on recruiting for all UAF sports. With these explanations, UAF has met its burden of articulating a legitimate reason for termination.

In fact, this was the only reason given by the university for dismiss-ing Richardson. Judge Wilson also noted that according to numerous witnesses, Richardson had made those comments often, beginning in 1995. Yet Richardson was never challenged or questioned by univer-sity administrators about this apparently common statement. Anyone who has been around coaches—especially older coaches—knows that this "Why the hell do I do this for a living?" sentiment is as common as a 2-3 zone. Saying it into a microphone at a press conference at the University of Kentucky, however, is not.

Sid Simpson believes the *hiring* of Richardson was tinted with racism, because the coach's race was the only issue to Frank Broyles. However, he thinks race actually had less to do with Richardson's fir-ing. "Broyles's ego got Nolan Richardson fired," he says. "Nolan would have gotten fired even if he were white. Broyles had been wanting to get rid of him for years. Nolan had become bigger than Broyles. He'd won a real national championship, not a fictional one," Simpson says, refer-ring to Broyles's disputed 1964 title. "Then Nolan damn near won the NCAA championship again."

"The firing of Coach Richardson was not a black-or-white story," Arkansas sportswriter Chip Souza says. "But if you don't think race was involved, you're sadly mistaken."

Charles Prigmore, former Medical Center boss, says: "I don't think the race issue had anything to do with it. Nolan was grasping at straws when he sued the university. If he'd been Chinese or German I think he still would have been gone." Prigmore thinks the real problem was Richardson having a boss who thought he knew basketball. "I was the head football coach at three high schools, and I know you don't want a principal who used to be a head coach," he says. "Frank Broyles was an enemy of success, and Richardson had gotten too successful."

Carrol Williams (no relation to Lonnie Williams) was Black Alumni Society president at Arkansas when Nolan Richardson was fired in 2002. "There was great discussion at that time about what had happened to Nolan Richardson," Williams says, "especially when we heard about the testimony of the board of trustees."

Specifically, it was the use of the "N word" in jokes and the realization that Frank Broyles might sit quietly and listen to those jokes. "At one time, we were going to go ahead and recommend, as a group, our BSA, that Frank Broyles be fired. But then we thought, 'We have to get real, John White is not going to fire Frank Broyles.' So instead we asked Chancellor White to step up and make a commitment to the African-American faculty and staff."

Bill Clark and Gary George, the members of the board of trustees at UA who used the word "nigger," eventually left the board. Broyles remained as AD until his retirement in the spring of 2007. But the BSA was mortified that any board member would use that kind of language and not be instantly cut loose from the school.

Judge Wilson's final summary makes it clear that he admires Richardson, not just for his obvious accomplishments but also for the coach's against-all-odds journey. In the end, Wilson sided with the University of Arkansas, but not before admonishing the administration for their clumsy collective management styles.

> Richardson should have been counseled about his sometimes intemperate remarks, and UAF administrators should have made more timely and direct responses to his complaints . . . I am inclined to believe that the firing could have been avoided, or postponed considerably, if there had been more and better communication by his supervisors.

Judge Wilson was troubled regarding what he clearly saw to be a difficult decision, and his sympathy for Richardson's situation is obvious:

> Although I have found against him on those points, his belief was clearly not unreasonable. In other words, while I do not believe that evidence of racial bias or impingement of free speech preponderates in favor of Plaintiff, the record is a long way from devoid of incidents which could cause him to hold these beliefs.

When Richardson's career crashed, the media almost invariably backed the University of Arkansas. Nearly always, his poor graduation rate from 1990 to 1994 was trotted out. When *Sports Illustrated* interviewed *SI* basketball writer Seth Davis, the title of the article was "Richardson Brought It Upon Himself"—although in the piece, Davis did conclude, ". . . it's clear from his behavior there was someone who didn't want him around."

John Smallwood of the *Philadelphia Daily News* wrote, "The University of Arkansas, Razorbacks fans and even the media that cover the athletics program didn't deserve what Nolan Richardson did to them . . . he was wrong to transport the image of Arkansas back to that of the racially intolerant 1950s and 1960s."

Without understanding the context, the history of the state, the university, and Frank Broyles, by taking Richardson's comments from his confusing Monday press conference at face value, people like Smallwood might find Richardson an ungrateful millionaire.

The coach, who had spent his professional life in an often-lonely confrontation with college sports' racist past, primarily was blamed for *reminding* the public about racism. "Why can't Nolan just get over it?" was the typical take from college basketball insiders. Wasn't America beyond racism, the reasoning went, if a black man was making a million bucks a year?

Yet was racism "over in America," as Newt Gingrich declared in 1995, if the board of trustees at a state's major university could put their feet up and ask, "Did you hear the one about the three niggers who went fishing?" How much of this racism was communicated, however subtly, to John White or Frank Broyles? Broyles claimed that in the 1960s, the board of trustees was the reason he was one of the last coaches in America to find qualified black players for his football team, and it's no stretch to think that, at the very least, the board's backwoods racism could influence Broyles again.

TWENTY-TWO

YOUR BLUES AIN'T LIKE MINE

In October of 2004, Frank Broyles lost his wife, Barbara, to complications from Alzheimer's disease. The couple had been married for fifty-nine years. Broyles continued working tirelessly on fundraising for Alzheimer's research and began writing a book about the disease.

Even with the lawsuit over, Chancellor John White felt like the Sisyphus of college administrators. In 2004, UA instituted a program where employees—on a voluntary basis—might learn to be more accepting of diversity. The program was called "Our Campus: Building a More Inclusive University of Arkansas."

Cynics pointed out that his training program in tolerance was instituted around the same time Richardson's suit for racial discrimination was filed. Barbara Taylor told the *Democrat-Gazette*, "Chronologically, they certainly coincided. But before the Nolan Richardson controversy and conflict arose, the diversity task force had already made that recommendation."

The university's enrollment today is still only 5 percent African-American, while the overall population of the state remains 16 percent. The faculty at UA is only 3 percent African-American. Yet it's undeniable that the school has attempted to diversify.

In January of 2005, the University of Arkansas hired an African-American woman named Carmen Coustaut as their first associate vice chancellor for diversity and education. In the spring of 2006, the University of Arkansas hired an African-American woman, Cynthia Nance, to be dean of the law school. Several key black university administrators and 43 percent of black faculty members have arrived since John White was hired in 1997. Of course, the ways in which an African-American championship basketball coach would have influenced that statistic are impossible to measure.

White said, when Richardson's removal was announced, "I'm strongly committed and I'm very concerned that the African-American community within the state not think that this is in any way a step back with respect to our commitment to that agenda." If not progress, there has been movement at University of Arkansas, and it's movement in the right direction.

Val Gonzalez, who conducted the workshops for the National Conference for Community Justice, was much more direct. "Discrimination is a real problem, right here at the University of Arkansas. Some of what we learned is not very pretty."

Nolan Richardson lost his appeal in the Eighth U.S. Circuit Court during May of 2006, in St. Louis. Judge Arlen Beam wrote, "The record amply supports a conclusion that Richardson's statement had a detrimental impact on the effective functioning of the public employer's enterprise—namely, the university's total athletics program. This public interest clearly outweighs any First Amendment privilege Richardson may have allegedly had in the making of the comment."

———

In February of 2007, Congressman Bobby Rush (D-Illinois) hosted hearings involving the NCAA, Congress, and experts on the struggles faced by African-American coaches. Rush called Nolan Richardson back to the battle.

Other witnesses who participated were NCAA President Myles Brand, Jesse Jackson, new BCA boss Floyd Keith, and Richard Lapchick from the Institute for Ethics and Diversity in Sports.

Bobby Rush stressed that legislation to correct the shocking lack of black football coaches would be appropriate. But NCAA President Myles Brand begged off any direct responsibility, saying, "The colleges and universities will not cede to the NCAA the authority to dictate who to interview or hire in athletics."

Richard Lapchick, one of the nation's foremost authorities on race and college sports, favors the NCAA using a policy similar to the "Rooney Rule," which had been put in effect, to make certain that every NFL coaching search would include at least one candidate of color. In his written statement, Lapchick suggested that legislation and lawsuits should both be options. "It's pretty clear that embarrassment hasn't been enough," he wrote.

The problem, Brand pointed out, was with the results of the searches.

Richardson cited the good ol' boy club of boosters who would almost certainly favor white coaches. The influence of well-heeled boosters over athletics departments—and thus entire universities—is a given today. The head coaching jobs in college football may be the last place where boosters can cling to white leadership.

At the time, fewer than 3 percent of head football coaches at all NCAA institutions were black, although more than half of the athletes were. Men's basketball, where over 60 percent of the players are black, was better, since nearly 30 percent of its head coaches were black.

Frankie Allen, now the basketball coach at historically black Maryland–Eastern Shore, knows the biggest reason that college basketball is decades ahead of football. "Basketball coaches *organized* a lot sooner, with the BCA," Allen says. "The guys at the top of the profession were all doing great—Thompson, Chaney, and Richardson. We had big-name people behind us, and they weren't afraid to speak out."

Richardson pushed his teams to play at a furious pace.
(*Copyright © Aynsley Floyd*)

Colorblind coach Don Haskins began an avalanche of desegregation.
(*Courtesy of UTEP*)

Rose Richardson, 1885–1968. "Ol' Mama" was Richardson's de facto mother. (*Courtesy of Nolan Richardson*)

Richardson's scoring average at Texas Western College plummeted under Haskins's slowdown system. (*Courtesy of UTEP*)

New York Nirvana: Tulsa's 1981 NIT championship put Richardson in the national spotlight. (*Courtesy of University of Tulsa Sports Information*)

High-flying Ralph Brewster: from Bowie to Texas Tech. (*Southwest Collections, Special Collection Library, Texas Tech University*)

Yvonne Richardson (*left*), Rosario Richardson (*middle*), Nolan Richardson.
(*Courtesy of Nolan Richardson*)

Leading the faithful:
Frank Broyles, University
of Arkansas football
coach and director of
athletics for fifty years.
(*Wesley Hitt/Getty Images*)

"He could have had a
PhD in psychology":
Nolan Richardson and
three-point ace Pat
Bradley. (*Jonathon
Daniel/Getty Images
Sport/Getty Images*)

Nolan Richardson and his
wife, Rosario, celebrate
after beating Duke for the
1994 NCAA title.
(*Damian Strohmeyer/
Sports Illustrated/Getty
Images*)

Throwing the book away:
Razorback substitute Ken
Biley climbs to the top.
(*Hawgs Illustrated*)

"A whole lot of courage":
Arkansas football walk-on Darrell Brown.
(*Courtesy of Darrell Brown*)

Unofficial Arkansas high school
touchdown leader Bob Walters
(*above*); nephew Danny Walters
(*right*) became one of the
greatest Razorbacks ever.
(*Courtesy of the Walters family*)

"We can recruit, motivate, and teach, but can we coach? I never hear that": Nolan Richardson and TV analyst Billy Packer. (*Hawgs Illustrated*)

"He seems to make a system out of anger": Richardson in the late 1990s. (*Brian Bahr/Getty Images Sport/Getty images*)

Vamanos! Richardson returned to the border to coach the Mexican National Team. (*El Paso Times/ Victor Calzada*)

The most important African-American coach in history: a pensive
Richardson before the championship team reunion in 2009.
(*Eric Howerton, Now Creative Inc.*)

TWENTY-THREE

BROTHERS AND KEEPERS

Arkansas fired Stan Heath in the spring of 2007, and the timing was obvious. With the conclusion of the Nolan Richardson lawsuit, Heath was expendable. His teams struggled his first three seasons, but in his fourth and fifth years, Arkansas finally qualified for the NCAA Tournament again. Heath's teams won over those five seasons, in order, nine, twelve, eighteen, twenty-two, then twenty-one games.

"Maybe I didn't do enough to protect myself," Heath says. "It was set up to be a pacifying situation after Nolan. [Frank Broyles said] ticket sales were down. But I can read. In 2006–07, we had more fans than the year before." Indeed, in 2006, the Razorbacks were twelfth in the nation—out of over three hundred schools—in overall attendance. In 2007, Heath's last season, they were ninth.

Arkansas would embarrass itself that spring by offering the job to a succession of five coaches—all white—who would consecutively turn down the job. Dana Altman left Creighton for a day before changing his mind and returning to Omaha. Finally, after the fifth rejection, Broyles found Arkansas their white coach in John Pelphrey, who had *not* led South Alabama to the NCAA Tournament. (Pelphrey quickly hired Rob Evans, Richardson's longtime friend.)

Heath noticed the parade of white coaches Arkansas fawned over that April. "I have no problems with the new coach, but if you just look at [Pelphrey's] résumé, the measuring stick had changed. I was an Elite Eight coach, and they hired a coach who had come from the NIT."

Unaware of the swirl of politics and maneuvering around him, Heath was focused on his quickly improving team. "I never felt that Dr. White was trying to manage the athletics department; I just thought he was a cheerleader. Dr. White's a nice guy, but it wasn't his decision [to fire Heath]. I can tell you, that is a fact."

Heath believes White made every effort to try to wrestle control of athletics from his supposed subordinate, Frank Broyles. "My second or third year," Heath says, "Dr. White wanted to make a change in the athletics director's job. What I remember came back to us—and this was a rumor—was this. If you try to change [Broyles's] job, you're going to lose yours. The lesson was that Broyles is going to run the athletics department."

Heath's point—the unchecked power of Broyles—echoes the feelings of many within the state: The University of Arkansas, in their decades of silence, condoned Broyles's behavior. "Even when a federal judge criticized him harshly for racially insensitive comments last summer, nobody from the university offered even the mildest censure," the *Chronicle of Higher Education* would write. "Not one peep of public reproach has been heard from any other state or university officials."

Heath is also quick to point out all Broyles has accomplished and his high regard in the world of college sports. Broyles, however, continued his pattern by meddling with Heath's basketball team. "He had opinions on the staff he wanted me to hire," Heath said.

That didn't bother Heath so much, since Broyles was admired for uncovering great assistants. Rather, it was his boss's basketball ideas and his management style. "Broyles never was a guy who told me to run this play or that play, but he certainly had his opinions on *style* of play. That was where he wanted to have some input. There were times when he had his opinion, but we had difficulty because he was almost like an overseer. We struggled with our communication."

Heath's timing in taking the job put him in an awkward place stylistically. He simply didn't play at the same pace as Richardson. "But Broyles was pushing us into a full-court press," he says. Heath thinks this was a matter of expedience for Broyles. "In the early part of his career, he wanted Nolan to play more Eddie Sutton's style. The fans were used to that. At the end of the day, Broyles wanted to make the fans in Arkansas happy. He wanted me to *replace* Nolan by playing Nolan's style."

Each year Heath's team improved, even getting to the championship game of SEC in his final season. By the conclusion of the 2007 season, Heath was itching with anticipation. His Razorbacks had consistently done better, and had no seniors.

Then the crimson rug was ripped from beneath his feet. "There are coaches going to the NIT, and they get raises. Bill Self lost in the first round of the NCAAs in 2007," Heath points out. Self's Kansas team won the national championship the following year.

Heath says there was one constant motivator for Broyles, which became apparent at the SEC conference meetings each spring. The league meetings involve university presidents, athletics directors, head coaches, and faculty representatives.

The young head coach and veteran AD, who was closing in on eighty years of age, would sit together. "During the basketball meeting, Broyles would sleep through the whole thing," Heath says. "People would be looking around, smiling at me."

Only one thing could awaken Broyles, Heath claims. One year the SEC bosses said they wanted Arkansas to give up a home game in basketball to play in something called "The SEC Challenge." Each home game was worth at least $300,000 to Arkansas. "He immediately woke up and snapped to attention," Heath says.

At certain times, though, money could be tossed around freely at Broyles's discretion. Both Nolan Richardson and football coach Houston Nutt were paid piles of money *not* to coach the Razorbacks. Richardson's payments finally ended in June of 2008.

Stan Heath handled his firing gracefully, and he bounced back within weeks, landing as the coach of the University of South Florida. In retrospect, he sees his time in Fayetteville differently. "Nolan made the job easier for me," he says. "People went out of their way to be kind to me." When things went badly for Heath, Richardson reached out and shared one of his favorite lines from Ol' Mama: "All sickness isn't death." Richardson also stuck up for the embattled Heath publicly.

"I wanted to sort of take the baton from Nolan," Heath says. The baton Heath would get came in the form of the same pink slip. "But it was only one person that led to my change," Heath says. "There was only one direction I was looking as to what happened to me."

"Frank Broyles fired everybody," one longtime Arkansas athletics department employee says. "Nolan Richardson lasted seventeen seasons, far longer than any football coach. [Football coaches] Lou Holtz, Ken Hatfield, Jack Crowe, Joe Kines, Danny Ford, and Houston Nutt were all either fired, forced out, or made to feel unwelcome by Broyles."

A common refrain heard around Fayetteville, Arkansas—athletics staff, faculty, waitresses, Wal-Mart execs among them—is how loved Nolan Richardson was during his tenure at the university.

Yet the criteria white people in Arkansas use to determine what constitutes racism is fuzzy. When Arkansans are presented with the obstacles Richardson had overcome in his career—reared in racist El Paso, "don't hire that nigger" sentiments at both Tulsa and Western Texas, dogs being brought in to black fraternity parties—these are dismissed with a shrug.

Frank Broyles—the face of the University of Arkansas since the early sixties—urging media representatives to use the word "nigger" in print? That was poor judgment. Board of trustees members telling nigger jokes? Well, it wasn't as though they'd lynched Nolan Richardson, or anyone else.

Hiring a black man to replace Richardson, keeping him in the post as long as the lawsuit was alive, then dumping him despite his team's dramatic improvement—that wasn't racist either, folks in Fayetteville said. That was the nature of college sports.

NABC director Jim Haney, whose column caused Richardson to reexamine his role as a "token" assistant athletics director, thinks obliviousness to Richardson's struggle indicates a poor sense of the past. "Just hiring an African-American to be a coach was at one time a huge step," Haney says. "Then there was that image of the recruiter who couldn't possibly understand the intricacies of the game. Next was, can we hire a black coach at a large state university? In Richardson, Thompson, and Tubby Smith, we've seen African-Americans lead teams to the NCAA title."

Haney also sees the firing of coaches of color as potentially a good thing. "At the end of the day, you want to be judged on the merits of what you do. Winning, fan base, academics, those things, just as a human being, not based on age or race. Guys like Nolan, John Thompson, Reggie Minton, they were trailblazers."

Despite the progress, today the Black Coaches Association is at a crossroads. Richardson, Chaney, and Thompson are no longer coaching. A lack of direction in the late 1990s—along with allegations by the BCA that its former executive director Rudy Washington had misused BCA funds—nearly led to the BCA's demise. The BCA itself sued Washington, seeking an accounting of funds, and there was an out-of-court settlement.

The BCA's influence has waned, but it may be on the rebound. They've changed their name to Black Coaches and Administrators. Their current director, Floyd Keith, has struggled to restore confidence and financial stability and has pushed the BCA coaches to get involved with at-risk kids.

The BCA was also the force behind the Football Hiring Report Card, which rates each college that hires a new football coach and evaluates their interest in considering candidates of color.

No matter how many basketball games Clarence Gaines, John McClendon, Dave Whitney at Alcorn State, or Don Corbett at North Carolina A&T won, nobody within the white power structure moved to offer them a job. Head coaches at historically black colleges today likely earn one-tenth of what their counterparts are paid at mostly white state universities.

Perhaps the most disturbing example of this is football legend Eddie Robinson, who coached at Grambling State University in Louisiana, only twenty-five miles from the Arkansas border. Robinson served at Grambling, a historically black college, for fifty-six years, lasting through eleven United States presidents. He could boast more football wins than any other coach and sent more than two hundred players to the NFL. He had a graduation rate of 80 percent (when football graduation rates were around 50 percent nationally). For his first fifty seasons, Robinson never had a player get in trouble with the law.

Despite being the winningest football coach of all time, Eddie Robinson was never even offered an *interview* for a major university head coaching job. Robinson, of course, is not the only man to be overlooked. To this day, in the history of major college football, there have been fewer than thirty black head coaches.

Some schools have been surprisingly progressive in their hiring.

The University of Mississippi has had two black basketball coaches. Texas schools like SMU, Texas A&M, Rice, and Houston have as well. Texas basketball, though, is still behind the curve. Don Haskins's historic team remains the only Texas school that has ever won the NCAA basketball championship.

"Integration in sports—as opposed to integration at the ballot box or in public conveyances—was a winning proposition for the whites who controlled the sports-industrial complex," wrote William Rhoden in his book, *Forty Million Dollar Slaves.* "They could move to exploit black muscle and talent, thus sucking the life out of black institutions, while at the same time give themselves credit for being humanitarians."

Rhoden laments that while the integration of sports often benefited the black athlete, the historically black colleges received a major blow as their talent pool thinned. The same was true of the Negro Leagues once Jackie Robinson opened those floodgates. Integration was ultimately not seen as a challenge to white coaches and administrators.

Nolan Richardson eclipsed Frank Broyles in popularity, and that may have been seen as a threat to the director of athletics' power within the state and school. Whenever black men were put in positions of power—as head coaches, for example—it meant a drastic difference from simply having black athletes on the court.

Haskins's 1966 championship returned to the national mindset with the release of the movie *Glory Road.* Stories appeared across the country, and retro Texas Western jerseys became popular. The *Nation*'s David Zirin called the 1966 game "the Selma Bridge of sports."

The Texas Western Miners' season was a coincidence of events that writers dream of discovering. The acerbic and crusty Haskins was the accidental hero and fine literary and artistic material. Instead of using the real Haskins, though, Disney coated him in cliché. It's hard to figure why the film's director encased its celluloid Haskins in plastic, when the real one was so much more interesting.

Glory Road is filled with deliberate inaccuracies, which was unfortunate, since the true story was more compelling. The movie even missed Haskins's real innovation, aside from his being color-blind—getting inner-city playground players to play slower offensively. Texas Western slowed down the run-and-gun Kentucky Wildcats, contrary to the movie's portrayal.

Haskins likely could never have considered starting five blacks at any other major school in Texas, and some credit would have to go to the Hispanic-majority El Paso that abolished its Jim Crow laws in 1962—after Nolan Richardson and Bert Williams were refused service in a popular restaurant.

Glory Road is nonetheless a finely constructed film. The banter and camaraderie between the players is perfect in this happily-ever-after story. But it all felt a little too feel-good.

UTEP, now a school with a Hispanic majority, had countless black athletes who have, like the 1966 Miners, brought fame and money to the school. Yet by 2005, UTEP had not had a black coach in any major sport. (Only women's basketball had a black head coach—they could claim Wayne Thornton, who coached for fifty dollars a month during a single season in 1978–79.) UTEP's road ran one way. Black athletes were welcome. Black leaders were not.

Since that glorious 1966 game, Richardson's alma mater has had seven athletics directors, eleven football coaches, four men's track coaches, and three other basketball coaches. (Don Haskins finally retired in 1999.) That's *twenty-five positions of leadership* for some deserving coach.

Every single one of those twenty-five jobs was filled by a white male. Obviously, Don Haskins was not doing the hiring. Three white coaches—all assistants with no wins on the major college level—followed Haskins. On two of those hires, UTEP even passed over Nolan Richardson.

One allegation that the University of Arkansas made at the trial was that Richardson was not really trying to find another job. They mentioned those two openings at UTEP since Richardson's termination. While Richardson may have been happy at times to collect his $500,000 a year from Arkansas (which would end if he accepted a coaching spot elsewhere), he was, in fact, interested in the UTEP job in 2006. But Richardson claims that the interest was not reciprocated.

"They brought Nolan in for an interview," Haskins said, "and they told him they were going to hire a black coach, but the athletics director didn't want Nolan."

UTEP finally did hire a black man in 2006, when Tony Barbee, an assistant coach from the University of Memphis, was named basketball coach. Forty years had elapsed since Haskins's historic win.

Firing coaches is part of college basketball. A study of what happens to coaches—both white and black—after they have been terminated is instructive.

New BCA boss Floyd Keith claims this is where racism still prevails. "Classic example. Here's Nolan Richardson," Keith told Skip Myslenski in a widely syndicated column. "He proved himself. He had no violations. Then I look around, I'm not going to name names, but here's a coach that, at Iowa State, hugged and kissed coeds, got drunk, and he's working again. There's something wrong here."

Keith was referring to Larry Eustachy, whose demise became a national story when photos of him at Big Twelve parties surfaced on the Internet. Eustachy resigned and acknowledged his addiction to alcohol. He was hired at the University of Southern Mississippi within a year of leaving ISU.

Young black coaches like Randy Ayers and Wade Houston got very brief chances, then never resurfaced, despite the fact that college sports is a business that possesses a limitless ability to recycle white coaches. Eustachy, Tom Penders, Bob Huggins, Eddie Sutton, and Bob Knight were all rocked by controversy.

Eddie Sutton, who represented the good old days to the good old boys of Arkansas, left Fayetteville for Kentucky. Things went terribly wrong at Kentucky, and Sutton resigned amid accusations of cash payments made to a top recruit. Sutton's career was renewed at Oklahoma State, and he led his alma mater to a couple Final Fours. His time at Oklahoma State would come to an end with a bizarre DWI. Campus cops hoisted the drunken coach—whose blood alcohol level was three times the legal limit—into his car at the Gallagher-Iba Arena. Minutes later, he swerved across four lanes of traffic, slammed into the rear of another vehicle, then crashed into a tree. Sutton was able to find work again, resurfacing for most of a season as the head coach at the University of San Francisco.

The well-documented case of Bob Knight is interesting as well. Knight and Richardson are nearly the same age, and both men played for coaches who won NCAA titles—Knight for Fred Taylor at Ohio State. Although Richardson was not a member of Haskins's 1966 team, he was certainly the better player. By the time Knight was only twenty-four, he was the army's head coach at West Point. With not a single black man coaching a major college team, Knight simply would not have been given the chance if he had been black. Richardson, of course, toiled at an obscure high school and junior college for over a decade, at a time when Knight was landing a plum Big Ten job.

Both Knight and Richardson won NCAA titles, although Knight won three. Knight's controversies at Indiana were reported nationally. He was dumped by Indiana in September 2000, but despite the negative publicity, Knight quickly resurfaced at Texas Tech. A group of alumni and fans—not Knight—sued IU soon after he was fired. Knight waited until he was hired and secure at Texas Tech, and then finally filed suit in November 2002, after negotiations for a settlement collapsed.

One of Richardson's former assistants, Wayne Stehlik, admitted to ESPN.com that part of the reason Richardson was untouchable was that he had sued Broyles. "Athletics directors and chancellors or presidents are probably a little bit nervous," Stehlik said, "because of how it turned out there at Arkansas."

The firing of Nolan Richardson remained a source of controversy in Arkansas when Razorback football coach Houston Nutt was let go. Nutt became the head football coach at Arkansas in 1998. His 2006 team was 7-1 in SEC play, and 10-4 overall. Going into the 2007 season—his tenth—Nutt had plenty to be proud of, although he hadn't approached the success that Richardson had in basketball.

Then a Freedom of Information Act request revealed that Nutt, who is married with children, sent close to a thousand text messages to an attractive TV anchorwoman. Arkansas was 3-4 then in the SEC, going into the last game in 2007, and five SEC teams had better records. Yet Chancellor John White and Frank Broyles stood by him, at least publicly.

During that tumultuous autumn, Stanley Reed, the new chairman of the board of trustees at UA, claimed the public had lost confidence in Coach Nutt. The fickle fans were ready for a change, and the "lost confidence" excuse clearly echoed the removal of Richardson, but Reed insisted Arkansas did not want to fire Houston Nutt. "It would look bad," he said.

What happened next would look worse. In a dramatic season finale, Arkansas beat the #1-ranked LSU Tigers in Baton Rouge. It appeared as though all might be forgiven and Nutt would remain a Razorback. But behind the scenes, boosters started the ball rolling on removing Nutt. A monstrous $3-million buyout was assembled through the Razorback Foundation. And they wouldn't have to fire the football coach. Houston Nutt resigned.

Chancellor John White stated at the ensuing press conference that UA wished to remove the "golden handcuffs" that were so invasive in Nutt's life. Since Nutt was resigning, the university should have been free of any financial obligation to him, but clearly there had been an agreement. White publicly encouraged the Razorback Foundation to shell out over $3 million to Nutt.

Stanley Reed was then quoted as saying, "It gets to the point of fairness and equity. We did not want to fire Houston Nutt. He had done a great job . . ."

Nutt had a conference record of 42-40. He never won an overall conference championship and, of course, no national championship, or the equivalent of a basketball Final Four. A day later, Nutt took a lucrative job at the University of Mississippi. Nutt wouldn't have to return any of the $3 million—he was free to coach at another school.

Richardson had been terminated in Fayetteville for essentially *suggesting* the same thing that the UA would later *do* for Houston Nutt: "If they go ahead and pay me my money, they can take the job tomorrow." Yet Richardson's buyout included a strict provision—he would lose any subsequent money if he took another job.

Richardson's overall winning percentage—70 percent—was far better than Nutt's overall percentage, not to mention the conference titles, Final Fours, and the 1994 NCAA title. When the University of Arkansas decided to dump Richardson, there was no talk of "fairness and equity" and whether firings would "look bad." Richardson seems to only have ground his heel into the sense of decorum that made it possible for Nutt to walk away with enough money to fill a Wal-Mart truck.

John White points out that Richardson was given the opportunity to resign in 2002. "Houston Nutt didn't come out and say that 'If they pay me my money I'm gone tomorrow.' We actually treated Houston the same way as Nolan, but there was no way from a public relations perspective that, nationally, people would understand why would Arkansas fire Nutt after the seasons he's just had. We couldn't fire him if we wanted to recruit another coach. There was an IRS rule change that meant Nutt couldn't afford to leave."

Whenever Richardson's firing resurfaced, his graduation rate from 1990–1994 was always mentioned as justification. That argument should have changed dramatically on October 4, 2007.

The Northwest Arkansas *Morning News* ran their usual "Briefly" column on page two of the sports section. The first three short pieces were these important issues in Arkansas:

- Tony Parker was taking time off from the French Olympic team to concentrate on his spot with the San Antonio Spurs.
- Knicks coach Isiah Thomas focused his mind on basketball during his sexual harassment trial.
- Lakers center Kwame Brown was charged with disorderly conduct.

The last section of the column was titled "Graduation Rates Increase Slightly." Most of the brief story on the NCAA's latest study—from 1997 until 2002 this time—discussed how overall graduation rates for all athletes were on the rise.

Then, this single sentence: "Arkansas' football team had a graduation rate of 53 percent, and the men's basketball team was at 50 percent."

Richardson's name was not even mentioned, although those were his final years coaching.

Why wouldn't Arkansas—which was embarrassed by his published graduation rates from 1990 to 1994—be shouting about this great academic improvement at the end of Richardson's tenure?

There had to be a big story the next day, when everyone at the

UA athletics department had a chance to plan a press conference to get their story out. *UA basketball had a respectable graduation rate in Richardson's last five years!* But the next day, there was nothing.

For most of Richardson's tenure, *Morning News* sports editor Chip Souza was an hour away, in Fort Smith. He had no excuse as to why the "new and improved" graduation rate was not a front-page piece. And he wonders why Richardson was constantly hammered for his older graduation rate after he was fired. "Nobody mentioned it when he was winning the national championship," Souza says. "It was just never an issue, until he lost and then had that press conference."

The story line about the new graduation rate was so small that almost nobody noticed, even in Arkansas.

Judge Wendell Griffen knows why the new study has never been publicized. "Frank Broyles and John White *wanted* to get rid of Nolan," Griffen says. "White was on the 'Graduation Rate Bandwagon,' thinking that graduation rates are somehow indicative of how people are doing their jobs. But athletics' function is to win games, not produce Nobel scientists. If Nolan had graduated every player and won half of his games, he would have been fired a long time ago."

Still, why not publicize the latest study, which exonerated the basketball program and shed a good light on then-embattled football coach Houston Nutt? "It would be an admission they were wrong," former UA administrator Lonnie Williams says. "You don't pick someone up that you've been kicking."

Griffen thinks that in many ways, the NCAA even speaking about graduation rates is hypocritical. "The coach of the basketball team does not have an obligation to graduate anybody, and there's not a performance feature in most contracts. The fact is that not even the dean of a college or a department head has an obligation to graduate people at a certain percentage. For the NCAA to suggest that coaches have to do what nobody else is required to do is a kind of lunacy. But that's what you get from this good old boy network, when everybody knows [college sports] is about dollars."

Forty years after the passage of the Civil Rights Act, which prohibited racial discrimination in hiring, the Southeast Conference hired its first African-American football coach. Sylvester Croom was named the Mississippi State coach in 2004.

College basketball remains far more progressive. One of the last college leagues to desegregate their teams was the glamorous Atlantic Coast Conference. Today, the ACC sets the national standard for black basketball coaches.

With twelve members in its fold, the ACC—perhaps the best league in the country—had seven black head coaches in the 2008–09 season: Boston College (Al Skinner), Georgia Tech (Paul Hewitt), Florida State (Leonard Hamilton), Clemson (Oliver Purnell), Miami (Frank Haith), Virginia (Dave Leitao), and North Carolina State (Sidney Lowe).

Not a single black head coach was employed in the ACC when Richardson won his NCAA title in 1994 (although Bob Wade had been the Maryland coach in the late 1980s).

Perhaps what lifted Nolan Richardson to greatness—his unwavering us-against-the-world attitude—might have contributed to his downfall. But Judge Wendell Griffen points out that Richardson had an important task at hand. "A brain surgeon doesn't have a chip on his shoulder," he says, "he simply uses a scalpel and is insistent on helping patients." What happened to Richardson left Griffen miffed. "We talk about opportunity," he says, "but we denigrate people who challenge the barriers."

"Nolan has the irony of being uncommonly good and universally misunderstood," Griffen says. "Nolan's battle has been in the cause of inclusion and equality but because he's a black man of action and courage—without apology or timidity—he's misunderstood as being angry or having a chip on his shoulder."

Stan Heath thinks each African-American coach needs to be taken on his own merits and politics, regardless of age. "You can't put us in the same box. Those guys [Chaney, Thompson, and Richardson] I have tremendous respect for. They voiced concerns and broke barriers in those early years and were instrumental in my development. For any coach, though, you don't become politically involved until you have success. Then you have a microphone in front of you. Were they as vocal their first years?"

Todd Day, Arkansas's all-time leading scorer, says, "When Nolan was young, he believed everything was against him. If you didn't agree with him, then you were against him, too. As he got older, he kept that edge, but that's what made him an incredibly successful coach."

Many are perplexed that Nolan Richardson could still feel disrespected or insecure when he was making so much money. Frank Broyles could be said to equate dollars and respect, but for Richardson respect had little to do with income.

Former UTEP All-American Fred Reynolds tells a story that would resonate with Richardson. Reynolds had a long pro career in Europe, returned to El Paso, and used his degree in criminal justice to become a highway patrolman. He also married a successful doctor.

For the last few years, he's bought season tickets for UTEP basketball. In 2007, an athletics department employee phoned to inform Reynolds of a new plan for season-ticket holders. Reynolds would not only have to pay for his seats, but was now required to make a donation to UTEP athletics. Although he didn't mind buying tickets, Reynolds said his career on the court was enough of a donation.

"I know your wife is a doctor," he says the UTEP employee told him. Meaning, of course, that the couple had plenty of money.

When Reynolds complained about this to the UTEP athletics director a week later, he got a similar response. "It's not like you're poor, Fred," he says he was told.

Reynolds believes his wife's status and their jobs were irrelevant. He gave great years on the court at a crucial time in UTEP basketball history. To the white people asking him, he believes, this contribution meant too little. Asking him to contribute money, even though he could well afford it, was a form of disrespect.

The long history of racism affected black athletes and coaches to varying degrees. Bob Walters was just one of countless black athletes in Arkansas whose career was stolen.

Negro schools didn't count, so his ninety-six career touchdowns were never listed as the state record. Instead, the Arkansas Activities Association for years listed a player from Osceola who scored eighty-eight touchdowns.

Walters was first diagnosed with cancer in the late 1970s, when Danny Walters was in high school. He had three brutal bouts. First, colon cancer. Then it spread, necessitating the removal of one lung in 1984. The cancer finally metastasized to his brain and kidneys. Walters never complained about the cancer that slowly ate him alive—or the racism that ruined his playing career.

"That was just Bob," his widow, Sheryl, says. "He didn't harbor bitterness."

While Walters was being devastated by the disease, though, he became keen on having his star guard Tim Hardaway join Don Haskins. "Bob liked the man," Sheryl says, "and he felt Haskins was someone who would see a person as a person, and an athlete as an athlete. Tim wound up in El Paso because Bob had both an admiration for, and trust in, Don Haskins."

Walters—who'd steered his nephew to Arkansas to play football—pushed Hardaway to sign early rather than wait until the later signing period, when there would no doubt have been a long line. "Bob liked the idea of people recognizing skills," Sheryl says, "rather than the whole black-white bit. He saw that in Haskins, I guess. There were so many places Bob went where he felt he didn't get a good shake because he was black."

Walters was able to both forgive Arkansas through his nephew and honor his own battles with segregation by sending Hardaway to Haskins.

"Bob Walters understood history," Tim Hardaway adds. "That's why he was happy to see me with Don Haskins."

Walters passed away in 1985 at the age of forty-three.

The challenges for the new generation of African-American coaches pose a different set of problems. "There are struggles that are common to the human condition," Judge Wendell Griffen says, "but it's a special experience for coaches of color. Coaches of the Stan Heath era are dealing with different facts, but they're still dealing with the issues of inclusion that Nolan had. One of the privileges of being white is that you never have to worry about boosters not supporting you, or the trustees of the institution wondering if you are white enough to head the program."

Griffen provides a simple analogy of what it has been like for blacks to navigate through American society. "I'm right-handed, but I never wake up and think about it. When I sit down at one of those preformed desks in a college lecture hall, I can fit." To those right-handers who are comfortable, everything seems fine. "Only left-handed people are aware of the fact that these desks are set up differently," Griffen says.

In May 2008, Griffen lost his reelection campaign. An ordained Baptist minister, he had been an appeals court judge in Little Rock for over a decade. During his tenure he had to appear before an ethics panel, where he was successful in fighting for his right to free speech. Griffen was highly critical of more than the way the University of Arkansas had treated minorities and Nolan Richardson. Griffen had pointedly criticized President Bush and also endorsed an increase in minimum wage in Arkansas.

Although his successor, Judge Rita Gruber, did not bring up Griffen's comments during the campaign, she told the Associated Press, "I think it's fair to say there were a lot of people in the community who were disappointed with the statements he's made over the years."

Even in defeat, Griffen was defiant. "I would much rather have maintained my integrity," he said, "and experienced these results than sacrificed my integrity for political expediency."

Ed Beshara died in Tulsa in the spring of 2007 at the age of ninety-one. The son of immigrants, Beshara often felt the strain of being an outsider. While Beshara and Richardson looked comically different standing side by side, Richardson believed he and Beshara were two of a kind. Beshara's background provided him with empathy for the underdog, something Richardson always found endearing. For twenty years, hardly a week would pass without Beshara and Richardson talking.

The month before Beshara's death, Richardson drove from Arkansas daily—four hours round-trip—to spend time with his friend. Beshara would hold Richardson's thick hand and call him "my adopted son," while a stream of nurses and doctors came and went. It was the first time Richardson made the trek to Tulsa on a regular basis since Yvonne had been sick.

"They were friends until the end," says Ed Beshara Jr., who took over his father's business. "My dad loved Nolan a great deal. Nolan is extremely loyal and will remember you forever if you try to help him."

Richardson's eulogy in tribute to Beshara brought the mourners to their feet, applauding through their tears. "I'd never seen people cheer at a funeral," Beshara Jr. says, "but they did that day."

TWENTY-FOUR

ANOTHER COUNTRY

Panama convinced Nolan Richardson to coach its national team in 2005. Richardson was thrilled to lead a national team where his fluency in Spanish would be useful, even if it meant coaching in obscurity. Panama posted its best finish in twenty-six years, but the news was hardly mentioned in the States.

Richardson's next crack at leading a Spanish-speaking squad was a homecoming of sorts. He was named the Mexican National Coach in the spring of 2007. The Mexicans, who had hopes of an Olympic bid, set up training camp across the Rio Grande from El Paso in Juárez, Mexico.

Today's Texas-Mexico border is radically different from the one Nolan Richardson grew up on. Juárez is now home to somewhere around two million people and a vast sprawl of poverty. The bridges that connect El Paso to Juárez are teeming with window-washers, accordion players, and trinket salesmen hustling like walk-ons at varsity tryouts. NAFTA's "free trade" has damaged the already-troubled Mexican economy—half-built concrete structures sit uncompleted all over town. Post-9/11 security measures and a rash of violence have discouraged tourism, one of the few steady sources of cash. Hundreds of women have been murdered in Juárez during the last decade and the crimes remain unsolved. If there was ever a city that should have "Us Against the World" as its motto, it's Juárez.

The Mexican team accepted Richardson without hesitation, as though he had simply been stuck in traffic on the bridge for a few decades. Richardson's squad featured players with both NCAA credentials and Mexican passports.

The players who did *not* participate for Mexico, however, devastated the team before Richardson ever coached a game. Eduardo Najera had an impressive run during his nine years in the NBA, but Najera claimed he would not represent Mexico under the current leadership of the Olympic committee. Earl Watson, whose mother was born in Mexico, may have made a bigger impact for Richardson. Watson was a solid NBA point guard, and Richardson's scrambling-and-trapping style would have been the perfect showcase for him. While Watson never officially declined, he didn't join the team either.

Nolan Richardson remains surprisingly fit for a man in his late sixties. He has a trim waist, muscular shoulders, and he's thirty pounds lighter than when he prowled the sidelines at Arkansas. His hair has gone gray, and he's let it grow out, along with a mustache that has evolved into a goatee. He leans forward when he walks, the way a young Mike Tyson did when he answered the bell.

Richardson appeared to reverse the aging process at practice in Juárez, morphing into a younger man. He hopped out of the way to avoid a collision. Grabbing the ball, he demonstrated the correct way to jump-stop. He was quick to halt play and hammer home a point. Occasionally he laughed along with his team, sometimes even at mistakes, as if they all shared the same secret—it's great to be back on the basketball court.

The most impressive aspect of his coaching comeback was how Richardson ran his practice with his fluent border Spanish—and Spanglish. He switched back and forth as easily as he had traversed the border as a boy. It didn't take him long to recall the words for "trap" and "fast break."

His "Forty Minutes of Hell" depended on a brutally fast pace. During the first week of training, nearly every player was bent over, hands to knees, and gasping for breath. *"Qué pasa, hórale, muévanse!"* Richardson said, but they couldn't move at the pace he was demanding.

Even after surrendering a layup, the Mexicans were required to racehorse the ball back down the court. "If you want to take the other team's heart, *no hay nada como hechar una canasta enseguida de la de ellos,*" Richardson says. Scoring quickly after his own teams' defensive breakdowns. Attacking the attacker. A Richardson trademark.

The Mexican National Team would take the floor the last day of May 2007.

It wasn't at Bud Walton Arena. Instead, it was a meaningless exhibition game in a dank Juárez gym. Meaningless with one exception— it was Mexico's first game with Nolan Richardson as coach. Ninety minutes before the match was to begin, the gym was jammed and the atmosphere was festive. Musicians, busking for pesos, set up outside the entrance. Inside, dozens of autograph-seekers and cell-phone-wielding photographers formed a queue, but the target wasn't the players.

A few minutes later, in a decaying locker room deep in the bowels of the building, Richardson gathered the red-white-and-green-clad players. *"Vamos a empezar* a half-court defense," Richardson said, but as the game progressed, he'd turn up the pressure with his *"Cuarenta minutos de infierno."*

After a few brief reminders, the players rose to their feet.

"Vámanos," Richardson hollered, and the team gathered around him in a tight circle, every hand reaching forward. "This is a new beginning for us," Richardson said, and the coach indeed looked new in his all-white attire. Clean, fresh, and young. Then he led the chant—*"Uno, dos, tres . . . México!"*

With the reborn Richardson guiding them, the undermanned Mexican team put on a valiant showing in Las Vegas in the summer of 2007, hoping to qualify for the Olympics for the first time in decades. They opened with an upset over bronze winner Puerto Rico, and it appeared as though Richardson might have to recall the Spanish expression for "Hollywood ending."

The Mexicans beat Venezuela later, but stumbled in games against Canada, Argentina, Uruguay, and Panama. In the end, Mexico did not win enough to qualify for the Beijing Olympics. Despite these disappointments, the Mexican team earned a measure of respect against the overstocked Americans—a monstrous team good enough for a Wheaties box, a team that had been winning by an average of 47 points. In his pregame talk, USA (and Duke) coach Mike Krzyzewski lectured his young squad on the historical importance of Nolan Richardson.

Mexico converted time and again off fast breaks, often after made baskets, and in the third quarter Mexico pulled within a dozen. Richardson's team would run 100 points on the Americans, the most the USA team allowed the entire tournament. That wasn't nearly enough. In the end Mexico lost by 27 points.

———

"**Nolan Richardson was one** of the best five coaches in the nation," Don Haskins said shortly after the Mexican team was eliminated. "It's terrible that he's not coaching in college. I don't even care about that black coach stuff," he added. "All I know is he was one hell of a coach."

Don Haskins died in September of 2008. The funeral services were held at the Methodist church near downtown El Paso, where Richardson had hustled parking cars on Sundays during his college days. Within a week of Haskins's death, Richardson's first wife, Helen, who had been on dialysis for years, passed away as well.

A few months later, Nolan Richardson was inducted into the College Basketball Hall of Fame in Kansas City. Other inductees included Charles Barkley, Danny Manning, and television commentators Dick Vitale and Billy Packer.

Richardson and his wife, Rosario, arrived early, and were quickly surrounded by a crew of Razorback supporters and ex-players. Just then, there seemed to be some sort of disturbance; the Arkansas group turned back toward the street, with big eyes.

Frank Broyles was getting out of an SUV.

Broyles looks more like a basketball man than a football coach. He's well over six feet, long-armed, and moves gracefully. For a man in his eighties, he looks fantastic. Broyles had no official responsibility to be at Richardson's Hall of Fame night; he had retired from the university nearly a year earlier.

Richardson helped Rose remove her red leather coat. She said something to him about the surprise guest. Richardson didn't seem too worried, though. "Let's just enjoy ourselves," he told her.

Several of Richardson's players were there. Ken Biley. Scotty Thurman. Corliss Williamson. Clint McDaniel. So was his attorney in the lawsuit, John Walker. Former assistant coach Wayne Stehlik and longtime basketball secretary Terri Mercer were there, as was his old boss from the junior college, Sid Simpson, and Arkansas's new AD, Jeff Long.

The press conference was jammed, with close to five hundred fans and media in attendance. Each inductee was given five minutes to speak.

Richardson is still a powerful public speaker and has an incredible sense of drama. His voice didn't crescendo with the power of a storefront preacher this time. Instead, he sounded reflective. Richardson mentioned Ol' Mama, Sid Simpson, and Don Haskins. His public talks often refer to his inevitable reckoning some day with Saint Peter at the Pearly Gates. This time he brought up somebody else.

"I noticed Frank Broyles is here," Richardson said, "and I appreciate him coming."

The Arkansas faithful in attendance saw it as a profound moment—Broyles took a small step; Richardson took one as well.

Scotty Thurman was surprised but not shocked. "They both know they could have handled it differently," he says. "People who have a lot of power play those battles. Deep down they don't really like each other, but they respect each other."

When all the inductees had spoken, master of ceremonies Reggie Minton invited anyone who wanted to interview or congratulate the inductees to come forward. Lines quickly formed in front of each honoree. Frank Broyles, who was sitting at the very back, got in line to shake hands with Nolan Richardson.

The next morning at breakfast, Richardson talked about his mixed emotions after both receiving a great honor and seeing Broyles. Richardson's tone had mellowed again. He admitted that he had noticed Broyles waiting patiently at the back of the line and said that Broyles was complimentary and congratulatory when he finally got his turn.

In February 2009, the school finally honored the 1994 NCAA title team—and coach. It marked the fifteenth anniversary of their championship and would be Richardson's first time on campus since he was fired. The ten-year anniversary had come and gone without mention because of the ongoing lawsuit. Frank Broyles had retired a year earlier and been replaced by Jeff Long, who seemed genuinely interested in bringing Richardson back into the Razorback family.

Northwest Arkansas had been rocked earlier in the month by vicious ice storms. Trees were torn out at their roots, buildings damaged, and power lines were dead all over the Ozarks. The lack of power had hit Madison County, just south of Fayetteville, especially hard. With no phone service or electricity functioning in this mountainous part of the state, a hundred workers were sent from Pennsylvania to assist the local electric cooperative in restoring power. Nearly a third of the conscripted workers from the North were African-American.

Madison County is virtually all-white, and the ice storm exposed an archaic mindset that still lives on in Arkansas, only minutes from the state's university.

The Pennsylvania workers were harassed by gangs of white men driving around them, hollering racial epithets, waving Confederate flags and guns. The imported workers figured they'd better call the sheriff's office—not in Madison County, though. They phoned nearby Washington County instead.

Madison County was in the national news after Barack Obama was elected in November, as well. In Huntsville, the day after the election, the owners of the Faubus Motel removed the Stars and Stripes and raised the Confederate flag. American voters, the owners claimed, had turned their backs on the principles of our founding fathers. The motel was at one time owned by the former governor but no longer had any connection to the Faubus family.

Even after the phone and power lines had been repaired, the

mangled trees and busted branches remained all over northwest Arkansas.

The Razorback basketball team had won just a single SEC game going into this final home contest. It was their worst season since joining the SEC.

Ken Biley would have walked to the reunion from Kansas City, where he works for H&R Block. "I've had all kinds of excitement in my life," says the surprise starter of the 1994 champs. "I've witnessed my wife giving birth to our kids. But my starting in that championship game, that honor did more for me than anyone could imagine."

Today, Biley still needs a few more classes for his college diploma. He's continued to watch sports in the fifteen years since Arkansas won it all, especially championship games, looking for a story that would mirror his own. He has uncovered nothing even close. "This wasn't a fourth down gamble in football," Biley says. "This was the NCAA championship on national TV. What would the critics say about Nolan if we had lost the game?"

The reunion weekend began with a Richardson staple—the team, along with wives, family, and friends, were invited to his home for a colossal barbecue. The players went out on the town afterward, but managed to be up the next day by nine a.m. for another typical Richardson event, a free basketball clinic at the Yvonne Richardson Community Center. The center, situated in Fayetteville's tiny traditional black neighborhood south of downtown, was opened in Yvonne's honor a few years after her death.

The players from the 1994 team were the guest coaches, but for the first few minutes of the clinic, they sloughed about and yawned, arms crossed and shirts untucked. Former Razorback assistant Wayne Stehlik tried to bring the kids and coaches to life with a warm-up drill, a simple relay race for the youngsters. Even that couldn't motivate the former NCAA champs, who were no longer subject to curfews to ensure a good night's sleep.

When the relay was just a minute old, Richardson appeared at the entrance. The parents noticed, then some of the campers—none of whom were born yet when Richardson led the Razorbacks to the title. A couple of his former players noticed, too.

Corliss Williamson leaped into a basketball stance. "Hey, I want to win this!" he shouted to his team, pacing up and down his line, bending at the waist to attempt a chest bump with one kid.

Clint McDaniel took Williamson's cue and began pushing his young campers, too. "We're not going to let them beat us!" McDaniel said. Then Ken Biley and the rest of the Razorbacks jumped in the kids' faces, high-fiving, fist-bumping, and taunting the nearest competitors. When it was over, the winning line jumped up and down and exchanged hugs, as though they were champions as well. The clinic had undergone an astonishing transformation. Richardson hadn't said a word.

College basketball is a business—that's a refrain repeated any time a coach is fired. If it is indeed true, then firing Nolan Richardson was a bad business decision. The Razorbacks have never been the same. Seven years after Richardson's removal, it's nearly impossible to conclude that Broyles's judgment was correct, since the Razorbacks have never come close to approaching his success.

With the current Arkansas team struggling, Nolan nostalgia gripped the state, and the reunion of the 1994 champs allowed Razorback fans a brief glimpse of their past glory—and an opportunity to reconsider what had transpired with their iconic coach.

"It was a sad day for the University of Arkansas," former chancellor John White says, in retrospect. "Nolan Richardson is just an absolute icon. He's not only an asset for the University of Arkansas, he's an asset for this nation. I just hated that it came to that kind of conclusion." White wasn't alone in his sentiments, and the weekend festivities would go a long way toward building trust between Richardson and the school.

There's also the "What if?" factor. Richardson's infamous press conference in 2002 began with the sports information director reading an encouraging letter from the parents of a recruit. The recruit was Andre Iguodala, who never enrolled at Arkansas because of Richardson's removal. Iguodala went to Arizona instead, then was the ninth pick in the NBA draft, made the All-Rookie team, and became an NBA All-Star. Joe Johnson was the only player of Richardson's ever to rise to that status in the NBA. Razorback fans could only speculate how good they might have been with Richardson coaching Iguodala.

The reunion banquet had the glitz and glamour of the Grammy Awards. The posh hall was packed with a crowd of nearly a thousand people who'd paid a hundred dollars each. Full-size color photos decorated the walls. Souvenirs from the title run were being hawked at the door. If Arkansas had at one time been viewed as backward, you wouldn't have known it this night. The expenditures would have made a Wall Street CEO blush.

Each player was given a minute to speak. Richardson was last, and praised some of the most obscure players effusively. Just before he was finished, he said, "I'm the only coach in America who was fired and still stayed in town." It was his way of saying both that he still loved Arkansas and that his firing was unjust.

One of the first things anyone entering Bud Walton Arena sees in the main lobby is a seven-foot cutout of Nolan Richardson, in a trophy case with a plaque that reads, "Arguably the most popular coach in any sport in Razorback history."

Two entire trophy cases commemorate "The Nolan Richardson Era." Another one is devoted to the 1994 NCAA title team. Just to the side is a miniature theater, where you can push a button and learn about the Razorbacks. Above the entrance, a sign proclaims: THE NOLAN RICHARDSON THEATER. On the side is a plaque dedicating the theater to Yvonne Richardson. All of these displays were built before Richardson was dumped in 2002, and all of them have remained, even through the contentious lawsuit.

Ralph Brewster, Richardson's first great player from Bowie, has little remorse about his own career. Brewster's impulse—to go along with what was best for his coach, instead of what might have been best for himself—is an indicator of the charisma of his coach, he says. Today he is proud of his role in Richardson's life. "Nolan will stand the test of history," Brewster says. "A lot of changes in the view of Nolan are going to come with time. He is an original who spoke the truth and stood on righteousness."

The leading scorer in Arkansas history, Todd Day, concurs about the test of time. "Nolan Richardson is the greatest African-American coach in history," he said days before Richardson came back to campus.

The 2009 SEC season had been a disaster for second-year coach John Pelphrey. The only league game Arkansas won leading up to the reunion was the day after Richardson had privately addressed Pelphrey's Razorbacks.

The Georgia game was a return to the best days and a chance for the fans to remember. Richardson addressed the crowd of 19,724 at halftime, and their reaction was deafening. "If a Phantom fighter jet had flown through Bud Walton [Arena] right then," Wally Hall wrote, "it would not have been seen or heard." There was still plenty of history that Richardson could invoke that made Razorback fans happy.

The overflowing emotion found its way into the current team. Arkansas won, 89-67, a rare win for the 2009 team that would finish 2-14 in the SEC—dead-last place.

TWENTY-FIVE

GO TELL IT ON THE MOUNTAIN

Nolan Richardson began his career determined to be different from his college coach. Nobody could have predicted all the ways he'd wind up like Don Haskins.

Haskins and Richardson won historically important NCAA championships, and it's difficult to invoke the name of either man without an ensuing discussion of race. Both were attacked for their graduation rates of black players on those title teams. In the end, both men did better in this regard than originally perceived.

Richardson even drove a pickup truck, although he surely had his choice of any car in town. The Razorbacks innocently began referring to Richardson as "The Bear" in the 1990s.

Haskins remained at UTEP for nearly forty years and may have been the last of that breed of coach. Richardson never applied for another job while coaching the Razorbacks.

"Nolan fell in love with Arkansas," longtime athletics trainer

Dave England says. "I know it hurt him those times when it seemed like Arkansas didn't love him back."

Richardson has done more than win championships to earn that love. He has been involved in over thirty charities during his time in Fayetteville. Sometimes Richardson used his name in hosting fundraisers; sometimes he put up his own money. His annual golf tournament in El Paso honors his daughter while raising thousands of dollars for leukemia research. After Yvonne's death, his empathetic antenna for the downtrodden became even more sensitive; he'd hand out large sums of cash like Halloween candy if sick children were involved. Sid Simpson says, "That's the direction Nolan seems to be going. He'd pick up a load of crippled kids and take them to a game, but he'd never tell anyone." Shortly after Yvonne died, Richardson learned there was a child in Paragould, Arkansas, who had cancer. "He wrote out a check for fifteen thousand, and had it delivered to the family," Simpson says.

Yet another aspect of Richardson's life that mirrors Don Haskins is his selective memory. Even as detailed evidence of his humanitarian giving mounted, he claimed to have no recollection of specific stories of generosity. He either has terrible recall, is too humble, or he's helped so many people he really has lost track.

Arkansas was the punch line of jokes and a source of national embarrassment at one time. Today, despite the recent raising of the Confederate flag and intimidation of the black repairmen after the ice storm, race relations are improved.

Elizabeth Jacoway, the author of two books about race and Arkansas, was born there in the 1940s. "My sense is that Arkansas has changed dramatically," Jacoway says. "People who lived through the Civil Rights movement understand the very slow nature in which change can come about."

Are Americans and Arkansans better off being reminded of that great distance and remembering that slow nature of change? Does discussing the racist history of the nation help us move forward or keep us stuck in the past? Does Richardson's outspokenness open wounds or help close them?

Anyone taking a close look at Nolan Richardson's life should understand how both memory and his sense of justice have haunted him. The austere woman who raised Richardson had an archive of stories about her own parents' enslavement. The poorest Mexican-Americans in segregated Texas could sit at lunch counters, splash in swimming pools, and lean back in air-conditioned movie theaters. He could not.

Standing toe-to-toe with American racism became unavoidable for Richardson.

By simply asking for a Coke, he had an inadvertent hand in ending Jim Crow laws in El Paso. At the time he began his career, there was not a single black man coaching major college basketball. Powerful people thought of him as the "nigger coach" upon his arrival in Snyder and Tulsa. In Arkansas he toiled at a campus where police dogs bared their teeth at black fraternity brothers and sisters. The most powerful man at the school spent a decade as the proud front man of segregation in Arkansas athletics, and later tried to prod a table full of journalists into using the word "nigger" in print. Being the first black at every outpost rubbed Richardson raw, especially in Arkansas, a state where sundown towns thrived, George Wallace triumphed, and, even into the new millennium, the state university board of trustees felt that "nigger jokes" were funny.

His refusal to keep quiet makes a lot more sense in that context; the long arc of his life puts that fateful 2002 press conference in perspective.

Richardson understood that Broyles wanted to fire him for years. Today, if the entire text of that 2002 news media gathering is read aloud, a few things become apparent. One, it's clear that Richardson was mostly talking to and about Frank Broyles—although he allowed that he has to "answer to" Broyles and the UA administration. Knowing Broyles preferred that he fail in order to facilitate his firing became an unbearable strain. Also apparent is that Richardson, under the extreme pressure of coaching a fledgling college basketball team, reverted to his own history and memory by quoting Ol' Mama.

After winning the NCAA title in 1994, Richardson's cause and his passion changed, and he obsessed about equality for black coaches, himself included. He continued to talk about race because racism was not over. In the world of college sports, one has only to count the number of black athletics directors and head football coaches to deduce that something is still wrong. Richardson's error was to think that trotting the elephant of racism out in front of a room full of white reporters and television crews during a mediocre season was a good idea.

Did he always comport himself in the best manner for his cause during the five decades that he coached? Of course not. But if the world was going to change, somebody had to follow Ol' Mama's advice. Nolan Richardson kicked down the damn door.

Richardson's ranch is a ten-minute drive west of Fayetteville, among the rolling hills that rest on the edge of northwest Arkansas. The town blends first into suburbs, then to farms. Just before the road turns to gravel, the land unfolds into a scenic panorama, calm and peaceful in every direction. At the end of the road there is an iron gate that reads RICHARDSON RANCH. The house is simple, understated, and rustic. It's much more a cabin than a castle.

The kitchen is also the dining room and the epicenter of all activity at the Richardson ranch. On any given weekend, and not just championship team reunions, their home is filled with ex-players, family, neighbors, and friends. His wife, Rosario, will be cooking; maybe green chile caldillo. Richardson will man the taco station expertly, folding in diced tomatoes and shredded cheese.

And there are kids, kids everywhere. School groups and church groups. Nieces and nephews and grandkids. And especially the children of former players.

One recent Fourth of July weekend, the five kids there just happened to be young girls, between two and ten years of age. The ex-Razorbacks at the ranch that holiday weren't very good players or even on great teams. That didn't matter to Richardson, who waited on them as if they were All-Americans.

While the adults were still feasting, the girls invented a game. They would run in a loop about the size of the center-jump circle. Then the lead one, the oldest, would turn a dramatic dance move into a split or somersault. The younger girls would imitate the first, then they'd all fall down, dissolving in laughter. Occasionally, they'd return to the table to trade bites and share bowls.

A hero of the Irish Civil Rights movement once said, "Our revenge will be the laughter of our children." This is the philosophy of the Richardson ranch, where the sound of young kids' laughing resonates.

Rose Richardson moved to the couch to watch the dance routine digress into silliness. Nothing makes the Richardsons happier than having children around, and during the girls' chaotic tumbles a palpable happiness descended on everyone. Rose was having as much fun as they were, although she courteously declined to try the cartwheels and flips.

When the dishes were done, Richardson roared, "Who wants to see the animals?" and the girls erupted into pandemonium. They formed a line behind Richardson, who led them outside.

Richardson roams his ranch these days with his giant Great Dane, Billy, at his hip. One of the girls walked up to Billy and reached to scratch his belly. The barn was nearby, but most of the horses were out in the pasture. So were the llamas. The youngest girl clung to Richardson's leg, and he hoisted her up. Then the coach bellowed, and his horses came running. She hugged his neck and hooted with joy.

The Horse Whisperer has nothing on Nolan Richardson. His thoroughbreds, Tennessee walkers, and quarter horses respond to anything he shouts. The kids were enthralled, shadowing Richardson as he directed the animals. Across the rolling hills, goats, lambs, and some pot-bellied pigs lazed about.

The animals have been a big part of Nolan and Rose Richardson's life since losing Yvonne in 1987. "Some people need someone or something to depend on them and she is one of those people," Richardson told the *Tulsa World* about his wife, but he could have been talking about himself as well.

A wide wooden porch surrounds most of the house and affords the best view. As sunset approaches, the ranch becomes bathed in a light that a religious person might call heavenly. Around the "U" of the porch on the north side of the house is a garden about the size of half a basketball court. The garden is filled with statues of kids jumping in puddles, running, skipping rope. Laughing. It's as if the Richardsons have tried to distill and freeze childhood—and memory—to protect and preserve it after losing Yvonne.

Something became clear that holiday weekend. Richardson *did* love Arkansas too much. He should have packed his boxes and loaded up the moving vans soon after carving his place in history in 1994. But even outsiders eventually need a place to rest, a home. Something else became clear, too. Nobody could remind people of where they came from, cross borders, or inspire players to believe in a cause like Nolan Richardson. Those were his gifts; his career a type of bridge.

Richardson has let his Afro grow gray and long, and he really does look like a historical figure—like Frederick Douglass with a goatee. Maybe that's fitting. Richardson attended a school named after the former slave who kept reminding America of its sins.

John McLendon never got the shot he'd earned at a big university. Neither did countless other black coaches. Other coaches of color of his era had terrific teams, but what distinguishes Nolan Richardson is the nature of his trailblazing career, as the first black coach to go into the old Confederacy—and the embers of racism—and have astonishing success. Richardson—outspoken, passionate, and righteous—is the most important African-American coach America has known.

Despite his garden full of statues of children at play, he could not freeze time. Memory, though. Memory endures, because Nolan Richardson, as relentless as forty minutes of hell's full-court pressure, won't let us forget. He has begun to fulfill his former chancellor's request to be happy, even if he's still an outsider, on the wrong side of the fence at the university where he won the championship. The basketball court where he finally returned belongs to him—although you won't find his name on it. Regardless, Richardson's shadow and history remind, admonish, and exhort Arkansas.

ACKNOWLEDGMENTS

Robert Boswell and Antonya Nelson have provided advice, books, friendship, beer, gourmet meals, and parenting tips for the last fourteen years. They are the best friends a writer could hope for.

Barry Pearce is a loyal and unselfish friend, as well as a fine writer.

Several people gave me great suggestions on the manuscript: Carol Capitani, Tom Spieczny, Josh Wheeler, Barry Pearce, Jeff Vance, Connie Voisine, Robert Boswell, Sheila Black, Tracy Sherrod, and Candice Morrow.

Thanks to: Geoffery Stark at University of Arkansas Special Collection.

Thanks to American sports heroes David Meggyesy, Dave Zirin, Doug Harris, Michael James, Steve and Tracey Yellen, and Ben Jobe.

Thanks also to John Conroy, Dennis Daily, Henry Thomas, Ken Olsen, Garrett Hongo, Austin Hoover, Keith French, Mike Thomas, and Modzel "Bud" Greer.

For help steering me around the UA campus, thanks to: Jim Harris, Donita Ritchie, Terri Mercer, Findlay Edwards, Robbie Edwards, and Wayne Stehlik.

Thanks also to Rosie Dixon and Frank Fellone at the *Democrat-*

Gazette, Glen Guthrie, John Podesta, David Shields, Dagoberto Gilb, Jennifer Grotz, Sharon Ord-Warner, Michael Collier, and Chris Engskov.

Big thanks to New Mexico State's Lou Henson, Duncan Hayse, Tama Garski, Chris Burnham, Harriet Linkin, Monica Torres, Pam Jansma, Bill Conroy, and Dr. Waded Cruzado.

Interviews were conducted with the following people: Ballard Shapleigh, Jimmie Tramel, Darren Ivy, Marc Spears, Wally Hall, Bob Holt, Chip Souza, David Hargiss, Steve Narisi, Joe Neal, Charles Robinson, Carrol Williams, Bob Carver, Fred Vorsanger, Dave England, Dr. John White, Rudy Keeling, Dick Versace, Tony Barone, Steve Green, Kelly Green, Pat Foster, Lanny Van Eman, Sid Simpson, Bob O'Day, Kenny John, Alvis Glidewell, Manny Placillas, Dwight Williams, Andy Stoglin, Mike Anderson, Earnest Starks, Phillip Trapp, Lyell Thompson, Otto "Bud" Zinke, Reggie Minton, Judge Thomas Spieczny, Don Haskins, Eddie Mullens, Lou Henson, Jim Haney, Almer Lee, Scotty Thurman, Alex Dillard, Clint McDaniel, Pat Bradley, Ben Daggett, Jeremy Rose, Ralph Brewster, Melvin Patridge, Tim Hardaway, Larry Gipson, Ed Beshara Jr., Alan Mantooth, Norris Stevenson, Charles Prigmore, John Phillips, Frankie Allen, Thomas Trotter, Jay Jennings, John Chaney, Stan Heath, Charles Martin, Richard Pennington, Lonnie Williams, Wendell Griffen, Darrell Brown, Sheryl Walters, Shelton Walters, Danny Walters, Irv Cross, Milton Katz, Bert Williams, Madalyn Richardson, Rosario Richardson, and Nolan Richardson.

Nearly a dozen people were interviewed who insisted that their names not appear. Thanks to them, as well.

Frank Broyles turned down repeated requests to be interviewed.

Thanks to the *Democrat-Gazette* for allowing me access to their archives.

Lonnie Williams gave me sage advice. Both Wendell Griffen and Darrell Brown not only made themselves constantly available, but were inspiring. Just as inspiring was the Walters family, whose stories of Bob Walters still resonate. Meeting Bert Williams was an honor.

The research and suggestions of Charles Martin, Richard Pennington, and Milton Katz were invaluable. All three have authored important works on race and college sports. Richard Lapchick's research was also helpful.

Ben Osborne at *SLAM* magazine first published my piece on Nolan Richardson, and his encouragement was vital. Thanks also to Khalid Salaam and Susan Price at *SLAM*.

oyles's segregated teams at the University of Arkansas in the mid-
50s.

Broyles: Icon of Arkansas sports; his association with UA as
tball coach and director of athletics lasted fifty years. He hired an
d Richardson.

Cash: First black basketball player in the Southwest Conference at
CU.

haney: Outspoken African-American basketball coach at Temple.

ark: University of Arkansas Board of Trustees member who
nitted using the word "nigger" in conversation and jokes.

nnors: Iconic Tulsa sportswriter who covered Richardson's time a
sa.

"Rose" Davila: Richardson's longtime wife; mother of the late
nne Richardson.

Davis: Richardson's coach for his first season at Texas Western
lege.

ay: Leading scorer in Arkansas history, helped lead team to their
Final Four.

illard: Hot-shooting sub who scored in bunches for Richardson's
4 team.

unne: Wealthy Tulsa booster who was originally opposed to
ng Richardson.

ans: Texas Tech assistant in the 1970s and 1980s, who recruited
ph Brewster in 1977. Later the head coach at Mississippi; now an
stant at Arkansas.

aubus: Governor of Arkansas during the Little Rock Central
is.

Fry: Former Arkansas assistant coach under Frank Broyles, then
d coach at SMU who brought the first black player (Jerry LeVias)
he Southwest Conference.

e "Big House" Gaines: Highly successful coach at historically
k Winston-Salem State.

Galarza: El Paso icon and Bowie High School star whose three-
t heroics predated Richardson's by a decade.

eorge: University of Arkansas Board of Trustees member who
itted using the word "nigger" in conversation and jokes.

idewell: Longtime El Paso high school basketball coach after
m Richardson modeled his first pressure defenses.

Special thanks to Christina Morgan, who championed this project initially.

Bobbito Garcia and Jesse Washington at *Bounce* magazine gave me encouragement, as did Alexander Wolff of *Sports Illustrated*. Dan McGrath and Barry Temkin of the *Chicago Tribune* were also supportive.

Thanks to Don Johnson, Scott Peterson, and everyone in the Sports Literature Association.

Glory Road, Dan Wetzel's book about the 1966 Texas Western team and Don Haskins, was terrific help. So was Frank Fitzpatrick's book *The Walls Came Tumbling Down*. Barry Jacob's book *Across the Line: Profiles in Basketball Courage* was a wonderful resource.

The quote "Our revenge will be the laughter of our children" is from the Irish Republican hero Bobby Sands.

UTEP, Tulsa University, Western Texas College, Eastern Arizona Junior College, Bowie High School, the *Democrat-Gazette*, and the University of Arkansas all provided information, photos, or media guides.

Eric Howerton at Now Creative Inc. and *Hawgs Illustrated* provided great help with photos.

Big thanks to Nolan Richardson and his family. Nolan was always available and willing to talk.

What I miss most about college basketball is the sense of optimism sometimes lacking in the book business. My amazing agent, Andrew Blauner, is an exception, and he has been a fantastic help. Thanks, Bird!

Thanks to editor extraordinaire Dawn Davis, Maya Ziv, Van Luu, and everyone at HarperCollins and Amistad.

Finally, thanks to my incredible wife, Connie Voisine, and to our daughter, Alma Bradburd, for their love and patience.

WHO'S WHO IN
NOLAN RICHARDSON'S

Mike Anderson: Longtime assistant to Richardson, h
guard for him at Tulsa. Now the coach at Univers

Jim "Bad News" Barnes: Born in Arkansas, Barnes w
player in Texas Western (later UTEP) history. Ri
recruit him to TWC.

Ed Beshara: Tulsa clothier and close friend of Richard
in 2007.

Ken Biley: Benchwarmer; a surprise starter in the NC
1994.

Jim Bowden: Former UTEP director of athletics who
Richardson to apply at Tulsa University.

Pat Bradley: Best three-point shooter in Arkansas hist

Ralph Brewster: Richardson's best player at Bowie Hig
Paso. Went to Texas Tech in exchange for their rec
Richardson for a junior college job.

Charlie Brown: First black player at Texas Western Co
UTEP).

Darrell Brown: First black football player to attempt t

Judge Wendell Griffen: University of Arkansas double graduate, civil rights and justice advocate, friend of Richardson.

Wally Hall: Longtime sportswriter for the Arkansas *Democrat-Gazette*.

Jim Haney: Head of the National Association of Basketball Coaches (NABC); his articles on the lack of black administrators enlightened and infuriated Richardson.

Tim Hardaway: Star guard at UTEP for Don Haskins in the 1980s; his high school coach, Bob Walters, was from Arkansas.

David Hargiss: Former Arkansas football player in the mid-1960s who defended and befriended black walk-on Darrell Brown.

Don Haskins: Richardson's college coach, he was the first man to start five blacks and win an NCAA basketball title in 1966.

Stan Heath: African-American coach who replaced Richardson at Arkansas in 2002; now at the University of South Florida.

Orville Henry: Iconic Arkansas sportswriter and close friend of Richardson.

Nemo Herrera: Longtime Bowie High School coach who mentored Richardson.

Darren Ivy: Penned most of the articles in *Untold Stories*, the collection of articles about black athletes in Arkansas during the time of segregation.

Ben Jobe: Politically conscious college coach who led historically black Southern University to the NCAA tournament.

Kenny John: Richardson's workout partner at Fort Bliss, played at UTEP, outstanding high school coach in El Paso.

Jimmy King: Tulsa basketball coach whose firing opened the way for Richardson.

Almer Lee: First black basketball player to letter at Arkansas.

Jerry LeVias: First black football star in the Southwest Conference, recruited by Hayden Fry, former assistant to Frank Broyles.

Charles Martin: UTEP professor; one of America's top scholars on the integration of college sports.

Wilson Matthews: Former Little Rock Central football coach; joined Frank Broyles's first staff at Arkansas.

Lee Mayberry: Star guard on Richardson's first Final Four team at Arkansas.

Terri Mercer: Longtime Arkansas basketball secretary.

Clint McDaniel: Defensive star of Richardson's NCAA champs in 1994.

John McLendon: Legendary black coach; won three consecutive national titles at Tennessee State; the godfather of black coaches and fast break basketball.

Oliver Miller: Center on Richardson's first Final Four team at Arkansas.

Reggie Minton: Groundbreaking black basketball coach at Air Force; now codirects the NABC.

Gordon Morgan: First black professor at University of Arkansas.

Steve Narisi: Arkansas native and TV journalist who has studied the desegregation of the Southwest Conference.

Joe Neal: Leader of progressive movements in Arkansas.

Melvin Patridge: Bowie High School basketball star on Richardson's final teams there.

Paul Pressey: Richardson's best player at Tulsa; went on to a long NBA career.

Helen Richardson: Richardson's high school sweetheart and first wife; mother of Madalyn, Notes, and Bradley.

Jon Richardson: First black scholarship football player at Arkansas, no relation to Nolan.

Madalyn Richardson: Richardson's first child.

Nolan "Notes" Richardson III: Richardson's son and former assistant coach.

Yvonne Richardson: Richardson's daughter; died of leukemia in 1987.

Will Robinson: the first black coach in Division I at Illinois State.

Sid Simpson: Richardson's athletics director at Western Texas College in Snyder.

Andy Stoglin: Teammate of Richardson at UTEP, assistant at Tulsa and Arkansas, later the head coach at Jackson State.

Eddie Sutton: Arkansas coach whose departure opened the door for Richardson in 1985.

John Thompson: First black coach to win NCAA title in Division I, at Georgetown.

Lyell Thompson: Professor at Arkansas for decades who pushed for desegregation.

Scotty Thurman: He made the decisive "3" to beat Duke for NCAA title in 1994.

Phillip Trapp: Longtime UA psychology professor who pushed Frank Broyles to desegregate.

Ken Trickey: Oral Roberts University coach in the 1970s whose fast-breaking teams had great success.

Lanny Van Eman: Arkansas basketball coach in the early 1970s, before Eddie Sutton.

Fred Vorsanger: Former Fayetteville mayor and manager of Bud Walton Arena at UA.

Duddy Waller: Arkansas basketball coach who signed the first black players at Arkansas in the late 1960s.

Bob Walters: Scored ninety-six touchdowns in high school in Arkansas but was ignored by the segregated teams of the South. Later was Tim Hardaway's high school basketball coach.

Bert Williams: Former El Paso city alderman (later mayor) who wrote the anti–Jim Crow legislation in El Paso after being denied service at a restaurant with Richardson.

Carrol Williams: Head of University of Arkansas black alumni group.

Dwight Williams: Key guard on Richardson's first junior college teams; transferred to Texas Tech.

Lonnie Williams: Longtime Arkansas administrator; now at Arkansas State.

Corliss Williamson: Center on Richardson's 1994 champs.

Judge William Wilson: Presiding judge in Richardson's court case.

Otto "Bud" Zinke: Senate Council member at UA, antiwar activist, quiet leader of desegregation movements on campus.

BIBLIOGRAPHY

Allen, James, Jon Lewis, Leon Litwack, and Hilton Als. *Without Sanctuary: Lynching Photographs in America*. New York: Twin Palms Publishers, 2000.

Brodie, Ralph, and Marvin Schwartz. *Central in Our Lives: Voices from Little Rock Central High School, 1957–1959*. Little Rock: The Butler Center for Arkansas Studies, 2007.

Broyles, J. Frank. *Hog Wild: The Autobiography of Frank Broyles*. Memphis: Memphis State University Press, 1979.

Dailey Jr., Maceo and Kristine Navarro, eds. *Wherever My People Chance to Dwell: Oral Interviews with African-American Women of El Paso*. Inprint Edition, 2000.

Dowling, William. *Confessions of a Spoilsport*. Harrisburg: Penn State University Press, 2007.

Edwards, Harry. *The Revolt of the Black Athlete*. New York: Free Press, 1969.

Ellsworth, Scott. *Death in a Promised Land: The Tulsa Race Riots of 1921*. Baton Rouge: LSU Press, 1992.

Encyclopedia of Arkansas History and Culture, encyclopediaofarkansas.net.

Fitzpatrick, Frank. *The Walls Came Tumbling Down*. Lincoln: University of Nebraska Press, 2000.

Frei, Terry. *Horns, Hogs, and Nixon Coming*. New York: Simon & Schuster, 2002.

Graves, John William. *Town and Country: Race Relations in an Urban Rural Context, Arkansas, 1865–1905*. Fayetteville: University of Arkansas Press, 1990.

Halberstam, David. *The Fifties*. New York: Villard Books, 1993.

Ivy, Darren. *Untold Stories: Black Sports Heroes Before Integration*. Little Rock: Wehco Publishers, 2002.

Jacobs, Barry. *Across the Line: Profiles in Basketball Courage*. Guilford, CT: Lyons Press, 2007.

Jacoway, Elizabeth. *Turn Away Thy Son*. Fayetteville: University of Arkansas Press, 2008.

Jacoway, Elizabeth, and C. Fred Williams. *Understanding the Little Rock Crisis*. Fayetteville: University of Arkansas Press, 1999.

Jennings, Jay. *Carrying the Rock*. Emmaus, PA: Rodale Press, 2010.

Katz, Milton. *Breaking Through: John B. McLendon, Basketball Legend and Civil Rights Pioneer*. Fayetteville: University of Arkansas Press, 2007.

Kenan, Randall. *The Fire This Time*. New York: Melville House, 2007.

Kriegel, Mark. *Pistol: The Life of Pete Maravich*. New York: Free Press, 2008.

Madigan, Tim. *The Burning: Massacre, Destruction, and the Tulsa Race Riot of 1921*. New York: St. Martin's Griffin, 2003.

Maraniss, David. *Clemente: The Passion and Grace of Baseball's Last Hero*. New York: Simon & Schuster, 2007.

Meggyesy, David. *Out of Their League*. Lincoln: University of Nebraska Press, 2006.

Morgan, Gordon. "The Firing of Nolan Richardson." Unpublished.

Morgan, Gordon, and Izola Preston. *The Edge of Campus: A Journal of the Black Experience at the University of Arkansas*. Fayetteville: University of Arkansas Press, 1990.

Onoda, Hiroo. *No Surrender: My Thirty-Year War*. Annapolis: U.S. Naval Institute Press, 1999.

Pennington, Richard. *Breaking the Ice: The Racial Integration of Southwest Conference Football*. Jefferson, NC: McFarland Publishers, 1987.

Powers, Elia. "Mulling Ways to Add Minority Coaches." Inside Higher Education, March 1, 2007.

Reed, Roy. *Faubus: The Life and Times of an American Prodigal.* Fayetteville: University of Arkansas Press, 1997.

Remnick, David. *King of the World: Muhammad Ali and the Rise of an American Hero.* New York: Vintage, 1999.

Rhoden, William. *Forty Million Dollar Slaves: The Rise, Fall, and Redemption of the Black Athlete.* New York: Three Rivers Press, 2007.

_____. "Sports of the Times; For Black Coaches, New Direction Needed." New York Times, February 19, 1995.

Riffel, Brent. "The Body Count: Lynching in Arkansas." Historymatters. gmu.edu.

Romo, David. *Ringside Seat to a Revolution.* El Paso: Cinco Puntos Press, 2005.

Roy, Elizabeth. *Bitters in the Honey: Tales of Hope and Disappointment Across Divides of Race and Time.* Fayetteville: University of Arkansas Press, 1999.

Shields, David. *Black Planet: Facing Race During an NBA Season.* Lincoln, NE: Bison Books, 2006.

Wetzel, Dan, with Don Haskins. *Glory Road.* New York: Hyperion, 2005.

Zirin, David. *What's My Name, Fool? Sports and Resistance in the United States.* Chicago: Haymarket Books, 2005.

_____. *Welcome to the Terrordome: The Pain, Politics, and Promise of Sports.* Chicago: Haymarket Books, 2007.

_____. *A People's History of Sports in the United States.* New York: New Press, 2008.

FILM, MEDIA, AND PERIODICALS

Black Magic, directed by Don Klores, ESPN Films, 2008.

UTEP, University of Arkansas, and Tulsa University all provided media guides for basketball and football.

The following magazines and newspapers were helpful: *Arkansas Times, Democrat-Gazette, Morning News, Chronicle of Higher Education, Sporting News, Sports Illustrated, USA Today.*

ABOUT THE AUTHOR

Rus Bradburd is the author of the acclaimed *Paddy on the Hardwood: A Journey in Irish Hoops*. A college basketball coach for fourteen seasons, he teaches writing classes at New Mexico State University and lives in Las Cruces, New Mexico, with his wife, the poet Connie Voisine, and their daughter. Visit rusbradburd.com.